W9-ASB-629

Hitler

Legend, Myth & Reality

-WERNER MASER

TRANSLATED FROM THE GERMAN BY
PETER AND BETTY ROSS

-HARPER & ROW, PUBLISHERS
NEW YORK, EVANSTON, SAN FRANCISCO, LONDON

FOR EVA MASER

First published as *Adolf Hitler: Legende, Mythos, Wirklichkeit,*
copyright © 1971, Bechtle Verlag, Munich and Esslingen.

ISBN: 0-06-012831-3   MAY   3 '74

LIBRARY OF CONGRESS CATALOG CARD NUMBER: 72-9136

Contents

List of Illustrations

Acknowledgements

Hans-Peter Kruse: 5, 6, 9, 10, 18; Ullstein Bilderdienst: 11, 12, 38, 45; Süddeutscher Verlag, Bilderdienst: 13, 43, 44; Marquess of Bath: 22, 27; Bildarchiv Heinrich Hoffmann: 31, 32, 33, 34, 36, 46, 47, 48, 49; Dr Erwin Giesing: 35; Radio Times Hulton Picture Library: 37; Dr Robert M. W. Kempner: 50, 51, 52.

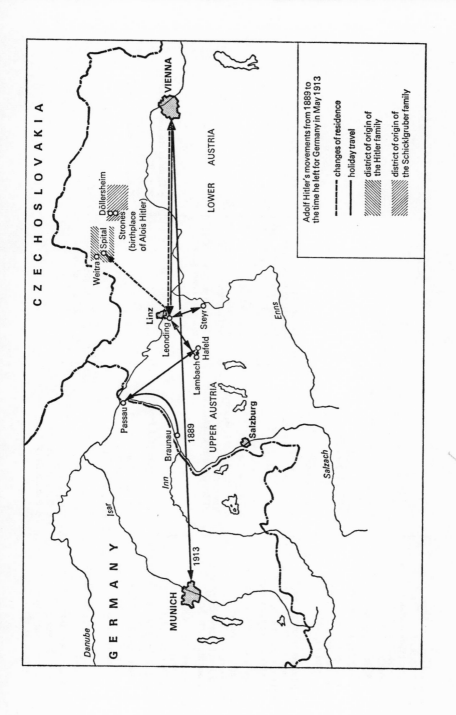

Adolf Hitler's movements from 1889 to
the time he left for Germany in May 1913

- - - - changes of residence
——— holiday travel
district of origin of
the Hitler family
district of origin of
the Schicklgruber family

CZECHOSLOVAKIA

Döllersheim
Strones
Weitra Spital
(birthplace
of Alois Hitler)

VIENNA

LOWER
AUSTRIA

Linz
Leonding
Lambach Hafeld Steyr

Enns

GERMANY

Danube

Isar

Inn Braunau
Passau
1889

UPPER AUSTRIA

Salzburg

Salzach

1913

MUNICH

FOUR GENERATIONS OF THE HITLER FAMILY

1. Adolf Hitler
   b. Braunau am Inn 6.30 p.m. 20.4.1889
   baptised Braunau 3.15 p.m. 22.4.1889
   d. Berlin 3.30 p.m. 30.4.1945

2. Alois Schicklgruber,
   imperial customs official
   b. Strones 11.30 a.m. 7.6.1837
   baptised Döllersheim 7.6.1837
   legitimised Döllersheim 1876
   as Alois Hitler
   d. 3.1.1903
   buried Leonding
   m. Braunau am Inn 7.1.1885
   as his 3rd marriage to

3. Klara Pölzl
   b. Spital 12.8.1860
   d. Leonding 21.12.1907

4(=14). Johann Nepomuk Hüttler,
   farmer
   b. Spital 19.3.1807
   d. Spital 17.9.1888

   Liaison with

5. Maria Anna Schicklgruber
   b. Strones 15.4.1795
   m. Döllersheim to J. G. Hiedler
   10.5.1842
   d. Klein-Motten 7.1.1847

6. Johann Baptist Pölzl, farmer
   b. Spital
   baptised Spital 25.5.1828
   d. Spital 9.1.1902
   m. Spital 5.9.1848 to

7. Johanna Hüttler
   b. Spital 19.1.1830
   d. Spital 8.2.1906

8. Martin Hiedler, farmer
   b. Walterschlag
   baptised Gross-Schönau 11.11.1762
   d. Spital 10.1.1829
   m. Spital c. 1786 to

9. Anna Maria Göschl
   b. Spital
   baptised Spital 2.12.1767
   d. Spital 7.12.1854

10. Johannes Schicklgruber,
    farmer
    b. Strones 29.5.1764
    d. Kleinmotten 12.11.1847
    m. Döllersheim 5.2.1793 to

11. Theresia Pfeisinger
    b. Dietreichs
    baptised Döllersheim 7.9.1769
    d. Strones 25.11.1821

12. Laurenz Pölzl, farmer
    b. Spital 15.7.1788
    d. Spital 10.4.1841
    m. Spital 20.2.1827 to

13. Juliana Walli (later Walli)
    b. Gross-Wolfgers 25.12.1797
    d. Spital 23.2.1831

14(=4). Johann Nepomuk Hüttler,
    farmer
    m. Spital 3.11.1829

15. Eva Maria Decker
    b. Thaures 16.12.1792
    d. Spital 30.12.1873

Martin Hiedler = Anna Maria Göschl

Johann Georg Hiedler = Maria Anna Schicklgruber = Johann Nepomuk Hüttler = Eva Maria Decker
(brother of J. N. Hüttler)

Johanna Hüttler = Johann Pölzl

illegitimate

Franziska Matzelsberger = (2) Alois Schicklgruber = (3) Klara Pölzl
(1876 leg. Hitler)

Alois Hitler

Angela Hitler
= Leo Raubal

3 others

Patrick
Hitler

Angela Raubal
known as 'Geli'

Leo Raubal

Adolf Hitler   Edmund   Paula
              Hitler   Hitler

Preface

Books on the subject of Adolf Hitler are legion. As much as a decade ago some fifty thousand serious studies of the Second World War had already been published. Yet there have been comparatively few actual biographies. Too much in Hitler's life has hitherto been regarded as unascertained or unascertainable. His biographers have, according to taste, either passed over in silence important stretches of his career, or have used their imagination to fill in the gaps and contented themselves with placing new interpretations and different emphases on already familiar details. Neither the documents in the Federal Archives at Coblenz nor the other Hitleriana to which most authors have had recourse can supply what is missing. Other sources very seldom come to light. Some were believed to be inaccessible if not actually lost – as, for instance, the complete text of the depositions made by Hitler's medical advisers, which is not to be found in any archive. Former members of his entourage remained silent – often with good reason – as did his sister, his half-brother and half-sister, his cousins and his nephews and nieces, all of whom were in a position to help the historian. The publication of my books *Die Frühgeschichte der NSDAP, Hitlers Weg bis 1924* (1965) and *Hitlers Mein Kampf* (1966) was to open up a veritable goldmine of information. Important witnesses came forward – school-fellows, childhood and army friends, comrades from the days of political struggle, opponents and enemies, relations and heirs. In the attic of one of Hitler's cousins I discovered, neglected and forgotten, some of the material which biographers had been seeking in vain for close on half a century. For the first time large numbers of letters and notes in Hitler's own hand have been made available for study, as have the depositions and statements made by his doctors.

The entire course of Hitler's life can now be traced without interruption. Much of what is already known I have either omitted or merely mentioned in passing, going into greater detail only where the material served to shed additional light on the new portrait here presented.

CHAPTER ONE

Family and Antecedents

On a dull and cloudy Easter Saturday a son was born to Klara and Alois Hitler at the Gasthaus zum Pommer in the small Austrian town of Braunau am Inn. Two days later, on Easter Monday, Father Ignaz Probst christened the child Adolf.

The Braunau parish register, Volume xix, 30 June 1881–91, contains two entries relating to Adolf Hitler made by Catholic priests of two successive generations, one recording his birth, the other his death.

From the first entry we learn that he was born at 6.30 p.m. on 20 April 1889, that he was helped into the world by his aunt, Johanna Pölzl, that he was a Catholic and the legitimate offspring of Alois Hitler, a customs official, and Klara, daughter of Johann Pölzl, farmer, of Spital, Lower Austria, and Johanna, née Hüttler.

The second entry, relating to his suicide on 30 April 1945, was made twelve years after the event by the then parish priest, Father Ludwig. It reads: 'Declared dead, *in fid. publ.*, in accordance with the ruling made by the Berchtesgaden District Court on 25 October 1956, II 48/52. Parish Presbytery, Braunau, 11 January 1957. Johann Ludwig.'

Had Hitler been an ordinary run-of-the-mill Catholic like countless others this latter entry would hardly be a matter for comment, nor would any interest attach to the particulars relating to Alois Hitler which were subsequently appended to his son's registration of birth in the Braunau parish register, namely:

The certificate of baptism issued in respect of Alois Hitler by the Döllersheim Presbytery on 7 June 1876 and signed by Father Josef Zahnschirm states that the said Alois Hitler was born on 7 June 1837, the legitimate son of Georg Hitler of Spital and Maria Anna, his wife, legitimate daughter of Johann Schicklgruber, farmer, of Strones, and his spouse Theresia, née Pfeisinger, all being of the Catholic faith. Alois Hitler was born in Strones 3 and was baptized on the day of his birth by Father Ignaz Rueskuefer in the presence of Johann Trummelschlager and his spouse Josefa as godparents. First marriage to Anna, née Glassl-Hörer, deceased 6 April 1883 in this parish. Second marriage to Franziska Matzelsberger, solemnized 22 May

1883. Marriage Register XIII in Ranshofen 268. Third marriage to Klara Pölzl, solemnized on 7 January 1885, I Marriage Register T. XIII. P. 68, p. 281.

From the outset Hitler's origins have been shrouded in obscurity, for certain of the entries in the Braunau Catholic parish register are distinctly misleading. Alois was not born legitimate. Maria Anna's husband was called Hiedler, not Hitler, and he was not the father of her child. Indeed – and this despite a great deal of research on the part of numerous historians, genealogists and biographers – the identity of Alois's father has hitherto remained a mystery.[1] Various candidates have been suggested, among them a 'Graz Jew' by the name of Frankenberger, a scion of the seigneurial house of Ottenstein and even a Baron Rothschild of Vienna. But if there is one fact on which at least some biographers are agreed, it is that Adolf's paternal grandfather was not the man officially regarded as such, namely the journeyman miller Johann Georg Hiedler. It has further been established that Adolf's father, Alois, did not adopt the surname Hitler until 1876 when he was already thirty-nine years old.

Hitler's paternal grandmother, Maria Anna Schicklgruber, has remained till now a figure hardly less shadowy than the man who fathered her son. Indeed nothing has been known about her save for the information contained in the church records, namely that she was born in 1795, that at the age of forty-two, as yet unmarried, she gave birth in Strones to her only child, Alois (Adolf's father), that she married Johann Georg Hiedler five years later and died five years after that.[2] According to most of Hitler's biographers her life with Johann Georg Hiedler was a wretched one.[3] But in fact there was nothing wretched or pitiable about Maria Anna. After her mother's death in November 1821, 74·25 gulden became due to her from the parental estate. According to handwritten documents which wrongly describe her as 'A. Maria',[4] she left this sum in the Orphans' Fund until 1838. Here it earned five per cent interest so that by 1838, shortly after the birth of her son Alois, it had increased to 165 gulden, more than twice the original amount.[5] At that time a cow, for instance, would have cost 10 to 12 gulden, a brood sow 4 gulden, a bed with bedding 2 gulden and an inn with stabling from 450 to 500 gulden.

Maria Anna's parents (Adolf Hitler's great-grandparents), Johannes and Theresia Schicklgruber, came of peasant stock and, like their daughter, were of a determined disposition. The Lordship of Ottenstein's business records for 1793[6] contain their marriage contract, drawn up in January of that year, whereby they bound themselves until 'solemn consummation' to abide by the following terms.

1. If so be the bride weds her betrothed she is to provide along with proper love and fidelity the portion inherited from her mother viz. 100 florins. Next from her father she shall receive an unencumbered dowry: 200 florins therewith goods and chattels viz: 1 bed 20 fl., 1 chest 7 fl., 1 coffer 1 florin 30 kr, 1 cow 20 fl., 70 skeins of flax @ 6 kr. 7 fl. In all 355 fl. 30 kr. Against which 355 florins 30 kronen

2. The bridegroom shall set the unencumbered marriage apportionment from his parents viz. 100 fl. and their savings of 100 fl., in all 200 fl. so that everything they presently bring together along with any wealth that may by God's Grace accrue to them in marriage shall be their common property and shall so be termed and so remain.

3. In the event of death and failing the existence of heirs between them two begotten, the nearest kith shall receive a third part of the full inventory; and if there be issue, one or more, one half.[7]

By 1788, at the age of twenty-four, Johannes Schicklgruber had already taken over the house in Strones (No. 1) previously held in fee by his father, Jakob Schicklgruber.[8] In 1817, when his wife Theresia (née Pfeisinger) inherited 210 gulden out of her father's total estate of 1054 gulden,[9] he felt prosperous enough to retire although only fifty-three years old at the time. He therefore sold the farm to his son Josef for the sum of 3000 gulden. According to the contract of sale, the property comprised 'a yoke of oxen, a plough, a harrow, a shed and implements, therewith 1¼ yokes arable land in Franzen [a village near Strones]'. In return for this Josef Schicklgruber undertook to provide his parents with free flour, straw, potatoes and other stores, and also with services in the form of manual labour and the provision of draught animals. A further condition was that the purchaser should set aside a plot of land and build thereon a chamber to serve as a free lodging for the vendors for the remainder of their days.[10]

By all accounts their daughter, Maria Anna, was a thrifty, reserved and exceptionally shrewd peasantwoman. Yet not even the most exhaustive research has succeeded in bringing her properly into focus. When her son Alois was born she did not reveal the identity of the child's father, nor would she do so at the christening, thus obliging the priest to baptize the child Alois Schicklgruber and to enter the word 'illegitimate' in place of the father's name in the baptismal register.

Had Johann Georg Hiedler been the father, Maria Anna would certainly have named him as such on the occasion of their marriage if not before. But she did not do so, for the simple reason that he was not the father. An entry made much later in the Döllersheim baptismal register according to which the 'child's mother' named Johann Georg Hiedler as the father casts an unjustifiable slur on her; for it was not she, already thirty years dead at the time, who was responsible for the untruth, but her brother-in-law Johann Nepomuk Hüttler and the illiterate witnesses at Alois's legitimation in 1876. And if, despite her relative affluence, Maria Anna allowed her son to be brought up in her brother-in-law's household instead of keeping him with her, it may well have been because her husband, who spent his days loafing about at home, objected to the presence in the house of a child that was not his own.

Though shorter-lived than her forebears, Maria Anna Schicklgruber must have remained in passable health at least until 1837 for in that year she gave birth to her only child at the then unusually advanced age of forty-two. She died on 7 January 1847, not in Strones, but in the neighbouring village of Klein-Motten where she and her husband, having no house of their own, had been living with the related Sillip family.

Hitler himself was always notably reticent about his own family, and he never complied with the clause in the NSDAP programme[11] stipulating that all Germans must provide documentary evidence about their ancestry – a clause which was to have such tragic consequences for those of Jewish extraction. Among close associates he would often speak of his mother but seldom alluded to his father and never, except indirectly, to Johann Nepomuk Hüttler, the brother of his 'official' grandfather, Georg Hiedler. Virtually the only information he vouchsafes about his parents in *Mein Kampf* is that his father was an Austrian customs official, 'a dutiful civil servant' and 'the son of a poor cottager'.[12] Of his mother, he says that she was a devoted wife and a kindly and self-sacrificing parent whom he had loved.[13] All else is devoid of substance, its sole intention being to promote the growth of the legend and to serve the purpose of National Socialist propaganda.[14]

From 1921 onwards Hitler consistently obscured and misrepresented his origins in a deliberate attempt to detach himself from his immediate family background. In this way he hoped to appear both as the emissary of history and as the incarnation of what in his view was the 'commendable and legitimate desire' of the German people. He was remarkably *au fait* with the history and culture of antiquity and the numerous gods and heroes of its mythology. He also knew his Bible, being particularly well versed in the Old Testament. Among close associates, and this more especially during the Second World War, he would hark back to certain aspects of his past in a manner calculated to awaken a sympathetic response in an already appreciative and devoted audience. Ingeniously he presented his own person, his antecedents and his social background within a framework that lent itself readily to adaptation as 'history'. This image was reinforced by the leading men of his entourage who systematically evoked the great figures of history and mythology to create a veritable fabric of analogies. Though Hitler would sometimes protest that, unlike the mythological figures of Greek and Roman antiquity, he was not endowed with supernatural powers, he made no effort to prevent the embarrassingly vociferous attempts of a Hess, a Goebbels or a Himmler to ascribe these to him. In a context of this nature small purpose would have been served by entering into the minutiae of family relationships, even where these comprised – as they did in Hitler's case – connections with figures well known in the world of literature and scholarship.* Indeed circumstances would hardly have permitted more than the passing allusions he accorded his father and paternal grandfather. This was quite sufficient for Hitler's purposes. A man of power, he wove his own legend in accordance with well-thought-out principles, and woe betide any objective historian who sought to demolish it.

His more immediate relations were expected to keep well in the background, as his nephew, Patrick Hitler, the son of his half-brother Alois and an Irishwoman, discovered after he had given unauthorized interviews to the British Press about the uncle he then still greatly admired. The resulting fracas was later described by Patrick in an article in *Paris-Soir* of 5 September 1939, from which we learn that, after furiously denouncing his nephew's indiscretion, Hitler exclaimed:

I've always taken such care to keep my private affairs out of the press! These people are not to know who I am. They're not to know where I come from

* E.g. the genealogist, Rudolf Koppensteiner and the Austrian poet, Robert Hamerling.

or what my family background is. Even in my book I never mention a word about these things, not a word! And now they've gone and lit on my nephew. Inquiries are set on foot and people sent to pry into our past!

If we read between the lines of Patrick's article it becomes evident that he was something of a thorn in his uncle's flesh. On one occasion, no doubt in the hope of ridding himself once for all of his importunate nephew, Hitler told him angrily that they were in no way related, since Alois (Patrick's father) had been merely adopted into the family. But Patrick was not to be so easily shaken off. In the summer of 1933 he went to Austria to search for proof of their relationship, and returned triumphant. 'There could be no doubt,' he writes. 'I was indeed Adolf Hitler's nephew.' On another occasion, when he asked his uncle for money, Hitler replied 'that he could not give help to everyone who happened to bear his name. . . . Though a mere wave of the hand would have sufficed to fill the pockets of his immediate relations, he didn't so much as lift a finger.' Nevertheless he would appear to have made Patrick at least two presents of money – one of 100 and one of 500 marks – and to have continued to tolerate his importunities and feck-lessness until 1938 when he insisted that his nephew should settle down to work. 'I was to earn 125 marks a month,' the young man writes, 'not a starvation wage, but not a living wage either . . . [by] working in a bank. But I couldn't send any money to my mother [in England] since German regulations forbade it. . . . At last I wrote to Hitler personally. . . . He replied: "I regret that I cannot accord you any privileges." ' Whereupon Patrick left Germany for good.

Hitler had another nephew towards whom his feelings were much more avuncular. This was Leo Raubal, the son of his half-sister Angela. Indeed when Leo, then a second lieutenant in the engineers, was captured after the fall of Stalingrad, Hitler so far forsook his policy of withholding favours from his family as to propose an exchange for Stalin's son Jakob, who had been in German hands since 1941. But Stalin refused. In 1967 Stalin's daughter, Svetlana Alliluyeva, wrote in her book *Twenty Letters to a Friend*: 'After Stalingrad, in the winter of 1943–44, my father said to me suddenly during one of our rare meetings: "The Germans have proposed that we exchange one of their prisoners for Yasha. They want me to do a deal with them! But I won't do it. War is war!" ' Svetlana could not have guessed that 'one of their prisoners' was Hitler's favourite nephew, nor did Leo Raubal himself know anything about this episode until told by the author in 1967.

Hitler was always at pains to eschew nepotism which he considered to have been one of Napoleon's gravest shortcomings.[15] This explains at least in part why, after becoming committed to politics in 1919, he tended to keep his family at arm's length, though he had previously enjoyed frequenting his relations in the Waldviertel (known after the Anschluss as 'the ancestral region'). Before 1914 he had sometimes stayed with them for his summer holidays and during the war he spent two periods of leave in Spital – the second, in September 1918, being the last occasion on which he visited his Waldviertel relations. The few members of his family who had access to him thereafter were – apart from his nephews Patrick and Leo – his half-sister Angela Raubal and her daughter Geli, the great love of his life. Also his younger sister Paula. None, save Patrick, made any demands on him though towards the end of her life, Paula – by then his sole legatee – hoped to benefit under the terms of his will. 'My dearest wish', she was to write on 10 January 1960, 'is that I may at long last get the probate certificate which would enable me to move into a nice, sunny flat so that for the remainder of my days I could perhaps enjoy the warmth and comfort I have so long craved in vain.'[16] She died the following June without ever entering into possession of the two-thirds share of his estate to which she was entitled.[17] The wheel had turned full circle.

The only places associated with Hitler's childhood for which he felt any real affection were Linz and the neighbouring hamlet of Leonding where his parents lay buried in the Catholic cemetery almost opposite their former home. He often referred in glowing terms to this village, which he revisited three times in all, actually spending the night there in 1938.[18] A well-known picture-postcard of the time depicts him standing pensively beside his parents' grave. Even in private conversation he never showed any interest in the other haunts of his boyhood. On entering Braunau after the invasion of Austria in March 1938 he gave no indication of a desire to see the house where he had been born. Nor did he ever visit Strones near Döllersheim, the birthplace of his paternal grandmother.

There is, however, no foundation whatever for Franz Jetzinger's suggestion that Hitler himself may have ordered the destruction of the village of Döllersheim,[19] where his father had been baptized in June

1837, because documents relating to his origins were stored there. Fancifully Jetzinger asserts that:

Döllersheim and many of the surrounding localities [including Strones where Alois Hitler was born in June 1837] no longer exist. The whole of this once flourishing and fertile region was turned into a military exercise area and is today a ghastly desert where malevolent death lurks in the form of unexploded shells. Its former inhabitants have been dispersed to all points of the compass. For several years Hitler was able to gloat over the fact that the place where his father had been born and his grandmother buried was being pounded and crushed by the Wehrmacht. Whether the choice of this particular spot was dictated by military considerations may be doubted, more especially since the Land Registry offices in Allentsteig and Weitra received instructions to value the land in mid-May 1938, barely two months after the occupation of Austria. . . . It looks very much as though Döllersheim was destroyed on the direct orders of the Führer – out of insane hatred for his father, whose father before him may have been a Jew.[20]

Far from being a 'fertile, flourishing region' the country round Döllersheim, with its heavy soil, produced wretched harvests, while in spring and autumn it became virtually impassable. Nor is it correct to say that the plan to turn the locality into an exercise area was adumbrated as early as 1938. In the *Register of Austrian Parishes*[21] there is specific reference to a special issue of the Lower Danube Region's *Official Gazette*:[22] 'The former Döllersheim military training area was established in 1941. On the authority of the then governor of the Lower Danube, the following parishes and parts of parishes were declared to be War Department property with the name "Döllersheim Military Training Area".'[23] Up till 1945 many of the individual houses and farms purchased in the villages by the German Resettlement Association on behalf of the Wehrmacht[24] remained virtually intact. It was only after Hitler's death that they were stripped of all usable building material by the inhabitants of the surrounding countryside. The final work of destruction was carried out by the Russians in the course of their occupation, which lasted until 1955. During this time a number of Hitler's male relatives, unmistakably peasants, who bore only a superficial likeness to him and had never derived any benefit from the connection, were arrested and deported to Russia.[25] The full absurdity of Jetzinger's allegations becomes manifest when we consider that after the Anschluss Maria Anna Schicklgruber's grave was adorned with a memorial stone and cross bearing the legend: 'Here lies the grandmother of the Führer – Maria A. Hitler, née Schicklgruber.'[26] The burial-place was invariably tended with special care and was much visited by schools and Hitler Youth groups.[27] In Döllersheim party officials carried hero worship to such lengths that a plaque was affixed to the school building, proudly but untruthfully proclaiming that 'Alois Hitler, the Führer's father', had been to school there.

In 1941 the inhabitants of Döllersheim and Strones were removed to other districts[28] such as Krenglbach in Upper Austria where Hitler's relatives, the Sillip family, were resettled.[29] Before the evacuation, instructions were given for the removal of all church, local government and court records from Döllersheim and the other villages involved. The baptismal register containing the entry relating to Alois Schicklgruber (after 1876 Alois Hitler) was first lodged in the Lower Austrian Provincial Archives in Vienna and later transferred to Rastenfeld, a small village not far from the former parish of Döllersheim. The register recording Adolf Hitler's baptism always remained at Braunau am Inn.

Again there is no substance in the much canvassed view that after 1938 the original entries were tampered with, even to the extent of removing whole pages from the register. The records remained unaltered excepting for one addition: the registration, in compliance with a court order, of Adolf Hitler's death.

It has been suggested that Hitler may have been anxious to cover up his genealogical traces because he had Jewish blood in his veins. Already in the early twenties, when he was scoring the first decisive victories of his political career, a number of his more ingenious political opponents were loudly demanding where this self-styled 'apostle of the purity of the German race' had actually come from, who his paternal grandfather was and whether he could prove that he was not partly Jewish. Those hostile to Hitler and his rabid antisemitism would have been only too delighted to find incontrovertible proof of his father's Jewish descent. Shortly before he took over the party[30] in late July 1921 (when Hermann Esser introduced him as 'our Führer') a number of the NSDAP chiefs put it about that he had Jewish antecedents. Ernst Ehrensperger, one of the first party members, wrote a leaflet which was reproduced in the *Münchner Post* with a ten-line commentary. Part of this leaflet reads: 'He [Hitler] believes the time has come to introduce disunity and dissension into our ranks at the behest of his shady backers . . . and thus to promote the interests of Jewry and its henchmen. . . . And how is he conducting this struggle? Like a real Jew.'[31] Between July and December 1921 there were frequent rumours in Munich about Hitler's Jewish descent. After 30 January 1933, by which time he had seized power and was systematically consolidating it, his origins necessarily ceased to be a matter for public conjecture in Germany.[32] Nevertheless articles and rumours concerning his Jewish provenance continued to be surreptitiously circulated, among them a story from the *Daily Mirror* of 14 October 1933 which was accompanied by a picture of a grave whose headstone was inscribed with Hebrew characters and the name 'Adolf Hitler'. Some ingenious journalists had discovered the existence of this grave (no. 9, row 7, section 18)[33] in the Jewish cemetery in Bucharest and had at once jumped to the conclusion that its occupant was the grandfather of the Führer and Reich Chancellor. The *Mirror*'s allegation that the grave belonged to 'the grandfather of Germany's antisemitic chancellor'[34] was taken up by the Polish Jewish newspaper *Haynt* and the American Jewish *Forward*.

Neither the fabricators of this story nor those desirous of believing them were troubled by the real facts, namely that the man, whose Jewish name was Avraham Eyliyohn, had been buried at the expense of the Jewish Filantropia Society in 1892 and that, since both headstone and death certificate gave his date of birth as 1832 (thus making him only five years older than Adolf's father), he could not possibly have been the Führer's grandfather. *Forward*'s comment on the story was as follows: 'A short time ago we received a cable from our Warsaw correspondent informing us that the local Jewish newspaper *Haynt* had published a photograph of the grave of Hitler's Jewish grandfather. . . . It is now clear that the story about the Jewish origins of this latterday Haman, Adolf Hitler, was not incorrect.'[35] Those Jews who happened to be called Hitler – no rarity in Eastern Europe – were filled with dismay. A number of them followed the example of Abraham Hitler, a Polish Jew from Sosnowice, and adopted another surname.[36]

None of this escaped the notice of his fellow National Socialists. Thus on 19 September 1934 the training officer of the National Socialist Women's Organization (Weser-Ems region), sent a copy of the *Daily Mirror* article to the NSDAP Reich Training Office with the comment that it might be of 'some value to the Party archives'.[37] Highly placed and influential members of the party grew restive, among them Himmler who, even at this early stage, had already opened a highly confidential 'Führer file' containing information which he thought might one day come in useful.[38] He was to have recourse to that file years later when he was planning to arrest Hitler with the help of the S S before offering his services to the Western Allies for a joint war against the Soviet Union.[39]

Eighteen months after Hitler's death the old allegations were resuscitated by fresh evidence plausible enough to convince even serious historians and biographers. The source of this material was Hans Frank, Hitler's sometime legal adviser, who had been a National Socialist Reichstag deputy in 1930 and Governor-General of Poland from 1939 to 1945. In his final speech at Nuremberg Frank assured the International Military Tribunal that he did not wish to leave behind him any 'secret and unatoned guilt'.[40] Shortly before this Frank had written a document in his prison cell with the 'invaluable help' of an American Franciscan army chaplain, Sixtus O'Connor,[41] a document which, since its publication in 1953, has presented students of Hitler with an almost insoluble problem. Frank, who embraced Catholicism while in Nuremberg, handed his manuscript to the priest, requesting him to pass it on to the archives of a monastery. Part of the document runs as follows:

One day, it must have been towards the end of 1930, Hitler sent for me. ... He showed me a letter which he described as a 'disgusting piece of blackmail' on the part of one of his most loathsome relatives and said that it concerned his, Hitler's, antecedents. If I am not mistaken it was a son of his half-brother, Alois (born of Hitler's father's second marriage), who was gently hinting that 'in view of certain allegations in the Press it might be better if certain family matters weren't shouted from the roof-tops'. The Press reports in question suggested that Hitler had Jewish blood in his veins and hence was hardly qualified to be an antisemite. But they were phrased in such general terms that nothing could be done about it. In the heat of the political struggle the whole thing died down. All the same, this threat of blackmail by a relative was a somewhat tricky business. At Hitler's request I made some confidential inquiries. Intensive investigation elicited the following information: Hitler's father was the illegitimate son of a woman by the name of Schicklgruber from Leonding near Linz who worked as cook in a Graz household. In accordance with the law which laid down that an illegitimate child must bear its mother's surname, he was called Schicklgruber up to the age of fourteen. But when his mother (Adolf Hitler's grandmother) married a Herr Hitler, he was formally legitimated as the offspring of the Hitler–Schicklgruber marriage, by means of the instrument *per matrimonium subsequens*. Up to this point all is perfectly clear and really nothing out of the usual. But the most extraordinary part of the story is this: when the cook Schicklgruber (Adolf Hitler's grandmother) gave birth to her child, she was in service with a Jewish family called Frankenberger. And on behalf of his son, then about nineteen years old, Frankenberger paid a maintenance allowance to Schicklgruber from the time of the child's birth until his fourteenth year. For a number of years, too, the Frankenbergers and Hitler's grandmother wrote to each other, the general tenor of the correspondence betraying on both sides the tacit acknowledgement that Schicklgruber's illegitimate child had been engendered under circumstances which made the Frankenbergers responsible for its maintenance. For years this correspondence remained in the possession of a woman living in Wetzelsdorf near Graz who was related to Hitler through the Raubals. . . . Hence the possibility cannot be dismissed that Hitler's father was half Jewish as a result of the extra-marital relationship between the Schicklgruber woman and the Jew from Graz. This would mean that Hitler was one quarter Jewish.[42]

It has often been suggested that, had Frank's story become generally known in 1930, it would have put an end to Adolf Hitler's career as leader of the party. This is exceedingly improbable, even though the NSDAP programme laid down that Jews and 'persons of Jewish descent' were to be denied German citizenship (Point 4), that their status in Germany was to be merely that of 'visitors' (Point 5) and that they were to be debarred from public office 'irrespective of its nature, whether in Reich, province or parish' (Point 6). When Konrad Heiden, himself the son of a Jewess, suggested in his widely read and highly thought-of biographies of 1932 and 1936 that certain evidence pointed to Hitler's Jewish descent, nothing whatever came of it.

Hans Frank's allegations (and the deductions drawn from them) presuppose firstly that there was a Jew by the name of Frankenberger living in Graz in 1836, secondly that in 1930 there was 'a woman living in Wetzelsdorf near Graz who was related to Hitler through the Raubals', and thirdly that Hitler's grandmother, Maria Anna Schicklgruber, had been employed in Graz in 1836. None of these things is demonstrable.

The assertion that Hitler's grandmother had corresponded with a Frankenberger family for a number of years and that their letters had subsequently been in the keeping of a woman related to Hitler through the Raubals,[43] is dismissed by the Raubal family as pure fantasy.[44]

Moreover none of the Frankenbergers known to have lived in Graz could have been the father of Alois Schicklgruber, nor does there appear to be any trace of a German Jew bearing this name or any variant thereof in the nineteenth century.[45] Indeed, from the end of the fifteenth century until a decade after Maria Anna Schicklgruber's death, no Jews were resident in Graz.[46] Under the terms of the treaty concluded on 19 March 1496 between the Emperor Maximilian I and the Styrian towns,[47] all Jews were to be expelled from the province by 6 January 1497, in return for which the Emperor was to receive from the Landtag a first and final indemnity of 38,000 gulden. Not until 1781 in the reign of Joseph II were they allowed to re-enter the Duchy of Styria and then only for a few weeks at a time, at mid-Lent and the Feast of St Giles, when they were admitted to the annual fairs in Graz, Klagenfurt, Laibach and Linz, against payment of a fixed sum. But as early as 9 September 1783 the rights of the Jews were again curtailed, a measure that was reinforced by further discriminatory regulations in 1797, 1819, 1823 and 1828. This situation remained unchanged until the beginning of the 1860's, save for the period of the Napoleonic Wars when a number of Jewish army contractors resided temporarily in Graz in order to trade with Jewish merchants from Munich, Augsburg, Stuttgart and Amsterdam.

There is, of course, no reason why a Frankenberger should not have attended the 1836 September Fair in Graz and there met Maria Anna Schicklgruber. Alois Schicklgruber (later Hitler) was born on 7 June 1837. Hence there might conceivably have been an encounter in September of the previous year but this would seem unlikely in view of the fact that Maria Anna did not live in Graz. Neither, evidently, did she visit the town at this time. From 1821 to 1838 the Allentsteig area court,[48] whose authority extended to Strones where her child was born in 1837, kept a record of the interest accruing to her from her parents' estate. Yet the books of the Orphans' Fund show no change of address either in 1836 or 1837.[49] Moreover, as a subject of the 'Lordship of Ottenstein', she could not have absented herself for any length of time in order, say, to make her way to Graz for the purpose of keeping an assignation. Finally, since she was not working in Graz in 1836, she could not possibly have entered into a relationship such as Frank describes. Her name does not appear either in the town's domestic service register or in the municipal register.[50]

Hans Frank's account has not only preoccupied a ¦whole generation of biographers but has also succeeded in firing their imaginations. For instance we might cite Franz Jetzinger's allegation that in his *Paris-Soir* article Patrick Hitler described his uncle as the grandson of a Graz Jew called Frankenreither. *Paris-Soir* no longer exists; the 1939 article has not been reprinted elsewhere, and none of Hitler's biographers (Jetzinger included) has probably ever set eyes on it. During a visit to Paris in 1969 I succeeded in unearthing that particular issue of the paper which devoted two pages of text and six illustrations to Patrick Hitler's story. It contains no allusion whatever to the possibility that Hitler might have had Jewish antecedents nor, since Maria Anna Schicklgruber is not even mentioned, to her supposed employer, one Frankenreiter, of Graz.[51] There was, it is true, a forty-two-year-old butcher and tripe-boiler called Frankenreither resident there in 1836. A native of Stadtberg near Passau, he was the son of Josef Frankenreither, shoemaker, and Margarethe Frankenreither of Tiefenbach, whose names appear in the Tiefenbach parish register.[52] But there is no proof whatever that Maria Anna Schicklgruber was ever acquainted with this Frankenreither or, indeed, with any other.

All this inevitably raises the question why, on the eve of his execution, Frank should have made such momentous allegations. While in Nuremberg under the tutelage of Father O'Connor, Frank was patently remorseful and devout.[53] Hence he may conceivably have been seeking, not only to disembarrass his fellow Catholics for all times of Adolf Hitler, the Catholic mass-murderer, but also to foment unrest, anxiety and a lasting sense of guilt among 'the Jews'. The assertions he made 'face to face with the gallows' were so confident as to disarm most sceptics. Yet a comparison with established facts reveals that none of his statements withstands close analysis. Indeed the extent of their reliability can be gauged from the following example. At the time of the blackmail attempt, he maintains, Hitler told him that from conversations with his father and grandmother he knew 'his father had not been born as a result of sexual intercourse between the Schicklgruber woman and the Jew in Graz'. The suggestion that Adolf Hitler had ever conversed with his grandmother is utterly absurd since she had already been dead for forty-two years by the time he was born. When his father died he was not yet fourteen years old.

Since, then, all suppositions regarding Hitler's Jewish provenance can be shown to be unfounded, we must look elsewhere if we are to solve the puzzle of the identity of his paternal grandfather. That puzzle is inextricably linked with the question of his father's legitimation.

By his own account, Alois had been legitimated when his mother married Johann Georg Hiedler, who had then officially acknowledged him as his child.[54] This is wholly untrue. Nor is there any justification for the assumption that Alois Schicklgruber sought legitimation in 1876 because, as a Catholic and a public servant, he could not afford the taint of illegitimacy. His career up to that time shows plainly enough that such was not the case. Moreover he himself was by no means narrow-minded where morality was concerned, as is evident from his conduct towards his first and second wives, and from his willingness to accept as his son the child born to him out of wedlock by Franziska Matzelsberger.

At the time of his legitimation, some twenty years after his putative father's death, he was, as we have seen, already thirty-nine years old. The fact that he now signed himself Hitler would seem to have signified more than just a change of name, for within a year he broke off all relations with the Schicklgruber family. We know, however, that he had still been using his old name in 1874 for on 21 September of that year he acted as witness at the wedding of Karl Fischer, a senior revenue official, and signed his name Alois Schicklgruber in the Braunau parish register.[55] But a later volume of the same register reveals that by June 1876 he had already changed his name to Hitler.[56]

There was nothing fortuitous about Alois's failure to adopt the name his mother had acquired thirty-five years previously by her marriage to Georg Hiedler. In the autumn of 1876 his name was recorded as Alois Hitler in the Döllersheim parish register. This was done either with the assent or at the instance of Johann Nepomuk Hüttler, Georg Hiedler's brother, by Father Josef Zahnschirm who had only recently moved to the parish. The priest appended neither signature nor date to the entry which reads:

The father, entered as Georg Hitler, who is well known to the competent witnesses, has acknowledged that he is the father of the child Alois, as claimed by the child's mother, Anna Schicklgruber, and has applied for his name to be recorded in this baptismal register. Attested by the competent witnesses: Josef Rommeder, witness Johann Breiteneder (his mark), Engelbert Paukh (his mark).

Being illiterate these witnesses did not notice the priest's mistake in entering Alois's father's name as Hitler instead of Hiedler. Obviously

Johann Nepomuk did not say 'Hiedler' as his brother had always done, but 'Hüttler', intending that Alois should call himself by that name, a variant which Zahnschirm might easily have misheard as Hitler.

Admittedly there is nothing, either in the entry or in the choice of witnesses, to betray the identity of the person behind this move. What is indubitable, however, is that both Johann Nepomuk Hüttler and Alois himself had decided on the change of name in compliance with the wishes of Maria Anna who had died in 1847. For in 1876 Franz Schicklgruber, the administrator of his sister Maria Anna's estate, made over to his nephew Alois what was then the considerable sum of 230 gulden.[57] It is no longer possible to ascertain what family discussions had preceded this event; but in view of the interest taken by the Schicklgrubers in Alois, of whose successful career they had good reason to be proud, there is every likelihood that at an early stage some hard and fast agreement would have been reached by Johann Nepomuk Hüttler, his brother, Georg Hiedler, Alois Schicklgruber, his mother, Maria Anna Schicklgruber, and other members of her family.

Bracher is wrong in assuming that Alois Schicklgruber's 'retrospective legitimation' had been brought about 'by the illegal machinations of his step-uncle with the aid of a gullible village priest'.[58] It is true that the applicants failed to comply with the official regulations which required that either Johann Georg Hiedler should appear in person or that a legally binding document signed by him be produced;[59] for Hiedler had died in 1857 without ever having recognized Alois as his child, and since the legitimation took place so long after his death there seems no good reason to regard it as the posthumous execution of his will. Nevertheless the authorities duly approved the priest's procedure. The documents show that having been promptly informed of the legitimation the district commissioner's office in Mistelbach notified the Braunau finance department; they also wrote to the episcopal secretariat in St Pölten and the governor's office in Vienna requesting confirmation of the legality of the procedure in Döllersheim. In both cases an affirmative answer was received. A communication addressed to the Governor's Office in Vienna dated 6 October 1876 reads: 'On 6 September 1876 we addressed an inquiry to the Imperial District Finance Department in Braunau as to whether the customs official Alois Schicklgruber should be permitted to adopt the name of "Alois Hitler".[60] The Governor's Office forwarded the letter on 16 October to the Episcopal Administration in St Pölten, having appended a minute in which they asked for written proof of the legitimation and sought an assurance that the procedure adopted by the priest concerned had been 'in accordance with the regulations laid down on 12 September 1868 by the Minister of the Interior'.[61] The reply dated 25 November and signed by Bishop Matthaeus Joseph reads:

In reply to your esteemed minute . . . the Episcopal Administration has the honour to . . . inform you that the registration of the legitimation of Alois Schicklgruber, born 7 June 1837 to Georg Hitler and his spouse M. Anna Hitler née Schicklgruber . . . was entered in the baptismal register of the parish of Döllersheim by the parish priest within his competence and in accordance with . . . the regulations laid down on 12 September 1868 by the Minister of the Interior.[62]

On 30 November the Governor's Office wrote to the Mistelbach District Commissioner's Office:

In accordance with the minute of 25 November 1876 from the Episcopal Administration in St Pölten . . . and by virtue of the registration of legitimation, the customs official Alois Schicklgruber is fully entitled to bear his father's surname, 'Hitler'. The matters raised in your letters of 6 October and 2 November of this year are hereby settled and we would request you to communicate the same to the party concerned.[63]

On 8 December, however, the Mistelbach District Commissioner's Office sent a further inquiry to the Governor's Office seeking guidance as to whether the name on Alois Schicklgruber's papers might now be amended to 'Alois Hitler'. In reply they received a communication dated 27 December to the effect that 'the questions raised yet again in your letter of 8 December 1876 . . . were answered on 30 November 1876'.[64] The matter was now closed.

The real motive behind Alois Schicklgruber's legitimation has hitherto remained a mystery. The key to that mystery is also the key to the identity of Adolf Hitler's grandfather.

It has sometimes been suggested that this man was the illegitimate son of a Strones farmer called Trummelschlager, since it was in his house and not in her parental home that Maria Anna Schicklgruber gave birth to her son. Görlitz, for example, writes: 'While still a child Alois Schicklgruber went to live with Johann Georg's brother [Johann Nepomuk Hüttler]. . . . Was his brother the father of Maria Anna's child . . . or could it have been the peasant Trummelschlager in whose house in Strones the ageing spinster gave birth to her baby?'[65] Koppensteiner may have been hinting at the same thing when in 1937 he suggested that 'the child's mother had been in service with its godfather'.[66] Trummelschlager did indeed stand godfather at the child's baptism and, being illiterate, appended his mark to the baptismal register, but there are no grounds whatsoever for supposing that he was Alois's father. In his will he left nothing either to the mother or to her child. There is a more plausible explanation for the fact that Alois was born in his house. Twenty years earlier, as we have already seen, Maria Anna's parents had sold their holding to their son Josef and gone to live in the 'free lodging' provided for them under the contract of sale. There would have been no room in this tiny dwelling for the forty-two-year-old mother and her new-born child, and she was thus compelled to seek asylum elsewhere. Again it must be said that there is no substance whatever in the theory, first propounded by Frank, that Maria Schicklgruber did not return to Strones until just before the birth of her child.

In this context particular significance attaches to the fact that in *Mein Kampf* Hitler's father is described as 'the son of a poor cottager',[67] a description which has misled unsuspecting National Socialist biographers to describe Alois Hitler as the son of a Spital farmer. Hitler paid several visits to Spital – in 1905, 1906 and 1908, and again when on leave during the First World War. He knew a great deal about his family history and his allusion to the 'small cottager' was patently neither a mistake nor an accident. Indeed his relations in Spital have stated that, during his last visit there, a discussion took place in the course of which it transpired that Johann Nepomuk Hüttler was their common forebear.[68]

Hüttler died in 1888 and today not even his direct descendants know what he looked like.[69] The most that can be said is that there is a distinct family resemblance between Hitler's relations in Spital, Mistelbach and Langfeld, the Schmidts and Koppensteiners, who can be shown beyond doubt to be directly descended from Johann Nepomuk. The fact that some of them look surprisingly like Adolf Hitler is readily explicable, for his mother, Klara Pölzl,[70] was a granddaughter of Johann Nepomuk Hüttler and the sister of Theresia Schmidt, a Pölzl from Spital and the forebear of the present Waldviertel Hitlers. Again, Leo Raubal, born in 1906 to Adolf Hitler's half-sister Angela, herself the issue of her father's second marriage to the (wholly unrelated) Franziska Matzelsberger, bears an astonishing likeness not only to Adolf Hitler who, through his mother, was descended from Johann Nepomuk, but also to the latter's proven descendants in the Waldviertel. This fact must be regarded as one of the most important links in the chain of evidence; for the resemblance can only be traced back to a common ancestor – in the case of Leo Raubal through Adolf's father, Alois Hitler, and in the case of the Waldviertel Hitlers, through Adolf's maternal grandmother, Johanna Pölzl, née Hüttler. That ancestor was Johann Nepomuk Hüttler.

A careful evaluation of all the relevant documents – most of them as yet unpublished – and of the information supplied by Hitler's relations, has made it possible to determine the identity of Adolf's paternal grandfather with some degree of certainty. Here again all the evidence points to Johann Nepomuk Hüttler, the brother of Adolf's putative grandfather, Georg Hiedler. In other words Johann Nepomuk was not only Adolf's paternal, but also his maternal great-grandfather, while Adolf himself was the issue of a union between Alois Hitler and the woman who was both the latter's niece and the daughter of his half-sister.

If, then, Johann Nepomuk was the father of Alois Schicklgruber there is a perfectly plausible explanation for the otherwise inexplicable postponement of the latter's legitimation until the ripe age of thirty-nine. Such a step was clearly out of the question during the lifetime of Hüttler's wife, Eva Maria, a domineering, matriarchal peasant woman whom he had married in 1829 when he was twenty-two and she thirty-seven. Until this woman's death, therefore, Alois had to retain his mother's name. Yet it might well be asked how Alois was able to live in the Hüttler household until the age of sixteen without its mistress either suspecting or discovering that he was her husband's illegitimate offspring, and adulterously engendered at that – a fact galling to any wife, even one living in Lower Austria where forty per cent of all children were born out of wedlock.[71] This question is easily answered. There can be no doubt that Eva Maria Hüttler believed Alois to be the child of her fifty-year-old brother-in-law, Georg Hiedler, who cohabited with Maria Anna Schicklgruber, first in Strones and then in Klein-Motten. She could not have known that her husband had urged his brother to marry Alois's mother so that he, Johann Nepomuk, could without difficulty introduce the child into his own household on the pretext that he was his nephew.

During his thirty-five years of prosperous retirement in Spital, Hüttler furthered the fortunes of his family by an astute policy of marriage alliances and the acquisition of the only inn in the village.[72] When he died on 17 September 1888 his heirs were surprised to find their expectations disappointed, for the executor's statement simply contained the entry, 'Liquid assets: none to hand'.[73] The cash had presumably been made over a short while previously to Alois Hitler, the man who, by 1876 at the latest, had come to be regarded as sole heir by Nepomuk's daughter, Walburga, and her husband Josef Rommeder amongst others. But there is no reliable evidence to show whether in fact he received the money as Johann Nepomuk's descendants suppose – no doubt correctly, for in the year of Hüttler's death Alois was able to purchase what was, even by present standards, a comparatively imposing dwelling in Wörnharts, a hamlet tucked away in a valley not far from Spital. He acquired this substantially built house with large courtyard, stables, barn, garden and additional land from Franz Weber, a farmer, for the price of some 4500 gulden.[74]

Now it can be shown that, until the windfall of 1888, Alois Hitler had not possessed any private means. True, he was a comparatively well-paid official, but the vicissitudes of family life had constituted a steady drain on his earnings. At the time of his early retirement on grounds of health, seven years after Hüttler's death, his annual salary was 1100 gulden,[75] together with a local allowance of 220 gulden in Passau and 250 gulden in Linz. He continued to live in rented premises until 1892, for he did not move to Wörnharts on acquiring the house there in 1888. How much rent he paid is not known but it was probably between 8 and 10 gulden a month, which would have left him about 1000 gulden a year. Taxation was negligible.[76] In 1895 Alois, with his wife and two children, Alois and Angela, were able to live comfortably on his salary, which was a good deal higher that that, for instance, of the headmaster of a private school, who was then regarded as typical of the prosperous upper middle class. Nevertheless his expenses between 1884 and 1888 must have made heavy inroads into whatever savings he may have had. During this period his second wife, Franziska Matzelsberger, fell ill and died. He also lost three of his children – Gustav and Ida, both at the age of two and, shortly before Adolf was born, a baby son, Otto. The undertakers' bills,[77] combined with the cost of medical attendance, medicaments and hospital treatment, must have completely swallowed up the 230 gulden Alois had received from his uncle Franz Schicklgruber in 1876. For by 1888 he would seem to have found it necessary to borrow 800 gulden from the trust fund of his children, Alois and Angela.[78] It was only after Hüttler's death that his situation changed dramatically. Thenceforward Alois never wanted either for money or for property. In addition to the house at Wörnharts he also acquired houses and land at Lambach and Leonding.[79] In October 1892, three years before his retirement at the age of fifty-eight, he was in a position to offer a mortgage of 4000 gulden to Johann Hobiger, the farmer who bought his Wörnharts property for 7000 gulden.

Thus Alois, whose Hitler and Schicklgruber forebears had all been of peasant stock, was the first of his line to seek to rise in the world and to escape from a tradition which continues to this day in the ancestral village of the Hitler family.

CHAPTER TWO

Childhood and Youth

The conditions in which Adolf Hitler grew up differed materially from those experienced by his father, whom in other respects he so much resembled. Both were of a markedly domineering disposition which, however, manifested itself differently in either case; both possessed exceptional charisma; both ruthlessly cast off their origins. Again, the son – like his father – was singleminded, extremely intelligent, impatient, restless and endowed with an intellectual curiosity which enabled him to acquire with ease a fund of knowledge that astonished laymen and specialists alike. Both were consistent in the pursuit of their aims and both exercised an authority that was cold and calculating; they knew how to gain power and how to wield it; knew, too, how to make a convincing and lasting impression on their immediate associates whom at the same time they despised. Both were outstanding, successful. Alois, the illegitimate son of a middle-aged peasant-woman, started life in a small village where only a few of the inhabitants could so much as write their own names. At first handicapped by an inadequate education, he rose to become a respected official who could afford to disregard the social conventions of the localities where he lived and to ignore the opinions of his neighbours. Adolf, the civil servant's son, born in a small frontier town, and likewise inadequately educated, was to become for a time the most powerful man in the world.

But during their earliest years – a period psychologists hold to be of supreme importance in a child's development – the influences at work in either case could hardly have been more different. Until his fifth year, Alois lived in the tiny village of Strones, where he was looked after by a grandfather in his seventies and a mother in her early forties. On reaching school age he moved to Spital and a more normal life in Johann Nepomuk's family.

The circumstances in which Adolf grew up were totally different. His mother was only twenty-nine years old when he was born and her love for him was deep and tender. In Strones, Alois had felt himself an outsider in a middle-aged world, whereas in Braunau Adolf was cosseted, the apple of his mother's eye – a comparatively young mother who, having lost three of her children in a single year,[1] concentrated all her devotion on this one child. Always alert and intelligent, he soon discovered how to twist her round his little finger.

For Alois, the move from Strones to Spital marked a happy turning-point. There for the first time he experienced the warmth of a home and the loving guidance of Johann Nepomuk, a man only thirty years his senior who, to his sorrow, had no legitimate male heir to perpetuate his name, but only three daughters. In his house, Alois enjoyed the stimulating company of young playmates while the pretty village provided him with opportunities for self-development. All these advantages his son enjoyed from birth. Believing Adolf to be sickly and delicate, his mother watched over and protected him with anxious solicitude.[2] If his father sometimes let fly and if, on occasion, his hand was heavy, this in no way signified any deprivation of love. Alois himself had learnt early on how to hold his own against an elderly and not very flexible world, against his old grandfather, against his middle-aged mother and latterly, at Strones, against an embittered, frustrated stepfather, forty-five years his senior. His early years had been spent among illiterates, but he had eagerly taught himself reading and writing, eventually becoming proficient in both, whereas Adolf was only six years old when he learnt to read and write. His father read books and newspapers and was fond of discussing the technicalities of bee-keeping. He is even said to have contributed to professional journals, though there is no documentary evidence for this. His relations in Spital and Linz know of it only by 'hearsay'. Even as a young boy, Adolf used to hear about 'what was going on in the world', and his father's dogmatic pronouncements stimulated him to interpret events after his own fashion.

The family, consisting of the baby Adolf, his elder half-brother, Alois, and his half-sister, Angela, enjoyed almost ideal conditions. They occupied the upper part of the Gasthaus Zum Pommer the most imposing house in that part of Braunau. Behind the building there was a large open space for the children to romp in, while the banks of the River Inn provided yet another playground. The house itself was so solidly built that none of the noise from the public rooms below could penetrate to the Hitlers' living quarters. Yet it would not appear that Braunau exerted any lasting influence on Adolf, despite the opening words of *Mein Kampf*: 'Today it seems to me providential that Fate should have chosen Braunau on the Inn as my birthplace. For this little town lies on the boundary between two German states which, we of the younger generation, at least, have made it our life work to reunite by every means at our disposal.'[3]

Until 1892 nothing of note happened in the Hitler household. Then, in May of that year when Adolf was just three, his father went to Vienna[4] and remained there until 6 June. There are no documents or witnesses to tell us what he was doing there, and his journey was, perhaps, less significant than the fact that at this time he borrowed 600 gulden, or nearly half a year's salary, his collateral being his property in Wörnharts.[5] Now, besides his wife, Alois always kept a mistress, and it seems probable that he handed over this sum to Therese Schmidt, his illegitimate daughter, on the occasion of the birth at Schwertberg of her son, Fritz Rammer who, incidentally, bore a striking resemblance to Alois junior.[6] It is conceivable, of course, that his visit to the capital may have had some connection with his promotion to the rank of Customs Officer Grade I (Acting) in August of that year. Since there was no provision for that grade in Braunau where twenty-one years of his life had been spent, this entailed a move to Passau in Bavaria.

While serving in Braunau he had occasionally abandoned his family for a month or more during the summer and stayed in lodgings in Braunau Altstadt so as to be within easy reach of his hives in the valley nearby.[7] In Passau, too, he spent little time at home, for he made daily excursions to Hailbach in Austria where his bees were kept, returning home late at night. Adolf cannot have seen very much of his father. Indeed it may have been at this time that Klara adopted the habit, noted by August Kubizek after Alois's death, of emphasizing her words and injunctions by pointing to a rack of her husband's pipes which stood on the kitchen shelf.[8]

Another son, Edmund, was born on 24 March 1894, not long before Adolf's fifth birthday. The arrival of this younger brother may for a time have ousted him from the centre of the stage. A week later his father was again transferred, this time to Linz, while the family remained behind in Passau, no doubt because Klara was unwilling to travel with so young a baby.

For a whole year the Hitler children were virtually deprived of their father's company, seeing him only during his rare visits. This meant that Adolf was removed from his immediate sphere of influence.

Young Alois and Angela, now in the senior classes at school, were expected to help with the household chores under their stepmother's supervision, while Adolf was left to do very much as he pleased. To this period spent on German soil can be attributed his predilection for the Austro-Bavarian dialect, a form of speech with which he was later to hold millions literally spellbound. His use of local idioms when talking to Bavarian building workers some forty years later was no affectation designed to curry favour, but a completely natural and spontaneous relapse into his 'home' dialect.

In April 1895 the Hitler family were reunited in Linz before moving to Hafeld near Lambach on Traun[9] where Alois had bought a house and nine acres of land.[10] This marked an important stepping-stone in Adolf's life, for on 1 May of that year he entered the single class primary school at Fischlam near Lambach.[11] This meant not only a perceptible curtailment of his independence but also his submission to discipline outside the parental home, as well as the acceptance of other children on an equal footing. Another change was the premature retirement of his father as a result of ill-health on 25 June, after forty years of service. Despite his bee-keeping and farming, Alois now had far more time to devote to his son who, he hoped, would one day acquire sufficient qualifications to enter the civil service.[12] These ambitions were encouraged by Adolf's undoubted aptitude at school. His teacher, Karl Mittermaier, awarded him top marks. In 1896 he entered the second class of the denominational school of the ancient Benedictine foundation at Lambach, where he was to remain until the spring of 1898. Here again he invariably got top marks from his teacher, Franz Rechberger. He was, as he later liked to recall, also a choir-boy in the Junior Choral Institute where he joined in the singing lessons in his spare time.[13] As a server and a member of the foundation's boys' choir he must have heard a great deal about Abbot Hagen who was well known to everyone in Lambach. The abbot's coat of arms, like the ring on his finger, contained a stylized swastika which he had also had carved on the pulpit. In *Mein Kampf* Hitler states that the refinement and solemn splendour of the glittering church festivals led him to believe that the Catholic priesthood was 'the highest and most desirable ideal'.[14] Some of his fellow pupils and school friends in fact followed the career to which Adolf had briefly aspired, among them Balduin Wiesmayr who subsequently became abbot of Wilhering near Linz, and Johann Haudum who officiated at Leonding from 1938 to 1943. The latter was responsible for looking after Hitler's parents' grave which had been purchased 'in perpetuity' and hence was exempt from levelling.[15]

The family home in Hafeld, sold in the spring of 1897 to the Viennese nobleman Ritter Conrad von Zdekauer, was an imposing one and as its owner Alois Hitler was treated with awe and respect by the villagers; indeed the whole family was held in high esteem. At the same time, Adolf's own attainments had earned him the praise of his school teachers at Fischlam and Lambach. All this gave him an early insight into the important political role played by factors such as property, attainments, influence, appearances and prestige. In later years Hitler seldom referred to Lambach, but he always retained a soft spot for Fischlam where, between 1895 and 1896, he had first learned to read and write. In 1939 he revisited the place, sat at his old desk and subsequently bought the school house so that a new building might be erected in its stead.[16]

On 21 January 1896 Adolf's sister Paula was born, thus ousting Edmund from his position as youngest child, a change that can only have been beneficial to Adolf's development. Throughout his life he remained singularly attached to this sister. He looked after her during his mother's illness in 1907 and later made over to her the whole of the monthly orphans' pension of 25 kronen. His paternal interest in her affairs persisted, even though in later years, when he was the most powerful man in Germany, she would covertly, and within the limit of her meagre resources, help those who had been condemned in his name.[17] Under the pseudonym 'Paula Wolf' she was in charge of Hitler's household from 1936 onwards.

By 1896 there were five children in the Hitler ménage – seven people in all – which must have meant a lively existence for young Adolf. His father often took refuge at the local inn where he would sit drinking wine or beer, reading the newspapers, and enjoying the pleasures of an early retirement after his forty years of successful service. A selfmade man he proudly sported moustaches modelled on those of his emperor. In carving out his own career he had spared neither himself nor his family, and his resulting self-confidence was reflected in his speech, which was interlarded with foreign terms. Like many selftaught and selfmade men with pretensions to learning, he believed it necessary to make known his attainments by using Latinisms. His son, however, with his fine ear for dialect and idiosyncratic turns of speech, never succumbed to this particular weakness. He used foreign words correctly and then only for the sake of precision, as an alternative to the vague circumlocutions often found in German.

Alois's holding in Hafeld amounted to nine acres. Farming it was no easy task, since for thirty-five years or more he had had little direct connection with the land, and his children were still too young to be of much help. Consequently, during Adolf's first years at school, his father grew increasingly short-tempered. Indeed he made life such a misery for his fourteen-year-old son Alois that in 1896 the boy was finally driven away from home. Thereafter Adolf, though not the eldest of the Hitler children, was treated as such by his father, who feared he might turn into a good-for-nothing like his half-brother.[18] As the centre of his father's attention he was subjected to ceaseless pressure. Yet it would seem improbable that the boy was influenced in any way by his father's criticism of political developments in Austria at a time when the Germans living there were beginning to feel anxious about their status.

There is little to indicate what part was played by Angela and her brother Alois in young Adolf's development. Angela, whose daughter Geli was later to become the love of his life, continued for some thirty years to enjoy his confidence. Indeed she was to be his unobtrusive and self-effacing housekeeper from 1928 until 1935 when she disappeared from his entourage as it were overnight, having, it would seem, blotted her copybook by helping Göring to acquire a plot of land opposite Hitler's in Berchtesgaden.[19] Adolf had never felt any affinity for his halfbrother, Alois, who had become a waiter on leaving the family fold. After a chequered career,* he settled in Berlin where he opened a restaurant, the 'Alois'. Hitler, by this time in power, refused to have anything to do with him and forbade all mention of his name.

In July 1897 Hitler's father sold his property in Hafeld and settled in Lambach am Traun, a place of some 1700 inhabitants.[20] He and his family lived for about six months at No. 58 (later the Leingartner Inn), and then moved into a house belonging to Zoebl, the miller, where they remained until 1898. Next door were the premises of the

---

*Between 1900 and 1902 he was twice imprisoned for theft and eventually left Germany for Paris. In 1909 he went to Ireland, married and later moved to Liverpool where his son William Patrick was born. Back in Germany during the twenties he was convicted of bigamy and again went to prison, after which he returned to England.

blacksmith, Preisinger,[21] so that every day young Adolf was subjected to the noise and bustle of the mill and to the din from the smithy. The new surroundings may have suited his father who now embarked on a life of sociability, though he probably missed his bee-keeping. But Adolf, sensitive as he always was to noise, does not appear to have retained particularly happy memories of this period. Whether these circumstances were responsible for his lifelong and otherwise inexplicable aversion to horses and horse-riding can only be surmised.

It was at this time that Hitler, to quote his own words, 'became more and more enthusiastic about everything that was in any way connected with war or military affairs'.[22] Kubizek's assertion, that Hitler as a youth was utterly averse to anything connected with war or even soldiers,[23] was a piece of propaganda intended to present his former friend as a peace-lover. Hitler's own recollection is corroborated by a classmate, Balduin Wiesmayr, who said: 'What he liked best was playing at war.'[24] After 1939 his school friend of Leonding days, Franz Winter, would often recall that 'as a boy he used to chase us, and now he's doing it again'.[25] Another of his classmates, Johann Weinberger, also testified to Hitler's boyhood predilection for warlike games. On these occasions he would initiate 'wars' between the boys of Leonding and those of Untergaumberg when, said Weinberger, 'we Leondingers, with Hitler for our captain, were the Boers while the Untergaumbergers were the English'.[26] There can be little doubt that even in those days Hitler was conscious of his magnetic personality. His allusions to his outstanding gift for oratory when still a schoolboy are corroborated without exception by his fellow pupils. He writes in *Mein Kampf*: 'I believe that even then my oratorical talent was being developed in the form of more or less violent arguments with my schoolmates. I had become a little ringleader.'[27]

In November 1898 Alois bought a house close to the cemetery at Leonding near Linz.* At the end of the following February the whole family moved in. Adolf was then not quite nine years old, and soon after the move he started going to the Leonding – his third – primary school, which he continued to attend until September 1900.

---

*After the Anschluss in 1938 an American wanted to buy the Leonding house in order to transport it to the United States and put it on exhibition there. For the place was long regarded as the Führer's parental home and after 1938 the 'Hitler House' became an object of pilgrimage for thousands of people from all over the world.

On 2 February Edmund died of measles. Adolf was now Alois's only surviving son by Klara and he thereafter concentrated all his hopes on the boy. In September 1900 he began attending the state secondary school in Linz. There are in existence two school photographs from which we can deduce how greatly this new turning-point affected Adolf. One is of the fourth form at the Leonding Primary School, the other of the first form at the Linz Secondary School. In the Leonding picture we see a very self-possessed, almost 'Führer-like' young Hitler, evidently anxious to attract attention. He is standing above and behind his teacher, proud and erect in the middle of the back row, his arms crossed over his chest, with a hint already of his famous quiff of hair. Little of this self-confidence is to be seen in the Linz photograph in which he is again standing in the back row, but this time at the far end, with a sulky expression on his face. He looks hunched up, as though not really caring whether he is noticed or not.

During the first years of his attendance at the secondary school Hitler continued to live at home in Leonding. Then his father died suddenly and quite unexpectedly in January 1903, and in the spring of that year Adolf went to live in the school hostel in Linz. Here he made friends with Fritz Seidl, later to be a civil servant, and with the Haudum boys, one of whom eventually became priest of Leonding. Together they used to concoct 'epics'[28] which, twenty years later, Hitler described in *Mein Kampf* as the typical expression of his character.[29]

Until the end of his life he continued to make appreciative remarks about Leonding, that extraordinarily compact agricultural village with its mill and its smithy, situated in close country some three miles from Linz. On moving there, Alois thought he had at last attained his heart's desire. Not only was he within easy distance of a town but in addition possessed a fine house and a pretty garden and was no longer compelled, as in Passau and Braunau, to walk miles in order to visit his hives which could now be kept almost underneath his bedroom window. He also had a lodger, Elizabeth Plöckinger,[30] whose rent helped to pay his monthly household bills.

Many of Hitler's remarks in later years reveal the fact that his critical attitude towards the Church originated at this time when he began to share his father's view of certain of its aspects which, in Lambach, had commanded his awe and admiration.

In his primary schools at Fischlam, Lambach and Leonding he had done exceptionally well, and when he joined the first form at the secondary school in Linz he made good progress in history, geography and drawing, at all of which, according to his master Sixtl, he was a good deal more proficient than many a teacher.[31] Nevertheless at the end of the year he did not move up into the next class. Forty years later, in the Wolfsschanze, he said with reference to Sixtl:

I was fifteen or sixteen, an age at which one still writes poetry. I used to go to all the shows and so on labelled 'Adults Only'. There's a time when you're curious about everything. Then, one evening, I went to the cinema in the Südbahnhof at Linz. Absolute rubbish! It was a charity show put on by the Red Cross – dubious films. Nothing but filth, really. Oddly broadminded, the Austrian government, in some respects! My teacher, Sixtl, was there too. 'So you're spending in a good cause, too, are you?' he asked me. 'Yes, sir!' I answered and he laughed. But I felt a bit uncomfortable in that murkey spot.[32]

The move from a small, familiar school in a village to a large, strange one in a town did not suit Hitler. The only thing he liked about it was the walk of four or five miles between his home and the school in the Steingasse.[33] From his report at the end of his first school year both Adolf and his parents learnt that his work had been 'uneven' and that he had not done well enough in mathematics and natural history to move up into the next class. He therefore had to remain in the first form. In *Mein Kampf* he writes of this period:

My report cards at this time, depending on the subject and my estimation of it, showed nothing but extremes. Side by side with 'laudable' and 'excellent', stood 'adequate' or even 'inadequate'. But far my best accomplishments were in geography and even more so in history. These were my favourite subjects, in which I led the class.

His explanation for this is perfectly straightforward and probably tallies with the facts: 'What gave me pleasure, I learned. . . . What seemed to me unimportant . . . or was otherwise unattractive to me, I sabotaged completely.'[34]

Alois Hitler, having made his own way up in the world and been disappointed in his eldest boy (Alois jun.), who had shown himself neither able nor willing to follow in his father's footsteps, now put so much pressure on his intelligent younger son that he killed what pleasure in his work the boy might have had. 'It was decided that I should go to high school,' Hitler later wrote in *Mein Kampf*.

From my whole nature, and to an even greater degree from my temperament, my father believed he could draw the inference that the humanistic

Gymnasium would represent a conflict with my talents. A *Realschule* seemed to him more suitable. In this opinion he was especially strengthened by my obvious aptitude for drawing; a subject which in his opinion was neglected in the Austrian *Gymnasiums*. Another factor may have been his own laborious career which made humanistic study seem impractical in his eyes, and therefore less desirable. It was his basic opinion and intention that, like himself, his son would and must become a civil servant. It was only natural that the hardship of his youth should enhance his subsequent achievement in his eyes, particularly since it resulted exclusively from his own energy and iron diligence. It was the pride of the selfmade man which made him want his son to rise to the same position in life or, of course, even higher if possible. . . . It was simply inconceivable to him that I might reject what had become the content of his whole life. Consequently my father's decision was simple, definite, and clear; in his own eyes I mean, of course. Finally, a whole lifetime spent in the bitter struggle for existence had given him a domineering nature, and it would have seemed intolerable to him to leave the final decision in such matters to an inexperienced boy, having as yet no sense of responsibility. . . . This would have seemed a sinful and reprehensible weakness in the exercise of his proper parental authority and responsibility. . . . I was forced into opposition for the first time in my life. Hard and determined as my father might be in putting through plans and purposes once conceived, his son was just as persistent and recalcitrant in rejecting an idea which appealed to him not at all, or in any case very little. I did not want to become a civil servant. . . . All attempts on my father's part to inspire me with love or pleasure in this profession by stories from his own life accomplished the exact opposite. I yawned and grew sick to my stomach at the thought of sitting in an office deprived of my liberty; ceasing to be master of my own time.[35]

Twenty years later Hitler was to declare that he deliberately did badly at school in order to frustrate his father's wishes, for only downright failure would enable him to get his own way and obtain permission to become an artist. 'I believed', he writes, 'that once my father saw how little progress I was making at the *Realschule*, he would let me devote myself to my dream, whether he liked it or not.'[36]

Alois Hitler's insistence that his son should become a successful civil servant like himself had the effect, as Adolf was later to point out, of forcing him, at the age of eleven, into 'opposition' and recalcitrance.[37] Whatever he himself may have had to say about the matter – and it was certainly not for want of intelligence or talent that he failed to earn better marks at school – all the circumstances go to show that young Hitler already regarded systematic and intensive study, unless self-appointed, as an intolerable imposition. Hence he never shone at subjects requiring a combination of talent and solid spadework, but only in those which demanded no initial effort. His achievements were determined solely by his inclinations, his interests and passing enthusiasms.

During his year in the second form at Linz, Adolf lost his father. Alois had been carried home after collapsing at the inn. In *Mein Kampf* Adolf Hitler writes that, despite tensions and squabbles, he was very fond of his father.[38] Beside his bier he broke down and sobbed uncontrollably.[39] Subsequently, in compliance with his mother's advice, proffered out of a desire to fulfil her husband's last wishes,[40] Adolf continued to go to school, but in his own mind he was more than ever determined to become an artist rather than a civil servant. Shortly before his death, Alois had accompanied Adolf to Linz and shown him round the Central Customs Office where he intended his son to work one day.[41] The pointlessness of that visit was now more than ever apparent to the boy. It seems clear that in many ways Adolf was liberated by his father's death. He grew lazy and was sometimes uncooperative in class. At home in Leonding he was the only 'man' in a house full of women – his mother, his aunt, Johanna Pölzl, the lodger Elizabeth Plöckinger, and his sister Paula.

Klara attempted to solace her grief for the loss of her husband by paying a visit to her parents in Spital and by busying herself with her beloved children, Adolf and Paula. Fate had not treated Frau Hitler very kindly, nor had her marriage to her cousin, a childhood friend and neighbour twenty-three years her senior, come up to expectations. Clever, vigorous and domineering, Alois had completely overshadowed the young peasant girl so that her own personality had never had a chance to develop. Kubizek describes her manner as modest and reserved. When he first met her she was in her middle forties and only recently widowed. She had borne Alois six children, of whom only Adolf and Paula had survived. Her son's friend noted that her features were careworn and that she seemed very tired.[42]

In April 1904, at the age of fifteen, Adolf was in his final term in the third form at secondary school. On 22 May he was confirmed and afterwards saw a film show for the first time in his life. Being determined always to remain 'his own master' he was not interested in the fact that in Austria four years' attendance at secondary school entitled a pupil to a state grant enabling him to enter an officer cadet training college. As before, he went unwillingly to school, his most hated subject being French. His total lack of interest inevitably affected the quality of his work and, in order to qualify for entry into the fourth form at the beginning of the new school year, he had to retake the French examination. This he did in the autumn of 1904 under the supervision of Dr Eduard Huemer. Although this teacher regarded Hitler as 'distinctly talented', he made him promise that, after passing his examination, he would enter the fourth form at a different school.[43] Huemer had taught him German as well as French and knew his pupil well, as is shown by his testimony at Hitler's trial in Munich in 1924. The boy, he said, had been 'distinctly talented, if in a rather narrow sense, but he lacked self-discipline, being generally regarded as obstinate, high-handed, intransigent and fiery-tempered. It was obviously difficult for him to fit in at school. He was not a hard worker, for otherwise, with his undoubted gifts, he could hardly have failed to do well.'[44] Why he changed schools long remained a secret upon which the wildest rumours thrive. Thus in 1923 certain political opponents maintained that Hitler had been expelled because, at a school Communion service, he had spat out the Host and put it in his pocket. Three days after this allegation had appeared in the *Münchner Post*, on 27 November 1923, the *Bayerischer Kurier* added the highly fanciful comment that the occurrence had created a 'considerable uproar in Linz'.[45]

In September 1904 Hitler entered the fourth form of the Steyr Senior Secondary School under the headship of Alois Lebeda. He lodged in a house in the 'Thursday Market' (later the Adolf Hitler Platz), where his landlord was Conrad Edler von Cichini.[46] Thirty years after leaving school he described his lodgings:

To me, Steyr seemed a horrible place. Linz was national [Pan-German], Steyr red and black [Socialist and Clerical]. I shared a small room at the back with a schoolmate called Gustav; what his surname was I don't remember. The room was nice enough, but the courtyard was a sinister spot. I used to take pot shots at the rats there. Our landlady was very fond of us; actually she always seemed to like us better than her own husband. It wasn't *him* that wore the trousers. She'd go for him like a hellcat. Once there was a real row. I'd already asked her if she would mind not giving me such hot coffee, as I was always in such a hurry in the morning that I couldn't drink it. One morning I pointed out that, though it was already half past the hour, I still hadn't got my coffee. She told me it wasn't half past yet, whereupon her husband said: 'It's true, Petronella, it was half past five minutes ago.' Then she really flew off the handle. Things had just begun to simmer down that evening when the real disaster happened. He had to go outside. . . . While he was out she bolted the door. We looked at each other and said: 'Now there'll be a rumpus!' We quite liked her. He shouted: 'Petronella, open the door!' She laughed, and wandered up and down humming to herself but did nothing. Having tried exhortation he fell to beseeching her. 'Petronella, do please open the door! Petronella, you wouldn't do a thing like that to me, would you?' – 'Wouldn't I just!' And then he changed his tune. 'Adolf! You're to open the door at once!' – 'I forbid you to!' she told me. 'Your wife has forbidden me to!' I replied. She left him out there until seven in the morning. All he did, when he came in with the milk, was to look reproachful. We didn't half despise him. She was about thirty-three. As for him, his beard made it difficult to tell, but I'd put him at about forty-five. He came of impoverished aristocratic stock. . . . Austria's positively crawling with impoverished aristocrats. . . . His wife was always giving us little extras. In Austria the students' landladies were called *Crux*. Ah, those were the days! But it wasn't all jam for me. Wriggling out of my work at school was pretty difficult, especially when exam time came round. . . . I learnt how to ski on the Damberg. At the end of term we always used to have a big celebration. They were pretty riotous affairs with a lot of drinking. On one of these occasions I got drunk for the first and last time in my life. We'd been given our reports and were supposed to leave for home. Now that term was over, our landlady got a bit smarmy. We went out on the sly to a country inn where we drank and had a high old time. Just what happened I don't know, I had to piece it together afterwards. . . . I'd been carrying my report in my pocket. The next day I was woken by a dairymaid, who found me lying beside the road. I must have looked a dreadful sight because when I got home my landlady exclaimed: 'For goodness sake, Adolf, what a pickle you're in!' I had a bath and she gave me some black coffee to drink. Then she said: 'Tell me, what was your report like?' I felt in my pocket. The report wasn't there! 'Heavens!' I said to myself, 'I've got to have something to show my mother!' And then I thought, 'You can tell her you showed it to someone on the train and the wind blew it out of your hands.' But my landlady was insistent: 'Where can it have got to?' 'Someone must have pinched it!' I said. 'Then there's only one thing to be done. You must go back and get a duplicate. Have you any money left?' 'Not a bean!' She gave me five gulden. I went to see the head, who kept me waiting for quite a while. Then he told me that in the meantime the report had been returned to the school torn into four pieces. In a fit of absent-mindedness I'd mistaken it for toilet paper. It really rattled me. What the headmaster said is unrepeatable. It was awful. And I swore by all that was sacred I would never touch drink in my life again. I was given the duplicate. . . . I was horribly embarrassed! When I got back my landlady said: 'And what did he say to you?' 'I'm afraid I can't tell you that. But there's something else I *can* tell you. I shall never drink again in my life.' It certainly taught me a lesson and I never did drink again. Then, light at heart, I set off for home. Not really light at heart, though, because that report wasn't all it should have been.[47]

To say that his report of 11 February 1905 was 'not all that it should have been' was gross understatement. His work in German, French, mathematics and shorthand had been deemed 'not satisfactory'. With the exception of freehand drawing (commendable) and gymnastics (excellent) the report contained nothing above 'fair' or 'satisfactory'.[48] During his first six months at the school he was 'absent without reason' for thirty days in all. On 3 March 1942, talking to his companions in the Wolfsschanze, he repeated the sentiments he had expressed earlier in *Mein Kampf*:

On the whole I probably didn't learn a tenth of what the others did. My preparation was always very quickly done. All the same, I got on all right in history. I often felt sorry for my schoolmates. 'Coming out to play?' 'No, still got work to go.' They sit the exam. They pass! But what indignation if someone comes in by the back door! What's this? We're the ones who worked! – Well, that's how it is. Either you've got it in you or you haven't.[49]

In Steyr Hitler's conduct was no less rebellious and disrespectful than it had been in Linz. Reminiscing on the night of 8 January 1942, he said:

If we hadn't had a few teachers who were prepared to speak up for me, I might have fared badly. . . . One of the masters, König, who taught us French, had been an official inspector of boilers. . . . An explosion had left him with a speech impediment so that there were certain things he found difficult to say. At the first class he took with us I was sitting at the front. He began reading out our names. When he got to mine I didn't budge, just sat and looked at him. Angrily he took me to task. 'My name is not Itler, sir,' says I, 'my name is Hitler!'[50]

Nevertheless, in the autumn of 1905 König's assessment of his attainments in French was no longer 'unsatisfactory', as in February, but 'fair'. On 16 September 1905 Hitler's end of term report was as follows:

Moral behaviour, satisfactory. Application, adequate. Religious instruction, fair. Mathematics, fair. Chemistry and physics, fair. Geometrical drawing

and descriptive geometry, fair (after retaking the examination). Freehand
drawing, excellent. Gymastics, excellent. Singing, satisfactory.[51]

And with this he seems to have been well content.

As a young child Hitler had had his adenoids removed and had also
had measles, but in general his health had been reasonably good.[52]
During his year at this school his teachers noted that he looked unwell,
as though 'sickening for something', and that he remained an outsider.
On 29 January 1941 Professor Gregor Goldbacher, the geometry and
geometrical drawing teacher, stated that 'no doubt as a result of his
father's death and because he was away from home . . . Hitler appeared
somewhat timid and depressed', and further that 'the young student
seemed unwell at the time'. As a newcomer to the town and school,
Goldbacher went on, he was evidently finding it difficult to find his
feet.[53]

What he looked like then can be seen from a sketch made by Sturmlechner, one of his school friends, who drew him in profile. The face in
this portrait seems much too old and grave for a boy of fifteen. Here we
have a slim adolescent with a high, receding forehead, a sharply jutting
nose, and a distinctly prominent chin. The eye is the most dominant
of these ascetic looking features. The ill-combed hair, parted on the
right, hangs down over the forehead. Kubizek's pen portrait of Hitler
as an adolescent, 'a remarkably pale, skinny youth . . . with glistening
eyes',[54] corresponds closely to Sturmlechner's amateurish effort.

Despite his reluctance to continue at school, Adolf could do little
else but obey his mother and try for matriculation. That, at least, is
what he promised to do, though it may be doubted whether he took his
promise seriously. When he finally left school in the autumn of 1905 it
was on account of an ailment which has remained unspecified but was
undoubtedly genuine. As he himself significantly wrote in *Mein Kampf*:

Then suddenly an illness came to my help and in a few weeks decided my
future and the eternal domestic quarrel. As a result of my serious lung ailment, a physician advised my mother in most urgent terms never to send
me into an office. My attendance at the *Realschule* had furthermore to be
interrupted for at least a year. The goal for which I had so long silently
yearned, for which I had always fought, had through this event suddenly
become reality almost of its own accord. Concerned over my illness, my
mother finally consented to take me out of the *Realschule* and let me attend
the Academy.[55]

Hitler was overjoyed. In the meantime he and his mother, herself not in the best of health, travelled by train to Gmünd where they were met at the station by their Spital relations in an ox-cart.[56]

While in Spital he was attended by Dr Karl Keiss of Weitra. He ate well, drank plenty of milk,[57] and made a quick recovery. But he kept himself to himself and spent his time playing the zither, drawing, painting, exploring the beautiful countryside and watching his relations at work in the fields, though never offering to help them. He felt drawn neither to his aunt (on his mother's side) nor to the village children whose interest in the 'grammar school boy' from the city he in no way reciprocated.[58]

He had finally left behind him the school for which (as we learn from Kubizek's account of their many conversations) he nourished so profound a hatred.[59] However his education and his final school report entitled him to apply for entrance to the Vienna Academy of Fine Arts. But now, having at last attained at the age of sixteen the end for which he had vainly striven during his father's lifetime, he was in no hurry to make his application. Nor, because he had been ill, did his mother at first bring any pressure to bear on him. Indeed even if he had wanted to take the entrance examination in the autumn of 1905 it was too late for him to do so. Meanwhile he considered sitting for the next one in the following autumn, and, during May and June of that year, spent some time in Vienna visiting museums and other places of note in the capital.[60] But he did not remain there long enough to take the examination, a step which he put off until the following year. On 7 May he wrote to Kubizek: 'Well, I have arrived safely . . . and am busy exploring. Tomorrow I am going to the Opera to see *Tristan* and the day after that *The Flying Dutchman* etc. Although I find everything very beautiful, I am homesick for Linz. . . .'[61] His confidence may perhaps have been shaken by the works of art he saw in Vienna.[62] But it would seem more probable that he was reluctant to give up his leisurely existence so soon in order to submit, as at school, to a programme that was not self-appointed.

After selling the house in Leonding in June 1905, Frau Klara had moved to Linz where she lived with her two children at No. 31 Humboldtstrasse. Thus Adolf no longer had to walk to town, as he had been doing up till the spring of 1903. In Linz he joined the libraries run by the *Volksbildungsverein* and the *Musealverein*;[63] from 2 October 1906 until 31 January 1906 he took piano lessons with the former military bandmaster, Prewatzky-Wendt;[64] he regularly attended the theatre[65] where he never missed a performance of Wagner's operas; he drew, painted, wrote poetry, composed music, designed bridges, streets, theatres and other buildings, and discussed grandiose and fantastic projects with his friend Kubizek. No longer subject to an imposed routine, he could decide for himself what and what not to do.

Meanwhile his mother's health was deteriorating and she had aged visibly. On 18 January 1907 she entered the Hospital of the Sisters of Mercy where she underwent an operation for cancer of the breast.[66] Though she appeared to recover she was to survive for only eleven months, a period made wretched by the knowledge that her son would continue on his way as ruthlessly and pig-headedly as if 'he was alone in the world'.[67] Meanwhile Adolf left for Vienna in the hope of entering the Academy of Fine Arts. When Kubizek went to see her in the autumn of that year he was shocked by her appearance. 'Frau Klara,' he wrote,

seemed more depressed than usual. Her face was deeply lined, her eyes were lifeless and her tone of voice was weary and resigned. She gave me the impression, now that Adolf was no longer living with her, of having completely let herself go, and she looked older and more of an invalid than before. To make it easier for her son to go she had undoubtedly concealed her condition from him. . . . But now that she was on her own she seemed to me an old and ailing woman.[68]

CHAPTER THREE

Artist and Architect

In September 1907, when his mother's health seemed to improve a
little, Hitler left for Vienna 'armed with a pile of drawings' to sit the
examination for the General School of Painting at the Academy of
Fine Arts – an examination which, he felt convinced, would be 'child's
play'.[1] He was then eighteen years old.

Unlike the majority of the hundred and twelve other candidates[2]
with whom he foregathered at the Academy in the Schillerplatz on the
appointed day, Adolf was full of optimism. Because of the high standards it set the examination was rightly regarded by most entrants as
an ordeal. A glance at the truly formidable list of set themes suffices to
show that the traditionally minded Academy demanded of its aspirants
not only considerable promise but also a high degree of technical skill.
The candidates had to choose two subjects for composition to be
executed in two sessions of three hours each.[3]

On the first day of the examination they were required to select from
the following:

1. Expulsion from Paradise, The Chase, Spring, Building Workers,
   Death, and Rain.
2. The Return of the Prodigal Son, Flight, Summer, Woodcutters,
   Mourning, and Fire.
3. Cain killing Abel, The Return, Autumn, Carters, Joy and Moon-
   light.
4. Adam and Eve discovering Abel's Body, Farewell, Winter, Shepherds, and Dance and Thunderstorm.

The second day's subjects were:
1. An Episode during the Flood, The Ambush, Morning, Mer-
   cenaries, Music, and Prayer.
2. The Magi, Flight (pursuit), Midday, The Beggar, The Fortune-
   teller, and Shipwreck.
3. The Good Samaritan, Pilgrims, End of the Day's Work, The
   Fisherman, The Story-Teller, and The Treasure Hunters.

4. The Binding of Sampson, An Excursion, Night, Slaves, Peace, and The Teacher.[4]

There is no documentary evidence to show which of the themes Hitler chose nor who his examiner was. More significant than either of these questions is the fact that Hitler succeeded where thirty-three of his fellow candidates failed. Having got over the first hurdle, an entrant had then to present what were known as 'sample drawings'; in other words he had to give proof of his abilities other than in the examination room. Hitler showed his 'pile of drawings' made in Urfahr and Linz. This contained relatively few heads, a shortcoming which decided the examining professor to exclude him from the Academy. His discomfiture on this occasion may have prompted his remark many years later to the effect that 'only a genius can get inside the skin of another genius'.[5]

Hitler failed this examination in company with fifty-one other fellow candidates. One of them, Robin Christian Andersen, was later to have a distinguished career in art and to hold leading positions in the very Academy that had once rejected him.

Of the 113 candidates only twenty-eight passed both sections of the entrance examination. In *Mein Kampf* Hitler writes: 'Downcast, I left von Hansen's magnificent building on the Schillerplatz. . . . For what I had just heard about my abilities seemed like a lightning flash suddenly revealing a conflict with which I had long been afflicted, although until then I had no clear conception of its why and wherefore.'[6] What the world might have been spared if Hitler had included a few more 'heads' in his portfolio can only be conjectured. Today there still exist portraits and studies for portraits drawn at this period which would undoubtedly have satisfied the Academy's requirements.

When Hitler went to see the Rector of the Academy, Siegmund l'Allemand, he was told, he relates, that the work he had submitted showed beyond all doubt that he had little aptitude for painting, and that his ability clearly lay in the field of architecture.[7] This judgement is borne out by his surviving drawings. His street scenes, often technically excellent and clearly owing much to the work of the Austrian landscape artist, Rudolf von Alt, contain practically no human figures. Those he does include are not intrinsic to the picture. They stand stiffly and unnaturally in the street like dummies in a shop window. By comparison with Rudolf von Alt, whose streets and buildings form a background to an animated scene peopled by dogs, horse-drawn vehicles and striding figures, Hitler depicts only the buildings. His evident pastiche of Alt's style may well have focused the examining professors' attention on the comparative lack of animation in his work. After his rejection by the Academy's General School of Painting, Hitler applied for admission to the Architectural School, although lacking the necessary qualifications, one of which was matriculation – a fact which he was to lament sixteen years later in *Mein Kampf*.[8] Thus his plans were temporarily thwarted. Moreover it would appear that the acquaintances with whom he was staying were urging him to return to Linz in order to try for his matriculation.[9] Whether Hitler in fact ever seriously contemplated doing so would seem unlikely in view of his profound hatred of school, his aversion to systematic work and his distaste for certain school subjects. However it may have been, he remained in Vienna for a few weeks longer, visiting the city's buildings and museums, an activity he found much more congenial than attending compulsory lessons.

In November 1907 he returned to Urfahr near Linz to look after his mother whose life was now despaired of by her Jewish physician, Dr Eduard Bloch. Hitler took charge of the household, supervised his sister Paula's homework, washed, scrubbed and cooked for the three of them and at the same time assumed the position of head of the family. Dr Bloch, who was personally acquainted both with Adolf and with his mother, declared in November 1938: 'His attachment to his mother was deep and loving. He would watch her every movement so that he might anticipate her slightest need. His eyes, which usually gazed mournfully into the distance, would light up whenever she was relieved of her pain.'[10] On 23 December, the day before Christmas Eve, Hitler accompanied his mother on her last journey to the cemetery at Leonding, where she was laid to rest beside Alois. Bloch recalls: 'In all my forty odd years of practice I had never seen a young man so broken by grief and bowed down by suffering as young Adolf Hitler was that day.'[11] The *faire part* was printed by the Linz firm of Kolndorffer at Hitler's behest:

We, Adolf and Paula Hitler, hereby announce, both in our own names and those of her other relatives, the passing away of our deeply loved, never-to-be-forgotten mother, and/or stepmother, grandmother and sister, Frau Klara Hitler, Senior Customs Officer's widow, who fell asleep . . . on 21 December 1907 at two o'clock in the morning.[12]

Adolf and Paula were now orphans in the full sense of the term. But Hitler was exaggerating when he later wrote in *Mein Kampf*: 'Poverty and hard reality now compelled me to take a quick decision. What little my father had left had been largely exhausted by my mother's grave illness; the orphan's pension to which I was entitled was not enough for me even to live on, and so I was faced with the problem of somehow making my own living.'[13] After describing the years in Vienna as a time 'of study and suffering',[14] he wrote: 'I owe it to that period of my life that I grew hard and am still capable of being hard. And even more I exalt it for tearing me away from the hollowness of that comfortable life.'[15] Now, certain self-styled witnesses would have us believe that Hitler's years in Vienna, which he himself described as the 'most thorough school of my life',[16] were aimlessly frittered away among tramps and petty thieves, the down-and-out flotsam and jetsam of humanity – and this story has been uncritically adopted by all his biographers.[17] Kubizek, too, advanced the same thesis when writing of the period after 1908, although he had ceased to keep company with Hitler in the autumn of that year when he himself was called up. Hence he knew nothing of his friend's subsequent existence save for what he learnt at second hand. His phrase, 'It was the road into the wilderness',[18] bears the stamp of indirect reportage. Nor did Hitler himself ever disclose the truth of the matter.

In the first place his assertion that what little money his father had left had been largely exhausted as a result of his mother's illness is quite untrue.[19] Moreover he neglected to mention the appreciable sum inherited from his mother in 1908. In June 1905, two and a half years before her death, Klara Hitler had sold the house in Leonding for 10,000 kronen, of which she in fact received only 7,480 kronen because of the mortgage still outstanding on the property.[20] Even when depleted by Adolf's and Paula's share of the inheritance,[21] this still left her with 5500 kronen, yielding an annual interest of at least 220 kronen, besides which, since 1903, she had been drawing an annual widow's pension of 1200 kronen. Hence she had more than enough cash in hand to cover the cost of supporting herself and her two children. The sum at the disposal of Frau Hitler and her children, Adolf and Paula, (discounting the proceeds from the sale of the house) was some 120 kronen a month,[22] to which must be added the interest she would have been receiving on the capital inherited from her aunt, Walburga Rommeder, née Hitler, of Spital.[23]

After her marriage in 1853, Walburga had lived at No. 36 Spital where, wealthy and childless, she eventually died. Her handwritten will,[24] drawn up between 1897 and 1903 by a clerk of the court at Weitra in the Waldviertel, was discovered (and identified by the author) in August 1969 in the possession of one of Adolf Hitler's cousins. In this will the testatrix left her entire estate to her sister Johanna (born 1830). She further directed that, in the event of this sister predeceasing her, the estate should pass to Johanna's three daughters, Klara, Johanna and Theresia. When Walburga's sole heir, Johanna, died on 8 February 1906, her three daughters inherited the estate. One of the beneficiaries, Klara, died in 1907 so that her part of the inheritance fell to Adolf and Paula Hitler.

Adolf's share of his father's inheritance produced a monthly income of 58 kronen, in addition to which he was receiving an orphan's pension of 25 kronen. With the large amounts also coming in from Walburga, (Hitler's legacy through his mother and his aunt Johanna Pölzl), he was thus very comfortably off. The rent he paid in Vienna amounted on average to some 10 kronen a month.

At that time a lawyer's salary, after one year's practice in court, was 70 kronen a month, that of a teacher during the first five years of his career, 66 kronen. A post office official earned 60 kronen while an assistant teacher in a Vienna secondary school before 1914 received a monthly salary of 82 kronen.[25] Benito Mussolini who in 1909 lived in Trentino (then Austrian territory) and was both editor of *L'Avenire del Lavoratore* and secretary to the Chamber of Labour, received a combined salary of 120 kronen.[26] Thus 'the hard fate' so often mentioned by Hitler when referring to his years in Vienna can have had nothing to do with straitened circumstances.

The house in which Klara had lived with her two children till the time of her death was owned by a well-to-do woman who began to take an interest in Hitler when, at the beginning of 1908, he was concerning himself with the affairs of his inheritance. Of her own accord, she offered to secure him an introduction to the well-known stage designer, Professor Alfred Roller of the Vienna Handicrafts School (now the Academy of Applied Arts), with whose brother her mother was personally acquainted. The resulting letter is of interest because of the light it sheds on Hitler's character at the time: 'My Dear Mother,' it runs,

I am going to ask you a favour and hope you will forgive me if it is too much of an imposition. I should be immensely grateful if you could write a letter of recommendation to Professor Alfred Roller on behalf of the son of one of my tenants. He wishes to become a painter and has been studying in Vienna since the autumn. He had intended to enter the Academy of Fine Arts but, not having been accepted there, he had recourse instead to a private establishment. . . . He is a serious and ambitious young man of nineteen, mature and sensible beyond his years. He is nice, steadygoing, and comes of a very respectable family. His mother died just before Christmas. . . . The family name is Hitler and the son on whose behalf I am writing to you is called Adolf.

Not long ago we were discussing art and artists and he happened to mention the reputation enjoyed by Professor Roller in the artistic world, a reputation which, he said, was not confined to Vienna alone but could almost be described as worldwide . . . and he went on to speak of his own admiration for the professor and his work.

Hitler had no idea that Roller's name was familiar to me, and when I told him I had known the great man's brother and asked whether it would be a help if he was given a letter of recommendation to the stage director at the *Hofoper*, the young man flushed deeply and his eyes grew bright. . . . I would very much like to help this boy; there is no one, you see, to put in a good word for him or to advise and encourage him. When he went to Vienna he was a stranger and entirely on his own. He had no guide or mentor and had to conduct all his own negotiations when he was trying to find a place that would accept him. He is firmly determined to undertake a regular course of study. From what I know of him so far he won't fritter away his time, since his aim is a serious one. I feel sure that you won't be putting yourself out in an unworthy cause. Indeed you may be doing something really worthwhile.

If you feel able to do so, mother darling, I do beg you to write a few lines of recommendation to Alfred Roller . . . and hope that you will not be vexed if the favour I ask is burdensome to you. . . . He is now waiting for the Board of Guardians to confirm the pension due to him and his sister.[27]

Her request was granted and in due course Professor Roller declared himself willing to receive Hitler. On 8 February the daughter wrote to thank her mother:

You would have thought yourself well rewarded for your pains if you could have seen the boy's radiant face when I sent for him and told him that you had recommended him to Professor Roller and that he would now be able to call on him.

I gave him your card and allowed him to read Professor Roller's letter. I wish you could have seen him! He was beaming as he read the letter in silence and almost with awe, lingering over every word as though he wanted

ARTIST AND ARCHITECT

to learn it by heart. Then, thanking me sincerely, he returned it to me and
asked whether he might write to you to express his gratitude. I told him that
he might.

May heaven reward you for your kindness!... Although nothing has yet
been decided by the Board of Guardians, Hitler is determined to wait no
longer and will be returning to Vienna in a week's time. His official guardian
is a simple-minded innkeeper, a good enough fellow but, I believe, somewhat
limited. He doesn't live here but in Leonding. The boy has to attend to all
the business that really should be dealt with by his guardian. I return
Professor Roller's letter herewith. If you should happen to see him, please
tell him how grateful I am for his kindness in agreeing, despite his busy
life and important engagements, to see young Hitler and give him his advice.
Such good fortune does not befall every young man, a fact which I feel sure
Hitler fully appreciates.[28]

No more than two days later Adolf wrote to thank the old lady.

I wish to offer you, dear madam, my most sincere thanks for your intervention in securing an introduction for me to the great master of stage
design, Professor Roller. It was, I feel sure, overbold on my part to expect
you to put yourself out like this for a complete stranger. So I would beg you
to accept my heartfelt thanks for the steps taken by you which have met with
such success, and also for the card which your much respected daughter was
kind enough to put at my disposal. I will at once take advantage of this most
happy opportunity.

Once again, therefore, with my sincerest thanks, I sign myself very
respectfully yours.

Adolf Hitler[29]

A few days later he again left for Vienna, having regulated at least
part of his affairs in Linz by signing a probate document at the behest
of his official guardian Josef Mayrhofer, the burgomaster of Leonding.
From this time until September he and his friend August Kubizek
lodged at No. 29 Stumpergasse with their Polish landlady, Frau
Zakreys. In *Mein Kampf* Hitler relates that his mood was defiant and
that he was determined to become an architect.[30] That this was no
mere bombast can be shown from other documentary sources.

At nineteen, therefore, Adolf still cherished his dream of one day
making his mark in the world of art, despite his failure to pass the 1907
entrance examination. He now undertook what he had deliberately
shunned while at school – a bout of hard, unremitting, and singleminded work. With the intention of putting his time to profitable use
before sitting the next entrance examination to the Academy, he took

painting lessons from the Viennese sculptor Panholzer, an art master at a senior secondary school and a very experienced teacher.[31] How he made Panholzer's acquaintance, we do not know. Perhaps he had been sent to him by Roller whom he mentioned some thirty years later as having been one of his teachers.[32] Early in 1942, when Hitler learned that Roller's son had been killed on the Eastern Front, he remarked that artists were irreplaceable and reproached Baldur von Schirach for having allowed the young stage designer to be sent into action. 'To think of such a man having his head blown off by some idiot of a Russian!' he said angrily. 'A chap like that's irreplaceable!'[33]

In the autumn of 1908 he again sat the entrance examination to the Academy. Neither the Rector nor any of the other faculty members had changed since the previous year, and their recollection of his earlier attempt would have impaired rather than favoured his chances. This time he failed in the first part of the examination, the part he had successfully completed in 1907. Hence he was not allowed to show the work he had done with such painstaking care and enthusiasm during his year under Panholzer. According to the classifying list for the year 1908–9, he 'was not admitted for the test'.[34]

The abrupt changes that had taken place in his family circumstances since December 1907 had not left him unscathed. The death of his mother while still relatively young had meant that he had 'suddenly' and almost unexpectedly had to 'grow up' and become 'independent', assuming responsibility both for himself and for his sister Paula, seven years his junior. Moreover he had deliberately repudiated the rest of his family and thereby completely isolated himself. The emotional strain of all this profoundly affected the quality of his work and during the examination he went to pieces. Another contributory factor was the unwontedly rigorous and conventional training he had received in Panholzer's studio, which had held back rather than developed his natural artistic talent. His bent for architecture, noted by the Academy professors in 1907 as being worthy of encouragement, was now more apparent than ever, both in his line-drawing and in his compositions.

Nevertheless, Hitler did not allow himself to become discouraged either by the cruel blow fate had meted out to his family or by his more recent personal failure. On the contrary, his faith in himself was unimpaired, nor did it so much as occur to him to change his lodgings although he must have realized that, in the eyes of his landlady, he would necessarily forfeit some of the prestige he had enjoyed as a comfortably-off 'young gentleman' from the provinces. It was only when his room-mate, August Kubizek, was about to return from his brief spell of military service that Hitler moved away from the Stumpergasse. Having suffered such a traumatic experience, he obviously felt reluctant to face a friend who knew so much about his innermost ideas and ambitions. He did not even leave an address,[35] but fled the world that had known him and hid himself where none could find him – not least the Austrian military authorities who were thus unable to conscript him into the army.[36]

The setbacks he had suffered did not prevent Hitler from confidently setting up as an 'academic painter', *tout court*. From 1909 onwards he also did a certain amount of writing.[37] His drawings and paintings were sold in Vienna – a city which, throughout his life, he never ceased to detest. Not until 1913 did he move to Munich where, six years later, he was to embark on his astonishing career.

Up till the middle of 1910 he painted countless small pictures, sometimes as many as six or seven a week,[38] mostly of buildings[39] which he would copy from postcards and old prints. Besides these he also produced landscapes and portraits in oil, ink or watercolour and even undertook technically difficult work for reproduction in print (usually engravings), mainly for posters or illustrations for advertisements of cosmetics, face powder, footwear, shoe polish and ladies' underwear. Hitler's facile but not unpleasing drawings and paintings – mostly watercolours – were sold to dealers and private individuals by Reinhold Hanisch whom he had met during a short stay in a dosshouse in Meidling. The takings were shared equally between the two of them.[40] In *Mein Kampf* Hitler relates: 'In the years 1909–10 my own situation had changed somewhat in so far as . . . I was . . . working independently as a small draughtsman and painter of watercolours.'[41] This is borne out by Hanisch's remark that he 'managed to get quite a lot of custom', thus enabling them both to live not 'too badly'.[42] The partnership lasted for eight months, to their mutual profit. Hanisch relates:

Since he [Hitler] told me he'd been to the Academy I told him he ought to paint picture postcards. I went out selling them. He painted views of Vienna as well and I sold them to picture dealers and interior decorators. I managed to get quite a lot of custom so that we didn't live too badly. But the better businesses in the art trade always refused to buy any pictures. I went on at Hitler about working harder. To help him get on we used to visit museums.

It was architecture he really got worked up about. I could have stood and listened for hours when he talked about Gottfried Semper.[43]

Hitler, however, did not mean to become a painter but an architect. As business prospered, so his work grew careless and superficial – in fact, he let himself go. He would draw and paint merely to supplement his already ample resources. Meanwhile Hanisch, with no kind of private income to fall back on, urged his partner to step up his artistic output. But his plea fell on deaf ears. Hitler showed no compunction whatever for his plight and finally Hanisch was driven to seek other means of sustenance. 'About this time,' he was to write later, 'I was given a few commissions for engravings and decided to try doing them myself since Hitler had given up working altogether.'[44] Eventually in the summer of 1910 their association came to an abrupt end. At the beginning of August Hitler went to the Brigittenau police station in Vienna to lodge a complaint against his partner, whom he accused of having illicitly made off with a picture and of having withheld his (Hitler's) share of the takings.[45] He maintained that Hanisch had embezzled nineteen kronen due from the sale of a watercolour of the Parliament building, 'a painting executed with photographic exactitude which lends a three-dimensional effect to the architectural and decorative detail'. He further accused his partner of purloining another watercolour valued at nine kronen. These misdemeanours earned Hanisch a week in jail.[46] In May 1933 he wrote: 'I didn't deny the allegation because the private customer who bought "Paliament" had given me a commission covering several weeks and this would have gone to Hitler if I said where I'd sold the picture.'[47] It is an unconvincing explanation and almost undoubtedly untrue.[48]

Hitler signed his pictures in a number of different ways – 'A. Hitler', 'A.H.', 'Hitler Adolf' or just plain 'Hitler'. From the time of his break with Hanisch, he often delivered his work personally to his clients, many of whom were intellectuals or Jewish businessmen.[49] He also sold a number of his pictures through the agency of a dealer called Neumann, a Hungarian Jew who from time to time lodged in the hostel in the Meldemannstrasse. Now that he no longer had a partner Hitler painted less and read far more than hitherto, devoting to politics an increasing amount of what had once been his working time. As a result his output declined even further, though it did not dry up altogether.

In 1913, while Hitler was delivering a watercolour to a customer, a chance encounter took place between the two former partners.[50] It was

to be their last. Subsequently, in the years before 1933, Hanisch was
to take a cheap revenge for his eight days in prison and the loss of his
job as middleman by spreading libellous stories about his one-time
associate. These were concocted out of the man's experiences as a
tramp and were sold to Konrad Heiden and Rudolf Olden, as well as to
the innumerable journalists who subsequently wrote about Hitler. In
an undated letter to Franz Feiler, with whom he had been friendly
since 1924, Hanisch complains of being down and out, with only a
pittance to live on and nothing over for the rent. How it would all end,
he went on, he did not know 'and anyhow, what does it matter where a
bloke pegs out?'[51] But hardly had Hitler seized power in May 1933
than Hanisch began to approach prominent NSDAP members,
insinuating that, in return for a suitable reward, he could help them
'please the Führer by airing first hand knowledge' about the latter's
artistic tastes and more especially his admiration for Gottfried Semper.[52] Hanisch had prostituted himself in vain. In 1936 he was brought
to book by the Gestapo for his earlier tittletattle about the Führer, being
arrested on Bormann's instructions immediately after the Wehrmacht
had marched into Austria. On 11 May 1938 Feiler, in a courageous
endeavour to save his friend's good name, wrote to the authorities,
asserting that Hanisch had died of pneumonia while on remand.[53]
(Bormann's version, however, put out on 17 February 1944, was that
'Hanisch hanged himself after the annexation of Austria'.[54]) 'I knew,
of course,' Feiler's letter continues, 'that Hanisch was often questioned about Adolf Hitler by certain journalists who then proceeded to
fill out the true facts with such lies as they thought fit. And now,
because of all this, Hanisch has been compelled to forfeit his good
name.'

Nevertheless, most of the lies about Hitler's life in Vienna before
1913 can be traced back to Reinhold Hanisch who, after Hitler's rise
to fame, also palmed off his own pictures as the work of his former
partner. It was he who was responsible for the dissemination of tendentious stories which were taken up, not only by journalists, but also
by biographers and historians.[55]

*

Hitler was later to develop certain traits which can be attributed, at
least in part, to these years in Vienna: his predilection for ostentatious
displays of power, for instance, or for the commissioning of monumental

buildings and works of art, his habit of impatiently brushing aside the views of experts in favour of his own, his excessive meticulousness in matters of secondary importance and, last but not least, his ruthlessness, cruelty and malevolence towards other people. Though his *Weltanschauung* had already been largely determined by the time he left Linz, it acquired a negative orientation when his hopes of embracing an artistic career were so rudely shattered – a trauma for which he held Vienna responsible. His reaction to that culturally selfconscious and much stratified city, contemptuously described in *Mein Kampf* as 'Phaeacian',[56] was not primarily that of a politically committed young bourgeois but rather the reaction of an unsuccessful art student who, while aware of his temporary loss of caste, refuses to look disagreeable facts in the face and lays the blame for his predicament on others. After he had failed his examinations in 1907 and 1908 he began to nurture an articulate hatred for the imperial capital, as though it alone were to blame for his lack of success in the enterprise on which, as a child with illusions as yet intact, he had set his heart in the face of parental opposition. He still hoped, however, to follow a regular course of study for which he prepared after his own particular fashion by concerning himself with literature, art and architecture. 'In this period there took shape within me', he was to write in *Mein Kampf*, 'a world picture and a philosophy which became the granite foundation of all my acts.'[57] He felt convinced that the world had failed to appreciate his gifts. 'If our schoolmasters generally fail to detect incipient genius,' he remarked on 10 May 1942, 'it is because genius is evident only to people of equal stature.'[58] His belief that he had been wrongfully rejected by the Academy appeared, moreover, to be justified by his discovery that he could, if needs be, live on the sale of what were mere ephemera. The unpalatable fact that reputable dealers would often refuse to buy his careless and amateurish work was never really brought home to him because middleman such as Hanisch and Neumann acted as buffers. Thus he developed an attitude of wishful thinking. Later on, when he had the means and the power to do so, he sought to demonstrate that he could build as no one else had ever built. In the Austrian capital he had discovered that neither his artistic attainments nor his educational qualifications sufficed for the realization of his dream. A quarter of a century later he set out to show that he, and he alone, knew 'best'. When, in 1942, he expressed the view that 'real artists' are not the product of traditional academic schooling but of training in the work-

shops of the great masters,[59] he was harking back to his experiences in
Vienna. No historian can determine whether his more ignoble manifestations were merely deepseated reactions to his experiences in Vienna
and elsewhere or whether, as variations of a substitute satisfaction, they
also betrayed traumatic prenatal disturbance resulting in a character
narcissistically distorted in early childhood.

The nature of what he once called his 'bread-and-butter occupation' inevitably led him to regard himself as a painter, if only a minor
one.[60] Like so many other artists since the turn of the century, particularly those living in Paris and Vienna, he adopted a highly uncon-
ventional mode of existence as a token of his refusal to conform to the
established order. Hitler, the self-styled 'academic painter', now
openly demonstrated his unwillingness to identify with a society which
he despised as retrograde and outmoded.[61] But as regards his personal
appearance, he never went to the extremes described by Hanisch and
Greiner, who allege that at this time Hitler epitomized everything
which in the eyes of the respectable world goes to make up an artist –
unruly locks, hirsute and unwashed countenance, dirty and dilapi-
dated clothing.[62]

From December 1909 to May 1910 Hitler lived in a men's hostel
where he drew and painted during the daytime. When at work on his
pictures he habitually wore a shabby suit, thus presenting an appearance which in no way conformed to the real state of his finances.[63] An
artist who works for preference in oil and watercolour is unlikely to
dress smartly at all times and on all occasions. And even if he had
wished to be as stylishly dressed as his father or, for that matter, as he
himself had always been in Linz, complete with cane, top-hat, frock
coat and kid gloves, his occupation would seldom have permitted it.
During these early days in Vienna when Hitler, now twenty years old,
was busily engaged in painting, he continued to regard himself as an
aspiring architect, a fact which he not only willingly divulged to anyone
who asked him about his plans for the future, but also sought to convey
by his manner and bearing in general. In May 1913, when he moved to
Munich, he took lodgings with a Herr Popp who, being a tailor, noted
with satisfaction that his new lodger was far from shabby. Both Popp
and his wife recall that Hitler's frock coat, overcoat, suits and personal
linen were in impeccable order.

By August 1914, if we are to judge by his subsequent comments on
the subject, he felt himself to be on the eve of attaining the goal he had

kept in view throughout his time in Vienna and Munich. In his head-quarters on 10 May 1942 he declared that, had it not been for the war, 'I should certainly have become an architect, perhaps even one of the leading architects, if not the foremost in Germany'.[64] This career, he thought, would wipe out all memory of his setbacks in Vienna, a city towards which his attitude always remained negative. Thus, even after 1938, he had very few changes in mind for the Austrian capital. His remark of 26 April 1942 that he had no intention of 'reducing Vienna's status' was unequivocal enough, even if he had not endorsed it two weeks later when he said that the Viennese had no reason to be con-cerned about their monopolistic position and their cultural tutelage of the Alpine and Danubian regions.[65] On the other hand, when speaking of the German capital on 11 March 1942, he said: 'Berlin will become a world capital comparable only to ancient Egypt, Baby-lon or Rome',[66] the tacit assumption being that it would become so only with the realization of his plan for a vast monumental building for which he had made a sketch in 1924.[67] The only city ever to tug at his heartstrings, and to do so right up to his dying day,[68] was Linz, which he planned to make into the most beautiful town on the Danube within ten years of winning the war.[69] Ever since his time in Vienna – during which, incidentally, he became an antisemite despite the fact that many of his customers and patrons were Jews[70] – he had con-stantly proclaimed his intention of performing great things. Under-lying that intention were hatred and rejection, an unbounded will to power, and a craving for ostentatious display, all of which are dis-cernible in his urge to reshape reality in so far as he had not already succeeded in doing so. When Hitler moved to Munich in May 1913 at the age of twenty-four his *Weltanschauung* was already firmly en-trenched.

In this German city for which, as an artist, he felt an understandable attraction, Hitler was for a time quite on his own. He was no longer living in a hostel with a perhaps distasteful routine imposed on him by both management and inmates, but was free to do as he pleased; he could come and go, burn the candle at both ends, work, read or simply loaf about. Those who had immediate contacts with him – the tailor, Herr Popp and his family – could see 'with their own eyes' that their uncommunicative lodger was a 'serious artist' who sold his pictures, but until August 1914 they did not know whether this was his sole means of livelihood. He would sit by the window overlooking the school playground on the opposite side of the Schleissheimerstrasse and copy photographs, usually in watercolour but sometimes also in oils.[71] The resulting pictures he sold with some success – mostly to the Kunsthandlung Stuffle in the Maximilianstrasse. His taxable income of 100 marks a month testifies more, perhaps, to his artistic ability than to his business acumen.[72]

He still preferred architectural themes and in Munich these necessarily differed from the subjects of his Vienna paintings. What particularly attracted him, he tells us in *Mein Kampf*, was 'this wonderful marriage of primordial power and fine artistic mood, this single line, from the Hofbräuhaus to the Odeon, from the October Festival to the Pinakothek'.[73]

It has not been possible to ascertain precisely how many pictures he painted and sold over this period of approximately thirteen months. More than two dozen survived the days of their creator's obscurity. On 12 March 1944 Hitler told Heinrich Hoffmann: 'I didn't want to become a painter. I only produced these things so that I could earn my keep and go on with my studies. . . . I only painted as much as I did in order to obtain a bare living.'[74] It is no coincidence that few of the pictures found on the walls of Hitler's customers were of architectural subjects. He treasured these drawings as his 'most valuable possessions'[75] and refused to dispose of them along with his other pictures which, as their dimensions clearly show, were produced expressly for sale.[76]

After 1918 Hitler's work was sometimes sold for him by his former army friend, Hans Mend, as had been done by Hanisch and Neumann in Vienna before 1913.[77] In 1942, by order of the Ministry of the Interior, his pictures were declared 'works of art of national importance' and made subject to registration. This meant that they could not be sold abroad without the express permission of the Minister of the Interior.[78]

Nothing of the slightest value on Hitler as an artist is to be found in any of his biographies, whether these are full length works or brief thumbnail sketches. Accounts range from fulsome adulation to untutored criticism, and the judgements they express are far too sweeping to be admissible. One or two typical examples will suffice to demonstrate this. For instance, Hermann Nasse, lecturer at the Academy of Fine Arts in Munich, writing in 1936 about the watercolours Hitler painted while serving in France, declared that they 'testify to his artistic gifts, not only as a draughtsman but also as a painter'. He singled out for special commendation two paintings done in 1914, 'Defile near Wytschaete' and 'Ruined Monastery, Messines': 'Here we find the powerful experience of destruction translated into colourful vision. This is not the romanticism of ruins or of war but rather, because of its fluid and painterly treatment, a most grave and moving memorial.'[79] Some of Hitler's other front line aquarelles, published in full colour by Professor Hoffman, 'Reich Photographer to the NSDAP', are indeed undeniably good. Of these Nasse writes:

The painting 'Dressing Station, Fromelles' belongs to the year 1915. It is rendered in light, sparkling pigment and the buildings with their overhanging eaves are depicted in the most delicate shades and gradations of colour. The watercolour 'Haubourdin' of 1916 is truly entrancing. Seen through the eyes of a German painter, the foreign landscape is experienced as something intimate, familiar and animate, indeed even poetic. One is as if transported to the walls of Nuremburg or Rothenburg. The painting here is exceptionally easy, fluid and full of movement. His superb pencil drawing 'Ardoye in Flanders' belongs to the summer of 1917. Besides these dated pictures there are two undated ones, 'Dugout at Tournes' and 'House with a White Fence'. All these pieces betray the hand of a trained and naturally gifted architect. The master builder of the Third Reich puts to shame the Vienna Academy of that day. What moves us above all in every one of these pictures is the genuine German sense of dedication, upright, honest and loving, both to the whole and to every minutest detail.[80]

Some twenty years later Franz Jetzinger was to write of Hitler's work in Vienna that his 'drawings and paintings were not original, but copies', and that there was no evidence that he ever painted from life.[81] The implication is unjust. Hitler made copies, not because he lacked talent, but simply because he was too lazy to go outdoors and paint. He was taking the easiest course although well aware that 'pictures painted in a studio . . . are worthless by comparison with those painted in the open air'.[82] And in fact the few paintings he made from nature betray quite uncommon talent. But this was a matter of comparative indifference to him. His assertion that he did not want to be a painter but an architect, and that he painted only in order to earn extra money is undoubtedly true. Moreover, as others besides Heinrich Hoffmann have confirmed, he himself often said that he was not a good painter. Thus in 1941–2, Hitler told the well-known German stage designer, Siewert, how much he admired his work. Its excellence, he went on to say, put his own pre-1914 efforts to shame, despite the fact of his having been Roller's pupil. Nevertheless his best watercolours, which were not copies but painted from nature, are thoroughly competent, if not outstanding, as he himself was undoubtedly aware.[83] Indeed he sometimes speculated about what he might have achieved as an artist – emulating Rudolf von Alt, for instance, whom he looked on as his master – if he had seriously taken up painting after 1907, despite his rejection by the Vienna Academy.

That those who write about Hitler show small concern for a proper evaluation of their subject's artistic talent is evident from the works they select for reproduction. An instance of this can be seen in Joseph Wulf's book, *Die Bildenden Künste im Dritten Reich* (*The Fine Arts in the Third Reich*) in which two drawings are reproduced. These in fact were mere ephemera. The drawing of a head designated by Wulf (and numerous other writers) as a 'portrait', was scribbled on a scrap of paper while he was telephoning. When bored by telephone conversations he would distract himself by drawing heads, many of them, surprisingly enough, in the Cubist manner. These might be caricatures of Richard Wagner, Heinrich Schliemann, Wallenstein or of Hitler himself, sometimes bearded.[84] The second drawing reproduced in Wulf's book is of an SA man. This again was merely a rough sketch, drawn to show his subordinates what he thought an SA man should look like.

The fact that works by Hitler painted before 1914 have survived for decades is evidence enough of their presentability and, indeed, a number of them were acquired by connoisseurs and collectors. Again, we may be sure, that the Jewish physician, Dr Bloch, who had been presented with several watercolours after attending Hitler's mother, did not retain them for some thirty years simply because Adolf and Klara Hitler had been his patients until 1907. Gordon Craig, the writer, theatrical designer and producer, was particularly interested in Hitler as an artist. After studying his First World War paintings he described them in his unpublished diary as remarkable artistic productions.[85] Alfred Rosenberg, who had studied architecture in Moscow, wrote of these watercolours while in Nuremberg: 'They betrayed an innate talent, an understanding of essentials and a marked feeling for painting.'[86] Indeed not a few great painters have left behind pictures inferior to those of Hitler, who is nevertheless debarred from a permanent place in the history of art by the fact that he never produced one really major work.

From 1907 onwards he took an increasing interest in historical buildings, their relative architectural merits and the techniques and craftmanship they embodied. His intensive study of the subject helped to broaden and consolidate his knowledge of architectural detail, the more so since he copied the same picture or photograph many times over. Some idea of his work in this respect can be gained from a catalogue of the pictures owned by a Dr Alfred Detig of Vienna in 1939, namely *Heiliger Kreuzerhof*, *Rotenturmtor*, *Michaeler-Platz and Dreilauferhaus*, *Hofburg and Old Passageway 1890*, *Michaelerkirche*, *Minoriten-Kirche*, *Fisherman's Gate* and *Kärntnerthortheater*. Other examples are the *Alte Burgtheater*, the *Auersperg Palais* and the *Schönbrunner Linie*, all of which belonged to Dr Walter Lohmann of Vienna, who worked for the Central Archives of the NSDAP.[87] So often did Hitler depict the Parliament building in Vienna and the Munich Hofbräuhaus that he was finally able to draw them from memory, in photographic detail. One result of this practice was his ability to reel off the dimensions of famous bridges, towers, gateways and façades, a fact confirmed not only by Speer but by men such as Arno Breker. Between 1924 and 1934 Breker, a sculptor, architect and connoisseur of French art, had spent much of his time in Paris where he produced some of his most important work. In 1937 he was elected by international vote to the jury of the World Exhibition. When summoned to Paris by the Führer in June 1940 to act as his artistic guide and mentor, Breker was amazed by Hitler's extensive knowledge of architecture:

We drove round the Opéra [he recalls] and drew up beside the steps in front of the main façade. As a result of his concentrated studies, Hitler was intimately acquainted with the stylistic elements of Garnier's Second Empire building. We at once began our tour. . . . We walked round the exterior of the building before going inside. . . . He was familiar with the ground plan and knew the measurements both of major features and of details . . . a Baedeker could hardly have been more informative and precise. . . . We were treated to one long hymn of praise to Garnier. This was not the raving of an enthusiastic layman; rather, it was the voice of one who is thoroughly conversant with the problems of architecture.[88]

Breker goes on:

As we passed the Hôtel de Cluny, Hitler pointed at a dome on the left and asked me whether it belonged to the Chamber of Commerce. I said no, thinking it was the dome of the Institut de France. A few minutes later, when we drove past the actual building, Hitler turned towards it remarking smugly: 'There you are! It says "Chambre de Commerce"!' I, an old Paris hand, had been put right by someone whose knowledge of the city derived solely from books![89]

While touring the Opéra with his retinue of German and French experts, Hitler asked to be shown the 'Oval Salon' and was in no way deterred when told that such a 'salon' did not exist. From his reading on the subject he was sure that it did, and when he actually indicated the spot where the door to the Salon should have – and indeed once had – been, his companions were thunderstruck. Neither Germans nor French knew that the 'Oval Salon' described in Hitler's out-of-date textbooks, had since been subdivided and the door in question walled up.

There is ample evidence to show that his knowledge was not confined to Parisian architecture. After the *Anschluss*, for instance, when Dr Martin, the Nuremberg police chief, returned from Austria, he told Hitler about a visit he had made to the theatre in Graz. Though he had never been to the town, the Führer was able to point out a defect in the theatre's planning known only to a few experts, namely the unsatisfactory nature of the transition from stage to auditorium.[90] The following ancedote shows Hitler's extensive knowledge of such matters (as also the store he set by such knowledge). During a banquet in March 1938 Neubacher, the Burgomaster of Vienna, was asked by another guest how wide the Danube was at a certain point in the city. Neubacher said he did not know, whereas Hitler immediately came out with the correct answer. But the Burgomaster's ignorance had dispelled the Führer's high spirits and, although he had just received confirmation of political victory, he remained in a bad mood for the rest of the evening.[91]

Hitler's dreams of becoming an architect went back at least as far as the autumn of 1907 when his lack of the necessary qualifications had debarred him from a regular course of study. Thereafter his ideas were mainly concerned with structures of a massive and monumental kind. Till 1945 his designs followed the neoclassical style of nineteenth- and early twentieth-century architecture in Europe, but transposed on to a vastly magnified scale which represented an extreme expression of the alienation of man from nature then so prevalent in contemporary building.

His point of departure was neither the groundplan nor the organization of space, but rather the exterior of the building, itself dominated by the symmetry of the Classical Orders. In his treatment of individual features he favoured the purely geometrical at the expense of the organic. Straight lines, broad planes and a formal austerity characterize his elevations. Movement and ornamentation played little part in his ideas. It is significant that it should have been Austria, in the person of Adolf Loos, which gave birth to the axiom that ornaments are a 'crime' indicative of 'sexual perversion'.[92] Hitler's 'romantic-classical' rationalism (an all-embracing term for his ideas) reflects the rebellion against the *Jugendstil** then fashionable in Viennese architectural circles. Hitler was never to outgrow this phase, even after becoming the 'patron-in-chief of Germany's best architects'.[93] Human beings, in his view, were no more than the uncritical, obedient slaves of the lone genius, puppets without any will of their own. Typical of his ideas are the designs made during his time of detention in Landsberg, for a triumphal arch and great assembly hall in Berlin. Speer, who from 1933 onwards was in charge of Hitler's architectural projects, said of these two designs some forty years after their conception: 'I thought them both a bit overpowering, though not in the sense of their cost or – to use an overworked expression – of their monumental size. There have been monumental buildings at every period of architectural history.'[94]

'The true value of every era', Hitler was to declare when he opened the Exhibition of German Architecture, Arts and Crafts in 1938,

finds definitive expression in its buildings. For a great era has to be experienced inwardly by a people if they are to give it outward form, when it will speak more convincingly than language itself. It is the word made stone. . . . This exhibition coincides with the turning-point of an era and records the beginning of a new age. . . . For the first time since the building of our cathedrals we see on display a truly great architecture, in other words not an architecture expending itself on commonplace tasks and needs, but an architecture which goes far beyond those tasks and needs. It can claim that it will withstand the critical scrutiny of millennia and that, for millennia, it will remain the pride of the people who created such works. . . . There are things that do not admit of discussion and among these are the eternal values. Who could presume to apply his puny, commonplace intellect to the creations of truly great, divinely endowed natures! Great artists and master builders are entitled to exemption from the critical scrutiny of their lesser contemporaries. In the final analysis their work will be judged in the light

* The German and Austrian equivalent of Art Nouveau.

of centuries and not in that of unimportant and transitory phenomena. . . . This is the hour when the curtain is drawn aside to reveal for the first time to the eyes of the general public works which are destined to leave their imprint, not just on tens of years, but on hundreds of years! For them this will be a moment of consecration like that so beautifully conveyed in the *Meistersinger*: 'Here a child was born.' These are architectonic achievements which possess enduring value and which, by human standards, will last for ever, strong, immutable and imperishable in their beauty and their harmonious proportions.[95]

Hitler wielded a unique power and, like most dictators, experienced the need to express it symbolically in architecture. By thus realizing his early architectural projects he felt he was asserting himself as an artist and making up for what he had missed in the years before 1933. But since he was not in a position to carry out his plans in person he had, as he wryly put it, to resign himself to the role of 'patron-in-chief of Germany's best architects'.[96] He drew no distinction between power and its reflection in a work of art – itself a reflection of reality. Schopenhauer's dictum that art should represent the nature of existence in such a way as to proclaim: 'Look! That is how life is!' was, like many another philosophical, historical and biological doctrine adopted and reformulated by Hitler. In his view it was the task of art to express with photographic exactitude the laws of nature or whatever he himself might choose to designate as such. It was primarily to these 'eternally valid Laws' that he appealed when justifying the claim to 'immortality' of certain works of art and architecture. He believed that life could be maintained only by dint of ruthless struggle, brute force and consistently unscrupulous brutality, and regarded these as natural laws which could not be flouted with impunity. Thus it was only logical that he should require the visual arts to confine themselves to a faithful rendering of readily assimilable norms. He would not allow the existence of contradictions. In 1933, for instance, at the cultural conference of the NSDAP rally in Nuremberg, he said:

Just as the preservation of any human society is dependent on the observation of certain principles, regardless of whether they are accepted by all, so too a people's cultural image has to be shaped in accordance with its best elements and with those who, by reason of their nature, are the only born representatives of culture.[97]

Architecture was clearly the medium best suited to the dissemination of Hitler's ideas, and one which enabled him to impose them on all and sundry. Hence he regarded it as the highest form of art. Sculpture and painting followed in that order, and here again Schopenhauer's influence is discernible.

Hitler also shared Schopenhauer's view that, like a prince, a work of art should be approached humbly and should be looked upon as a revelation of existence; in other words the individual should wait and see what a given work of art has to say to him. Because he had always felt himself to be an artist, Hitler had from the beginning regarded this 'response' as the very cornerstone of artistic creation. He wanted to be both Atlas and master of the world, to carry the globe on his shoulders and to shape it in accordance with his own ideas. Indeed Albert Speer has rightly pointed out that, as Führer and Reich Chancellor, Hitler saw in politics and political power a means of putting his artistic ideas into practice.[98] Thus at the opening of the Exhibition of German Art in 1939 he declared:

The monuments of architecture today bear powerful witness to the strength of the new German phenomenon which is making itself felt in the political as well as the cultural field. In the same way that political malcontents were eliminated with each successive stage of our national resurgence, whose proud culmination was the creation of the Greater German Reich, so too cultural malcontents will be eliminated with the building of the new Reich's imperishable edifices. But there can be no disputing the fact that sculpture and painting are coming to play an increasingly valuable role as complements of architecture.[99]

Because Hitler regarded power as a tangible reflection of natural laws he rejected abstract painting, a branch of creativity diametrically opposed to architecture. Dictators have never tolerated attempts at individual self-expression. People who inquire into the meaning of the shadows on the wall, as did the prisoners in Plato's allegory of the cave, have invariably acted as grit in the rigidly controlled machinery of power apparatuses. Hitler officially designated them 'consumptive aesthetes',[100] whose opinions must without exception be eradicated. His own personal view, which he would occasionally voice when under no compulsion to influence anybody, was not always in strict accord with his official and semi-official pronouncements made for propaganda purposes. Though, like Mussolini and Stalin, he officially rejected abstract art, his own pictures betray a certain tendency in that direction. Indeed, if some of his portraits or his pictures of people with animals were not signed and fully authenticated, they might well be attributed to abstract painters. His conservatism and traditional outlook did not extend to every field of art. For instance he once ordered some cutlery to be made to his own specification; in the fifties virtually the same designs in the shape of souvenir pieces bearing the names of towns were successfully placed on the market as examples of modern cutlery. Whether these were in fact deliberate copies of Hitler's designs or genuinely original work is of little or no importance in this context.

His taste for the most part was extremely conservative and adhered strictly to bourgeois ideas of traditional elegance. Though fond of old pictures, fine carpets and impressive antique furniture, he was not averse to modern furnishings, provided they were not too extreme. In the period preceding 1914 the traditionally minded social and cultural élite had already turned towards Impressionism if not indeed Expressionism. Although by his own admission his *Weltanschauung* had taken shape during that time, Hitler remained unaffected by this development. To what extent his ideas were influenced by the 1907 manifesto of the *Deutscher Werkbund* in Munich is not ascertainable, though he did in fact share some of its members' likes and dislikes. For instance, he rejected constructional and stylistic features such as balconies, windows flanked by columns, and the use of stucco in place of natural stone.

The opinion he sometimes expressed that we should look to Greek and Roman antiquity for 'our ancestry' was consistent with his conviction that painting and sculpture had reached their apogee in the art of Greece and Rome. He rejected the futurism of the modern Italian painters on the grounds that it was too similar to Expressionism and Impressionism, movements which, he alleged, owed their renown solely to the machinations of the Jews.[101] For it was his belief that true art had been largely confined to classical antiquity and the Romantic and Baroque eras. He was particularly proud of having acquired Hans Makart's 'Plague in Florence', for instance,[102] or the famous copy of Myron of Eleutherae's 'Discobolus' (fifth century B.C.) this last with Mussolini's help.[103] The Renaissance he regarded as too closely linked with Christianity and he disliked Gothic art because of its intensely mystical connotations. Nor did he appreciate contemporary German pictures, though he sometimes bought them to encourage living artists.[104] Indeed, he refused to recognize any development in the field of painting which, as opposed to technological development, requires some measure of discrimination. Among his favourite painters, on whose pictures he would make expert comments, were Carl Spitzweg (1808–85), Hans Thoma (1839–1924), Wilhelm Leibl (1844–1900) and Eduard Grützner (1846–1925). He instantly recognized as fakes some Spitzwegs bought by Heinrich Hoffman, but refrained from pointing this out in order not to spoil his pleasure.[105] He was at pains to build up a reputation for rediscovering near-forgotten artists. Thus he acquired over twenty paintings by Friedrich Stahl and more than a dozen by Karl Leipold.[106] He never lost his interest in pictures of which he was an inveterate buyer.

His views on art and architecture – views which he held to be permanently valid – were formed in the years before 1914 at a time when he was also building up his knowledge of literature. It was no coincidence that throughout his life he continued to believe that the greatest works of art in the German-speaking countries had been produced before 1910.[107] Hitler's real architectural aims only became clear to Albert Speer while the latter was serving his twenty years' sentence as a war criminal in Spandau gaol. 'His notions', Speer said in 1966, 'corresponded roughly to those current in artistic circles shortly before the First World War. While I was in Spandau I sent for back numbers of German architectural journals published between 1890 and 1916 so as to study this question.'[108] Hitler's world was primarily that of the nineteenth century and its heritage, which he liked to confront with the historical and artistic testimony of Greece and Rome. His artistic judgement, which he regarded as absolute and immutable, was formed by his copious but narrowly orientated reading, his petty bourgeois origins, the kind of life he led and the nature of his experiences in Vienna, all of which imposed limits he was never to transcend.

His provenance is plainly discernible in his proposal to provide special galleries where contemporary artists could study the art of the nineteenth and twentieth centuries.[109] Throughout his life his artistic judgement was determined by what he had seen and learnt to value and admire in the Austrian capital. In 1924 he expressed the view that by 1900 art had already begun noticeably to decline. 'Even before the turn of the century', he wrote in *Mein Kampf*, 'an element began to intrude into our art which up to that time could be regarded as entirely foreign and unknown.'[110] As opposed to occasional 'aberrations of taste in earlier times' this was, he thought, a form of 'spiritual degeneration' in which the 'political collapse' was already beginning to manifest itself culturally.[111] Eighteen years later, by which time German art had been forced onto a Procrustean bed, he was prepared to advance this 'spiritual degeneration' by a quarter of a century. On 27 March 1942 he said: 'Up till 1920 our artistic achievements remained at a remarkably high level. Since then it has unfortunately shown an increasingly rapid decline. . . . What has been foisted on the German people from 1922 [until 1933] is just one miserable scrawl.'[112] Amongst many who were condemned as 'degenerate' and who suffered expulsion from the world of art, if nothing worse, were artists such as Emil Nolde, who had joined the NSDAP not long after Hitler, Karl Schmidt Rottluff, Erich Heckel, Otto Dix and Conrad Felixmüller, each one of whom has his assured place in the annals of art.

We know both from Hitler's own account and from the numerous pictures and sketches that have survived, what models he used in order to increase his knowledge of art, architecture and art history. The style of the buildings he drew – and sometimes tentatively re-designed – and the cultural status of their architects provide not only valuable clues but also answers to questions which hitherto few if any have troubled to ask. One source of architectural inspiration was the Ringstrasse in Vienna. Built between 1858 and 1865, it is three miles long, nearly two hundred feet wide and comprises such important buildings as the Museum of Applied Art, the Opera, the Natural History Museum, the Museum of Art, the Neue Burg, the Parliament, the Rathaus, the University, the Burgtheater, the Bourse and the Gartenbau building. Hitler studied them all.

Describing the period up to 1908 Kubizek writes:

Gradually I came to understand my friend's strong predilection for the Ringstrasse buildings, although it seemed to me that the style of older structures such as St Stephen's Cathedral or the Belvedere was far more genuine, vigorous and convincing. But Adolf did not care for Baroque architecture which he regarded as altogether too florid. The pretentious Ringstrasse buildings dated back no further than the second half of the nineteenth century, having been erected on the site of the fortifications which up till that time had enclosed the inner city, and their style was far from uniform. Quite the contrary, in fact. Practically every style evolved in bygone times was represented here. Parliament was in the classical, or rather pseudo-Hellenic style, the Rathaus neo-Gothic, the Burgtheater . . . late Renaissance. Yet they all had one feature in common which particularly appealed to my friend – their size and ostentation. But what drew him again and again to these buildings and led him to describe the Ringstrasse as, so to speak, a practical training ground for his profession, was the comparative ease with which he could study the history of their construction at the hands of the preceding generation, redraft their plans and, in his mind, rebuild each edifice afresh, identifying himself the while with the lives and achievements of the great architects of the time, men such as Theophil Hansen, Semper, Hasenauer, Siccardsburg and van der Nüll.[113]

Much though Hitler admired the Parliament building and the museums, he was particularly attached to the Burgtheater, where he scarcely ever missed a performance. The building had originally been the Court ballroom. In 1741, with Maria Theresa's permission, the lessee of the old Kärntnerthortheater set about converting the ballroom to Weisskern's design. Hitler liked to copy early prints of the building whose architecture no less than the art treasures it displayed provided the young autodidact with an awe-inspiring field for study. The parapet above the main building was crowned with a huge and much-admired group of statuary depicting Apollo with the tragic and comic muses. Decorating the frieze above the main entrance was Rudolf Weyr's triumphal arch of Bacchus and Ariadne. The side elevations displayed allegories by Benk, personifying many of the passions and virtues by which both drama and life are governed. Niches in these façades contained Viktor Tilgner's statues of Prometheus and Genoveva, Josef Gasser, Hanswurst, Falstaff, Phèdre and the Judges of Zalamea. Hitler's interest in cultural history was aroused by these memorials which prompted him to delve further into the subject in public libraries and bookshops. Always a voracious reader, his intellectual curiosity was guided along definite channels by his contemplation of Tilgner's busts of great writers set above the windows of the main building and depicting Calderón, Shakespeare, Molière, Schiller, Goethe, Lessing, Halm, Grillparzer and Hebbel.

These studies were interrupted by his move to Munich and the outbreak of the First World War. After the armistice, in the early summer of 1919, Hitler returned to the Bavarian capital, where he was soon singled out for important duties with the Bavarian Army of which he remained a member until the spring of 1920. Though in many respects more experienced than in 1908, he had not yet abandoned the dreams of his childhood and youth, dreams which he continued to cherish as late as April 1945 and now made a further attempt to realize. His intention was not to study architecture but rather to follow a regular course of study in art. For a time he worked with Ernst Schmidt (later mentioned in *Mein Kampf*)[114] with whom he discussed art and architecture.[115] Schmidt, Inkhofer, Mend and other army friends owned oil paintings, pastels and drawings in charcoal, pencil and ink made by Hitler during the war.[116] They were convinced that he possessed artistic talent and urged him to develop it. At about this time he asked the well-known and highly esteemed artist, Max Zaeper, to give an opinion on his recent work. Zaeper was so impressed by the quality of Hitler's watercolours and drawings that he sought a second opinion from Professor Ferdinand Staeger, a colleague of Czech extraction. Staeger's romantic-mystical pictures painted in a naturalistic style had first come to Hitler's attention at the Vienna Secession's exhibition held in 1898 at No. 12 Friedrichstrasse in protest against the conservatism of the artistic 'establishment'. His verdict on Hitler's work was: 'It shows quite exceptional talent.'[117] Over the course of years Hitler bought six of Staeger's pictures, though he did not actually meet the artist until after 1933 when he consented to sit for his portrait. On that occasion, however, he made no reference to the events of 1919.[118]

Despite the favourable verdict of the experts, Hitler could not be persuaded to make up for the opportunities he had missed in the past. By now he was too much immersed in the army political education course he was attending at Munich University[119] to take more than a half-hearted interest in art. Thereafter he appears to have been wholly preoccupied with his political duties in the Reichswehr, and his painting was relegated to second place. When Heinrich Heim first met him in July 1920, the impression he gave was not at all that of an artist whom the outcome of the war had driven temporarily and almost involuntarily into active politics.[120] Only on rare occasions, when relaxing, or again at moments of tension – waiting for a meal in a restaurant, for instance, or speaking on the telephone – would he draw on a menu or on scraps of paper. To the very end of his life pencils and paper always lay ready to hand for this purpose on his desk.

There were some who believed, as Speer still does, that at heart Hitler always remained an artist. After his release from Spandau gaol Speer told the author that not only he himself, but other architects such as Troost, Gieseler and Breker, not infrequently saw in Hitler a 'colleague', a frustrated artist and architect whose 'misfortune it was to have to take part in politics and wage war'.[121]

On the night of 25–26 January 1942, speaking to his companions in the Wolfsschanze, Hitler said:

I became a politician against my will. To my mind politics is just a means to an end. There are people who think that at some future date I shall find it hard to be less active than I am at present. Not a bit of it! The finest day of my life will be the day I quit politics and leave all cares, worries and annoyance behind. That's what I shall do as soon as I have completed my political tasks after the war. Then I want five or ten years to think my thoughts and set them down. Wars come and go. The only lasting things are cultural values. Hence my love of art. Are not music and architecture the forces that will guide the footsteps of future generations?[122]

Similar thoughts had already found expression in Part I of *Mein Kampf*. In 1924, at a time when he was already engaged in making calculations and sketches for the largest building of all time, he wrote:

What in antiquity found its expression in the Acropolis or the Pantheon now cloaked itself in the forms of the Gothic cathedral. Like giants these monumental structures towered over the swarming frame, wooden, and brick buildings of the medieval city, and thus become symbols which even today, with the tenements climbing higher and higher beside them, determine the character and picture of these towns. Cathedrals, town halls, grain markets and battlements are the visible signs of a conception which in the last analysis was the same as that of antiquity. Yet how truly deplorable the relation between state buildings and private buildings has become today! If the fate of Rome should strike Berlin, future generations would some day admire the department stores of a few Jews as the mightiest works of our era and the hotels of a few corporations as the characteristic expression of the culture of our times.[123]

On occasion one might feel tempted to think that Hitler only became a politician in order to realize his vast and extravagant architectural projects. That his true vocation was indeed architecture is evident from the fact that, even during the Second World War, he was constantly working at new and, in the circumstances, wholly irrelevant plans and endeavouring to reshape old ones. Christa Schröder relates that 'even in the midst of the excitements of political life he found time to practise his skill. On his desk there was always a pile of drawing-paper within easy reach, and at idle moments he would draw whatever came into his head.'[124] After Stalingrad he discontinued the evening gramophone concerts of music by Beethoven, Bruckner, Wagner, Liszt, Brahms, Hugo Wolf, Lehár and Johann Strauss; some of these records he had heard more than a hundred and forty times.[125] But he continued to indulge in painting and architectural planning. Even in March 1945, four weeks before he committed suicide, he became engrossed in a wooden model of Linz depicting the town as he had one day hoped to reconstruct and expand it.[126]

There are biographers of Hitler whose prime concern is not to open up new sources and to discover historically verifiable facts, but rather to 'reinterpret' earlier assumptions which have long since been exposed as false. If such methods were adopted in discussing Hitler's attitude to architecture it could be argued that his launching of the Russian campaign in 1941 was an extraordinary measure designed to safeguard his architectural daydream. For Stalin's intention to honour Lenin with a Congress building more than 300 metres high appears to have caused Hitler more concern before June 1941 than the not exactly negligible problems arising out of the war. Such was his attitude to architecture that he regarded the Russian dictator's project as a challenge to his own longstanding plans for the erection of the largest building in the world. He had first conceived this immense domed structure in 1925, when he had been at work on *Mein Kampf*. The building, 220 metres high, was to have a dome with the almost incredible diameter of 250 metres, and a roof lantern measuring 46 metres across. The hall was to provide standing-room for 150,000 to 180,000 people and would have been big enough to accommodate St Peter's, Rome, nearly seven times over. Not until the Russian campaign had begun did Hitler breathe easily again. Then as Speer was to recall thirty years later, he remarked with evident relief: 'That puts paid once and for all to Stalin's building.'[127]

In the same context Speer said of the Feldherrnhalle scheme: 'In no way was this hall a crazy and unrealizable project', though in retrospect its proportions seemed to him preposterous. Speer was speaking in 1966, at which time a domed hall, described in professional circles as 'remarkable even by American standards', was under construction in Houston, Texas.[128] It was hailed with superlatives such as the 'first' and the 'biggest', yet its dimensions fell far short of those of the domed structure planned by Hitler forty years earlier, and the whole effect was modest and unimposing in the extreme by comparison with the German project.

The proposed width of Hitler's hall was 250 metres; the width of the Houston Astrodome is 214 metres. The Berlin building, which could have accommodated a fifty-six storey tower-block, would have had an overall height of 220 metres, the dome alone being 122 metres high. The height of the Texas building from ground level to the top of the dome is no more than 70 metres. And whereas the hall in Berlin would have held 150,000 to 180,000 people, the capacity at Houston is 66,000.[129]

Work on Hitler's monumental structure was to have begun in 1940 and to have been completed ten years later. It is well known that he concerned himself not only with the overall effect of the building but also with technical and architectonic matters in which he showed an interest that was often both practical and shrewd.[130] A few years after he had designed his domed hall, a bridge-building firm was entrusted with the task of investigating the respective merits of steel and reinforced concrete as constructional material for vaulting a hall of these dimensions. Speer proposed that the dome should be erected without the use of steel. As the man responsible for the new Reich Chancellery in Berlin, the Party Rally building in Nuremberg and the German pavilion at the 1937 Paris World Exhibition he was considered an architect of genius – and not by Hitler alone. Yet it was the latter who realized that a dome without a steel framework could not be repaired if damaged, say, in an air raid. Speer finally appreciated his point and took note of it in his calculations.[131]

A number of eminent architects who worked with and were influenced by Hitler from 1933 onwards thought highly of his abilities in this field, an opinion they continued to express even after 1945. Paul Troost, Paul Giesler and Albert Speer, to name only a few, were surprised no less by his very real knowledge than by his intuitions and ideas. Though naturally anxious, so soon after his release from Spandau, to avoid contradicting his earlier statements at the Nuremberg trial, Speer nevertheless remarked of Hitler in 1966: 'I would not deny that he . . . might have been well above the usual run of architects. He was not without talent.'[132] One of Hitler's secretaries, who had been present at numerous discussions, formed the impression that he had an 'astounding' knowledge of architectural matters. Her remark that she had seen 'eminent architects literally staggered by his expertise' is of some significance.[133]

For some twenty-five years there is evidence of a restraining influence in the realization of his architectural projects, but the year 1937 marks a distinct turning-point. Now he began to let his 'genius' run riot and to translate into reality the visionary ideas of his youth, ideas which had first germinated between 1906 and 1913 in the Vienna Ringstrasse and were to recur thirty years later in greatly amplified but technically viable form. Thus the influence of such notable architects as Paul von Troost inevitably declined. Four years in power had been enough to turn Hitler into an architect and master-builder whose unparalleled self-confidence was only matched by his lack of restraint. Albert Speer, an architect as talented as he was ambitious,[134] submitted so completely to Hitler's tutelage that he appended the remark 'prepared in accordance with the Führer's ideas'[135] to his own designs for outsize buildings and, despite subsequent experiences, continued to refer to them thirty years later as 'our' projects.[136]

At this time [he wrote in 1969] my designs became increasingly disassociated from what I regarded as 'my style'. This departure from my beginnings was evident not only in the pretentious size of my buildings but also in the absence of the Doric simplicity I had striven to achieve in my earlier work. . . . Sheer riches, the inexhaustible resources that were placed at my disposal, no less than Hitler's party ideology, had impelled me towards a style more suited to the palace of an oriental despot.[137]

Speer was not the only one thus affected. In the Third Reich official architecture, like official painting and official sculpture, bore the stamp of a man who, in effect, had never been a pupil in any of these fields, but always and only a teacher.

In *Bruder Hitler* Thomas Mann asks with some scepticism 'whether the superstitious ideas commonly associated with the concept "genius" still have sufficient force to prevent us from describing our friend [Hitler] as a genius'.[138] Mann was aghast to find that his own idea of the true nature of art was basically in agreement with that of Adolf Hitler.

CHAPTER FOUR

Soldier for the Reich

'In the spring of 1912 I came at last to Munich', Hitler wrote in *Mein Kampf*.[1] After his assumption of power a large plaque was affixed to the wall of No. 34 Schleissheimerstrasse in that city. Adorned with an eagle and swastika, it bore the legend: 'Adolf Hitler lived here from the Spring of 1912 until August 1914 when he volunteered for military service.'[2] Neither statement tallies with the facts.[3] Until 24 May 1913 Hitler continued to live at No. 27 Meldemannstrasse in Vienna. On that date he left the Austrian capital for Munich with 80 kronen in his pocket, and two days later found lodgings in the house of a tailor called Josef Popp.[4]

In the meantime, on the night of 24 May, Colonel Alfred Redl, Chief of Staff of the Austro-Hungarian VIII Corps, had shot himself in Vienna. Redl, a homosexual, had been blackmailed into spying for the Russian Intelligence service and for years had been providing them with important military secrets. The news, which Hitler read in the Munich Press, seemed to confirm his view[5] that the Austrian Army was not worth joining, and he was delighted.[6] Even at this early stage his quick grasp and original interpretation of political events had already made an impression on his new landlord Josef Popp who, as a young man, had worked in some of the best Parisian tailoring establishments, spoke French and prided himself on his cosmopolitan outlook. Every evening he would talk politics with Hitler whose fellow lodger and room-mate, finding these discussions insufferable, ended up by giving notice.[7]

During the early part of his stay in Munich Hitler busied himself with acquiring firsthand knowledge of the city and comparing it with what he had learnt from books. In 1924 he wrote in *Mein Kampf*: 'The city itself was as familiar to me as if I had lived for years within its walls. This is accounted for by my study which at every step had led me to this metropolis of German art. . . . Not only has one not seen Germany if one does not know Munich . . . above all one does not know German art if one has not seen Munich.'[8]

In Munich Hitler's circumstances were as good as, if not better than, they had been in Vienna. It was not without reason that he later wrote: 'This period before the war was the happiest and by far the most contented of my life.'[9] As a painter his average earnings amounted to the then considerable sum of a hundred marks a month. We know this from a letter he wrote to the Linz magistrates in reply to a summons issued after his repeated failure to report for military service. In that letter, dated January 1914, he enclosed a tax certificate in support of his statements.

I earn my living as a self-employed artist [he wrote], but I do so only in order to continue my education, being otherwise quite without means (my father was a civil servant). I can only devote a very small part of my time to earning as I am still learning to be an architectural painter. So my income is very modest and only just enough to meet my expenses. In proof of this, I enclose my tax certificate which I should be grateful if you would return to me without delay. My income is estimated on the high side at 1200 marks, which should not be taken to mean that my monthly income is exactly 100 marks.[10]

The tenor of the letter agrees with the following passage in *Mein Kampf*, written some ten years later:

Even if my earnings were still extremely meagre, I did not live to be able to paint, but painted only to be able to secure my livelihood or rather to enable myself to go on studying.[11]

Even so, his minimum annual income, officially assessed at 1200 marks, was higher than his average earnings in Vienna. Moreover conditions were more favourable in Munich. In Vienna Hitler would have spent some 25 kronen a month if he had lunched daily at a medium-priced restaurant, as compared with only 18 to 25 marks in Munich. The rent for a room in a private house in Vienna amounted to 10 kronen (or perhaps 15 kronen for a short let) whereas Hitler was charged 20 marks for his room in the Schleissheimerstrasse, which was well-furnished and had a separate entrance.[12] After deducting the cost of his breakfast and evening meal, he still had at least 30 marks a month to spend. This was more than enough since his tastes were not extravagant. In Munich at that time a bank clerk of the same age would have earned about 70 marks a month. Speaking to Heinrich Hoffmann on 12 March 1944, Hitler said that he had never needed more than 80 marks a month, one mark a day being sufficient for lunch and supper.[13]

Thus, as Popp relates, he could always afford to give the son of the house a tip or sweets for fetching his books or running some other errand for him.

In Munich as in Vienna Hitler remained a lone wolf. The fact that he was misunderstood and unappreciated was wholly immaterial to him. Being reluctant to open his heart to anyone he desired neither acquaintances nor friends. In the eyes of ordinary citizens he was an artist leading an aimless and dilatory existence. He spent most of his time reading books and pamphlets, and might also paint for an hour or two, but only during the day. From time to time he visited the local café where he read the daily papers and ate pastries, while in the evenings he would expound his views and ideas to his landlord or else, having co-opted Popp's son as prompter, recite by heart passages from military works.[14] He was not interested in a career, or what is normally understood as such, and in this he differed little from other painters – Oskar Kokoschka, for instance, who, on the occasion of his eighty-fifth birthday, described himself as having 'always been a vagabond' from youth up.[15]

Despite his Bohemian existence, Hitler was invariably dressed with such care that his appearance never jarred on his landlord. The latter's wife and his son, Josef, relate that the young artist liked to wear an immaculate frock-coat which Josef Popp senior would press for him. Even at that time Popp sensed that his lodger promised great things and it was no coincidence that as early as 1919 he became member no. 609 of the German Workers' Party of which Hitler was already chief propagandist.[16]

Hitler realized that he was regarded as a crank by those around him.[17] He read voraciously and applied himself to painting only when he had orders to fulfil or when circumstances made it imperative. He was passionately interested in politics and possessed an uncommon ability to convince others by means of oratory, argument and gesture, as people who had known him in Linz, Spital, Leonding, Vienna and Munich all confirm. However, it would seem that in the face of his gesticulations and impassioned eloquence they were often left poised uncertainly between laughter and amazement.[18] According to relations and acquaintances his nature betrayed violent contrasts. Moreover his need to assert himself, his aggressiveness and his striving for power seemed excessive, as did the impulsiveness and egocentricity of his actions. He permitted no one to take liberties with him. To friends and enemies alike he would appear by turns unrelenting, obstinate, hypersensitive, capricious and quarrelsome, or again, secretive, reserved and gauche. He would sometimes startle his immediate associates by his overweening ambition, the extravagance of his plans, his apparently unshakeable self-confidence and his indefatigable energy. Even before 1914 critical observers held many of his ideas to be crude and grossly inflated.

Contemporary eye-witness accounts would seem to indicate that even in his youth Hitler showed marked psychopathic tendencies. The assumption found in numerous biographies that he 'was simply abnormal' derives from a view that is not only prejudiced but also, as often as not, crudely simplistic and unbalanced. The effects to which psychopathy may give rise have been described by Wilhelm Lange-Eichbaum whose generally accepted analysis includes the following passage:

A psychopathic affectivity may provide the impulse for the development, expansion and deepening of a natural talent. A psychopath will respond to the minutest of stimuli and his experience is thereby enlarged. The inner turmoil in his blood, his restlessness, and his ever changing moods enable him to experience many things and to see them in as many different lights. Thus the psychopath acquires a keen eye for what is recurrent, permanent and essential. The extreme versatility of his imaginative life, his perpetual thirst for stimulation, his craving for novelty, impel him to explore numerous fields. This enlarges his horizon, develops his psychic potential, and may even tap unsuspected talents. Thus widely separated fields can be united in one psyche – peripheral areas, peripheral sciences and arts, suddenly become sources of extreme significance. The relentless force of the emotional life, the greater measure of unreason, the lack of self-control and all that this implies, give rise to experiences such as never come to other people.[19]

Whether Hitler was capable of artless humour or possessed any truly likeable human qualities will never be known. Years later he was to recall that in his Linz and Steyr days he had been a malicious youth with a cold and calculating eye for other people's weaknesses. The majority of those who knew or met him at the time take a subjective view, but significantly they all agree that he could be very pleasant whenever he cast off his self-consciousness along with the cold and pompous manner he had assumed from his schooldays onwards. Dr Bloch, for instance, to whom his young patient had always seemed secretive and unapproachable, was taken aback by his sudden display of human feeling after his mother's death. However his piano teacher, Prewatzky-Wendt, never saw him in an expansive or a confiding mood.[20] And when, after leaving school, Hitler visited his relations in the Waldviertel in Lower Austria, he seemed to them distant rather than friendly.[21] They were not alone in regarding him as a precocious boy who stood overmuch on his dignity, gave himself too many airs and graces and would never in any circumstances admit to gaps in his knowledge or to personal failings. At the age of twenty-five Hitler was described by Josef and Elizabeth Popp as an 'Austrian charmer' who, though always pleasant, helpful and generous, tended to be eccentric and to keep himself to himself. They and their parents were, to use their own words 'very fond of the young man', but they never discovered what was really going on in his mind: 'You couldn't tell what he was thinking. He never spoke about his parents, nor yet about his friends. Most of the time he sat at home with his nose buried in heavy books. In between times he painted.'

While Hitler was in Munich during 1913-14 neither Popp nor his family ever knew who his associates were. Yet he was very fond of the children and always mentioned them in his letters from the front, calling them by their pet names, and greeting each one individually.[22] He never received visitors, though by doing so he would not have disturbed the family as he had his own front door. Nevertheless he is known to have had other acquaintances in Munich besides the Popps – the lawyer Ernst Hepp and his wife, for instance, with whom he was evidently on very friendly terms as can be seen from a long letter to Herr Hepp from the front (reproduced later in this chapter).

In 1924 he was to write in Mein Kampf: 'I had left Austria primarily for political reasons. . . . I did not want to fight for the Habsburg state.'[23] Only much later was it discovered that this circumlocution concealed a painful episode that occurred while he was living in Munich. On 29 December 1913 the Austrian police had applied to their German colleagues inquiring whether Hitler had registered in the Bavarian capital. Their communication ran: 'Adolf Hietler, born 1889 in Braunau am Inn . . . artist officially domiciled in Linz, removed from Vienna to Munich on 24 May 1913. – We shall be grateful if you will inform us whether the above-named has registered there.' The Munich police traced him and on 10 January 1914 wrote to Linz: 'The subject of your inquiry has been registered as living c/o Popp 34/III Schleissheimerstrasse with effect from 26 May 1913.'[24] Eight days later Hitler received a summons from the Munich police, directing him to present himself for enlistment in Linz on 20 January. On 19 January they escorted him to the Austrian Consulate where a statement was taken. At the interview, Hitler – clad, no doubt, in an old, paint-spattered suit – complained of being ill and clearly succeeded in arousing the sympathy of the consular official, thus inducing him to write in support of the veracity of his statement:

From the observations made by the police and the impression gained in this office, it would seem that the excuses put forward in the enclosed letter are entirely in accord with the truth. It would also seem that this man is suffering from a complaint which renders him unfit for military service.... As Hietler seems very deserving of considerate treatment, we shall provisionally refrain from handing him over as requested and have instructed him to report on 25 January without fail to the Special Conscription Panel in Linz. ... Hietler will therefore proceed to Linz unless you feel that the circumstances described above and his lack of funds justify his being allowed to report in Salzburg.[25]

Hitler telegraphed the Linz magistrates requesting them to postpone the date to 5 February 1914. The Austrian authorities refused his request and replied, obviously in high dudgeon: 'Essential you appear',[26] a message which did not reach Hitler until 21 January. He then inquired from Linz whether, in view of his financial situation, he might be allowed to report in Salzburg, which was closer to Munich. His very courteous letter ends:

I am sending this letter independently of the statement I signed at the Consulate today. I also request that further instructions be sent to me through the Consulate and beg you to rest assured that I shall not fail to execute them promptly. Finally, with regard to my statements concerning the summons, these are being confirmed by the consular official, who very kindly gave me reason to hope that it might be possible for me to enlist in Salzburg. I trust I may make so bold as to hope that you will be kind enough not to make things more difficult than necessary for me.

I most humbly request that you give my letter your kind consideration and sign myself.

Your very humble servant, Adolf Hitler, Artist.[27]

His boldness in hoping that things would not be made too difficult for him was rewarded. On 5 February 1914 he travelled to Salzburg to enlist and, in accordance with his expectations, was exempted from

military service. As the Registrar of the Upper Austrian Provincial
Government confirmed in 1932:

According to the relevant enlistment roll, Adolf Hitler, born 20 April 1888
at Braunau am Inn and domiciled in Linz, Upper Austria, son of Alois and
Klara, née Pölzl, presented himself on 5 February 1914 in Salzburg before
the Recruitment Panel dealing with men overdue for enlistment in Age-
Group 3 and was found to be 'not strong enough for combatant and non-
combatant duties' and registered as 'unfit for military service'.[28]

The Austrian official's cautiously worded comment in his letter of
19 January, 'It would also seem that he is suffering from a complaint',
suggests that at the interview Hitler had invoked his old lung trouble,
long since cleared up, which had induced his mother to take him away
from school in the autumn of 1905.[29] At all events Adolf Hitler, the
draft-dodger, was not brought to book for his repeated failure to enlist.
He now proposed to practise what he had preached in the late summer
of 1908 when his friend Kubizek had received his calling-up papers.
He did not wish to serve in the same army as Czechs and Jews nor did he
wish to fight for the Habsburg state. Nevertheless he was at all times
ready to die for the German Reich,[30] which offered him, a fanatical
Pan-German, a congenial home and one worthy of his homage. Hence,
if soldier he must be, better there than anywhere else. In 1914,
then, he was able to stay on in Munich, where he pursued a Bohemian
existence and vented his scorn on his Austro–Hungarian fatherland.

In Munich Hitler was not primarily concerned with antisemitism
and Marxism as he had been in Vienna, but rather with Austro-German
foreign policy and the attitude of the Germans towards Austria. Even
before moving to Munich, he tells us in Mein Kampf, he had regarded
as 'absolutely mistaken'[31] the Germany policy of alliances – the
Austro–German Alliance of 7 October 1879, the Dreikaiserbund of 18
June 1881, and the Triple Alliance between Germany, Austria–Hungary and Italy of 20 May 1882.[32] In Munich Hitler came to the conclusion that the Germans generally looked upon their ally, Austria–
Hungary, as 'a serious power' which, 'in the hour of need' would
surely rise to the occasion. But he, as an Austrian, did not share this view
since he believed that 'Austria had long ceased to be a German state'.
Indeed it seemed to him that 'internal conditions' in Austria–Hungary
were deteriorating 'from hour to hour'.[33] He mistrusted Austro-
Hungarian assurances, believing that 'in Austria the only exponents

of the alliance idea were the Habsburgs and Germans. The Habsburgs, out of calculation and compulsion; the Germans, from good faith and political stupidity.' He did not doubt that, in joining the Triple Alliance, Germany had chained herself to 'the corpse of a state' which would 'inevitably drag them both into the abyss'; and he was convinced that, 'better than the so-called diplomats', he knew the German policy of alliances to be as dangerous as it was futile.[34] In Munich this young Austrian with his Pan-German views was astounded by the general apathy towards the plight of Germans living in Austria: 'To my amazement, I could not help seeing everywhere that even in otherwise well-informed circles there was not the slightest glimmer of knowledge concerning the nature of the Habsburg monarchy.[35] In the same context he states that 'in the years 1913 and 1914, I, for the first time . . . expressed the conviction that the question of the future of the German nation was the question of destroying Marxism'.[36] That he was not simply being wise after the event is evident from his conversations with his landlord and others, and also from his correspondence at this time.

On hearing that the Austrian heir-apparent, Franz Ferdinand, and his wife had been murdered in Sarajevo on 28 June 1914, Hitler's initial reaction was, as he wrote later, concern lest the shots had been fired by

German students, who, out of indignation at the heir-apparent's continuous work of Slavization, wanted to free the German people from this internal enemy. . . . But when, soon afterwards, I heard the names of the supposed assassins, and moreover read that they had been identified as Serbs, a light shudder began to run through me at this vengeance of inscrutable Destiny.[37]

His feeling of unease was shortlived. There is in existence a photograph taken on 1 August 1914 in the Odeonsplatz in Munich of a crowd listening to the announcement of the declaration of war. Among them is Hitler, his eyes shining, his face radiant with gladness and excitement. Along with many of the German intelligentsia such as Thomas Mann, Ludwig Thoma and large numbers of university teachers, Hitler was overjoyed at the turn of events. 'To me those hours seemed like a release from the painful feelings of my youth. . . . Even today I am not ashamed to say that, overpowered by stormy enthusiasm, I fell down on my knees and thanked Heaven from an overflowing heart for granting me the good fortune of being permitted to live at this time.'[38]

Though only a few months previously he had been declared unfit for military service by an Austrian conscription panel he now hastened to lodge a personal petition with Ludwig III requesting that, though an Austrian, he should be permitted to enlist in the Bavarian Army. The very next day he was informed by the Chancellery that he might join a Bavarian unit. He chose 16 Reserve Infantry Regiment, later familiarly known as the List Regiment after its commanding officer, Colonel List, who was killed in action at the end of October 1914. On 16 August the popular *Berliner Illustrierte Zeitung* carried on its title page a picture of charging soldiers led by an infantry officer, complete with spiked helmet and drawn sword, shouting 'At 'em!' That same day Hitler reported to 2 Company of the 6th Recruit Replacement Battalion, 16 Bavarian Infantry Regiment at the *Elisabeth-Schule* in Munich where, on 8 October 1914, he took his oath of allegiance, first to the King of Bavaria and then to the Emperor Franz Joseph. In 1931 Hans Mend, who had been responsible for Hitler's initial training, recorded his impressions of the new recruit: 'I saw Hitler for the first time in Schwabmünchen. Though I didn't know who he was, I was struck in passing by his dynamic glance and by his unusual presence. I thought he might be an academic because a lot of them had joined the List Regiment.'[39] After a sketchy training Hitler was posted to France in the middle of October 1914. Nearly five months later, in February 1915, he wrote a highly informative letter to his Munich acquaintance Ernst Hepp in which his experiences are described with an artist's gift for observation:*

Glad to hear you got my last card, and thanks a lot for the kind letter you sent in reply.

This letter will bring up to date what I wrote in my last long missive. First of all I'd like to tell you straight away that on 2 December I was awarded the Iron Cross. Praise be, there were more than enough opportunities to win it. Our regiment did not go into reserve as we had expected but was sent into action straight away early on 29 October and for the last three [illegible] we've been mixing it with the English, as defenders if not as attackers. After a really lovely trip down the Rhine we arrived in Lille on 23 October. We came across the first signs of war as we travelled through Belgium. Liège was a mass of charred rubble. As

far as [illegible place name] our journey went smoothly and safely. But then there was one delay after another. In some places the rails had been loosened

---

*No attempt has been made to render in translation such spelling mistakes as occur in the letter, nor to reproduce the somewhat erratic punctuation. Spaces in the text indicate Hitler's original pages.

in spite of having been carefully guarded. More and more often we came across blown-up bridges and wrecked locomotives. Although the train was crawling along at a snail's pace, there seemed to be no end to the maddening stops. By now we could hear the monotonous rumble of our heavy mortars in the distance. Towards evening we arrived at a Lille suburb which had been rather badly knocked about by gunfire. There we detrained and waited about beside our piled arms. Some time before midnight we finally set off for the town itself. A never-ending monotonous road, squat factories on either side, nothing but soot and soot-blackened brick, the road filthy and rottenly surfaced. By 9 o'clock the street was empty of inhabitants but, for good measure, swarming with soldiers. At risk to life and limb we threaded our way through baggage trains and ammunition columns until at last we reached the gates of the inner town. Lille itself was certainly something of an improvement, but there really isn't very much to choose between the centre and the outskirts. My thoughts kept turning to Germany. We spent the night in the courtyard of the Bourse, a pretentious building which has not yet been completed. We didn't sleep very well because we had to bed down with our packs on as we were expecting an alert. Also the stone flags were very cold. The next day we moved into a billet, a huge glazed hall.

There was no shortage of fresh air since nothing was left but the iron ribs. The blast from German shells had shattered the glass to smithereens. In the daytime we trained for a bit, had a look at the town and were struck most of all by the power of the military machine. It has left its mark on the whole place and we gazed with awe at its enormous structures. At night we had sing-songs. For some of us it was to be the last time. At 2 a.m. on the third night we suddenly had an alert and marched off in battle order for our assembly area. No one knew anything for certain, but we thought it might only be a practice. It was a pretty dark night. We had hardly been marching for twenty minutes when we were ordered to move over to the verge so as to let through baggage trains, cavalry etc. The road was completely blocked but eventually we were able to start off again. Morning came at last. We had left Lille far behind. The thunder of the guns was gradually growing louder. Our column moved forward like a gigantic snake. At 9 a.m. we halted in the grounds of a château. Two hours' rest and then on again till eight in the evening. We weren't a regiment now but a whole lot of companies all seeking cover from air attack. At nine in the evening we were given our grub.

Unfortunately I couldn't get to sleep. There was a dead horse four feet away from my palliasse – at least a fortnight dead by the look of it. The thing was already half rotten. And on top of that one of our howitzer batteries was in position just behind us and every fifteen minutes a couple of shells went sailing over our heads into the darkness. They made a soughing, whistling

noise and then we'd hear, far off, two dull crumps. We all of us listened for
them. After all, we'd never heard anything like it before. And while we lay
huddled together talking in whispers and looking up at the stars a terrible
shindy began in the distance and then a rat-tat-tat coming nearer and
nearer and soon the shell bursts came so thick and fast that they merged into
one continuous roar. We all felt the blood throbbing in our veins. Word
went round that the English were making one of their night attacks. An-
xiously we waited. No one knew what was really happening out there. But
then things began to quieten down again till at last the hellish din stopped
altogether except for our own battery which every fifteen minutes thundered
its metallic greetings into the night. Next morning we discovered a big
shell-hole.

After much effort on our part the horse found its final resting place. We were
just starting to make ourselves comfortable when at 10 o'clock there was a
fresh alert and fifteen minutes later we were on the march. After a great deal
of toing and froing we arrived at a ruined farmhouse where we again
bivouacked. That night I was on guard. At 1 a.m. there was another alert and
at 3 we moved off. But first we drew more ammunition. As we were waiting
for the order to move, Major Graf Zech rode past. 'We'll be attacking the
English tomorrow,' he said. Our hearts leapt. At last! Having made this
announcement the major dismounted and walked to the head of the column.
At six o'clock next morning we joined up with the other companies outside
an inn and at seven the fun began. Moving by platoons, we wheeled to the
right and passed through a wood, arriving in good order at a clearing on
higher ground. Four guns had been dug in just in front of us. We took up
position behind them in some large craters and waited. By now the first
shrapnel was coming over and bursting at the edge of the wood, shredding
the trees as though they were wisps of straw. We watched curiously without
any real idea of the danger. None of us was afraid. We were all waiting

impatiently for the order to advance. The racket was getting worse and
worse. We heard that some of our people had already been wounded.
Suddenly everyone cheered at the sight of five or six chaps in dun-coloured
uniforms approaching on our left. Six Englishmen and a machine-gun. We
looked at their escorts who were marching proudly behind their quarry. As
for us, we had to go on waiting, hardly able to see through the fog and
smoke of the witches' cauldron ahead of us. At long last came the order
'Advance!' We swarmed out of our craters, came to some fields and raced
across them towards a small farmhouse. Shrapnel was bursting to right and
left of us and English bullets went singing in between but we took no notice
of them. We lay there for ten minutes after which we were again ordered to
advance. I was right out in front and no longer with our platoon. Suddenly

the word went round that Stöwer, our platoon commander, had been hit
Crikey, I thought, that's a fine beginning. But we were out in the open and
it was best to get a move-on. The captain was leading us. Now we had our
first losses. The English had brought their machine-guns to bear on us. So
we threw ourselves down and crawled slowly along a furrow.

Occasionally there'd be a hold-up; it happened whenever someone was
wounded and couldn't go on and had to be hauled out of the furrow. We
crawled on like this until the furrow ended and we were forced out into the
open again. Fifteen or twenty yards further on we came to a big pond. One
after the other we flung ourselves into it, took cover and got our breath back.
But we couldn't remain there for ever. So out we got and doubled towards a
wood about a hundred yards ahead of us. There we reformed after a fashion
but we were no longer very thick on the ground. Now there was no one left
to command us except a tall, lanky sergeant called Schmidt, a first-rate chap.
We crawled along the ground till we reached the edge of the wood. There
was a shrieking and whistling overhead, shattered trunks and branches
flying all over the place. Then more shells came crashing into the edge of the
wood sending up fountains of rock, earth and sand, tearing enormous trees
up by the roots and smothering everything in a foul stinking grey-green
vapour. But we couldn't stay here for ever and if die we must far better to
do it out there. Then our major turned up.

Again we advanced. Running and jumping as best I could, I crossed meadows
and beet-fields, leapt over ditches, struggled over wire and through hedges
and then ahead of me I heard someone shouting: 'In here! Everyone in
here!' There was a long trench just in front of me. A moment later, with
countless others ahead of me, behind me and to my left and right, I leapt
down into it. Alongside me were Württembergers, under my feet dead and
wounded English soldiers. The Württembergers had stormed the trench
before we arrived. And now I knew why I had landed so softly. 250–290
yards away on our left front the English were still entrenched and on our
right they still held the road to [illegible]. An uninterrupted hail of metal
went hurtling over our heads. At last, at ten o'clock, our own artillery began
to join in. 1-2-3-5 etc. continuously. Shell after shell began to strike the
English trenches in front of us. The blokes began swarming out like ants
out of an ant-heap and then we charged.

  We were across the fields in a flash and after some bloody hand-to-hand
fighting we cleared one trench after another. A lot of the enemy put their
hands up. Those that didn't surrender were

slaughtered. So it went on from trench to trench. At last we reached the
main road, coppices on either hand. In we went and herded the English
out in droves. In this way we came to the edge of the wood where the road

ran out into open country. Some farm buildings to the left of us were still in enemy hands and we came under ferocious fire. We started going down like ninepins. Then along comes our major calmly smoking and cool as a cucumber, and with him his adjutant, 2nd Lt Pyloty. The major took in the situation at a glance and ordered us to assemble on either side of the road and prepare to charge. We'd lost all our officers and most of our NCOs so anyone who still had any gumption turned back in search of reinforcements. When I came back for the second time after rounding up a party of Württembergers, the major was lying on the ground with a gaping hole in his chest, round him a pile of corpses. Now only one officer was left, his adjutant. We were boiling with rage. 'Lead us into attack, sir!' we yelled in unison. So we entered the wood on our left. It was impossible to advance up the road. Four times we tried and each time we had to withdraw. Of my whole section, only I and one other remained and soon there was only me. My right sleeve was ripped off by a bullet but miraculously I was not even grazed. Finally at 2 o'clock we launched our fifth attack and this time were able to occupy the edge of the wood and the farm buildings. At five in the afternoon we reassembled and dug in three hundred yards away from the road. So it went on for three days and on the third we finally dislodged them. On the evening of the fourth day we marched back to [illegible]. Only now did we realize how heavy our casualties had been. In four days our regiment had dwindled from three and a half thousand to six hundred men. Only three officers were left in the whole regiment and four companies had to be disbanded. But we were all very proud at having thrown back the English. Since then we've had an unbroken spell in the front line. I was put up for the Iron Cross – for the first time at Messines and for the second, along with [illegible] others, at Wytschaete – by Lt-Col. Engelhardt, our regimental commander. I finally got it on 2 December. I am now

a runner at headquarters. It may be a cleaner job but it's a good deal more dangerous. At Wytschaete, on the very first day of the attack, three men were killed out of our total of eight and one was badly wounded. We four survivors including the wounded man were decorated. It was this decoration that saved our lives. For while they were preparing a list of men recommended for the Iron Cross, four company commanders came into the tent or dug-out rather. To make room for them we had to go outside for a while. We had not been out there more than five minutes when a shell hit the tent, severely wounding Lt-Col. Engelhardt and either killing or wounding the rest of the headquarters staff. It was the worst moment of my life. We worshipped Colonel Engelhardt.

I'm afraid I must stop now and beg you to excuse this scrawl. I feel very shaky at the moment. Every day from eight in the morning till five in the afternoon we're under very heavy artillery-fire which in the long run is

1. The cradle of the Third Reich. The house in Spital where Hitler's mother was born and (*right*) part of the next door house in which his father grew up.

2. The home of the Hitler clan in Spital. It was here that Alois Hitler spent his childhood and Adolf his school holidays; here, too, that he came to convalesce from his pulmonary complaint.

3. All that remains of Strones, birthplace of Hitler's father (b. 1837).

4. Entrance door to the Catholic presbytery, Rastenfeld, close to the ruined village of Strones. It was here that the author discovered some of the Döllersheim parish records relating to Hitler's father.

5. Adolf Hitler's parental home from 1892 to 1895, at Hafeld near Lambach an der Traun.

6. The Hitler house at Leonding near Linz, now the home and surgery of the local doctor. Just across the road is the cemetery where Adolf Hitler's parents are buried.

8. Tomb of Adolf Hitler's parents at Leonding near Linz.

9. Alois Hitler, Adolf Hitler's father.

10. Klara Hitler, Adolf Hitler's mother.

11. Adolf Hitler as a baby.

12. Adolf Hitler as a ten-year-old primary school boy at Leonding.

13. Adolf Hitler as a grammar school boy in Linz.

14. Paula Hitler, Adolf Hitler's sister (c. 1915).

bound to shatter the strongest nerves. Very many thanks for the two parcels which you and

Frau Hepp were kind enough to send me. I think about Munich very often and if there's one thing we all of us want, it's to settle accounts with this bunch once and for all, to get to grips with them, cost what it may and, if we're lucky enough to get home again, to find it cleaner, and cleansed of foreign elements. We further hope that the sacrifice and agony we suffer daily in our hundreds of thousands, the stream of blood shed day after day against an international world of enemies, will not merely destroy Germany's enemies abroad but also break our internationalism at home. That would be worth more than any territorial gain. As for Austria, things will turn out like I've always said they would.

Thanking you once again, and with respectful greetings to your lady mother and your lady wife,

I remain, in gratitude,

Your humble servant,

Adolf Hitler.[40]

Hitler's war record* – campaigns, decorations, wounds, periods in hospital and on leave – is fully documented.[41] In addition there is evidence to show that he was a comradely, level-headed and unusually brave soldier, and that a number of his commanding officers singled him out for special mention. Nevertheless political opponents at the time of the Weimar Republic put it about that he was not entitled to wear the Iron Cross 1st Class, a rumour which was revived after 1945.[42] He himself never told anyone how he had won this decoration, but is more forthcoming about his Iron Cross 2nd Class, which he was awarded as early as December 1914. Writing from the front in a hitherto unpublished letter to Josef Popp he said:

I was promoted Lance-Corporal and by a miracle haven't yet had a scratch. After three days' rest we were back in action again first at Messines and then at Wytschaete. There we made two attacks. But it was pretty hard going. In my company there are only 42 men left and only 17 in 11 Company. Now three drafts have just arrived, 1200 men in all. After the second battle I was recommended for the Iron Cross. But that same day the Company commander was badly wounded and the thing was dropped. Instead I joined headquarters as a runner. Since then, though I say it myself, I've risked my life every day and death has been staring me in the face. Then Lt-Col. Engelhardt himself put me up for the Iron Cross. But that same day he was badly wounded as well. He was our second CO – our first was killed on the

* See Appendix A.

third day. Next it was the adjutant, Lt Eichelsdörfer, who put me up for it and yesterday, 2 December, I was actually awarded the Iron Cross. It was the happiest day of my life. Of course my mates deserved it too, but they're nearly all of them dead. I beg of you, dear Herr Popp, to keep a copy of the newspaper with the announcement of my decoration. I'd like to have it for a souvenir, if so be the Lord spares my life.

Having delivered himself of his main item of news he concludes: 'I very often think of Munich and of you in particular, dear Herr Popp. . . . Sometimes I have a great longing to be home. I must close now, dear Herr Popp, and again beg you to forgive me for not having written for so long. For that, you must blame the Iron Cross.'[43] When Eichelsdörfer wrote his *Four Years on the Western Front. The Story of the 16th List Reserve Infantry Regiment* in 1932, he was unaware of the existence of this letter. He described Hitler as a level-headed front-line soldier whose courage and resolution had helped to prevent the regimental commander, Engelhardt, from being struck down by enemy fire like his immediate predecessor, Colonel List, who had been killed on 31 October 1914.

It is, of course, true that Hitler's descriptions of his war experiences are not altogether free of falsification and hyperbole. Thus he wrote to his landlord in Munich stating that in the space of four days his regiment had dwindled from 3600 to 611 men as a result of enemy action.[44] An examination of the casualty lists shows that on 29 October 1914, the day the regiment received its baptism of fire, it lost 349 dead, while the total number of men killed between 30 October and 24 November 1914 amounted to 373. In all 3754 officers, NCOs and men of the List Regiment lost their lives between 1914 and 1918.[45] We cannot tell whether Hitler's statements were deliberate exaggerations or miscalculations resulting from wrong or inadequate information. But where his decorations were concerned there was only one point of detail on which he failed to adhere strictly to the facts.

Most of the rumours and myths surrounding his Iron Cross 1st Class can be traced back to his wartime company sergeant, Georg Schnell, and to his corporal, Hans Mend. Schnell, for instance, maintained in a letter to the author that:

Hitler had no right to wear the Iron Cross 1st Class. On 8 August 1918 it was announced in Regimental Orders that 'Hitler, Adolf, Acting Lance-Corporal, 3 Company' was among those to be decorated with the Iron Cross 1st Class. When I discovered that his company had not put him up for this decoration I at once got in touch by telephone with the then regimental clerk, Sergeant Amann . . . [Later NSDAP Reichsleiter]. I also reported the matter to Rudolf Hess, his company commander at the time. Recommendations for the Bavarian Service Cross had to be in by the first of every month and those for the Iron Cross 1st Class by the fifth. These recommendation lists would go up to Regiment and Amann had added his own and Hitler's name to one of them. In other words it was a rotten swindle.

There is no truth in Schnell's allegations nor, for that matter, is he correct in stating that Rudolf Hess was a company commander in the List Regiment at the time. The other main source of rumour, ex-Corporal Hans Mend, was a farmer's son from the neighbourhood of Rothenburg ob der Tauber, whose audacity as a mounted orderly had earned him the admiration of his fellow-soldiers. After 1933, in what has come to be known as the 'Mend Report', he disseminated highly unflattering and invidious information, allegedly based on his personal knowledge of Hitler as a soldier. A story he concocted about how the latter won the Iron Cross 1st Class was later recounted by Dr Schmid-Noerr:

Having completed his military training Hitler received permission from Captain von Godin to accompany two runners on a mission in order to gain some practical experience. According to Mend, the three men had only just set out when one of them received a superficial wound and turned back. The other two noticed some movement behind a breach in a parapet. As they approached it the second man was killed. Hitler ran the last few yards to the abandoned trench where he found huddled together a party of frightened French soldiers. Having ordered them to stand up immediately and throw away their weapons, he marched them off at gunpoint and brought them back in good order. Captain von Godin listened to Hitler's inflated account and was so impressed by the heroic action of this relatively inexperienced recruit that he put him up for an immediate award of the Iron Cross 1st Class.[46]

The last sentence alone is enough to show that Mend did not know what he was talking about. Hitler won his Iron Cross 1st Class after four years and some three dozen engagements on the Western Front and could in no circumstances have been described as a 'relatively inexperienced recruit'.

Schnell's and Mend's allegations were made with an expressly political aim in view. They continued to be secretly disseminated in the years after Hitler had seized power and are even claimed by Mend's friends and acquaintances to have played some part in the plot of

20 July 1944.[47] They were intended to discredit Hitler and to counteract the propaganda which had extolled his courage as a soldier in the First World War and his military genius in the Second. Hans Mend's 'reminiscences' have no more connection with the facts of the matter than Hanisch's stories about Hitler's life before 1914. Mend, described by an acquaintance as 'a somewhat unpleasant . . . true-to-type, garrulous Franconian, with a coarse and ready turn of wit and a sometimes offensively blunt way of talking',[48] may well have heard these stories in Munich where, after the war, he earned his living partly as a riding instructor and partly as an art dealer.[49] However in 1931, while still unswayed by political considerations, he published a pamphlet entitled *Adolf Hitler in the Field, 1914–1918* in which he wrote: 'As one of his comrades, I often had the opportunity of hearing him talk about the war, of witnessing his bravery and getting to know his outstanding qualities.' He went on to describe him as a 'born soldier'.[50] Yet after 1933 the so-called Mend Report gave a very different version of the matter. Reconstructing part of the text from memory, Schmid-Noerr writes:

Soon after the outbreak of war Adolf Hitler, a volunteer, was allotted to me [Mend] as a general 'bottlewasher' . . . but first he had to be deloused. As a footloose Austrian . . . he had button-holed Prince Rupert, the heir-apparent, in Munich and had held forth about his German patriotic feelings and his ardent desire to volunteer. The Crown Prince told an ADC to direct the importunate man to the nearest military headquarters where he was accepted on the strength of his assurance that he had been 'directly recommended'. In the field he soon struck his comrades as a busybody with too many bees in his bonnet to be sensible. Off duty he would make long, muddled speeches to the men. He educated himself by diligently studying *Reclam* pocket editions. When he was serving in the trenches he made little clay figures, stood them in a row on the parapet and harangued them . . . about how, after the war had been won and the social order changed, a free people's state would be set up. More and more his comrades came to look on him as an absurd braggart and a crazy chatterbox whom no one could take seriously.[51]

Mend vanished suddenly and without trace but how – and whether – he lost his life is not known. Schmid-Noerr gives the following account of his disappearance:

Mend and I were walking along the Karlstrasse in Munich intending to visit some art dealers. A man came up to us and asked Mend in my hearing whether he could spare him a moment. They went away and I waited expecting to see Mend back at any minute. But he did not come back and I never saw him again. His landlady in Berg told me that the Gestapo had escorted him to Würzburg and brought him before the Gauleiter, who received him with the words: 'So you're here at last. We've been expecting you for a long time. What have you been up to?' Shortly afterwards Mend was taken to the Brown House in Munich and then to an unknown destination on the Chiemsee.... Here he was subsequently 'liquidated' on Hitler's orders.

Schmid-Noerr's contention that Mend was not taken to a concentration camp is refuted by the evidence. According to the relevant documents Mend remained in detention until Christmas 1938. On 23 January 1939, in reply to inquiries from the Central Archives of the NSDAP, the official at the Ministry of Justice responsible for the penal camp at Emsland stated that the 'convict Hans Mend' had been pardoned and 'released from confinement' on 24 December 1938.[52]

In the spring of 1922, at a time when there was as yet no compulsion to refer to Hitler in glowing terms, a number of officers described their former runner and bicycle despatch rider[53] as keen, dedicated, cool and unruffled. For instance, Lieutenant-Colonel von Lüneschloss said of him: 'Hitler never let us down and was particularly suited to the kind of task that could not be entrusted to other runners.'[54] And Major-General Friedrich Petz, a former commander of 16 Reserve Infantry Regiment, wrote: 'Hitler ... was mentally very much all there and physically fresh, alert and hardy. His pluck was exceptional, as was the reckless courage with which he tackled dangerous situations and the hazards of battle.'[55] On 20 March 1922 Colonel Spatny recalled that:

the intense and unremitting activity on the battle fronts in northern France and Belgium where the regiment remained throughout the war demanded the utmost of its members in terms of devotion and personal bravery. Here Hitler set a shining example to those around him. His pluck and his exemplary bearing throughout each battle exerted a powerful influence on his comrades and this, combined with his admirable unpretentiousness, earned him the respect of superiors and equals alike.[56]

Lieutenant-Colonel Anton Freiherr von Tubeuf (a Knight of the Order of Maximilian Joseph) also spoke very highly of him. He was, he said,

invariably obliging and helpful.... There was no circumstance or situation that would have prevented him from volunteering for the most difficult, arduous and dangerous tasks and he was always ready to sacrifice life and tranquillity for his fatherland and for others. Of all my men he was closest to me in the human sense, and I never failed to appreciate the views he expressed in our private conversations, views which testified to his profound love of his country and to his altogether upright and honourable nature.[57]

The recommendation for the award, which was signed by Lieutenant-Colonel Freiherr von Godin on 31 July 1918 and forwarded to the 12th Royal Bavarian Reserve Infantry Brigade, reads:

As a runner his coolness and dash in both trench and open warfare have been exemplary, and invariably he has shown himself ready to volunteer for tasks in the most difficult situations and at great danger to himself. Whenever communications have been totally disrupted at a critical moment in a battle, it has been thanks to Hitler's unflagging and devoted efforts that important messages continued to get through despite every difficulty. Hitler received the Iron Cross 2nd Class for gallant conduct during the fighting at Wytschaete on 1 Dec. 1914. I consider that he fully deserves to be awarded the Iron Cross 1st Class.[58]

The National Socialists were themselves partly responsible for the unsavoury rumours that proliferated round Hitler's award of the Iron Cross 1st Class. They refused to admit (in so far as they knew) that the decoration Hitler proudly wore right up to the end of his life had been awarded him at the instance of a Jew – at the instance that is, of Hugo Gutmann, the regimental adjutant. Hitler had earned this recommendation after he had carried a message to the German artillery under exceptionally difficult conditions, and thus prevented them from firing on their own infantry which in the meantime had taken up a more advanced position.[59]

As a runner at regimental headquarters he was in regular contact with a succession of officers of all ranks and hence in a position to see and hear more than did many of the battalion, company and platoon commanders. By all accounts his conduct was impressive. For instance, during the fighting south of Courthiezy on 17 July 1918 he saved the life of the commander of 9 Company when, having found him severely wounded by an American shell, he dragged him to the rear.[60] Two weeks later he was awarded the Iron Cross 1st Class and three weeks after that he went to Nuremberg on short leave. On 25 August he was awarded the Service Decoration 3rd Class. On 10 September he went on home leave to Spital, the Hitler family's place of origin.

In the course of four years fighting round Ypres, Fromelles, Messines, Wytschaete, on the Somme, in Artois, round La Bassée, Arras, the Chemin des Dames, on the Marne and near La Montagne, he gained inside knowledge of the way a regiment is commanded and accumulated insights and a fund of experience such as no General Staff officer could hope to acquire in peacetime. Later on, during the Second World War, this was to give him a certain advantage over many of his generals. But even as a strategist and warlord and despite his notable decisions based on intuition and inspiration, he always remained at heart a regimental commander who thinks it incumbent on him to know all, miss nothing and decide everything, down to the smallest detail himself.

The orders he issued as Supreme Commander of the Wehrmacht, as well as the arguments he put forward in support of his decisions, tended to reflect his own experiences in the First World War. Thus, during a discussion of air operations in Italy at his situation conference on the evening of 18 June 1944, he said:

During the Great War we were nowhere as weak in the air as we are now. I know that for a fact. At the time of our push during the Great Battle in France we actually chased every single British aircraft from the battle zone. During the Great War we were never faced with anything like the present situation. Even in 1917, at the Battle of Arras, the situation was such that the Richthofen Squadron was able to clear the sky of all enemy aircraft. Not one British squadron was able to get through – we fought them all off. I myself witnessed part of an engagement in which the last remnants of a formation of ten aircraft were shot down. We had the sky to ourselves. There was some murderous air fighting during the Flanders battles – major engagements by the standards of the day with seventy to one hundred machines on either side – but there was never any suggestion of the enemy flying around in complete possession of the sky. Obviously they were getting a bit cheekier by then, and in 1918 things got worse.[61]

On another occasion, towards the end of 1944, he is reported as saying:

That's how people are, as I myself well know from the time when I was a runner. For instance, a picture postcard would arrive for a commander up forward. Then – at least in our regiment between 1915 and 1916, until we finally got a sensible CO – a man would be sent up in broad daylight to deliver his card, which he knew had arrived because they'd told him by telephone. Sometimes that would cost a man his life, not to speak of endangering the HQs because anybody in the air could see where the runners were going. Sheer madness! It was only gradually that orders seeped down from above, putting a stop to this useless waste of life. It was the same with the horses. For instance someone would drive from Messines to Fournes to fetch a pound of butter, then back they'd come with their pound of butter from Fournes to Messines. I've seen the same kind of thing in industry. A four and a half ton truck is sent to pick up a minute piece of machinery weighting twenty pounds. But we're gradually putting a stop to that.[62]

Hitler's refusal to countenance the timely evacuation of positions that were no longer tenable, and the obstinacy with which he almost invariably opposed his generals' suggestion that defensive works be established to the rear, derived very largely from the knowledge he had gained twenty-five years earlier. In the spring of 1917, while in the Prussian military hospital at Beelitz near Stettin, he had heard that the withdrawal of German troops to the 'Siegfried position', undertaken to eliminate the salient between Arras and Soissons, had been rather more precipitate than the High Command had intended. Since then he had been convinced that the existence of fortifications and prepared positions to the rear had an unsettling effect on fighting troops, who were drawn to them as by a magnet.

One of the more important, and indeed fateful, lessons he learned at this time was in the field of propaganda. In *Mein Kampf* he wrote: 'It was not until the war that it became evident what immense results could be obtained by the correct application of propaganda. . . . For what we failed to do, the enemy did, with amazing skill and really brilliant calculation.' After enumerating the main points learnt from his observations namely that humanity can play no part in propaganda, that this must be 'popular' and that it is 'a means to an end' to which all else must be subordinated, he declares: 'The army gradually learned to think as the enemy wanted it to.'[63] During the Second World War, Hitler showed consummate skill in using propaganda to influence the Wehrmacht and the German people, but he made a fatal error in attempting similarly to influence enemy and world opinion, an end to which he was even prepared to subordinate his military decisions and actions. His notorious tendency to elevate his own notions, whether or not they had any factual basis, to the status of natural laws inevitably proved catastrophic in this context.

After his assumption of power and the position of 'Führer and Reich Chancellor', Hitler became Supreme Commander of the Wehrmacht and, to all intents and purposes, Foreign Minister and Minister for Propaganda as well. In December 1941 he also appointed himself Commander-in-Chief of the Army. Thus Goebbels, Ribbentrop and the soldiers were simply the tools through which he implemented his decisions and decrees in the fields of propaganda, politics and military affairs, the third being subordinated during the latter phase of the war to the demands of the first. The nature of the conflict and his position as Supreme Commander of the Wehrmacht necessarily meant that economics, politics and propaganda all had a part to play in his strategy, but to place so disproportionate an emphasis on propaganda was inadmissible. During the Battle of Stalingrad and the struggle for the Crimea, for example, he refused to order a withdrawal though from a military point of view this seemed imperative. His concern after 1942 with the possibly adverse propaganda attendant on a withdrawal caused him to neglect long-term planning and to abandon all flexibility in the conduct of military operations. In 1944 he insisted that the Crimea be held because he feared that its surrender and the resulting increase of Soviet pressure in the Black Sea area would induce Turkey to abandon her neutrality and throw in her lot with the Allies. Ultimately his strategy came to be governed almost solely by considerations of propaganda and it was to this that he geared his war machine. He was prepared to settle for specious victories, staged to influence world opinion, at the expense of genuine strategic victories, even if the effect he achieved was no more than transitory. Such undue emphasis on psychological warfare inevitably prevented him from making strategic decisions involving loss of territory, since he feared that at first sight the move might be interpreted as a defeat. It is obvious that in adopting a prestige strategy of this nature he embarked on the worst possible course and one which no effort, however heroic, on the part of soldiers and civilians could hope to remedy. 'In the long run,' Schramm writes, 'it is impossible to bluff in military affairs. Whoever tries it will not only find that the battle reveals the true balance of forces, but also that the next reverse, which – in a purely strategic action – might have been prevented, is made unavoidable.'[64]

Sometimes, however, Hitler not only disregarded but actually inverted the wholly realistic conclusions he had drawn from his First World War experiences. This is admirably illustrated by the following passage from *Mein Kampf*:

Since the September days of 1914, when for the first time the endless hordes of Russian prisoners from the Battle of Tannenberg began moving into Germany over the roads and railways, this stream was almost without end – but for every defeated and destroyed army a new one arose. Inexhaustibly the gigantic Empire gave the Tsar more and more new soldiers and the War its new victims. How long could Germany keep up this race? Would not the day inevitably come when the Germans would win their last victory and still the Russian armies would not be marching to their last battle? And then what? In all human probability the victory of Russia could be postponed, but it was bound to come.[65]

Yet in spite of the knowledge thus gained he hoped in 1941 to be able to overrun the Soviet Union within a matter of weeks or months.

Towards the end of the Great War a gas attack had rendered Hitler *hors de combat*. On 29 November 1921 he wrote: 'During the night of 13–14 October 1918, I was badly affected by mustard gas and at first was completely blinded.'[66] He was evacuated to the Bavarian field hospital at Oudenaarde and transferred on 21 October to the Prussian Reserve Hospital in Pasewalk in Pomerania. He was tormented not only by the fear of remaining blind or partially blind but also by anxiety about political developments in the war-weary Reich. For it seemed to him that, despite his medals and decorations, the changed circumstances resulting from a revolution would have nothing to offer a semi-trained artist with permanently impaired eyesight, and that he would be reduced to begging.

Unfavourable rumours were constantly coming from the navy, which was said to be in a state of ferment. But this, too, seemed to me more the product of the imagination of individual scoundrels than an affair involving real masses. Even in the hospital, people were discussing the end of the War which they hoped would come soon, but no one counted on anything immediate. I was unable to read the papers.

But his uncertainty was shortlived.

In November the general tension increased and then one day, suddenly and unexpectedly the calamity descended. Sailors arrived in trucks and proclaimed the revolution; a few Jewish youths were the 'leaders' in this struggle for the 'freedom, beauty, and dignity' of our national existence. None of them had been at the front. By way of a so-called 'gonorrhoea hospital', the three Orientals had been sent back home from their second-line base. Now they raised the red flag in the homeland.[67]

There followed:

terrible days and even worse nights – I knew that all was lost. Only fools, liars, and criminals could hope in the mercy of the enemy. In these nights hatred grew in me, hatred for those responsible for this deed. In the days that followed, my own fate became known to me. I could not help but laugh at the thought of my own future which only a short time before had given me such bitter concern. Was it not ridiculous to expect to build houses on such ground? At last it became clear to me that what had happened was what I had so often feared but had never been able to believe with my emotions.[68]

On 7 November 1918, while still in hospital in Pasewalk, he heard that the war was over and that Bavaria had become a republic.[69] Three years later he recalled: 'My blindness did not last very long and gradually my eyesight returned. Because of this and also because the revolution had begun, I applied to be transferred to Munich as soon as possible and by December 1918 I was back with the Replacement Battalion of 2 Infantry Regiment.'[70]

In much the same category as the assertion that Hitler had obtained his Iron Cross 1st Class by an underhand ruse, we may cite the insinuation, for which General von Bredow was largely responsible,[71] that his temporary blindness was due solely to hysteria. Even Morell (at least after 1945) thought that this might possibly have been the case.[72] In October 1918 Hitler was still envisaging a future of creative artistic activity and there can be no doubt that, after his eyes had been affected by mustard gas, his mental suffering was very real. 'Beneath the fear of going blind for ever,' he wrote, 'I nearly lost heart for a moment.'[73] There are, however documents and eye-witness accounts which prove irrefutably that Hitler was blinded in a gas attack at La Montagne and that he was admitted to hospital as a gas casualty along with a number of others. According to Adolf Meyer, some 400 such cases were admitted within the space of a few days.[74]

On 21 November 1918 Hitler was discharged from hospital, by which time he had, as he himself wrote in 1924, decided 'to go into politics'.[75] While still in France he had discussed future plans with his friend, Ernst Schmidt, whose name he misspells Schmiedt in *Mein Kampf*.[76] Thus it was not until after the war that he finally decided to become a politician rather than an architect.[77]

From Pasewalk he went to Munich, where he found a disturbing political situation. The unit to which he reported (7 Company, 1st Replacement Battalion, 2 Bavarian Infantry Regiment) had been 'in the hands of the soldiers' councils'[78] since 7 November, when Eisner, by means of what he himself ironically called a 'Cossack charge', had taken over the reins of government and proclaimed the Republic.

Kurt Eisner, according to his own description, a Berlin-born Jew,[79] was well known to the Bavarians if not to Hitler. A former Social Democrat and editor of *Vorwärts* who had made a name for himself as a journalist and theatre critic, he had been arrested after taking a leading part in the Munich strikes of January 1918 and had subsequently become involved in proceedings for high treason. In September of that year he resumed his political activities at the instigation of the Social Democrats who wished him to enter the Reichstag in place of an outgoing Social Democrat deputy.[80] The Bavarian king to whom Hitler had sworn his oath of allegiance on 8 October 1914 had abandoned his throne precipitately and without a struggle, while his supreme warlord the Emperor Wilhelm II had actually taken refuge abroad. On 13 November, a week before Hitler's arrival in Munich, the ex-king had excused 'all officials, officers, and other ranks from further service in view of present circumstances', and released them from their oath of allegiance.[81] As Hitler soon discovered after his arrival at the barracks,[82] the majority of the officers and NCOs were happy to continue serving under their new political masters. General Freiherr von Speidel, speaking in the name of the officers' corps, gave an assurance on 8 November that officers, 'in token of their conviction, will place themselves unreservedly and wholeheartedly at the service of the People's State'.[83] The political situation being what it was they had no choice but to bow to it and sever their official ties with the throne. Neither they, the police, nor anyone else in an official position saw fit to resort to arms on behalf of their hereditary rulers, but continued to carry out their duties as before.

To Hitler all this seemed 'repellent'.[84] Nevertheless he remained in barracks, where he and Schmidt were employed on guard duties. In order to supplement their pay, the two of them volunteered to sort military clothing.[85] Yet he still found time to pursue the studies which had been interrupted in August 1914. What he experienced in Munich convinced him of the rightness of the opinions he had formed in Vienna about the Jews.[86] While in Pasewalk in November he had finally eliminated from his *Weltanschauung* the figure which, from 1900 to 1914, had been for him the symbol of empire – the German Emperor. He had at the same time adopted the view first propounded some months earlier[87] and subsequently reiterated in *Mein Kampf*, namely that the German defeat had come about because Wilhelm II had been 'the first Emperor to hold out a conciliatory hand to the leaders of Marxism', never suspecting that 'scoundrels have no honour'.[88] Yet he did not ascribe sole blame to the Emperor. In his view Wilhelm II had been deceived and hoodwinked by the Jews. He accused the Marxists of clasping 'the imperial hand in theirs' while 'their other hand was reaching for the dagger'[89] in order to 'fulfil their Jewish mission', and went on to declare that 'nearly the whole of production was under the control of Jewish finance'.[90] It is, perhaps, significant that in the 1925 and 1928 editions of *Mein Kampf* Hitler, himself a 'socialist', still tended to equate socialists with Jews. It was only in the 1930 edition that he drew a distinction between socialists and Marxists.[91]

In Munich in 1918 he would have had ample opportunity to read leaflets and pamphlets of nationalist-racist origin which, having given an antisemitic twist to an already morbid patriotism, put forward the resulting view as a desirable attitude. In these writings the blame for the German defeat was laid at the door of the Jews, who with their 'lust for money and domination . . . had rendered Germany unpopular throughout the world', had made millions out of army contracts and wartime transactions, and had systematically preyed on Germany and paved the way for 'Jewish domination'.[92] Moreover they were accused of having staged the revolution with the sole intention of covering up these alleged facts. Not only in Bavaria but throughout the country militant antisemites were actively engaged in a neurotic attempt to find a scapegoat and so absolve German national sentiment, oppressed as it was by the defeat and its aftermath, from the charge of having been largely responsible for its own misfortunes.

As a soldier Hitler was not yet prepared to begin to 'talk about politics'.[93] Of his attitude during the war he wrote in *Mein Kampf*: 'At that time I wanted to hear nothing of politics but I could not help taking a position on certain manifestations.'[94] In barracks he attracted little attention. He read a great deal, observed the world around him and shunned close friendships either with civilians or with his fellow-soldiers, only excepting Ernst Schmidt.[95]

At the beginning of February 1919 during a roll call of 7 Company of the 1st Replacement Battalion[96] some twelve men were asked to volunteer for guard duties at the POW camp at Traunstein, since the elderly *Landsturm* members on duty there were about to be demobilized. Hitler and Schmidt stepped forward and were transferred to 2 Demobilization Company of 2 Bavarian Infantry Regiment which had been detailed for the task.[97] On 12 February they arrived at Traunstein to guard French and Russian prisoners, some of whom were engaged in work outside the camp. Subsequently the French left and only Russians remained.[98]

On 16 February 1919 Marshal Foch ordered the cessation of the German counteroffensive in Poland. He also laid down the demarcation line in the East which later largely determined the frontier as defined in the Peace Treaty. On 20 February 1919 the National Assembly at Weimar was compelled to bow to the Allied terms[99] and conclude the treaty which was to shape the destiny of the Weimar Republic no less than that of the NSDAP. The overwhelming majority of the German people was outraged by the unexpectedly harsh terms imposed by the Allies. Article 231 of the Versailles Treaty, for instance, reads: 'The Allied and Associated Governments affirm and Germany accepts the responsibility of Germany and her allies for causing all the loss and damage to which the Allied and Associated Governments and their nationals have been subjected as a consequence of the war imposed upon them by the aggression of Germany and her allies.' The text of the Treaty – with marginal annotations – usually accompanied Hitler on the lecture tours he devoted to the subject of 'the shameful peace'.[100]

On 21 February 1919, five days after the announcement of Foch's order, Kurt Eisner was shot in the back by Count Arco-Valley. This officer, the son of a Jewess[101] and nephew of General von Speidel who some four months previously had vouched for the loyalty of the officers' corps,[102] was hailed as a hero by much of the Press and described as a 'second Tell'[103] and 'another Charlotte Corday'.[104] During his trial the public prosecutor, Hahn, said of Arco-Valley: 'Were our youth as a whole to be inspired with such ardent patriotism, we should be able to face the future of our fatherland with joy and confidence.'[105] The count was condemned to death on 16 January 1920 but the following day his sentence was commuted to one of life imprisonment in the fortress of Landsberg-am-Lech – Hitler's future place of detention. Some four years later Arco-Valley was released on ministerial instructions.[106]

Hitler's reactions to Eisner's murder are not known but such evidence as is available would seem to show that he would not have condoned it, a view which is supported by his declaration in *Mein Kampf* that 'Eisner's early death only hastened the development and finally led to a dictatorship of the Councils ... to a ... rule of the Jews, as had been the original aim of the instigators of the whole revolution'.[107] On 7 March,[108] after the camp in Traunstein had closed down,[109] he was ordered to return to his unit in Munich. 'At this time,' he recalls in *Mein Kampf*, 'endless plans chased one another through my head. For days I wondered what could be done, but the end of every meditation was the sober realization that I, nameless as I was, did not possess the least basis for any useful action.'[110]

During the first two months of 1919 political turmoil reigned in Munich. Hitler did not take sides but remained a spectator; he looked to his own safety and left others to play an active role. In an endeavour to find his bearings he read all the pamphlets and manifestos he could lay hands on, particularly approving of one which had been issued some time before by the *Deutschvölkisches Schutz und Trutzbund*.[111] Adorned with a swastika, the pamphlet attacked the 'Jewish thirst for world power' and called for the banishment of the 'Oriental Jews' and for the death penalty for profiteers and bolshevist agitators.[112] And he took due note of the warning posted up by the Military Command of the Soviets on 7 April 1919 which read: 'Anyone who raises his hand against the representatives of the Soviet Republic ... will be shot.'[113]

At the beginning of March the machinery for the election of a new Bavarian prime minister had been set in motion at Nuremberg. On 17 March, ten days after his return from Traunstein, Hitler heard that after only a matter of minutes, the choice had fallen on the Social Democrat Minister of Education, Johannes Hoffmann, who had already made his name in imperial Germany as a Social Democrat deputy in the Landtag and the Reichstag.[114] In principle he approved of the fact that the first government to be elected after the fall of the Wittelsbachs had begun its rule without a parliament. This was the result of a private agreement between the Central Council of the Workers', Peasants' and Soldiers' Councils on the one hand and Hoffmann's cabinet on the other. Niekisch relates that 'the cabinet had been accorded special powers, on the personal responsibility of the chairmen of the fractions, to rule for a time without a parliament'.[115] By the end of the month the Councils, grown nervous, began to communicate their uncertainty and confusion to the other parties and to the population as a whole. The Communists and Independent Social Democrats believed that the impending crisis

could be averted only by setting up a Soviet government as had just
been done by Béla Kun in Hungary. Meanwhile demagogues were
busily fomenting discontent. Strikes were called and workers' meetings held. Many people regarded the proclamation of a Soviet Republic
as the only solution. On the night of 4 April there was a conference at
the War Ministry attended by some 80 to 100 delegates of the German
Socialist Party, the German Independent Socialist Party, the Bavarian
Farmers' League, the Central Council, the trade unions and a liberal
democratic opposition group. Also present were the ministers Schneppenhorst, Unterleitner and Simon. The Russian Communist, Eugen
Leviné, who did not appear until the debate was in full swing, made an
inflammatory speech in which he repudiated all idea of cooperation
with the German Socialist Party. After this speech the delegates
decided against the proclamation of a Soviet Republic. But on 6 April
the same delegates foregathered in the Wittelsbacher Palais and, after
a further sally by Leviné, it was ultimately decided that telegrams
should be sent out that night to all regional offices announcing that
Bavaria had become the first Soviet Republic.

At that moment Bavaria became a state with no effective political
leadership. Hoffmann and his Minister of the Interior, Endres, had
already repaired to Bamberg, while the Soviet government was composed of men who had yet to prove their competence as ministers (or
people's deputies, as they preferred to be known). From the start the
Soviets were heavily handicapped by their choice of people's deputies.
For example Dr Lipp, the foreign minister, had spent some time in a
mental home and, after he assumed office, his mind again became
deranged. He sent a telegram to Moscow in which he alluded to Kant's
treatise, *Perpetual Peace* (theses 2–5) and informed the Bolsheviks that,
as 'Prussian agents', the liberal bourgeoisie had been disarmed, that
at this eventful hour Hoffmann had made off with the 'key to the
water closet', that 'Gustav Noske's hairy gorilla's hands were dripping
with blood', and that Prussia desired 'an armistice in order to prepare
for a war of revenge'.[116]

But neither the hard-pressed prime minister Hoffmann in his Bamberg retreat, nor the war minister Schneppenhorst were prepared to
accept the aid offered them by Noske on 4 April 1919 in the name of
the Reich.[117] They prohibited the opening of recruiting offices for
private armies, the insertion of recruiting advertisements in the daily
papers, and the use of hoardings for the same purpose.[118] However,

the extreme right-wing anti-Bolshevist and antisemitic Thule Society's *Kampfbund* disregarded the prohibition and continued to attract hundreds of volunteers from Munich – including Rudolf Hess, later Hitler's deputy. They also procured weapons and lent their support to von Epp's Bavarian Freikorps which had been set up at Ohrdruf in Thuringia with the aid of Reich funds.[119]

The ambivalent Schneppenhorst did not want to 'cause any bloodshed'.[120] 'Calm and order' were not to be restored either by 'force of arms or by Prussia, or by von Epp'.[121] Schneppenhorst was waiting for the commandant of the republican *Schutzwehr* to carry out a coup-de-main against the Soviet government in Munich.[122] But his expectations were disappointed. A putsch was indeed staged on 13 April 1919, largely at the instigation of the Thule Society's *Kampfbund*, in the course of which Lipp, Mühsam, Hagemeister and Wadler, an extreme left-wing lawyer, were arrested.[123] But suddenly the Spartakists showed themselves ready to take up the cudgels on behalf of the 'pseudo-Soviet Republic' and their countercoup brought Munich back under the control of the Soviets.[124]

On 13 April the Works Councils, meeting in the Hofbräuhaus under Levin's and Leviné's leadership, proclaimed themselves the highest authority in Bavaria, abolished the Central Council and proclaimed the (second) Communist Soviet Republic. Dr Leviné placed himself at the head of the newly constituted Action Committee and was joined by two fellow Russians, Max Levin and Tobias Axelrod. Gustav Landauer was discarded, and Egelhofer, a twenty-one-year-old sailor, appointed City Commandant and Commander-in-Chief of the Red Army. Prohibitions of all kinds now followed each other in quick succession. 'Bourgeois' newspapers were banned. Hostages were arrested and then for no apparent reason, released again, food and fuel were withheld from the 'bourgeoisie', jewellery and houses commandeered, and old banknotes simply overprinted. Rents were made payable direct to the Soviet government. The baking of cakes was no longer permitted,[125] and milk was obtainable only on production of a medical certificate stating that a patient was critically ill. Leviné publicly declared: 'What does it matter if Munich goes short of milk for a week or two? After all, it mostly goes to the children of the bourgeoisie. Their survival is no concern of ours. It doesn't matter if they die, since they'll only grow up to be enemies of the proletariat.'[126] The bourgeoisie, but not the proletariat, were subject to a curfew which initially began at 7 p.m. and later at 9 p.m., a regulation which would have materially curtailed their freedom had there been adequate means to ensure its proper enforcement. All this, combined with the activities of looters and the effects of rapacious measures for which members of the Thule Society and not the Soviets were quite often responsible,* led to mounting unrest, uncertainty and resentment among the populace. Scarcely any food was coming into the capital from the country and soon hunger and want became so general that Hoffmann at last made up his mind to appeal to the Reich government for assistance.

Now, the raising of private armies had been forbidden in Bavaria and for this reason Colonel Ritter von Epp, a seasoned officer much admired for his loyalty to the Crown and his leadership of the Bavarian Bodyguard Regiment, had set up his own Reich financed Freikorps at Ohrdruf on the advice and instructions of Gustav Noske.[127] Large numbers of Bavarians were recruited on von Epp's behalf by the Thule Society. Noske offered the services of this Freikorps to Hoffmann who refused on the grounds that Bavarian popular feeling would not countenance the arrival in Munich of 'Prussian firing squads'.[128] On 14 April 1919 he called the Bavarians to arms. At the same time a 'proclamation' was issued, announcing the formation of *Volkswehren* (citizens' defence forces)[129] out of which *Einwohnerwehren* (home guard units) were intended to emerge.[130]

On the same day that Hoffmann made his call to arms, Egelhofer decreed that 'all citizens must hand in weapons of whatever kind to the City Commandant within twelve hours. Anyone who fails to hand in his weapons within this period will be shot.'[131] Also on the same day the Jewish writer Ernst Toller, who was in command of the northern sector, announced: 'All armed workers and all workers whose weapons are stored in their factories will report to their factories today, Sunday by 9 a.m.'[132]

In an attempt to anticipate the Soviets, Hoffmann sent in the troops from Bamberg. On 15 April the first clash occurred in the Freising and Dachau district. Hoffmann's battle-weary, undisciplined soldiers handed over their arms to the Soviet troops and went home. Rosen-

---

* In order to compromise the Soviets on the one hand and enrich themselves on the other, they issued confiscation orders bearing what appeared to be the stamp of the Communist City Commandant Egelhofer.

heim, Kaufbeuren, Schongau, Kochel and Starnberg fell to the Red Army. After this Waterloo even Hoffmann and Schneppenhorst were prepared to welcome 'the Prussians'. Hoffmann now climbed down and accepted the assistance of the Reich. Noske, von Epp and Captain Ehrhardt with their Prussians, Württembergers and Bavarians, 15,000 men in all,[133] advanced on Munich. As a result the situation changed dramatically. On 17 April a leaflet, to which all parties except for the Independent Socialists subscribed, called upon the Bavarians to join the volunteer *Volkswehr* without delay,[134] and, on 17 April Rudolf Kanzler, a surveyor, who for some months had been gaining wide experience of irregulars, was granted permission by the Hoffmann government to raise his own Freikorps.[135] From the archepiscopal see of Bamberg telegrams went out to all the clergy in Bavaria urging them to lend their 'most vigorous' support to the decrees of the Hoffmann government in accordance with Bishop Senger's recommendation of 19 April 1919.[136] Few Bavarians, however, responded to this call to arms by Church and government. The people of Munich had no intention of turning out at the risk of their lives, particularly since they trusted neither Hoffmann nor his troops. Hitler, too, did nothing. He remained in barracks awaiting developments. Only in a few places, such as Rosenheim, was there any spontaneous resistance to the Soviet forces. Now that the Catholic Church had come out publicly on the side of the Hoffmann Government, the 'High Command of the Red Army' threatened to take Cardinal Faulhaber hostage as a reprisal for ecclesiastical intervention.[137] They also issued a proclamation signed by Egelhofer calling for an immediate general strike and an armed struggle against the 'capitalists'. The proclamation further declared that the enemy was at the gates of Munich and that the revolution was threatened by officers, students, 'the sons of the bourgeoisie and the mercenary White Guards of capitalism'.[138]

Frightful excesses were perpetrated on both sides. Thus at Puchheim near Munich fifty-two workers – Russian ex-POWs who had been set free by the Soviets – were herded into a quarry and shot by the 'Whites', who also murdered about twenty of their opponents' medical orderlies at Starnberg. On 29 April in the Luitpold School Soviet troops shot ten members of the Thule Society[139] whom they were holding as hostages, among them Gräfin von Westarp, Baron von Westarp, Baron von Teikert, Professor Berger, Prince Maria von Thurn und Taxis and Baron von Seydlitz.[140] When this incident became known there was widespread indignation in anti-Soviet quarters and among the 'White' troops.

Munich was taken after a series of hard-fought engagements. On 1 and 2 May Noske's forces entered the town. As always in civil war, both sides were guilty of the most appalling atrocities.[141] On 4 May the Soviet regime was overthrown. But the killing was not yet over; intoxicated by victory, the liberators of Munich dealt with the 'Reds' in barbaric fashion. With bestial cruelty they clubbed, shot or stabbed their victims regardless of whether these were communists, Russians or innocuous citizens. Twenty-one artisans were dragged out of the Catholic hostel in which they lodged and taken to the prison in the Karolinenplatz where, on 6 May, they were murdered out of hand by members of 2 Guards Division.[142] On 4 and 5 May in Munich members of Lützow's Freikorps apprehended and shot twelve innocent workers from Perlach.[143] According to a communiqué issued by von Oven's headquarters, seventy-seven Germans and fifty-eight Russians were shot in Munich on 16 May 1919 after being found in possession of weapons. The same source alleged that 433 of Egelhofer's men had been killed or wounded.[144] Irresponsible accusations led to the arrest of 180 people who were brought before the Bavarian emergency courts and illegally condemned to death and executed, many being murdered virtually without trial.[145]

After Noske's troops had taken Dachau, where Egelhofer had assented to the shooting of forty hostages,[146] they advanced on Munich while Ritter von Epp and the Württembergers launched their attack from the south. By now the Soviets were prepared to negotiate with Hoffmann. But it was already much too late and, as the regular troops and the Freikorps closed in, Egelhofer called on the Munich garrison to side with the Red Army in the defence of the city against the 'Whites'. In some units the matter was put to the vote, as was done in Hitler's barracks after a sergeant, Rudolf Schüssler, had expressed a definite opinion on the subject. While the soldiers were still considering how they should vote, Hitler climbed on to a chair and said: 'We aren't a revolutionary guard for alien Jews, comrades! Sergeant Schüssler's quite right when he says we should stay neutral.'[147] The general reluctance to follow Egelhofer's call is evident from the fact that Hitler's brief harangue was enough to dissuade his comrades from placing themselves at the disposal of the Soviets.[148]

In 1921 Hitler maintained that his name 'had been on the conscrip-

tion list [sic] during the period of the Soviets'[149] and in *Mein Kampf*
he alleged that he had 'acted in such a way as to arouse the disapproval'
of the Soviets in consequence of which the Central Council in Munich
had issued orders for his arrest on 27 April 1919.[150] But this could not
have been so in view of the fact that the Central Council had ceased to
exist a fortnight previously. Ernst Niekisch, who resigned as president
of the Central Council on 7 April writes: 'Hitler's contention that
certain deputies of the Central Council ... wanted to have him arrested
on 27 April 1919 is sheer moonshine. After 7 April the Central Council
ceased to function. Moreover I can say with certainty that, all the time
I was a member, the Central Council never issued instructions for
Hitler's arrest.'[151]

From 7 March 1919 until the day when the regular troops, together
with von Epp's and Noske's Freikorps, entered Munich and put an end
to the supremacy of the 'Reds', [152] Hitler remained in the Maximilian
II Barracks in Munich-Oberwiesenfeld. He could only have done so
by adapting himself to the prevailing circumstances. Red brassards
were worn by the soldiers in the Communist Red Army and, no doubt,
also by Hitler,[153] as indeed his arrest after the arrival of von Epp's
Freikorps would seem to suggest. He owed his release to the intervention of some of his officers.[154] Subsequently, when this episode might
have compromised him in the eyes of his chosen political associates,
he concealed the truth, alleging that those who had attempted to arrest
him had been Egelhofer's Red Army men. Ernst Deuerlein has claimed
that before the overthrow of the Soviets Hitler vainly attempted to
join both the Independent Socialists and the Communists.[155] This
has never been corroborated and, even if Hitler had tried to join these
parties, it would hardly signify. At the time there were very few people
who did not put up a false front in an attempt to save their skins.

Once Munich had been liberated political, military and administrative power effectively passed into the hands of 4 Reichswehr Group
Headquarters. Hitler was now ordered to report to the commission
investigating revolutionary activities in 2 Infantry Regiment,[156] an
assignment which, according to that generally reliable source Ernst
Schmidt, had probably been arranged by the same officers who had
engineered Hitler's release after his arrest by von Epp's soldiers.[157]
This marked the definitive beginning of Hitler's 'purely political
activity'.[158] One of his former admirers, Adolf Viktor von Koerber,
speaking of the task on which Hitler was engaged immediately after

the overthrow of the Soviets, said: 'After joining the investigating commission, he produced indictments which threw a merciless light on the unspeakably depraved military betrayals perpetrated by the Jewish dictatorship at the time of the Munich Soviets.'[159]

Hitler had no legal training and the tasks with which he was entrusted by the Bavarian military courts cannot therefore have been of a purely legal nature. He himself never subsequently discussed his work in any detail, nor did he talk about it to his friend Ernst Schmidt who, now discharged from the army, was living in Munich.[160] Hence it was small wonder that he should have aroused the suspicions of his enemies who described him as an 'informer', a 'spy' and an 'agent'. There can be little doubt that Hitler's assigment was to track down the NCOs and men who had supported the Communist Councils at the time of the Soviets. This task he carried out to the complete satisfaction of his superiors who eventually ordered him to attend an education course between 5 and 12 June 1919 at which repatriated prisoners of war and soldiers due for demobilization were to be 'instructed in the fundamentals of civic thinking'.[161]

These courses, designed to combat Bolshevism, were financed severally by Reichswehr Headquarters in Munich, the Reichswehr administration in Berlin and private contributions;[162] they were intended for specially picked officers and men. The principles were set out as follows:

Under the protection of the youthful Reichswehr new and meaningful foundations must be laid for all internal relations within our fatherland; only when the State is again master in its own house will it be possible to bring about an improvement in relations with other countries. Thus the Reichswehr is the cornerstone upon which the . . . last remnants and . . . first beginnings of our social, economic and political right of self-determination must rest. It is therefore essential to inculcate into the men of the Reichswehr a high sense of responsibility and selflessness on the one hand and, on the other, national self-confidence and an appreciation of the fundamentals of political thought. Political education in the Army must be above all party and within the scope of everyone while remaining scientifically unexceptionable.[163]

'For me,' Hitler wrote, 'the value of the whole affair was that I now obtained the opportunity of meeting a few likeminded comrades with whom I could thoroughly discuss the situation of the moment.[164] Foremost among these 'likeminded comrades' was Gottfried Feder, a right-wing lecturer who for the past six months had been contributing to the periodical *Süddeutsche Monatshefte*. Feder, a qualified engineer, was regarded as a financial expert and had begun his political career in the Thule Society. In his lectures on economic questions he endeavoured to put across his theory about 'breaking the thraldom of usury'.[165] Other university lectures and seminars attended by Hitler dealt with the following subjects and problems:

1. German history after the Reformation (Professor Karl Alexander von Müller).
2. The political history of the war (by the same).
3. Socialism in theory and practice (Karl Graf von Bothmer, a writer and journalist).
4. German economic conditions and the peace terms (Dr Michael Horlacher, Superintendent of the Central Office of the Bavarian Farmers' Unions and Agricultural Industry).
5. The correlations between domestic and foreign policy (Graf von Bothmer).

There was a second course from 26 June to 5 July which he may well have attended. The lectures included 'Foreign policy since the end of the war' by Bothmer, 'Russia and Bolshevist rule' by Dr Pius Dirr, 'State control of bread and cereals production' by Dr Hasselberger, 'Germany from 1870 to 1900' by Professor Erich Marcks, 'The Significance of the Reichswehr' by Captain (General Staff) Karl Mayr, 'Prices policy in the economic system', by Dr Merz, and 'Bavaria and the Unity of the Reich' by Professor Zahn.[166]

Of these courses Hitler later wrote in *Mein Kampf* that for the first time in his life he heard an analysis of the principles of 'international stock exchange and loan capital'.[167] It was a subject with which he had not grappled when studying Marxism in Vienna and indeed in later years he always tended to fight shy of financial problems. What he had hitherto merely suspected or 'sensed' was now presented in easily assimilable form and shown to be 'scientifically unexceptionable'. Moreover the lecturers, especially Feder, provided formulae and blueprints which, if put across with confidence and conviction, were bound to make an impression on those sections of the populace to whom the war had spelt ruin. Some of the more prominent members of this group, in particular Hitler and Feder, were agreed that 'Germany could no longer be saved from the impending collapse by the parties of the November crime – the Centre and the Social Democracy'.[168]

They therefore discussed 'the formation of a new (social revolutionary) party'.[169] If it was to have mass appeal such a party must be given a name which in itself seemed to open up new horizons. 'Thus we arrived at the name of "Social Revolutionary Party"', as Hitler later recalled.[170] But nothing came of the scheme which had first been adumbrated after one of Feder's lectures.[171] However this milieu provided him with ideas and, more important still, opened up avenues which were largely to determine the future course of his life.

In 1918 Hitler, who later maintained that he had become a politician against his will,[172] had not as yet put down any roots. Without either recognized professional qualifications or a position in civilian life, he now began to think seriously of taking up politics and perhaps becoming a professional speaker.

One of his lecturers, Professor von Müller, early noticed Hitler's natural talent for rhetoric, an occasion which he describes as follows:

My lecture and the lively discussion that followed it were over and the students had already begun to leave when my attention was caught by a small group of people. They were standing spellbound round a man who was vehemently haranguing them in a curiously guttural voice and with ever mounting passion. I had the peculiar feeling that he was responsible for their excitement, which in turn stimulated his eloquence. His face was pale and thin, his forehead partially concealed by an unmilitary lock of hair. He wore a close-cropped moustache and his strikingly large, pale blue eyes shone with a cold fanatical light.[173]

A decisive factor in Hitler's life was his total commitment to anti-semitism. 'One day', he writes, '. . . one of the participants on the course felt obliged to break a lance for the Jews and began to defend them in lengthy arguments.'[174] Hitler thereupon asked permission to speak and proceeded to demolish his comrade's case in a way that astonished his listeners. Here was an opportunity to show what he had read and learnt in Linz, Vienna and Munich and inwardly digested during the war. So convincing and impressive were his antisemitic arguments that the head of 4 Reichswehr Group HQ Education Section selected him for political duties within the Reichswehr. Hitler writes: 'The result was that a few days later I was sent into a Munich regiment as a so-called "education officer".'[175] In 1921 he described his activities as follows:

Both in this regiment [41 Rifle Regiment] as well as in other units I gave numerous educational lectures about the madness of the Red dictatorship of blood and had the pleasure of seeing my first group of supporters take shape from among members of the armed forces demobilized in consequence of the general reductions in the Reichswehr.[176]

Hitler was not in fact an 'education officer' but a political agent in Captain (General Staff) Karl Mayr's Section I b/P, variously known as Information Section, Press and Propaganda Section and Education Section.

On 22 July 1919 Group Headquarters issued instructions for the formation of an education detachment under the command of Rudolf Beyschlag at Lechfeld, a transit camp for repatriated prisoners of war. Part of the order signed by Major von Prager, the Chief of Staff, reads:

Lechfeld Transit Camp is expected to receive a regular flow of men returning from abroad. Present conditions in the camp . . . leave something to be desired. The camp is freely accessible, and neither the repatriated prisoners of war nor the many civilians employed there . . . are believed to be reliable. . . . The unit on guard duty in the camp . . . will be allotted an Education Detachment. . . . It is requested that the following men, all of whom attended the Group HQ course, be transferred. . . . The aftercare of ex-POWs is of special importance both in their own interest and in that of the Reichswehr and particular emphasis is therefore placed on the necessity for these postings.[177]

The seventeenth entry in the list of twenty-three names reads: 'Inf. Adolf Hitler, 2. Inf. Regt., Postings Section, (IAK).'[178]

The activity of the Education Detachment is well documented, as is the part played by Hitler who, on 10 September 1919, received a letter from Captain Mayr in which the form of address is markedly respectful.[179]

The Bavarian military authorities were not disappointed in their protégé. Hitler carried out his duties with extreme competence and eventually a soldier was put at his disposal to relieve him of the more mechanical duties, such as the distribution of leaflets.[180] In a report to headquarters one of his colleagues wrote: 'He proved to be an outstanding and fiery speaker, able to grip the attention of his listeners',[181] while another mentioned his ability to carry away his audience by his dialectical skill.[182] On 23 August 1919 Lorenz Frank wrote: 'Herr Hitler is a born popular orator, whose fanaticism combined with the common touch . . . unfailingly compels his audience's attention and commands their sympathy.'[183] Similar opinions were expressed by the commander of the guard unit, Lieutenant Bendt, in his reports dated

21 and 25 August 1919 to 4 Group Headquarters.[184] Other colleagues
have recorded that he knew how to arouse real enthusiasm among the
men,[185] and that 'the lion's share'[186] of the credit must go to him for
his ability to make contact with war-weary and demoralized soldiers
in whom, once he had secured their fanatical allegiance, he succeeded
in instilling not only fresh hope but also impatience, hatred and a
thirst for revenge.

In a secret speech before officer cadets on 30 May 1942, Hitler
recalled his activities at this time:

> When in 1918 the flags were lowered, my faith raised its head. But not my
> faith alone. My defiance, too, rose against the idea of capitulation to a
> seemingly inevitable fate. Unlike the rest, I did not believe that the history
> of the German people could have reached its term unless, that is, the German
> people were prepared to renounce their entire future. Thus, within the limits
> of my circumstances and abilities, I at once resumed the struggle which
> tallied wholly with my conviction that only an internal struggle within our
> people could ensure the victorious emergence of the movement which would
> ultimately restore the German people in the eyes of other countries.[187]

War, fighting, ruthlessness, unrelenting hardness, the absolute determination to survive and conquer, the rejection of humanitarianism –
such was the substance of his thinking. By 1914–18 at the latest his
Weltanschauung had begun to pivot on the view gleaned from his
studies of Malthus, Darwin, Bölsche, Ploetz and Tille that history was
a combination of pitiless interracial warfare on the one hand and
the victory and survival of the strongest, cruellest, most ruthless on the
other. On the same occasion, he also said:

> In one of the profoundest maxims a great military philosopher has asserted
> that fighting, and hence war, is the father of all things. One only has to look
> at nature to see that this maxim holds good for all living creatures and for all
> happenings. . . . The entire universe seems to be governed by this one
> thought that a continuous process of selection is taking place whereby the
> stronger survives and retains the right to live, while the weaker falls. Hence
> some may consider nature to be cruel and pitiless, while others understand
> that this same nature is only obeying the iron law of logic. . . . Anyone who
> believes that his suffering, his sensitivity or his principles entitle him to rebel
> against that law will not do away with the law but merely do away with
> himself. History shows that peoples grow weak. They have not done away
> with the law . . . but they have vanished without trace. . . . It is essential that
> this fundamental insight should govern the actions of anyone . . . who, in

confrontation with the all-powerful creator of these worlds, is compelled to appear before the court which pronounces on a man's goodness or weakness. . . . This struggle taking place all around us . . . which determines that when someone falls someone else immediately takes his place, which . . . gives every reason to suppose that, when peoples become weak, other peoples take over and which, even if the whole of mankind were to fail, would indubitably not allow this earth to remain empty or permit other beings to take their place – this struggle inevitably leads to . . . a selection . . . of the best and the hardest. Hence in this struggle we see one element of the general evolution of everything that is alive and animate. . . . We know that this struggle only eliminates the weakest while making the strongest even stronger and harder, and that this renders individual living beings . . . capable of progressive development. It is a world order of power and strength. There is no world order of weakness and submission. Submission is a fate and that fate spells extinction and obliteration. Since the beginning of time this law has been in force. . . . And hard though it may seem to the individual it is well for him to know that his fate is no different from the fate of preceding generations, that in theory the individual can choose to renounce this life but that by so doing he casts the load of his suffering upon others. Heavily though the burden may lie upon the individual man, it is incumbent upon him to realize that it has also been imposed upon countless generations and millions of others before him and that, had those others not been ready to bear the burden, he himself would not be in a position today to exist as a representative of his people . . . and to fight.[188]

Once the Soviets had been overthrown, 'saviours of the Fatherland' appeared all over Germany, rallying to the standards of antisemitism and anti-Bolshevism. Strikes, attempted communist coups, economic distress, the unfamiliar political order, the population's resentment against the victors, the new class relations and the influx of paramilitary organizations all combined to foment discontent and ensure that antisemitism and chauvinism were kept constantly on the boil. Political parties, associations, societies and organizations, frequently of a military or quasimilitary nature, sprang up everywhere. There was no shortage of willing hands to put antisemitic and anticommunist ideas and programmes into effect. Germany, and more especially Bavaria, had become one large armed camp for militant Freikorps units and self-defence organizations, most of which could be described as extreme right wing. Bavaria alone housed among others the Thule Oberland League, the *Deutschvölkisches Schutz- und Trutzbund*, the Escherich and Kanzler organizations, the Old Reich Flag Association, the National Association of German Officers, the Black, White and Red League, the Young Bavarians, the *Volkswehr*, the Iron Fist, von Epp's Freikorps,* the Bogendörfer and Probstmayr Detachments, the Würzburg, Bayreuth, Berthold, and Wolf Freikorps units, and numerous cavalry and artillery associations. In Munich alone Section I b/P kept watch on no less than forty-nine registered political parties and organizations.[189]

Prominent amongst the organizations disseminating the 'new' formula at the 'right' moment, was the Thule Society whose Bavarian membership numbered over two hundred. This society, to all intents and purposes the forerunner of the NSDAP, served as a cover for the Teutonic Order which had been founded in 1912, and which significantly paid homage to Wotan, the god of war and death worshipped by the Western and Northern Teutons. Rudolf Freiherr von Sebottendorff had been responsible for inaugurating the Bavarian branch of the Order in the summer of 1918, and launching it under the unequivocal formula: 'Now we shall declare the Jew to be our mortal enemy and as from today we shall begin to act.'[190] Up till 1919, when Sebottendorff had to leave the country, the Thule Society demonstrated on numerous occasions not only that it would stop at nothing but that it was quite prepared to take the law into its own hands. A letter from Sebottendorf to the Munich Chief of Police demanding immunity from arrest for members of the Thule Society, clearly reveals how dangerous was the power wielded by that organization. Threatening to unleash a reign of terror should the police fail to comply with his demand, Sebottendorff declared that 'my men will pick up the first Jew that comes along, drag him through the streets and let it be known that he has stolen a consecrated wafer. Then, my dear Sir, you'll have a pogrom on your hands that will put paid to you as well.'[191]

Sebottendorff chose to surround himself with an aura of mystery and, like the head of a secret service, always remained a legend, a rumour, rather than a man of flesh and blood. His real name was Alfred Rudolf Glauer.[192] Born in Saxony in 1875 of lower-middle-class parents, he had emigrated to the Near East where he was adopted by a Freiherr von Sebottendorff. During the Balkan Wars of 1912–13 he played an important role as head of the Turkish Red Crescent and, under the auspices of a Jewish merchant, Termudi, became a Magus of

*In July 1919 the Haack Regiment, the Herrgott Regiment and the *Bund Oberland* were incorporated into von Epp's Freikorps.

the Society of Rosicrucians. He returned to Germany in 1917 a wealthy man, but was compelled to leave again two years later and went back to Turkey. A further visit to Germany after Hitler's rise to power ended after the publication – and banning – of Sebottendorff's book, *Before Hitler Came*. He is said to have refused a request from Himmler, with whom he felt little affinity, to set up a German espionage headquarters in Vienna.[193] During the Second World War, now a self-styled baron, he operated as an agent in Istanbul, under the well chosen code name of 'Hakawaki', meaning 'Teller of Tales'. According to his chief, Rittlinger, he was wholly unsuitable for employment in Canaris's *Abwehr* and may have been also working for the British. Rittlinger further relates that, although a 'Nazi hater', Sebottendorff drowned himself in the Bosphorus on the day Germany capitulated:

Though still hale and hearty the baron, who lived by himself, had grown old and I think he had come to the end of his tether – in a purely material sense, I mean. He had no money left, he was completely cut off, and there was not the slightest prospect of his being able to support himself, however modestly. The signing of the armistice, with its implications of total defeat, can only have added to his depression.[194]

In 1917 – and indeed even after his departure from Germany two years later – Sebottendorff's ideas were fundamentally in agreement with those of the *völkisch** movement. This is amply illustrated by one of his articles published in the newspaper – later the NSDAP's *Völkischer Beobachter* – which he is said to have bought for the sum of a thousand marks:[195]

With the encouragement of Christianity people had disseminated the doctrine of the equality of all men. Gypsies, Hottentots, Botocudos, Teutons are all said to be equal. Unfortunately Nature . . . teaches us otherwise – namely that this equality is nonsense. . . . There are higher and lower races. To equate that racial hotchpotch, the Chandalas, with the Aryans, those human aristocrats, is to commit a crime against mankind. For to attain higher development, mankind needs leaders as well as leading nations. Of all the races on this earth, it is the Teutonic race . . . which is called upon to play that leading role.[196]

After November 1918 the Thule Society became a hive of activity. It harboured Hans Dahn's reconstituted National Liberal Party, Rohmeder's *Deutscher Schulverein*, the Pan-Germans, the *Fahrenden*

* *Völkisch* may be roughly defined as 'nationalistic with racist overtones'.

Gesellen and the *Hammerbund*. In short, the Society extended its hospitality to any Munich organization that represented nationalist interests.[197] It provided the first platform for Gottfried Feder's theories, gave full scope to the talents of Lehmann, leader of the Munich Pan-Germans, and placed its hotel the *Vier Jahreszeiten* at the disposal of nationalist circles. In addition the Society sponsored the emergence of a large number of political clubs with innocuous sounding names, and gave financial support to antisemitic and anti-Bolshevist publications as well as to other enterprises of a costly nature. Under its aegis Walter Daumenlang founded a

circle for genealogical and heraldic research; Walter Neuhaus . . . expanded his circle for North German culture; Johann Hering formed a circle for the study of ancient German law [joined in 1919 by Hans Frank, later a prominent National Socialist]. In December 1918 the Society distributed antisemitic leaflets in addition to its regular periodicals. In July 1918 Sebottendorff acquired the *völkisch* organ, the *Münchener Beobachter*. On 7 December 1918 Dietrich Eckart [Hitler's friend and mentor] brought out the first number of his violently antisemitic journal *Auf gut deutsch. Die Rote Hand* also appeared at this time and it was now that Dannehl began writing his first pamphlets.[198]

At the end of 1918 Sebottendorff and the Thule Society played a key role in the founding of the *Bürgerwehr* which was incorporated into the Society's sabotage and intelligence organization. With the financial assistance of the Munich paper manufacturer Theodor Heuss,* one of the earliest members of Hitler's Party, Sebottendorff also raised the *Oberland Freikorps*, a body of some political and military significance. In short, any group that was prepared to combat the Jews found ready encouragement from the Society.

After the fall of the monarchy and the overthrow of the Communist government those Bavarian reactionaries who favoured military measures pinned their hopes mainly on von Epp, von Möhl, Mayr, Escherich, Kanzler, Xylander, Pittinger and, until he left the country, on Sebottendorff, a man with his finger in every pie. The less militaristically minded looked to Heim, Kahr, Held and Bothmer.

In September 1919 a trial took place in Munich which aroused considerable interest throughout Bavaria, for the prisoners in the dock stood accused of responsibility for the death of hostages murdered by

---

*Not to be confused with the first President of the German Federal Republic.

Red Guards during the fighting earlier in the year. On 18 September 1919 six of the accused were condemned to death and shot the following day.[199]

At the beginning of September the German Workers' Party, another offshoot of the Thule Society, numbered some four dozen members. After a period of stagnation under the Soviets it was showing signs of revival, for the turn of events had removed the left-wing extremists by whom its activities had hitherto been inhibited. But this alone was not enough to ensure its progress. The real history of the party began on 12 September 1919 with Hitler's first attendance as an army political agent and with his offer to become the party's chief propagandist. Hitler himself has related in *Mein Kampf* how, long after normal political conditions had been restored in Munich, this momentous encounter between himself and the German Workers' Party took place:

One day I received orders from my headquarters to find out what was behind an apparently political organization which was planning to hold a meeting within the next few days under the name of the 'German Workers' Party' – with Gottfried Feder as one of the speakers. I was told to go and take a look at the organization and then make a report.[200]

Forty-five persons were assembled in the 'Leiber' room of the *Sterneckerbräu* in Munich. Apart from five whose occupations are not specified, they comprised a doctor, a chemist, two businessmen, two merchants, two bank employees, a painter, two engineers, a writer, the daughter of a district judge, sixteen artisans, six soldiers and five students. Hitler arrived in civilian clothes and described himself in the register not as an education officer or a military representative but simply as a 'lance-corporal'; for address he gave the name of his unit.[201] The lecturer was Gottfried Feder, whose acquaintance Hitler had made a few months before while attending the political course for demobilized soldiers. The address bored him and he only stayed because he was anxious to hear the ensuing discussion. But he pricked up his ears when a professor by the name of Baumann began advocating Bavaria's secession from the Reich and her union with Austria. 'At this point', he writes in *Mein Kampf*, 'I could not help demanding the floor and giving the learned gentleman my opinion on this point.'[202] Two days previously, on 10 September 1919, the Peace Treaty had been signed at St Germain-en-Laye between German Austria and the countries of the Entente, setting the seal on the separation of

Hungary and Austria, banning the use of the name 'German Austria' and enforcing the recognition of Czechoslovakia, Poland, Hungary and Yugoslavia as independent states, with a concomitant loss of territory for Austria. The disintegration of the Austrian 'political corpse', so ardently desired by Hitler in his Vienna days, had finally come about as a result of the war. Yet now a German professor, of all people, was proposing the secession of part of Germany from the Reich and its union with Austria, a country which even before the war Hitler had held to be a moribund political structure. As a convinced Pan-German he was outraged; in an impassioned contribution to the discussion, which silenced most of those present, he put the abashed professor to flight. This brilliant display of virtuosity so impressed Anton Drexler, the first chairman of the German Workers' Party and a tool-maker by trade, that he followed Hitler out of the hall and handed him a copy of his pamphlet, *My Political Awakening*. Hitler read it when he returned to barracks, finding it unadventurous but otherwise acceptable.[203]

A few days after the meeting at the *Sterneckerbräu* he received a postcard from the party's committee inviting him to attend a committee meeting at the Altes Rosenbad inn, 48 Herrnstrasse on 16 September, and informing him that he had already been made a party member.[204] 'After two days of agonizing pondering and reflection', he wrote in 1924, 'I finally came to the conclusion that I had to take this step. . . . From here there was and could be no turning back. And so I registered as a member of the German Workers' Party and received a provisional membership card with the number 7.'[205] Thus he became a member of a party which existed nowhere but in Munich and which on 16 September 1919 numbered in all fifty-five members, counting himself.[206]

As he himself put it, he had made the most important decision of his life. By now his military superiors had become so impressed with his apparently unlimited capacity for absorbing knowledge and his ability to present it in simplified form that they were prepared to give serious consideration to his political ideas, even to the extent of regarding them as worthy of publication.[207] Thus on 10 September 1919 Captain Mayr wrote commending Hitler for an analysis he had made of resettlement problems and added: 'This Headquarters proposes . . . to release your official report to the Press.' Then in surprisingly deferential terms he went on to request a written exposition of his views on the Jewish question. Hitler handed this in on the same day that he attended the German Workers' Party committee meeting. Before passing it on Mayr appended the following comment: 'I am in complete agreement with Herr Hitler's view that what is termed governmental Social Democracy is indissolubly linked with Jewry.... All harmful elements must, like viruses, either be eliminated or "encysted". This also applies to the Jews.'

The ideas embodied in this paper are so central to Hitler's thinking at the time that, before embarking on an analysis of his intellectual background, it seems pertinent to conclude this chapter by quoting the following passages:

In so far as the danger with which Jewry threatens our people today finds its expression in an undeniable aversion experienced by the majority of our people, the cause of that aversion is not generally to be found in a clear awareness of the Jews' systematically destructive effect, whether conscious or unconscious, on our nation as a whole, but arises mainly from personal intercourse and the impression made by the Jew as an individual. . . . Thus antisemitism all too easily takes on the character of a mere manifestation of emotion. And that is wrong. As a political movement antisemitism cannot and must not be determined by emotional motives but by a recognition of the facts . . .: To begin with, Jewry is incontestably a race and not a religious community. And the Jew himself never describes himself as a Jewish German, Jewish Pole or, say, a Jewish American, but always as a German, Polish or American Jew. In no case has the Jew ever . . . assimilated very much more from other nations than their language. . . . Even the Mosaic faith . . . is not the final word on the question of Jew or non-Jew. . . . By a thousand years of inbreeding, often occurring within a very small circle, the Jew has generally kept his race and type more sharply defined than the peoples among whom he lives. The result of this is that we have in our midst a non-German, foreign race neither willing nor able to sacrifice its racial characteristics or to renounce its own way of feeling, thinking and striving and which nevertheless has just the same political rights as us. If the Jew's very feelings are concerned with the purely material, how much more so his thinking and striving. The dance round the Golden Calf becomes a merciless struggle for all those possessions which to our way of feeling ought not to be the only and ultimate things worth striving for. The value of an individual is no longer determined by his character, by the importance of his achievements to the whole, but exclusively by the size of his fortune. . . . A nation's stature is no longer to be reckoned by the sum of its moral and spiritual forces but only by the profusion of its worldly goods. From this feeling there arises that thinking, that striving after money and after the power to protect it, which leads the Jew to be unscrupulous in his choice of methods, and pitiless in applying them. . . . In an autocratically governed State he whines to gain the 'majesty's', the prince's, favour which he abuses [by battening] on his subjects like a leach. In a democracy he goes whoring after the favour of the masses, crawls before the 'majesty of the people' and knows only the majesty of money. He destroys the prince's character by Byzantine flattery, and national pride – the strength of a people – by mockery and the shameless promotion of vice. His weapon is public opinion . . . which he guides and distorts by means of the Press. His power is the power of money which in his hands proliferates unceasingly and effortlessly in the form of interest. . . . Everything that induces men to aspire to higher things, be it religion, socialism, or democracy, is to him only a means to an end – that of satisfying his lust for money and domination. He acts on the peoples like racial tuberculosis. And as a consequence anti-semitism arising out of purely emotional reasons will find its ultimate expression in the form of progroms [sic]. Antisemitism based on reason, however, must lead to a systematic and legal campaign to deprive the Jew of the privileges which he alone of all the foreigners in our midst enjoys (Aliens Legislation). But its final goal must always remain the removal of the Jews as a whole.[208]

CHAPTER FIVE

Intellectual Background

At thirty years of age Hitler considered that in the course of the First World War he had learnt more about the 'problems of life' than he could have done 'during thirty years at university'.[1] This opinion voiced in Munich was based upon a view of the world which was already complete in its essentials. While in Landsberg he wrote in *Mein Kampf*: 'Yet Vienna was and remained for me the hardest though most thorough school of my life. . . . In it I obtained the foundation for a philosophy in general and a political view in particular which later I only needed to supplement in detail, but which never left me.'[2] His 'philosophy' or, to use a term constantly on his lips[3] even before 1908, his *Weltanschauung*, had been formed by his early environment, by his parental home and his schooling and studies in Linz, Steyr, Vienna and Munich. Other determining factors were his study of literature from 1905 onwards, his exposure during his last three years in Vienna to the often very extreme views of his variegated fellow lodgers in the men's hostel, and his experiences first as a soldier in the field during the First World War, then as a political agent in the service of the Reichswehr and finally as leader of a political party. His reading after 1919, and particularly during his detention in Landsberg which he described as 'higher education at state expense', merely served to give him a deeper knowledge of certain subjects upon which he had long since made up his mind.

During his trial in Munich after the putsch of November 1923 he declared: 'I left Vienna a confirmed antisemite and a mortal enemy of the whole Marxist view of life. My outlook was Pan-German.'[4] And his statements in court reveal, as does *Mein Kampf* which he began to write soon afterwards, that his *Weltanschauung* was based on negative attitudes and insensate pugnacity. When he left Austria for Germany in 1913 he hated not only his own country but also the Jews, Social Democracy, the trade unions, parliament, democratic rule, the 'masses' and humankind in general. He hated everything – and was devoid of compassion. It was no coincidence that he failed to make any friends during his 'autodidactic forays' in the vicinity of the Meidling dosshouse. The only things that impressed him were ruthlessness and brute force. 'If the power to fight for one's own health is no longer present,' he wrote in *Mein Kampf*, 'the right to live in this world of struggle ends.'[5] And four years later on 2 April 1928 he declared: 'Whatever goal man has reached is due to his originality plus his brutality.'[6] The views thus expressed have been attributed by biographers and others to his unpleasant experiences with the riffraff he encountered in the dosshouse, a theory which leaves no room for the possibility that he may have reached his conclusions as a result of intensive reading, although there is ample evidence to show that such was indeed the case. Hitler digested what he read and, by a process of careful selection and rearrangement, eventually laid down fundamental principles both for himself and for others. Hence it is of crucial importance to discover what he read, what he believed and disbelieved and what were the sources of his self-education. Hitherto his biographers have almost invariably considered that his reading was confined to light literature and the writings of a handful of thinkers. They have shown themselves all too prone to accept his own dicta which, though expressed in the form of 'firm convictions', positive 'decisions' and 'intentions', or 'authentic versions', were frequently at variance with his real way of thinking. Moreover the views he held in Vienna are often found embodied, if in modified form and with wholly different intention, within ideas propounded at a much later date. Only very few authors have taken the trouble to make an unbiased analysis of the books he read and of his intellectual background. Among those who have done so are Ernst Nolte and P. E. Schramm, but even they take too narrow a view. With a few rare exceptions it is impossible to discover, either from Hitler's biographies or from his own writing, what he read during the course of his life. He has left behind virtually no information on the names of books or their authors. Writing about his childhood reading in *Mein Kampf* he mentions only a popular history of the Franco–Prussian War of 1870–71 and a few books of a military nature.[7] He also mentions the names of newspapers which influenced or interested him after he had left school, among them the Austrian *Neue Freie Presse*, the *Wiener Tageblatt* and the *Deutsches Volksblatt*.[8]

August Kubizek confirms Hitler's general statements when he says that Adolf 'read prodigiously' both in Linz and in Vienna:[9]

That's how my friend was. It was always books and more books! I cannot imagine Adolf without books. At home he would have them piled up all round him. If he was really interested in a book he always had to have it with him . . . even if he wasn't actually reading it. When he went out he would always carry at least one book under his arm. Sometimes there were too many for him to manage. Then, rather than give up his reading, he would give up . . . the open air. Books were his whole world. In Linz he subscribed to no less than three libraries in order to be able to get all the books he wanted. In Vienna he frequented the Hofbibliothek so assiduously that I once asked him if he intended to work his way through the entire stock, whereupon of course he flew out at me. He once took me along with him to show me the main reading room. The sight of those walls lined with row upon row of books almost overwhelmed me and I asked him how he was able to find what he wanted in all that superabundance. He then tried to explain the workings of the catalogue which only served to confuse me still further. When he was reading hardly anything disturbed him. Rather, he disturbed himself, for no sooner had he taken up a book than he would begin talking about it. Then I would have to listen patiently, whether the subject interested me or not.[10]

But Kubizek gives no more than a vague idea of the books and authors Hitler preferred. Apologetically he writes: 'I would be hard put to it to say which of the enormous number of books he read . . . influenced him most.'[11] Since Kubizek's own knowledge of literature was then distinctly limited, he could hardly be expected, after an interval of some forty-five years, to shed very much light on the subject or to recall the names of more than a handful of writers. Among those he mentions are Frank Wedekind, Otto Ernst, Schopenhauer, Nietzsche, Stifter, Schiller, Lessing, Peter Rosegger and, finally, Ibsen. Though Hitler was later to inveigh against what he described as 'corrupt bourgeois society' – while in fact remaining one of its staunchest supporters – it would seem that the Norwegian dramatist failed, at least until 1908, to make any noticeable impact on him. Clearly at this stage the message of plays such as *The Pillars of Society* eluded him, for he was unable to see that they had anything to do with reality. Kubizek's remark that his otherwise unlimited intellectual curiosity did not embrace natural science tells us nothing except the fact that, at the age of nineteen, he had not as yet developed any interests in this direction.[12] In a book by Josef Greiner, purporting to be a firsthand account but whose total absence of objectivity absurdly misrepresents his subject's character, we find a list of reading matter compiled from information provided by Hitler's associates. Greiner writes:

Hitler immersed himself in translations of classical literature such as Sophocles, Homer, Aristophanes, Horace and Ovid. He showed a particular preference for early Germanic mythology and he was better acquainted than many academics with the 250,000 verses of *Parzival*. Martin Luther and the history of the Reformation in general aroused his keen interest as did the Dominican, Savonarola. He knew all about Zwingli's activities in Zurich and those of Calvin in Geneva and was conversant with the times and teachings of both Confucius and Buddha. His wide reading, which comprised the work of Renan and Rosalti, familiarized him with the teachings of Moses and Jesus and the origins of the Judaeo-Christian faith. Of the classics he read Shakespeare, Goethe, Schiller, Herder, Wieland, Rückert and Dante and, later, Scheffel, Stifter, Hammerling, Hebbel, Rosegger, Hauptmann, Sudermann, Ibsen and Zola.[13]

Otto Dietrich recalls Hitler's addiction to Karl May, an addiction that was not confined to his childhood and adolescence, for it would seem that between 1933 and 1934 he reread all the sixty or more books written by this author.[14] To him Karl May was more than just light entertainment, as is borne out by the fact that he presented his nephew, Heinz Hitler, with a collected edition while the latter was studying at a National-Political Education Centre.[15]

Hans Zeverus Ziegler, whose admiration for Hitler was as unqualified as Kubizek's, speaks of his mastery in subjects such as music, the history of art and 'considerable areas of world history, comprising not only the history of Germany and Europe, both ancient and modern, but also of America in which he showed an unusual grasp of detail. Indeed it was American history which interested him above all.'[16] From Hans Frank we learn that while in Landsberg Hitler read a great deal, in particular Nietzsche, Treitschke, Houston Chamberlain, Ranke, Marx and Bismarck (*Reflexions and Reminiscences*) as well as the war memoirs of German and Allied soldiers and statesmen.[17]

While Hitler himself often referred to the extensive range of his reading and studies it was almost invariably in terms so vague that no conclusions of any import can be drawn from them. For instance on 29 November 1921, after he had spent two years working his way through the comprehensive and virulently antisemitic 'national-socialist library' belonging to his Munich sympathizer Dr Friedrich Krohn, he wrote:

Between the ages of twenty and twenty-four I began to devote more and more time to politics, not so much by attending meetings as by making a thorough study both of political economy and of all the antisemitic literature I could lay hands on at the time. . . . From the age of twenty-one onwards I threw myself enthusiastically into the study of military and political writings and never since then have I allowed my interest in the various aspects of world history to flag.[18]

In earlier years, he went on to say, he had studied the history of art, civilization and architecture and had concerned himself with political problems. According to well-authenticated accounts by those who knew him, Hitler had begun his self-education while still at school with the help of books whose matter and outlook had little if anything in common with official curricula. Thus even before 1905 the satisfaction of his intellectual needs depended on his own efforts, the more so since his father had died two years earlier and no real rapport existed between himself and his teachers, either in Linz or Steyr. Between 1910 and 1914 his discussion ranged over a very wide field, as did his discourses after 1919. Before his move to Munich in 1913 he had been at pains to further his literary education. He read German lyric poetry and also the classics which he saw performed in the theatres of Linz and Vienna. As a fifteen-year-old boy he wrote poems, short stories, and plays,[19] one of these about the Linz 'Separated Couples Club',[20] and a libretto for an opera derived from Richard Wagner's *Ring* for which he composed the overture.[21]

In 1919 at the latest his interest turned to literature of a pragmatic kind. Once he had taken up politics he regarded novels as a waste of time and poetry of any kind as superfluous, at least so far as he was concerned. The fields he eventually came to know best were those of architecture, art, military history, general history and technology; but he also felt at home in the spheres of music, biology, medicine, and the history of civilization and of religion. Indeed he was often able to surprise his listeners with his detailed and thorough knowledge of these subjects. Thus on 11 November 1945 Dr Erwin Giesing, for a short time his ear, nose and throat specialist, recorded that:

Hitler knew his way about . . . in medical matters as I discovered once when discussing a book on aural medicine. . . . His general knowledge of medicine . . . was quite remarkable. He recognized that there was a connection between coagulation of the blood and thrombi and also knew about the effects of nicotine on the coronary vessels and the possible connection between an inflammation of the maxillary cavity and the dental system. He was familiar, too, with the most important properties of the sulphonamides and penicillin.[22]

Hitler had an infallible instinct for the gaps in other people's knowledge and would deliberately steer the conversation round to matters with which they were not conversant. On the other hand he was perfectly prepared to enter into discussions with recognized experts and it was by no means rare for architects, artists and professional soldiers to acknowledge him their equal if not their superior. In so far as they knew better than he, it was very often 'after the event'. He was often better informed than his experts about architecture, art, warfare and technology, and had done most of his reading on these subjects before coming to power. His method of study has been described both by himself and by well-informed observers. He would first leaf through a book, most often backwards, to discover whether it was worth reading. If so, he would search through it to find additional confirmation for the opinions he had formed in his Vienna and Munich days. Thus he would only give close attention to a work if it seemed likely to provide ammunition for later arguments. And of such ammunition he had a goodly store. Reliable witnesses have endorsed his claim that he was able to read one substantial book a day by setting aside the early morning and the late evening for the purpose.[23]

He never undertook a definite programme of study, and what he read would invariably provoke him either to anger or to enthusiasm. He could only assess calmly what he had already accepted, while anything objectionable he simply dismissed. After 1945 his personal physician Dr Morell made a deposition entitled 'Psychiatric Data' in which he wrote: 'Hitler's lack of a formal academic training was counterbalanced by the vast fund of general knowledge he had gained from books.'[24] Indeed he was astonishingly well-informed as a result of his reading, one example being the range and quality of his knowledge of literature. General Jodl, as Chief of the Wehrmacht Operations Staff, came into contact with Hitler almost as frequently as did Morell, and knew him both in triumph and disaster. Shortly before his execution at Nuremberg Jodl said: 'His knowledge and intellect, his rhetoric and his willpower triumphed in the end in every spiritual conflict over everyone.'[25] It can be proved beyond doubt that even as a young politician, Hitler did not confine his reading to trivia. For instance in 1924 a pamphlet was published entitled *Bolshevism from Moses to*

Lenin. Dialogue between Adolf Hitler and Myself, an unfinished essay by his close friend Dietrich Eckart, whose writings had already acquired an antisemitic slant by 1916 at the latest. This pamphlet cites no less than six major works on the subject of the Jews in such a way as to postulate that both protagonists were familiar with them. The books in question were Otto Hauser, *Geschichte des Judentums* (*History of Jewry*); Werner Sombart, *Die Juden und das Wirtschaftsleben* (*The Jews and the Economy*); Henry Ford, *The International Jew*; Gougenot des Mousseaux, *Le Juif, le judaïsime et la judaïsation des peuples chrétiens* (translated into German by Alfred Rosenberg in 1920); Theodor Fritsch, *Handbuch der Judenfrage* (*Handbook of the Jewish Question*) and Freidrich Delitzsch, *Die grosse Täuschung* (*The Great Deception*). In the same context Eckart cites the *Archives Israelites,* the *Jewish Chronicle* and the *Jewish World.*

The hitherto neglected *Dialogue* also contains a number of references to the Old Testament and the Talmud which further confirm the remarkable extent of Hitler's knowledge of these texts, a knowledge of which he had already given ample proof both in public and private discussion. On the other hand we have no means of knowing to what extent he was conversant with the work of the other authors quoted in the *Dialogue* – Cicero, Thomas Aquinas, Fourier, Luther and Goethe – though to judge by his subsequent comments on the last two he appears to have had some knowledge of them. By 1923 he had almost certainly made a close study of *Der Rassenkampf* (*The Racial Struggle*) by the Austrian Jew, Ludwig Gumplowicz, which was published in Innsbruck in 1883, and perhaps also of Georges Vacher de Lapouge's *L'Aryen, son rôle social.* The influence of Lapouge's axioms, 'The notion of justice . . . is a lie. Only force exists' (p. 349) and 'Race, the nation is everything' (p. 340), is discernible in Hitler's thinking from 1919 onwards.

Le Bon's *The Crowd, a Study of the Popular Mind*[26] and McDougall's *The Group Mind, A Sketch of the Principles of Collective Psychology*[27] were also early sources. From these he clearly derived his successful methods of propaganda – admired even by his opponents – his contempt for the masses and the unexampled sway he exercised over them.

Hitler's familiarity with the *Lebensraum* theories of Ratzel, Haushofer and Mackinder dates from 1924 at the latest. This is evident not only from the many allusions to the subject in *Mein Kampf* and the views he expressed on world hegemony, but also from his subsequent policy towards Japan. On the other hand the fact that he more than once described the Jews as 'a ferment of decomposition'[28] a phrase which he borrowed from Mommsen, does not necessarily imply any knowledge of Mommsen's work. Nor is it possible to show beyond doubt how well he knew the work of Treitschke, Fichte or Nietzsche or to what extent he wittingly adapted and exploited the latter's ideas. Despite all that they have in common ideologically and intellectually, despite the similarity of their affects – vindictiveness, hatred, disgust, ambition, jealousy, vanity, envy and cruelty – and of their pronouncements about God, the soul, Christianity and man, and notwithstanding the personal pretensions they shared, Nietzsche cannot be described as Hitler's mentor.

During the latter part of 1913 his landlord Josef Popp often found him reading the works of Schopenhauer and Plato,[29] the former being the philosopher to whom Hitler is known to have referred more often than to any other.[30] He would praise his style,[31] knew by heart passages from his writings and would sometimes quote them without any indication of their provenance. According to Hans Frank, Hitler told him that even during the First World War he had never been without the Reclam pocket edition of *The World as Will and Idea*.[32] This story would seem to be corroborated by the statement of a fellow-soldier, Hans Mend, to the effect that Hitler spent a great deal of time reading Reclam books during off-duty periods in the line.[33]

There is no such evidence so far as his knowledge of Plato is concerned. Yet he cannot possibly be assumed to have derived that knowledge solely from the numerous quotations found in Schopenhauer or from the latter's exegeses of the Greek philosopher's work. Indeed as a young man Hitler, who regarded himself as an artist well versed in philosophy and literature, must surely have felt impelled to sample Plato's writings if only because, in the preface to the first edition of *The World as Will and Idea*, Schopenhauer states that the reader who had 'tarried awhile in the divine Plato's Academy'[34] would be especially fitted to understand his own work and hence ready to follow him. Even the subtitle of Book III of *The World as Will and Idea* contains allusions to Plato's forms and his view of the purpose of art of which Schopenhauer goes on to make an authoritative analysis.[35] Plato's concepts[36] also played a major role in Schopenhauer's interpretation of the intrinsic nature of art and his 'observations on the aesthetics of the fine arts'.[37] From both of these Hitler would borrow when talking about a work of art which conformed to his views – views which indeed, Schopenhauer had helped to shape.[38]

According to Plato, art is no more than the imitation of Nature and the reflection of copies of the form which alone is real Being. Because these doctrines were completely incompatible with Hitler's conception of nature and his views on painting and architecture, he considered them to be of secondary importance and hence incapable of serving as criteria. Hence we cannot gauge the extent of his knowledge though certain of his remarks, at least during the years after the publication of *Mein Kampf*, betray some familiarity with Plato's works. For instance on 13 December 1941 while conversing at table he said: 'Like the body, mind and soul undoubtedly return . . . to a general reservoir. Thus we are the basic material that fertilizes the stock from which new life springs.'[39] This briefly sums up certain of the ideas developed in the *Timaeus* and the *Phaedo*. According to Plato the soul, having overcome corporeality, returns to its 'original state', and the cycle of life inevitably comes to an end when the alternation between life and death and death and life finally ceases. Hitler's 'stock from which new life springs' corresponds to Plato's 'world soul', the principle that moves the universe, the power that moves all things, the ideal entity and world-consciousness. In speaking of art or education, Hitler would sometimes paraphrase the passage in the *Symposium* on 'absolute beauty' proclaiming this to be his own objective. Thus on 11 November 1941 he said: 'If beauty is to maintain its sway it must have power over men',[40] and again, on 3 March 1942: 'When Greek culture was at its height, its ideal was certainly to inculcate beauty into man.'[41]

Hitler laid himself open to attack in philosophical and literary discussion only through his fanatical insistence on the rightness of his opinions and his tendency to think in terms of absolutes. If, therefore, he failed to identify the source of his propositions it may have been because he feared that, in the unlikely event of his being mistaken, his authority would be impaired. This circumspection is evident even in personal correspondence, as can be seen from his reply of 20 May 1931 to a letter from an unidentified 'Excellency' who had obviously criticized him for having sanctioned the publication of Rosenberg's *Mythus des 20. Jahrhunderts*. Hitler maintained that, as a poet, Goethe had been 'at liberty to advance what might be regarded as anti-clerical opinions without coming into conflict with the Grand Duke' although

he was also one of the latter's ministers. 'I could cite', the letter continues, 'dozens of such cases involving writers who also held political
office.' His reticence extended even to fictional and mythological
characters. For instance during a discussion about Stalin with General
Zeitzler on 27 December 1943 he obviously had the Greek god Antaeus
in mind when he said: 'We shouldn't assume that a man's a classical
giant just because he grows stronger every time he topples to the
ground.'[42] No doubt, too, he wanted to pass off the fruits of his
studies as the product of his own original thinking, and in this he was
largely successful.

Now Hitler, however much he might deny it, was a counterrevolu-
tionary and an extreme conservative[43] who considered that the key to
an understanding of history and politics was to be found in the existence of 'the Jews' and what he supposed to be a 'true knowledge' of
them. Consequently his analyses of historical events are sometimes so
unusual as to cloak the identity of his sources. Thus in Eckart's *Dialogue* he refers to Isaiah 19:2–3 and Exodus 12:38 from which he
deduces that the flight from Egypt under Moses's leadership occurred
after a perfidious revolutionary plot on the part of the Jews against the
Egyptian ruling class, and that Moses was the first Bolshevist leader.
Some twenty years later, on 15 May 1942, he was to place a no less
curious interpretation on these same biblical passages which he cited
to prove his assertion that 'like parasites' the Jews were the 'most
climatically adaptable people in the world' and, in contrast to Aryans
everywhere, were able to make themselves at home, whether in the
tropics or in Lapland. According to his reasoning the account in the
Old Testament proved conclusively that 'nothing could harm the
Jews, neither residence in the desert nor the passage through the Red
Sea'.[44]

Dietrich Eckart's influence on Hitler's intellectual and social
development up till the time he wrote *Mein Kampf* cannot be overrated. None of his other educated friends or followers played so
important a role. By his own admission Hitler was also to some extent
indebted to Gottfried Feder whose lectures he had attended during the
Reichswehr's anti-Bolshevist education courses at Munich University
in 1919.[45] On the other hand Hitler never admitted the extent to
which his view of history and his oratorical technique had been influenced by the Munich historian, Alexander von Müller, another
lecturer on the Reichswehr course.[46] To Hitler as to Müller 'the root,

intertwined in female passivity with the soil' was one of the principles that underlie all things.[47] Hitler also shared with Müller the view (already put forward by the latter before 1914) that not only 'dynasties' and 'human beings' but also all positive products of civilization such as 'education' are rooted in the 'soil' – the all-nourishing substance, the *völkisch*, well-tilled, 'national soil' (*Volksboden*).[48] Although Müller regarded himself primarily as a man of letters, he would often affect a distinctly unliterary form of speech richly interlarded with the Bavarian vernacular. Hitler, who was particularly fond of this dialect, used the same idiom as Müller – and this not simply when lecturing to the troops in 1919 or speaking before Bavarian audiences. Like Müller he was fond of using words with emotive connotations – for instance, 'rooted in the soil', 'convinced', 'healthy' or 'ardent' (this last often qualifying the word 'German', e.g. 'ardent German'). Another favourite was 'demoralize', as in the 'demoralizing influence of Jewry',[49] a phrase used by Müller in an essay on Freiherr von Stein in 1912 and by his alumnus Hitler in September 1919.

There is no justification for the theory sometimes put forward that, while Hitler was working on Volume I of *Mein Kampf* in the so-called 'warlord's' wing at Landsberg, his ideas were noticeably influenced by Hermann Kriebel, formerly of the General Staff, as also by the veterinary surgeon Dr Weber. Nor, for that matter, were they influenced by another of his fellow prisoners, Rudolf Hess, who was later to become Deputy Führer. Before his committal to Landsberg Hess had been an organizer of National Socialist student groups[50] and assistant to Professor Haushofer, the geopolitical expert at Munich University. Though he was responsible for making certain minor emendations to *Mein Kampf* he exerted no ideological influence whatever on Hitler. From the beginning the leading members of the NSDAP – Hess, Göring, Esser, Streicher, Rosenberg, von Scheubner-Richter, Luedecke, Amann, Röhm and Frank[51] – were never Hitler's teachers but invariably his pupils. Yet they rendered him invaluable service in providing him with important introductions to people of affluence such as his early patrons and benefactors – Bruckmann, Bechstein, von Seidlitz, Hanfstaengl, Borsig, Grandel, Thyssen, Kirdof, Prince Arenberg, Heinrich Class and Prince Kyrill Coburg. Other important contacts included manufacturers, wealthy members of the nobility, senior statesmen, diplomats, politicians, and influential personalities and organizations abroad.[52] At Elsa Bruckmann's house alone he had the opportunity of meeting Professor Müller, Ludwig Klages, Geheimrat Domhöfer, the director of the Pinakothek, and Ludwig Troost (who was later entrusted with the extension of the Munich Brown House). However he did not visit the Bruckmann's house to listen to the talk of others but rather to talk and be listened to himself.

Voluminous though Hitler's reading may have been during the last ten to fifteen years of his life, his interests as reflected in his choice of books, and the composition of his library would appear to have been comparatively specialized and not primarily of a practical political nature. Nor, according to his secretary, did his private library contain either classics or any works whose character was predominantly humanistic or literary.[53] He himself is said to have lamented the fact that he had been forced to give up reading belles-lettres in favour of scientific works,[54] and contrasted this situation with his earlier years when he had read whatever he could lay his hands on. He once told Christa Schröder that, when in Vienna before 1913, he had devoured indiscriminately all the five hundred volumes which went to make up stock of one of the city libraries.[55] According to Ernst Hanfstaengl, the volumes on Hitler's shelves included:

a history of the Great War by Hermann Stegemann, and Ludendorff's book on the same subject; German histories by Einhardt and Treitschke; Spamer's *Illustrated Encylopedia*, a work dating from the nineteenth century; Clausewitz's *Vom Kriege*, and a history of Frederick the Great by Kugler, a biography of Wagner by Houston Stewart Chamberlain and a potted world history by Maximilian Yorck von Wartenburg ... also a tome called *Geographical Character Pictures* by Grube, a collection of heroic myths by Schwab and the war memoirs of Svan Hedin.[56]

Hanfstaengl further noted some thrillers as well as the *History of Erotic Art* and the *Illustrated History of Morals* by Eduard Fuchs, a Jewish author.

After becoming Führer and Reich Chancellor Hitler's innumerable responsibilities necessarily restricted the scope of his interests. He was no longer at pains to shine in literary conversation. At the same time he avoided topics properly the concern of a politician within the context of an industrial society – legal, constitutional and administrative questions, for example, or public finance. Consequently his lieutenants, Gauleiters and senior officials were free to do very much as they pleased and this enabled Martin Bormann, for instance, to rise to a position of incalculable power in the State. By 1930 if not before many of these men had come to regard themselves as little tin gods and to conduct themselves accordingly. For in that year the new edition of *Mein Kampf* Volume I, departing fundamentally from the 1925 editions, laid down categorically that the leaders of local groups, districts, regions and provinces should be appointed by the 'next highest leader' and invested with 'unlimited powers and authority'.[57] And just as the German middle classes in the reign of Wilhelm II had deliberately identified with the monarch by flaunting the same style of beard so, for a period of twenty-five years, many National Socialists affected the kind of toothbrush moustache worn by Hitler, a style he had originally adopted to offset his broad nose. Though his moustache (probably copied from Dietrich Eckart) did not at first meet with the approval of his close associates, no less than nine of his Gauleiters subsequently grew one of the same type.

Even during the Second World War, despite the toll on his nerves and the illnesses which ultimately undermined his physique, Hitler always found time to read. According to one of his physicians, Professor von Hasselbach, hardly a day went by without his having read at least one major work,[58] such as Franz Petris's scholarly *Germanisches Volkserbe in Wallonien und Nordfrankreich* (*The Germanic National Heritage in Wallonia and Northern France*), Karl Pagel's *Geschichte der Hanse* (*History of the Hanseatic League*), Wilhelm II's speeches in four volumes edited by General Scherff, Ernst Kantorowicz's biography of the Hohenstaufen Emperor Frederick II or, perhaps, a book on medicine.

Biologism, especially of the pseudo-Darwinian variety, religious monotheism and vulgar anticlerical liberalism all played an important role in Hitler's *Weltanschauung* and/or the view of history he happened to hold at the time. He was undoubtedly right when he said that by 1914 his intellectual standpoint was already firmly established. Outside the field of technology, anything that accrued after the period of his self-styled 'Viennese education' was incorporated into his ready-made *Weltanschauung*, sometimes by means of over-simplification, sometimes by sheer brute force. Occasionally this led to discrepancies if not to gross distortions as, for example, when he refashioned the doctrines of Darwin, Bölsche and Malthus to suit his own ends.

Because of his belief in the lasting validity of the ideas and opinions formed by his early reading, Hitler was unable to accept the fact that any part of the knowledge thus gained could ever become obsolete or unreliable,[59] a fact that applies particularly in the field of natural science. So far as the arts were concerned he rated his own 'intuitive genius' above the conclusions of scholars and experts should these happen to clash with his own theories; in this way he would reject the findings of prehistorians and archaeologists in favour of his own interpretation of myths and legends, an interpretation derived from the Stoa. Throughout his life his face was turned to the nineteenth century, that breeding-ground of genius. To him the thinking and ideas of its intellectual giants (save in the fields of religion and the Church) provided the final confirmation of his own era, and also its touchstone.

Hitler's intellectual affinity for the nineteenth century and his consequent indebtedness to Hegel is plainly evident in his concept of Europe's historical role and what in his case was an exaggeratedly contemptuous attitude towards America and Russia. Hegel's doctrine of the state as 'the deity made manifest' permeated the philosophical thinking of the nineteenth century and inspired its historiography, while his dialectical method laid the foundations for the historical materialism of Marx and Engels who in turn were to determine the history of the twentieth century. Hegel, Marx and Hitler, each in his own particular way, relegate Russia and America to a secondary position. In his *Lectures on the Philosophy of History* Hegel excludes America from the theatre of world history: 'What has taken place here up till the present is no more than an echo of the Old World and the expression of an alien way of life.'[60] He held Russia to be of secondary importance because 'hitherto she has not made her appearance as an independent force in the ranks of the forms of Reason in the world'.[61] Hitler, too, despised America, considering her to have no share in the cultural history of a world which he believed to be both creative and 'preservative',[62] while he regarded the Russians as fundamentally lacking in the qualities required to build a state.[63]

Schramm has rightly pointed out that 'throughout his life Hitler remained an inland-orientated German, his imagination untouched by the sea. . . . He was completely rooted within the cultural boundaries of the old Roman Empire.'[64] His unfamiliarity with English history and its implications – which was to have ominous consequences – was more than matched by his ignorance of American history, an omission he only began to make good when forced to do so by the political contingency he had himself contrived. As late as the autumn of 1939 none of the leading German politicans save Göring envisaged the role America might play if she entered the war against Germany[65], an eventuality Hitler himself refused to take into account. He believed that a rapid victory over Great Britain and his continental foes followed by the establishment of a German-dominated European bloc would drive America even further into isolationism, thus precluding her intervention in Europe. Hence it was not until the summer of 1940 that possible American reactions began to play a material part in his calculations.

Some ideas of the intellectual background from which Hitler sprang can be gained from the answers to a twenty-seven point questionnaire which appeared in the *Berliner Illustrierte Zeitung* towards the end of 1898 when Hitler had almost completed his schooling at Leonding and was about to move on to his secondary school in Linz. This, perhaps the first nationwide survey, met with response from over six thousand readers through whom the publishers and editors hoped to discover, not only what Germans were thinking about the nineteenth century and its prominent personalities in the fields of science, literature and art, but also what they expected of the twentieth century. The views of the majority of the *Illustrierte*'s middle-class readers give a picture of the cultural climate into which Hitler, himself a member of the middle class, was about to emerge. Nevertheless it would appear from his own evidence that the ideas he formed as a result of his schooling and self-tuition, more especially in Linz and Vienna, differed materially from those held by the majority of *Illustrierte* readers at the turn of the century. Despite the fact that he welcomed the 1914 war and at one time admired the German emperor, he would never have rated Helmuth von Moltke (1200 votes to Kant's 1000, Darwin's 800 and Schopenhauer's 700) 'the greatest thinker of the century', nor have regarded Wilhelm I (2400 votes to Bismarck's 1600) as its hero. His *Weltanschauung* after 1919 is reflected in the hopes he then expressed which bear a close similarity to the political demands of two of the *Illustrierte* readers, demands so excessive that the pair were rapped over the knuckles by the editors who wrote: 'That there are also wicked people in the world is proved by one of these readers who desires nothing less than "the conquest of the United States of America".' The second culprit they described 'a braggart and fire-eater' whose demands were even more exorbitant since he hoped 'for nothing less than the overthrow of England and France as well as of Austria and Russia, the containment of further American expansion and the ultimate domination of the world by Germany, not to speak of the rapid demise of Social Democracy'.[66] Thus what were regarded as the absurd and unrealistic views of a tiny minority (two in six thousand) in the German Reich when Hitler was ten, came to be accepted through his agency by large numbers of Germans and Austrians, and continued to be so accepted even after his death and the catastrophe he had brought down on the world. In 1968 a study group set up by the Göttingen Teachers' Training College collected data from 5000 primary and secondary school children and 5000 student teachers, university tutors, teachers and members of parliament. The findings disclosed prejudice in forty-five per cent of the schoolchildren whose intolerance of minorities led them to propose that gypsies, for instance, should be 'put in special camps' and either 'shot' or 'gassed' and that foreign workers should be 'chucked out of the country'.[67]

 By his tireless reading Hitler had accumulated a vast fund of specialized knowledge which he was able to call on when necessity arose. Not infrequently his superior command of certain technicalities would reduce the professionals to exasperated silence, professionals such as Speer, Dönitz, Keitel, Jodl, Heye and Engel.[68] Heye recalls that those whose duty it was to brief the Führer on naval matters 'never felt quite at their ease' because he always had everything so much at his finger-tips.[69] And in 1967 Dönitz wrote:

Naval officers who had spent any length of time in Hitler's immediate entourage – for example his naval aide, Rear Admiral Von Puttkamer – have told me that Hitler had an extraordinary grasp of the technicalities of the vessels listed in Weyer's *Handbook of the World's Navies*. Thanks to his excellent memory he knew more about the displacement, armament and protective armour of these vessels than the naval experts in attendance on him.[70]

 He had studied the background of all the larger military units, could identify them in any circumstances and, throughout the war, always knew where they were employed.[71] He was familiar not only with every detail of the structure of the Wehrmacht but also with the units of the Fleet, including their equipment.[72] At the time of the Polish campaign he astonished his otherwise well-informed generals by revealing his superior knowledge of the types of artillery used by the Poles and the French.[73] 'His technical knowledge', Schramm writes, 'his mastery of modern military science, placed him in a strong position at conferences with his generals and the General Staff. In this respect he was their equal if not their superior.'[74] Even Field-Marshal von Manstein admitted that:

Hitler possessed an astoundingly retentive memory and an imagination that made him quick to grasp all technical matters and problems of armaments. He was amazingly familiar with the effect of the latest enemy weapons and could reel off whole columns of figures on both our own and the enemy's war production. . . . There can be no question that his insight and unusual energy were responsible for many achievements in the sphere of armaments.[75]

The foundations of this knowledge had been laid before the First World War. Josef Popp relates that in 1913 and 1914 his twenty-four-year-old lodger was constantly sending him out to the Munich University library and other libraries and to bookshops to fetch him the books he needed. These dealt primarily with political economy, art history, foreign policy and warfare, this last category including Clausewitz's *Three Confessions* and *On War*, as well as the *Illustrated German Naval Almanack* published by Wilhelm Köhler of Minden.[76] Schramm was told by reliable informants that:

when in 1942 it was thought essential to provide the infantry fighting round Narvik with anti-tank guns, the only means of transporting them was by U-boat. However the navy reported that the type of gun in question . . . could not be loaded through a U-boat's hatch. To this Hitler replied that during the march into Austria he had seen an anti-tank gun whose dimensions he felt sure would permit it to pass through the hatch. After a series of telephone calls and teleprint messages the gun was located and Hitler was found to be right. After the Allied invasion in the summer of 1944 the infantry kept complaining that they were completely immobilized by the box barrages laid down by enemy warships on the positions behind the coast. When Hitler was told about this at his situation conference he asked how far inland the enemy's shot could fall. Of the three naval officers present none was able to enlighten him. Angrily Hitler demanded they should supply the answer by the following day; at the same time he called their attention to the fact that, owing to differences in draft, some enemy vessels could approach closer inshore than others; he also reminded them to take note of the depth of water off the coast and the varying calibres of the enemy's weapons. These he then proceeded to enumerate from memory. The complex calculation appeared in a flash before his mind's eye.[77]

But his knowledge of technology and natural science was not confined to war and architecture. About motor cars and their engines he knew almost as much as the experts. For example when, shortly before his seizure of power, a director of Mercedes was showing him a model he had not as yet seen, Hitler wagered that he could guess the vehicle's weight.[78] It came as no surprise to his entourage that he won the bet. Erich Kempka, his head chauffeur, tells of the time Hitler examined him on his mechanical knowledge prior to engaging him. 'His questions came so thick and fast that I had to react like lightning. It wasn't all that easy, because I hadn't expected a man like him to know so much about it.'[79] When a well-known car manufacturer told him about the proposed shape of the Volkswagen, which was then in course of development, Hitler declared himself dissatisfied with the design and proceeded to deliver a lecture on the subject. 'It should look like a beetle,' he said. 'You've only got to look at nature to find out what streamlining is.'[80] The manufacturer objected that when its wing-cases – its 'garage' as he termed it – were closed, a beetle could only crawl along very slowly, whereas in flight it was capable of high speeds. Hitler's rejoinder astonished many of those present. 'And where does the beetle leave its garage when it takes off? On the ground?'[81] With the observant eye and graphic imagination of a painter he would seek in natural forms models for technological creations, believing that this was the best way of exploiting the laws of nature. For example, he approved of the bicycle whose spokes, when the wheel was moving forward, he compared to a man's natural gait, whereas he regarded a zeppelin's construction as wrong, indeed 'utterly crazy', since no bird had ever been equipped by nature 'with an air-bladder on the lighter than air principle'.[82] The influence of biology was particularly apparent in his theories about ships and aircraft whose lines and methods of propulsion, he believed, should be modelled on those of birds and fish.[83] For this reason he criticized naval architects for having overlooked the fact that nature, that source of ideal forms, instead of endowing fish with a pointed forepart similar to the bows of a conventional ship, had shaped their heads like a 'falling droplet' and had, moreover, refrained from equipping them with a 'propulsive device' at the rear. On 2 June 1942 he told Admiral Krancke, the Navy C-in-C's permanent representative at Führer headquarters, that the naval experts must have erred in their calculations if a battleship of over 45,000 tons with engines of 136,000 h.p. was capable of 30 knots while the maximum speed of an aircraft carrier of half the tonnage but with engines of 200,000 h.p. was no more than 35 knots. In his view the fact that a 32 per cent increase in power and a reduction of 50 per cent in weight resulted in a gain of a mere 5 knots provided the best proof of his contention[84] that naval architects had failed to grasp the laws of nature. He further maintained that the fish's method of propulsion by the action of its fins and the expulsion of water through its gills plainly showed how a ship ought to be driven, namely by the suction of a vacuum at the bows and the thrust from the water built up astern. Propellers, he asserted, through being mistakenly located at the stern, produced suction and hence a vacuum, thereby retarding the forward movement of the hull which was further impeded by the mass of water built up at the bows.

Hitler had not reached these conclusions solely as a result of observing nature however. He had read a great deal of the relevant technical literature and as a boy had in all probability been familiar with such technically knowledgeable authors as Jules Verne; he knew at once what was practicable in any given circumstances. Among his projects were double-decker railway trains operating to the Donets Basin on a four metre gauge at speeds up to 200 k.p.m., autobahns eleven metres wide and new cities, with imposing gubernatorial palaces for the German overlords, in the conquered eastern territories.[85] Other plans were the establishment of rubber plantations over an area of more than one and a half million acres, the systematic exploitation of hydraulic power for the chemical industry, the use of Norway as a central power-house for Europe, the production of domestic gas from sewage, the harnessing of the winds and the seasons for the purposes of technology[86] and the transformation of entire regions by changing their climate.[87]

Hitler's technical knowledge, however, did not extend to the more abstruse areas of physics and chemistry. He was reluctant to turn his attention to these subjects and would do so only when absolutely necessary. Thus he refused until it was too late to take any interest in nuclear physics or high frequency technology, despite the endeavours of the scientists to make him see the importance of research in these fields and the potential of the atom bomb as a decisive factor in the war. It was not until the beginning of 1945, when even the most starry-eyed could no longer seriously believe in a German victory, that Hitler began to extol the atom bomb which he described as a 'victory weapon'. In conversation with Dr Giesing in February of that year he said:

I shall be unleashing our victory weapons in the very near future, and then there'll be a glorious outcome to the war. The problem of nuclear fission was solved long ago and development has now reached the stage when we can put the resulting energy to military use. That will knock them into the middle of next week. This is the weapon of the future and it means that Germany's future is assured. Providence has already given me a glimpse of this final way out.[88]

Although he professed so great an interest in science, Hitler never bothered to consult scientific works when his encyclopedias failed to supply the information he wanted. He would turn to these, even on crucial historical occasions such as the Munich Agreement. Colonel von Donat, who was present at the conference, relates: 'It began with a discussion about frontiers. Eventually it was agreed that the ethnographic map of Austria–Hungary in the 1908 *Brockhaus Encyclopedia*, showing the German and Czech speaking areas and ethnographic boundaries, should be used in determining which of the Sudeten German zones were to be handed over.'[89] While encyclopedias were perfectly adequate for looking up items of information such as historical dates, the dimensions of buildings, the composition of medicines or the symptoms of diseases, their usefulness in the field of the exact sciences was distinctly limited.

Even when considering predominantly scientific problems, Hitler was ever alert to the implications of history about which his thoughts and discourse constantly revolved. 'If a man has no sense of history', he said on 27 July 1941, 'it's as though he were deaf or lacked a face'.[90] He always saw himself as 'making history', as part and parcel of it. Hence he was for ever seeking to interpret his ideas, decisions, and plans in terms of history and to see his achievements as intrinsic to and presaged by it, or else as ingeniously woven into its fabric. To him history was a continuous process from which, however, he excluded prehistory, even though the latter's chronological sequence had been established with some degree of certainty during the nineteenth century. Hitler's remark to the effect that mythology might well provide conclusive information on prehistoric times[91] requires further elucidation since it might all too easily tempt us to assume, like Schramm, that his 'knowledge of prehistory was obviously very slight'.[92] For instance, on the night of 25 January 1942 he remarked: 'I've been reading a book about the origins of the human race. It's something I've thought about a great deal in the past, and I must say that if you take a closer look at some of the traditional legends and fairy-tales, you come up with some pretty strange conclusions.'[93] He himself described his conclusions as 'strange' because he knew that they differed widely from the accepted academic view; nevertheless he continued to stand by them. In the same context he refused to admit, despite the lip-service he paid to Darwin, that man 'from his earliest origins has not always been the same as he is today'.[94] True, he conceded the possibility of 'change and development in the realm of plants and animals',[95] but at the same time insisted that 'in no species is there any sign of a development such as the leap forward man must have made if he had evolved from the simian state to become what he is today'.[96] He narrowed down his perspective so as to comprise mankind only in so far as it had wittingly made and purposefully shaped its own history. 'If we look at the Greeks,' he said, 'we find a beauty far above what modern times have to show. This applies to the world of thought as much as . . . to the representation of phenomena. . . . The Egyptians of the previous era attained to an equal stature.'[97] Hitler was at pains to discover evidence that would place prehistoric man within the context of 'manmade' history. The result was a ragbag of fact and fiction which included mythology, Bible stories,[98] the relative durability of stone and metal implements, the accessibility of 'only one-eighth of the earth's surface' to scientific research[99] and Hanns Hörbiger's glacial cosmogony. 'I am inclined to favour Hörbiger . . .', he said.

Maybe that twelve thousand years ago there was a collision with the moon. It's quite possible that at that time the earth forced the moon into its present orbit. Maybe too that the earth then appropriated whatever atmosphere there may have been round the moon so that the conditions under which men were living on the earth underwent a fundamental change. It's conceivable that at that time there were beings capable of living at any altitude or depth because of the absence of atmospheric pressure. Again it's conceivable that the earth burst open and that the rush of water into the crater led to tremendous explosions and torrential downpours from which only one human couple managed to escape by taking refuge in a cave on higher ground. I believe that these questions will only be solved when a flash of intuition enables someone to put two and two together, and thus point the way for the exact sciences. In no other way can we lift the veil which has fallen between us and the historical world as a result of this cataclysm.[100]

Four years earlier certain astronomers who had had the temerity to describe 'glacial cosmogony' as an already outmoded concept had been severely criticised by Himmler for dismissing discoveries which in his view could be of use to mankind. 'I advocate unrestricted research of whatever kind and that includes unrestricted research into glacial cosmogony,' he wrote on 23 July 1938 to SS-Oberführer Dr Otto Wacker, a departmental head of the Reich Ministry of Education.

I intend [he went on] to encourage that research and in so doing I find myself in the best of company ... as the Führer, too, is a convinced supporter of this theory so much abominated by scientific hacks. I would again repeat ... that the Ministry ... must put these opinionated schoolmasters in their place. There are a great many things we should like to see researched, even by non-scientists.[101]

On occasion Hitler was not above doing violence to his material. Because the biblical myth of the cataclysm,[102] for instance, happened to fit in with his theory, he attributed it to the Babylonians and Assyrians rather than to the Jews and went on to draw a comparison with the Nordic legend of the fight between the gods and giants.[103] He was convinced that science would never be able to provide the key to everything man desired to know. Rather it was like a ladder which the seeker after knowledge must climb rung by rung yet without ever reaching the top. At best he could hope to know only what he was able to survey from the particular rung he had happened to reach.[104]

Because he desired to extend the boundaries of history beyond the traditionally accepted limits he deplored the fact that documentary evidence covered no more than some 'three to four millennia'.[105] This compelled the man of insight to have recourse to legends or 'sagas', a word whose derivation from '*sagen*' [to say] indicates that 'those who passed on these traditions were men of the same stamp as ourselves'.[106] It was no coincidence that, seventeen years after leaving school, he urged the need for a 'completely revised outlook on history' that would link historical scholarship to the Roman Empire and to Greek Antiquity.[107] On 26 July 1942, for instance, he suggested that in teaching history analogies should be drawn between 'Alexander the Great and his father Philip on the one hand and Frederick William I and his son Frederick the Great on the other'.[108] Hence he had little difficulty in appreciating the classical culture of the Mediterranean and the important achievements of Roman statesmanship in the millennium between 500 BC and AD 500. On 7 July 1942 he declared: 'At a time when our forebears were producing the stone troughs and clay vessels about which our archaeologists have made such a to-do, the Greeks were building the Acropolis.'[109] Picker also records him as saying:

Caution must be exercised in making specific assumptions about the cultural level reached by our forebears in the first millennium BC. The discovery, for instance, of an ancient Bible in East Prussia is no proof whatsoever that East Prussia was its place of origin ... quite possibly it had been acquired from the South in exchange for amber. The real centres of civilization, not only in the last few millennia BC but also in the first thousand years AD, were the Mediterranean countries. To us this may sometimes seem implausible since we judge the Mediterranean countries by the conditions we find there today.... North Africa was once a thickly wooded region and so was Greece. At the period of Greek supremacy and of the Roman Imperium, there were dense forests in Italy and Spain. Great caution is also needed in assessing Egyptian history. At the peak of its glory Egypt, like Italy and Greece, was altogether habitable and enjoyed a good climate. It is yet another symptom of a people's cultural decline when they cut down their trees without heed for reafforestation and hence destroy the very means whereby nature in her wisdom conserves water.[110]

Hitler regarded the ancient world as his true spiritual home and, at the height of his power, would often meditate on its decline, which he saw not only as an historical process but also as holding out a lesson for the future. Instead of consulting professional historians he tried to find the answer himself,[111] reaching the conclusion that the decline had been due to the passivity of the ruling class and their desire not to disperse their accumulated wealth – and hence undermine their power – by engendering too many children;[112] in this way they became outnumbered by their slaves who represented part of that wealth. He also suggested that Christianity had contributed to the process by 'obliterating the demarcation lines between the classes.'[113] There could conceivably be some connection between his proposition and Gibbon's thesis that Christianity was responsible for the decline of Rome. This might explain why, in assigning an analogous place in history to the Jews and Bolshevism, Hitler claimed that it was an historical lesson he had early learnt and acted upon.

Sometimes, indeed, he would attribute the destruction of the ancient world to the Mongols[114] and Huns, whose hordes had harassed the German people ever since the latter 'had entered the charmed circle of historical knowledge'.[115] By 1920 at the latest he began to fear that history would repeat itself in the shape of an armed onslaught by Bolshevism which he described in 1942 as 'a new organization of Cen-

tral Asiatic humanity'.[116] No less curious is his explanation in the
same context of the racial origins of the Eastern European peoples
from which it would seem that the Bulgarians are descended from the
Turcomans and the Czechs from the Mongols.[117] He regarded the
medieval Empire or, to use his own all-embracing term, 'the history
of the German Emperors', not only as an historic phase during which
'German' rulers had skilfully and presciently warded off attacks from
the East but also as justification for his *Ostpolitik*. 'If we want to claim
our place in the world', he remarked at a time when the German
Wehrmacht had come to a standstill on the Eastern Front,

we must invoke German imperial history . . . the mightiest epoch after that
of ancient Rome which the world has ever seen. Just imagine the daring of
those chaps and the number of times they crossed the Alps! They were men
all right! And they even ruled from Sicily. It's been our misfortune never to
find a dramatist who has really entered into the spirit of German history.
And then Schiller, of all people, elects to glorify that Swiss franc-tireur
[Wilhelm Tell]. The English may have Shakespeare, but all their history
has been able to produce is barbarians and nonentities.[118]

Nevertheless he professed a certain admiration for Henry VIII and
Oliver Cromwell.

Charlemagne, whom Heinrich Himmler and other leading Nazis
even after 1933 still continued to describe as 'the slaughterer of the
Saxons', receives no mention in *Mein Kampf*, though Hitler regarded
him as 'one of the greatest men in world history, a man who succeeded
in federating the squabbling Germans'.[119] But he also greatly admired
Charlemagne's successors who, he asserted, had 'dominated the world
for a period of five hundred years'. Smugly he continued: 'When I
encounter leaders of other tribes in the Teutonic territories . . . my
country of origin places me in a marvellous position. I can point out
that, though it had been a powerful empire . . . for the space of five
hundred years, I did not hesitate for a moment to sacrifice it to the concept of Empire.'[120] In saying this he was passing judgement on Henry
the Lion, whom he decried as a rebellious 'smallholder'[121] with little
understanding of history and one, moreover, who had 'slavicized
German blood'.[122] And yet some prominent National Socialists
regarded this monarch (as also Henry I and Lothair of Saxony) as the
forerunner of their party's *Ostpolitik*, preferring him to Charlemagne
who had turned his face to the south.

Hitler, who had once remarked that 'he would rather travel on foot

to Flanders than on wheels to the east',[123] justified the imperial preference for the south on the grounds of Europe's political structure and
climatic conditions in antiquity and the Middle Ages. On 4 February
1942 he said:

Today we know why our forefathers did not make their way eastwards but
southwards. In those days the whole region east of the Elbe was no whit
different from what Russia is to us today. It was not for nothing that the
Romans shuddered at the idea of climbing the Alps and not without reason
that the Teutons went down to those parts. Formerly Greece was one great
forest of oaks and beeches; the olive groves only came later. . . . The Teuton
yearned for a sunny climate. . . . It was only in Greece and Italy that the
Teutonic spirit could expand! In the course of many centuries he eventually succeeded in creating a decent human existence in northern climes.
. . . To a Roman a posting to Germania must have been rather like what a
spell in Posen at one time was for us . . . never-ending rain and the whole
place a morass. . . . In an age when others already possessed metalled roads,
our country showed no sign of culture. Only the coast-dwellers made any
contribution to culture. The Teutons who stayed behind in Holstein
remained lackeys for two thousand years while their brethren who emigrated
to Greece succeeded in acquiring culture. . . . I'm always sceptical about
archaeological finds in our territories. . . . These things were obtained by
the coast-dwelling Teutons in return for their amber. They had reached no
higher cultural level than the Maori of today.[124]

'I feel sorry for anyone,' he openly admitted, 'who is condemned
constantly to suffer the inhospitability of certain regions. What we've
got is the Bavarian highlands. That's what we have to put up with.'[125]
And in *Mein Kampf* he wrote:

And so we National Socialists consciously draw a line beneath the foreign
policy tendency of our pre-war period. We take up where we broke off six
hundred years ago. We stop the endless German movement to the south and
west, and turn our gaze towards the land in the east. At long last we break
off the colonial and commercial policy of the pre-war period and shift to the
soil policy of the future. If we speak of soil in Europe today, we can primarily
have in mind only Russia and her vassal border states.[126]

Hitler's assertion that the Teutons moved exclusively southwards and
westwards could only be justified if the period of migration from 375
to 568 comprised the whole of Teutonic history. But this is not the
case, as is immediately apparent if we recall the history of tribes such
as the Veneti, the Mordvinians or the Ostrogoths, and more especially
that of the Heruli and the Aestii who penetrated as far as the Black Sea

and the Caucasus respectively. No less tendentious and, indeed, typical of his deliberate manipulation of history, is his assertion that German expansion towards the East had been abandoned 'six hundred years ago', an assertion which one look at the *Ostpolitik* of the Habsburgs and Hohenzollerns is enough to disprove. We need only cite here the three partitions of Poland in the eighteenth century.[127] In 1771 Prussia acquired West Prussia, the Bishopric of Ermland and the Netze district, in 1793 Danzig, Thorn, Posen and Kalish and, finally, in 1795 Masovia and Warsaw, part of the Cracow region and the territory between the rivers Vistula, Bug and Nieman. His assertion is further disproved by Germany's foreign policy as reflected in the Treaty of Brest-Litovsk (March 1918) which compelled Russia to renounce her sovereign rights, first in Poland, Lithuania and Courland and, as a result of a supplementary treaty concluded on 27 August, in Latvia and Esthonia as well.

Hitler maintained that 'for more than a thousand years', in other words roughly since the end of the Carolingian Empire, the Germans had shown themselves incapable of planning their policy with a view to the future.[128] 'Only three phenomena', he wrote in *Mein Kampf* could be claimed as the positive results of:

clearly defined actions in the field of foreign and general politics.

(1) The colonization of the Ostmark, carried out mostly by Bavarians;

(2) the acquisition and penetration of the territory east of the Elbe; and

(3) the organization by the Hohenzollerns of the Brandenburg–Prussian state as a model and nucleus for crystallization of a new Reich.[129]

Hitler's violation of historical fact is so manifest that it would be otiose to provide further examples here. It may well be assumed, however, that such aberrations were due to inadequate historical knowledge, for at that time his horizon appears to have been bounded by the notion of the dominant role played by 'the Aryans' and by 'German blood' in the fields of culture and history.[130] He had returned from the First World War without any of that keen interest in the navy and the sea which he had evinced in Munich before 1914. Nevertheless he continued to advocate the idea, originally derived from the Pan-Germans in Linz and Vienna, of Germany as a world power, a view which had already been publicly professed by, amongst others, Wilhelm II and a number of the influential politicians of the monarchy such as Admiral Tirpitz and the Reich Chancellor, Bethmann Hollweg. Hence it was only logical that Hitler should regard the demand for the restoration of Germany's prewar frontiers not only as inadequate but as absurd.[131] In *Mein Kampf* he wrote: 'In contrast to the conduct of the representatives of this period, we must again profess the highest aim of all foreign policy, to wit: to bring the soil into harmony with the population.'[132]

In November 1923 he attempted to 'make history' by staging a putsch that was to bring about a 'national revolution' and place him at the head of the new government. The attempt met with a bloody reverse. There followed a period of mental depression during which he was assailed for the first time by doubts as to his own infallibility. Yet when, during his detention in the Fortress of Landsberg, he re-examined his ideas about the future of the Reich, he came to the conclusion that they did not require revision. This is hardly surprising since, as has already been seen, his political outlook had been definitively shaped by his early experiences in Linz, Vienna and Munich, and by his study of history in the years immediately preceding the war. Later he came to feel that it was his mission to rectify the mistakes of his predecessors. Hence his concept of international affairs was based on his view of the earlier European system of alliances and on a consideration of the roles played by Britain and France before the First World War.[133] His meditations on the Dual Alliance, the Triple Alliance, the Dreikaiserbund and the Reinsurance Treaty led him to see Britain and Italy as possible allies for Germany, and France as an enemy to be neutralized either diplomatically by a policy of alliances or, if needs be, by war, while he looked to Russia to provide the *Lebensraum* deemed essential to the development of the German Reich.

Hitler's plans for the future did not evolve pragmatically out of current events but rather were rooted in history, and they were strongly coloured by his *Weltanschauung*. This led him to inveigh intemperately in *Mein Kampf* and elsewhere against the Weimar Republic's foreign policy which he denounced as the machinations of 'Jews'.[134] The Social Democrats he regarded as 'anti-German opportunists' who, seeking to win the victors' favour by 'voluntary submission'[135] had only succeeded in damaging their own nation. In order to highlight the 'decay' for which he held the 'Jews' responsible, he invoked the period of Prussian history between 1806 and 1813, a 'time-span which sufficed . . . to imbue a totally collapsed Prussia with . . . new determination for struggle'. This he compared with the seven-year period after the war which had led not only to 'an ever-greater

weakening of our state', but also to the Treaty of Locarno whose terms
are described as 'oppressive measures' and 'edicts of enslavement'.[136]
The more positive aspects of that treaty are wholly disregarded. There
is no mention of the security pact between Germany, Belgium, France
and Italy, for instance, or of the agreement confirming the inviola-
bility of the Franco–German and Belgo–German frontiers and the
demilitarized zone of the Rhineland. Germany's arbitration conventions with Belgium, France, Poland and Czechoslovakia are likewise
passed over in silence.

The question posed in *Mein Kampf*: 'What form must the life of the
German nation assume in the tangible future, and how can this
development be provided with the necessary foundations and the
required security within the framework of the general European
relation of forces?'[137] was the necessary outcome of Hitler's studies of
German and Austrian history. Indeed he claimed to be better informed
about the political structure of Austria than were the professional
diplomats whom he accused in *Mein Kampf* of blindly rushing 'towards catastrophe'.[138] He also criticized German prewar foreign
policy which was, he alleged, based on a confused view of history combined with a lack of insight into the 'psychology of nations', for
otherwise 'they [the Germans] would not have been able to suppose
even for an hour that the Quirinal and the Vienna Hofburg would ever
stand together in a common fighting front'. Italy, he went on, had
chosen to ally herself with Austria while preparing for war against her.
Since Russia and Austria were at that time drifting ever closer to 'a
military clash, the German alliance policy was as senseless as it was
dangerous'.[139] His accounts of the historical relationships between
Austria and Germany on the one hand and Italy and Russia on the
other are riddled with discrepancies. In 1928, for example, he asserted
that the 'Dual Alliance with Austria . . . had resulted in enmity with
Russia',[140] going on to say that 'this enmity with Russia . . . was the
reason why Marxism, while failing to endorse German foreign policy,
did its best to prevent any other real alternative'.[141] In fact, however,
the Dual Alliance between the German Reich and Austria–Hungary
was intended as a safeguard against attack by Russia or Russian supported aggression; it did not precede this 'enmity' with Russia but
rather was a consequence of the deterioration in Russo–German relations after the Congress of Berlin in 1878. Again, Hitler's interpretation
of history is controverted by the fact that the entry of Italy into the

Dual – thenceforward the Triple – Alliance, far from driving a wedge between Russia and the Central Powers, led to a rapprochement. His comment on Marxism is more than dubious since, out of some four hundred Reichstag deputies in 1881, only twelve were Social Democrats while in 1884, six years after the introduction of the Socialist Law (repealed in 1890), they numbered no more than twenty-four. The Reinsurance Treaty concluded by Bismarck with Russia in 1887 as compensation for the *Dreikaiserbund*, which had lapsed as a result of the tension between that country and Austria–Hungary, was considered by Hitler to be a ploy on the part of the Chancellor aimed at relieving Germany of her obligations to Austria–Hungary in the event of war between the latter and Russia.[142] In reality the treaty provided for the neutrality of the partners in time of war, save in the case of an attack by Germany on France or by Russia on Austria–Hungary. Hitler accused the House of Habsburg of having, in the course of centuries, sinned grievously 'against Italian freedom and independence',[143] although nothing deserving of the name occurred until after 1820 with the intervention of Austrian troops at Rieti in 1821 and in Piedmont, Bologna and Parma in 1831. Like the majority of the eight million German Austrians in the German hereditary lands, confronted as they were by forty-two million non-Germans, Hitler always remained convinced that the Habsburgs, and more especially Franz Ferdinand, had failed to treat all the thirteen peoples of the Dual Monarchy impartially and had been guilty of discrimination against their German and German Austrian subjects. This was not so.

In 1920 at the latest Hitler began to stress the need for an Italo–German alliance, regarding this as one of the most important tasks confronting German diplomacy.[144] The project was as yet unconnected with Mussolini whose 'march on Rome', however, was to prove crucial to Hitler's career as Führer;[145] indeed as early as 3 November 1922 it led a prominent National Socialist to describe him as the 'German Mussolini'.[146] Ever since 1922 the Fascist régime had been doing its best to achieve in Italy the kind of solution Hitler had already begun to envisage for Germany and he therefore gave the Duce his public support by accusing the Jews and the Marxists of concentrating on Italy their hostility to authoritarian régimes.[147] The alliance with Mussolini was the result of, not the precondition for, political developments in Italy, and could only be welcomed by Hitler, who on 22 May 1939 was to see his hopes finally realized in the Italo–

German treaty of friendship and mutual assistance, the 'Pact of Steel'.
Despite the fact that the Duce consistently let him down, Hitler continued to regard him as far and away the best man in Rome. Indeed he
was to cling to his prematurely formulated concept of foreign policy
right up till 1945 and even at moments when the vagaries of his Italian
ally made it positively burdensome. Thus in 1939 Mussolini remained
neutral and only decided to enter the lists after the French had sued
for an armistice on 17 June 1940. His 'French campaign' came to an
inglorious end after a few cheaply won victories had taken him no
further than Menton. In November 1942 it was the Italians and
Romanians who gave way at Stalingrad, thus enabling the Russians to
break through and encircle the Sixth Army. And finally, in 1943, the
Badoglio government declared war on the Third Reich. Hitler's con-
stancy in the face of all this only goes to prove that even here reality
meant less to him than the insights he had gained in the years before
the First World War. Not until the beginning of 1945, when there was
no longer any room for doubt, did he admit that the alliance had not
come up to expectations. In February of that year he laid the blame for
the defeat at Mussolini's door when he wrote:

The alliance with Italy has clearly been of greater benefit to our enemies
than to ourselves. While I was on my way to Montoire, Mussolini took
advantage of my absence to launch his ill-starred campaign in Greece. We
were compelled willy-nilly to intervene by force of arms in the affairs of the
Balkans, and by so doing calamitously delayed our attack on Russia. Had
this begun on, or shortly after, 15 May, everything would have turned out
differently.[148]

Hitler's view of an Anglo–German alliance as a means of securing
Germany's rear while she was engaged in her 'necessary' eastward
expansion, was largely the result of wishful thinking. At best it was no
more than indirectly related to historical fact. The purpose of previous
Anglo–German treaties had been the containment of French expansionism – the alliance, for example, concluded during the Spanish
War of Succession (1701–14) between William of Orange, the Holy
Roman Emperor, Prussia, the Empire and, later, Portugal and Savoy,
or again, the alliance between England and Prussia during the Seven
Years War (1756–63). Hitler regarded France as Germany's hereditary
enemy, but his aims differed from those pursued in the past by Britain
and Prussia, for the earlier alliances had been designed to prevent
precisely what he hoped a pact with Britain would enable him to per-

petrate – aggression. He believed he was historically justified in assuming that, at the time of the monarchy, Britain would have been prepared to enter into an alliance with Germany on a *quid pro quo*[149] basis thereby permitting the Reich to pursue her European policy – an attack on Russia[150] – with impunity. It seemed to him that in the past Germany had had only two alternatives with regard to Britain. The following extract from *Mein Kampf*, written in 1924, reflects views he had already held for ten years or more: ' If a European territorial policy was only possible against Russia in alliance with England, conversely, a policy of colonies and world trade was conceivable only against England and with Russia.' [151] In either event the inevitable corollary must have been the abandonment of the Austrian alliance, an alliance whose every aspect Hitler deplored.

There is no saying precisely when he began to envisage the possibility of an alliance with Britain. On 1 August 1920, the first occasion on which he publicly advocated an Italo–German alliance, no such possibility was mentioned.[152] It would seem probable that it first occurred to him some two and a half years later when he noted with satisfaction that on 4 January 1923 Britain had not endorsed the Reparation Commission's vote of censure on the Reich for having failed to maintain its coal deliveries. In addition the United Kingdom had thereafter conspicuously disassociated itself from all reprisals against Germany, including the occupation of the Ruhr by France and Belgium on 9 January. Hitler also assumed from his reading of eighteenth-century history that, notwithstanding the Entente Cordiale of 1907 and the fact of having fought side by side in the First World War, Britain and France were enemies at heart. Hence he believed that by openly proclaiming his hostility to France he would inevitably win over Great Britain who would undoubtedly be anxious to prevent any of the continental powers from rising to a position of world political importance, least of all France whom she could in no circumstances allow to take possession of the 'West European iron and coal deposits'.[153] Thus when laying down guidelines for a German foreign policy that would be both sensible and farsighted, he concluded that while Britain was reluctant to see Germany become a world power, France was 'reluctant to see her become a power at all.' 'Today,' he went on, ' we are not fighting for a position as a world power; today we must struggle for the existence of our fatherland, for the unity of our nation and the daily bread of our children. If we look about us for European allies . . . there remain only two states: England and Italy.'[154] The first of these alliances he never succeeded in concluding. Among the chief obstacles were his pronouncements on foreign policy in *Mein Kampf*, pronouncements he came to regret.[155] When the book appeared in translation in 1939 there was no mistaking the attitude of the British Press. It was plain from the comments in The *Daily Telegraph* of 23 March and The *Times* of 25 March that the British public no less than their political leaders had understood very well what role Hitler proposed to allot to them. The despatches which the foreign minister von Neurath had been receiving since December 1936 from Ribbentrop, his ambassador in London, should have left Hitler under no illusions as to Britain's readiness to fight if Germany were to start a war.[156] Moreover he had been specifically warned of this eventuality by Ribbentrop on 2 January 1938.[157] And when Britain declared war on 3 September 1939 he was forced to realize that he had been badly mistaken. Yet on 23 May 1939, the day after the signature of the Italo–German Pact of Steel, he had already shown signs of deviating from his earlier policy in declaring that Germany must 'burn her boats' and prepare for war against England.[158] There is no knowing whether this had anything to do with Ribbentrop's conclusion that, since Britain would not tolerate Germany as a major power in Central Europe, she would fight the Third Reich as soon as she was strong enough to do so.[159] After the collapse of Poland, Hitler tendered his peace offer to the Western Powers in the hope that he could pick up where he had left off and strike a bargain with Great Britain. In other words he proposed to renounce all political objectives in the West in return for freedom of action in the East. But once more he found he had been mistaken. Again, his hope that the fall of France would eventually drive Britain into his arms proved to be as empty as his wholly illusory expectation that the Russians would refuse to fight under a Bolshevist leadership.

Since his earliest days as a politician Hitler's attitude towards France had been one of mistrust and hostility.[160] This marked, indeed violent, anti-French sentiment characterizes many of his utterances about international affairs even in the period before he wrote *Mein Kampf*, as is evident, for example, from his attacks on the peace terms after the First World War, his demands for the return of ceded German territory, and his choice of potential allies for Germany. As early as 6 June 1920 he remarked: 'So far as we're concerned the enemy is just across the Rhine, not in Italy or some such place.'[161] Later he publicly accused France of seeking to destroy Germany by splitting her up into small states and of aspiring to European hegemony.[162] In *Mein Kampf* he further charges the French with having endangered 'the existence of the white race in Europe' by contaminating the Rhine with 'negro blood'.[163] He continues:

What France, spurred by her own thirst for vengeance and systematically led by the Jew, is doing in Europe today is a sin against the existence of white humanity and some day will incite against this people all the avenging spirits of a race which has recognized racial pollution as the original sin of humanity. For Germany, however, the French menace constitutes an obligation to subordinate all considerations of sentiment and hold out a hand to those who . . . will neither suffer nor tolerate France's desires for domination. In the predictable future there can be only two allies for Germany in Europe: England and Italy.[164]

He was convinced that, with her fundamentally anti-German attitude and her hegemonic aspirations, France must be destroyed if Germany was to preserve her unity and be in a position to secure her rear when the time came to acquire by force of arms the space she required in the East. This is confirmed in his *Zweites Buch* in which he writes:

When it comes to choosing between France and Italy . . . Germany can only choose Italy. For a Franco–German victory over Italy would mean the South Tyrol for us, but also an enemy in the shape of a now stronger France. A victory over France with the help of Italy would give us Alsace-Lorraine at very least and, best of all, . . . the freedom to put into effect a really far-reaching policy of expansion.[165]

Hitler never materially altered the views on France he had publicly expressed for the first time shortly after the First World War.[166]

Because of his deep-rooted prejudices he consistently repudiated the idea of a Russo–German alliance, and this not only in the mid-twenties when he was dictating *Mein Kampf*. From 1920[167] until 1939, and again between 1941 and 1945, the arguments he constantly invoked against it remained virtually the same. When on occasion he appeared to deviate from this line, it was always for tactical reasons. For example on 23 March 1933 he informed the Reichstag: 'The Reich government is willing to cultivate friendly relations with the Soviet Union. . . . The government of the National Revolution finds itself in a position to pursue a policy of a positive nature.'[168] And in a telegram to Stalin on 20 August 1939 he even went so far as to say: 'The conclusion of a non-aggression pact with the Soviet Union will mean that I can embark on a long-term policy for Germany. This country will thereby resume a political line . . . which will be of benefit to both countries for centuries to come.'[169] Since he did not really care whose hands held the reins in the Soviet Union, his decisions were not materially affected by the fact that the Russian rulers were Bolshevists and hence, by his own definition, also Jews. In *Mein Kampf* he expressly states that 'present-day Russia, divested of her Germanic upper stratum, is . . . no ally for the German nation's fight for freedom',[170] since Slavs lack the energy to form a state. He goes on to accuse their leaders of being the tools of 'world Jewry' who are seeking to establish a 'Jewish world hegemony. . . . In Russian Bolshevism we must see the attempt undertaken by the Jews of the twentieth century to achieve world domination'.[171] Shortly before his execution at Nuremburg Ribbentrop stated that, after his return from Moscow in September 1939, he and Hitler often discussed the supposed Jewish Bolshevization of the world. It then seemed to Ribbentrop that the Führer's views, at least in 1939 and 1940, were beginning to draw closer to his own. 'However,' he writes, 'his opinions constantly varied and it is impossible to say to what extent he was motivated by tactical considerations in talking to me thus. . . . As the war went on the Führer reverted to his notion of an international conspiracy and was most insistent about its supposed efficacy.'[172]

In September 1944, some eight months before Hitler's suicide, the end of the war was already in sight: in Russia, the entire southern front right down to the Black Sea had collapsed, the Red Army had been in occupation of Bulgaria since 9 September, a Finnish armistice delegation was already in Moscow, the Germans had evacuated the Peloponnese and the Ionian Islands and on every front the Wehrmacht was in rapid retreat. Yet on 17 September Hitler told his physician, Dr Giesing:

In June 1941 . . . I began the struggle against the Moloch of Bolshevism and I shall bring that struggle to a victorious conclusion. My only real adversary is Stalin and he is more or less my equal. I can only express my admiration for what he has made of Russia . . . and for his military achievements. But in the end the wave of Bolshevism will break on the unshakeable world-view of National Socialism and I shall grind this East Asiatic brood under my heel. Militarily and politically Churchill and Roosevelt, my two other adversaries, are factors of no importance. In the same context Britain will be entirely shattered and nothing whatever will remain of her empire. What remains will be annexed by the United States, and the British Empire will be erased from history. I can't understand the stupidity of these people. They just can't see how dangerous Bolshevism is, or that they're sawing off the branch they're sitting on. I'd like to see these two powers realize, before it's too late, that they're fighting on the wrong side, and I can clearly foresee the time when it's I who'll be holding the balance in the issue between the Russians on the one hand and the Anglo-Americans on the other. Providence has shown me that there's no coming to terms with Bolshevism, and I shall never offer my hand to Russia.[173]

The Soviet–German Pact which involved a temporary diplomatic volte-face on Hitler's part, was a purely tactical measure in face of the political situation immediately before the Second World War. He chose to overlook the warning he had uttered in *Mein Kampf* for the benefit of the then German government to the effect that a Russo–German alliance would constitute a challenge to the Western Powers who, in case of war, would be in a position to concentrate their air attacks on Reich territory – an area that was not within reach of effective Russian aid.[174] In provisionally jettisoning his *Weltanschauung* for the sake of present reality, Hitler was motivated primarily by his impatience to begin his Polish campaign and by his hope of coming to an understanding with Britain. Other considerations were the increasing role played by Poland's eastern neighbour the Soviet Union, in the European balance of power and Japan's reluctance to comply with his urgent demand that her existing treaty obligations be extended to comprise active intervention against the USA should the latter go to war with Germany. He may have temporarily silenced his conscience by recalling his earlier reflections on the subject of Russia, when he had seen her as the only ally that could help Germany pursue a global policy in opposition to Britain.[175] When on 22 June 1941 he not only reverted to the policy he had advocated ever since becoming a politician but also proceeded to implement it, he believed himself to be secure in the West and was visibly relieved that he no longer had to make an outward show of swallowing his own words. But he made a grave error when, instead of advising caution, he urged Japan to take immediate action against the USA.[176] For the Japanese attack on Pearl Harbour on 7 December 1941, some six months after Hitler had first marched against Russia, brought about the armed intervention of the USA and Germany's consequent declaration of war on her. This marked the beginning of the Allies' ascendancy in what had become

the Second World War. It should perhaps be said that, since Japanese
foreign policy was so devious as to be almost impenetrable, Hitler can
hardly be accused in this instance, either of over-optimism or of
having deliberately disregarded the true circumstances.

In 1939, when he embarked on the final phase of his world-power
programme with his first Blitzkrieg, the line-up of the powers bore
little resemblance to the constellations which since the early 1920s, he
had regarded as a necessary prerequisite if Germany was to fulfil her
destiny and embark on the expansionist programme he believed indispensable. While in Vienna and Munich in the years before 1914 he
had believed that Germany and Austria had been guilty of impardon-
able diplomatic blunders through having pursued a mistaken and
historically ill-judged policy of alliances.[177] Yet now, on the threshold
of war, he refused to recognize that he himself had been guilty of
similar blunders, nor for that matter could he have done so, being
incapable (saving only perhaps in the case of Stalingrad) of perceiving
and admitting his own mistakes. Indeed to him a mistake was by
definition anything that failed to agree with his own dogmatic ideas.
Hence he persisted in laying the blame for the failure of his foreign
policy exclusively on his European allies.[178] His attitude towards the
past combined with his firmly held conviction that he had learnt a great
deal from history, which he alone was capable of understanding, was
bound to have catastrophic consequences – and that not only in the
field of foreign policy.

Neither Hitler's *Weltanschauung* nor his character permitted him
to take a dispassionate view of history or to express even remotely
unbiased opinions on the subject of the different social classes, the
churches or the various professions. Even after he no longer had any
need to do so, he would inveigh in scornful if not violent terms against
the 'upper crust', against royalty and what he called the 'Hohenzollern
brood'. He would aim sarcastic barbs at the teaching profession in
general and at primary school-teachers in particular. Lawyers he
execrated, regarded financiers as rogues, and despised the clergy
of both confessions. But his contempt did not extend only to the middle
classes who had flocked to his political standard and quickly become
the backbone of the NSDAP; he also despised the masses to whom
he had consistently turned for support between 1919 and 1933. The
only bourgeois elements he was prepared to tolerate were the Hamburg patricians, whose manner of speech he could and often did mimic

admirably. And whereas Karl Marx in his *Communist Manifesto* had conceded that the bourgeoisie had played a highly revolutionary role in history,[179] Hitler refused to admit that they had ever served a useful function. 'No section of the population,' he said in 1942, 'has shown itself more stupid in political matters than this socalled bourgeoisie.'[180] What particularly aroused his ire and sarcasm was their failure, as he thought, to understand or even genuinely accept antisemitism in the form in which he himself practised it.[181]

An attempt to evaluate Hitler's historical knowledge by academic standards would be neither pertinent nor psychologically justifiable, were it not for the special place allotted to history in his scheme of things. Repeatedly he insisted that he had understood history correctly and that his policy was the best and most logical manner of putting that understanding into practice. 'If mankind would only study history,' he asserted categorically on 27 January 1942, 'just think what the results would be!'[182] Hitler, who prided himself on being a thinker, regarded his interpretation of history as the very cornerstone of his political thoughts and actions which, he hoped, would in turn, be seen as statesmanship of the 'kind that makes history'. That interpretation, which he held to be the objective reflection of reality, evinced grossly distorted and arbitrarily accentuated features and ruthlessly ignored the recognized findings of historians. The consequent inconsistencies were not evident to the generals, the officers from the front line units and the artists who came to visit him at his headquarters, nor to members of his entourage – Bormann, Speer, Morell and Heinrich Hoffmann, for instance. None of these men possessed sufficient historical knowledge to question his frequent pronouncements on the subject. What they heard was new to them and was put across with such assurance that they believed they were being vouchsafed a privileged glimpse behind the veil of history. But even historians would sometimes have been hard put to it to correct him on points of detail or, indeed, to advance a convincing alternative. For example Hitler once maintained that the Roman Extern stones in the region east of the Elbe 'were certainly not places of worship but places of refuge'[183] to which the Romans retreated at times of emergency. Since this was a point on which opinions were divided, he could safely have overridden anyone who sought to dispute it.

His view of the medieval empire, in support of which he advanced seemingly plausible arguments, differed from that of most historians in that he saw it as a kind of Germanic republic and approved its electoral system. Hereditary monarchy, on the other hand, he believed to be conducive to degeneracy, which in turn could lead to children and idiots becoming heads of state. Meditating on this theme in March 1942, he wondered what would happen if Marshal Antonescu had not been at the side of twenty-one year-old King Michael of Romania, 'an abysmally stupid and hopelessly spoilt'[184] youth whose education had been entrusted by King Carol to women. Again, he expressed doubt as to Peter of Yugoslavia's capacity to rule since, when told that a *coup d'état* had placed him on the throne, the new king had 'gone down to the cellar and blubbered'.[185] An electoral system, he thought, was less liable than an hereditary monarchy to produce a head of state who was a 'total idiot', and of this the best proof was the history of the German emperors. For whereas in hereditary monarchies at least eight out of ten rulers had been 'nincompoops', not one of the elected German 'Titans' could be described as such.[186] He also differed from accepted academic opinion in regarding Napoleon's downfall not as the result of his Russian campaign but as arising inevitably out of his typically Corsican sense of family and his 'want of taste' in accepting the imperial crown, thus making 'common cause with degenerates'.[187] Hitler himself eschewed nepotism on the grounds that it was a form of 'protection of the ego'[188] conducive to inefficiency; Napoleon's indulgence in nepotism he regarded as evidence of human weakness if not of hubris for which history had exacted her own revenge.

Hitler would adopt generally accepted historical facts and opinions and proceed to give his own version of them, supporting that version with instances drawn from impeccable sources, quotations from the correspondence of such rulers as Peter the Great and Napoleon,[189] and references to the publications of obscure Austrian dissidents* many of whose names were unknown to German scholars. Thus he was able to dazzle his audience with a display of erudition on a variety of topics. Academics, on the other hand, would find themselves completely nonplussed by the dogmatic, pertinacious and sometimes ridiculously overemphatic views this autodidact had derived from his studies – views which remained unmodified since they never met with any serious opposition. Save in a few instances, he was impervious to argument. Six weeks after Hitler's death Giesing wrote:

---

*In Austria this is customary even among serious historians.

Despite scientific proof to the contrary, he refused to believe that there was such a thing as minimum protein requirement, and that this was the reason why he often felt hungry. He preferred to allay his pangs by drinking tea and eating three of four slices of cake twice daily. His opinions and pronouncements, even on minor matters such as these, were all of so tenacious and absolute a nature that it was usually hopeless to try and make him see reason. Yet he was quick to understand medical innovations of which he had not previously heard.[190]

Hitler often spoke disparagingly of the Teutonic cult,[191] contrasting it with the culture of ancient Greece and Rome, which he regarded as 'our spiritual home'. He derided as foolish those who failed to understand that the Teutonic races had been comparatively late arrivals so far as the history of civilization was concerned. After 1933 he waxed so critical of *Deutschtum* that his credibility would have suffered had his views on the subject ever become generally known.

Why [he asked angrily] do we call the whole world's attention to the fact that we have no past? It isn't enough that the Romans were erecting great buildings when our forefathers were still living in mud huts; now Himmler is starting to dig up these villages of mud huts and enthusing over every potsherd and stone axe he finds. All we prove by that is that we were still throwing stone hatchets and crouching around open fires when Greece and Rome had already reached the highest degree of culture. We really should do our best to keep quiet about the past.[192]

Hitler never modified his 'world power programme'[193] which comprised among other things 'the peaceful conquest' of European territory, the establishment of a German continental imperium by means of a series of Blitzkriegs, the acquisition of colonies in Africa, the creation of maritime bases and a strong navy and, finally, the development of a war economy capable of sustaining a global conflict. This programme, which incongruously enough owed certain of its aspects to his idiosyncratic interpretation of the cosmopolitan outlook of Stoic philosophy, had already begun to occupy his mind in his Vienna days. Then a 'fanatically committed' German Austrian, he read publications such as *Grossdeutschland* and *Deutsche Weltpolitik* some of whose themes later recurred when, as a member of the German army, he discussed war aims with his comrades. The German Pan-Germans, who had a not inconsiderable influence on the shaping of Hitler's *Weltanschauung*, claimed that the German Empire should consist of the Lesser German Reich along with Luxemburg, Holland

and Belgium, German-speaking Switzerland and the Austrian Empire.[194] As early as 1895 (the year in which Hitler started school at Fischlam) Ernst Hasse, a well-known professor of statistics at Leipzig University and president of the German Pan–German League, had called for the extension of the Greater Reich to the shores of the Persian Gulf.[195] Further Pan-German demands included the whole of Switzerland, the Balkan Peninsula, Asia Minor and the seven eastern *départements* of France.[196]

The main lines along which Hitler was to develop his theory of history had already been laid down while he was a schoolboy in Linz. Later it betrayed the influence of, amongst others, Malthus, Darwin, Kjellén, Bölsche, Gobineau, Carlyle, Ploetz, Alexander von Müller and, perhaps, also Edward Gibbon. His history teacher in Linz was Dr Leopold Poetsch, a member of the Linz municipal council and a militant German Nationalist whose political views had been formed in the German and Slav speaking region of southern Austria. He indoctrinated his pupils with the theories of the Pan-German League and deliberately manipulated various aspects of history to make them fit in with a preconcieved ideological view. By this means he turned the boys into true 'children of Germany' and enemies of Austria. 'For who', Hitler asked in *Mein Kampf*, 'could have studied German history under such a teacher without becoming an enemy of the state which, through its ruling house, exerted so disastrous an influence on the destinies of the nation?'[197] Later, however, at the height of his power, he was to single out for commendation one member of that house, Rudolf von Habsburg, because he had secured possession of certain hereditary lands, had defeated Ottokar of Bohemia, had skilfully avoided complying with a number of the Church's demands, and had restored the unity of the Empire.[198] Hitler also conceded that the Habsburg monarchy, to which by 1924 he vouchsafed little more than contempt, 'had continued to uphold the German idea at a time when . . . the empire had disintegrated into separate states and was literally torn asunder by dynastic interests'.[199]

Of Poetsch he wrote in *Mein Kampf*:

Perhaps it affected my whole later life that good fortune sent me a history teacher who was one of the few to observe this principle in teaching and examining. Dr Leopold Poetsch . . . embodied this requirement to an ideal degree. This old gentleman's manner was as kind as it was determined, his dazzling eloquence not only held us spellbound but actually carried us away.

Even today I think back with emotion on this grey-haired man who, by the fire of his narratives, sometimes made us forget the present; who as if by enchantment carried us into past times and, out of the millennial veils of mist, moulded dry historical memories into living reality. On such occasions we sat there, often aflame with enthusiasm, and sometimes even moved to tears. What made our good fortune all the greater was that this teacher knew how to illuminate the past by examples from the present, and how from the past to draw inferences for the present. As a result he had more understanding than anyone else for all the daily problems which then held us breathless. He used our budding nationalistic fanaticism as a means of educating us. . . . This teacher made history my favourite subject. And indeed, though he had no such intention, it was then that I became a little revolutionary.[200]

This fact was all too patent to those teachers he happened to dislike. Speaking to his visitors in the Wolfsschanze on the evening of 8 January 1942 he recalled an incident involving his scripture teacher:

The moment Schwarz entered the room the class was as though transformed. A new spirit entered into it, a general mood of rebellion. . . . So as to annoy him I got hold of some pencils in the Greater German colours, black, white, red. 'Get rid of those disgustingly coloured pencils at once!' Schwarz exclaimed. There was an 'Ooh!' from the whole class. 'They stand for nationalist ideals!' I cried. 'I forbid you to cherish nationalist ideals. There is only one ideal and one alone, and that is our fatherland and our own House of Habsburg.'[201]

Even as an adolescent Hitler had little affection either for Vienna or for the House of Habsburg. His aversion for Vienna, an aversion shared by a great many other Austrians, whether from Innsbruck, the Vorarlberg, Graz or elsewhere, would seem to have had its origins in Linz. But it was only after he had actually lived in the capital between 1908 and 1913 that he grew to hate it and to detest the Viennese dialect which, save for one or two idioms, he never used. Hitler's *Weltanschauung* as well as his attitude to history and to Austria was to a large extent moulded by Linz, then a semirural, middle-class town governed by freethinking German Nationalists. Its industrialization came only with the Anschluss and it was never to become the unrivalled centre of art and culture such as Hitler had planned once victory was his. The authorities turned a blind eye to the gatherings of the banned 'Gothia' or 'Wodan' Societies frequented by the pupils (young Adolf among them) from the school in the Steingasse, an establishment of Pan-

German persuasion. Not only was he exposed, therefore, to the ideological influence of these gatherings, but he also witnessed the intolerent nationalism of the citizenry, whose anti-Czech sentiment even led them to protest against the appearance of the eminent violinist, Jan Kubelik, and to demonstrate against Father Jurasek's use of the Czech language in church. These memories are plainly in evidence in *Mein Kampf*. Indeed they are at the root of his attacks on the Habsburgs for their 'Slavization' of the Austrians, and of his constant harping on the undue influence exerted by the Catholic clergy. Again, his early experiences in Linz may well account for his morbid nationalism with its predominant strain of Pan-Germanism and antisemitism.

In *Mein Kampf* Hitler relates that, during his schooldays in Linz, he 'learned to understand and grasp the meaning of history',[202] and again that 'to "Learn" history means to seek and find the forces which are the causes leading to those effects which we subsequently perceive as historical events'.[203] This assertion not only presupposes the virtual infallibility of a *Weltanschauung* that seeks to explain historical cause and effect in highly stereotyped terms; it also tenders the experiences and insights he gained at that time as historical lessons applicable to the future of the Reich. For example, throughout his life his plans and decisions consistently reflect the impressions made on him by the British, French and Russian policy of encirclement, of which he had heard so much in Linz and Steyr between 1904 and 1907. The hysterical terms in which he subsequently expressed his fear of a renewed encirclement of the Reich can be partly attributed to his voracious reading, at this impressionable age, of the nationalist press, the *Südmark-Kalender* and the Linz *Fliegende Blätter*.[204]

Hitler admitted in 1942 that when in Linz he had not yet been capable of grasping doctrines of any complexity or of drawing conclusions therefrom. Again speaking of Father Schwarz, his scripture teacher, he relates: 'I would drive him to such desperation that he often didn't know whether he was coming or going. I had read a lot, much of it free-thinking stuff, and when I came out with my half-baked scraps of erudition it really drove him wild.'[205] Even in *Mein Kampf*, twenty years after he had left school, his historical dissertations were still so generalized and so tendentious that it is difficult to credit him with any real familiarity with history. He would undoubtedly have written in much greater detail had he possessed the knowledge of which he later gave evidence – in his table-talk for example. What he wrote in 1925, while consistent with his later opinions, was encumbered with irrelevant detail and gave no more than a vague idea of the concepts on which his *Weltanschauung* was based. He speaks, for instance, of the 'colonization of the Ostmark' for which the Baiuvarii had been mainly responsible,[206] of the 'organization of a Brandenburg–Prussian state as a model and nucleus for crystallization of a new Reich',[207] of the 'acquisition and penetration of the territory east of the Elbe'[208] and of the need for a historiography which would not only give a proper account of the 'growth, of the activity and – the decline – of the true culture-founders of this earth, the Aryans themselves', but would also elevate the racial question to a 'dominating position'.[209] Too many of his pages are filled with empty phrases and generalizations interspersed with a few names, the whole often couched in language which merely betrays the triteness of his judgement.

In Hitler's view, history was the work of great men; among them Arminius the Cheruscan, Theodoric, Charlemagne, Rudolf von Habsburg, Wallenstein, Frederick the Great, Peter the Great, Napoleon, Bismarck, Wilhelm I, several emperors of the German Imperial period and one or two popes. These were some of the pre-eminent figures whom he regarded as 'makers of history' in the sense used by Thomas Carlyle and the idealistically inclined historiographers of the nineteenth century – figures who must 'always be understood in the context of their time', as he put it on 31 March 1942.[210] 'Who knows,' he went on to ask, 'whether some mad schoolmaster a thousand years hence, some poor simpleton . . . won't come along and say: "Hitler may have meant well but, when all's said and done, what he did in the East turned out to be sheer folly"?'[211] To him history was not, as it was to Marx and Engels and their followers, the history of class struggle, but rather the history of racial struggles whose outcome was always determined by men of major stature; it was the sum total of struggle and war, waged by each against all[212] with no room for either mercy or humanity. Citing Moltke he said that the most drastic methods of warfare,[213] by helping to curtail its misery, were in fact the most humane, and that anyone who was not prepared to countenance such methods would thereby eliminate himself from history. In nature, he believed, there was an 'iron law of logic' which ordained that there should be a perpetual process of selection through a life and death struggle in which the stronger always overcame the weak and thus secured the 'right to exist'.[214] Applying this idea to the future of the German people he said on 28 January 1942:

If this war costs us a quarter of a million dead and a hundred thousand cripples, the loss will have been made good by Germany's high birth-rate since we came to power. They will be replaced several times over in the settlements I am creating for German blood in the East. . . . The fact that we have too many children is to our advantage. For that gives rise to want or necessity which in turn compels people to bestir themselves. We are not in danger of remaining stuck at the stage of development which has brought us superiority today. Necessity compels us always to be in the van as far as technological progress is concerned, for only by that means can we retain our lead. . . . The price that has to be paid for life is blood, and this begins at birth. If anyone says he doesn't like that kind of life I can only advise him to do away with himself.[215]

On 1 December 1941, when recuperating from six months of severe illness during which he had suffered from an agonizing heart condition, attacks of dizziness, constant stomach ache and debilitating bouts of shivering, he remarked:

Some people might be horrorstruck by the way creatures devour each other in nature. The fly is killed by a dragon fly, which is killed by a bird which in turn is killed by something bigger. The biggest creature, when it grows old, falls a prey to bacteria, and fate finally catches up with these as well. . . . Hence all we can do is to investigate the laws of nature in order not to go against them . . . otherwise it means rebellion against the heavens! If there is one divine commandment I could believe in it is this: Preserve the species.[216]

Jacob Burckhardt regarded nations as biological organisms subject to natural laws, as did Hitler and Alexander von Müller who further saw them as 'rooted in the earth and, like the earth, restricted to certain natural limits'.[217] But whereas Burckhardt applied biological laws to the history of peoples, assigning to each a lifespan of up to 1200 years, Hitler took the view that a country's history came to an end only when its people ceased to fight, thus ignoring 'the natural law upon whose observance their survival depends'. Holding forth on this subject on 27 January 1942 he said: 'So long as a few thousand men are willing to go to prison for an idea, their cause is not lost. It's only done for when the last man despairs of it. . . . On this point I am absolutely adamant: If the German people is not prepared to take active steps to preserve itself, well and good – let it disappear.'[218] Thus overpopulation, fighting and war were to him the principal means of safeguarding the continued existence of the German people.

Sixty-five years before Hitler was born, Malthus had advanced a theory which rapidly gained popular support, namely that the world's population was outgrowing the soil's capacity to provide for it, so that overpopulation would inevitably entail famine, war and pestilence. There was, he believed, a twofold solution: firstly, control of the birthrate by means of late marriage and continence and, secondly, the intensive development of agriculture. Hitler, on the other hand, saw the solution exclusively in ruthless struggle, in a predatory war of annihilation, not for the sake of glory but solely as a means to an end – an historically all-important act in response to natural law and necessity, an act in which his ideology was translated into practice. Unlike Malthus, Hitler did not see overpopulation as a threat but rather as desirable because conducive to 'necessity' which in turn would compel the nation to 'bestir itself'[219] and overthrow other nations. The dangers inherent in such an interpretation were greatly enhanced by Hitler's affectivity and his ability to arouse uncontrollable and irrational forces in the people – an ability which derived from his exceptional gifts as an orator and from his unexampled expertise in the manipulation of power.

Recent research into problems of overpopulation has revealed certain modes of behaviour which appear in an exceptionally interesting light when seen in relation to Hitler's reactions on a number of occasions. At the 8th Conference of the International Planned Parenthood Federation at Santiago de Chile in 1967,[220] the Scottish psychiatrist, Professor G. M. Carstairs of Edinburgh University, cited studies which demonstrated that various species of animals show disorganization of their normal behaviour patterns when confined to overcrowded pens; among other changes, the frequency of combats tends to increase. Hitler's markedly emotional reactions when dealing with the problem of war and territorial expansion bear a close parallel to those of the animals described by Carstairs. Whenever he broached the subject of *Volk und Raum* (people and space) in relation to war, he would for a time become alarmingly and distressingly vehement, so that the impression he gave was of a fanatically committed psychopath acting instinctively in a state of bellicose exaltation. The blood rushed almost visibly to his head, his features became congested, his body rigid, he threw out his chest and thrust forward his arms as though to seize or strike down an adversary. At the same time he shouted menacingly and looked the very image of aggression. To what extent this behaviour was due to high blood pressure and the effects of constant medication is not readily ascertainable.

The particular interpretation Hitler put on war and his brutal attitude towards 'invalids and weaklings' reflect his view of the world and of history. The sources of the ideas he adopted and reshaped are not difficult to trace. One such was Alfred Ploetz, a doctor of medicine, whose book *Die Tüchtigkeit unserer Rasse und der Schutz der Schwachen* (*The Efficiency of our Race and the Protection of the Weak*)[221] Hitler had obviously read while still in Vienna. Ploetz expressed concern over the threat 'to the efficiency of our race',[222] more especially the 'Aryan race',[223] a threat inherent in 'the protection of the weak'. The doctor, who was appointed an honorary professor in 1933, introduced eugenics (now dubbed 'racial hygiene') into Germany. There is a striking similarity between his ideas and those of Hitler, as the following passage shows:

Advocates of racial hygiene will have little objection to war since they see in it one of the means whereby the nations carry on their struggle for existence. .... In the course of the campaign it might be deemed advisable deliberately to muster inferior variants at points where the main need is for cannon fodder and where the individual's efficiency is of secondary importance.[224]

Since war occupied so central a place in Hitler's thinking, the question arises whether his study of Clausewitz's work was ever profound enough to play any real part in shaping his *Weltanschauung*. Military historians have either avoided the subject or accorded it no more than a casual mention. There can be no doubt that his works were already known to Hitler before the outbreak of the First World War. And in the early twenties Hanfstaengl recalls having seen *Vom Kriege* among Hitler's books. He could, Hanfstaengl says, quote Clausewitz 'by the yard', and from the same informant we learn that in his early days as a party leader Hitler professed an unbounded admiration for his writings.[225] There is also evidence to show that, in quoting from Clausewitz's work, he was not motivated solely by the desire to demolish hostile criticism or to impress others. Though a number of sources have noted his familiarity with works on military science none,[226] save Hanfstaengl, name specific authors.[227] The fact that (unlike Halder, for instance) Dönitz, Blumentritt, Gause, von

Manstein, Liss and Warlimont[228] can none of them recall ever having heard Hitler refer to Clausewitz at his conferences or in lectures, is of little import.[229] His willingness expressly to cite him, both as a source and in justification of his decisions, is in marked contrast to his reluctance to acknowledge the intellectual parentage of his other concepts, and would seem to indicate a certain familiarity with the master's works.[230]

Nevertheless, apart from Keitel's statement at Nuremburg and Hanfstaengl's[231] account, there are only three distinct published references that would seem to substantiate Hitler's claim to have actually studied, and not merely read, Clausewitz. The first is his reproachful and somewhat self-righteous remark on 8 November 1934 in the Munich *Bürgerbräukeller*. 'Not one of you,' he said, 'has read Clausewitz, or if you have read him, you haven't known how to relate him to the present.'[232] The second is found in an address to his senior officers on 23 August 1941 when he said: 'My generals know Clausewitz but understand nothing of the economics of war. Come to that, I also know Clausewitz and his axiom: One must first destroy the enemy's armies in the field and then occupy his capital.'[233] Finally Hitler's Chief of the General Staff, Heinz Guderian, quotes him as saying in 1944: 'I have studied Clausewitz and Moltke and read the whole of the Schlieffen Plan.'[234]

Like his one-time teacher, Alexander von Müller, Hitler regarded the Jews as a 'ferment of decomposition' and incorporated them as such into his general view of history. He drew on biological terminology to express his antisemitism, which he envisaged as part of the ruthless struggle for existence. 'Can it be', he asked on 1 December 1941,

that nature created the Jew so that, by his decomposition, he should set other peoples in motion? If that be the case, then Paul and Trotsky are the most estimable of Jews for having done more towards this end than anyone else. Their activity sets up a resistance. This follows their action as the bacillus follows the body it is seeking to destroy.[235]

He further regarded 'the Jew' as the 'mortal enemy of all light' who 'poisons the blood of others',[236] 'sucks them dry' and deceives, misleads and subjugates them; who distracts them from the necessary struggle for existence and strives to achieve 'the victory of democracy'[237] using the latter as a means to destroy the peoples.

How Hitler came to adopt this crude and perverted attitude, which he significantly describes as the victory of reason over feeling,[238] is plainly discernible from the following passage in *Mein Kampf*:

Today it is difficult, if not impossible, for me to say when the word 'Jew' first gave me ground for special thoughts. At home I do not remember having heard the word during my father's lifetime. I believe that the old gentleman would have regarded any special emphasis on this term as cultural backwardness. In the course of his life he had arrived at more or less cosmopolitan views. . . . Likewise at school I found no occasion which could have led me to change this inherited picture.

At the *Realschule*, to be sure, I did meet one Jewish boy who was treated by all of us with caution . . . but neither I nor the others had any thoughts on the matter.

Not until my fourteenth or fifteenth year did I begin to come across the word 'Jew' with any frequency, partly in connection with political discussions. This filled me with a mild distaste, and I could not rid myself of an unpleasant feeling that always came over me whenever religious quarrels occurred in my presence.

At that time I did not think anything else of the question.

There were few Jews in Linz.* In the course of the centuries their outward appearance had become Europeanized and had taken on a human look; in fact I even took them for Germans. The absurdity of this idea did not dawn on me because I saw no distinguishing feature but the strange religion. The fact that they had, as I believed, been persecuted on this account sometimes turned my distaste at unfavourable remarks about them into horror. . . .

Then I came to Vienna.

Preoccupied by the abundance of my impressions in the architectural field . . . I gained at first no insight into the inner stratification of the people in this gigantic city. . . . Not until calm gradually returned and the agitated picture began to clear did I look around me more carefully in my new world, and then among other things I encountered the Jewish question. . . . For the Jew was still characterized for me by nothing but his religion, and therefore, on grounds of human tolerance, I maintained my rejection of religious attacks in this case as in others. Consequently, the tone, particularly that of the Viennese antisemitic press, seemed to me unworthy of the cultural tradition of a great nation. I was oppressed by the memory of certain occurrences in the Middle Ages, which I should not have liked to see repeated. Since the newspapers in question did not enjoy an outstanding reputation . . . I regarded them more as the products of anger and envy than the results of a principled though, perhaps mistaken, point of view.[239]

* This statement is false; cf. also Kubizek pp. 112 f.

So much for Hitler's own account. Kubizek, however, declares that, to the best of his recollection, Adolf's father was not a broadminded cosmopolitan, but rather an out-and-out antisemite and follower of Schönerer.[240] He further contests Hitler's assertion that there was virtually no antisemitism in his secondary school at Linz. In fact, Kubizek maintains that when they first met in 1904 – at a time, that is, when Hitler was attending the school – his friend's attitude was already 'distinctly antisemitic'.[241] Some other points may be worth mentioning in this context. For instance on 8 January 1903 the free thinking Linz newspaper, *Tagespost*, published an obituary of Hitler's father, Alois, which described him as 'a progressive-minded man' of comparatively wide culture, 'a warm friend of the freethinking school' and a champion of 'probity and justice'. On this point Hitler's account appears to be more accurate than that of Kubizek. Not so his ensuing remark to the effect that he was acquainted with only one Jewish pupil in his secondary school at Linz. In fact out of the school's 329 pupils fifteen were Jewish, 299 (including Hitler himself) were Catholics, fourteen were Protestant and one was Greek Orthodox. At the beginning of 1902 Hitler's class, 1B, consisted of twenty-eight Catholics, six Jews and five Protestants.[242]

From this we may conclude either that Hitler was deliberately falsifying the facts or that his assertion about the comparative absence of antisemitism among his fellow pupils was true. For had he encountered any definite antisemitic manifestations at school he would surely have stressed in *Mein Kampf* that six of his classmates had been Jews. On the night of 8 January 1942, reminiscing in the Wolfsschanze about his former German teacher Siegfried Nagel, he said:

At Steyr we had a Jewish teacher. One day we locked him into the laboratory. [In his classes] the racket was terrific. . . . He had no control at all. I was told that at one time the boys had been afraid of him because of his terrifying bellow. Then someone saw that he was laughing up his sleeve, so that was that. . . . Once when I was reading a book on fungus disease he strode across the room, snatched the book out of my hand and tossed it away shouting: 'Why don't you do as I do and read tripe?'[243]

It seems highly improbable that, before going to Vienna, Hitler should not as he alleges have even suspected 'the existence of an organized opposition to the Jews'. Undoubtedly, however, the question would have been more acute and hence more obtrusive in the capital. From *Mein Kampf* we learn that the Viennese papers he read before his 'conversion' to antisemitism were the Jewish-owned *Neue Freie Presse* and the *Wiener Tageblatt*, both of which appealed to him because of 'their exalted tone and the objectivity of individual articles'.[244] What displeased him, he goes on to say, was the excessively servile attitude of these papers which 'made the most obsequious bows to every rickety horse in the Court, and flew into convulsions of joy if he accidentally swished his tail. . . . Another thing that got on my nerves was the loathsome cult for France which the big press, even then, carried on. A man couldn't help feeling ashamed to be a German.'[245] Hitler therefore turned to newspapers that expressed opinions rather more to his liking. He began to read the markedly antisemitic *Deutsches Volksblatt* and came to the conclusion that this paper was 'somewhat more appetizing'[246] than the national press if only because it refrained from attacking Wilhelm II whom he regarded 'not only as the German Emperor, but first and foremost as creator of the German fleet'.[247] Later he was to maintain that at first he was repelled by the *Volksblatt*'s virulent antisemitism. Nevertheless it stimulated his interest in Lueger and the Christian Social Party which, on his arrival in Vienna, he had regarded with hostility. But from being Lueger's enemy he succeeded in transforming himself into his admirer, a process which, he relates in *Mein Kampf*, represented a marked improvement in his understanding of Jewry:[248]

My views with regard to anti-Semitism thus succumbed to the passage of time, and this was my greatest transformation of all. At the time of this bitter struggle between spiritual education and cold reason, the visual instruction of the Vienna streets had performed invaluable services. There came a time when I no longer, as in the first days, wandered blindly through the mighty city; now with open eyes I saw not only the buildings but also the people. Once, as I was strolling through the Inner City, I suddenly encountered an apparition in a black caftan and black hair locks . . .[249]

Kubizek, who is at pains to substantiate and fill out a number of his friend's descriptions, tells us that Hitler once appeared as a police witness after the arrest on a begging charge[250] of an Eastern European Jewish peddler of bootlaces, braces and the like. The man, who wore a caftan and high boots, was alleged by the police to have had 3000 kronen on his person at the time of his arrest.[251] Hitler's own description of this encounter in the Inner City has been much embroidered by a number of his biographers. He himself maintains that, after observing the 'apparition in the black caftan' he zealously studied all available antisemitic literature to find out as much as possible about the Jews. The antisemitism expounded in the pamphlets he bought for a few hellers 'seemed to me so monstrous', he wrote, and 'the accusations so boundless, that, tormented by the fear of doing injustice, I again became anxious and uncertain'.[252] He goes on to say that, though he could not always follow the arguments in antisemitic publications since these 'unfortunately ... all proceeded from the supposition that in principle the reader knew or even understood the Jewish question to a certain degree',[253] he no longer believed the difference between Germans and Jews to be a purely religious one.

According to Wilfried Daim, the publications in question were copies of the *Ostara*, a periodical not infrequently adorned with a swastika, which had been founded in 1905 by a fanatical racist who called himself Georg Lanz von Liebenfels. It was claimed that on occasion sales of this periodical had reached as many as 100,000 copies. No. 29 (autumn 1908), after calling attention to statements of policy in previous issues, goes on to define the publication's task as follows: 'The *Ostara* is the first and only periodical devoted to investigating and cultivating heroic racial characteristics and the law of man in such a way that, by actually applying the discoveries of ethnology, we may through systematic eugenics ... preserve the heroic and noble race from destruction by socialist and feminist revolutionaries.'[254] This extract speaks for itself. In 1905 Lanz von Liebenfels founded the 'Order of the New Temple' whose membership was restricted to fair-haired, blue-eyed men, all of whom were pledged to marry fair-haired, blue-eyed women. In 1908 Liebenfels, an uncommonly prolific journalist, produced his *magnum opus*, which was reprinted in the *Ostara* between 1928 and 1930, in the form of a pamphlet entitled *Theozoology or the Science of Sodom's Apelings and the Divine Electron. An Introduction to the Earliest and Most Recent World View and a Vindication of Royalty and the Nobility.* 'Sodom's apelings' were the dark-skinned, 'inferior races' whom Liebenfels described as the 'bungled handiwork' of demons in contrast to the blue-eyed, fair-haired 'Aryo-heroes', the masterpiece of the gods. These latter beings were equipped with electric bodily organs and built in electric transmitting and power stations. They were the archetypes of the human species and the human race. By means of 'purifying eugenics' he proposed to awaken the gods who, he alleged, continued to slumber in the 'fleshy coffins of men's bodies'.[255] At the same time he proposed to help the new human race, about to emerge out of the Aryo-heroic race, to regain their former divine 'electro-magnetic-radiological' organs and, thus equipped, to become 'all-knowing, all-wise and all-powerful'[256] as in the primeval era of the gods.

Liebenfels claimed a number of world-famous politicans as his alumni, among them both Hitler[257] and Lenin. He also maintained that, together with Kitchener, Lenin had been the only one to understand his teaching 'before the war and to have drawn his conclusions from it'.[258] These absurd claims require no further comment. Adolf Josef Lanz (1874–1954), alias Lanz von Liebenfels, the son of a Vienna schoolmaster, had once been a Cistercian monk. In 1899 he left the Heiligenkreuz monastery in the Wiener Wald, assumed the title of baron, awarded himself a doctorate, and falsified both the place and date of his birth, amending the latter to 1872. According to Daim this impostor was not only the author of the publications which caused young Hitler such a mental struggle, but also 'the man who gave him his ideas'.[259] There is no substance in either of these assumptions. If, as seems probable, Hitler came across Lanz's pamphlets during his time in Vienna, his development as an antisemite can have been little affected by them. After the Wehrmacht's occupation of Austria he prohibited their publication.[260]

The sources of the ideological arguments upon which Hitler's anti-semitic ideas were based can be traced back at least as far as September 1919. These consisted in innumerable books, periodicals, pamphlets and articles, all of very similar content. Their authors, whether eminent or obscure, set a disastrous example both before and immediately after the First World War, particularly in the German-speaking countries. While in Linz Hitler read not only *Fliegende Blätter* and *Das Alldeutsche Tageblatt*, but also and more especially the *Südmark-Kalender*, a paper much favoured by his schoolmates and by the Nationalist-minded townspeople. This paper pleaded the cause of the Südmark Frontier Defence Association, and consistently promoted a 'German-conscious' policy. Thus during the course of 1904, the year in which Hitler left Linz for Steyr, it advocated a 'greater German consciousness', the recognition not only of 'the conditions necessary to our nationhood' but also of 'the goal assigned by Providence to the Germanic people', the 'training of strong *völkisch* natures' and the acceptance of 'the profound lesson of history as the lodestar' for all action affecting the 'weal or woe' of the 'Great German National Community'. The *Südmark-Kalender* was the source of much of Hitler's vocabulary, in particular the term *Volksgenosse** which frequently recurred in its columns.[261]

It has already been shown that, while still at school in Linz, Hitler had fallen under the influence of the Austrian Pan-Germans, more especially that of their leader, Georg Ritter von Schönerer, whose strong pro-German bias he shared. Even before 1908, the year in which Hitler finally left for Vienna, Schönerer's movement was beginning to show antisemitic tendencies[262] such as had manifested themselves in the German Pan-German League as far back as 1897 with the publication of Ernst Hasse's book *Deutsche Weltpolitik*. In this work the leader of the League declared that 'our future lies in our blood' and went on to say how remarkable it was that 'this apparently obvious fact has gone so long unnoticed'.[263] Following the publication of Houston Stewart Chamberlain's *Foundations of the Nineteenth Century* and the appearance in German translation of Gobineau's mid-nineteenth-century *Essai sur l'inégalité des races humaines*, racism made rapid headway in the Pan-German League. It was finally endorsed by the unanimous election in February 1908 of the antisemitic lawyer, Heinrich Class, as leader of the League in Hasse's stead. As Werner put it in 1935: 'The prevailing liberal doctrine of the equality of all who have a human face was replaced by an appreciation of the importance of a nation's racial composition.'[264]

As a follower of Schönerer in the years preceding the Great War Hitler had taken careful note of developments in the Pan-German League, both as regards its organization and its literature – information which later was to stand him in good stead. Thus, by the time of the Pan-Germans' Bamberg conference in February 1919, he had been familiar with the League's arguments and programmes for more than ten years. And, indeed, the thoughts expressed in his paper on the Jews written six months later are consistent with the following passage from Point 5 of the League's 1919 manifesto: 'To combat the disruptive, subversive influence of the Jews – a racial question which has nothing whatever to do with questions of religion.'[265]

This manifesto marked the launching of biological antisemitism. Though familiar with that theory's intellectual sources, Hitler could

---

*A rough equivalent might be 'comrade and fellow countryman', a term having distinct racial overtones and frequently used by Hitler at the beginning of a speech. (trans.)

not at this time have handled its terminology with any confidence. The memory of his struggle, not only in Linz and Steyr, but also no doubt in Vienna, to understand what he had once described as 'freethinking stuff', long continued to inhibit him and it was not until 1921 that he began to overcome those inhibitions. Indeed he could hardly afford 'not to understand things' if he was to head a party which, because of its platform, contained 28 per cent officials and white-collar workers (some with academic qualifications), 20 per cent merchants and independent business men and 7 per cent academics.[266] Three years later, writing of the Jews in *Mein Kampf*, he made use for the first time of expressions such as 'parasite',[267] 'parasite in the body of other peoples',[268] 'bacillus',[269] 'germ-carriers',[270] 'vampire',[271] and 'fission fungus of mankind', going on to assert that 'if the Jew is victorious over the other peoples of the world . . . this planet will, as it did thousands of years ago, move through the ether devoid of men'.[272] In this new departure we can discern the formative influence of, amongst others, the 'Darwinians' Ernst Haeckel and his henchman Wilhelm Bölsche though they are not, of course, mentioned by name. In 1899 Bölsche had written a book called *Vom Bazillus zum Affenmenschen* (*From the Bacillus to the Apeman*)[273] in which he had described the 'naked struggle for dominance between the zoological species "Man"'[274] and 'the lowest form of organic life'. In the nineteenth century, Bölsche held, man had found himself on the threshold of 'total domination of the earth',[275] and in the twentieth he would fight his 'last decisive battle' against the 'third Reich' of the bacillae,[276] a battle which 'in all human probability'[277] he would win. The theory that the bacillus constituted a threat to man who, a few decades before, had not even been aware of the existence of his 'most dreadful living enemy',[278] was incorporated by Hitler, after his own fashion, into his *Weltanschauung*. From then on his antisemitism was expressed in such terms as to deprive 'the Jew' of all human attributes. At dinner on the evening of 22 February 1942 he said:

The discovery of the Jewish virus is one of the greatest revolutions the world has seen. The struggle in which we are now engaged is similar to the one waged by Pasteur and Koch in the last century. How many diseases must owe their origin to the Jewish virus! Only when we have eliminated the Jews will we regain our health.[279]

In *Mein Kampf*, whose very title may derive from Hitler's study of Bölsche, he wrote:

The Jew . . . was always a parasite in the body of other peoples. . . . His spreading is a typical phenomenon for all parasites; he always seeks a new feeding ground for his race . . . a sponger who, like a noxious bacillus, keeps spreading as soon as a favourable medium invites him. And the effect of his existence is also like that of spongers: wherever he appears, the host people dies out after a shorter or longer period.[280]

To Bölsche may be attributed, not only Hitler's ideas about the Jews and his manner of expressing them, but also his monstrous anti-Jewish policy which culminated in his destroying them like vermin with the pesticide *Cyklon B*. In addition Hitler's fear of personal contamination and infectious disease as well as his morbid preoccupation with the cleanliness of his hands, which he was continually washing, can likewise be traced back to the same source.

Again in *Mein Kampf* he wrote: 'Hence today I believe that I am acting in accordance with the will of the Almighty Creator: by defending myself against the Jew, I am fighting for the work of the Lord.'[281] From this it is clear that he ultimately came to regard himself, not as the effective murderer of countless Jews, but rather as the saviour and redeemer of mankind. And from 'mankind' he excluded not only the Jews but the Russians who, in the debased vocabulary of the Second World War, became 'dogs' and 'pigs'.[282] There is no real evidence to support the widely held view that Hitler had lost all inhibitions about the taking of human life and, indeed, it seems doubtful whether he himself could have performed the drastic actions he automatically demanded of others – for instance, the deliberate killing at Hadamar of Stuka crews who had suffered psychological damage, and of other hopelessly crippled German servicemen. Even during his period of struggle when he was constantly becoming involved in brawls, he never himself took part in the fighting, though he invariably carried a ferocious-looking leather dog-whip. Only once, on 9 August 1921, was he known to strike a political opponent.[283] He never attended either a killing or an execution. Indeed, when several of his comrades had been shot down on the afternoon of 9 November 1923 in front of the Feldherrnhalle in Munich, he contemplated suicide and fell victim to the nervous tremor which was to trouble him intermittently for years, but more especially following the Stalingrad defeat. When, after the attempted coup of 20 July 1944, he was overcome by rage and a merciless lust for revenge, he gave orders that the execution of those responsible be carried out in the most humiliating manner possible, that afterwards they be hung up on meathooks like butcher's carcasses and that the whole process be filmed and photographed.[284] His entourage, believing he intended to use the film to deter potential waverers or opponents, were surprised when he eventually watched it himself,[285] especially since they thought him too squeamish even to stand the sight of a bombed city. In fact, he is said to have asked one of his doctors in 1945: 'Do you think I haven't the imagination to envisage what it's like?'[286]

During the campaign in the East he was notoriously reluctant to visit either the forward areas or the headquarters of his army groups. In this he was motivated neither by fear for his own safety, nor by the desire to preserve, despite his own secret doubts, the last shreds of his belief in victory; and his argument that he was kept fully informed by the representatives of the army groups and lower formations who visited his headquarters was no more than a pretext. Many members of his immediate entourage, both soldiers and civilians, were firmly convinced that the only reason for his refusal to visit the battle areas was that he could not stand the sight of dead and wounded,[287] and this despite the fact that he felt no particular bond between himself and his soldiers. Rather he looked on them as tools and, on occasion, would count the cost in bald terms of 'rounds pooped off',[288] German tanks destroyed and German aircraft shot down. It is relatively easy to describe in general terms how Hitler's antisemitism came into being and how it subsequently developed, but rather more difficult to discover how a man so talented, well-read and self-opinionated could have succumbed to such a dreadful aberration. Of all the factors – some more easily discernible than others – which went to make up this outlook one in particular stands out, namely the truly appalling tradition of antisemitism in Germany and Austria. Thus there are some important historical parallels to the grisly martyrdom of the Jews for which Hitler was responsible.

On 1 April 1933 a boycott of Jewish business houses was proclaimed in Germany. Uniformed SA men picketed Jewish shops and held up placards informing passers-by and wouldbe shoppers that German *Volksgenossen* should not buy from Jews. In the summer of 1935 the sign 'Jews not welcome' began to appear in public gardens, cafés, hotels and business establishments. And after 10 October 1941 Jews wishing to leave their dwellings or to use public transport were required to obtain a special permit.

On 14 December 1821 all Jews living in Carlsbad were ordered 'under pain of the statutory penalties to remove their persons and their goods and chattels from the town . . . not later than the twentieth of this month'. Failure to comply with the order entailed the confiscation of their belongings, expulsion from the town and severe penalties for householders who continued to let their premises to 'these Israelites'.[289] Similar instructions were issued to the citizens of Reichenberg.[290]

By the spring of 1939 some 250,000 German Jews had left the country, most of them penniless. The deportation to the East of German Jewish notables began on 19 June 1941.

A century before, on 9 December 1836, fourteen Jews were expelled from Carlsbad and on 16 February 1839 another ten were ordered to leave the town within forty-eight hours.[291] In 1866, after the Prussians had defeated the Austrians and Saxons at Königgrätz, the Jews of Romania were declared foreigners.[292] From 17 August 1938 onwards, a few months after the *Anschluss*, all male Austrian Jews were compelled to call themselves 'Israel' and all females 'Sarah', to both of which derogatory connotations attached.

In the eighteenth century a great many Austrian Jews still went without a surname and in the following century restrictions were placed on the choice of names. For example an Austrian edict dated 18 February 1802 forbade Jews to adopt the names of noble families[293] and in 1887 further regulations prohibited the use not only of Austrian place names but even of names from 'the Jewish language', i.e. from the Old Testament.[294]

Yet despite the wealth of information gained from an analysis of all the available data on Hitler's medical, intellectual and social backgrounds, there is still no really satisfactory explanation for his anti-semitism.

When he declared that by defending himself against the Jews, he was fighting 'for the work of the Lord',[295] Hitler was expressing one of his deepest convictions. Yet it would seem that during the 'small hours' he was sometimes troubled by doubts about his doctrine and his 'mission'; at the height of his power and military success in 1941 he confided to some of his closest associates the fear that, from an historical standpoint, he might have erred in his policy towards the Jews. Similar and hitherto unpublished remarks such as, for instance, the apprehension he once expressed that his Jewish policy, in running counter to history, was inevitably doomed to failure,[296] amount to very little by comparison with the historical facts, and only serve to heighten the enigma. Indeed, in the course of the conversation mentioned above, he described the existence of the Jews as representing a dialectical antithesis to all the other peoples and went on to express concern lest his policy towards that race be misunderstood by future generations who, in the circumstances, would no longer have any first-hand knowledge of 'Jews'. This remark can hardly be said to indicate doubt. Rather it reveals a Hitler fully determined to leave behind him a Reich without Jews and already preoccupied with his posthumous position in German history. We can say with absolute certainty that Hitler never seriously doubted the rightness of his Jewish policy. In the political testament which records his thoughts immediately before his suicide, he invokes his official doctrines when addressing his successors. 'Above all I bind the leadership of the nation and their followers to scrupulous observance of the racial laws and to merciless resistance to the universal poisoners of all the nations, international Jewry.'[297] Although at the eleventh hour he modified certain of his long held convictions about racial matters, his concept of Jewry remained unaltered. 'If I regulate my life in accordance with my god-given insight,' he said on 13 December 1941, 'I may make mistakes, but I act in good faith.'[298]

This leads on to a consideration of Hitler's attitude to religion and the Church, an attitude in which ideas derived both from the Stoa and from the Enlightenment play an undeniable if somewhat indeterminate role. The matter is not a little complicated by the fact that, while rejecting the Church, he approved of religion as such and, indeed, regarded himself as an 'intrinsically pious' man.[299] Yet to all appearances he was wholly irreligious and, though he continued to belong to the Church till the day of his death, made no secret of his contempt for that institution whose teaching he declared to be 'utterly crazy'.[300] He threatened the Church, publicly opposed her and derided her clergy. While assuming that modern man, with his knowledge of natural science, could no longer take the Church seriously,[301] he nevertheless repeatedly spoke of religious faith as a blessing to mankind. In October 1941, tormented by a variety of ailments and more than ever convinced that he had little longer to live, he said: 'The fact is that we're creatures without wills and that there is a creative force. It's stupid to attempt to deny it. To believe wrongly is better than not to believe at all.'[302] And a month later, when the fortunes of war were beginning to turn against him, he remarked: 'Religiosity is a really wonderful boon to mankind.'[303] Indeed, he hoped to see what he described as 'true piety' in the form of man's belief in the divine take root from 'a most profound knowledge of human insufficiency'.[304] Where religion was concerned he did not seek to impose his views on others. 'I would not force my philosophy on some wretched peasant woman,' he is recorded as saying:

The teaching of the church is also a kind of philosophy, though not one that seeks the truth. Since people are incapable of taking in great thoughts, it doesn't much matter. Somehow it all leads up to the recognition of man's helplessness in the face of the eternal law of nature. That can't do any harm so long as we eventually realize that man's salvation lies in attempting to understand divine Providence, not in believing that he can rebel against the law. If man humbly complies . . . with the laws, that's wonderful.[305]

As he grew older he tended increasingly to substitute the term 'Providence' for 'God', and to speak of a 'creative force'. He used the term Providence in the same sense as did the Stoics, to whom it denoted the power that holds sway over men's lives, a power that foresees everything and preserves and guides the world it has created. There is ample proof that Hitler's belief in a supreme divine power was not merely simulated. Both in public and within his most intimate circle he never hesitated to interpret either failure or success in the light of that belief. For example on 23 April 1944 when talking to his physician, Dr Giesing, about the defeat at Stalingrad – a defeat for which he assumed full responsibility – he said: 'The fortunes of war often deal out rabbit-punches of this kind and I know that Providence has already given the enemy more than a full share of them and will continue to do so.'[306] Six months later, speaking of the July plot, he told the doctor: 'If I ever harboured any doubts about the task entrusted to me by Providence, I have none left now. Every day it seems to me a miracle that I came out of the wreckage alive.'[307] And shortly before his suicide, he reverted to the same topic: 'Providence has guided me safely until now', he told Giesing, 'and I shall continue unerringly on my appointed way, whatever the circumstances.'[308] Because of his negative attitude towards the Church and what he thought to be her abuse of God's name, and also because of the humanist influence of the Enlightenment on his religious outlook, he avoided equating the terms 'God' and 'Providence' in public. Among close associates, however, he would sometimes refer to the deity. For example on 24 October 1941 he said: 'When people say that lightning is made by God, they're not far off the truth. But we can be quite sure that lightning isn't guided by God, as the Church would have us believe. That's a falsehood manufactured by the Church for secular ends.'[309] In Hitler's view religion could not be regarded as the product of any particular moment in human history. Rather he sought its origins in myths and sagas, believing that religion resulted from 'man's conceptualization of remembered images which have faded to mere outlines', and that the ideas thus formed 'helped to keep the church in power'.[310] This interpretation is not far removed from that of Engels, itself the outcome of his criticism of Feuerbach's concept of the nature of religion. Like Hitler, Engels regarded comparative mythology as a source of information on the Indo–European peoples – the Indians, Persians, Greeks, Romans and Teutons and also, 'in so far as material was available', on the Celts, the Lithuanians and the Slavs. While conceding that there was some degree of truth in religion, Engels saw it as 'the fantastic reflection in men's minds of those external forces which control their daily life, a reflection in which the terrestrial forces assume the form of supernatural forces'.[311] In his view religion first came into being 'in very primitive times from erroneous, primitive conceptions of men about their own nature and external nature surrounding them'.[312] For a time religion had played a positive role in the evolutionary process but as a result of radical economic changes it would, Engels believed, necessarily be superseded by the historically inevitable advent of communism. It was a view Hitler did not share, nor would he have welcomed such a development. In his opinion religion had been 'more human in its early stages' and he desired its survival – not least as a means by which to subjugate others and to bolster up and expand his own power.[313] On the other hand he felt that the Church had not made any positive contribution to history and remarked of her role in the Middle Ages: 'In the period between the middle of the third and the middle of the seventeenth century, that most cruel of epochs, humanity certainly sank to its lowest level. It was a period dominated by blood-lust, baseness and falsehood.'[314] At the end of 1941 Hitler related how, in his youth, he had considered it imperative to rid the world of the Church – instantly, forcibly and mercilessly, as if 'by dynamite'. But now, he went on, he intended to arrange things in such a way that the pulpits would be manned exclusively by dunderheads preaching to a bunch of old women, so that the Church would rot away 'like a gangrenous limb'.[315] Yet at heart he remained convinced that it would one day be necessary to eliminate the Church by force. In 1942 he declared:

I don't hold the view that just because something exists it's got to stay. Providence has endowed man with intuition so that he can act in accordance with that intuition. My intuition tells me that the dominion of falsehood will be broken. But it also tells me that the time is not yet ripe. So as not to connive in that falsehood, I've kept the party free of ecclesiastics. When the time comes, I won't shrink from the struggle and I will act as soon as it has been shown that action is possible.[316]

Up till the turn of the century and during his primary schooldays in Lambach and Leonding the Catholic Church had not only been accepted by Hitler but had exercised such a sway over him that at one time he had actually dreamt of becoming an abbot.[317] There is some evidence that this uncritical attitude began to wane in Linz under the influence of his 'progressively minded' father who, it will be recalled, was described in his obituary as 'a warm friend of the freethinking school'. Moreover there is good reason to believe that it was not Alois alone who influenced his son against the Church. A major part was also played by Father Schwarz. This priest was regarded as stupid and unfeeling by Hitler and his schoolmates, one of whom later blamed him for the fact that 90 per cent of the pupils at the Linz Secondary School became at least temporarily estranged from religion and the Catholic Church.[318] On the night of 8 January 1942 Hitler gave a revealing description of Schwarz's teaching methods. The account, which was taken down verbatim by Heim, is reproduced here almost unabridged since it shows the Führer in one of his comparatively rare moments of jocularity. 'Our religious instruction was given entirely by priests,' he recalled:

I was eternally asking questions. When it came to examinations, I did better than anyone else, which put me in a strong position. My scripture reports were marked 'good' and 'excellent' though for conduct all I got was 'unsatisfactory'. I'd specially pick out the dubious passages in the Bible and then ask, 'Please, sir, what does this mean?' to which I'd get an evasive reply. But I'd keep on at Schwarz until he'd finally lose patience and shout: 'That's enough! Sit down!' One day he asked me whether I said my prayers three times day. 'No, sir,' I told him, 'I don't say them; I don't suppose that God cares much whether or not a schoolboy like me says his prayers!'

Schwarz had a big blue handkerchief which he used to fish out of the lining of his cassock; when he unfolded it it crackled. One day he left it lying about in the classroom. Just when he was joining the other teachers I went up to him, holding the handkerchief gingerly by its corner: 'Please sir, you've forgotten your handkerchief,' I said. He glared at me and took it. Uproar in the class! At that moment Herr Hueber came in. 'Now then, Hitler, next time you return someone's handkerchief, don't do it like that!' 'I couldn't help doing it like that, sir!' says I.

One of Schwarz's female relatives ran a shop in the Steinstrasse. . . . We used to go in and ask for the most impossible things like ladies' drawers. When she said she hadn't got them we'd go out shouting 'What a miserable hole. Never has anything!' At Easter we had to go to confession. Beforehand there was a written exercise. It was a great joke. Our confessions consisted of one of us saying: 'I have thought ill of my teacher,' 'I have annoyed X,' etc. When Schwarz arrived he told us we'd been guilty of a grave sin because we hadn't searched our hearts. Then we decided we'd each draw up an enormous list of sins. Only nasty little boys could have invented all the crazy things we thought up. During break I wrote on the blackboard 'To be copied' and underneath some crazy nonsense such as you'd hardly credit a thirteen-year-old with. I was still scribbling away when I heard a whistle from the lookout we'd posted and I hastily turned the blackboard round and rushed back to my desk. . . . Next day was Easter confession. The holidays went by and we'd forgotten the whole business. Then someone had to write on the blackboard. He lifted it, turned it round, and there the thing was! 'I have indulged an unnatural . . .' The teacher took one look at it and blenched. 'I know that writing,' he said. 'Are you the culprit, Hitler? What could have come over you?' 'It's just an example, sir. To show I was searching my conscience properly like Father Schwarz told us to do.' 'Well, I'd advise you to keep your examples to yourself, or it's you I'll make an example of – by locking you up!' I was always making resolutions to be more restrained, but it was never any good. What I loathed was his dishonesty. I can see him today with that long nose of his, and it irritated me so much that I forgot my resolutions and got up to my tricks again. Once, when my mother came into the classroom, he rushed up and told her I was damned. To me, he said: 'Oh you poor, unfortunate boy!' 'Please, sir,' I answered, 'I'm not at all unfortunate!' 'Just you wait till you get to the next world!' 'Please, sir, I've heard tell that there's no such place . . .' 'If there's one place you'll never see it's heaven!' 'But, sir, supposing I do penance?' I was very fond of visiting the cathedral – perhaps because of the architecture, though I didn't realize it at the time. Somebody must have told him about it. He couldn't imagine what I did there and must have thought I was up to no good. In fact I walked around very reverently. Coming out I bumped into

Lance-Corporal Adolf Hitler wearing
e Iron Cross, Class II.

17. Adolf Hitler (with dog) and two comrades, after their award of the Iron Cross, Class I[

8. The author of *Mein Kampf* (1925).

19. Men's hostel in the Meldemannstrasse, Vienna, where Hitler lodged from December 1909 to May 1913.

20. 'Schliersee', an oil painting by Adolf Hitler, 1913.

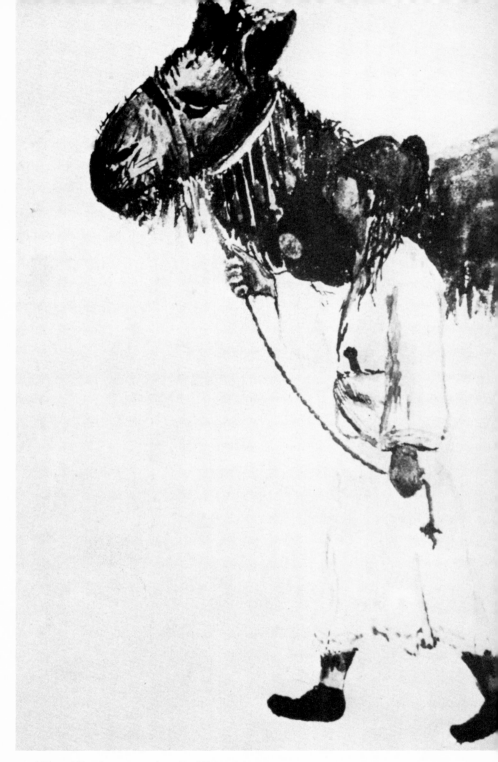

21. 'Camel Boy', water-colour by Hitler, Linz period.

22. Water-colour by Hitler: 'Karlskirche', Vienna, 1912.

23. Water-colour by Hitler: 'Auersperg Palais', pre-1913.

24. Water-colour by Hitler: 'Feldherrnhalle', Munich, 1913/14.

25. Water-colour by Hitler: 'Alter Hof', Munich, 1914.

26. Sketch by Hitler: 'Dugout at Fournes', France, World War I.

27. German infantry playing draughts in the trenches. Pen and wash drawing by Hitler, 1914.

28. Water-colour by Hitler: 'Haubourdin', World War I.

29. Portrait sketches made by Hitler while telephoning.

30. A sketch-design by Hitler for an imposing public building. Sketch-designs of this kind were often accurately drawn and not infrequently accompanied by precise details and calculations. Much of the work planned and/or executed by the architects, Giessler, Troost and, in particular, Speer, were based on them.

31. On his fiftieth birthday (1939) Hitler inspects a model of a triumphal arch, nearly 4 metres high, made by Speer after a 1925 drawing of Hitler's.

32. Hitler's study in the Berghof. Not only did he design the lay-out but he was responsible for the exact specification of every detail.

33. The main reception room in the Berghof.

34. Adolf Hitler and Eva Braun inspecting the presents made to him on his birthday on 20 April 1933.

35. Hitler greets his ear, nose and throat specialist, Dr Erwin Giesing, a few weeks after 20 July 1944.

36. Angela (Geli) Raubal.

37. Unity Mitford.

38. Margarete (Gretl) Sle.

39. Sigrid von Laffert.

40. Eva Braun.

Schwarz. 'And I believed you to be damned, my son,' he said. 'But you aren't after all!' It so happened that I needed his good opinion just then because we were about to get our reports, so I didn't put him right. When I was fifteen I dictated a play to my sister. In Linz there was a Society of Separated Couples, there being no such thing as divorce in Austria. The society used to demonstrate against this uncivilized state of affairs. Public demonstrations were prohibited, but not what were known as Clause 2 assemblies, in other words meetings attended by members only. I went into a meeting after signing a membership form at the door, and what I heard put me into an unholy rage. The speaker told us about monsters of depravity whose wives were prevented by law from ever breaking away from them. I said to myself, everyone's got to know about this. No one could read my writing, so there and then I rushed off and began dictating the thing to my sister. It had hundreds of scenes and I gave full rein to my imagination.

When Frau Hammitzsch saw it she said: 'Come now, Adolf, this could never be put on!' I could only agree with her! And then one day my sister went on strike and refused to do any more writing. I never finished the thing. It was just the subject to get Father Schwarz's goat. Full of righteous indignation I broached it next day. 'I'm at a loss to know, Hitler, how you manage to get hold of such ideas!' 'It's because they interest me, sir.' 'What business have you to be interested? Your much respected father is dead . . .' 'I'm a member of the Society!' 'You're what? Sit down at once.' We had him [Schwarz] for three years. Before that it was Silizko . . . He was a real enemy of ours.[319]

During his time in Linz, when his *Weltanschauung* was beginning to take definitive shape, Hitler was much impressed by Schönerer's strident slogan 'Break with Rome!' This he described as 'a most powerful . . . mode of attack which could not fail to demolish the enemy's citadel'. It was then, too, that he first became acquainted with the anti-Catholic arguments of the chauvinist Pan-Germans. But during his formative years he made little attempt to criticize the Church's doctrines and dogma since he was not really equipped to do so. Nor was his knowledge much greater in 1924, as can be seen from the relevant passages in *Mein Kampf* such as that in which, discussing the 'Break with Rome' movement, he speaks of 'Czech pastorates and their spiritual shepherds'.[320] In fact the butt of his hostility in this passage is still what he describes as the 'unscrupulous ruling house of Habsburg' which is censured for its anti-German attitude and for its systematic 'Slavization of Austria',[321] a process allegedly aided and abetted by the Church of Rome through the agency of the nationalistically-minded Czech clergy. It was only when he realized he had made a political blunder in publishing *Mein Kampf*[322] that Hitler became really outspoken in his criticism of Catholic teaching. Up till the end of his life, however, he not only refrained from criticizing but actually expressed admiration for 'the constitution' of the Catholic Church, her organization, the dignity of her priesthood and the splendour of her ceremonial. His attitude was fundamentally the same in 1945 as it had been forty years earlier. He was impressed by the cohesion and historical continuity of Catholicism which had never been seriously endangered either by its own mistakes and shortcomings or by the actions of political or religious opponents – always excepting Martin Luther. Despite numerous crises and 'a thoroughly crackpot intellectual basis', Hitler alleged on 31 March 1942, the Papacy's 'constitution' had stood the test.[323] Needless to say the Third Reich could hardly have accommodated the Catholic Church as a hallowed institution, nor have fitted her into a 'German church', a state-controlled organization whose creed and attitude towards religion corresponded to Hitler's own. And he had obviously not forgotten Schönerer's teaching when on 6 April 1942 he announced his intention of considerably reducing the state subsidy to the Catholic Church at some time in the future.[324]

The circumstances of his life at home, at school and elsewhere up to the age of twenty had precluded any closer acquaintance with the Protestant Church[325] which did not seem to him an ally of sufficient stature[326] to be of much assistance in a struggle against Catholicism. As early as 1924 he had ceased to regard it as a potential church for National Socialists. While recognizing that the Protestant Church was more patriotic than its Catholic counterpart, he accused it of putting its ideology above the national interest and, worse still, of combating 'with the greatest hostility any attempt to rescue the nation from the embrace of its most mortal enemy, since its attitude towards the Jews ... happens to be more or less dogmatically established. Yet here we are facing the question without whose solution all other attempts at a German reawakening ... [must] remain absolutely senseless and impossible.'[327] He never saw any reason to revise these views, since neither his reading of history nor his personal experience had revealed any real unity in German Protestantism. From the time of the Reformation until 1918 there was no Protestant Church as such but only *Land* churches whose denominations and religious practice corresponded to those of their respective rulers. During the nineteenth century the *Innere Mission*, the Gustavus-Adolphus Association and the Evangelical League were regarded by German Protestants as a kind of substitute for the Evangelical German National Church they so greatly desired. Hitler was aware of the history of these organizations which seemed to him to present no genuine alternative of the kind he envisaged. Hence when he was eventually in a position to do so he did not smooth the way for an amalgamation of the *Land* churches, although the collapse of the Imperial Reich and of the sovereignty of the *Länder* in 1918 had made this perfectly feasible. For a time he had hoped to realize his project for a German Evangelical Church by enthroning Reich Bishop Ludwig Müller as 'Pope of the Protestant Church',[328] but came in the end to see the impracticability of this scheme. After his assumption of power he ceased – as Napoleon had done before him – to extend his sympathy to German Protestantism and postponed the solution of the 'Church question' until the day of ultimate victory. When, after Hitler was dead and gone and his Reich with him, German Protestantism finally achieved unity* in the shape of the Evangelical Church in Germany (EKD), it was the direct if quite unintentional result of his policy. Hitler blamed Luther's successors, indiscriminately dismissed as 'epigones', for having provided opportunities for the renewed expansion of the Catholic Church which, in the twentieth century, had grown more liberal.[329] Luther himself he described as a 'powerful man',[330] but criticized him for having translated the Bible into German, thus making it generally available along with 'all its Jewish pettifoggery' which in turn had fostered 'mental disorders' and thrown open the door to 'religious mania'.[331] While, like Marx and Engels, he commended Luther for having 'rocked the foundations'[332] of the Catholic Church, he maintained that the reformer had failed to understand the absolute historical necessity of persisting on the course upon which he had embarked before the Peasant War.

'It is our misfortune', Hitler remarked on 1 December 1941 with a wistful eye on Greek antiquity, 'to be saddled with a religion that destroys our delight in beauty.† There's a kind of Protestant grundyism

* Of no more than twenty years' duration.

† Hitler's need to have 'beauty' around him even extended to his aides and orderlies who had to be reasonably presentable. A notable exception was his personal physician, Dr Morell.

that's even worse than Catholicism.'[333] And from the viewpoint of a
scientifically-minded neoclassicist, he went on to bewail the fact that
the standard of 'religious philosophy, which is largely based upon the
views of the Ancients, is inferior to that of presentday science'.[334] He
also expressed the doubt that scientific discovery could make people
happier, pointing out that in the nineteenth century 'liberal science'[335]
had foolishly and importunately persuaded man that he was lord and
master. Yet, throughout his life, he continued to assume that a diversity
of faiths was conducive to human happiness, as also to propound, even
when almost at the height of his power – and in striking contrast to his
practice – the theory that as a politician he should be tolerant in religious
questions and leave the solution of confessional and ecclesiastical
problems to reformers better qualified than he. As the situation
deteriorated in the East and his health grew worse, the opinions he
expressed on ecclesiastical matters became ever more aggressive. Thus
in December 1941 he declared: 'I don't meddle in matters of creed,
nor will I tolerate any meddling by priests in secular matters. Organized
falsehood must be utterly smashed so that the State remains absolute
master.'[336] At the end of January 1942, when the Wehrmacht was in
the throes of its struggle against the appalling Russian winter, he
remarked that he would not shrink from open conflict with the Church
when the time came. Yet little more than a year earlier he had assured
his close associates: 'Since any upheaval is undesirable, I think the best
thing of all would be if we could gradually and painlessly do away with
the institution of the church by means of intellectual enlightenment.'
Nevertheless, as soon as victory had been won, he intended to make it
quite clear to the leaders of the church that, as he put it, 'their kingdom
was not of this world'.[337] On 23 September 1946 Ribbentrop
wrote:

After the outbreak of war Hitler instructed the Foreign Office to ignore all
protests by the Vatican relating to Church matters in the occupied territories
since the Vatican did not recognize German control of these territories. . . .
Bormann, who was responsible for persecuting the Christian Churches,
persuaded Hitler that the Foreign Office had been too compliant both in its
dealings with the Vatican and in its replies to protests from that quarter.
Things went so far that one day the Führer was on the point of taking all
matters connected with the Vatican out of the hands of the Foreign Office and
making them the responsibility of the Party Chancellery, or even of Rosenberg, in order to ensure a more aggressive policy.[338]

On 11 December 1941, at a time of crisis on the Eastern Front, Germany declared war on the USA after Japan's entry into the conflict, thus fulfilling Hitler's historical concept of 'a situation . . . in which every individual knows he must live and die for the preservation of the species'.[339] Two days later he declared: 'The war will come to an end. Then we must consider that the last great task of this era is to solve the problem of the Churches. Only then will the German nation be really secure.'[340] His confidence was, perhaps, more assumed than real. Indeed he was not wholly indifferent to the way in which the Catholic Church might react to his measures, as is betrayed by his remark to members of his immediate entourage to the effect that he would rather suffer temporary excommunication than be indebted to the Church.[341]

During the war he was more than ever troubled by the puzzle of existence – a problem which, because of his ill-health, had increasingly preoccupied him after his rise to power. He was unable to find peace of mind in the contemplation of the vision he had conjured up for others, that of living only for the preservation of the species. From the religious point of view he always remained a seeker. He flirted with Islam, more especially with the theories of the Mu'tazilites or 'Separatists', sometimes also described as rationalists. Their belief that man, having no will of his own, could not be held responsible for his actions by a just god, was invoked by Hitler in self-exoneration. For it enabled him to argue that, if his decisions were based on god-given insights and knowledge, any mistakes he might commit must be attributed not to bad faith but to genuine error. Other elements of Islam of which he approved were the Prophet's avowed hostility to the Jews, his idea of a pre-Mosaic revelation, his insistence on the need for military preparedness and his renunciation (with one exception) of all dogma. He once remarked that 'Mohammedanism might still succeed in arousing my enthusiasm for Heaven'.[342] It is impossible, however, to say how much Hitler knew about this faith since his allusions to the subject are comparatively rare.

Christianity he would sometimes compare unfavourably with other beliefs. For instance on 8 June 1942 he declared:

It's enough to make a sensible German tear his hair to see Germans reduced by Jewish muck and priestly drivel to the sort of behaviour we find so ludicrous in negroes and howling Turkish dervishes. And what is particularly infuriating is that, while religious teaching in other parts of the world – that of Confucius, Buddha and Mohammed, for instance – has provided religious-minded people with a broad spiritual basis, Germans have been landed with theological expositions lacking all real depth.[343]

The Christian doctrine of 'transformation' originated by St Paul in 2 Corinthians 5:17 was derided by Hitler as 'the maddest thing that ever an aberrant human brain had thought up', and he described such metamorphosis as a 'mockery of all that is divine'.[344] Of Houston Stewart Chamberlain, Wagner's son-in-law and a writer much esteemed in National Socialist circles, with whom Hitler was personally acquainted, he said that not only had he failed to understand the nature of Christianity but had also misguidedly believed it to be a spiritual reality.[345] Though Hitler described Jesus as an Aryan and greatly admired him as a man, he did not believe he was the Messiah, nor did he believe in the Trinity or the Christian 'hereafter'. In November 1941 he said: 'I know nothing about the next world and am honest enough to admit it.'[346] Yet on another occasion he voiced the somewhat astonishing argument that 'a hereafter conceived in physical terms is impossible if only for the reason that it would be torture for anyone who was forced to look down on this earth and watch mankind continually making mistakes'.[347]

It is impossible to discover what took place in Hitler's mind during the final hours of his life. Ilse Braun, who had many opportunities of observing and talking to him and had learned a great deal about him from her sister, is convinced that he and Eva prayed together before they committed suicide.[348] On 24 October 1941, five days after Stalin had declared a state of siege in Moscow and demanded that the now rudderless city be defended to the last man, Hitler remarked: 'The Bolshevists imagine they've triumphed over creation. . . . Whichever we may turn to – the catechism or creation – we have a last recourse whereas they, with their wholly materialistic outlook, are bound to end up by mutually devouring each other!'[349]

Without grossly distorting the facts it would be impossible to depict Hitler's *Weltanschauung* as reflecting any one doctrine or coherent part thereof, or again as following the tradition of a readily recognizable school of thought. Nor can he be seen as the disciple of any one specific thinker, scientist or writer.[350] Summing up his view of the man, Schramm writes:

Hitler can be explained neither in terms of his social origins nor his school or early environment, and not on the basis of the fact that he originated among a particular people. At best, only aspects of the problem can be understood with reference to these factors. The Hitler problem simply cannot be forced into that frame of reference. Seen as a whole, Hitler was not petty bourgeois at all, nor was he Catholic, or even German. His most essential characteristics ... were singular and unique, shaped by his own capacities and talents, by certain fateful events in his life, by certain decisions for and against him, and by certain strokes of good fortune which made possible an extraordinary rise to power (for no matter how gifted and ruthless he was, he might well have been stopped – and more than once he almost was). Only through all these circumstances taken together, which converged only on this one man alone, can Hitler be understood.[351]

In so far as he believed the fruits of his reading to represent objective knowledge capable of realization, Hitler would seek to put them into practice, thus forcing reality onto the Procrustean bed of his own misconceptions. So optimistic were his ideas as regards science and technology that he seldom doubted the feasibility of his projects. This sanguine attitude clearly betrays the influence of the Enlightenment as well as that of the nineteenth century with its artistic and scientific achievements and its concept of genius.

Hitler adopted long-accepted norms and basic concepts only to subject them to radical and dramatic revision. Having formulated new precepts and principles, he intimated that his insights were god-given and he himself the instrument of Providence. He got the war he wanted, but in the event too soon. He exterminated a vast number of Jews, deprived men and women of their freedom, castrated and sterilized them and murdered the sick. In addition he persecuted the churches, made justice his executioner, regimented the Press, art and architecture, manipulated the masses and promoted the decay of civic morality. Before throwing down the gauntlet to the world, he had committed a series of gross errors and had wrongly assessed objective factors both inside and outside his sphere of influence. Despite all this he achieved the most astonishing success. For many years the scales were tipped, not so much by reason and a grasp of reality, as by certain more imponderable factors: his unexampled charisma and his incredible strength of will, for instance, or his ability to manipulate power, to deceive the world and, last but not least, to win people's allegiance and fill them with hope and pride – not only by offering them positive inducements and holding up the prospect of a new and better world, but also by presenting himself as the incarnation of the national will he had shaped in his own name.

Before concluding this survey of Hitler's intellectual background it would seem pertinent to ask what languages he understood and whether he knew them well enough to be able to read them. During his five years at secondary school in Linz and Steyr he attended five French lessons a week. The fact that in July 1904 at the age of fifteen he could not be admitted to the fourth form at the school in Steyr without retaking his French examination would seem to confirm that French was one of the subjects which he describes in *Mein Kampf* as 'unattractive'.[352] We may suppose, however, that he was not completely hopeless at this subject, for otherwise his geometry master at Steyr, Gregor Goldbacher, would almost certainly have refrained from making explicit reference to this particular French examination on 29 January 1941. Kubizek recalls that 'French was the only foreign language Hitler ever tackled or, to be more precise, was forced to tackle, at least in the junior classes'.[353] Hans Mend relates that during the Great War Hitler's knowledge of French never failed him, even in situations fraught with danger. Moreover during his four years as a headquarters runner he would have had every chance of improving that knowledge by mixing with the population in the rear areas. There can be no doubt that he had read, in the original French, books and other writings published in France before 1914, as may be verified by comparing the dates of publication with the dates of Hitler's comments on the works in question.

Neither his school timetables nor his reports give any indication that he ever learnt English as a boy. It would seem, however, that by 1913 he had acquired some knowledge of the language. No one knows where or when he applied himself seriously to the subject. Fifty-three years later Josef Popp junior, who had emigrated to America, stated emphatically that Hitler was conversant with English, for on numerous occasions between 1913 and 1914 he had sent young Popp to Munich libraries in search of English books and publications.[354] And indeed, Hitler's remarks in Chapter 11 of *Mein Kampf* and elsewhere about the organization of crowds clearly betray the influence of McDougall's *The Group Mind*[355] published in Cambridge in 1920 and as yet not translated into German. It is well known that later, and particularly after he had become Führer and Reich Chancellor, Hitler enjoyed watching English and American films and that he read French and American newspapers.[356]

In his highly subjective book, *Adolf Hitler aus dem Leben darge-*

stellt, Hans Severus Ziegler, a fluent English speaker, who had known Hitler personally for more than twenty years, writes: 'One would not expect a student of English, even after several terms at university, to have as good a knowledge of the language as Hitler.'[357] In view of his intellectual attainments it is not surprising that he should have sometimes discussed, and this in some detail, the spirit and structure of English, French and Italian. For instance on 7 March 1942, when considering the relative merits of German, English and Italian, he remarked that English, 'though the simplest and clearest in expression and at the same time the most masculine in tone', did not lend itself to the expression of generalities and abstract ideas;[358] Italian, on the other hand, was a musician's language which sounded 'marvellous phonetically' but in translation was apt to prove 'mere froth'.[359] Of Mussolini he said that he spoke beautiful Italian, better even than his own German.[360]

Associates who knew Hitler before 1924 maintain that prior to writing *Mein Kampf* he had tackled Yiddish and Hebrew. There is no documentary evidence for this, though in his dialogue with Eckart, which betrays an above-average knowledge of the Bible, he uses philological arguments in support of his antisemitic views.[361] For instance he traces back the names of Jewish historical personages to their original Hebrew form, as he was sometimes to do later in the course of his table-talk. Again, speaking of St Paul he remarks that he had first gone by the name of 'Shaul', subsequently adopting the more Roman sounding 'Saulus' which he had finally altered to 'Paulus' – 'food for thought',[362] Hitler comments, suspecting this to be a typical piece of Jewish artifice. He goes on to point out that Paul himself, the Jew of Tarsus (Acts 21:39, 22:3), testified to the fact of his own Jewishness when he described himself as a 'Hebrew of the Hebrews, as touching the law of a Pharisee' (Philippians 3:5). And again his source is undoubtedly The Acts of the Apostles when he remarks that St Paul had been a 'candidate for the rabbinate' and had sat at the feet of the Rabban Gamaliel I, or the Elder.

His largely irrelevant reference to Shaul in this context is of interest not only as a case of special pleading but also as an instance of the way his mind worked. St Paul's parents belonged to the diaspora and lived in Tarsus, the capital of Cilicia. The family possessed both Tarsian and Roman citizenship and were accordingly exempt from degrading punishments and entitled at any time to appeal to the emperor. As

HITLER

H. J. Schoeps put it: 'Roman citizenship had been attainable since Augustinian times and in Paul's day it meant a great deal; it differentiated him, the son of well-to-do parents, very materially from the poor Galileans who were the leaders of the original community.'[363] These few facts are in themselves enough to show how Hitler would distort well-documented historical events so as to bring them into line with his own views. In this particular instance he used a smattering of Hebrew to draw a curious parallel between the unconverted 'Shaul's cruel persecution of the as yet barely-fledged Christian community'[364] and ('food for thought') Paul's change of name. There is no proof that Hitler ever studied Hebrew etymology despite his occasional references to it and his use of Hebrew terms when relevant to a particular discussion (such as his dialogue with Eckart in which he used the Hebrew word 'rea' for neighbour[365] in much the same way as he would refer to Germans as *Volksgenossen*). Undoubtedly Eckart was right when he maintained that Hitler's knowledge in this respect derived from the antisemitic periodical *Auf gut Deutsch* founded by Eckart at the end of 1918, a publication misleadingly and pretentiously subtitled *The Weekly of Law and Order*. Being a painter endowed with a strong visual imagination and, in addition, an astonishing memory, Hitler would not have taken long to learn as many Hebrew words as he needed – and, of course, the Hebrew alphabet.

In the period between 1919 and 1924 his friends Esser, Eckart and von Scheubner-Richter,[366] all of whom were experienced linguists, could have adequately explained anything that was unclear to him in foreign publications. This was confirmed some twenty-five years later by Hermann Esser, the only one of the trio to have survived the events of 1923.[367]

Hitler liked using words of foreign derivation and his use of them was correct, though his spelling might leave something to be desired. In the course of a conversation in the Wolfsschanze on 7 March 1942 he declared that:

we ought to be grateful to imported words for providing us with such subtle means of expression and giving scope for variation in tone and colour. . . . Suppose we were to start extirpating words of foreign origin, we shouldn't know where to stop, not to mention the risk we'd run of mistaking a word's real root. . . . If a foreign term creeps in and makes itself at home here, and providing it sounds all right, we should be grateful for the contribution it makes to the richness of our language.[368]

So that others might be spared the spelling difficulties he himself had experienced, he wanted to see foreign words written as they were spoken. This in turn, he thought, would ensure their correct pronunciation.[369]

Hitler believed that men in prominent positions lost face if they admitted to incomplete knowledge or other deficiencies. Hence he never divulged his knowledge of foreign languages save when he confided to his secretary, Christa Schröder, that he could follow conversations in English and French provided they were conducted slowly enough.[370] The fact that he was able to hoodwink the more important members of his entourage on this score is evident from a remark made by his chief interpreter, Paul Otto Schmidt: 'Hitler seemed somehow to sense when an interlocutor's interest began to wane.'[371] He could usually catch the gist of what an English or French speaker was saying, so that instead of listening to the interpreter, he would spend the interval devising an appropriate answer. He was anxious to be regarded as a politician who not only makes 'snap' decisions but is able to formulate them with the utmost precision. Yet he would often appear to stray from the point and raise what seemed to be irrelevant questions.

Though as he grew older Hitler's spelling improved, his punctuation always remained erratic. In his youth there were certain words which he spelt correctly only if he wished to make a good impression or gain some other personal advantage. Indeed the quality of the handwriting reveals the nature of a letter at first glance; if the writing is good, the spelling will be as correct as he can make it, if bad, it will be deliberately careless. By the beginning of the 1920s at the latest such discrepancies are no longer in evidence. Why he should deliberately have misspelt words is a matter for conjecture. Perhaps it was out of unconscious protest against hard and fast rules as representing an order for which he himself was not responsible. At all events it is the expression of a distinctive side of his character, a character to whose analysis his handwriting provides some valuable clues. By the time he left school Hitler was capable of spelling correctly but his punctuation still left something to be desired. In this he resembles the majority of artists, irrespective of education, whose punctuation and spelling is unconsciously determined by purely visual standards.

The letters and postcards[372] written in the period before 1908 to his friend Kubizek vary in quality. Although an assiduous playgoer, he usually spells *Theater* without the 'h'. Other typical mistakes are *nähmlich* for *nämlich*, *dan* for *dann*, *gieng* for *ging* and *lies* for *liess*. However, amongst his early correspondence one letter stands out and that is his note of thanks to the woman who secured his introduction to Professor Roller in 1908; it does not contain a single mistake. His letters written while on active service between 1914 and 1918, though comparatively long, are better spelt than the generally short missives he wrote before the war. And this despite the fact that they contain not only French place names and other proper nouns but also unfamiliar terms and phraseology. Yet strangely enough he consistently misspells *Quartier* (*Quatier*) and *tot* (*tod*).

Mein Kampf was taken down at Hitler's dictation by several of his fellow detainees in Landsberg during 1924 and 1925.[373] Hence no one individual can be held to blame for the large number of spelling mistakes in the manuscript, nor was Hitler entirely responsible for all the other errors, mostly stylistic, which necessitated some 2500 corrections in the various editions of his book up till 1939.[374] His ability to make vivid thumbnail sketches of a situation, to render ideas tangible to his readers and to persuade them to fall in with his judgements had always been remarkable. For the most part his correspondence betrays a surprisingly sure eye for essentials. In a letter to his landlady in Munich, for instance, he describes his first encounter with French prisoners-of-war in 1914. 'They stared at us in amazement. Those blokes never imagined that there were so many of us. Incidentally most of them were big powerful fellows, French élite troops captured right at the beginning of the campaign.'[375] He was for ever 'minding other people's business' and taking to heart matters that were entirely beyond his control. His behaviour in this respect was of a kind he would never have tolerated in others for, besides continually carping and criticizing, he proffered advice and suggested decisions in areas quite outside his competence. 'We shall hold out here,' he wrote from the front, 'until Hindenburg has worn Russia down. That will be the day of reckoning.'[376] A letter written four years earlier to his friend Kubizek betrays a similarly dogmatic mood:

Have you read the council's latest about the new theatre? It looks as though they're going to patch up the old place again. They've not much hope, since they haven't got the authorities' permission. – At any rate all this clap-trap goes to show that these toffs know as much about the job as a rhinoceros about violin-playing. If my architectural manual wasn't so tattered I'd feel tempted to wrap it up and post it to them . . . .[377]

Up till 1914 Hitler's mind – sceptical, imaginative, speculative and ceaselessly fertile – was busy with designs for the construction of bridges, buildings and squares. Such was his mentality that he could be flexible only on minor questions of detail, but fundamentally his approach was rigid to the point of intransigence. During the First World War his interest was necessarily centred on military matters and here again his judgement betrayed the same doctrinaire rigidity as his earlier attitude to architecture and the fine arts.

Hitler's letters between 1905 and 1918 reveal a singular lack of warmth. They are obviously written by a person who pays heed to others only in so far as they can be of service to him and are prepared to act in accordance with criteria determined by him alone. He seldom asked after his correspondents' health save by way of conventional courtesies, nor did he ever seek their advice. He had no desire to enter into an exchange of ideas and regarded his own opinions as sacrosanct. All that he wanted, and indeed succeeded in finding, was a responsive audience prepared uncritically to accept his view of things. Thus criticism was usually suppressed – at least until it was too late. His style of writing was of a kind rarely found save in painters who combine a talent for reproducing their environment in simplified and abstract form with an ability to describe it vividly in words. For instance in a letter to his Munich landlord – an unusually slipshod letter as it happens – he describes a sector of the front between Messines and Wytschaete:

The landscape is partly flat and partly undulating. Everywhere there are hedges and trees in straight rows like avenues. Because of the continuous rain (we've had no winter), the closeness of the sea and the low level of the land the fields and meadows are like a bottomless morass while the roads are ankle-deep in mud running through this swamp are the trenches belonging to our own infantry, a maze of dugouts, main trenches, firing-steps, saps, barbed wire entanglements, pits and fougasses. . . . Often at night the thunder of the guns begins to roll along the whole of the front first in the distance and then nearer and nearer. Then gradually at first the small arms' fire starts up after half an hour things gradually calm down, except that the lights of a great many flares can be seen in the distance and to the West the beams of large search-lights and we can hear a continuous roll of thunder from heavy naval guns.[378]

 In considering Hitler's intellectual background we should not over-look the importance of the handwritten notes he made for his speeches during the early part of his career. Of these, 250 sheets still survive and a glance at any of them is enough to show that their originator was a man with a remarkable memory and truly astonishing mental resources, a man who knew how his speech was going to end even before he had completed the first sentence. Hitler used notes merely to remind him of the sequence of his arguments. For this he needed no more than isolated nouns and an occasional short sentence or idiomatic phrase. The mere sight of one of his key-words was enough for the rest to follow automatically. He invariably carried in his head the details he needed: names, figures, facts, illustrations, examples, turns of phrase – in short everything that distinguishes a first class orator. His notes for his speech on 'Jewish Domination and the Starvation of the Nations' (See Appendix C) show how he set about planning his speeches in the early days. From 1930 onwards, and more especially after his accession to power, he dictated his speeches straight on to the typewriter, sometimes in one continuous session and without recourse to notes.

After the war Hitler's secretary, Christa Schröder, gave a detailed account of his procedure to Alfred Zoller, the Frenchman who interrogated her.[379] Usually, she said, Hitler put off dictating his speech until the very last moment. Again and again she would have to drop hints and finally remind him tactfully that it was time he began his dictation. Invariably he prevaricated, pointing out that he must first have up-to-date reports from his ambassadors so that he could take stock of the international situation. Up till the last minute – carefully shielded from interruption – he mulled over the points he intended to make, jotted down catch phrases and notes, and considered various alternative formulations.[380] At a given moment two fresh, well-rested secretaries, usually Christa Schröder and Johanna Wolf, had to be ready to answer his bell. Before starting his dictation he would pace restlessly up and down, rearrange some of the many small pieces of sculpture he possessed, pause in front of Franz von Lenbach's portrait of Bismarck, move on, stop in his tracks and at last begin dictating. Now he started to pace up and down again and, as he dictated, ran through the whole gamut of the emotions he was to display in public, so that his secretaries witnessed even the outbursts of rage which punctuated so many of his speeches. He began, as he would in public, with quiet concentration, tense as a runner at the start of a race. Next, in a spate of impassioned oratory, he gave vent to his natural talent. He forgot his surroundings, one sentence following hard on the heels of another as if eager to plunge into the fray.

When the last words had fallen from his lips and the inspiration had left him it was as though he had cast off a burden. He regained his tranquillity, praised his secretaries who were usually in a state of total exhaustion, paid them compliments and sometimes invited them to a meal. Now that it was all over he returned to normality and his staff were able to resume their daily round, freed at last from his tyrannical pressure and from the fear that his energy might be discharged upon them. Many secretaries were, indeed, incapable of typing for Hitler. Inhibited and confused, they would literally tremble with nervousness and find it impossible to keep up with him. As soon as he noticed this he would break off his dictation but in such a way as not to make his secretaries – or 'typing force' as he liked to call them – feel that they were to blame. A few hours later, to all appearances calm and poised, he would make handwritten corrections to the manuscript,[381] continuing on occasion to do so right up to the time of his public appearance.

CHAPTER SIX

Women

'I can't describe ... what I have to go through on the Führer's account',[1] Eva Braun wrote to her friend Herta Ostermayr on 22 April 1945. The following day she asked her sister Gretl to collect together all the letters Hitler had written her over the years and wrap them up in waterproof material so that they could be buried if need arose.[2] For many years Hitler kept Eva as his mistress, only marrying her at the very last moment. During all this time the rivalry of other women and their adulation of the man she loved made her life a misery. He was not always faithful to her. Indeed the only woman to whom he always remained true was one of her predecessors, his attractive niece Geli Raubal. He would sometimes tell his secretaries and Frau Winter, his Munich housekeeper,[3] that already in Linz he had been fond of the company of pretty girls, even if chaperoned by their mothers.[4] This would seem somewhat implausible, more especially since Hitler admitted on 10 May 1942 that in Vienna he had still been exceptionally self-conscious and had never had the courage to assert himself in any way.[5] There is no evidence of any close acquaintanceship with girls either in Linz, in Vienna or, before 1914, in Munich. Kubizek relates that in Linz Adolf nourished an undeclared passion for a pretty blonde called Stephanie, a girl somewhat older than himself, with whom he never exchanged a word[6] and who only came to hear of his devotion a quarter of a century later. To her seventeen-year-old admirer she seemed the very epitome of feminine beauty around whose image his immature and as yet untutored imagination constantly played. He never directly approached Stephanie, whom he would sometimes see flirting with young army officers, for he realized the hopelessness of such a move. He did, however, write her a letter in which he said he was a student who greatly admired her and who intended to ask for her hand as soon as he had completed his studies.[7] Hitler's infatuation for Stephanie differed little from the calf-love felt by most adolescents for seemingly unattainable young women.

There are numerous firsthand accounts of his life in Linz and

Vienna,[8] and he himself wrote of his time in the capital: 'I believe that those who knew me took me for an eccentric.'[9] Yet neither he nor anyone else apart from Kubizek has anything to say on the subject of women. From Kubizek we learn that after the two of them had attended a performance of Wedekind's *Frühlingserwachen* in Vienna, Hitler proposed that they should pay an 'educational visit' to the Spittelberggasse where prostitutes in various stages of undress displayed themselves behind their windows to male passers-by. But this educational stroll through the 'sink of iniquity' would not appear to have been repeated. They had already had a not dissimilar experience while seeking lodgings for Kubizek, who describes the episode as follows:

Seeing a 'Room to let' notice in a house in the Zollergasse . . . we rang the bell and the door was opened by a very smartly dressed maid who led us into a very elegantly furnished room which contained two magnificent double beds. 'Madam will be here directly,' said the maid with a curtsey and disappeared. We both thought it was a bit too classy for us. But at that moment 'madam' appeared in the doorway, a real lady, no longer particularly young but very elegant. She was wearing a silk dressing-gown and very dainty slippers trimmed with fur. She smiled as she greeted us, looked us up and down, first Adolf then me, and offered us a seat. My friend asked which was the room that was to let. 'This one!' said the lady, indicating the two beds. Adolf shook his head and said briefly: 'One of them will have to be taken out to make room for my friend's piano.' The lady was visibly dismayed that it was I and not Adolf who wanted the room and asked him whether he already had accommodation. When he said he had, she suggested that I and my piano should move into his room and he should take this one. While speaking she had become very animated and a sudden movement loosened the cord of her dressing-gown. . . . She at once readjusted the garment but the brief moment had been enough to show us that underneath the silk dressing-gown she was wearing nothing but a diminutive pair of knickers. Adolf went as red as a turkey-cock, stood up, and took me by the arm saying: 'Come on, Gustl!' I don't really know how we got out of the house. All I remember is that when we at last found ourselves in the street, Adolf blurted out angrily: 'Potiphar's wife!'[10]

Ever since the publication of *Mein Kampf*, with its references to prostitution in the Austrian capital and to venereal disease, ingenious if ill-informed commentators have assumed that Hitler contracted syphilis from a Viennese prostitute and that it continued to afflict him for the rest of his life. After 1942 even Himmler, according to his masseur Felix Kersten, was prepared to subscribe to this cock-and-bull story and to use it in furtherance of his intrigues. Hitler certainly never suffered either from syphilis or from creeping paralysis, as we know from other evidence besides the results of the Wassermann, Meinicke and Kahn tests carried out on 11 and 15 January 1940.

No less inaccurate are the equally hoary tales about Hitler's homosexual tendencies. These received fresh impetus after the Second World War, and more especially in 1953 when Kubizek recounted the following episode:

One evening, at the corner of the Mariahilfer Strasse and the Neubaugasse, we were approached by a well-dressed, very respectable-looking man who questioned us about ourselves. When we told him we were students – 'of music and architecture', Adolf volunteered – he invited us to have supper with him at the Hotel Kummer. He let us choose what we wanted. . . . Meanwhile we learnt that he was a manufacturer from Vöcklabruck and that he shunned female company because women were only interested in money. I was particularly pleased by his remarks about chamber music for which he seemed to have a very good ear. After we'd thanked him he saw us out of the hotel and we went home. Back at our digs Adolf asked me what I thought of the man. . . . 'He's a homosexual,' said Adolf baldly. . . . It seemed to me quite natural that he should feel horror and disgust at this and other sexual aberrations encountered in the capital and that unlike most adolescents he did not indulge in frequent masturbation – adhering, indeed, in all sexual matters to the rigid code which he prescribed both for himself and for the future state.[11]

In 1952 a doctor who had X-rayed Hitler before the war declared: 'As a homosexual I was fascinated by Hitler's eyes, speech and gait but I could tell at once he wasn't one of us,'[12] – a remark which speaks for itself.

The Munich period from May 1913 to August 1914 is even more scantily documented as regards Hitler's relationships with the opposite sex. What little information he himself provides is conflicting. For instance, in the Wolfsschanze early in January 1942, he remarked that as a young man he had met 'lots of beautiful women',[13] whereas in the same context six weeks later he described himself as having been 'a lone wolf' with little need for companship.[14] According to his Munich landlord, Josef Popp, who was able to keep an eye on his twenty-five-year-old lodger despite his having his own private entrance, Hitler never took a girl up to his room or made assignations with the kind of woman with whom he might have been sexually intimate. During the hours of daylight he painted, and his evenings were spent discussing politics and war with the Popp family. Neither Herr Popp nor his wife can recall ever having seen Hitler in the company of a woman or having heard him refer to a girl friend.[15]

The absence of information is in itself no proof that Hitler was completely without sexual experience right up to 1914. In the period preceding the First World War, the rigid observance of class distinctions meant that the unmarried middle-class male tended to be secretive about the women with whom he associated sexually. A survey carried out by Meirowsky and Neisser[16] in 1912 – the year before Hitler left Vienna – revealed that 75 per cent of the young doctors[17] who completed the questionnaire had experienced their first sexual intercourse with prostitutes, 17 per cent with domestic servants and waitresses and only 4 per cent with middle-class girls who might qualify as potential wives. By birth, occupation and fortune Hitler belonged to the middle classes, so that fear of social ostracism would have made him naturally reticent about casual encounters with prostitutes and the like. Though we have no reliable information on the subject we are probably justified in assuming that while in Vienna between 1908 and 1913 he indulged in heterosexual relationships.

From August 1914 until the end of 1918 he was serving on the Western Front. His spells in hospital (9 October to 1 December 1916 and 16 to 21 October 1918)[18] as well as his periods of leave in Nuremberg (23 to 30 August 1918)[19] and with his relatives in the village of Spital in Lower Austria (30 September to 17 October 1917 and 10 to 27 September 1918),[20] would certainly have afforded opportunities for sexual encounters. However, there is no reason to believe that anything of the kind took place in Spital, for a liaison with one of the very few available girls could not have escaped the notice of his relatives.[21] None of his army friends have anything to say about his relations with the opposite sex. Nevertheless, since the enforced celibacy of army life makes women a topic of absorbing interest to soldiers, he must undoubtedly have acquired a great deal of fresh information on the subject.

After the end of the war Hitler, like most of his fellow soldiers, was eager to make up for past deprivations. However nothing definite is known about his reputed affairs, even that with Jenny Haug, his chauffeur's sister. Little can be learnt from his own remarks on the

subject. Talking to his guests in the Wolfsschanze on the evening of
16 January, for instance, he said: 'I knew a lot of women at that time.
A good many returned my affection.'[22] The fact that after 1945 some
of his better-informed friends of those days expressed the intention of
revealing to the world the inside story of his numerous love affairs may
be of some significance in this context.[23] In the early twenties he was
once described as the 'king of Munich',[24] a lady-killer at whose feet
the wealthiest and most beautiful women were said to 'prostrate themselves'. Indeed, he may well have been indirectly responsible for a
number of attempted suicides; and was undoubtedly so for one that
succeeded. His mistress, Eva Braun was twice prompted by jealousy
to attempt suicide, once by shooting herself and once by taking an
overdose of sleeping-pills.[25] In 1927 Maria Reiter, daughter of the
co-founder of the SPD in Berchtesgaden, tried to hang herself
because of her love for Hitler.[26] Unity Mitford shot herself twice in the
head when Britain declared war on Germany and, in 1943, Inge Ley,[27]
a former actress, threw herself out of a window after writing Hitler a
letter that is said to have affected him deeply. Other would-be suicides
were Martha Dodd, daughter of the American ambassador in Berlin,
an Austrian girl, Susi Liptauer,[28] and an 'unknown beauty' who,
according to Hitler's friend Hoffmann made an unsuccessful attempt to
hang herself in a hotel bedroom.[29] Finally and more tragically, Geli
Raubal, who went to live with him in Munich in 1928 and became the
great love of his life, shot and killed herself on 18 September 1931.[30]
It has been alleged that she was pregnant by him at the time.

He is reputed to have been on intimate terms not only with a number
of dancers and actresses, but also with Munich society women such as
his wealthy patronesses, Helene Bechstein, wife of the piano manufacturer, and Gertrud von Seydlitz. Also Viktoria von Dirksen, privily
regarded by knowledgeable National Socialists as the 'mother of the
revolution', Elsa Bruckmann, the wife of a well-known publisher, and
Frau Carola Hoffmann, a headmaster's widow. Hitler himself has
confessed his admiration for Erna Hanfstaengl, the sister of his friend
Ernst (a friendship that ended after the Führer had played a sinister
practical joke on him).[31] Other names associated with him at various
times were those of a Finnish woman, Frau von Seydl, a divorcée,
Princess Hohenlohe, Frau Scharrer, wife of the Bulgarian Consul
General[32] and Sigrid von Laffert of whom Ciano wrote: 'For the first
time [22 May 1939] I have heard a reference in the Führer's confiden-

tial circle to his tender feelings for a beautiful girl. She is twenty years old, has regular features, a pair of limpid eyes and a wonderful body. . . . They meet frequently, and sometimes tête-à-tête.'[33] At one time there was even a former nun, Eleonore Bauer, whose passion for him led her to take part in the march on the Feldherrnhalle in 1923 and who thereafter continued to be closely associated with the National Socialist movement.[34] There would appear to be no real substance in any of these rumours and, indeed, some of the women mentioned above later maintained that their interest in him had been purely maternal.

He was aware of the emotions he aroused in women. For instance, reminiscing on 10 March 1942, he said:

Of all my older women friends, Frau Hoffmann was the only one who was invariably kind and considerate. Even Frau Bruckmann was no exception. She stopped inviting one of the Munich society women at the same time as me after intercepting a look her guest had given me in the drawingroom as I was bowing my farewells to her. The lady was very beautiful and I daresay she found me interesting, but there was nothing more to it. I know one woman whose voice grows hoarse with agitation if I so much as say a few words to another member of her sex.[35]

It is not surprising that women should have been among Hitler's most important benefactors. Thus on 3 April 1923 the *Münchener Post* carried a story about women who, 'infatuated with Hitler', lent or gave him money. Their contributions, however, did not always take the form of cash. Numbers of wealthy patrons presented him with valuable objets d'art and jewellery to dispose of as he pleased. According to the hearing conducted at Munich Police Headquarters on 27 May 1924, Helene Bechstein stated that, besides the regular financial support given by her husband to the leader of the NSDAP, she had herself made appreciable contributions – 'not, however, in the form of money,' as she put it, 'but rather of a few objets d'art which I told him he could sell or do anything he liked with. The objets d'art in question were all of the more valuable sort.'[36] On 13 December 1923 Gertrud von Seidlitz told the Munich police that she herself had helped Hitler financially and had, moreover, persuaded others, both at home and abroad, to do so.[37]

As a rule Hitler would raise loans on the valuables presented to him by his 'infatuated' admirers, using the money to keep his party afloat in times of difficulty. The following extract from the loan and transfer agreement concluded in the summer of 1923 between the NSDAP's financial controller, acting for Hitler, and the coffee merchant Richard Frank of the firm Korn-Frank of Berlin, will serve as an example:

As security for the loan [of 60,000 Swiss francs] Herr Adolf Hitler will make over to Herr Richard Frank the undermentioned property presently in the keeping of Heinrich Eckert, Bankers, of Munich. . . . A platinum pendant set with an emerald and diamonds on a platinum chain. . . . A platinum ring set with a ruby and diamonds. . . . A platinum ring set with a sapphire and diamonds. . . . A diamond ring (solitaire), a 14-carat gold ring with diamonds set in silver. . . . A piece of *grospoint de Venise*, hand-stitched, six and a half metres long and eleven and a half centimetres wide (seventeenth century). . . . A Spanish red silk piano runner with gold embroidery.[38]

Speaking in private, when no women were present, Hitler would talk contemptuously and slightingly of marriage and the female sex in general. For instance on 25–26 January 1942 he declared: 'The worst of marriage is that it creates demands. That's why it's far better to keep a mistress' – a statement he qualified by going on to say that 'only outstanding men' should do so.[39] 'A man,' he further opined, 'should be able to leave his stamp on a girl. It's what women like.'[40] And on 1 March 1942 he declared: 'When a woman starts thinking about the problems of existence that's bad . . . it's apt to get on one's nerves.'[41] Ten days later he was saying: 'A man's world is big compared with a woman's. . . . The man is all her world. Only occasionally does she think of anything else. . . . A woman's love is deeper than a man's. Her intellect is of no great consequence.'[42] Again, on 10 April 1942, holding forth to his military guests, he suggested that a woman's 'overriding desire' was to be admired 'by every presentable man'.[43] Some time previously he had also maintained that:

when a woman goes to a good deal of trouble to make herself look nice, it's often because she gets a secret pleasure out of annoying another member of her sex. One thing woman can do that we men can't is to kiss a woman friend and at the same time stick a needle into her. It's quite hopeless to want to reform women in this respect. Better ignore these little failings! If it makes them happy, well and good. It's an infinitely preferable occupation for a woman than dabbling in metaphysics![44]

Despite his low opinion of the sex, he always gave a woman the impression that he thought her beautiful and worthy of his admiration and esteem. With a display of Austrian charm he would kiss her hand, a courtesy he extended even to his married secretaries.[45] He never shouted at his 'typing ladies', however serious their mistakes, and he never behaved crossly towards them, addressing them instead as 'my pretty' or 'dear child'. He would greet them politely, allow them to precede him when entering or leaving a room and invariably ask them to sit down first. (In this last respect he was not always so punctilious with foreign statesmen – for example on the occasion of his meeting with Chamberlain and Daladier in 1938.) When women were present his harsh voice became soft and caressing so that many who had ex- pected to find a boorish vulgarian came away charmed and delighted. The tiniest scratch, if suffered by a woman, was enough to elicit his sympathy and concern. The strict rules observed even by such highly placed members of his entourage as Goebbels, Speer and Bormann – the ban on smoking in his presence, for instance – could occasionally be infringed by a woman, although the culprit might not invariably emerge unscathed. One evening after Hitler had retired, Max Schmel- ing, Speer, Goebbels and Ilse Braun settled down to a game of cards; some of them were smoking. On the Führer's unexpected reappearance, the cigarettes vanished. Ilse Braun dropped hers, still burning, into an ashtray and sat on it. This did not go unnoticed by Hitler who went and stood beside her and asked her to explain in detail the rules of the game they were playing. Then he left. The next morning Eva Braun asked her sister 'how the blisters on her bum' were getting on.[46]

Women could say things to Hitler that would have cost a man his freedom at the very least. Thought processes of a relativistic and dialectical nature were foreign to him and hence he tended to be distant, critical and impatient towards intellectuals – especially those of the male academic variety – who ventured to express opinions different from his own. But towards women he always showed himself receptive, long-suffering and attentive even if they broached an unpalatable topic. For instance when Henriette von Schirach once tried to remonstrate with him upon his treatment of the Jews, it earned nothing worse than a sharp reprimand.[47] And a similar remark from Ilse Braun merely elicited the sardonic rejoinder that every German was obviously entitled to his own pet Jew, except that there were not enough Jews to go round.[48]

There is no truth in the widely accepted theory that Hitler was incapable of deep and tender love. When his niece and mistress Geli, nineteen years his junior, committed suicide in 1931 he was so badly shaken that he attempted to shoot himself. At no other time did his close relatives see him so depressed. On 23 December 1931 he sent his favourite nephew, Leo Raubal (Geli's brother), a sum of money as a Christmas present, accompanied by a note that read: 'Dear Leo, My most affectionate greetings to you and Aunt Marie at this sad Christmastide ... Your Uncle, Adolf Hitler.' He did not attend Geli's interment in Vienna, for he was neither mentally nor physically fit enough to do so.[49] Withdrawing from his associates, he became a prey to self-reproach, and from then on never touched meat or food prepared with animal fats. No one might enter Geli's room in his Munich flat at No. 16 Prinzregentenplatz save for himself and his housekeeper, Frau Winter.[50] He commissioned a bust of Geli from the sculptor Josef Thorak and subsequently had it placed in the Reich Chancellery. Adolf Ziegler, whose political views had earned him Hitler's approbation, was commissioned to paint her portrait which later occupied a place of honour, permanently decked with flowers, in the Berghof drawingroom. He was even mindful of his dead mistress in his private will of 2 May 1938: 'To my sister Angela I entrust the appointments of the room in my Munich flat formerly occupied by my niece Geli Raubal.'

Barely fifteen months after Geli's suicide, Eva Braun attempted to take her own life. She had first met Hitler in 1929 at No. 50 Schellingstrasse in Munich where she worked as an assistant to his comrade in arms and official photographer, Heinrich Hoffmann. Eva, the convent-educated daughter of a Munich teacher, was then seventeen, an ingenuous, fair-haired girl to whom he immediately took a liking, although still in love with Geli, his mistress of barely a year's standing. Whenever he visited Hoffmann, which was often, he always made a point of seeking out Eva Braun whose enthusiasm for him was not shared either by her father or by her elder sister Ilse who worked as a receptionist for a Jewish doctor called Martin Levi Marx. From 1930 onwards their meetings became ever more frequent. He saw her only in the daytime, however, when they would go to the cinema together, eat at the Osteria Bavaria, visit the opera and take picnics into the surrounding countryside.[51] It was clear that he was growing steadily more enamoured of Eva, despite the determined advances of Hoffmann's daughter Henriette, who later married Baldur von Schirach the Reich Youth Leader. Henriette Hoffmann was an attractive buxom girl but she entirely failed to captivate Hitler.[52] Though he enjoyed her company and used to escort her to museums and joke with her, he never forgot her father was his friend Hoffmann to whom he owed responsibility.

His evenings and nights belonged to Geli Raubal who quickly sensed, indeed knew, that her uncle had another girl friend whom he did not wish her to meet. Geli was in love with Hitler and Hitler was flirting outrageously with Eva Braun. Though neither girl knew the other, both were aware of the circumstances, suffered accordingly and reacted each in her own way. When Angela, driven to despair, committed suicide in September 1931, Eva Braun saw her chance and took it. Hitler was in a state of deep depression. By her love and devotion she was able by degrees to revive his flagging spirits and thus make him entirely her own. Hitler took her to live in his flat and finally, at the beginning of 1932, made her his mistress.[53] Thereafter she remained with him through thick and thin, though she occasionally suffered from bouts of well-founded jealousy. On 1 November 1932 she attempted to commit suicide by shooting herself in the throat and three years later, during the night of 28 May 1935, she made a second attempt, this time by taking an overdose of sleeping tablets.[54]

Even when writing to her sister, Eva Braun always referred to Hitler as 'the Führer'.[55] Under his careful tutelage she gradually attained maturity. In compliance with his wishes she kept out of the limelight and meanwhile educated herself as she thought fit, took slimming courses, went in for gymnastics, made occasional appearances at the Berghof. Always she remained a shadowy figure behind the Führer whose photograph she would place on the table in front of her whenever she ate alone.[56] For thirteen years she had to endure his disparaging view of marriage. On 1 March 1942 he said: 'One has to remember that it is given to very few to find in wedlock the fulfilment they expected – the fulfilment of life's great craving. The greatest happiness results when two people find each other who naturally belong together.'[57]

For some while after Geli's death Joseph and Magda Goebbels, whose hospitality Hitler often enjoyed, made unobtrusive attempts to introduce him into the company of attractive women. One of these was thirty-year-old Gretl Slezak, daughter of the celebrated opera singer, whom they invited in the hope that she might cheer him up and distract him. We have no means of knowing whether his relationship with this fair-haired granddaughter of a Jewess really prospered. All that can be said is that Goebbels provided them with frequent opportunities to converse in complete privacy.[58] Next he engineered a series of meetings between Hitler and Leni Riefenstahl, the beautiful and talented actress to whom he was later to accord exceptional privileges, not least that of filming the 1936 Olympic Games in Berlin in preference to such experienced and internationally famous directors as Luis Trenker.[59] Nothing definite is known about the exact nature of Hitler's relations with Leni Riefenstahl[60] or with another reputed favourite, the clever, fair-haired, eccentric actress Mady Rahl, who has maintained an impenetrable silence since his death.[61]

The much canvassed view that Hitler was sexually impotent is entirely unfounded. According to the findings of the Soviet Medical Commission – who claimed in May 1945 that the corpse in their possession was 'presumably' that of Hitler – the dead man's 'left testicle' could not be found 'either in the scrotum, or on the spermatic cord inside the inguinal canal, or in the small pelvis'.[62] The publication[63] of these findings has led to a number of inadmissible conclusions.[64] Morell several times examined Hitler's genitalia about which he wrote: 'The sexual organs showed no sign of abnormality or pathology and the secondary sexual characteristics were normally developed.'[65] Moreover the doctors who tested Hitler for syphilis on 11 and 15 January 1940 discovered no anomalies.[66] Even if he had in fact had only one testicle, his capacity for sexual intercourse would not necessarily have been impaired. Monorchism and cryptorchism, more common than might be supposed, do not as a rule inhibit sexual activity although they may be prejudicial to fertility. Röhrs's allegation that Eva Braun had been pregnant by Hitler[67] is refuted by Ilse. 'My sister was certainly never pregnant,' she maintains:

And if she had become pregnant, she would in no circumstances have had her pregnancy terminated. It would have been contrary to her whole outlook on life. And in the same way as she insisted on staying with Hitler in Berlin in April 1945 – and dying with him – so she would certainly have refused to have her pregnancy terminated.[68]

There is no doubt, however, that Hitler led a normal sexual life, as is plainly apparent, for instance, from an entry in Eva Braun's diary for March 1935. 'He needs me only for certain purposes . . .' she complains, 'it can't be otherwise. . . . When he says he loves me, he only means it at that moment.'[69] In 1945 when Morell, Hitler's personal physician, was under investigation by the United States Commission, he wrote a report in which he stated that the Führer had indubitably had sexual intercouse with Eva Braun.[70] He also confided to one of his former patients, Dr Paul Karl Schmidt, that when on visits to the Führer, Eva had often pressed him, Morell, to give Hitler drugs that would stimulate his sexual desire. In later years his sexuality was impaired by prolonged ill-health,[71] overwork, the burden of duties and responsibilities, and a succession of major military reverses.[72]

Another common and equally farfetched misconception is that Hitler associated for preference with 'dumb blondes'.[73] But Geli Raubal, for instance, had black hair and a distinctly Slavonic appearance and it would seem in fact that he was equally attracted by blondes, brunettes and redheads. Stephanie, his early flame, was blond. So was Eva Braun, although in the words of Blaschke, the dentist she shared with Hitler, 'there was a touch of peroxide. She wasn't exactly fair-haired. She'd done something to help it along a bit.'[74] Physically Hitler preferred the full-bosomed type such as Maria Reiter, Sigrid von Laffert and Unity Mitford.[75] The comparatively small-bosomed Eva Braun, well aware of Hitler's tastes in this respect, used at first to stuff handkerchiefs into her brassière.[76] On 10 May 1935 she morosely recorded in her diary: 'As Frau Hoffmann sweetly and tactlessly informed me, he has now found a substitute for me. She's called Valkyrie and looks like one, legs and all. But that's the kind of measurements he likes. If it's true, irritation will soon whittle her down – unless, that is, she's clever enough to wax fat on her troubles.'[77] Most of Hitler's inamoratas were some twenty years younger than himself. Geli was born in 1908, Maria Reiter in 1909, Eva Braun in 1912, Unity Mitford in 1914, and Sigrid von Laffert in 1916.

Obviously then, Hitler enjoyed the company of pretty women, and this was particularly the case between 1921 and the outbreak of war. On 10 March 1942 he said: 'I can't stand being alone now. Best of all I like to have my meals in company with a woman.'[78] In his remote headquarters in East Prussia he would reminisce about earlier encounters with the opposite sex. 'What beautiful women there are!' he exclaimed one evening (26 January 1942), and continued enthusiastically:

We were sitting in the Ratskeller in Bremen when a woman came in. It almost seemed as though Olympus itself had opened up! She was absolutely dazzling. Everyone stopped eating and all eyes were riveted on her. Then there was that other time in Brunswick. How I cursed myself afterwards! No one in my suite showed any more gumption than I did. A blond piece came

tripping up to my car to give me a bouquet. Everybody saw what was going
on but it didn't enter anyone's head to ask the girl for her address so that I
could send her a note of thanks. She was a wonderful girl, tall and fair! But
there it was! There was such a crowd – and besides, we were in a hurry. But
I regret it to this day. Once in the Bayrischer Hof I was at a function that
positively glittered with beautiful women and diamonds. Then in comes a
woman so beautiful that she put all the rest into the shade (she wore no
jewellery). It was Frau Hanfstaengl. I once saw her and Mary Stuck
together at Erna Hanfstaengl's place. What a picture! Three women, each
more beautiful than the other![79]

In the years before 1933, whenever Hitler needed a change from the
'bunch of louts'[80] who were constantly in attendance on him, he
would order them to find him some female company. His personal pilot
Hans Baur relates that he once commiserated with him for having to
keep aloof from women to which the Führer replied:

I can't afford to behave otherwise. All women do is boast about me and, as a
man who's continually in the limelight, I have to guard against that. If you,
Baur, spend a night on the tiles, no one'll think twice about it, but if I tried
to do the same, I'd soon be unable to show my face in public. Women just
can't keep their mouths shut. Whenever I discussed Hitler with women,
[Baur continues] they were either enthusiastic, fanatical or hysterical. . . .
On one occasion when our conversation revolved entirely round Hitler,
my companion confessed that she was in love with him and was afraid she
would never marry . . . since she compared every man she met with the
Führer and not one of them ever measured up. I couldn't help passing on
what he had told me. . . . She stared at me aghast. 'Did he really say that?
Tell him from me that I'd never breathe a word – I'd sooner let my tongue
be torn out! . . .' When I told Hitler about it the next day he merely laughed.[81]

As the years went by, and more especially during the war, his private
encounters with women became ever fewer. Even Eva Braun was not
permitted to visit the Wolfsschanze, his headquarters in East Prussia.
The only women he saw there were his secretaries and his personal
cook. When at the Berghof he would sometimes sit and converse with
the wives of his guests. There could no longer be any real question of
sexual relationships, particularly in view of the strict security measures
obtaining at that time. The subject of women, however, continued to
recur in conversation. On such occasions it was sometimes possible to
deduce what was really going on in his head. For instance in March
1942 when Rommel's triumphant progress in North Africa still gave

Hitler reason to hope that there was a future for his ideology, he discoursed upon the subject of legitimate and illegitimate children (the latter a commonplace in his family) in a manner that hardly tallied with his ultra-conservative outlook. 'To my mind,' he said, 'a girl who has a child and cares for it is superior to an old maid. Social prejudice is on the wane. Nature is again asserting herself. It's the best course we can follow.[82] Hitler's origins are plainly discernible behind this view and the reasons he adduced are illuminating. 'For centuries', he alleged,

the Catholic Church has taken this circumstance into consideration by tolerating the so-called 'rehearsal'. . . . As the time of birth approaches the priest draws the prospective father's attention to his marital obligations. Unfortunately Protestantism has broken with this admirable custom and smoothed the way for the sort of moral hypocrisy which, if a marriage is concluded because a baby's on the way, frowns on the union and discriminates against it by laws both written and unwritten.[83]

His attitude to women is reflected in his view that a 'great man' should 'keep a girl'[84] for the satisfaction of his sexual needs and treat her as he deems fit, without compassion or a sense of responsibility, as though she were a mere chattel possessing no rights. As Eva Braun so aptly put it: 'When he says he loves me, he only means it at that moment.'

Throughout his life Hitler was an introvert and for this not only he, but also those closest to him, had to pay a high price. Save only in respect of his mother, Geli and Eva Braun, he was incapable of deep attachments. For whatever Kubizek may say about the closeness of their early friendship, he was simply cast aside like a suit of wornout clothes as soon as it suited Hitler's book. After Geli's death his aloofness became even more pronounced and from 1937 onwards, when he believed himself to be seriously ill, he ceased to have any close rapport with the men who had worked with him and fought at his side. Women he tended to regard as physical objects, if sometimes also as sympathetic listeners. Even Eva Braun had cause to complain of this, as we know not only from her sister but also from Hitler's secretaries and his housekeeper, Anny Winter.[85]

Hitler's reserved and impatient nature prevented him from exploiting to the full the fascination exerted by his 'Austrian charm' which might otherwise have enabled him to establish deeper ties. The fact that he sometimes tried to suppress this tendency, more especially when signs of approaching senility (primarily physical) began to make themselves manifest, is readily explicable in psychological terms. His self-esteem – and this significantly enough even at the height of his political and military success – was still up in arms against the treatment meted out to him in childhood by his energetic and mercurial father, an ambitious civil servant of Lower Austrian peasant stock. As a boy Hitler may not have had to grovel before his parent and kiss his feet as his great examplar Frederick the Great had been compelled to do after his early attempt to run away from home, but if we are to believe *Mein Kampf* he was frequently beaten and was 'forced into opposition'.[86] According to Anny Winter, Hitler often told her that the last time his father had beaten him he had received no less than thirty-two strokes.[87] Except during the period up to 1903, and again from 1914 to 1919, he was never compelled to do violence to his own personality and hence he made a fetish of his unusual mode of life, overlooking the fact that his equally unusual tendencies, as in the case of most neurotics, hindered his consistent development and prevented him from coming to terms with his childhood and adolescence. Because he was cut off from others his experiences did not help to promote normal development. Though supremely able to appeal to and exploit the emotions, he rated these far inferior to the will – a will by which his whole existence was governed. No matter how hard the blows of fate, whether in the form of sickness, personal setbacks or bitter disappointments and frustrations, he seldom felt moved either to replace the men in whom he had put his trust or to revise the objectives he had set himself. In this respect he showed himself persistent to the point of pigheadedness. His conviction that he would attain his goal remained unshaken either by initial adverse experiences such as the early loss of his parents, his rejection by the Vienna Academy, his homelessness after Germany's defeat, the disastrous failure of his Munich putsch, the near ruin of his political career and his detention in Landsberg, or by the many tribulations of later years. Throughout he remained unchastened and his ideas underwent no fundamental change. Yet almost without exception he achieved the victories for which he strove.

On two occasions, however, he was prepared not only to jettison the views he regarded as permanently valid but even to take his own life – a life he believed to be the embodiment of Germany's future. The first occasion was in 1923 with the failure of his putsch. The second in 1931 when he heard that Geli, the great love of his life, had committed suicide.

CHAPTER SEVEN

The Ailing Führer

In 1925, after his release from imprisonment in the Fortress of Landsberg, Hitler expressed the view in the second volume of *Mein Kampf* that 'the mind ... if it is healthy, will as a rule and in the long run dwell only in a healthy body'.[1] When he dictated that sentence he was not healthy. He was suffering from a tremor in the left arm and leg, and movement of the left forearm was limited. Twenty years later his personal physician declared that the complaint might possibly have been of a psychosomatic nature.[2] The abrupt conclusion of his putsch outside the Feldherrnhalle in Munich, his own share of responsibility for the death of some twenty people, the dissolution of his party, and his arrest – all these had left their mark on him. Political friends and fellow combatants – Rudolf Hess, Hermann Esser and several other arrested putschists – succeeded in convincing him that he was blameless and that, being absolutely indispensable, he must on no account do what, in his state of deep depression induced by the catastrophe, he was threatening to do, namely take his own life.[3] While his leg ceased to trouble him relatively soon,[4] the tremor in his left arm was to persist for several years.

In 1931, with most of his 'lean years' behind him, he received a further serious blow: Geli Raubal, his mistress and daughter of his half-sister Angela, shot herself on 18 September in her Munich flat. Again, as in 1923, he fell into a state of deep depression, and again he sought to take his own life. Rudolf Hess only just succeeded in grabbing his arm and snatching away the revolver which he was about to turn on himself. There was, it is true, no recurrence of the tremor but thenceforward he refused to touch meat though he not infrequently complained about this diet. 'A man is supposed to keep alive on that ...! Then **how am** I going to exist?'[5] he asked Albert Speer as early as 1935. Nevertheless he persisted for another year with the diet he had devised for himself, a diet which had long since proved inadequate. From 1931 onwards he was a confirmed vegetarian. The man who had hitherto consumed relatively large quantities of meat and beer and for whom, since 1914, no exertion had been too great – he could spend a whole day making speeches without any sign of tiring – now foreswore all forms of protein deriving from butcher's meat or animal fats.

In 1934, some twelve months after his appointment as Chancellor, he entered the Westend Hospital in Berlin for a thorough check-up. The doctors who examined him certified that he had no organic disease, a finding to which he himself lent little credence. By 1935 at the latest he had become firmly convinced that he was seriously ill, and this conviction appeared to be confirmed by recurrent bouts of gastric pain and flatulence, troubles attributed by his doctors to his self-imposed and inadequate diet. He was sleeping badly and sometimes complained of heart trouble.[6] As yet, however, there was nothing seriously the matter with him.[7] All that could be diagnosed was a persistent hoarseness which not unnaturally worried him, for he would almost certainly never have achieved what he did without the immense range of his voice. Nearly fifty years later Ernst Hanfstaengl, who had heard him speak for the first time in 1922, was to write:

There was still a mellowness and resonance about his baritone and he could bring gutturals into play which sent a shiver down one's spine, for at that time his vocal cords were still in prime condition and enabled him to produce subtleties of tone that were extraordinarily impressive. Of all the many gifted speakers I have heard in the course of my life – three of the most outstanding being Theodore Roosevelt, the blind Senator Gore from Oklahoma, and Woodrow Wilson, the man with the silver tongue – none was capable of achieving an effect comparable to Hitler's superlative performance which was to prove so fateful both to himself and to us.[8]

Hitler feared that he would suffer the same fate as the Emperor Frederick III, but a throat specialist, Professor von Eicken, found only benign polyps of the vocal cords, which he removed. The knowledge that he was not after all suffering from cancer lifted a great weight off Hitler's mind. But other worries still remained. He was tormented by stomach cramps and pain in the region of the right kidney as also by flatulence and a swollen condition of the upper abdomen, the latter being attributed by Dr Morell to enlargement of the hepatic lobe.[9]

A grateful patient, Heinrich Hoffmann, had been responsible for introducing this doctor to Hitler. Albert Speer, who shared the dislike felt by most of the 'Nazi bigwigs' for Morell, relates in his memoirs that when Hoffmann fell 'critically ill' in 1935, the doctor cured him with sulphonamides.[10] It would seem improbable that anyone – even

Hitler – knew what had been wrong with Hoffmann. After 1945 Morell broke his professional silence and placed on record that, prior to becoming the Führer's physician, he had treated Hoffmann for gonorrhoea.[11]

Born in 1886 in Traysa, Hesse, Morell had set up as a specialist in 'skin and venereal diseases' in Berlin's fashionable Kurfürstendamm. When first introduced to Hitler at the Berghof, he already had a chequered career behind him. He had studied at Giessen, Heidelberg and Paris. Between 1912 and 1914 he had held appointments as house physician at Munich and Bad Kreuznach, and had worked as a ship's doctor in the employ of the Hamburg–America Line, the Norddeutscher Lloyd and other companies. In 1914 he set up a small general practice at Dietzenbach near Offenbach. A year later, when even inexperienced doctors were being entrusted with responsible duties in the fighting zones, he was employed as surgeon on the Western Front – though possessing no special qualifications in surgery – and subsequently at a number of hospitals at home. And in 1918, again without any specialized training, he set up in practice as a specialist in electrotherapy and urology. Despite his lack of qualifications in this field he had, by 1920, become a doctor highly esteemed in certain circles in Berlin and had even treated eminent members of the Inter-Allied Commission. So much did his practice prosper throughout the economically and politically turbulent twenties that he could afford to turn down lucrative offers of employment from foreign countries.[12] However this prosperity may well have been due to a combination of avarice and business acumen, since it would seem that Morell was better versed in the current rates of exchange than in up-to-date medical teaching – though glib enough when it came to citing the names and addresses of distinguished colleagues and medical institutes. Up till 1936 he was what might be called a society doctor, consulted by those prominent party functionaries and stage and film personalities who went to make up the fashionable world which he delighted in frequenting but whose style he failed to reflect.

It was not long before Hitler became convinced of Morell's ability. The knowledge that this bespectacled man with the bulging eyes, who so rapidly alleviated his aches and pains, had only joined the NSDAP after 1933, was of small concern to him. Nor, despite his almost morbid preoccupation with cleanliness, was Hitler ever seriously troubled by the fact that his physician was regarded by his entourage in general as evil-smelling and filthy, and by Eva Braun in particular as downright disgusting.[13]

In 1936 Hitler, who figures in Morell's files and correspondence as 'Patient A', weighed about 11 stone, his height being just under 5 feet 9 inches. His blood group was A, his pulse, temperature and respiration normal. An eczema on his left leg was eventually diagnosed as the result of a digestive disorder. Morell requested Dr Nissle's Bacteriological Institute in Freiburg in Breisgau to use Hitler's faeces for the cultivation of bacterial colonies in order to discover the condition of the intestinal flora. The findings confirmed that their condition was abnormal, whereupon Morell prescribed *Mutaflor* for his patient.* Morell was in no way disturbed by the fact that in the eyes of many orthodox medical men Nissle was a sectarian and a monomaniac whose methods of treatment, consisting almost exclusively in the regulation of the intestinal flora, were hardly worthy of serious consideration. In an attempt to inhibit the flatulence caused by a vegetarian diet Morell also prescribed Dr Köster's Antigas Pills, which contained strychnine and belladonna. The dosage – two to four tablets a day – was frequently exceeded by Hitler. Neither of these medicines, *Mutaflor* or Dr Köster's Antigas Pills, was analgesic. Indeed, Dr Brandt and Dr Giesing who, with Morell's permission, attended Hitler as surgeon and as ear, nose and throat specialist respectively, both objected to the administration of the antiflatulence pills on the grounds that the cumulative effect of the strychnine would of itself induce pain.[14]

From 1935 onwards Hitler had to wear spectacles; he also suffered from inflammation of the gums which was treated with antiseptic mouth wash and Vitamin C. His tongue was frequently furred and his blood pressure fluctuated. The left ventricle was enlarged, while auscultation revealed aortic murmurs. His features were distended and puffy. *Mutaflor* had proved to be no more than a palliative. At times, and particularly after meals, he continued to suffer from violent stomach cramps which Morell hoped to combat with intramuscular injections of *Progynon*.[15]

Hitler trusted his doctor implicitly, although he was beginning to feel increasingly unwell. By 1937 he was already convinced that there was something seriously wrong with his heart. Those closest to him were struck by the feverish sense of urgency which he now revealed for

* See Appendix D for alphabetical list of drugs prescribed by Dr Morell, dosages and periods over which they were administered.

the first time.[16] He was tormented by the fear of leaving something undone, of dying, perhaps, before he had accomplished all that he had set out to do. His oft-reiterated 'peace policy' which, ever since 1933, had been taken at its face value both at home and abroad, was now suddenly – or so it seemed to many – abandoned in favour of undisguised expansionism. He pressed his architect, Speer, to put into effect the projects he had devised more than twenty-five years earlier, and he hinted to Eva Braun, his mistress since 1932, that before long she would have to live without him.[17] Indeed, on 5 November 1937, anxiety drove him, not only to mention the possibility of his own death in an exposé of his ideas for the future, but also to formulate his political testament,[18] which was followed on 2 May 1938 by a detailed, handwritten private testament.

In the meantime he had withdrawn from the entourage he capriciously ruled onto a lone and lofty pedestal where not even former fellow combatants such as Frank, Rosenberg, Hess and Esser ventured to join him. Thus the party leader, who had once extolled comradeship and loyalty between friends, had elevated himself to the status of an unapproachable idol. Argument was no longer tolerated and advice only when solicited. Thenceforward anything that Hitler thought, planned or did was determined by the conviction that he was a sick man with only a short time to live. His foreign policy now betrayed a new sense of urgency arising out of the determination to realize in the shortest possible time what he had originally planned to achieve step by step over a period of years. Ultimately this was to prove his undoing.

From 1937 onwards Hitler avoided all physical exertion. As an Austrian from the Linz area he had once been a good skier, but not even Eva Braun could persuade him to go ski-ing with her. Luis Trenker, the world-famous actor and producer, was permitted to accompany her instead,[19] a fact which in itself is significant. For Trenker was notoriously a Casanova, whereas Hitler was known to be jealous and, moreover, acutely sensitive to the merest breath of scandal.

Morell was far from satisfied with his eminent patient's condition and continued to prescribe a wide variety of drugs, while Hitler himself at long last consented to an X-ray examination. In the early part of 1940 his conviction that he was mortally ill led him to demand that his personal physician, in consultation with independent specialists, should provide him with a straightforward report on the state of his health. After Morell had made the necessary arrangements there followed a detailed medical check-up which lasted for several days. The most important investigations took place on 9, 11 and 15 January and the whole was not concluded until 18 January when the results of Dr Nissle's tests on the intestinal flora became available – results which both Morell and Hitler believed to be of paramount importance.[20]

The doctors' opinion of 'Patient A' was as follows:

9 January 1940: Blood count normal. Pulse 72, blood pressure 140/100.

11 January: Sugar and albumin content of urine = negative, urobilinogen = increased, Wassermann (test for syphilis) = negative, urinary sediment: slight, calcium carbonate. Isolated leukocytes.

15 January: Sugar content of urine = negative. Meinicke Clearing Reaction II, to syphilis = negative, Kahn (test for syphilis) = negative.[21]

The blood pressure was much too high. Morell found a systolic pressure of 170 to 200 mm with 100 mm diastolic pressure when his patient was excited and 140 mm when relaxed.[22] A diastolic pressure of up to 90 mm would have been in normal range. Morell, anxious about Hitler's heart, advised him to take great care of himself.

Except for the marked increase in blood pressure and consequent damage to the heart (enlarged left ventricle and aortic murmurs) and the intermittent stomach and digestive disorders (flatulence), Hitler was in good health; believing himself to be a very sick man, however, he tended increasingly to leaf through professional medical journals and to read books on medical subjects. On 21 December 1940, he again underwent a detailed medical examination. The results were as follows: Urine albumin test = slightly opalescent (i.e. just positive), urobilinogen = small increase, in the urinary sediment – very occasional leukocytes; some magnesium ammonium phosphate. Although little different from the January findings,[23] they seemed to Hitler to provide confirmation of his hypochondriacal fears, with the result that his doctor appeared more than ever indispensable to him.

When in 1941 oedema developed in the region of the calves and shins Morell prescribed ten drops weekly of *Cardiazol* and *Coramine*.[24] Neither of these drugs with their action on the circulation was medically indicated in this case, and from a medical standpoint might even be considered improper; Hitler's blood pressure was too high, and others besides Morell knew how easily he became excited. But *Coramine* and *Cardiazol* were not the only stimulants used. Morell also prescribed caffeine and *Pervitin*. Under the impact of this treatment, his patient's habits would sometimes undergo a complete change. His eyes, which had always excited such fascination, would flash dangerously, he became peremptory if not actually aggressive, and would sometimes make outrageous remarks. For instance, in the course of an otherwise brilliant and well-thought-out speech in the Sportpalast on 4 September 1940 he called Churchill, Eden, Chamberlain and Duff Cooper 'cacklers' and 'broody hens'. He went on to threaten Britain with a night raid in which 'a million kilograms of bombs' would be dropped, a figure which, however, he amended before publication to '400,000 kilograms or more'[25] because the quantity he had named while under the influence of drugs now struck him as excessive. During discussions he would occasionally put forward projects so wildly unrealistic as to obliterate all memory of that grasp of technical detail which had once commanded the admiration of his expert advisers. For now he began to urge not only the realization of what was possible, as indeed he had been doing since 1935, but also the realization of what exceeded the bounds of possibility.

It was at this time that instructions were issued concerning the 'final solution' of the Jewish question in Europe. On 2 April 1941, Rosenberg was Hitler's guest. The subject of discussion was such that Rosenberg did not dare commit it to his diary. 'Something I do not wish to record today but shall never forget',[26] he noted, after a two hours' conversation with Hitler who had obviously been informing him of his plan for the extermination of the Jews. Within less than two months Adolf Eichmann had been notified of that plan. On 20 May his Bureau IV B 4* sent out instructions to police stations throughout the Reich and France to put a stop to all Jewish emigration out of France and Belgium and, 'in view of the now imminent solution of the Jewish question',[27] to keep open last minute facilities for the passage of Jews out of the Reich.

At this time Hitler was confiding his growing fears about his heart condition to people such as Eva Braun,[28] Speer[29] and Goebbels. In July 1941, during a heated discussion with Ribbentrop after the inception of Operation Barbarossa, he suddenly clutched his chest and expressed the fear that he was about to have a heart attack with possibly fatal results.[30] On 31 July 1941 Göring entrusted to Heydrich

*'"IV" stood ... for the Gestapo, "B" ... for the religious and cults division, and "4" for the subdivision specializing in the Jewish religion': Reitlinger, *The Final Solution*, p. 29 (Trans.).

216   HITLER

the task of implementing the 'final solution'.[31] At Auschwitz Eichmann and Höss proceeded to investigate various methods of extermination and to discuss the relative advantages of shooting and of
asphyxiation, whether by carbon monoxide or some other form of
gas.[32] Meanwhile Heinrich Himmler had been keeping a wary eye on
Hitler whom he had long known to be a sick man. Despite severe pangs
of conscience he began in the spring of 1941, if not before, to put out
feelers through contacts in Switzerland in an attempt to discover how
the British might react to a proposal for a conditional peace, with himself and not Adolf Hitler as negotiator on the German side.[33]

    After dinner on the evening of 2 August Hitler, although evidently
out of sorts, discussed a wide range of topics, including political
ideologies, agriculture and technology.[34] Heinrich Heim, who was then
keeping a shorthand record of his table-talk, remarked on his pallor,
lassitude, depression and general air of ill-health,[35] comments which
are borne out by photographs of Hitler taken four days later, immediately after the fall of Smolensk.[36] Until 9 August he took his meals
separately. When he returned his talk consisted of a series of allusions
of a marked testamentary character.[37] He was still clearly unwell and,
indeed, complained to his doctor of stomach troubles, bouts of nausea,
shivering fits, debility, and attacks of diarrhoea and dysentery.[38] On
14 August an electrocardiogram revealed rapidly developing coronary
sclerosis.[39] Morell's answer was to prescribe yet more drugs.

    Harassed by concern for his own health, the irascible and impatient
Führer railed against the high command whom he reproached for
their failure to advance rapidly enough in the East. Righteous indignation characterizes his directive of 21 August 1941 which opens with
the declaration: 'The Army's proposal concerning the future conduct
of operations in the East does not accord with my intentions.'[40]

    After a renewed absence from the communal table the 'Chief', as
Hitler's closest colleagues called him, put in an unexpected appearance on 8 September. No one noticed that his monologues on 8, 9 and
10 September were of a decidedly 'testamentary' nature and that,
unlike those of 2 and 9 August, they dealt with geography in continental and politics in global terms.[41]

What India has been to Britain [he asserted], the eastern territories will be
to us. If only I could make the German people understand what this space
means to our future! . . . Norwegians, Swedes, Danes and Dutch must be
encouraged to emigrate to our eastern territories, which will be incorporated

into the German Reich. .... Though I shall no longer be there to see it I rejoice on behalf of the German people who will one day see Britain and Germany united together against America. .... If there is one man who is praying for the success of our arms, it is the Shah of Persia. He'll have nothing more to fear from Britain ... once we've arrived down there. What, I ask you, is the potential of America by comparison with the creative forces latent in the European area – Germany, England, the Scandinavian countries, France and Italy? There will be only one army, one S S, one administration to cover the whole of the new Reich and the effect of this will be tremendous.[42]

By degrees Hitler's health began to improve although, as 1941 drew to a close, the situation in Africa failed to develop along the lines he would have wished. On 28 November 23,000 men, the last of the Italian forces, surrendered at Gondar in Abyssinia. And in other parts of the continent, too, the Allies began to gain the upper hand. On 10 September the British occupied Tobruk. Benghazi was evacuated on 26 December. The loss of Bardia on 3 January 1942 was followed by that of Sollum fifteen days later. Yet these setbacks did not hit him hard enough to leave any lasting physical effects. Indeed his bodily afflictions did not recur until the spring of 1942 when Rommel, having retaken Benghazi and Gazala, was preparing his attack on Bir Hachim which fell to the Germans on 11 June. Hitler now began to complain of severe headaches and admitted for the first time that his memory was failing him. Nevertheless he seemed cheerful and in good health on 4 July 1942 when he remarked in the Wolfschanze that, since he could take nothing with him into the grave, he might as well pay his headquarters expenses out of his own pocket.[43] Shortly before transferring his headquarters from south-east Prussia to Vinnitsa he succumbed to a severe attack of influenzal encephalitis,[44] the glaring sunlight of the Ukranian summer was particularly trying to him, for the sparse woodland surrounded by acres of sunflower fields afforded scant shelter, and it was not until his return to the Wolfschanze in the autumn that his health began to improve. But the improvement was only temporary. No sooner was he back in Vinnitsa in February 1943, than he was again afflicted by some form of influenza. Moreover he was now visibly affected by the disaster at Stalingrad (for which he assumed sole blame)[45] and the defeat in North Africa. In a very short space of time he became quite literally a changed man. His eyes grew lustreless, protuberant and staring. Red blotches appeared on his cheeks. A slight curvature of the thoracic spine induced a stooping posture, somewhat aggravated by slight scoliosis (lateral curvature of the spine), but neither defect caused more than a minimal distortion of his bodily symmetry.[46] As in November 1923 after his putsch, he now suffered from a tremor of the left arm and leg and when walking he dragged his left foot. His movements were abrupt and jerky. He became more touchy than hitherto and reacted violently if annoyed by some situation or argument. With dogged tenacity he clung to his ideas and inspirations, even though these might sometimes appear erroneous or inappropriate to those around·him. However, he remained as alert as ever, and his answers to questions came no less promptly.[47]

Himmler, on whom Hitler had conferred additional powers as recently as August,[48] had long harboured doubts about the ability of the ailing Führer to bring the war to a successful conclusion. Indeed he had been planning to negotiate a separate peace with the Allies, a fact of which Count Ciano, for one, had been aware since April.[49] While Hitler had been at Vinnitsa, Gestapo agents had been sent to Austria to investigate his genealogy[50] with, however, wholly negative results. Himmler stowed away his S S spies' nugatory findings in his safe,[51] but he also had other irons in the fire. While his agents had been at work in Austria, the Reichsführer-S S had initiated a further investigation, this time into the nature of Hitler's illnesses. According to Felix Kersten, Himmler's personal physician, the Gestapo chief claimed to possess a twenty-six page dossier proving that Hitler was suffering from a syphilitic complaint which threatened him with creeping paralysis.[52] If such a 'dossier' ever in fact existed, it can have been no more than a collection of phantasmagoria. At least on this point there can be no doubt that Himmler was mistaken. Hitler certainly never contracted syphilis, nor did he ever suffer from creeping paralysis.[53]

In the course of time the Führer had become as well informed about certain drugs, symptoms of illnesses and their circumstances as his doctor, whom he occasionally tried to catch out, sometimes with success. Nevertheless, he obeyed Morell and took the drugs he prescribed though only, as a rule, if he knew – or thought he knew – what their effect would be.[54] Christa Schröder recounts that:

Morell exclaimed: 'My Führer, it is my responsibility to watch over your health. But suppose something were to happen to you?' To this Hitler responded by fixing him with his uncanny eyes in which there flickered a demoniacal flame. Stressing every word, underlining each individual syllable with cruel glee, Hitler replied: 'Morell, if anything happens to me, your life won't be worth a brass farthing!'[55]

Though convinced that he was capable of looking after his own health, Hitler made constant calls on his doctor,[56] and Morell took advantage of his privileged position to acquire considerable influence, becoming, in addition, the owner of several pharmaceutical concerns.

In February 1944 Hitler began to complain of a sudden deterioration in the condition of his right eye. He had experienced a stabbing pain and for about a fortnight afterwards had seen everything as though through a veil.[57] Morell called in Professor Walter Löhlein the ophthalmic specialist and head of the Berlin University Clinic.[58] Löhlein diagnosed vitreous haemorrhage and sensitivity and clouding of the eye, though on examination the fundus proved to be normal. This indicated that Hitler's high blood pressure was not malignant.[59] The specialist recommended ray treatment of the eye and prescribed *Homatropin* for the right eye and *Veritol* for the left.[60] After long consultations with Morell he advised – somewhat impractically having regard to the state of hostilities at the time – that Hitler be spared undue excitement. He also recommended that the patient take only a limited amount of tranquillizers and that he should do some light reading before going to sleep at night.[61]

Although Löhlein prescribed a new pair of glasses, he advised against any further ophthalmic examinations on psychological grounds, but said he would again inspect the right eye in some six to eight weeks' time.[62] The new spectacles were equipped with bifocal lenses, then something of a novelty by reason of the different refracting powers they possessed. For distant vision (upper half) there was plain glass on the left hand side, on the right $+1 \cdot 5$ dioptres; for near work (lower half) left $+3$ and right $+4$ dioptres,[63] a normal enough prescription for his age. In order not to have to wear spectacles all the time, he would use an exceptionally large magnifying glass which gave him a relatively extensive field of view when studying maps or documents.

That Hitler was almost blind in the right eye, as David Irving for one, maintains,[64] is untrue. His eyesight remained passable except during these few weeks early in 1944, and then it was only the right eye that was affected.

The sudden if temporary disturbance in the vitreous body of the right eye had a lasting psychological effect. And it was now that Hitler's mistrustfulness, always a predominant characteristic, began to manifest itself in alarming ways. Diplomats attuned to the niceties of protocol were not the only ones to be shocked by his outrageous and unfounded accusations; in March 1944 on the Obersalzberg he overwhelmed the Hungarian Regent, Nicholas Horthy, with accusations and insinuations which culminated in the assertion that the Hungarian government was negotiating not only with the Americans and British but also with the Russians.[65] His hysterical criticism went far beyond what was called for in the circumstances. Though at the time the attitude of the Hungarian Government and a significant part of its high command[66] was somewhat ambivalent, and though there may have been doubts about the army's preparedness, neither circumstance could justify such coarse and to all appearances politically inept accusations. Löhlein's sensible advice that for 'psychological reasons' the Führer should be spared undue excitement was evidently not superfluous.

Meanwhile anyone who had occasion to see Hitler either standing or walking was struck by his pronounced stoop. After his declaration on 12 December 1942 that Stalingrad, once lost, could never be regained,[67] he had begun to feel, if not to know, that time was catching up on him. As he put it on 31 August 1944: 'If my life had come to an end on 20 July 1944 . . . it would have meant, to me personally . . . no more than my liberation from cares, sleepless nights and a grave nervous disorder.'[68]

Life had indeed become a torment to him. His illness, severe suffering and the effects of medication were compounded by the oppressiveness of his prolonged sojourn in the bunker, the monotony of his vegetarian diet and the news of defeats at the front and of air raids at home. Not only was he under constant mental and physical strain but towards the end he was getting no more than two to three hours sleep a night, a regime which poisoned his mind and took steady and visible toll of his physique.

The Crimea fell on 14 May 1944. Two days later Hitler ordered that missile attacks on England were to begin in the middle of June.[69] His physical exhaustion now became increasingly apparent and he was tortured by stomach pain. Since the early part of the year the tremor in his left hand had become worse than it had ever been before. Morell continued to administer injections of *Testoviron* (sex hormone preparation), *Tonophosphan* and glucose, and to prescribe not only heart and liver extracts and Vitamultin tablets containing *Pervitin* and caffeine, but also Dr Köster's Antigas Pills. In addition he made Hitler breathe pure oxygen two or three times a day and, basing himself perhaps on the opinion expressed by Löhlein in early March that the patient's high blood pressure was not malignant, he allowed him the unlimited use of *Cardiazol*, a drug acting on the circulatory centre in the brain, the respiratory centres and the vascular nerves.

On 1 January Hitler, now a sick and tired man, declared: 'The year 1944 will make severe and heavy demands on all Germans. During the course of this year this momentous war will approach its climax.'[70] On the night of 20 July, immediately after Stauffenberg's unsuccessful attempt on his life, he issued his much quoted order of the day: 'A small clique of unscrupulous saboteurs have attempted to assassinate myself and the Operations Staff of the Wehrmacht in order to seize power. Providence has defeated their criminal intentions.'[71] Hitler had not emerged unscathed, however. His skin was riddled with wooden splinters, more than a hundred being removed from his legs alone. His face had been slightly cut. There was an abrasion on his forehead and bruising of the right elbow and left hand. His right hand was sprained and the hair on the back of his head singed. Injury to the eardrums had caused haemorrhage in the auditory canals, temporary deafness in the right ear and diminished hearing in the left. He complained of a taste of blood in his mouth, of severe earache and later insomnia, but he was surprised to find that, as if by a 'miracle', the shock had virtually banished his 'nervous complaint', namely the tremor in his left leg.[72] This improvement was only temporary. Quite soon the tremor returned, affecting not only his left hand and leg, but the whole of his left side. He dragged his feet as he walked, his actions being performed as it were in slow motion. During a short stroll he was seen to lurch suddenly to one side – the first indication that his sense of balance was seriously disturbed. The injuries to Hitler's ears were being treated by Dr Giesing. Without anaesthetic (at Hitler's own request) he cauterized the edges of the tympani which he then massaged, discovering at the same time that the patient's nose was not quite normal. The organ was anatomically constricted, the middle left concha being unusually large and deformed; the septum, which deviated in several places, was much thickened on the left near the root.[73] Apart from frequent colds and congestion of the nasal passages, the condition of Hitler's nose had never bothered him, although he

always gave a wide berth to anyone suffering from a cold. Trevor-
Roper is not entirely correct in maintaining that 'the events of 20th
July 1944 . . . though they represent a military, political, and psycho-
logical crisis, had little physical significance in the life of Hitler'.[74]

By September he had still not been cured of the pains in the head
(and more especially the forehead) which had been continuously
plaguing him since August and were being combated by Dr Giesing
with cocaine. Then he succumbed to jaundice, his skin becoming
discoloured, the whites of his eyes yellow, and his urine dark brown
with traces of bile pigments.[75] He complained of pain in the region of
the gall-bladder and was treated by Morell with Gallestol.[76] He never
left the bunker and sensed danger everywhere. The headaches and
jaundice had a debilitating effect such as he had never experienced
before, his heart was troubling him and he was suffering from tooth-
ache. And on top of all this the war situation was giving him cause for
serious concern. On 15 August the Allies had landed on the Riviera;
ten days later General de Gaulle's forces marched into Paris, and by
the end of the month Toulon and Marseilles had been lost. On 17
September, at the time of the Arnhem and Nijmegen landings, Hitler
suffered a heart attack and was confined to bed. After 1945 his dentist,
Blaschke,[77] was to recall: 'When I arrived he was in bed. . . . He spoke
in a low voice, saying no more than was absolutely necessary. I washed
out the socket daily [Blaschke had previously extracted a tooth]. A few
days later I found him sitting in a chair and shortly after that he was
up and about.'[78]

At about this time three X-ray photographs were taken of Hitler's
head[79] and an electrocardiogram, reproduced below, was made on

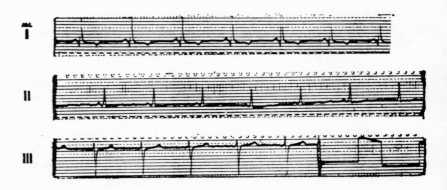

24 September. This latter document, found among Morell's papers after the War, was evaluated in October 1970 at the author's request by the Heidelberg University Clinic. The ECG confirms that, besides sclerosis of the coronary vessels, there was also disturbance of conduction and hypertrophy with damage to the left ventricle. Whether the above-mentioned collapse was attributable to myocardial infarction cannot be deduced with any certainty from the tracings of electric currents from the heart. But it seems a plausible explanation.

Morell passed the electrocardiogram for analysis to Professor Karl Weber, head of the Bad Nauheim Heart Research Institute. After studying Weber's conclusions the Führer's personal physician could find no better advice to give his evidently listless patient than to avoid physical exertion even more carefully than hitherto.

The X-ray photographs reveal an inflammation of the left maxillary antrum and of the ethmoidal cells which form part of the paranasal sinus system. Hitler was treated by Professor von Eicken who, as in October 1935, again removed polyps from his vocal cords. The patient now seemed very weak. His voice was feeble and he remained lying apathetically on his camp bed, no longer, it seemed, having any will to live. A common cold gave rise to inflammation of the frontal sinuses, in addition to which he was suffering from attacks of dizziness and outbreaks of cold sweat. Barely able to eat anything, constantly thirsty and tormented by stomach cramps, he lost six pounds in weight between 28 and 30 September.

By this time the British and Americans were already on the borders of the Reich. On 1 October shortly after 5 p.m. Dr Giesing examined Hitler and found that his pulse was rapid and faint. Indeed, he actually lost consciousness for a time, a dramatic interlude of which Giesing wrote the following account in 1945, a few weeks after his patient's suicide:

Hitler turned down the bed-clothes . . . and pulled up his nightshirt for me to . . . examine his abdomen. . . . [This] was generally somewhat distended and percussion revealed distinct meteorism [the accumulation of gases in the intestine, distending the loops of the intestine]. No sensitivity to pressure was apparent in the abdomen. Neither the right epigastrium nor the region of the gall-bladder gave pain on pressure. . . . I then used a . . . safety pin to test the abdominal reflexes . . . which seemed very lively. I next asked Hitler if I might check on his neurological condition. . . . [He] agreed. I drew down the nightshirt to cover his abdomen and pulled the bed-clothes right back.

... The genitals ... showed no abnormalities. The prepuce was drawn back, the glans ... showed no signs of irritation, or pyramid signs. ... Babinski, Fordon, Rossolimo and Oppenheim [reflexes] ... negative. As the patient was in bed, I did not apply the Romberg test ... to judge from previous results, [it would also] probably have been negative. I then asked Hitler to take off his nightshirt ... which he did, helped by myself and Linge. Again I noticed that the ... white skin on his trunk ... was rather dry, and I could feel no sweat in the axillae. Triceps and brachio-radial reflexes [arm reflexes] on both sides were very lively, spastic reflexes in the upper extremities (Léri, Meyer and Wartenberg) ... negative. Adiadochokinesia was ... not present, nor were other cerebellar symptoms. ... Tapping anterior to the parotid gland to test the facial reflex ... elicited a hint of a spasm of the type known as Chvostek's sign; Kernig and Lasègue were definitely negative, no signs of rigidity in the neck muscles. Head movements unrestricted. It seemed to me that the muscles of the upper arm showed a certain rigidity on flexion and extension. ... Hitler followed the neurological examination with great interest and finally remarked: '... Apart from this nervous overexcitability, there's nothing wrong with my nervous system and I hope everything will be all right again soon. I had a motion ... yesterday and the day before, after Morell had given me chamomile enemas, and presently he's going to give me another one. ... In the last three days I've hardly been able to eat anything, so my intestine's practically empty now ... and hasn't had much to do during that time.' Linge and I helped Hitler to put on his nightshirt again. ... Then Hitler said: 'If we go on talking like this we'll forget the treatment. Would you please have another look at my nose and put in that cocaine stuff. My larynx is certainly a bit better, but I still feel hoarse.' I then [treated] ... the left nostril with the 10 per cent solution of cocaine ... with the patient lying down. Afterwards I examined the ... ears again and ... the larynx. Some moments later Hitler said: 'My head is almost clear again now and I feel nearly well enough to get up. But I feel ... very weak what with all this colic and eating so little.' A few moments later I noted that Hitler's eyes were closed and that ... his face, previously rather flushed, had turned pale. I took his pulse which was ... rapid and weak. The pulse rate was about 90 and the quality seemed to be very much softer than at other times. I asked Hitler how he felt and received no reply. He had obviously suffered a slight collapse ... and was not responsive. Linge had gone ... to open the door that led into Hitler's small sitting-room, because someone had been knocking on it. ... I can only have been alone with Hitler for a very short time since I was still treating the left nostril with cocaine when Linge returned ... Linge stood at the foot of the bed and asked how much longer the treatment would take. His question startled me. 'I've almost finished,' I said. Just then Hitler's face grew even paler and for a moment his features twitched convulsively as he drew up his knees. Seeing this, Linge murmured: 'The Führer's getting colic again. Better leave him alone. He probably wants to sleep now.' Making as little noise as possible we packed up my instruments and quickly left the bedroom.[80]

After this episode on 1 October Hitler's physical condition deteriorated more rapidly than hitherto, although his hearing showed some improvement which at least made it easier to communicate with him. In September Giesing and Brandt had discovered to Morell's mortification that he was prescribing Antigas Pills, a form of medication they regarded as dangerous.[81] After a lengthy discussion with Dr Giesing about Morell's treatment, Hitler came down firmly on the side of Morell. Dr Brandt (condemned to death by the Führer in April 1945) and his deputy, Dr von Hasselbach, were dismissed while Giesing was called in for the last time on 7 October. Hitler had no desire to be treated by a bunch of wrangling doctors. On being asked by the Führer to suggest a replacement for Brandt and von Hasselbach, Himmler recommended Ludwig Stumpfegger. A capable doctor and astute courtier, Stumpfegger was the devoted and subservient disciple of the S S chief's own physician, Karl Gebhardt, described variously by members of Himmler's inner circle as repulsive, unscrupulous, egotistical, corrupt and greedy.[82] What Himmler had in mind when, on the advice of his infamous henchman, he sent Stumpfegger to the Führer in East Prussia, can only be surmised. No doubt he hoped that in Gebhardt's protégé he would possess a tool with which to eliminate Hitler whenever it suited his book. If such was his intention, he had counted his chickens before they were hatched. Stumpfegger, arriving at Hitler's quarters for the first time on 31 October, immediately threw in his lot with the Führer who, for his part, enjoyed taking walks with his new doctor. Indeed on 21 April 1945, when even Morell was permitted to leave for Berchtesgaden, Hitler kept Stumpfegger with him.

As yet he knew nothing of Himmler's plans; but he was mistrustful and not even the condition of his health could induce him at this stage to relinquish a fraction of his personal control. He kept a jealous eye on the conduct of the war in the different theatres, lest anything should be done without his knowledge if not actually against his wishes. By the end of 1944 his decline, which had been manifest to all, appeared to have been temporarily arrested. On 20 November he left East Prussia for the last time. For some three weeks his headquarters were in Berlin, the city which, from 1933 to 1939, had been the scene of his greatest triumphs. In December he moved to the Adlerhorst, the Führer headquarters which had been constructed as far back as 1939 at Ziegenheim in the Taunus. The early successes that followed the launching of the Ardennes offensive on 16 December induced in him the gratified feeling that he was not yet 'a dead man'. When Dr von Eicken again visited him on 30 December in the Adlerhorst, he was astonished to find that Hitler's voice sounded normal and that he seemed both lively and confident.[83] But the improvement was more apparent than real. Though he could stand up straight he needed all his strength to do so, for the curvature of his spine was irremediable. His face was ashen grey. He moved by dragging himself forwards and the whole of his left side trembled continuously. When he wanted to sit down someone had to move up a chair behind him since he was no longer capable of drawing it up himself. His eyes pained him when he faced the light. Only his mind seemed fresh and alert, though apt to tire on occasion. His memory was still remarkable and he could reel off figures, names and dates at will. But he was no longer in full control of his intellect which had lost its flexibility. Moreover the state of his health was such that major achievements were now beyond him. 'The outstanding commander of the early part of the war', as Field-Marshal von Rundstedt once described him, 'had become a second-rate architect where military planning was concerned.'[84] In the space of five years his appearance had changed so much that visitors who had known him before the war now found him scarcely recognizable. Even Dr Giesing, seeing him in February 1945 after an interval of only five months, was surprised at the change.

He seemed to me to have aged [he wrote], and to stoop much more than before. His face was as pale as ever and he had great bags underneath the eyes. He spoke clearly but very softly. I was immediately struck by a marked tremor in his left arm and hand, which invariably increased when his hand was unsupported, so that he always kept his arm resting on the table, or his hand on the chair arms. . . . I got the feeling that he was somewhat absent-minded and no longer able to concentrate. The impression he gave was of complete exhaustion and abstraction. The skin of his hands was also very pallid and the finger nails completely bloodless.[85]

Thenceforward Hitler went rapidly downhill. An elderly staff officer, who had not seen the Führer for many years, was shocked by his appearance when he met him again on 23 March in the Reich Chancellery bunker. 'Before I went to the Reich Chancellery for the first time', he was to relate after 1945,

I was told by a staff officer that I must be prepared to find a man quite different from the one I had known hitherto, either in the flesh or from photographs and newsreels, for he was now old and worn out. The reality exceeded by far what I had been led to expect. I had seen Hitler briefly twice before. The first time in 1937 at a state ceremony in memory of the fallen and the second on the occasion of his birthday parade in 1939. The Hitler of those days was in no way comparable to the wreck of a man to whom I reported on 25 March 1945 and who wearily stretched out a nerveless, trembling hand towards me. . . . It was a ghastly physical image he presented. The upper part of his body was bowed and he dragged his feet as he made his way slowly and laboriously through the bunker from his living room to the conference room. He had no sense of balance. If anyone happened to stop him during this short walk (some fifty or sixty yards), he was forced either to sit down on one of the seats placed along the walls for the purpose, or to catch hold of the person he was speaking to. . . . His eyes were bloodshot and, despite the fact that certain documents were typed out for him on special 'Führer typewriters' with letters three times the normal size, he needed strong lenses to read them. Often saliva would dribble from the corners of his mouth . . . presenting a hideous and pitiful spectacle. . . . In contrast to his physical decay, Hitler's mind was still active. And, though he sometimes showed signs of weariness, his remarkable memory was still much in evidence . . . he could pick out what was essential from the innumerable, diverse and sometimes conflicting documents submitted to him and he possessed a keen nose for incipient danger.[86]

But in fact his remarkable memory had also begun to deteriorate though this might not have been apparent to the officer, who did not really know Hitler and had little idea of his former abilities. As early as February Giesing had already been struck by the fact that Hitler would sometimes repeat a question to which the doctor had already given the answer. This could never have occurred even in the autumn of 1944. Indeed, after February 1945, the Führer was little more than a wreck. In spite of his neurotic inflexibility now patent to all, he would overlook contradictions and objections which he would previously have tolerated, if at all, only in exceptional circumstances and within very narrow limits. Thus on 13 February 1944, a day or two before his interview with Giesing, he had an argument with Guderian which lasted for two hours. Guderian describes it as follows:

His fists raised, his cheeks flushed with rage, his whole body trembling, the man stood there in front of me, beside himself with fury and having lost all self-control. After each outburst of rage, Hitler would stride up and down the carpet-edge, then suddenly stop immediately before me and hurl his next accusation in my face. He was almost screaming, his eyes seemed about to pop out of his head and the veins stood out on his temples.

Guderian, however, continued to uphold his opinion, whereupon Hitler 'suddenly said with his most charming smile: "Now please continue with the conference. Today the General Staff has won a battle."'[87] With the war almost over, the General Staff had 'won a battle' against their ailing Supreme Commander, and he was content to leave it at that. Heinrich Himmler had never dared to enter the lists openly against the Führer. Now, incensed by the humiliation of the S S* and aware of the grave condition of Hitler's health, he sought to influence the course of events indirectly. At the beginning of April Schellenberg had paid a visit to his friend Max de Crinis, head of the psychiatric section of the Charité hospital, who told him that the Führer (whom he had never treated) was clearly suffering from Parkinson's disease.[88] This fitted in very well with Himmler's plan to rid himself of Hitler at the first opportunity, either by way of enforced abdication, or by placing him under arrest or even, if necessary, by assassination. Nevertheless he was reluctant even at this stage to take such drastic measures though he agreed when de Crinis offered to prepare some medicine to be administered to Hitler by Stumpfegger. But the latter had fallen so much under his patient's spell that he failed to cooperate. Neither conspirators nor disease, neither drugs nor his mode of life, were able to kill the Führer. He lived for a few days longer and then died by his own hand.

On 21 April Morell departed from Berlin, leaving behind his 'Patient A' who was preparing himself for the end. Until then, even without Morell's dispensary, he would have at his disposal the drugs he needed to keep him going during the final days. He knew the nature of those drugs and took what he held to be necessary. No one who has read about his behaviour during this time or about his pronouncements at the situation conferences on 23, 25 and 27 April 1945, then

* The Führer had ordered the *SS Leibstandarte Adolf Hitler* to remove their distinctive armbands after the failure of their attack in the region of the Upper Danube.

still being recorded,[89] can fail to recognize what it was that made him conjure up in all good faith such patently hair-brained schemes. The rapid alternation of depression and euphoria, exhaustion and artificially induced buoyancy clearly reflect Hitler's dependence on the stimulants prescribed by Morell. On 22 April Eva Braun wrote to her friend Herta Ostermayr: '. . . he has lost faith', and on the following day when the situation was even more hopeless: 'I believe that even he is able to see more clearly than he did yesterday what the future holds in store.'[90]

A few days later he took his own life. Bezymenski's assertion in 1968 that Hitler poisoned himself cannot be substantiated.[91] Morell did not long survive the Führer. Hitler's threat that his personal physician's life would 'not be worth a brass farthing'[92] if anything should happen to himself, was in a sense fulfilled.

When Dr Paul Karl Schmidt visited Morell in the American POW hospital at Dachau, he found him lying on a camp-bed, paralysed, exhausted, depressed and complaining of heart trouble. In tones of lachrymose self-pity, and struggling with a speech impediment, he told his story to his erstwhile patient.[93] He died in 1948 in a hospital beside the Tegernsee, after having handed over to the American military authorities papers which comprised diagnostic records, indications, medical reports, his correspondence with colleagues about Hitler's case, and his own recollections of his famous 'Patient A' with whose physical and pyschological constellation he was more familiar than any other man.[94]

Dr Morell's treatment of Adolf Hitler has been widely censured and the remedies he administered have been variously described as 'quick drugs',[95] 'inadequately tested medicines',[96] 'harmful prophylactic measures',[97] the 'disastrous experiments of a charlatan',[98] 'quackery'[99] and 'fancy nostrums'[100] never precisely specified and not even identifiable by Hitler's physicians, Giesing,[101] von Hasselbach and Brandt. Few of these accusations can really be substantiated. Between 1936 and 1945 Morell prescribed some thirty different medicaments[102] for his patient more than half of which are still in current use. If given in wrong dosage or for the wrong indication they could, of course, be dangerous. The doses prescribed by Morell, however, were not only correct but often very conservative and this also applies to his prescriptions for quick-acting drugs. It was only in the case of Cardiazol and Coramine that he had obviously arrived at the wrong indication.

Hitler, who neither drank nor smoked, liked to use pharmaceutical stimulants. For instance, before a public speech or some demanding function he would take pep pills in the form of Kolz-Dallmann tablets, a preparation containing cola, caffeine and sugar which is still obtainable today. Dr Giesing once had occasion to paint the inside of his patient's nose with cocaine. Discovering that this cleared his head, Hitler asked for more frequent applications, despite the fact that cocaine is known to be harmful if extensively used. Again, although the immoderate consumption of caffeine and Pervitin, both of which were contained in Morell's product Vitamultin, can damage the nervous system, it would seem that Hitler absorbed alarming quantities of these drugs – if, that is, we are to believe Professor Ernst-Günther Schenk. Professor Schenk, a specialist in internal diseases and at that time adviser to the Reich Health Department, writes:

One day in 1942 or 1943 I received from a reliable quarter some small 'golden' tablets – i.e. wrapped in gold foil. They were about an inch square and about an eighth of an inch thick. I was told that these 'golden' Vitamultins were provided exclusively for the Führer by Morell. . . . I myself pounded them in a mortar and sent the powder with a covering note to one of the institutes of the Academy of Military Medicine . . . to be analysed for its alkaloid and drug content. I learnt that the powder contained caffeine and Pervitin in what seemed to me a truly horrifying concentration.[103]

Brandt's allegation that Morell prescribed 'secret nostrums' for the Führer, is at most applicable to these 'golden' Vitamultin tablets, the more so since Morell refused to divulge either the concentration or the quantity prescribed.

As Hitler's personal physician, Morell earned some 60,000 marks a year. His position was not an enviable one, however. Quite often he would complain how difficult it was to be the Führer's doctor since more often than not it was the patient who laid down the law to his physician.[104] This necessitated constant compromise. Morell could not, for instance, simply declare that Hitler was sick and confine him to bed or send him away on holiday. And he had to provide him with stimulants whenever he needed or demanded them. Hence Brandt's assertion that Morell deliberately gave Hitler too many prophylactic injections carries little weight.[105]

As we have seen, de Crinis of the Charité Hospital had declared his conviction that Hitler was suffering from Parkinson's disease, a diagnosis based solely on the Führer's appearance in newsreels. Brandt's successor, Dr Stumpfegger, who had attended Hitler since October 1944, did not share this opinion.[106] Nor, after 1945, would either Dr Brandt or Dr Hasselbach make any definite comment on the subject.[107] Though Morell had hinted at the possibility of psychosomatic disease, he had never been prepared to commit himself.[108] 'It would be useful to know,' Schramm wrote, 'whether Morell used antispasmodics and, if so, whether it was because he suspected Parkinson's disease.'[109] This question is now settled. While Morell prescribed antispasmodics in the form of Eukodal and Eupaverin, he did so not because he suspected Parkinson's disease, but in order to alleviate Hitler's stomach cramps. Belladonna 606, which was then used for the treatment of Parkinson's disease, was never prescribed. Morell's analysis of the activity of the central nervous system and the major reflexes reveals no indication of morbidity,[110] evidence that he excluded the possibility of this disease. The activity of the cerebrum he described as normal, and discounted any suggestion of 'euphoria' and 'personality change'. As regards the motor sphere, he alleges that the patient was free of 'spasms' and convulsions, and that there was no evidence of 'paralysis of the vocal musculature'. Morell's diagnosis also shows the cerebellum and spinal cord to be free of disease.[111] He expressly emphasized that he had never had cause to revise the results of his reflex tests.[112] Moreover Hitler himself had described his tremor as a serious nervous complaint.[113]

During the last three years of his life, there were certain indications that might have denoted Parkinson's disease: his shuffling gait and short steps, the increasing jerkiness of his movements, his stooping posture, masklike features, his difficulty in speaking, the evident rigidity both of habitus and of thought processes and the degeneration evinced by his handwriting. The tremor in his left arm and leg might be regarded as evidence, although as a symptom it is far from conclusive in view of the fact that Parkinson's disease seldom affects one side of the body only. Nor, like Hitler's tremor, does it lapse only to recur a number of years later. There are two possible causes of the disease – severe influenzal encephalitis and cerebral sclerosis – and Hitler is known to have suffered from the former in 1942.

An evaluation of Morell's neurological findings, however, disposes once for all of the allegation that Hitler suffered from Parkinson's disease.

The first instance of tremor in Hitler's left arm and leg occurred after the failure of his putsch, when his life seemed about to take a negative turn. In due course the tremor disappeared completely and it was not until twenty years later, that the same reflexes were again triggered by the extreme tension engendered at a situation conference in December 1942 when Hitler ominously remarked: 'In no circumstances must we surrender Stalingrad. We would never be able to retake it.'[114] This tremor, which ceased for a time after the traumatic occurrence of 20 July 1944, was quite clearly a symptom of the nervous palsy resulting from the condition known, during the First World War, as war neurosis, a psychosomatic illness from which frontline soldiers frequently suffered and which was diagnosed as an extreme and primitive reaction on the part of the instinct of self-preservation.[115] And just as this neurosis would disappear as soon as a soldier felt himself to be out of danger, so the tremor which affected Hitler after the events of 1923 disappeared when his existence no longer seemed under threat. Its recurrence at the end of 1942 was closely connected with the changing fortunes of war and their probable consequences to himself.

CHAPTER EIGHT

The Politician*

Mein Kampf contains a description of the deep and widespread feelings of disappointment and uncertainty that prevailed during the latter part of 1918, shortly before the revolution. It was then that Hitler 'decided to go into politics',[1] a decision which came as no surprise to his wartime associates.[2] For despite his avowed opinion of politicians as men whose only 'real conviction is lack of conviction',[3] he was known to have considered entering politics once he had been demobilized.[4] Such a course meant relinquishing his long cherished dream of becoming a famous architect – a dream which in any case, given the circumstances, now appeared 'ridiculous'.[5] His decision to embark on a political career followed logically from the view he early adopted of himself as a genius, above all a political genius, and of other people as merely a means to an end.[6] In 1918 it was evident to others besides Hitler that all statesmen and politicians of world standing were similarly actuated – or 'programmed', to use an expression frequently on his lips in later years. Thinking as he did so largely in historical and always in messianic terms, his *Weltanschauung* – conventional enough at the time – no less than his as yet unrecognized talents and proclivities, necessarily constituted a source of danger. He could not have foreseen that his basic political concept, formed in the course of his self-tuition, would remain unchanged or that, carried to extremes, it would precipitate the final disaster.

From the start of his political career Hitler was firmly convinced that he was a chosen instrument of the 'Providence' he so constantly invoked and that, holding as he did the key to history, the role he would come to play in it would not be that of an ordinary politician. He never once considered the possibility of tailoring his political actions and knowhow to 'the practical reality of the moment' in return for that transitory fame which, in *Mein Kampf*, he describes as the politicians' lot.[7]

* For a chronological table of Hitler's political career see Appendix A.

As his power grew, so his health deteriorated; he was haunted by premonitions of death, which induced in him a feverish impatience to get results before it was too late. Goals which in similar circumstances would have seemed unattainable to other politicians, he regarded as well within his reach. Thus even in 1924 when under arrest, with his party in ruins and himself relegated to the political sidelines, he interpreted Bismarck's famous description of politics as 'the art of the possible' in such a way as to make it fit his own concept of a policy based almost exclusively on force. In *Mein Kampf* Bismarck's successors are castigated for the aimlessness of their domestic and foreign policy and their limited aspirations, while the Bismarckian view of politics is described as 'somewhat modest'[8] – by comparison, doubtless, with Hitler's own, which he wished to be regarded as the epitome of wisdom. 'For Bismarck', he wrote, 'only wanted to say that for the achievement of a definite political goal all possibilities should be utilized or, in other words, that all possibilities should be taken into account.'[9] In Hitler's view politics, rightly understood, assumed the form of a ruthless, ideologically orientated contest for power within the framework of the naked struggle for existence prescribed by natural law. Behind his political negotiations there was always the threat of force, for at no time was he intent on gaining allies in the conventional sense of the term. In order to attain secondary goals that were no more than incidental to his ultimate ideological aim he was prepared to stake everything he – or indeed others – had already gained. For instance in 1936 he abrogated the Treaty of Locarno – regarded by Stresemann a decade previously as an important step towards Germany's reinstatement as a great power. In March of the same year he occupied the Rhineland and restored the military sovereignty of the Reich, despite the fact that France could have crushed him singlehanded and at little cost to herself. In March 1938 he occupied Austria and, in the following October, the Sudetenland. A year after the Anschluss he invaded Czechoslovakia and annexed Memel. Six months later, having gained the support of the overwhelming majority of Germans by the unexpected magnitude of his successes, he launched an attack on Poland, knowing the Wehrmacht to be equipped only for a short Blitzkrieg. Anything that differed from his own brand of politics he ascribed to a false reading of history, to the personal failings of politicians or to the fact of their being the tools, witting or unwitting, of 'international Jewry' for the execution of its fell designs.[10]

His scant regard for international pacts and treaties is illustrated by his cynicism in concluding a non-aggression pact with Poland in 1934 and by his assurances that his intentions towards that country were entirely peaceful. Indeed he had already made it clear in *Mein Kampf* that 'an alliance whose aim does not embrace a plan for war is senseless and worthless. Alliances are concluded only for struggle.'[11] Such a policy, if successful, inevitably begets grave injustice. For it cannot succeed unless its exponents eliminate all security risks, gain a complete ideological hold over their own people, conquer other nations and thereafter maintain them in total subjection. The foregoing is in no way invalidated by the fact that Hitler's downfall was so long delayed. On the contrary, this simply proves his ability to pursue, over an unbelievably long period, a policy that by rights should not even have been viable (let alone enduring) and to pursue it for the most part with alarming success.

His first taste of failure in 1923 was of crucial importance to his career as a politician.[12] Instead of reverting to obscurity, as had been generally anticipated, he was able to make a comeback. And when he did so, he was neither chastened nor humbled but instead disputed the right of his critics to pass judgement on him. Indeed it is clear from *Mein Kampf*, composed during his period of eclipse, that he held himself to be that rare historical phenomenon – a politican and theoretician rolled into one or, to use his own words, a 'pole star of seeking humanity'.[13] The theoretician as such, he explains, is inevitably misunderstood, because he works for the future. And whereas it is he who lays down the aims of a movement, it is the politician who brings them to fruition. The one must think in terms of eternal truths while the other concentrates on present reality. 'The greatness of the one,' he wrote, 'lies in the absolute abstract soundness of his idea, that of the other in his correct attitude towards the given facts and their advantageous application; and in this the theoretician's aim must serve as his guiding star.'[14] Hence, in his capacity as theoretician, Hitler regarded the end as more important than the means. To him it was self-evident that the theoretician must take account neither of 'utility' nor of 'reality'. He held that the stature of a theoretician, unlike that of a politician, could not be judged by tangible successes since the attainment of his ultimate goal must inevitably be frustrated by human limitations. Indeed, 'the more abstractly correct and hence powerful the idea . . . the more impossible . . . its complete fulfilment'. Hence, in the final analysis, the theoretician could never be properly assessed by his contemporaries.[15] Hitler claimed to be a past master in both capacities and ultimately he was to fail in each of them. Nevertheless there can be no disputing his influence, for the mark that he has left on history is unique. He translated into reality the most inhuman ideas, presented a radical challenge to conventional modes of thought and action and set the stage for a drastic realignment of powers.

All that remains of the German Reich and of Hitler's dream of a world power without precedent in history is a country divided into two parts, neither of which enjoys major status. This elimination of Germany from the group of powers capable of shaping European politics has diminished the status of Great Britain and led to the predominance of the United States and Soviet Russia. Neither Britain – wooed by Hitler for nearly two decades with a view to establishing German world hegemony – nor Germany can now be numbered among the great powers. Hitler, the professed Anglophile and German 'European', put an end, most probably a definitive end, to European world domination, and eliminated Germany as an autonomous force in the field of major diplomacy. And had it not been for him, the colonial and 'semicolonial' peoples he despised might not so soon or so confidently have put forward their demands for emancipation, nor the Third World have become a political force which even the United States and the Soviet Union cannot afford to ignore.

To some extent Hitler's ideas would appear to be endorsed by what has happened since 1945. For example his view of politics as power politics pure and simple still remains valid, as does the maxim that power politics can best be implemented by war. His thoughts on morality in relation to international affairs have not in practice been superseded. Whenever and wherever, since the time of the Nuremberg trials, an opportunity has arisen to infringe international law, that opportunity has been taken. This alone is enough to make Hitler's political ideas seem a little less out of the ordinary than some historians would have us suppose. For instance, one of his major aims, namely world hegemony for the Reich, belongs to a German tradition, which can count among its protagonists some of the great figures of the country's past.

The history of the Reich from its creation by Bismarck in 1871 until its destruction in 1945 covers a span of some eighty years. Throughout that period there runs a distinct and continuous thread linking the

Bismarckian and Wilhelmine eras, the Weimar Republic and the Third Reich, all of which have important characteristics in common. Since 1945 the older school of German historians has chosen either to disregard this aspect or to dismiss it as historically incorrect, a state of affairs which, where Hitler is concerned, has led to gross distortion if nothing worse. Nor is our argument in any way weakened by the consideration that Hitler's *Weltanschauung* not only determined every one of his aims in the field of foreign policy, but also provided the prerequisites, the impetus and the justification for each successive phase of the National Socialist policy of aggression after 1939.[16] Jacobsen has suggested that the National Socialist line before 1933, Germany's diplomatic moves up till 1939, and her aims in the field of foreign policy prior to 1943 were the logical outcome of the National Socialist outlook, so that German foreign policy after 1933 would better be described as 'National Socialist foreign policy'.[17] This view is untenable, though it must be conceded that never, before Hitler, had German policy comprised such activities as the deliberate corruption of men's minds, the systematic extirpation of opponents, and the endeavour to subject Europe to a radical New Order based on racial-ideological concepts. Again, in stating that the year 1933, 'and the subsequent course of German history up to the end of the war should be seen, not so much as a continuous process, but rather in the light of a revolutionary upheaval', Jacobsen has allowed himself to be unduly swayed by the evident consequences of Hitler's policy which, he holds, has 'encumbered Germany for all time with an onerous historical mortgage'.[18]

While still a schoolboy Hitler had learnt from textbooks, Pan-German manifestos and other sources that the most cherished desire of the German people was to see their country become a mighty empire. Even before the 1914 war he ardently supported the expansionist views of Admiral Tirpitz,[19] Secretary of State for the Imperial Navy from 1897 to 1916. The admiral's approach to foreign policy and his reactionary attitude to social reform at home derived from the then current vulgar Darwinism that was also at the root of certain aspects of Hitler's political thinking. Tirpitz wished to see the Reich become not merely a great European power, but a world power equal in status to the British Empire. Even in 1924 he continued to adhere to these ideas, if in a form somewhat modified by Germany's defeat six years previously.[20]

On 20 June 1915, not long before Tirpitz's resignation, a 'strictly confidential' memorandum signed by more than a thousand eminent professional men was laid before the Chancellor, Bethmann Hollweg.[21] Part of the text runs:

We seek full and universal recognition commensurate with our cultural and economic greatness and military strength. It may not be feasible, in view of the preponderance of our enemies, to attain at one blow all the goals required to safeguard the nation. But the military victories achieved at such great sacrifice must be exploited to the very utmost limits.

For centuries we have been under threat from France and in the periods from 1815 to 1870 and 1871 to 1915 our ears have been assailed by an unceasing clamour for revenge. We wish to put an end to this danger once and for all. But not by means of inappropriate attempts at conciliation to which France has always responded with unbridled fanaticism. At this point we would stress most emphatically the need to beware of self-delusion. Our very existence depends on our ruthlessly undermining that country, both politically and economically.

Along our eastern borders, bastion and basis for the protection of our nation's growth, lies territory which must be ceded to us by Russia. It must be a region of agricultural settlements which will provide us with a healthy peasantry, that fountainhead of national and political strength.

Should we ever find ourselves in the position to exact reparations from Britain – a country ever parsimonious in the sacrifice of her blood – no sum would be too high. Britain has seen fit to use her wealth to stir up the world against us. The most vulnerable part of this nation of shopkeepers lies in its purse and, when we have the power to do so, it is this same purse that must be ruthlessly attacked.[22]

In the Imperial Chancellery, in the Foreign Office and within the General Staff the European status of the German–Austro–Hungarian bloc was debated exhaustively and with more than academic interest; the conclusions reached differed from those of Tirpitz only in degree. On the one hand the Chancellor, Bethmann Hollweg, inclined to the traditional view that the status of the bloc should be safeguarded; by this he meant complete freedom of action in the field of foreign affairs and the conservation of military superiority in relation to the other European powers. On the other, the school of thought represented by Ludendorff and the 3rd Supreme Army Command saw as their goal a self-contained territory of continental magnitude governed so far as possible by direct rule. In other words they envisaged the creation after the war of an enlarged Reich that would incorporate some of Russia's more economically important regions. So far as possible this new Reich would be self-supporting, immune to blockade, and capable of holding its own not only against Great Britain but, if needs be, against the combined sea-power of Britain and the United States. Thus it would form a strong base when the time came for the expected confrontation with the other great powers. To what extent Hitler's expansionist and hegemonic ideas derived from the 3rd Supreme Army Command and from Ludendorff's two-phase programme would seem relatively unimportant but, like Ludendorff, he advocated continental expansion followed by the acquisition of colonies. Moreover there is a direct and significant link between Hitler's own brand of power politics and the shortlived 'eastern solution' imposed by Ludendorff at Brest-Litovsk in 1918.

The emergence of Germany as a great power continued to be adumbrated by the leaders of the Weimar Republic no less than by Hitler who, we learn from Mein Kampf, had been convinced since the outbreak of the Great War, if not earlier, that what he was experiencing was a turning-point of history.[23] Thus, from the beginning of his political career he had been in no doubt that the small maritime nations, dependent on their navies, their overseas bases and the wealth of their colonies, had all but had their day. It was this conviction that moved him in the same context to describe the demand for the restoration of the 1914 border and the return of German colonies as mere 'wheedling and begging' and as inadequate, anachronistic and politically pointless.[24] Hence, only a few years after the war, when engaged in writing Mein Kampf, he was already dreaming, like the military, of a new kind of world power – his own kind – controlling a vast self-contained territory. The very fact that he could envisage such a power arising out of the rubble of defeat testifies to the strength of his convictions. He did not believe, however, either that the Weimar Republic could be its matrix or that Marxism could provide its dynamic. Nor did the restoration of the monarchy seem to hold out any prospect of steering future events to Germany's best advantage. Though himself an ultra-conservative he rejected monarchy as over-conservative and regarded it as an institution better qualified to maintain than to carve out an empire. This, he thought, could only be achieved by ideologically based revolutions of world historical significance. He looked on himself as a man who not only understood history but was also capable of 'making' it.

On 20 December 1918 the German military leaders met in the
General Staff building in Berlin to take part in the first conference on
policy to be held since the armistice. The subject of discussion was
General von Seeckt's plan which envisaged Germany's early re-
emergence as a great power and hence as a desirable ally. Because of the
Republic's impotence both at home and abroad, however, the conference proved fruitless and von Seeckt's proposal to overthrow Poland
with the help of Russia, thus freeing Germany's hands for an attack on
France, also came to nothing. It was not in any case a proposal Hitler
would have endorsed. From 1920 onwards his own expansionist
ideas were zealously, if quite unwittingly, nourished by a number of
the leading soldiers and politicians of the Weimar Republic, who
appear to have been in no way deterred by the real state of affairs.

As we have seen, Hitler had publicly demanded more than the mere
revision of the Versailles Treaty and no sooner had he become Chancellor, than he made known, in the inflated language of propaganda, the
Reich's determination to assert itself as a great power and to insist on a
fair say in European affairs. For he believed the prerequisites for any
viable policy to be the restoration of Germany's sovereignty, the
integrity of her frontiers and opportunities for economic expansion to
ensure the prosperity of the German people. Nevertheless his attitude
was rather more conciliatory than that adopted by some of the Chancellors of the Weimar Republic. For instance he stated officially that
he would not seek to exert any influence, whether ideological or otherwise, on foreign countries. In November 1933 he assured Joseph
Lipski, the Polish Ambassador, that he would never consider going to
war* over minor frontier disputes,[25] and in the following month he
even went so far as to hail Poland as a bastion against Bolshevist Russia.
Later, according to Jacobsen, he

reprobated any mention of the 'traditional enmity' between Germany and
Poland. The conclusion of the German–Polish Non-Aggression Pact in
1934 with its mutual renunciation of the use of force appeared proof enough
that Hitler intended to approach the frontier problem in a far more flexible
manner than that of the foreign ministers of the Weimar period, who had
persistently refused to conclude with Poland a frontier agreement similar to
that reached with the Western Powers at Locarno in 1925. . . . In view of
the Reich's precarious position, Hitler's method up till 1937 was one of

---

* In April 1933 he told the French Ambassador, François Poncet, that the
Reich could not indefinitely tolerate the existing eastern frontier.

peaceful change, which necessarily entailed the revision of the Versailles Treaty. With matchless virtuosity and admirable perseverance he proclaimed his desire for peace, continually harping not only on the German people's longing for peace and quiet but also on his experiences as a frontline soldier in the First World War, whose toll of blood he was thus especially well qualified to judge. These catchwords – greedily lapped up by all too many people – he would trot out on every possible occasion, whether in major speeches in the Reichstag or during interviews and conversations with foreigners. So far as German national interests were concerned the preservation of peace seemed to have assumed pride of place.[26]

Foreign affairs had always been accorded pride of place by German governments. But shortly before Hitler became Chancellor, the situation had caused General Schleicher to diverge from this policy and to implement a long-standing plan, one which he himself had been perfecting ever since the end of the war. Ultimately expansionist in intention, its initial aim was the restoration of order within the Reich followed by the revival of the country's economy. Having accomplished this he would, he hoped, be able to voice German demands in unequivocal terms and to concentrate on restoring the Reich to the status of a major power. One of his predecessors, Stresemann, the leader of the German People's Party, had already taken a major step in the same direction after temporarily solving the problem of reparations and boosting the country's economy. Indeed, this statesman, who was much influenced by Pan-German ideas, has gone down in history, not only as a conciliator, but also as a protagonist of economic expansionism.[27] It is hardly surprising that a man of his political complexion should have regarded the conclusion of the Treaty of Locarno in December 1925 as the first stage in the revision of the Versailles Treaty. His policy has been aptly described by Hillgruber as combining 'traditional secret diplomacy . . . overt activity on the stage of the League of Nations', and, finally, the 'maintenance of a balance between the country's economic potential and the demands of the military'.[28]

Each phase of this policy marked a step in the direction of National Socialism, for Hitler laid much the same stress on military power as the determining factor in foreign affairs. Until September 1933, however, he showed such circumspection with regard to his military and political programme that he incurred the criticism of the Foreign Minister, von Neurath, and the Minister for War, von Blomberg, both of whom were advocates of overt rearmament. He was not the first to infringe the rearmament clauses of the Versailles Treaty. Ever since 1929 the Reichswehr commanders, led by Streicher, had been taking advantage of the other powers' almost total preoccupation with the world economic crisis to free Germany from the military restrictions imposed upon her after the armistice. Again, during the final phase of Müller's Social Democratic government, Julius Curtius, the Foreign Minister, and some of his high-ranking officials including the Secretary of State, von Bülow, had expressed their aims in terms suggestive of an extreme chauvinism.[29] Like the great majority of the German people, Hitler demanded the repudiation of the reparations clause as well as equal military rights for Germany. Brüning's own sympathies lay in the same direction but, in view of the political situation, his Centre Party cabinet (1930 to 1931) could never have ventured to emulate Hitler's outspokenness.[30] On the other hand the rearmament programme, begun as a clandestine operation after the disbandment of the Allied Control Commission in 1927, was now being carried out with an increasing disregard for concealment on the part of the Reichswehr commanders. Brüning was overthrown as the result of the machinations of Schleicher, aided and abetted by the National Socialists. With the arrival of von Papen and his 'cabinet of barons'[31] Germany embarked on the course which had seemed too risky to Brüning, namely an accelerated and overt rearmament programme.

On acceding to power in January 1933 Hitler, whose foreign policy was dominated by the traditional methods of diplomacy and force of arms, at first displayed rather more reticence on the subject of rearmament than his immediate predecessors.[32] His reserve gave those who were unfamiliar with the man and his outlook some reason to believe that the new Chancellor would not fulfil the hopes he had aroused. On 17 May 1933 he made a speech before the Reichstag which largely concealed his true intentions, though it presaged Germany's withdrawal from the League of Nations and touched on economic and military problems as well as the Reich's position vis-à-vis other countries. His opening words echoed those of several earlier Chancellors:[33]

For long centuries the countries of Europe and the demarcation of their frontiers arose out of views which belonged solely to the realm of exclusively national thinking. With the victorious emergence of the nationalist idea and the nationality principle in the course of the last century, states that owed their origins to other circumstances failed to take these new ideas and ideals into consideration, thus sowing the seeds of innumerable conflicts. After the end of the Great War a peace conference, once having clearly recognized this fact, could have set itself no loftier task than the reconstruction and reordering of the countries of Europe along lines that would do justice to every possible aspect of this principle. . . . A territorial reshaping of Europe that took the true national frontiers into account would have provided a historical solution which, at some time in the future, might have made the sacrifices of the Great War seem not altogether vain either to the victors or to the vanquished. . . . A fresh conflict in Europe could bring about no improvement in the unsatisfactory state of affairs that prevails today.

On the contrary, the use of force in Europe could in no circumstances produce a situation that was either politically or economically more favourable than that of today. Even if the use of force resulted in a decisive victory the outcome could only be a further disturbance of the European balance of power, and thus the seeds of fresh contradictions would be sown. . . . Further wars, further insecurity and further economic distress would follow. If such unbridled madness were to erupt it would mean the collapse of social and political order as we know it today. A Europe foundering in communist chaos would precipitate a crisis of unimaginable dimensions and incalculable duration. . . . Germany has disarmed. All the terms imposed upon her by the treaty have been fulfilled, and fulfilled far beyond the call of justice, if not beyond the call of reason. . . . Should all nations agree to a universal and international control of armaments, Germany would always be prepared to submit to inspection . . . in order that the whole world might have irrefutable proof of her wholly unmilitary character. . . . These demands do not imply rearmament but rather our desire that other countries should disarm. . . . The only nation having good reason to fear invasion is the German nation which has not only been denied offensive weapons but whose entitlement to weapons of defence has actually been curtailed, while the construction of frontier defences has been forbidden her. . . . Germany is concerned not with aggression but with security.[34]

For the first nine months Hitler trod warily, representing himself as a man of peace. To all appearances he had departed from the doctrines dictated by his *Weltanschauung* which was centred on the, to him, indivisible and causally related concepts of struggle, war, racial-ideological antisemitism and the extermination of 'inferior beings'. But this was no more than a cloak assumed for tactical reasons. Five years later, having lost some of his reticence, he admitted as much in a secret speech before an audience of newspaper editors and other Press representatives:

For decades [he told them], circumstances have compelled me to talk almost exclusively in terms of peace. Only by constantly stressing Germany's desire for peace was I able little by little to restore freedom to the German people and provide them with the armaments which were the necessary prerequisite for each successive step forward. Obviously... peace propaganda of this kind has its undesirable side; for it can all too easily happen that a lot of people get it firmly fixed in their heads that the present regime is synonymous with the determination and the desire to maintain peace at any price. ... It was only under compulsion that for so many years my talk has been wholly of peace.[35]

A study of Hitler's military and political decisions and actions from the late 1930s onwards reveals how crucially they were affected by his deteriorating health. He had once summed up his political credo in the following terms: 'Every being strives for expansion and every nation for world dominion. Only he who keeps his eyes fixed on this latter goal will take the right path.'[36] Convinced that he alone was capable of attaining that goal, and that he had little time left to live, he felt impelled to put into effect as many of his ideas and projects as possible before it was too late. During his early years in office, however, no such compulsion had existed, for his health had been reasonably good. At that time there was an undeniable similarity between his professed aims and those (little changed since Bismarck's day) of the traditional ruling class, which in both cases plainly reflected the foreign policy advocated by the militant right-wing opposition during the Wilhelmine and Weimar periods. The concept of power politics which had taken root in Germany in the nineteenth century envisaged a strong central European power under German leadership, an expansionist programme in the East, an overseas empire and the inevitability of military confrontations with other major powers. With Hitler's assumption of office these ideas had received considerable impetus. It has been wrongly supposed by a number of historians that there was something fundamentally new about the scope of Hitler's aims and his means of achieving them. But the actions with which he encumbered German politics were modelled on the inhuman antisemitic measures he knew to be a fact of his country's history, and which with presumptuous messianism and morbid hate he translated into the present. No aspect of his racial-ideological policy – neither warfare nor the extermination of the Jews, neither the aspiration to transform the entire German people by eugenic methods, nor the proposal to extend the dominion of his new ruling caste outside the bounds of Europe – was altogether foreign to German or Austrian history.

As can be shown from *Mein Kampf* and certain of Hitler's earlier assertions, he was convinced even then that the conquest of the *Lebensraum* he claimed as so essential would be fruitless unless the Jews were simultaneously and systematically exterminated, not only within the Reich but throughout the conquered territories. In accordance with the policies he had laid down as Führer and Chancellor, extermination orders went hand in hand with the crucial attacks on Poland in 1939 and Russia in 1941.[37] In *Mein Kampf* he had declared how much better it would have been if 'twelve or fifteen thousand of these Hebrew corrupters of the people had been held under poison gas'.[38] Again, on 30 January 1939, seven months before his invasion of Poland, he uttered the following threat: 'If international Jewish finance inside Europe and elsewhere succeeds in precipitating the nations into another world war, the result will not be victory for Jewry, but the destruction of the Jewish race in Europe.'[39] Simultaneously with the attack on Poland he unleashed, with one stroke of his pen, a campaign for the extermination of human beings still officially under the protection of the law he represented. For instance, under the aegis of the victorious German armies, thirty million Jews and Slavs were to be killed off, thereby making territory available for Germans.[40] Again, on 1 September 1939 he ordered Reichsleiter Bouhler and Dr Karl Brandt, one of his physicians, 'to extend the powers of specified doctors so that invalids who, so far as can humanly be judged, are incurably ill may be accorded a merciful death subject to a critical assessment of their condition'.[41] In this way more than fifty thousand human beings died between September 1939 and the summer of 1941, including not only invalids, mental cases, Jews, half Jews, 'persons with Jewish blood', and foreigners (mostly Poles and Russians), but also German nationals incapable of work and even German servicemen severely wounded in both world wars. These 'mercy killings' took place between September 1939 and the summer of 1941 at Hadamar, Brandenburg, Grafeneck, Hartheim, Sonnenstein and Bornburg.[42] Medical certificates and notifications to next-of-kin were unscrupulously forged and produced by the thousand in accordance with set formulas.[43] Few of Hitler's oldest comrades-in-arms had dared believe that he would ever put this political concept into practice and, when he came to do so, he succeeded in drawing such a veil of secrecy over the operation that it went almost unnoticed.[44] Neither party officials nor such high-ranking soldiers as Keitel learnt very much more than was already suspected by the inhabitants of the localities where euthanasia was daily practised. But despite all precautions rumours proliferated, to the harassment of party functionaries, public prosecutors and doctors who found themselves unable to shed any light on the subject.[45] Letters were received at the Ministry of Justice requesting that a stop be put to the illegal practice of euthanasia.[46] The head of Rudolf Hess's staff was made responsible for dealing with these protests[47] which, 'on instructions from Berlin', were to be treated as top secret and were not to be answered.[48] Moreover, public prosecutors were forbidden to pursue such cases.[49] On 19 December 1940 Himmler told Walter Buch, the Chief Justice of the NSDAP: 'If there's been a leak, it means someone's slipped up.'[50]

Though we cannot know how often Hitler asked for reports on the progress of the undertaking initiated by him on 1 September 1939, there is no doubt that he was fully alive to all its implications – the more so, perhaps because he was pressed by his ministers to put these 'mercy killings' on a legal footing. This he refused to do. The same reluctance to consider such problems in the light of traditional legality was to manifest itself yet again in the spring of 1942 when interdepartmental strife broke out between the Head of the Reich Chancery, the Minister of Justice and the Minister of the Interior on questions relating, for instance, to the sterilization and killing of Jews, and the dissolution of marriages between half-Jews and Germans. By now Hitler was under extreme mental and physical strain and believed himself to be mortally ill. Hence, though himself the highest judicial authority, he felt unable to do more than promise his ministers to resolve their differences when the war was over.

There is no foundation for the thesis recently put forward[51] to the effect that he also intended to postpone the extermination of the Jews until that time.[52] Not only had he ceased by then to believe in a victorious outcome to the war,[53] but he was concerned if anything to accelerate the process of genocide. On 15 August of that year, while inspecting various lethal devices in a Polish extermination camp under the expert guidance of Himmler and SS-Gruppenführer Odilo Globocnik, he remarked irritably that the killings were proceeding too slowly and that 'the whole operation must be speeded up, considerably speeded up'. When another member of the party suggested that for reasons of concealment it might be better 'to burn the corpses instead of burying them'[54] Globocnik, who shared Himmler's visions of 'racial hygiene' practised on a vast scale,[55] replied that later generations could hardly be 'so feeble and cowardly' as not to appreciate 'such good and necessary work'. He went on to suggest that they should also bury 'bronze plaques recording that it was us that had the courage to complete this gigantic task'. To this Hitler replied approvingly: 'Yes, my good Globocnik . . . I think you're perfectly right.'[56]

During this summer his health deteriorated still further as the result of a severe attack of influenzal encephalitis, and for the first time he complained of lapses of memory. Fearing that he had only a short time left to live, he became increasingly stubborn and fanatical. On 20 August, at his headquarters in Vinnitsa, he dictated a new decree conferring special powers on the Minister of Justice. It ran:

A strong judicial system is necessary for the fulfilment of the tasks facing the Greater German Reich. I therefore charge and empower the Reich Minister of Justice and Head of the Reich Chancery and the Director of the Party Chancery to institute a National Socialist judicial system conforming with my principles and directives and to take all steps necessary to that end. In doing so he may depart from the law as it stands.[57]

On 19 March 1934 Hitler declared: 'The victory of a party means a change of government, and the victory of a *Weltanschauung* means a revolution which effects an intrinsic and radical change in the condition of a people.'[58] From the very beginning he had adopted an unequivocally belligerent stance. The ruthlessness, for instance, with which he and his eight hundred S A men had smashed popular opposition in the streets of Coburg[59] in 1922 had seemed to presage an equal ruthlessness in the pursuit of the aims and ambitions so blatantly proclaimed two years later in *Mein Kampf*. Hence any apparent deviation from his declared course or any failure to declare his intentions sowed confusion not only among his adherents, but also among his critics who, whether out of righteous indignation, ignorance or intellectual arrogance, have always tended to denigrate his statesmanlike qualities. Thus Jacobsen writes:

In so far as there is any question of firm principles, we can only cite those of expediency, continental power politics, self-righteousness and ideological evangelism. For in his day-to-day policy Hitler relied very largely on improvization, experimentation and the inspiration of the moment, but opportunism also played its part. At the same time his ruthlessness, determination and drive were always in evidence, more especially where his personal interests were involved.[60]

In a later chapter Jacobsen goes on to say:

When it came to stabilizing and extending their power, the National Socialists refused, more or less on principle, to select any one method. For everything depended on what course was open to them in a given situation or in a given set of circumstances. This was not without consequences for those National Socialist leaders who were concerned with foreign policy . . . and here a fundamental question imposes itself: Was the National Socialist 'system' of foreign policy planned or haphazard, intentional or unintentional? In all likelihood a combination of both; there seems every indication that, despite his revolutionary élan and his indisputable achievements, the organization of foreign policy was something Hitler had failed to master either in breadth or in depth. Moreover his attitude was often one of laissez-faire . . . even though at home he might promote the principle of struggle: namely that, in the long run, it is the stronger who always prevails.[61]

Certainly there is much in Hitler's career that may appear conflicting, obscure or fortuitous. When in 1923, at the height of the inflation, French and Belgian troops occupied the Ruhr, his attitude bemused even his staunchest supporters in the NSDAP. For whereas the militant Right and the extreme Left suddenly found themselves prepared to make common cause by turning the passive resistance invoked by the Cuno government into active resistance, Hitler held aloof together with his party whose SA formations, some 6000 men strong, constituted the most powerful striking force at that time.[62] To the astonishment of his supporters he announced that any party member taking part in active resistance to the occupying forces would be expelled. Hardly anyone understood his intention or suspected the reason behind these tactics. Two years later he was to write in *Mein Kampf*:

Just as in 1918 we paid with our blood for the fact that in 1914 and 1915 we did not proceed to trample the head of the Marxist serpent once and for all, we would have to pay most catastrophically if in the spring of 1923 we did not avail ourselves of the opportunity to halt the activity of the Marxist traitors and murderers of the nation for good. . . . No more than a hyena abandons carrion does a Marxist abandon treason.[63]

In 1923 it was not in Hitler's interest to see all militant movements united in support of the government. His attitude led both Left and Right to conclude that he was in the pay of the French.[64] Even at this early stage he was putting personal success and the imposition of his own views before the welfare of the country. This decision belongs to the same category as his remark, much quoted after 1945, that if the German people failed to fight as he thought fit, they deserved to disappear from history.[65] The difference is merely one of degree.

When convinced that his goal was unattainable by direct means, Hitler was prepared not only to compromise but sometimes to act in a manner that seemed wholly out of keeping with his *Weltanschauung*, a particularly glaring example being his shortlived agreement with the Soviet Union.[66] Now, when wielded by a man who despises the broad masses and public opinion,* dictatorial powers can be exceptionally dangerous. Hitler demanded of the people, with whose history he constantly and publicly identified himself, that they should believe what he said and trust him to do what was best for them and for the Reich, in accordance with his better knowledge and his mission. Until the end of his life he was able to use the power of words to persuade his supporters that he was acting correctly, even though there was much that might seem to them wrong or obscure. He would point to his extraordinarily long run of good luck as proof that he had been singled out by Providence. Again, speaking of the staggering nerve which had enabled him to carry off the occupation of the Rhineland in 1936, he said: 'I go the way that Providence dictates with the assurance of a sleepwalker.'[67] He made skilful use of speeches and interviews as instruments of foreign policy and throughout his political career preferred the spoken to the written word.[68] The former came to be almost an 'authoritative pointer and major act of diplomacy; above all it served, both at home and abroad, as a paradigm and dialectical method for the initiation of exchanges with other countries'.[69] The fact that many of these utterances were incompatible with *Mein Kampf* was of small concern to Hitler, who consistently refused to rewrite passages which were thought by many to have become anachronistic. For instance, upon being asked by Bertrand de Jouvenel in February 1936 why, in the new editions of *Mein Kampf*, he did not amend the anti-French sentiments expressed in the book so as to conform with his present views, he replied: 'Are you suggesting that I should correct my book like an author who is bringing out a revised edition of his work? I'm a politician, not a writer. My corrections are made in my

* As *The Times* of 25 March 1939 aptly put it, his comments on the masses showed him to be as cynical as any writer of advertising copy.

foreign policy which is directed towards an understanding with France. . . . My corrections are made in the great book of history.'[70] It was, of course, unwise to set down in *Mein Kampf*, at the age of thirty-five and without diplomatic experience, what a seasoned politician would rather have chosen to conceal.[71] Once he had become a statesman he was no longer always prepared to make his plans and aspirations publicly known, lest he might have cause to regret his frankness. But it was not till the tide had turned against him that he came to believe that a politician 'should learn to speak without saying anything'.[72]

After his rise to power there was obviously much that was still outside his control. For instance he could hardly have changed overnight the existing diplomatic machinery, geared as it was to the Weimar Constitution and to the Republic's responsibilities at home and abroad. Hence, before he could become sole arbiter and impose his racial ideological ideas in the spheres both of domestic and of foreign policy, there was bound to be a period of tactical compromise which in turn might have seemed to imply a lack of purpose. On questions of foreign policy, for instance, the final say still rested with the President, the Chancellor, and the Foreign Minister, who for their part had to take into account the views of the Reichstag, the Foreign Affairs Committee, the political parties and the public. Even after Hindenburg's death Hitler, though now Führer and Chancellor, could not afford to ignore certain influential groups within the old ruling caste and elsewhere. This inevitably gave an appearance of discontinuity to his policy, the more so since he had failed to fulfil many of the pledges given before 1933. Hence the accusation by numerous old party members that he had betrayed the National Socialist idea. Nor were they alone in believing that Hitler might allow himself to be deflected from his own aims.

Indeed Hitler himself cannot be absolved from contributing to the confusion. 'The goal was broadly defined,' Jacobsen writes of National Socialist foreign policy, wrongly inferring that the individuals or groups responsible for its implementation were at pains to 'give concrete shape to what they severally believed to be the "Führer's" intentions.'

Admittedly [he continues] they did not know how, when and in what circumstances the goal, once defined, could be attained, but within . . . their various spheres of activity they each made their . . . partial contribution.

Embroiled in hierarchical squabbles, limited by compromises born of expediency and by the tactical considerations governing day-to-day politics, they engaged in unremitting activity. Not knowing what their neighbour was doing . . . or the exact nature of the goal the 'Führer' was presently pursuing, they did their individual best . . . as it were, to steal a march on history by anticipating the 'Führer's' intentions and to gain by their actions the dictator's trust and favour which in turn were necessary if they were to consolidate and extend their own power internally. This gave rise to the building of many a castle in Spain and to not a little wishful thinking. . . . But Hitler remained wholly unimpressed; all that counted in his eyes was success and the fact of having everyone under his control. . . . It would have been easy enough to put an end to the confusion by uttering a word *ex cathedra*, by making decisions that were less equivocal and by delimiting spheres of influence. But he took care not to do so.[73]

One of the first historians to recognize Hitler's singleness of purpose in putting his ideology into practice was H. R. Trevor-Roper who has said:*

This consistency, this purpose has often been denied. It was denied at the time by those, in Germany and abroad, who wished to disbelieve it: whether, like some Western statesmen, they feared to contemplate this hideous new power, or, like some German statesmen, they hoped to harness it to their own more limited aims; and it has been denied since by historians who are so revolted by Hitler's personal character, by the vulgarity and cruelty of his mind, that they refuse to allow him such virtues as mental power and consistency. But in fact I believe that all these denials are wrong. The statesmen were proved wrong by events. The historians, in my opinion (though they include some distinguished names among my own compatriots – Sir Lewis Namier, Alan Bullock, A. J. P. Taylor), err by confusing moral with intellectual judgements. That Hitler's mind was vulgar and cruel I readily agree; but vulgarity and cruelty are not incompatible with power and consistency.[74]

Though a continuous thread composed of several different strands runs through Hitler's political career, contradictions and obscurities are not lacking. The very inception of that career was hardly typical of a political début for, as he himself said, he first entered politics against his will. From *Mein Kampf* we learn that as a soldier during the war he felt no desire to 'politicize' and that his 'first purely political activity'[75] was the result of express orders from his military superiors.[76] This,

*Professor Trevor-Roper very kindly supplied the English version of the text. (Trans)

added to the fact that, despite his not altogether flattering view of the DAP,[77] he passively accepted his co-option into the party* in September 1919,[78] might suggest an inclination to leave important decisions affecting himself to others whose authority he would then exploit with unprincipled opportunism. But this impression is deceptive: Hitler never entered into any commitment unless 'Providence' pointed the way, or a given 'task' corresponded to his ideas and aims.

Only those unfamiliar with the course of his life could maintain that it was a completely new man who emerged on to the political scene in the autumn of 1919. No sooner had he been thus removed from the anonymity of field-grey into the sphere of politics than he began to strive for goals he had long held to be both right and feasible, although others might deprecate his means as untimely and his ends as impracticable. Having once set foot on the political stage at the instance of his military superiors he never turned back. For though he repeatedly declared that his one ambition was to become an artist and architect, it is clear that he was pre-eminently fitted to undertake the task entrusted to him. He became an adept at his trade and as well versed in intrigue as any party official, ruthlessly exploiting the weaknesses of his fellow-members and playing off the leaders each against the other in the best Machiavellian tradition. Hitler's exceptional political gifts were already manifest in the earliest days of his commitment to the party which, under his impetus, emerged from its Arcadian existence to become a political force in its own right. Having carefully laid his plans he believed himself strong enough by July 1921 to confront the party with two alternatives: either they accepted him as undisputed dictator or they dispensed with his services – which in the circumstances they obviously could not afford to do.[79] By 1921, with the backing of influential associates, he had already acquired the title of 'Führer' and during the next two years he was to lay the foundations of the 'Führer legend'.

While detained in Landsberg he found time to do more than simply prepare his political ideas for public consumption. After his early release, when seeking to pick up the threads of the first four years of his political activity, he decided to eschew the risk of a violent coup and declared that he would seek to achieve power by 'legal' means. For the time being he made full use of the liberties guaranteed by the con-

* As member no. 555; the party comprised only fifty-four other members, for the numbering started at 500.

stitution, in order systematically to destroy them, setting the letter of the law against its spirit. Despite all that he had previously said and written about the National Socialist movement, he put up candidates for the *Land* parliaments and the Reichstag – contemptuously described by him as 'yapping shops'. Few people, it would seem, realized that this move was designed solely for the purpose of accelerating his rise to power, although he and Goebbels among others had never made any secret of it. For instance on 30 April 1928 Goebbels wrote in his newspaper *Der Angriff*:

We enter the Reichstag, that arsenal of democracy, so as to help ourselves to its own weapons. We become Reichstag deputies in order to cripple the Weimar mentality with its own crutches. If democracy is stupid enough to provide us with free travel and attendance allowances in return for this work of demolition, that's its own affair. ... So long as it's legal we don't mind what means we use to revolutionize the present state of affairs. If in these elections we succeed in planting some sixty or seventy agitators from our party in the various parliaments, our fighting machine will thereafter be state-equipped and state-subsidized. ... No one should imagine that parliamentarianism will tame us. ... We come as enemies! As a wolf irrupts into a flock of sheep, so too will we. Now ye have strangers in your midst!

The threat did not go wholly unnoticed. As early as the spring of 1922 Bavarian politicians and Social Democrat Reichstag deputies were demanding that Hitler, then still an Austrian citizen, should be expelled from the country as an undesirable alien. But in March 1922 Erhard Auer, a Bavarian Social Democrat to whom Hitler was simply a 'comic figure', insisted so strongly on the democratic principle of freedom that the expulsion order was never issued.[80] Six years later Hitler was again theatened with prosecution and expulsion, first by the Prussian Minister of the Interior, Albert Grzesinski, and then by his successor, Carl Severing. The political section in Berlin Police Headquarters received orders to investigate the extent to which Hitler and his subordinates in the NSDAP had contravened the law. The investigation was conducted by three jurists belonging to the police department of the Prussian Ministry of the Interior, Drs Schoch, Stumm and R. M. W. Kempner. In their report, a copy of which was sent to the Ministry of Justice, they concluded that Hitler and some of his subordinates had been guilty of indictable offences and that proceedings should be instituted against them. However, no action was taken either then or later, despite Kempner's attempts to recall

Karl Werner, the Attorney General, to his duty by means of a
pseudonymous article in a legal periodical.[81] In the same year, at the
so-called Ulm Reichswehr trial, Hitler was even able to get away with
perjury when he testified on oath to the legality of the NSDAP.
The Attorney General finally closed the files against the National
Socialists on 7 August 1932, two weeks after von Papen's coup had
brought down the Prussian Social Democratic government and thus
virtually ensured Hitler's rise to power.[82]

Indeed in February of that year a major obstacle had already been
removed from his path. Since his renunciation of Austrian citizenship
in 1925 he had been stateless and as such ineligible for high political
office. The first attempt, early in 1932, by influential party members to
provide Hitler with an official post that would obviate this difficulty
was unsuccessful; his lack of schooling precluded his appointment as
professor extraordinary of 'organic political and social studies' at the
Technische Hochschule in Brunswick. Moreover it was feared that
there might be repercussions among the students.[83] Finally, on 25
February 1932 he was appointed attaché to the Brunswick legation
thereby automatically acquiring German citizenship.[84]

Unlike most politicians, to whom reality is a yardstick, Hitler was
largely concerned with bringing reality into line with his own *Weltanschauung*. He despised and never ceased to combat the Marxist view of
history, according to which the economic base determines the ideological superstructure, a theory he was at pains to prove untenable
by endeavouring to mould the world in accordance with his own
grossly unrealistic pattern – an endeavour in which he was not wholly
unsuccessful. Since this could be done only with the help of carefully
trained, antidemocratic cadres, he set about from the very start creating
the apparatus with which he hoped to be able to attain his ends. He
disciplined his party – as he was later to discipline the state – like a class
in a Prussian school in the days of the Soldier King. Every member
owed instant obedience to his superior's commands. There was no
show of hands, no consultation and no contradiction. The organization
of the party along military lines had begun in July 1921 when its committee had replied to Hitler's ultimatum with the words: 'In recognition of your vast knowledge, of your rare gift of oratory and of the
services you have rendered with rare self-sacrifice and in a purely
honorary capacity for the advancement of the movement, this com-

mittee hereby accords you dictatorial powers.'[85] Thereafter committees served a purely ornamental purpose,[86] and there were to be no more alliances or coalitions with partners who demanded equal rights.

The postwar period had seen the emergence of innumerable small factions whose attitude tended to be parochial and self-important. With these Hitler would have nothing to do, nor did he welcome the advances of larger groups and political parties. It was a policy from which he was never materially to depart. As early as March 1921, when not even leader of the party, and in opposition to the wishes of its first chairman Anton Drexler, he thwarted its union with the German Socialist Party, founded the previous year in Hanover. Basically anti-semitic like the NSDAP, this party was, in other respects, relatively democratic. Unlike the NSDAP it took part in the Reichstag elections of May 1920 and, again unlike the NSDAP whose activities were confined to Munich, it had local branches in Leipzig, Berlin, Bielefeld, Duisburg, Kiel, Wanne-Eickel, Munich, Nuremberg, Düsseldorf and elsewhere. It also collaborated with National Socialists in Austria and the Sudetenland. At the Salzburg Interstate Rally, at which National Socialists from all the German-speaking areas foregathered in August 1920, it was decided that the River Main should form the boundary between the two parties' spheres of influence.[87]

From his first days as a politician Hitler resolutely repudiated not only the entire Left and Centre but also the whole of the Right, including even such parties and factions as were prepared to fall into step with him. Both on principle and for tactical reasons he was against the incorporation of the NSDAP into the general framework of the extreme Right, which included groups such as secret societies, lodges and paramilitary organizations. No one knew better than he that the NSDAP could never become a mass movement unless his aims and methods gained full acceptance. Once he had become leader of the party he dictated unconditional terms for membership. He also put a stop to the assimilation of other organizations and, unlike his predecessors, refused to collaborate with the *deutschvölkish* movement.

Later he was to apply the same principles to Germany and Europe. As Buchheim has aptly put it:

Just as the party had once been an instrument completely at his disposal, so now the German Reich; just as his aim had then been revolution and his tactics legality and terrorism, so now he aimed at the domination of Europe and sought to corrupt his adversaries with assurances of peace mingled with the threat of force. Just as he had ruthessly used the common weal as a weapon against the Weimar Republic, so now he ruthlessly speculated on the common interests of the European comity of peoples and on the weaknesses and particular interests of individual nations; he felt no scruple about poisoning international relations by means of gross dishonesty, nor did he hesitate to keep Europe perpetually on the brink of war.

In this way, though he was able within a short space of time to achieve brilliant successes such as no democratic politician could have hoped to attain, he impeded the incipient stabilization of Europe and made all the world his foe. He had always fought shy of coalitions lest they restrict his freedom of action; in the field of foreign affairs this anxiety manifested itself in an avoidance of multilateral alliances, pacts and institutions which would oblige him to treat with several partners at once, and where every agreement reached would be guaranteed by a plurality of powers. Instead he preferred to deal with one partner at a time and to conclude bilateral treaties so that in their observation he would have only one contracting party to contend with.[88]

When measured against traditional power structures and modes of leadership, whether of nation or party, Hitler's methods evinced certain lacunae. In order to make good these deficiencies, he had been accustomed from the start to play on the ambitions of others, their guilty secrets or penchant for intrigue, and to exploit the inordinate craving for approval of his subordinates many of whom had been forcibly ejected from their 'petit bourgeois rut' in 1918. For instance he would be intentionally vague in defining the powers he delegated to others, taking care to share them out among men who were at odds with one another and who, for preference, had compromised themselves in the past. From the outset he proved adept at using blackmail as an instrument of leadership. History had taught him that men divided by rivalry and burdened, perhaps, with a guilty conscience – whether civil servants, party officials, generals or ministers – would never combine against their 'liege lord'. Rather, wholly at the mercy of his unlimited powers, they would hang upon his every word and obey his slightest whim. In much the same spirit Göring told his counsel in Nuremberg:

Wicked men, with a skeleton in their cupboards, are accommodating people, on the qui–vive for threats, for they know how it's done. You can demand anything of them because you know they'll stand for anything. . . . And you can hang 'em, if they step out of line. Let there be cunning rogues about me – always provided I have power of life and death over them.[89]

At the same time Hitler was invariably at pains to keep at his side men who had proved their worth, being of the opinion that unless he did so he would not be able to plan ahead. The political fruits of that policy – as apparent in his relations with, for instance, Göring, Rosenberg, Goebbels and Speer – show beyond doubt that he knew his men and usually found the right ones. Throughout this period and at least until 1939, though he might occasionally be balked by *force majeure*, he was always able to adhere to his basic aims. Since events over the years had, if anything, endorsed his *Weltanschauung*, it is small wonder that he believed all political issues to be dependent in the final analysis on his will alone. For he had early formed the opinion that his accession to power would immediately place in his hands the reins of foreign no less than of domestic policy. That opinion was not without consequence since, as we have already seen, the question of the primacy of foreign over home affairs was debated in Germany with more than academic interest. But in Hitler's view the recognition of the primacy of foreign policy as a determining factor in policy generally was never more than a passing phase of history. In 1938 he turned his back on it.

All his measures, whether the shooting of Röhm and a number of other SA leaders on 30 June 1934, the amalgamation of the offices of President and Chancellor on 2 August 1934, or the execution of the men and women of the Resistance, were invariably presented by National Socialist propaganda in a positive light as great historical deeds, a task made easier by the fact that the official version could be neither openly criticized nor in any way contested. In the earliest days of his association with the NSDAP Hitler had shown himself to be an agitator and propagandist of the first water and it was not for his *beaux yeux* alone that the party made itself his instrument and creature. Its unquestioning obedience helped to bring about many of the manifestations of National Socialist Germany;* the presentation, for instance, of propagandist clichés as incontrovertible facts, or the transmogrification of government agencies into the convinced and compliant tools of murderers and 'deceivers of the people'.

*Before the outbreak of war Hitler forbade the use of the term 'Third Reich'. Cf. R. Bollmus, *Das Amt Rosenberg und seine Gegner*, Stuttgart 1970, p. 326.

Never before had there been in Germany a ruling politician and statesman so dependent on propaganda as was Hitler from 1933 to 1945. But nor had any been confronted with the task of transforming themselves overnight (after years of unbridled agitation as a party leader ruthlessly and violently opposed to the *status quo*) into a statesman pledged to put into immediate effect earlier undertakings which by their very nature could be fulfilled only with difficulty if, indeed, at all. In the circumstances, rather than give himself the lie, Hitler was compelled to trim his policy to the needs of propaganda. It was a practice that was to have disastrous consequences during the Second World War in the fields of diplomacy and strategy alike.

Nevertheless his ability not only to win over the majority of the German people, but to lead them so completely astray, has no precedent in history. His confession at his trial that it was not out of modesty he had originally chosen to be 'a drummer',* than which there was 'nothing finer',[90] has been generally misconstrued. From the outset it was not only the masses that rallied to his banner. In her essay 'Hitler as Ideologist', Edith Eucken-Erdsieck writes:

There is no doubt that . . . educated people cooperated with little enthusiasm if not with profound reluctance. . . . Nevertheless, the fact remains that intellectuals did cooperate. . . . The ideology of National Socialism did not merely fill beer halls and public arenas with its thunder but studies with its fog. It gave birth to a hesitant enthusiasm of the kind that transports people across the threshold of a new era. Here the fascination permeating the Hitlerian ideology is clearly in evidence.[91]

Hitler knew 'his' people and the 'masses' he so detested. More than that, he despised them and said so openly and without circumspection – and still they applauded him. But obviously he could not rest content with applause, for his intention had always been not merely to dominate the people but completely to refashion and, indeed, recreate their minds anew along racial-ideological lines. This is of some significance in the context of the question whether his rule was totalitarian or authoritarian, a question which still remains open despite voluminous research on the subject of Fascism and the wealth of authenticated data on Hitler, his *Weltanschauung* and the National Socialist regime generally. For instance it has recently been put forward that the Nazi regime was an authoritarian system because Hitler's aim had not been

* In the sense of one who drums for recruits or partisans.

'revolution in the sense of a radical change in the social structure'.[92] The theory of Fascism advanced immediately after 1945 in the Western countries followed the official pattern in using the term as a general description of the systems of government obtaining in those countries which had fought against the democracies during the war, namely Germany, Italy and Japan. After the Nuremberg trials and the onset of the Cold War, Stalinism was also subsumed under this heading while Italian Fascism and the Horthy and Franco regimes were redesignated authoritarian, as distinct from fascist and hence totalitarian. With the appearance of a thaw in 1960, Italian Fascism came to be regarded as fully fledged totalitarianism having nationalism as one of its variants. In 1959 Martin Lipset interpreted Fascism in terms of class, describing it as the extremism of the middle classes and an inevitable manifestation of Western society, while in the countries of the Eastern bloc it had already been identified with imperialism. Not until after 1960 did the proponents of linguistic analysis gradually make their voices heard, and it was through them that Fascism came to be accepted as a field of study in its own right.[93]

Hitler, an orator of genius, always able to present abstractions in readily assimilable if oversimplified form, owed his political career in large measure to the power of propaganda. Indeed propaganda was one of the mainsprings of his policy from 1919 onwards. It was not without reason that Goebbels said in 1935: 'What would have become of this movement without propaganda? And what would become of this state were it not for the truly creative propaganda which today still provides it with an intellectual face?'[94] The importance Hitler attached to propaganda is already discernible in certain statements in which hypothesis and fact are treated as one. For instance in *Mein Kampf* he professes the conviction that Germany only lost the war of 1918 because of the failure of German propaganda. And again, though Germany's military defeat had been publicly conceded by Hindenburg and Ludendorff, two of the most popular commanders of the First World War, Hitler simply chose to ignore it and to present his own version couched in propagandist terms. He knew that if, as a politician, he was to succeed in putting across his own view of life he must, as he himself expressed it, 'encroach . . . on man's freedom of will',[95] the more so since the war had been lost. His statement that propaganda is 'a means and must be judged with regard to its end'[96] provides a clue to his belief that with its aid he would be able to stand facts on their

head and achieve the virtually unattainable. Such aims naturally precluded 'the scientific training of the individual', he wrote in *Mein
Kampf*. Rather, its function lay 'in calling the masses' attention to
certain facts, processes, necessities, etc., whose significance is thus for
the first time placed within their field of vision'.[97] He believed that
political propaganda left no room for either aesthetic or humane considerations since its function was 'not to make an objective study of
the truth . . . and then set it before the masses with academic fairness,'
but to concentrate on the task in hand.[98] Hence in his view it was
'absolutely wrong' to discuss 'war guilt' as though Germany alone
were 'responsible for the outbreak of the catastrophe';[99] on the contrary 'it would have been correct to load every bit of blame on the
shoulders of the enemy'.[100] Fundamentally it was immaterial to him
whether or not his pronouncements accorded with the facts. He
wished to eliminate from political propaganda all qualified statements
and prevarications since these give rise to doubt and the drawing of
undesirable comparisons. He was firmly convinced that he must
address and treat the masses in accordance with the lessons he had
learnt from Le Bon, namely that a crowd feels neither doubt nor
uncertainty, nor any real concern about truth; it reacts in extreme
ways and is not receptive to logical argument.[101] Hence in Hitler's view
propaganda comprised only 'a positive and a negative; love or hate,
right or wrong, truth or lie, never half one thing and half the other'.[102]
Variations on a theme must not be made a pretext for differentiation,
but 'in the end must always say the same thing. For instance, a slogan
must be presented from different angles, but the end of all remarks
must always and immutably be the slogan itself.'[103]

Both Le Bon and McDougall agree that political propaganda must
be simple. Hitler accordingly assigned it the task of 'always and
exclusively' addressing itself to the masses whom he believed to be
fundamentally incapable of discerning 'where foreign injustice ends
and our own begins'.[104] Le Bon held firstly, that intellectual performance, unlike affectivity, is inhibited by the collective and, secondly,
that an individual becomes an automaton as soon as he is absorbed
into the crowd, an instinctual being without personal values, imbued
with primitive feelings of heroism and easily incited to action. Given an
eloquent political leader whose personality commands the masses,
such an individual can be hypnotized to the extent of believing himself
invincible.[105] He becomes a barbarian thinking only in images, easily

swayed by example and receptive to simple repetition and hyperbole. At the same time he has no objective sense of justice or any feelings of responsibility.[106] All this is reflected in *Mein Kampf*. Where Le Bon states that in the masses there is very little conscious intellectual life by comparison with unconscious emotional life,[107] Hitler, in slightly different form, declares: 'The receptivity of the great masses is very limited, their intelligence is small, but their power of forgetting is enormous.'[108] Again drawing on Le Bon he concludes that in practical politics 'all effective propaganda must be limited to a very few points and must harp on these' until every one of those present has absorbed the message. Any departure from this principle or attempt at diversification will so impair the effect that the crowd will neither digest nor retain what has been presented to it and thus 'the result is ... entirely cancelled out'.[109] As for 'the intelligentsia,' he writes sarcastically, '– or those who today unfortunately often go by that name – what they need is not propaganda but scientific instruction. The content of propaganda is not science any more than the object represented in a poster is art.'[110]

Since it was Hitler's aim to unleash a political mass movement he recognized that propaganda must be popular and its intellectual level 'adjusted to the most limited intelligence among those it is addressed to'.[111] But the larger the crowd – and hence the more important the goal – the lower the purely intellectual level of the propaganda must be, for its effect depends on its being addressed almost exclusively to the emotions of the crowd.[112] And this all the more since 'the people in their overwhelming majority are so feminine by nature and attitude that sober reasoning determines their thoughts and actions far less than emotion and feeling'.[113] It was in accordance with this view that Hitler surrounded his public appearances with paraphernalia specifically calculated to play on the emotions: banners, drum rolls, ingenious lighting effects, the walk to the rostrum through expectant crowds, the anthem.

As the fundamental principle of propaganda he lays down that 'it must confine itself to a few points and repeat them over and over. Here, as so often in the world, persistence is the first and most important requirement of success.'[114] Hitler was convinced of the significance of history and it is tempting to attribute to this the impatience sometimes so disturbingly manifest in his speeches. But that would be wrong; for the driving force behind his increasingly hectic political activity after 1937 was not the fear that he had missed his cue, but rather the conviction that he would not live long enough to complete the task set him by history and his *Weltanschauung*. For some twenty years he had shown his ability to bide his time if tactical considerations demanded it – in 1919, for instance, under Soviet rule in Munich, in 1921 when preparing to assume leadership of the NSDAP, in August 1932 when offered the position of Vice-Chancellor, and in the weeks preceding the Röhm putsch in 1934. But once he had come to believe himself a sick man, that ability left him. The sense of urgency thus induced caused him to draw up his political testament in November 1937, and his private testament some six months later. Thereafter, to the concern of his doctor and immediate entourage, his impatience became ever more marked. It first obtruded on foreign affairs during the Sudeten crisis when Chamberlain and Mussolini successfully prevented him from marching against Czechoslovakia, and was to manifest itself in even more alarming form at the height of the Polish crisis in 1939 when he expressed anxiety lest 'some fellow come along' and prevent him embarking on his first Blitzkrieg. From that time on his sense of urgency was exacerbated not only by his steadily deteriorating health but by the knowledge that the means at his disposal were not adequate to the fulfilment of his aims. True, he had occupied France, but Britain, under a premier determined to continue the war against Nazi Germany, still held out, Franco resisted his attempts to involve Spain in the war, Japan remained outside his sphere of influence and Russia showed no inclination to comply with the request made to Molotov in November 1940 that she should stir up trouble for the British in southern Asia. Hitler's change of personality was coincident with the progress of the Russian campaign launched in June 1941 under the code name Barbarossa, a campaign that proved to be anything but the Blitzkrieg he had anticipated. Thus the peace of mind for which he had hoped, and continued to hope until 1942, was denied him by the course of events.

Having passed the zenith of his career and knowing that he would not emerge victorious from the conflict, Hitler voiced the opinion that politicians should be judged by their positive attributes and achievements alone,[115] and should show as much courage in their own sphere as a soldier in the face of the enemy,[116] while the pessimists among them should be eliminiated.[117] Though he constantly harped on his wide political experience, he did not consider such experience essential to a statesman[118] nor, despite his own constant preoccupation with history, did he think a politician should meditate on, or endeavour to fulfil retrospectively, the decisions of the past,[119] or allow himself to be unduly influenced by historical precedents. And yet he prided himself on his historical knowledge and the prescience gained therefrom which, he believed, entitled him to plan his policy on a grand scale. Thus on 9 April 1942 he declared: 'If . . . the battle on the Catalaunian plains had not ended in the Romans' victory over the Huns, the flowering of western culture would never have happened, and the civilized world of the time would have suffered the fate held in store for us today by the Soviet Union.'[120] He clearly had himself in mind when he maintained that the ideal politician must be hard, bold, optimistic and tough.[121] The same does not apply to his remark that statesmen should not be overendowed either with experience[122] or knowledge.[123] He considered that, at moments of crisis, too close an acquaintance with unfortunate precedents might inhibit a politician's power of decision so that he would be far more likely to go to pieces than one who was less well informed.[124] Hence he was unwilling to confer high political office on men whose outstanding intellect would induce a critical attitude towards public affairs, for he believed that they would be too cautious and meticulous to fulfil their function adequately.[125] After 1942 he was accustomed to describe as 'wrongly programmed' those politicians who gave such undue weight to the little word 'if' that it paralysed their powers of decision.[126] Yet, as a strategist and military leader, his own decisions were not infrequently swayed by this same little word – so much so, indeed that a number of his generals later held it responsible for at least some of their country's setbacks and defeats. But this was not the least of Hitler's inconsistencies. In *Mein Kampf*, for instance, he had declared that a 'decent' politician must give up his political career, should he ever feel impelled to 'depart from the platform of his general philosophy . . . because he recognizes it to be false'.[127] Once he had acquired unlimited powers of life and death over his people, there would have been little chance of survival for anyone who had dared to invoke those words. Again in *Mein Kampf* he wrote: 'In an hour when a national body is visibly collapsing and to all appearances is exposed to the gravest oppression, thanks to the activity of a few scoundrels, obedience and fulfilment of duty towards them amount to doctrinaire formalism, in fact pure insanity.'[128] On 20 July 1944 a few men took action in the spirit of the foregoing passage and of the promises Hitler had uttered in 1933. Their attempt on his life failed. That night he described them as 'a small clique of ambitious, unscrupulous and criminally stupid officers . . .'.[129]

In the same way as before his accession to power, Hitler identified himself with the Reich – or rather the Reich with himself – whenever he spoke of 'Germany', so after that date he disregarded the will of the people despite the solemn pledges he had made. Thus on 10 February 1933 he had declared: 'People of Germany. . . . In office I shall follow the same path by which I entered it.'[130] Two weeks later he informed the German people that they 'must weigh, decide and judge and, should they conclude that I have failed in my duty, they are perfectly at liberty to crucify me'.[131] And, speaking at the Sportpalast the following November, he announced: 'If ever I go astray, or if ever the people believe they cannot endorse my actions, then they may execute me: I will face the music.'[132] Yet not once during the period of his resounding diplomatic and military setbacks did he ever consider honouring his promise. It would be otiose to speculate whether he might have done so had he not been a sick man whose personality had been severely warped by his physical condition. Whatever complexion his propagandists might try to put upon the country's plight they were powerless to alter the facts. By 1942 it had become difficult to believe in a German victory and, after 1944, impossible. Early in that year the Russians crossed what had once been Poland's eastern frontier. In April they reached the Romanian border. In June the German armed forces broke before their massed attacks. In July Vilna, Minsk, Pinsk, Grodno, Bialystok and Dvinsk fell to the Red Army. German divisions stationed in the Baltic states were in danger of being cut off as the Russians advanced towards the East Prussian border. German cities, villages, roads and railways were under almost constant air attack. In March 1944 the Americans carried out their first daylight raid on Berlin. In May the German troops in Italy were compelled to retreat. On 4 June the Allies entered Rome. Two days later the Allied landings in Normandy set the seal on Germany's fate.

Others besides Buchheim have held that, even after he had come to power, Hitler's outlook remained essentially 'Bohemian' and that he 'detested the discipline of day-to-day government business', doing his best to 'dodge his share of administrative chores'.[133] That this view is unfounded is evident from his regimen between 1939 and 1945, when he imposed upon himself a rigorous and exhausting discipline, often under conditions of considerable discomfort. It was neither 'inveterate bohemianism' nor self-indulgence that made him reluctant to tackle essential administrative questions and led him to adopt so cavalier an attitude towards certain aspects of political business. Rather it was the belief – for which he advanced a variety of reasons – that a statesman of his calibre was not really concerned with mastering the minutiae of routine political problems. But since he exercised jurisdiction over virtually every aspect of political life, his neglect of, for example, administrative and financial matters, was apt to have unfortunate repercussions, especially during the war when he was wholly preoccupied with the conduct of hostilities. Indeed so glaringly evident did this become that in 1943 Goebbels wrote in his diary: 'We are concerned too much with the conduct of the war and too little with politics. In the present situation, when our military successes have not been exactly thick on the ground, it might be a good thing if we tried to make better use of politics as an instrument.'[134] Now military historians from Polybius onwards have always emphasized the importance of politics in war. But Hitler chose to ignore this vital factor on ideological grounds for, unlike Bismarck, he did not regard war as a continuation of politics by other means, but rather as a necessary and historically vital step towards the realization of his *Weltanschauung*. Typical of this shift of emphasis is the remark he made on 4 May 1942 that Germany's war debts would present no real problem in view of the additional territory she would be acquiring,[135] – and this despite the alarming rise in the national debt since 1933.[136] Hitler stood reality on its head, insisting that the time was not ripe for a political solution. He argued, realistically enough from his own point of view, that the long series of military reverses precluded his paying any attention to politics.

True to his forecast in *Mein Kampf*, Hitler never abandoned his *Weltanschauung* or those categories of political thought with which he had identified as a solitary and eccentric youth. Now, a politician cannot be censured for seeking power which is, after all, the inevitable corollary of politics. And power once achieved cannot be retained unless it produces results. To achieve that end Hitler pursued a policy both at home and abroad that was based on the threat of force. Blind to the claims of humanity, he systematically abused the power he had gained, extending it beyond the limits of legality in order not only to impose his ideology, but also to obtain the tactical freedom that would enable him to repudiate obligations he would otherwise have had to honour. Moreover his appetite for power, morbidly stimulated by disease, became so insatiable that he finally concentrated into his own hands more of it than he was able to consolidate. An inevitable and disastrous result of that policy was his inability to place on a relatively stable and enduring footing either what he had inherited or what he subsequently achieved. Thus in the final analysis his political and military victories inevitably proved illusory and hence destructive of the very substance that had made them possible – a process aggravated by his unremitting attempts to find objectives for the propaganda machine upon which he placed such undue reliance.

CHAPTER NINE

The Strategist and Warlord

On 3 February 1933, four days after he had been appointed Chancellor, Hitler told the Reichswehr commanders: 'The most dangerous period will be during the reconstruction of the armed forces. Then we shall see whether or not France possesses any statesmen; if she does she'll give us no time and fall on us instead.'[1] Unlike Konstantin von Neurath and Werner von Blomberg,[2] who were advocates of overt rearmament, he remained unforthcoming on this subject up till September 1933, though on principle already prepared to assume the role of strategist and military commander. For his political success prior to 1933, the power this had brought him, and his belief not only in the rightness of his programme but in his own talents, knowledge and intuition had led him to envisage the possibility of one day trying his hand in the military field also. When war broke out in September 1939, he was by no means unprepared, a fact which right up to the end he continued to invoke as proof of his resourcefulness when in a tight corner. Hence he felt both entitled and empowered to make demands and to implement them if necessary by force.

Within a period of six years and six months he had passed the Enabling Act, the first of the measures that were to make life a hell on earth for Jews living in the territories of the Reich (24 March 1933),[3] abolished the trade unions (2 May 1933), forced the 'voluntary' dissolution of the political parties (June/July 1933), concluded the Concordat between the Reich and the Holy See (22 July 1933), promulgated the law 'concerning the reconstruction of the Reich' (30 January 1934), settled, in the Reichswehr's favour, the claims made against it by the SA leadership (30 June 1934), appointed himself Führer and Reich Chancellor (2 August 1934), and required the armed forces to swear an oath of allegiance to 'Adolf Hitler, the leader of the German people and the German Reich'.[4] At the Saarland referendum of 13 January 1935 he had won for himself and the Reich 91 per cent of the votes, having already secured 90 per cent of the poll at the plebiscite held on 19 August of the previous year (he counted

among his battle honours the decision of the League of Nations Council to return the Saarland to Germany). On 16 March 1935 he had
introduced compulsory military service and on 7 March 1936 estab-
ished full military sovereignty by occupying the demilitarized zone of
the Rhineland. Between March and October 1938 he had brought
Austria and the Sudetenland 'back into the fold', and in March of the
following year had occupied Bohemia and Moravia and established
the Reich Protectorate.

In the early years after his assumption of power he had constantly
declared his desire for peace and, even in 1939, was regarded by his
troops solely as a great statesman and politician possessed of a magic
touch, never as a strategist or military commander – titles to which,
indeed, he had as yet laid no public claim. The German soldiers who
fought in the Polish campaign did so in fact with little enthusiasm, yet
by far the greater majority took it for granted that anything which
furthered Adolf Hitler's interests must be defended with life and limb.
Jodl's words were no more than partially true when he told the International Military Tribunal at Nuremberg that in 1939 the military
leaders, and with them the whole of the Wehrmacht, had been confronted with an insoluble problem, 'namely how to conduct a war they
did not want under a Supreme Commander whose trust they did not
enjoy and whom they themselves trusted only to a limited extent'.[5]

Six years and six months prior to September 1939 there had been
no autobahns, no marriage grants or child allowances, no tours sponsored by *Kraft durch Freude*, no really favourable opportunities for
aspiring farmers. There had been no Adolf Hitler schools, or National-
Political Education Centres, or pre-military training for the young, no
Arbeitsdienst or 'reconciliation of the social classes'. Nor had there
been a Greater German Reich, a (pervertedly) proud national consciousness among the people, nor yet food and work for everyone. To
many all this spelt 'National Socialism', the achievement of one man
alone, Adolf Hitler. The troops – and the vast majority of their
generals – believed Hitler[6] when on 1 September 1939 he declared:
'The Polish state has rejected the peaceful settlement of neighbourly
relations for which I have been striving. Instead it has had recourse to
arms.'[7] Not once did they learn from him personally how matters
really stood, for as military commander and strategist no less than as
politician Hitler remained an opportunist where propaganda was concerned. As early as 1938 advocates of the 'liberal-imperialist' course[8]

and those who adhered to the conventional policy of a single German centre of power in the heart of Europe, had been removed from positions of responsibility, the opinions of eminent experts in foreign policy and military matters had been disregarded and German foreign policy had been purged of its dualism. Nor did he tell them in so many words – though he had proclaimed it plainly enough both in *Mein Kampf* and in innumerable public pronouncements – that his intention was the gradual expansion of German territory in Europe, initially by peaceful 'political' measures and, when no more such opportunities existed, by localized Blitzkriegs against one opponent at a time. Furthermore they could not have known that, contrary to his intention expressed in *Mein Kampf* of acquiring colonies in Africa, he was proposing to place the German economy on a war footing in preparation for a second 'world war' whereby the Reich would be forcibly transformed into a world power along racial-ideological lines.[9] In more than twenty years of experience he had learnt on occasion to disregard sober reality in favour of ideologically slanted dissimulation, and he would either lie or remain silent when circumstances demanded the outspoken truth. Thus during the course of the war he himself had started (earlier than planned and not entirely in accordance with his 'programme') he assigned the blame for it to others, to the Poles, the Jews, the Italians, the British, and the 1914–18 generation of Germans.[10] On 19 September 1939, three weeks after he had assured Sir Nevile Henderson, the British Ambassador, that the British offer to mediate in the dispute between the Poles and the Reich was acceptable and that he would be prepared to receive a Polish plenipotentiary in Berlin on 30 August, he declared: 'In what frame of mind the Polish government rejected these proposals, I do not know. . . . Poland's reply was . . . mobilization. Simultaneously a savage reign of terror began. My request that the Polish Foreign Minister visit me in Berlin to re-examine these questions was refused. He travelled not to Berlin but to London!'[11] What Hitler did not divulge, however, was the fact that his conclusion of an agreement with Russia on 23 August 1939 – regarded by the Japanese as a violation of the Anti-Comintern Pact – had preceded by two days the conclusion of the Anglo–Polish Mutal Assistance Pact.[12] On 21 March 1943 shortly after the catastrophic defeat at Stalingrad, he said: 'We were forced into a pitiless and merciless war by wandering Jewry.'[13] And on 29 April 1945, he wrote in his political testament: 'The war was willed and instigated exclusively by those international statesmen who were either of Jewish origin or working for Jewish interests.'[14] On 18 December 1940, some eight weeks after the occupation of Romania and four months after the conclusion of the Tripartite Pact with Italy and Japan which he himself had initiated, he charged Italy with responsibility for the war on the grounds that she had remained neutral in 1939 and thereby weakened his position between 1939 and 1940 in terms of the balance of power in Europe. 'Had Italy declared her solidarity with Germany [in 1939]', he surmised in 1940, 'war would never have broken out, for the British would have done nothing and the French would have done nothing.'[15] In February 1945, however, he was to confess that 'the alliance with Italy has clearly been of greater use to the enemy than to ourselves'.[16]

Up till the late autumn of 1941 the course taken by the war in Europe[17] had exceeded everyone's wildest expectations with the result that Hitler, along with a number of eminent officers, became convinced that he was a warlord and strategist of rare and outstanding ability. Field-Marshal von Rundstedt regarded him as such, at least during the initial phase of the war, as did General Jodl and Admiral Dönitz[18] who may even have continued to hold this view after the events in Stalingrad, Tripoli and North Africa. Both Field-Marshal von Kluge[19] and Field-Marshal Keitel hailed him as a military genius. In 1946 Keitel declared that the Führer had been 'so well-informed concerning organization, armament, leadership and equipment of all armies and . . . all navies of the globe, that it was impossible to prove any error on his part . . . even in the simple, everyday questions concerning organization and equipment of the Wehrmacht. . . . I must admit openly that I was the pupil and not the master.'[20] Major-General Walter Scherff, who liked to describe himself as the 'Führer's historian', saw Hitler as 'the greatest military commander and head of state of all time', a view which instilled in him the desire to immortalize the Führer in the war diary as a 'leader of armies, a strategist and a man to inspire unshakeable confidence'.[21]

But in view of the course taken by the war, its final outcome and the inevitable commitment of the chroniclers and 'assessors', these opinions cannot really be recognized as possessing universal validity, the more so since the concept of strategy as defined by Clausewitz, that is, the 'use of the battle to further the war,[22] has undergone a fundamental change. In terms of the war waged by Hitler this interpretation was already outmoded. Nor is the later definition of the words – a definition of Anglo-Saxon parentage – comprehensive enough to describe a sphere in which, as Andreas Hillgruber has so neatly put it, politics and warfare overlap.[23] In 1946, when discussing Hitler's concepts, Alfred Jodl, chief of the Operations Staff of the Wehrmacht, said: 'Strategy is the supreme leadership activity in warfare. It comprehends foreign and domestic policy, military operations and economic mobilization, propaganda and popular leadership, and must harmonize these vital aspects of the war effort in terms of the purposes and the political goal of the war.'[24] In such a context it is obvious that the terms military commander and strategist can no longer be synonymous, for it was not the field marshals and generals of the Second World War who were the strategists, but rather the supreme heads of state, the dictators wielding absolute power – Hitler in Germany, and Stalin in the Soviet Union. The military did no more than conduct operations in accordance with the directives of these men. Not only was Hitler statutory head of state and Supreme Commander of the Wehrmacht; after 1941 he was also in direct command of the army and, to all intents and purposes, sole leader of Germany's co-belligerents. His command of the Wehrmacht and his conduct of the war, whose every aspect, economic, military and political, he had himself minutely planned, were wholly consistent with his talents, personality and intellect – which is not to say, of course, that he possessed the prerequisites essential to a strategist and warlord.

During the Second World War the majority of senior officers in Germany never succeeded in reconciling themselves to the radical change that had come about in their profession, nor have they done so since, as is evident from a number of the books they have written on the subject in the postwar years. Even so eminent a soldier as Field Marshal von Manstein, in his expressively titled *Lost Victories*, declares not without bitterness:

In my opinion everything depended . . . on persuading Hitler . . . to leave the conduct of military operations in all theatres of war to *one* responsible Chief-of-Staff and to appoint a special Commander-in-Chief for the Eastern theatre. These attempts of mine . . . unfortunately proved unavailing. . . . Hitler knew full well that I was the very man many people in the army would like to see in the position of a proper Chief-of-Staff or as Commander-in-Chief in the East.[25]

There is a good deal of truth in Bezymenski's thesis that 'postwar writings have a strong tendency to attribute every defeat ... to the Führer's decisions and every victory to the O K W or the O KH.'[26] The ideological bias inherent in the works of Russian soldiers and historians in no way invalidates their view that 'a sorry figure was cut' by the German generals who, after serving Hitler for twelve years, inveighed against him after his death, decried his military decisions as fundamentally those of a dilettante, blamed him for the defeats, and maintained that the war would probably have ended quite differently had they and not he been responsible for its prosecution. The fact that Hitler's achievements in the fields of strategy and operations were very real provides further justification for the Russians' view.

In Germany historical research into the Second World War[27] is not, as in Anglo-Saxon countries,[28] generally acknowledged by scholars to be a field of study in its own right and most historians of note are reluctant to turn their attention to military history. Hence the gaps in this field are so large (not least because of lack of agreement on the definition of terms) that it would be presumptuous, in the space of a single chapter, to hope to give anything more than a disjointed account of Hitler's wartime role. This part of the book can only aim at presenting what, to a biographer, is an aspect of the utmost significance, namely the fact that during the War Hitler underwent a profound change as a result of illness, and that from 1942 onwards he came less and less to resemble the man who had ordered the attack on Poland in 1939. It is an aspect neglected by a number of historians whose view of the Führer in their studies of Hitler and the Second World War tends to be influenced by preconceived ideas.[29]

At the outbreak of war he was no longer in particularly good shape either mentally or physically. He had already passed his prime when he realized that he was still not adequately equipped, either from a military or an economic standpoint, to undertake even a localized minor campaign. It has frequently been argued that he intended to go to war in 1938 and that this was the sole reason why he drew up his private testament on 2 May of that year and put his papers in order for posterity. The argument has no factual basis. In 1938 no one knew better than he that it would be a long time before the Wehrmacht became a truly consummate instrument of battle, nor did he yet intend to embark on the next stage of his hitherto successful 'world power programme'. As one whose prognostication (on 5 November 1937)[30] of developments in Europe between 1938 and 1941 turned out to be more accurate than that of any other European statesman, Stalin not excepted,[31] he was still of the opinion in 1939 that such a step would be premature. When his Blitzkrieg in September 1939 sparked off the European conflict, he was convinced that the war had been thrust upon him. He argued firstly that he had not yet begun to think in terms of war with France and, secondly, that he had no intention whatsoever of waging war against Great Britain whose policy since the seizure of Prague had led him to hope that he would be permitted to subdue Poland[32] with impunity by means of a localized campaign. Hitler drew up his testament in 1938, not because he intended to go to war, but because he believed his health to be in a very much poorer state than did his personal physician.

There can be little doubt that even as early as 1939 a great many Germans would have hesitated to dedicate themselves to the Führer's cause had they known about the state of his health, his personality or structure and the general lines along which his character was developing.

Now, according to Clausewitz, military genius demands outstanding qualities, of which the first is courage both in meeting personal danger and in accepting responsibility, whether imposed by an external agency or by the dictates of conscience. It further requires the cultivation of mental as well as physical powers of endurance, which in turn presuppose a strong constitution. Finally Clausewitz postulates strength of mind balanced by judgement, inexhaustible energy, perseverance, tenacity and firmness of character as attributes indispensable in a distinguished military commander[33] who, however, need not attain equal excellence in every one of them.[34] Hitler was fond of citing these dicta and, from 1940 onwards, expected his generals, for whom he had scant respect, to regard him as a military genius.[35] Indeed, despite certain failings, he more than fulfilled a number of Clausewitz's criteria. Intellectually he had no need to defer to the field marshals and generals of the Second World War. And his powers of judgement no less than his courage, tenacity, energy and perseverance were exceptional. As he himself put it on 20 May 1943, he had a 'good nose' in strategic matters so that he could usually 'smell things out in advance'.[36] Moreover, being possessed of a keen intuition he could, as often as not, immediately detect an adversary's weaknesses and in most cases he knew far better than the soldiers when and where to exploit a situation.[37]

For years past he had been imposing his will on his subordinates in the party and on the ministers in his government, and he now adopted the same authoritarian approach towards the tradition-conscious military. The relatively ill-informed soldiers were no more capable of standing up to him than were the leading members of the civilian aristocracy and the middle classes. Jodl threw some light on this aspect at Nuremberg: 'Hitler was a leader to an exceptional degree. His knowledge and intellect, his rhetoric and his will-power triumphed in the end in every spiritual conflict over everyone.'[38] So powerful was his charisma, even in the final stages of the war, that disillusioned generals, having at last made up their minds to renounce their allegiance, found themselves unable to break with him. Eberhard von Breitenbuch, Field-Marshal Busch's aide-de-camp, tells us that in March 1945 the angry and exhausted field-marshal had travelled to Berlin, still in his battle-stained uniform, in order finally 'to speak his mind' to the Führer. When at last he emerged from the interview he seemed transformed and confident of final victory.[39] This highly experienced soldier, fresh from the front, who an hour before had been able to see the situation in its true light, was now utterly convinced of the 'rightness' of Hitler's arguments and actions though by that time these were little more than manifestations of grossly unrealistic wishful thinking.

In many important respects, however, the Führer's character fell markedly short of the criteria set by Clausewitz for 'military genius', particularly as regards an 'harmonious balance of characteristics'. Thus Hitler, whose contempt for human existence was rooted in his *Weltanschauung*, could fascinate his adherents to an almost incredible degree yet shun all human relationships, and this so thoroughly that by 1945 there was no one who could claim to be his friend.

His grasp of technology was remarkable, as Jodl testified in the following passage from his statement dictated in Nuremberg prison:

Hitler . . . created the Ministry for Weapons and Munitions under Todt, leaving only the building of airplanes and ships with the air force and navy. From then on Hitler determined the monthly quota as well as the direction and scope of all production of weapons and munitions down to the last detail. All the Operations Staff [of the High Command of the Wehrmacht] had to do was to give him the exact figures, inventory, utilization and production during the previous month. But beyond this, Hitler's astounding technical and tactical vision led him also to become the creator of modern weaponry for the army. It was due to him personally that the 75-mm anti-tank gun replaced the 37-mm and 50-mm guns in time, and that the short guns mounted on the tanks were replaced with the long 75-mm and 88-mm guns. The *Panther*, the *Tiger*, and the *Königstiger* [i.e. *Tiger II*] were developed as modern tanks at Hitler's own initiative.[40]

But though he combined the ability to procure the best weapons at the right time with a particular interest in innovations provided these did not conflict with his ideas, he closed his mind to other innovations that were both useful and comparatively easy to assimilate. Again, he would champion ideas which, if one considers his remarkable intellectual powers, can only appear unbelievably crude. And, while his tenacity could be unwavering in trivial matters, he would sometimes vacillate incomprehensibly where important issues were concerned. It can now be conclusively shown that his intransigence and obstinacy were the after-effects of disease, as were his intolerance, mistrust and persistent refusal to listen to advice – attitudes which overshadowed and, to some extent, neutralized his outstanding qualities as a military leader.

According to Hitler it was his vegetarian regime that enabled him, despite his serious ailments, to achieve his astounding wartime feats of mental and physical endurance and to act as the driving force of the gigantic military machine[41] (although it might be added that his success in this respect was qualified by a tendency to interfere unnecessarily). Dr Giesing, however, disagrees with the Führer's contention. He writes:

The facts do not really bear this out. Before his assumption of power he must have been . . . more efficient. According to the information supplied by Schaub and Linge Hitler particularly enjoyed (up to 1932) fatty pork . . . and even took animal protein for breakfast. . . . If, despite his vegetarian regime . . ., he remained tolerably efficient both physically and mentally, it can only be regarded as an exception, a phenomenon in fact.[42]

Some idea of the Führer's diet in 1944 (aside from fruit, vegetables and Morell's innumerable drugs; see Appendixes C and D) can be gained from a top secret communication sent by Himmler to Bormann some two weeks before Stauffenberg's attempt. It contains a requisition calculated on the Führer's 'estimated' requirements for one month, namely 20 packets of *Knäckebrot*, 20 packets of *Knusperbrot* (two varieties of crispbread), 3 packets of wheat flakes, 3 packets of oat flakes, 3 packets of *Keimdiät* (wheat germ), 15 packets of *B-Tropon* glucose, 2 tubes of vitamin A and R, 1 jar of *Philozythin* (yeast extract), 2 packets of *Endokrines Vollsalz*, 2 packets of dried rosehips or seedless rosehips, 4 packets of *Basica* (containing mineral cations to balance excess acid in foods), 1 kilo of linseed, camomile tea and 2 packets of *Titrosalz* (biologically balanced salt used instead of table salt).[43]

For the greater part of the war Hitler lived below ground underneath a thick slab of concrete at his headquarters in East Prussia, a place described by Jodl at Nuremberg as a combination of monastery and concentration camp. There he withdrew from reality to the extent that he shrank from confronting it even indirectly. His physician, Dr Giesing, writing in November 1945, points out that although Hitler was

decidedly a realist and an exceptionally strong-willed man he was no longer able to face up to the exigencies and horrors of the time as exemplified by the miseries of the fighting soldiers and the civilian population. He was not concerned for his own safety . . . on 15 September 1944, for example, while on his way to an X-ray examination with only a light escort, he walked through a large, unmarshalled crowd of bystanders. As they clustered round him he allowed them to take repeated snapshots. His flights to the front and his tours of factories had ceased as early as 1943. For a long time now he had been confined to his bunker where he kept himself informed of failure or success exclusively through the medium of radio and telephone, never by firsthand experience or by personal observation on the spot.[44]

Giesing's medical report dated 1945 is a revealing document since it deals with Hitler's behaviour in the period following 20 July 1944. 'Rarely,' he says, 'could one argue with the Führer.' Even in medical matters, 'when the facts plainly spoke against him', it was virtually impossible to do so.

His constitutional psychopathy induced the firm conviction that he was more capable and knowledgeable than anyone else, which in turn gave rise to severe neuropathy. His perpetual harping on his digestive and excretory functions was . . . only one symptom, others being his habit of frequently taking his pulse . . . and his obsession about dying before his time. In the autumn of 1944 he announced repeatedly that he had only two or three more years to live. . . . Of relevance, too, were his persistent insomnia, which hardly responded at all to medication, as well as his way of life which, by

turning night into day and day into night, conflicted with every physiological law. . . . Despite the two-hour tea period that followed the night
situation conference. . . and his extreme lassitude, he suffered from insomnia
[which] . . . he combated energetically . . . by taking fairly long walks in
order to induce a physiological need for sleep.[45]

Evidence of the correlation between Hitler's physical disorders and
the situation on the various fronts can be seen in his ever-increasing
tendency to extol the fanatical will and (from 1942 onwards) to rate
inflexible stubbornness and dogged pertinacity more highly than brilliant strategic ideas and the acceptance of operational risks. True, his
mind retained its incisive clarity and grasp up to the end of his life
but after 1942 it rapidly lost much of its elasticity. Even more ominously than hitherto, preconceived 'programmes' and opinions took
precedence over reality and the demands that reality imposed, so that
finally the only situations and events he would consider and accept
were those that fitted in smoothly with his preconceived ideas. The pass
to which he had come is revealed by the minutes of his situation conferences of 23, 25 and 27 April 1945 which quote him as saying: 'The
man who makes headway is the one who summons up all his strength
and then immediately starts charging forward like a lunatic!'[46] The
remark testifies alarmingly to the changes wrought by illness. Only
seven days or so before the Red Army finally broke through,[47] hoisted
the Soviet flag over the Reichstag building and began their search for
Hitler's body, the Führer had been invoking Clausewitz,[48] speculating
on strained relations among the Allies in the hope that these might
prove militarily advantageous to what was in effect a no longer extant
Reich, directing the operations of imaginary armies, worrying about
Austrian oil production, issuing trivial orders and planning strategic
moves which, in view of the situation, could have been devised
equally well by the inmates of a lunatic asylum.

Warlimont's assertion that as a leader Hitler suffered no loss of
efficiency when the tide of war turned against him is no more valid
than Schramm's attribution of the Führer's 'increased stubbornness
and intransigence – or as he himself would have said – "fanaticism"'[49]
to the change wrought in him by the crisis on the Eastern Front in the
winter of 1941–42, the catastrophe at Stalingrad, the evacuation of
North Africa, and other wartime setbacks.[50] It was not these that
wrought the change in Hitler; rather it was his deteriorating health
that affected the course of the war, a fact of which he was aware. This

explains his constant worry over Mussolini's 'physical constitution' which he regarded as 'crucial'[51] to the latter's views on future developments in Italy (and hence on the military alliance with Germany). At no time before the end of 1944 was the military situation really reflected in his demeanour. Thus he was sometimes noticeably weary, cast down, and oppressed by premonitions of death when he might have had occasion to be elated – as, for example, at the beginning of August 1941 after the capture of Smolensk. On the other hand he was not so hard hit by the serious reverses at Gondar in Abyssinia, or at Tobruk, Benghazi, Bardia and Sollum, as to suffer any physical effects. And by the time his afflictions returned in earnest early in 1942, Rommel had already won some major victories and was heading for Bir Hachim, which fell to the Germans on 11 June. A severe attack of influenzal encephalitis at Vinnitsa shortly afterwards marked a major turning-point. His inspiration in strategical matters deserted him for good, nor from then on was there any consistent military planning.

When defeats and setbacks temporarily deprived him of the power to act, the condition was never more than superficial. Save in the case of Geli's suicide he remained relatively unscathed by the major blows of life – his mother's death, his rejection by the Academy of Fine Arts, his disillusionment in 1918, the unsuccessful putsch of 1923, the electoral defeats under the Weimar Republic and, during the Second World War, a succession of serious military reverses. Though he was extensively injured by Stauffenberg's bomb, the shock brought a temporary alleviation of other symptoms, and he was able to shake the whole thing off as easily as Keitel had brushed the dust off his uniform after the explosion. When he received the Duce shortly after the attempt, the latter's interpreter heard him remark that if there was one thing he regretted it was the loss of a new pair of trousers.[52] Five weeks later the effects of 20 July 1944 had ceased to affect him in any way.[53]

By 1942 it had become evident to the more observant among his immediate followers that Hitler was no longer the man he had been when he created the NSDAP or when, having gained power in 1933, he proceeded energetically to extend it; nor was he the man who had unleashed the war and then conducted it for two years or more with undreamed of success. Some of them including, surprisingly, Heinrich Himmler, reached the conclusion that since Hitler was now in effect a totally changed man who could no longer properly be described as normal, the time had come to deprive him of office or even to do away with him. In the summer of 1942 members of the resistance began their search for an explosive best suited to the purpose of removing the now incurably 'degenerate' Führer.[54] Himmler, meanwhile, enquired of his personal physician, Felix Kersten, whether it was correct to say that Hitler was 'mentally ill'.[55] Obviously the latter was not aware of this when on 25 July 1942 the S S chief, with a profession of loyalty and devotion, reported that by his own efforts 4500 Dutchmen, 200 Swiss and 250 Swedes had been recruited for the Waffen-S S. Indeed barely three weeks later, on 18 August, the Führer issued his Directive No. 46 in which he made Himmler responsible for the collection and evaluation of information in the Reich Commissioner's territories, and also for the 'intensification of operations against bandits'.[56] Even as Hitler was dictating this order Himmler, at his field headquarters at Vinnitsa in the Ukraine, was hatching a plot with Schellenberg, his head of espionage,[57] to remove Ribbentrop, supplant Hitler and initiate peace negotiations with the West. It was not till the eleventh hour that the Führer discovered the disloyalty of the man he had once trustingly described as 'faithful Heinrich'.

On the morning of 28 April 1945, two days before he committed suicide, he learned from an intercepted despatch filed by Reuter's correspondent in San Francisco that the Reichsführer-S S had offered surrender terms to the Western Allies. In Hanna Reitsch's words (as quoted by Trevor-Roper) 'he raged like a madman' and later dictated the following proclamation:

Before I die I hereby expel Heinrich Himmler, the former Reichsführer and Minister of the Interior, from the Party and from all his Offices of State. . . . Göring and Himmler, by their secret negotiations with the enemy which were conducted without my knowledge and contrary to my wishes, as also by their illegal attempts to seize power in the State, have done incalculable mischief to the country and to the whole of our people, and this quite apart from their disloyalty to my own person.[58]

Hitler ordered Field-Marshal Ritter von Greim, whom he had appointed in Göring's stead, to leave Berlin immediately by air and arrest his predecessor, a mission that was frustrated by circumstances. Himmler survived until 23 May 1945 when he died by his own hand.

Hitler was not 'mentally ill' as Himmler had supposed, though his reasoning, his conduct and his decisions, particularly after 1943, may sometimes have given grounds for such suspicion. For disease had destroyed his flexibility of mind and had in certain respects consider-

ably speeded up the process of ageing. Thus he overrated the power
of his will which, though it had produced some outstanding successes
during the war, inevitably became a source of defeat when pitted
against the enemy without regard for the circumstances. An illuminating example is provided by his remarks at a conference with Keitel,
Rommel, Warlimont, Hewel, Schmundt, Scherff and others on 20
May 1943. When the question of the transfer of the Hermann Göring
Division from Sicily came up for discussion, Hitler categorically
declared that 'it's not the ferries that are the decisive factor; the decisive factor is willpower'.[59] At crucial moments he failed to take into
account the enemy's strength and probable intentions. And there is
no truth whatever in the contention that as a military leader his
decisions were without exception quickly arrived at and as quickly
executed. The intrepid and adventurous gambling spirit which, before
1939, had inspired his actions and decisions as a politician (such as the
occupation of the Rhineland and Austria), seems to have deserted him
as a military commander, if one excepts the Norwegian campaign. Far
from 'charging forward like a lunatic', he was both hesitant and
cautious. He seldom made a military decision if he thought that too
many risks were involved. And when the situation made a decision
imperative, he would procrastinate for as long as possible, so that the
enemy often had a chance to bring up reinforcements or make other
preparations. Any proposal to evacuate an untenable position met with
stubborn refusal. When he did reluctantly give way to the urgent
representations of his generals, it was usually too late. One example of
the extent to which his failing health determined his military decisions
was his attitude from the beginning of 1944 towards Manstein, des-
scribed by Liddell Hart as the Allies' most dangerous opponent. Manstein's dismissal occurred in conjunction with an eye complaint from
which, in addition to his chronic ailments, Hitler was suffering at the
time. Under the influence of his deteriorating health and his First
World War experiences he refused to permit even the temporary
evacuation of conquered territory or to weaken secondary fronts and
theatres in favour of sectors where a positive decision might possibly
have been achieved. The army's proposal to establish strong points and
defensive positions in the rear was rejected. The areas behind the lines
were without defences (at least until the autumn of 1944, by which time
it was too late), a blunder that was already having disastrous consequences in 1943. The exhausted troops, compelled to evacuate their

positions, found they had nothing to fall back on and that no arrangements had been made for their reception, with the result that the withdrawal, which Hitler opposed with all the means at his disposal, gathered even greater momentum. Refusing to take any share of the blame, he persisted in the view deriving from his experiences of the First World War that the generals' one idea was to give ground.

From 1941 onwards his wrong decisions in the field of technology – decisions affecting the air force and the armoured formations, for example – led to the exclusion of programmes which had hitherto been successfully incorporated in his planning as factors of decisive operational importance. Thus he declined to support the development of jet-propelled aircraft, on which work had begun in 1941 at the Heinkel factory in Rostock,[60] because he believed that he could subdue Russia with another Blitzkrieg. Indeed so certain was he of this that on the very eve of Operation Barbarossa he ordered a reduction in the output of armaments.[61] But what prompted him in September 1943 to demand that preparations for the large-scale production of the jet-propelled Me 262 be suspended[62] was his increasing obstinacy and a hitherto uncharacteristic mistrust of innovation, both attributable to the steady deterioration in his health since the middle of the previous year.

Six months before, when he returned to East Prussia from Vinnitsa, he was already an old man. A slight curvature of the thoracic spine induced a stooping posture, somewhat aggravated by minor scoliosis (lateral curvature of the spine). He was suffering from a tremor of the left arm and leg, and his eyes were protuberant and staring. He would fly into alarming rages when presented with proposals that failed to please him or agree with his own ideas, and would stubbornly uphold his own programme. Twice daily he took Intelan (a product containing vitamins A and D and glucose) to stimulate his appetite, combat tiredness and increase bodily resistance; to stimulate the smooth muscles and supplement his phosphorus intake he was given Tonophosphan. For a short period he also took Dr Köster's Antigas Pills and Mutaflor, the last-named being later replaced by the preparation, Trocken-Coli-Hamma. On top of these he was receiving Euflat to promote digestion and, on alternate days, two ampoules of Prostacrinum, an extract of seminal vesicles and prostate glands, to avert fits of depression. Also, and in combination with other drugs he was given Vitamultin-Calcium on alternate days.*

* For a full list of drugs taken by Hitler see Appendix D.

Striking confirmation of his doctors' diagnosis is provided by
Hitler's behaviour at the beginning of 1944 when he abruptly reversed
his decision of September 1943 (sabotaged, incidentally, by Speer who
was responsible for armaments) and suddenly began to press urgently
for the production of the maximum possible number of jet-engined
Me 262s in the shortest possible time.[63] Nor was that all. Many experts
believed that as a bomber the Me 262 was wholly unsuitable. But
despite their strong recommendation that the aircraft be employed in
a fighter role, Hitler obstinately insisted that it should enter service as
an unarmed bomber.[64] He hedged when German fighter pilots suggested to him that the aircraft should be used against the American
bomber formations and from then on refused to approve any such
experiment. Clinging obstinately to his decision he maintained that
with its greater speed the Me 262 would be at a disadvantage when
engaging the enemy's slower but more manoeuvrable fighters. And in
the autumn of 1944, after the Luftwaffe generals and the General Staff
had failed in yet another circuitous attempt to point out to him the
error of his ways, he forbade any further discussion of the matter.[65]
The Me 262 was a twin-engined aircraft with a top speed of over 500
m.p.h. and its rate of climb was then unequalled. According to Speer
it could have been put into large-scale production in 1944, as could a
ground-to-air rocket and a new type of naval torpedo. The ground-to-
air rocket was even faster than the Me 262 and homed on enemy aircraft with the aid of a heat sensor. The torpedo was guided by a sound-
locating device and was capable of finding its target, regardless of the
evasive manoeuvres of the vessel under attack.[66] But Hitler put a stop
to both these projects and thereby further weakened Germany's
position. 'To this day', Speer writes,

I think that this rocket, in conjunction with the jet fighters, would have
beaten back the Western Allies' air offensive against our industry from the
Spring of 1944 on. Instead [from July 1943 on], gigantic effort and expense
went into developing and manufacturing long-range (V-2) rockets which
proved to be, when they were at last ready for use in the autumn of 1944, an
almost total failure.[67]

Whereas Hitler's 'world power programme' was planned on a
relatively long-term basis his strategy was tailored exclusively to the
demands of the Blitzkrieg, a mode of warfare which between 1939 to
1941 had been a source of wonder to the entire world. As Bullock puts
it:

With a shrewder judgement than many of his military critics, Hitler realized that Germany, with limited resources of her own and subject to a blockade, was always going to be at a disadvantage in a long-drawn-out general war. The sort of war she could win was a series of short campaigns in which surprise and the overwhelming force of the initial blow would settle the issue before the victim had time to mobilize his full resources or the other Powers to intervene.[68]

The campaigns up till 1941 endorsed Hitler's theories. The operations against Poland and Norway lasted four weeks and eight weeks respectively; Holland was overrun in five days, Belgium in seventeen. He conquered France in six weeks, Yugoslavia in eleven days, Greece in three weeks. Prior to Operation Barbarossa, the formula had produced the results he had expected of it. But in Russia, a country he had hoped to subdue with yet another Blitzkrieg, it failed to work. And by the time Hitler discovered that the formula was bound to fail and that the war was in fact lost, it was too late.[69]

As a military leader and strategist he tended to be even less forthcoming than he was at other times and kept the General Staff[70] largely in the dark, telling them only what he thought fit. Thus, even in August 1939, they still believed that the Führer, despite his use of military pressure, was aiming at a political solution of the Polish question, similar to the agreement reached on Czechoslovakia in Munich in the previous year.[71] A further illustration of this attitude is provided by his remarks on 28 December 1944 in connection with the Ardennes offensive. 'Anyone who does not have to know about this operation', he told his commanders, 'should not know about it. Anyone who has got to know something about it, should know only what he needs to know. Anyone who has got to know something about it should not be told sooner than is necessary. That is vital. And no one who knows about it must be allowed up forward in case he goes into the bag. That is vital.'[72] He trusted no one more than was strictly necessary. Before the start of Barbarossa even Eva Braun did not know what was in the offing. Shortly before the attack he told her that he had to go to Berlin for a few days. In fact he went to East Prussia to supervise the final preparations for the launching of the eastern campaign.[73] Before the attack on Poland not one of the commanders, apart from Göring, had been aware of the exact position. The following passage is from a memorandum dictated in Nuremberg prison by General Jodl, the former Chief of the Wehrmacht Operations Staff:

No soldier could know whether the attack would take place, whether it would be provoked or unprovoked, a war of aggression or defence. . . . When the propaganda machine began to run and mobilization on the Polish border was ordered, all the leading soldiers were indeed quite clear about the operational questions confronting them, but the political, the strategic remained for them a veiled secret. . . . Was the mobilization backed by a serious determination to attack Poland, or was it only a means of exerting pressure for negotiation, as had been the case in 1938 with Czechoslovakia? Was this hope not confirmed when, on 26 August 1939, the ordered attack was halted? The details of the struggle of the Great Powers to preserve the peace were unknown to the Commanders-in-Chief and their staffs, with the exception of Göring.[74]

During the operations in Poland Hitler left military decisions to the General Staff, although he had intimated how he wished the German forces to be deployed in East Prussia before the attack.[75] With the unexpectedly rapid conclusion[76] of the campaign and the Allies' failure to intervene – interpreted by Hitler as an admission of weakness – he informed the OKH on 27 September 1939 (without first consulting the Army's Commander-in-Chief) that he was planning an autumn offensive in the West, however inadvisable it might appear to the military.[77] 'The Commander-in-Chief of the Army (General Walther von Brauchitsch) did not want to do it,' Jodl recalled.

To remain on the defensive on the border and along the *Westwall*, letting the war to go sleep, was his desire . . . which he sought to cloak behind military reasons, particularly the inadequate preparation of the army for so gigantic a task. . . . The generals all objected, there was not a single one who did not warn against it. But it did them no good at all.[78]

Underlying his Directive of 9 October 1939 is a plan which, though incomplete, was both ambitious and strategically astute:

Any further delay will not only entail the end of Belgian and perhaps of Dutch neutrality, it will increasingly strengthen the military power of the enemy, reduce the confidence of neutral nations in Germany's final victory, and make it more difficult to bring Italy into the war on our side as a full ally. . . . I therefore issue the following orders for the further conduct of military operations:

(*a*) An offensive will be planned on the northern flank of the Western Front, through Luxemburg, Belgium and Holland. This offensive must be launched at the earliest possible moment and in the greatest possible strength.

(b) The purpose of this offensive will be to defeat as much as possible of the French Army and of the forces of the allies fighting on their side, and at the same time to win as much territory as possible in Holland, Belgium and Northern France, to serve as a base for the successful prosecution of the air and sea war against England and as a wide protective area for the economically vital Ruhr.[79]

The OKH, whose Commander-in-Chief had by now been effectively relegated from military adviser to nominal C-in-C bound in obedience to the Führer, resigned themselves to Hitler's decision and set about drawing up orders for the operation. A number of senior members of the OKH, however, doubted whether the offensive would succeed.[80] They had in mind a paper, prepared towards the end of the Polish campaign by General Heinrich Stülpnagel on behalf of the OKH, dealing with the future conduct of hostilities in the West. Such was their professional bias that they attached more importance to the general's paper than they did to the strategic and tactical theories of the Führer. In their view Stülpnagel's conclusion that the Maginot Line could not be breached before 1942[81] was irrefutable. Thus they were all the more surprised at Hitler's intention to bypass the Maginot Line by advancing through Belgium and Holland. Had it not been for the weather, this plan would almost certainly have been put into operation as early as 1939. As Jodl commented:

Only the weather god was harder than Hitler, denying us the needed period of clear, freezing weather. It was necessary to wait until the dry spring. 10 May 1940 was correctly chosen. Hitler staged his breakthrough via Maubeuge toward Abbeville. He had overruled the General Staff's idea of effecting a broad encirclement through Belgium by initially careful but then increasingly tenacious and unhesitating intervention in the operational leadership.[82]

Hitler's plan, based on that of Manstein, departed from the traditional ideas of the General Staff, who wanted to break through on the right wing. He decided to violate the neutrality of Holland, Belgium and Luxemburg – despite his recent pledge to respect it – and to launch the attack at the centre in the direction of Sedan–Abbeville. On 13 February 1940 Jodl wrote in his diary: 'I would draw attention to the fact that in thrusting towards Sedan we may well fall into a trap of our own making.'[83]

At that time neither the general public nor the Allied intelligence services[84] were aware of the deplorable state of the German armaments industry. Despite Hitler's demand made in 1936 that the armed forces and the economy should be ready for war by 1940,[85] the armaments programme, in terms of Germany's industrial potential, had as yet barely got off the ground.[86] Before September 1939 there was little or no sign in any sector of the economy that production was being placed on a war footing.[87] Even in May 1940, when armaments still represented less than 15 per cent of total industrial production,[88] fewer than forty tanks a month were being produced (as compared with over 2000 a month in 1944). In 1939 aircraft production (including trainers and civil and transport aircraft) had not yet reached a thousand units a month, whereas in 1944, after years of heavy and destructive air raids, the monthly output of fighters alone was more than 4000. Thus when Hitler boasted on 1 September 1939 that he had laid out 90,000 million marks for armaments,[89] this can only have been intended to impress the uninformed. The higher echelons of the army knew that supplies of raw materials would suffice for twelve weeks of war at the most and that, of the country's total requirements, 95 per cent nickel, 50 per cent lead, 60 per cent mineral oil, 70 per cent copper, 80 per cent rubber, 90 per cent tin, 25 per cent zinc and 99 per cent bauxite had to be imported.[90] Hitler knew this too, of course, but he also knew that, in terms of strategy and the economy, the conclusion of the Non-Aggression Pact with Russia on 23 August 1939 had materially altered the position of the Reich.[91] Russian neutrality, once Poland had been defeated, would enable him to concentrate all his forces in the West without fear of attack from the rear. Moreover he could count both on economic support from Russia and on supplies of raw materials from south-east Europe and Scandinavia, while increasing the production of synthetic rubber[92] and synthetic fuels at home.[93]

Nevertheless, immediately after the Polish campaign, Hitler found himself in an awkward position. Both he and the General Staff knew from the cost of their Blitzkrieg just how long they would be able to go on fighting. Although about three months' supply of raw materials still remained, they could calculate that the war would be over in some fourteen days should the French and British attack in the West.[94] Yet to continue an offensive war was a hazardous undertaking, for the *Westwall* was woefully undermanned and ammunition supplies had been gravely depleted by the campaign in Poland. But it was a risk Hitler was willing to take. He knew that time was not on his side except in so far as his armaments programme was concerned. Whether he overestimated his own power and underestimated that of his enemies can only be surmised. The General Staff were sceptical, having learnt from the history of the NSDAP as well as from recent military experience that Hitler was a gambler who believed he was bound to win. By 1939 his declared requirement of 3,200,000 soldiers in case of war had still not been met.[95] Only four age-groups – those born between 1914 and 1917 – had been trained. But Hitler, better informed in many respects than his generals, surprised them[96] by declaring that his offensive, far from raising additional problems, would result in a rapid victory over France, and that Britain would be forced to call a halt to the war once her foremost ally on the continent had been crushed in a Blitzkrieg.

After his successful handling of the Sudeten crisis Hitler had grown more than ever convinced that the people of the 'Greater German Reich' would follow him through thick and thin. It was this conviction that led him to declare on 8 November 1938: 'If there is one man who is responsible for the German people, it is I.'[97] Since then even the more touchy generals had chosen to forget how, at the time of that crisis, he had ridden roughshod over the opinions of the OKH, pointing out to their Commander-in-Chief that the situation demanded not military, but political, decisions which he alone was qualified to take.[98]

On 12 December 1939 Admiral Raeder drew the Führer's attention to the dangers by which the Reich and its war economy would be threatened if the British were to occupy Norway, as Winston Churchill, First Lord of the Admiralty, had recommended in his memorandum of 19 September 1939.[99] To the horror of the generals, Hitler immediately relieved the Commander-in-Chief of the Army and the Chief of the General Staff and Operations Section of their responsibility for the control and deployment of the land forces.[100] Thenceforward, like Napoleon, and to the intense irritation of the military – even Göring felt insulted and angry[101] – Hitler proceeded to surround himself exclusively with men who were little more than minions, the executive instruments of his will. The generals were in fact in favour of a centralized command, if not in the form laid down by the Führer. Nor would they have objected to a unified OKW, particularly for an enterprise such as the Norwegian campaign involving all three Services, always provided one of their number were put at its head. But this was not Hitler's idea at all, as is evident from the opening sentence of his order dated 27 January 1940 to the effect that the study of operations in the North would thenceforward be carried out under his own immediate supervision and with close reference to the overall prosecution of the war. This decision was passed on to the Commanders-in-Chief of the three services by Keitel, who had been ordered to take charge of the preliminary studies. 'To this end,' the communication reads, 'a working staff will be set up within the OKW and will form the nucleus of the future Operations Staff.'[102]

Hitler was convinced that he himself must be responsible for every aspect of the campaign and lost no time in ordering that 'the Norwegian operation be kept in our own hands'.[103] An absolute dictator who knew his history, he was determined to avoid the tensions that arise when military necessity comes into conflict with the demands of diplomacy as had happened, for example, in the controversy between Bismarck and Moltke during the Franco–Prussian War of 1870–71 over the question of whether or not Paris should be bombarded. Since Hitler was effectively in control of foreign affairs and his Foreign Minister a mere puppet, he was already in a distinctly favourable position. But the concentration of power in the hands of one man only, despite its obvious advantages, was ultimately to prove a stumblingblock. For as time went on, Hitler's strategy came increasingly to be determined by the demands of prestige so that in certain cases his decisions were made without due regard for military considerations.

Confidently he took over the function of the OKH and, relying only on the cooperation of the Wehrmacht staff and other organizations expressly set up at the end of February 1940 within the framework of the OKW, proceeded to put his own interpretation on Raeder's ideas, originally purely defensive in character. Having then, after some hesitation, adopted the admiral's viewpoint, Hitler went on to reorientate it in an aggressive and expansionist sense. At the same time he became convinced that decision-making must rest with him alone, as supreme head of state, and not with the military. Ever since January 1940 he had been obsessed by the fear that the Allies might occupy Scandinavia, gain control of the Baltic, block the only reliable passage from the North Sea into the Atalantic and stop the shipments of the Swedish iron ore so vital to Germany.[104] A further cause of worry at that time was the thought that ill-health might prevent him from ever bringing his plans to fruition. On 9, 11 and 15 January 1940 he underwent a thorough medical examination. The result seemed to justify his fears, for his blood pressure was found to be far too high. But instead of following his doctor's advice that he should lead a less taxing existence, Hitler threw himself into ceaseless preparations for his next Blitzkrieg, a campaign which, from the time of its conception, the generals had regarded as overbold[105] if not thoroughly irresponsible. Once the Führer had made up his mind, however, there was no restraining him, the more so since he feared that political decisions by other powers might get in the way of his campaign. The view advanced by his military advisers that the conclusion of peace between Finland and Russia on 12 March 1940, had obviated the need to occupy the Scandinavian countries, since neither Germany nor Britain now had any cause to intervene, was as unacceptable to Hitler as the opinion of the naval chiefs that the best policy would be to uphold Norway's neutrality. Jodl's diary entry for 28 May 1940 in which he declares that 'a number of naval officers lack enthusiasm for Exercise Weser and could do with a shot in the arm',[106] undoubtedly reflected Hitler's own views, as did his further contention that the British would land in Narvik if the Germans occupied Belgium, Holland and Luxemburg.[107] The Führer was, indeed, in no doubt about his aim and he knew what he was doing. The campaign was to have the appearance of a 'peaceful occupation' intended to 'protect by force of arms the neutrality of the Northern countries'. At the same time he ordered that 'any resistance which is ... offered will be broken by all means available'.[108] In this way he hoped to make sure of his iron ore supplies from Sweden and to extend his naval and air bases, thus increasing his maritime power for the further prosecution of the war against Britain. Meanwhile the Allies had been making preparations for a similar operation and on 7 April 1940 they began embarking troops for the occupation of Norway.[109] In this they were anticipated by Hitler, literally at the eleventh hour.

On 9 April the Wehrmacht began its offensive both on land and sea. The occupation of Denmark, which forthwith placed herself under German protection, was followed by landings at Kristiansand, Stavanger, Bergen and Trondheim. After some hard and costly engagements* in the course of which the coastal artillery was neutralized, landings were also made in the Oslo Fjord. Further heavy losses were sustained when the flotilla of ten destroyers, which had transported Colonel

*Involving the loss of the heavy cruiser, *Blücher*, and the light cruisers, *Karlsruhe* and *Königsberg*.

Eduard Dietl and his mountain infantry regiment to Narvik, was destroyed by the British Navy on 10 and 13 April. So ominous did all this seem to Hitler that for a time he advocated both the evacuation of Narvik, the key point of the whole operation, and a total withdrawal from Norway.[110] He had perforce to admit not only that his experience in the First World War was now virtually useless to him and that as a military commander he still had much to learn, but also that the Führer mystique he had so carefully nurtured over the years was seriously at risk, and this in the very milieu which, for the furtherance of his future plans, he was particularly anxious to impress – that of the military. After what is described by Warlimont as 'a lamentable display of weakness lasting eight days or more', during which Hitler had appeared distraught and at his wits' end, he finally managed to pull himself together.[111] Although the entry in Jodl's diary for 17 April reads: 'The Führer is again talking as animatedly as ever', relations were still at times extremely strained and the situation at headquarters was often chaotic, largely as a result of Hitler's constant intervention both in matters of detail and in military decisions. Warlimont, whose Second World War experiences never extended to command in the field, talks of Hitler's failure to maintain the exemplary confidence and imperturbability shown by Moltke on the battlefields of France and Bohemia.[112] The remark is largely irrelevant. So far as the Norwegian campaign was concerned, Hitler was not the only one to lack experience in the conduct of operations involving the combined use of air, land and naval forces. His conviction that Norway might still have to be reckoned with as a theatre of war, even after an attack had been launched against France, Belgium, the Netherlands and Luxemburg, proved correct. The British did not finally evacuate Norway until 8 June, the day before the Wehrmacht reached the Seine and the lower Marne. Equally correct was his decision not to begin operations in the West until 10 May a decision which was put into effect despite Jodl's objection that a considerable proportion of the Luftwaffe was still tied up in Norway.

On 14 May, four days after the offensive had begun in the West – belatedly, owing to the Norwegian campaign and to unfavourable weather conditions – Hitler issued his War Directive No. 11 in which he laid down instructions for the future conduct of operations, thus clearly intimating to the OKH that henceforward he would keep the reins in his own hands. From now on he intended to abandon indirect in favour of direct command, and required no more of the Operations Staff than that they should proffer advice and translate into orders the decisions which he himself, as Supreme Commander of the Wehrmacht, had made. Although not personally responsible for the victory in Norway but only for its bold and brilliant conception he now saw himself as supreme warlord and the professional soldiers as mere humble advisers. There was no longer any trace of the reticence he had so wisely observed in military matters during the Polish campaign. Some twenty-five years later Warlimont was to criticize him for planning and initiating the offensive in the West without the usual preparatory staffwork, a stricture which the success of the campaign does not endorse.[113] Once again Hitler's decision proved correct, as did his surmise that the French would not fight as doggedly as they had done between 1914 and 1918.[114] 'Contrary to the expectations of the German High Command,' General Guderian was to write in 1953, 'the attack in the West led to rapid and total victory.'[115] And at Nuremberg Jodl said: 'Once more Hitler's will triumphed and his faith proved victorious. First the front collapsed; then Holland, Belgium and France collapsed. The soldiers were confronted with a miracle. They were ... amazed.'[116]

It now transpired, however, that Hitler had made no further strategic plans. Misled by his conviction that England, faced with the rapid surrender of France, would be prepared to break off hostilities, he had come to regard victory in the West as the virtual end of the war. Britain's failure to react as expected, despite the fact that he had spared her expeditionary force at Dunkirk, led him to consider the possibility of launching an attack against her. In Directive No. 16 of 16 July 1940 he declared:

Since England, in spite of her hopeless military situation, shows no signs of being ready to come to an understanding, I have decided to prepare a landing operation against England and, if necessary, to carry it out. The aim of this operation will be to eliminate the English homeland as a base for the prosecution of the war against Germany and, if necessary, to occupy it completely.[117]

Since Britain was not merely an island adjacent to the coast of occupied France and possessed of a Home Fleet, but also a strong maritime and world power with fighting forces in Canada, New Zealand, Australia, Egypt, India and South Africa, it would have been politic for Hitler, after the fall of France, either to implement his

Directive No. 16 without delay or to put into effect Raeder's plan to bring her to her knees by indirect attack. However, he now evinced a sudden disinclination to take the risk which an offensive against Britain would necessarily entail. He vacillated and was apparently incapable of paying attention when addressed. Hence even the doubts expressed by the naval chiefs – less assured than their military counterparts of a victorious outcome to this venture – seemed scarcely to get through to him. Sometimes his eyes would glitter in a way they had never done before and his habitual peremptoriness began to border on aggression.

He was no longer the man he had been four years earlier, and this applied not only to his external appearance. He himself, ever alive to his own physical condition, was aware of the change and redoubled his calls upon his personal physician. And when, three days after the armistice, he visited Paris, the impression he gave was not that of a man elated by victory – except perhaps to strangers. From the memoirs of Speer, Gieseler (an architect) and Breker (an architect and sculptor) who had been flown by special aircraft to join him in Paris for his tour of the capital, we learn that, while his entourage seemed drunk with victory, Hitler stood aloof and that there were tears in his eyes when the trumpet call, *Das Ganze halt*, was sounded.[118] Those tears were attributed by Speer[119] to the intense 'contradictions in his nature', and by Breker and Gieseler to his love of architecture and his desire for peace. They were wrong. Hitler's emotion was due, not to the thought of death and destruction, but rather to the conviction that, as a very sick man – then almost constantly under medication – he would never live to see the accomplishment of his aims.

Strategically, however, his prospects were bright indeed. France had been defeated, and Italy had entered the war on the German side, which meant that Britain could neither count on the support of the French fleet nor maintain her control of the central Mediterranean. Germany's U-boat and air bases now stretched all the way from North Cape to Bordeaux, enabling her to inflict telling blows on Britain herself, on Gibraltar and on Egypt. And Egypt meant the Suez Canal, one of the life lines of the British Empire, now more vulnerable than ever to attack because of Italy's entry into the war. Moreover operations in that region had been advocated severally by Admiral Raeder, General Kurt Student and General Rommel. But Hitler hesitated to accept the hazards involved. Indeed it was now that he showed the first signs of a general inflexibility and reluctance to take risks, although his staff was as yet unaware of any basic change of attitude.

It would be otiose for a historian today to debate whether or not an attack on England would have succeeded, even allowing for the assumption that there would have been little incentive for America to abandon her neutrality in favour of Britain either then, or in response to Churchill's warning to President Roosevelt that the German victories in North Africa and Crete might well entail the loss of the whole of the Middle East, with potentially adverse repercussions in Spain, Vichy France, Turkey and perhaps even Japan.[120]

Hitler seemed to have lost his impetus and to have exhausted his strategic inspiration, seeking refuge instead in an *Ersatz* strategy. Thus, on 12 November 1940 in his Directive No. 18 he ordered an investigation into the possibility of occupying Madeira and the Azores and declared that his policy for France was 'to cooperate with that country in the most effective manner possible for the future conduct of the war against England'. He considered intervening in the Iberian Peninsula so as to seize Gibraltar, and drive Britain out of the western Mediterranean. But these were no more than sand table exercises. His own particular war, the 'German march on the East', which had been the nub of his thinking ever since the end of the First World War, had constantly haunted his dreams about the future. In the middle of this respite, just 446 days after the conclusion of the pact with the Soviet Union, he decided 'that all preparations for the East for which verbal orders have already been given will be continued', and that further orders would follow with regard to the 'manner of execution and the timing of individual operations'.[121] This ran counter to the advice of Raeder, Rommel, Student and Korten for whom the prime objective was to drive Britain out of the Mediterranean and the Near East and to attack the Suez Canal and the Persian Gulf. Hitler's decision to disregard that advice and to march against Russia was determined ideologically by his *Weltanschauung* and strategically by the ideas he had evolved during the First World War on the battlefields of France, where he had first begun to think in continental terms. His attack on the Soviet Union in June 1941 made a mockery of his public asseverations over the past two years and marked a definitive return to his former doctrines. It shocked not only a section of the public but also some of the generals whose forebodings were due to other factors besides the ominous precedent set by the campaigns of Napoleon I and Charles XII, even though the Red Army, to judge by its performance in Finland, did not appear to be a very formidable foe.

On 4 May, a week before Rudolf Hess, the Führer's deputy, climbed into an Me 110 and flew from Augsburg to Britain, Hitler had made a speech before the Reichstag in which among other things he recalled his victorious campaigns, enumerated his 'peace offers', castigated Churchill as a warmonger, a fool, a liar and a criminal, and declared that the Third Reich was the only alternative to the 'Jewish demo-racies' and their political systems resulting from the 'Jewish-capitalis-tic obsession with class and status'.[122] His speech, however, was notably free of the customary virulent vilification of Bolshevism. Irritated though they might be, the generals could not but admit that Hitler succeeded in all he undertook and that, unlike themselves, he had hitherto very seldom been mistaken. Nevertheless they found him evasive and unpredictable, as Guderian clearly implied when he wrote: 'The [military] advisers' assessment of the enemy was by now no less muddled than their estimation of their Supreme Commander's strategic abilities.'[123]

As regards the conduct of the Russian campaign, the Führer's ideas diverged from those of the OKH who suggested that the main German effort should be directed against Moscow, so as to strike at the enemy's heartland and the seat of his power. Hitler's thoughts on strategy were determined primarily by economic and political considerations. He wanted to force a decision on the wings; in the north the objective was to be Leningrad, whence contact could be made with the pro-German Finns and control established over the Baltic, thus enabling rein-forcements to be brought up for the left flank of the army in the east. In the south his objectives were the Ukraine and its raw materials, the Donets basin and its armament industries and, finally, the Caucasus and its oil. Only when all this had been accomplished was Moscow to become an objective, and one of far greater importance than at the time of the Swedish or Napoleonic campaigns. In his Directive No. 21 of 18 December 1940, Hitler declared: 'The capture of this city would represent a decisive political and economic success, and would also bring about the capture of the most important railway junctions.'

With the rapid advance of the Wehrmacht and the collapse of the Russian centre, the high command and the generals in the field urged Hitler to take Moscow before Leningrad and not after it as laid down in the Barbarossa plan. But for six weeks Hitler vacillated between his original scheme of first taking Leningrad and the alternative of continuing the thrust towards the capital. He hesitated in spite of the knowledge[124] that the Red Army had lost large numbers of its generals, officers and commissars in a 'purge'* he himself had helped to engineer, so that the Germans were now infinitely superior to their Russian opposite numbers at staff and command level.[125]

On 21 August 1941, after the Wehrmacht had crossed the Beresina at Borisov and taken Smolensk, Hitler declared 'to the horror of all the officers concerned'[126] that strategically speaking the most important task before the onset of winter was not to capture Moscow, as they had advocated, but to safeguard the supply of Romanian oil, seize the Crimea and the industrial and coal-producing area in the Donets basin, cut off Russian oil supplies from the Caucasus, encircle Leningrad and effect contact with the Finns.[127] Abandoning the drive for Moscow, Hitler despatched elements of Army Group Centre southwards and even south-westwards, and ordered the seizure of the Ukraine. He disregarded the advice of the General Staff and contested their judgement not only in political and economic, but also in military matters. Heinz Guderian was ordered to march south and capture Kiev in concert with von Rundstedt, an operation which, to the surprise of most of the generals, not only succeeded but brought about the capture of 665,000 enemy troops and the destruction of the main body of the Russian forces in the south.

Hitherto the god of war had smiled on Hitler, despite the temerity of his campaign in the west which had not, as Jodl so much feared, called

* It would seem probable that in late 1936 Hitler and Himmler hatched a plan to cripple the Red Army, which was well equipped, technically efficient and numerically superior to the German army. On Heydrich's orders the SS Security Service forged thirty-two documents, purporting to be an exchange of letters between officers in the German army and Marshal Tukhachevsky, the Soviet Chief-of-Staff and Deputy War Minister (1931–37). The signatures of the German officers and those of Bankchek and Tukhachevsky were copied from documents obtained during the period of cooperation between the Reichswehr and the Red Army. A letter allegedly written by Tukhachevsky gave the impression that he was spying for Germany. On Hitler's instructions the material was leaked to the NKVD who in turn placed it before Stalin in the middle of May, thus providing him with an excuse to place on trial and ultimately liquidate such Red Army generals as he disliked. The arrests and shootings began as early as May 1937 (cf. Robert Conquest in *Der Spiegel*, vol. 7, 8 Feb. 1971).

down that deity's wrath. But now this happy state of affairs had almost run its course. After his great victory at Kiev, the Führer began to make mistakes which, before very long, were to prove disastrous. Some twenty-five years later Adolf Heusinger, chief of the Operations Section of the Army General Staff from 1940 to 1944, was to criticize his former Supreme Commander in the following terms: 'As early as August, the fatal turning-point had been reached. Hitler had abandoned all idea of immediately resuming the thrust towards Moscow, and thus our last chance was gone.'[128] Marshal Grigori Zhukov, Chief of the General Staff at the outbreak of war and commander of the Soviet forces in Leningrad until October 1941, did not share the German generals' low opinion of Hitler's decision:

In August [he wrote] the German forces were in no position to march on Moscow and capture the city, as planned by certain German generals. Had they embarked on an offensive, their position would have been even more serious than it was outside Moscow in November and December 1941. . . . Hence all attempts by German generals and historians to ascribe the blame for the defeat to Hitler . . . are unavailing.[129]

Even Marshal Konstantin Rokossovsky averred that, militarily speaking, Hitler was right in opposing the General Staff:

The position of the Soviet forces was highly involved . . . [he says]. Yet I am of the opinion . . . that there would have been no real opportunity for the German forces to continue a large-scale offensive against Moscow. What they needed above all was a breathing-space, and in August they got it.[130]

Marshal Vassily Sokolovsky who was Chief of Staff on the Soviet western front in the autumn of 1941, also argues against the German generals and in favour of Hitler's decision which, he believes, was the best solution from the German point of view.[131] Though these chroniclers have undoubtedly been influenced by a desire to emphasize the Soviet Union's 'invincibility', there is considerable substance in their argument.

Whether or not Hitler decided rightly in August 1941 can never really be proved. The mistakes he undoubtedly committed stemmed from the belief (shared by many of the experts in the OKW) that the Red Army was on the verge of collapse and that only one more effort was needed to send it toppling. Upon that misapprehension he based his military policy. At the beginning of September[132] he ordered an attack on Moscow, the seizure of the Caucasian oilfields and the encirclement and siege of Leningrad. However on 17 September he himself frustrated the plans for the capture of that city by withdrawing from the North both Hoepner's Panzer Group and the bomber units.

Nevertheless, Hitler seemed once again to have been right. On 7 October 1941, by which time Army Group Centre had already been vigorously pressing its offensive against Moscow for almost a week and had reached the Orel-Briansk-Viazma line, Hitler ordered the immediate pursuit of the enemy with all available forces, notwithstanding the warnings of experts on Russia who pointed out that the muddy season was at hand, and that this had already proved an almost insurmountable obstacle both to Charles XII of Sweden and to Napoleon. Directive No. 37 of 10 October 1941 reads:

After the defeat or destruction of the main Russian forces in the principal theatre of operations, there will be no compelling reason to tie down Russian forces in Finland by continued attacks. The strength and offensive power of the available German formations are inadequate, in view of the lateness of the season, to capture Murmansk or the Fisherman's Peninsula or to cut the Murmansk railway in Central Finland before the onset of winter. The most important task, therefore, is to hold what we have gained, to protect the Petsamo nickel fields from attack... and to make all preparations, beginning while it is still winter, for the final capture of Murmansk, the Fisherman's Peninsula, and the Murmansk railway next year.[133]

Hitler had no real knowledge of Russian weather conditions. On 24 September 1941, when Field-Marshal von Bock drew his attention to the difficulties inherent in an attack on Moscow at this season and suggested that the winter be spent in fortified positions, the Führer declared:

Before I became Reich Chancellor, I used to think that the General Staff was like a mastiff which required a firm hand on its collar to prevent it from attacking everyone within reach. Since becoming Reich Chancellor I have realized that the German General Staff is not in the least like a mastiff. The General Staff has always sought to prevent me from doing what I considered necessary. The General Staff opposed rearmament, the occupation of the Rhineland, the invasion of Austria, the occupation of Czechoslovakia and, finally, even the war on Poland. ... It is I who have always had to stir up this mastiff.[134]

Thus, in the conviction that it would be possible to reach Moscow before the onset of winter and confident in the belief that he could destroy Russia by means of a Blitzkrieg without having to stake his all, he ordered the attack to continue while denying the army and air force any appreciable reinforcements. The fact that the Wehrmacht had already lost much of its impetus was ignored. As in the past he continued to count on good, well-surfaced highways, keen, fresh troops, and weapons and machines that functioned without a hitch. The mud and dust of the Russian roads, which seriously impaired the efficiency of weapons if it did not render them entirely unserviceable, played as little part in his strategic and tactical calculations as did disease, lice, inadequate clothing or the stubborn fighting spirit of the Red Army. During the planning stage he had already underestimated the transport problem which, because of the vast distances to be covered and the unbelievably poor state of the roads, represented a factor of vital importance to the conduct of the operation. Moreover the gauge of the Russian railways was different from that of the German system and had to be altered. The locomotives were wood-fired and the primitive railway plant was totally inadequate for the rapid movement of troops, weapons and other war material so essential to the numerically inferior Wehrmacht. On top of all this the Luftwaffe was incapable of fulfilling the role demanded of it; for not only had it suffered severe losses in Crete and the Battle of Britain, but it also had commitments in the Atlantic area, southern Italy and North Africa.

As far as the campaign in the East was concerned, Hitler grossly overestimated the technological factor. This is evident, if only from the view he expressed in March 1941 that technological weapons, especially aircraft and armoured fighting vehicles, would enable him, despite the partial demobilization of the land forces,[135] to achieve in Russia the objective which had eluded both Charles of Sweden and Napoleon. This fatal misconception is in itself sufficient proof that, in spite of his exceptional knowledge of technological and military matters, he was not a true military leader. After 1941 his assumptions were only partially based on the real circumstances, even though he was more familiar with those circumstances than most of his advisers. The fact that he would weigh up a situation soberly only when it suited his book and that, as time went on, he would actually fabricate a 'show' situation with a view to impressing certain of his visitors cannot be considered normal in the strictest sense of the word and was, moreover, likely to have the most serious repercussions. As early as the autumn of 1940 and more especially when, in the spring of 1941, his medical adviser first began prescribing *Coramine, Cardiazol, Pervitin* and caffeine, it became clear that certain of his decisions and declarations were not subject to rational control. Under the influence of these drugs he would sometimes make fantastically exaggerated assertions which, when restored to a sober frame of mind, he would regret and perhaps amend. Again, he might issue directives of a horrifying nature – for the 'final solution of the Jewish question', for instance, or the implementation of the 'Commissar Order'.[136] Because such measures were sometimes included in memoranda that were otherwise unimpeachable, farsighted and sensible, his entourage, and more especially the military, remained almost wholly unaware that their author was not always *compos mentis*. Field-Marshal Erhard Milch, who had observed Hitler at very close quarters, stated in 1946:

The abnormality was not such that one could say 'this man is out of his senses' or 'this man is insane'; it would not have to reach that stage. It often happens that abnormalities are such that they escape both the public and the nearest associates. I believe that a doctor would be better able to give information on that subject.[137]

On 18 December 1941 Hitler assumed the additional role of Commander-in-Chief of the Army, a move later described as 'successful usurpation' by certain of the military whose vanity had been wounded. That same winter his lamentably ill-clothed *Ostheer* came to a halt in every sector, and he was faced with the urgent question of how, as an aggressor balked for the first time, he proposed to carry on the conflict during the coming year. He himself had been responsible for the course the war had taken since it was he who had initiated a wrongheaded ideological struggle, had declared the Russians to be outside the law and had drawn the USA into the conflict, thus unleashing in December 1941 what he had not planned to take place until the very end of his graduated programme, namely the Second World War. By now he had ceased to believe in victory. According to Jodl, who spent many hours with him each day, he declared that 'when the catastrophe of the winter 1941–2 occurred' it became clear to him that 'victory could no longer be achieved'.[138] He was further convinced that he had been gravely mistaken in turning the conflict into a global war after the Japanese attack on Pearl Harbour. When told of that attack by Heinz Lorenz, deputy press chief at Führer headquarters, on 8 December 1941, he is said to have remarked: 'Now the British will lose Singapore. That was never my intention. We are fighting the wrong people. We ought to have the Anglo–American powers for our allies. But force of circumstances has compelled us to make a world-historical error.'[139]

Everything he did thereafter was in effect directed towards prolonging the war and his own life. But his immediate strategic deliberations were concerned with the Wehrmacht's operations in the coming spring. Were he to remain on the defensive, this would suggest to world opinion – for his strategy had come increasingly to be dictated by the demands of propaganda – his own privily held idea that Operation Barbarossa had spelled defeat, the first defeat of the war. On 5 April 1942, when a muddy spell again precluded offensive operations, he issued his Directive No. 41 in which he stated that, since the winter battle was nearing its end, 'we must seize the initiative again and, through the superiority of German leadership and the German soldier, force our will upon the enemy. Our aim is to wipe out the entire defence potential remaining to the Soviets and to cut them off as far as possible from their most important centres of war industry.'[140]

At this stage of the war it became evident that, contrary to his own asseverations of 30 March 1940, and unlike the Russians, Hitler was overestimating the combat potential of Germany's co-belligerents whose strength, at that particular juncture, amounted to thirty-five divisions. In deploying unseasoned allied troops by the Donets and the Don, he was virtually inviting attack by the Red Army. Hence the disaster which began on 19 November 1942 when the Russians broke through the Third Romanian Army north-west of Stalingrad, and the Fourth Romanian Army south of that city. This proves beyond all doubt that the Führer was no military commander in the accepted sense of the term. From the sum total of his victories there emerges ever more clearly the figure of the blatantly aggressive power politician, depending wholly on force and his new tool, the 'Blitzkrieg', in order to implement his programme. The immense length of the front called for prolonged periods of defensive warfare – described, it is true, by Clausewitz as intrinsically the strongest form of strategy – but it was a form in keeping neither with Hitler's programme nor with his temperament. Hence in 1942 he again went over to the offensive in accordance with plans which he alone had thought out. The events of the summer were to prove him right again, although by all the canons of military orthodoxy his was a misguided conception.

In accordance with his orders, Army Group South launched its offensive in June 1942. The initial thrust was made from the Kursk area on 28 June by the 4th Panzer Army and the 2nd Germany Army.

After the opening stages of the attack Army Group South was split into two new Army Groups – A and B. The objective of Army Group A was the lower Don, while Army Group B was to advance to the Volga, forming a broad front on either side of Stalingrad. Before long, however, the left wing came up against strong Soviet resistance and failed to cross the Don save at the bridgeheads. The Russians, intent on maintaining an unbroken front, gave ground in order not to be encircled as had happened in 1941. Though the Germans inflicted heavy casualties on them, it was not a crushing defeat. Since Hitler was now demanding that Army Group A continue its advance towards the Caucasian oilfields and that Army Group B press on to Stalingrad so as to cripple its industries and disrupt communications along the Volga, the two Army Groups opened out thus overextending their front which finally stretched from Tuapse to Stalingrad and Voronezh. The result was that, out of a total eastern front of some 2000 miles, these Army Groups occupied a frontage 1500 miles long and an operational area 500 miles in depth. Having reached Stalingrad, the spearhead of General Paulus's Sixth Army formed a narrow wedge with inadequately protected flanks in the Russian defensive positions. In August 1941 Hitler had feared that a Russian flank attack might impede his seizure of the Crimea, an undertaking he had ordered against the wishes of the generals. Now he again flouted their opinion, although on this occasion they were to prove the better judges of the enemy's potential and intentions. Obstinately adhering to his belief in his luck, Hitler refused to pull out the formations which had so far failed to take Stalingrad, a city soon to become such a symbol of prestige that there could be no question of turning back. The disaster began on 19 November 1942. The Russians broke through the sector held by the Third and Fourth Romanian Armies (in action since October) and eventually the two prongs of the attack met behind the Sixth Army in the Don bend west of Stalingrad. On 22 November the city was surrounded. When Paulus requested that his forces be permitted to break out, Hitler refused. Göring's promise to fly in 500 tons of supplies a day could not be kept, and Manstein's attempt to relieve the city also failed, not least because of the mounting losses of the Luftwaffe. The Führer, who in mid-December had made the impassioned plea that 'once lost Stalingrad could never be regained', now began to realize the full implications of a prestige-orientated strategy. But it was too late. On 20 January 1943, ten years to a day after Hitler's seizure of power, the Sixth Army surrendered. Out of 265,000 men, 100,000 had been killed, 34,000 wounded and 90,000 taken prisoner.

Talking to Dr Giesing, his ear, nose and throat specialist, in the autumn of 1944, Hitler said:

It wasn't due to lack of information about the size of Russian troop concentrations on the left bank of the Volga, or to a surprise attack by the enemy, or to unfavourable weather conditions. I'd taken everything into account and it was my intention to fight and to force an issue here before winter. When the position began to deteriorate in Stalingrad in December 1942, the Luftwaffe left me in the lurch although Göring had assured me that he would guarantee supplies for the Sixth Army in Stalingrad for a period of six to eight weeks, if not longer. . . . In addition, just when things were at their most critical, with the Italians giving ground in the north and the Romanians giving ground in the south, I myself was incommunicado since I was travelling at the time in my special train. For twenty-four hours I was unable to direct the operation in person and when I came to hear of the disaster, it was already too late.[141]

Quite apart from the absurdity of trying to camouflage the defeat with an explanation of this kind, it should have already been plain to Hitler by the end of 1941 that the Luftwaffe could no longer be a decisive factor in the prosecution of the war, in spite of its success during the battle for the Russian capital in October when air raids had reduced the inhabitants to a state of near-panic. The fact that he trusted Göring's assurances and assigned them a place in his calculations argues against him, even though the airlift, as Field-Marshal Kesselring was to point out in 1945, had been promised 'only for a limited period and under specified conditions'.[142] Nevertheless he did not seek to absolve himself of the responsibility for the defeat at Stalingrad, a defeat which ushered in the defensive phase of the conflict. It is impossible to say, however, whether he shared Manstein's view (expressed twenty years later) that 'Stalingrad was certainly a turning point to the extent that the wave of German offensives broke on the Volga. . . . But grave though the loss of the Sixth Army undoubtedly was, it still need not have meant that the war in the east – and *ipso facto* the war as a whole – was irretrievably lost. It would still have been conceivable to force a stalemate.'[143] Whatever place may be assigned to Stalingrad in the overall picture of the Second World War, there can be no doubt that it marked a definitive turn for the worse. Now even true believers among the National Socialists began covertly to express their doubts, asking whether the Führer was in fact the military commander of genius he had always been held to be.

Hitler's illnesses were neither transitory nor imaginary; they were permanent factors which exerted an increasingly negative influence. At the end of 1942 his inspiration in the field of strategy left him, never to return, nor was there any consistent military planning after this time.[144] Thenceforward he shunned risky undertakings and, in the conduct of operations, would permit no flexibility where long-term objectives were concerned. He never voluntarily surrendered conquered territory, as circumstances after 1943 sometimes demanded, and he refused to weaken secondary fronts and theatres of war in favour of more crucial ones. Moreover he postponed unpleasant decisions for as long as possible, even where a rapid decision was called for. And whereas after 1935 he had pressed feverishly for action, now he had become an overcautious, obstinate, intransigent old man who, like Stalin in Moscow in 1941, based his conduct of the war on the sole principle that every inch of soil must be defended whatever the cost.[145] In 1942, however, Stalin abandoned these tactics which had so nearly sealed the fate of the Soviet Union. But Hitler, growing ever more mistrustful, remained immune to all the lessons of experience. Any proposal, irrespective of its provenance, he regarded not as an attempt to help or inform, but rather to outwit him. His all too palpable mistrust and suspicion, his increasingly frequent outbursts of rage and his aggressive dogmatism and obstinacy brought about the downfall of most of his senior officers. These included every Commander-in-Chief his army had possessed – von Hammerstein, von Fritsch and von Brauchitsch – four successive Chiefs of the Army General Staff – Beck, who took his own life on the occasion of 20 July 1944, Halder and Zeitzler who were dismissed, and Guderian (the last Chief, General Krebs, was killed in Berlin); also eleven out of eighteen field-marshals, twenty-one out of thirty-seven colonel-generals and (with the exception of Schörner) each successive Commander-in-Chief of Army Group North on the Eastern Front – von Leeb, von Küchler, Lindemann and Friedner.

Manstein's contention that Hitler was unwilling to incur risks in the military sphere is too sweeping and not wholly in accord with the facts.[146] The policy which inevitably propelled Hitler towards war was full of hazards, nor did he seek to avoid these during the first half of the conflict. Indeed Bullock goes so far as to say: ' It seems to me far more likely that the pattern which is unmistakeable after September 1939, using each victory as the basis for raising the stakes in a still bolder gamble next time, is the correct interpretation of his foreign policy before that date.'[147] True, Hitler recoiled from attacking Britain, yet later on he was prepared to face the risks involved in Operation Barbarossa. As a strategist he was a gambler in thought and action; not so as a commander responsible for tactical moves, when he tended to be hesitant, indeed sometimes over-hesitant and, by postponing a troublesome decision, would often forfeit the chance of success. After the beginning of the defensive war, procrastination became the order of the day. For weeks on end he refused to listen to the generals' plea to abandon positions which, like the Donets basin in 1943 and the Dnieper bend in 1944, had become untenable. However there is no factual basis for Manstein's suggestion that, because of his lack of a proper military training, he feared he might prove unequal to ventures of this kind. To admit such an idea, even to himself, would have been quite out of keeping with Hitler's character, for he was convinced that he was a match for any man and that he would be able to bend even the enemy to his will. He knew perfectly well what he was doing and what his orders implied. Thus, commenting on 2 June 1942 on reports in the Soviet Press of the battle south of Kharkov, he accused the Russians of camouflaging their defeats which, he said, proved that they had not the courage 'to abandon an operation which no longer promised any hope of success'.[148]

From 1942 onwards Hitler avoided taking military risks and even began to intervene in matters that would more properly have been the concern of a regimental commander, so morbidly mistrustful had he grown and so despairing of victory. A warlord and statesman of any moral integrity would, in a similar situation, have brought the conflict to an end. Hitler failed to do so because he himself wanted to go on living. But given the continuation of hostilities it is a moot point whether, once he had realized the war was lost, he could or should, as political leader and strategist, have aimed at achieving a different result by adopting some other course of action. Would it not have been better, for example, to employ in the East the troops, weapons and ammunition later committed in the Ardennes offensive? Or again, should not the last Panzer reserves, sacrificed in the German attack in the Lake Balaton area, have been preserved for the subsequent defence of the Reich? Such questions no longer admit of any answer.

In April 1943 the Supreme Commander, newly returned from Vinnitsa, celebrated his fifty-fourth birthday. He had aged considerably and could only be kept on his feet by the use of innumerable drugs. There was not the slightest prospect of his recovering his health, nor would he ever regain his flexibility, determination and drive. Some two months earlier he had agreed to the evacuation of the Rhzev salient, but only with the utmost reluctance, for during the First World War he had seen how rapidly a planned withdrawal could degenerate into a landslide. Now that the front had been stabilized the Chief of General Staff sought to convince him of the need to seize the initiative, destroy the Russian's combat potential and eliminate their westward-facing salient at Kursk. To this Hitler finally assented in the hope that the 'victory at Kursk would shine out to the world like a beacon'. Nevertheless, he had his reservations which, in the event, were to prove justified. The operation, code-named Citadel, was launched on 5 July with a simultaneous drive from north and south. While the southern assault force progressed satisfactorily, the attack from the north failed, with heavy casualties on the German side. In the circumstances the situation proved irrecoverable, especially as troops had to be diverted to Italy. On 13 July the operation was called off.

In 1943 Hitler's position was even less favourable than in 1942 when, it came to exploiting the captured Eastern territories as a strategic base for defensive operations or to bringing the conflict to a rapid conclusion by means of a compromise peace, a course which many of the generals held to be feasible. This he knew to be an illusion and was content that it should be so, having long since realized that he had lost the war. But it was his policy to inspire others with confidence in order that they should be prepared to make the final sacrifice for what they believed to be a great cause. As late as mid-February 1945, after an air raid on Berlin, he tried to persuade his former physician, Dr Giesing, that the war would culminate in victory.[149] His war directives, which were not intended for general consumption, clearly reveal the discrepancy between what he knew and what he hoped. His Directive No. 51 of 3 November 1943, for instance, reads: 'The hard and costly struggle against Bolshevism during the last two and a half years, which has involved the bulk of our military strength in the East, has demanded extreme exertions. . . . The danger in the East remains, but a greater danger now appears in the West: an Anglo-Saxon landing.' Aware that the war would very soon be over unless he succeeded in repulsing that invasion, he went on to point out that 'should the enemy succeed in breaching our defences on a wide front here, the immediate consequences would be unforeseeable'. Warlimont recalls that, towards the end of 1943, he repeatedly heard Hitler remark that the war would be lost if the landings were successful.[150] The Führer was also sceptical about the possibility of success in the East.

It was now the generals, the men he sometimes treated as though they were no more than humble privates, who proved to be the better commanders, at least where tactical and operational matters were concerned. But they were insufficiently versed in economics and foreign policy, both of which Hitler had to take into consideration when reaching his decisions. Moreover, they never succeeded in achieving vis-à-vis their Supreme Commander a status comparable to that of their British and American counterparts. 'My influence on the Führer,' Jodl was to admit before the military tribunal at Nuremberg, 'was unfortunately not in the least as it might, or perhaps even ought, to have been in view of the position I held.'[151] And Keitel conceded that from as early as 1938 onwards none 'of the really important decisions . . . had ever been formulated as a result of joint counsel. . . . It was the issuing of an order . . . but not a conference.'[152] Even in the years 1943, 1944 and 1945, Hitler's power was still such that the generals had to act secretly and with the utmost caution if, in the light of their own knowledge and for the benefit of their own particular sector, they wished to disregard any part of his orders, as was done, for example, in another field by the Armaments Minister, Albert Speer, immediately before the door slammed shut. That Hitler made occasional concessions – to Wilhelm List, for instance, or Guderian or Manstein – in no way alters the fact that, ever since the Norwegian campaign, he had repudiated the advice of military experts. When he did give way it was often done as a magisterial gesture and entirely of his own free will.

In April 1944 the Seventeenth Army, which had been encircled in the Crimea since 1 November 1943, was forced by Russian pressure to evacuate the Kerch Peninsula whence it withdrew to Sebastopol and took up defensive positions in the trenches and localities established by the Red Army in 1942. Hitler ordered that the town must be held, adding the comment that strategy must concern itself not only with military but also with political and economic questions – which, theoretically, was perfectly correct. In view of the actual military situation, however, and Hitler's privately held resolve to put off his

Hitler-Ludendorff trial, 1 April 1924. Since the failure of his putsch in November 1923, he had suffered from a nervous tremor of the left arm and leg. Movement of the left forearm was limited and he had to make an effort to control his left hand. This is plainly evident from the way he is convulsively gripping his hat and holding it pressed against his side.

2. Some nine months later, on 20 December 1924, Hitler leaves the fortress of Landsberg, the remainder of his sentence having been remitted. His state of health remains the same. Here again his left hand is convulsively pressed against his thigh, as though he were 'clinging' to his hat.

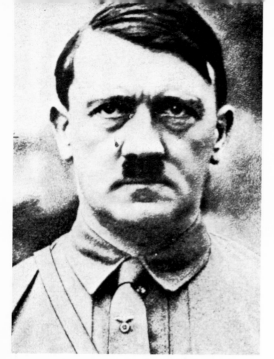

1933. He no longer suffers from a nervous tremor. He is in the best of health and fully up to the demands of his position, both physically and psychologically. His expression is expectant, his bearing alert and controlled.

44. Hitler in 1933 at Gut Neudeck, as the guest of Hindenburg.

45. Hitler on 29 September 1938 during the Munich conference. Despite his new-won political victory, he looks oppressed and worried. By now he already believed himself to be seriously ill and to have been suffering from an alarming heart-ailment for the past year. By comparison with his appearance on his accession to power, his features had become blurred and puffy. He was for ever taking his pulse and consulting his personal physician. As early as 5 November 1937 he had drawn up his political testament, and on 2 May 1938 had put his private affairs in order.

46. The ailing Führer examines a map at his headquarters. He first began to need spectacles in 1935. Early in 1944 he suffered a sudden vitreous haemorrhage, accompanied by sensitivity and clouding of the right eye which, however, proved on examination not to be morbidly impaired.

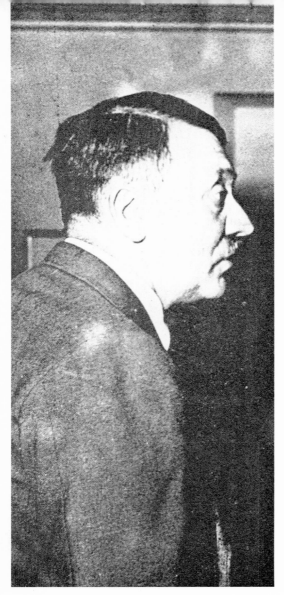

47. Within a short space of time, in the spring of 1943, Hitler became literally a changed man. His eyes grew lustreless, protuberant and staring. Red blotches appeared on his cheeks. A slight curvature of the thoracic spine induced a stooping posture, somewhat aggravated by slight scoliosis (lateral curvature of the spine), but neither defect caused more than a minimal distortion of his bodily symmetry. As in November 1923 after his putsch he was again suffering from a tremor of the left arm and leg and when walking he dragged his left foot. He became more touchy than hitherto and reacted violently if annoyed by some situation or argument. With dogged tenacity he clung to his ideas and inspirations, even though these might sometimes appear erroneous or inappropriate to those around him. When he spoke, his voice was comparatively toneless. He would repeat himself and, like an old man, keep harking back to his childhood and early political career.

48. Hitler, immediately after Stauffenberg's attempt on his life on 20 July 1944. Though he escaped with his life he did not remain unscathed. His skin was riddled with splinters of wood, more than a hundred being removed from his legs alone. His face had been slightly cut. There was an abrasion on his forehead and bruising of the right elbow and left hand. His right hand was sprained and the hair on the back of his head singed. Injury to the eardrums had caused haemorrhage in the auditory canals, temporary deafness in the right ear and diminished hearing in the left. He complained of a taste of blood in his mouth, of severe earache and of insomnia. Before long his sense of balance became seriously disturbed. He tended increasingly to drag his feet as he walked, his eyes twitched. His actions were performed as though in slow motion.

49. Six weeks before his suicide. Though only fifty-six years old he had long been no more than a wreck, physically an old man. He appeared distrait, and totally exhausted. His face was ashen grey, and there were large bags under his bloodshot and lustreless eyes. His lips were dry and cracked and saliva dribbled from the corners of his mouth. The skin of his hands was pallid, the fingernails completely bloodless. For months he had suffered from a tremor not only – as after 1923 and again 1943 – of the left hand and leg, but of the whole left side of his body. His sense of balance was gravely impaired and he had to lean forwards in a painful effort to drag himself along. He was unable to move more than twenty or thirty yards at a time without sitting down or seeking a helping hand.

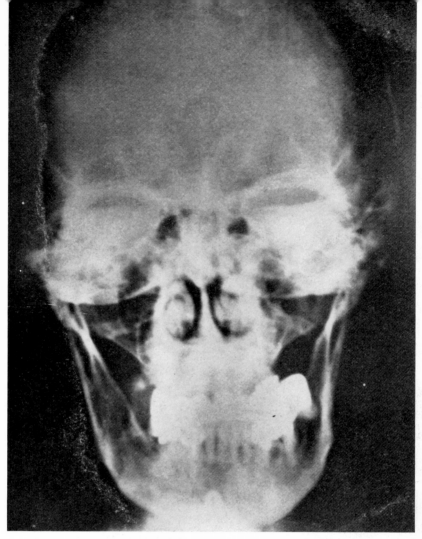

50. X-ray photograph of Hitler's head (19 September 1944). In the original (though less so in the above reproduction) the steel pin in the lower right incisor is plainly evident. The false teeth in the lower jaw of the corpse, believed by the Russians to be Hitler's, were not attached to the lower right incisor. Similarly the dentition of their corpse differed materially from that of Hitler, both in the number of the teeth and in the way the bridge was held in place in the upper jaw.

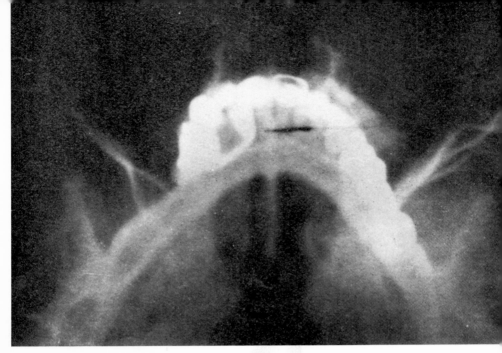

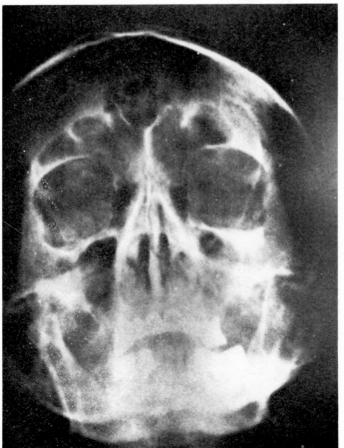

51. X-ray photograph of Hitler's head, taken from the thorax (19 September 1944).

52. X-ray photograph of Hitler's head (19 September 1944).

own end as long as possible, his every strategic, operational and tactical move after 1941–42 involved him ever more deeply in monstrous crime.

Withdrawal from the Crimea, at a time when this could have been effected without undue loss, had been rejected by the Führer on the grounds that Turkey, whose chrome iron ore supplies were vital to the German war economy, would abandon her neutrality as a result of Soviet pressure in the Black Sea area and throw in her lot with the Allies. This and other fears were confirmed by what happened after the retreat. The Romanian oil needed by the Wehrmacht ceased to be available.[153] Soviet aircraft were brought within effective striking range of targets in Romania. The Soviet navy regained the base it had lost in 1941–42 so that German and Romanian warships were confined to the restricted waters of the Bulgarian and Romanian littoral. Moreover the Crimea and the shores of the Caucasus were no longer within easy range of the Luftwaffe. Hitler's prediction that the evacuation of the Crimea by Germany would restrict Turkey's freedom of action also proved correct.[154] But of what avail were such insights, when his aims were determined solely by morbid egocentricity?

Hitler was no longer able to evaluate facts soberly unless they corresponded to his preconceived ideas, and he chose to ignore items of information which any other commander would have been eager to possess. Thus he brushed aside the intelligence reports submitted by the Foreign Armies (East) Section, which included not merely details concerning the Red Army's morale and fighting spirit but also precise data on the timing of future Russian attacks. Had he been in a more normal frame of mind, he would certainly have made dispositions to counter undertakings such as the Soviet Orel offensive in July 1943 or the attacks on the German positions in the region of Briansk in August, or again, the operations against the southern wing of the German Eastern Front in March 1944.[155] Yet he furiously rejected these predictions and, to his own detriment, refused to make use of them. He swept aside the generals' proposals for positive action to avert the dangers and continued to adhere unswervingly to the policy he had been following ever since the defeat at Stalingrad. He ordered that the imperilled Dniester front be held and justified his refusal to allocate forces for essentially hazardous undertakings on the grounds that an invasion was impending in the West.[156] His increased tendency to believe only what was plainly to be seen led him to equate the temporarily impaired vision of his right eye with a corresponding loss of personal power. However on 25 March 1944, when the treatment with *Homatropin* had cleared his vision of the film of blood so that he once again felt more at his ease, he suddenly gave way to Manstein's plea for reinforcements to enable the First Panzer Army, which was in danger of encirclement by the Russians, to break through to the West.[157] Nevertheless, shortly after this deviation from his normal military practice, he found a diplomatic solution to the problem by dismissing Manstein – a commander who had made repeated demands for operational freedom and the establishment of a clear focal point of effort.

But it was not solely because of his physical and psychological condition that he rejected the generals' proposal to revert to the positive operational policy of the early part of the war.[158] For he was aware that to do so at this stage of the conflict might involve not only considerable risks in other theatres and other sectors of the front, but also grave repercussions in the political and economic fields.[159]

Hitler was able to cope with the difficulties arising out of the Allied landings at Anzio–Nettuno in January 1944 but not with the Normandy invasion which began on 6 June. He knew it was useless now to pretend that defeat was not imminent and avoided private discussions with his principal generals. Nor was he prepared either to make peace or to abdicate.

The fate of the country and the people was bound up with his own life which for years had been a wretched one and of which he himself said on 31 August that, had the attempt of 20 July succeeded, it would have liberated him for ever from his cares, his sickness and his sleepless nights.[160] His thoughts were fixed on his end, yet he still hoped for another month or two of life. There were sufficient supplies of chrome iron ore to last out until the end of 1945, so that the fighting could if necessary continue until then. When, on 17 June 1944, Rommel and Rundstedt finally succeeded in obtaining an interview with the Führer, he reassured them[161] with optimistic talk about the V-1 and V-2. Schramm cites him as remarking on 31 August 1944:

I said right away that the time is not yet ripe for a political decision. That I am also in a position to achieve political successes I have, I believe, adequately proved in my life. That I would not let such an opportunity pass, I do not need to explain to anyone. But to hope, at a time of serious military defeats, for a favourable political moment, is naturally childish and naïve. Such moments can come when one has successes. . . . The time will come when the tensions between the Allies will become so great that the break will occur. . . . Throughout history coalitions have always gone to pieces sooner or later. One has only to wait for the moment, no matter how hard the going. . . . My task, especially since the year 1941, has been never to lose my nerve under any circumstances.[162]

It has often been said that, until the very end of his life, Hitler retained his faith in victory, but such is not the case. He had known that the game was up even before the end of March 1945 when, on General Josef Kammhuber's remarking that Germany had lost the war, he grudgingly replied: 'I know that myself.'[163] Indeed Hitler sensed and knew 'earlier than any other person in the world . . . that the war was lost', and he also knew just when it had been lost.[164] While in Nuremberg prison, Jodl wrote that the Führer had already ceased to believe in victory 'when the catastrophe of the winter of 1941–42 occurred'. And from the same source we learn that by the end of 1942 he was more than ever convinced that he would not live to see victory. 'When towards the end of the year Rommel, defeated before the gates of Egypt, fell back on Tripoli, as the Allies landed in French North Africa [i.e. November 1942], it was clear . . . to Hitler himself that the god of war had now turned from Germany and gone over to the other camp.'[165]

Towards the end of December 1944 Hitler's star rose above the horizon for the last time. Once more the generals seemed to see in him the warlord they had known between 1940 and 1942 – a man whose daring strategy had time and again astonished, if not alarmed and horrified, the professionals. When, after an interval of four weeks, Dr von Eicken visited him on 30 December in his Adlerhorst headquarters during the Ardennes offensive, he was amazed. Hitler seemed stronger and, on the whole, confident. He was also able to speak normally, in spite of relaxed vocal cords.[166] But the improvement was more apparent than real. Though he had recovered from the effects of Stauffenberg's attempted assassination and could again stand erect, he needed all his strength to do so. The curvature of his spine was irremediable, his complexion an ashen grey. He dragged himself along rather than walked. Seeing him for the first time in 1944, Dr Giesing was shocked. 'Hitler gave the impression of being prematurely aged . . . worn out and exhausted,' he later declared, 'a man who had to husband his strength. . . . His shoulders sagged, his chest was hollow and his breathing superficial', all of which indicated 'a slight admixture of asthenic leptosome, attributable at least in part to mental and physical exhaustion'.[167] It was not till later that he learnt from members of Hitler's entourage[168] how greatly over the past two years the Führer's appearance had changed by comparison with earlier photographs taken by Hoffmann.

From the end of 1942 Hitler was unable to tolerate intense light.[169] He wore a cap with a strikingly long peak to protect his eyes and, when travelling by train, would always keep the blinds drawn. His skin was flaccid and very white[170] and he was hypersensitive to certain tastes and smells, this manifestation being attributed by Giesing in 1945 to the effects of the strychnine contained in Dr Köster's Antigas Pills, which Hitler had been taking over a long period. His sense of balance was disturbed. 'I always feel as though I'm falling over to the right,' he said in July 1944 when he also complained of feeling even more unsteady in the dark.[171] As a man he became still more aloof and lonely, confiding in no one and abruptly breaking off a conversation when any distasteful topic was broached.[172] Music, in which he had once delighted, no longer held any charms for him. His hair was now grey and there were large bags under his eyes – eyes which had lost their power to fascinate; his lips were dry and slightly cracked.[173] But that he was still as keenly observant as ever is evident from his remarks to Giesing on 22 July about the nature of Stauffenberg's bomb. He had seen 'that infernally brilliant flash very clearly . . . and immediately thought that the explosive must be British since German explosives don't give off so harsh and intensely yellow a flame'.[174]

An attack was now in process of being mounted which Hitler had first conceived at the time of the Normandy battles and thereafter carefully elaborated in strictest secrecy. The Wehrmacht Operations Staff had not been asked for their opinion, nor had they been given the opportunity of subjecting the plan to a preliminary study.[175] This was the Ardennes offensive, launched on 16 December 1944, whose outcome was to illustrate yet again Hitler's tendency, in certain situations, to disregard the facts. Barely a fortnight later he was compelled to declare that 'the offensive no longer holds out any prospect of success'.[176] Not until 14 January 1945, however, the day before his headquarters returned to Berlin, did he finally concede that the initiative had passed to the enemy.

He had a hundred and six more days to live. As early as 6 August

1944, five days before Hitler announced that the time was not yet ripe for a political solution, Roosevelt had written in a minute to his Secretary for War: 'It must be made plain to the German people as a whole that the entire nation has entered into an unlawful conspiracy against all that is decent in modern civilization.' A bleak prospect for everybody, but bleakest of all for Hitler.[177]

On 21 April 1945 Professor Theodor Morell departed, leaving his patient, now a total wreck of a man, in the Reich Chancellery bunker. On the following day, meditating upon the subject of suicide, Hitler said: 'I should already have made this decision, the most important of my life, in November 1944, and should never have left my headquarters in East Prussia.'[178] He let fall this remark knowing perfectly well that the only reason he had kept the war going after the end of 1941 was to enable that decision to be postponed as long as possible. When five days later, like a bankrupted gambler, he decided it was time to 'be done with the whole beastly mess'[179] and to take his own life, he began to dramatize and glorify his imminent end before an audience of faithful followers. 'I should,' he said, 'regard it as a thousand times more cowardly to commit suicide on the Obersalzberg than to meet my end here.'[180] And again: 'In this city I have had the right to give orders: now I must obey the orders of fate. Even if I could save myself, I would not do it. The captain too goes down with his ship.'[181] On 13 April Eva Braun asked Lieutenant General Gerhard Engel, Hitler's former army adjutant, to advise her on the best method of shooting herself.[182] Despite the pleas of loyal followers, among them Hanna Reitsch and Hans Baur who wanted to fly him out of Berlin, the Führer remained in the capital where, when all was lost, he took his own life. Three days previously, having swallowed a strong dose of stimulants, he had grown 'a little calmer' and had gone to bed ordering that he should not be disturbed until a Russian tank was actually outside his bedroom door so that he could then 'take the necessary steps'.[183]

What happened next has been described so circumstantially and reliably by Trevor-Roper[184] in his book *The Last Days of Hitler* that there is no need to recount it here.

So far as Hitler's physical remains are concerned, the case is altogether different. In his book published twenty-three years after the event,[185] Lev Bezymenski clearly fails to take account of the facts when he states that the body, having been discovered early in May

1945, was identified by a commission of Russian experts a few days later, and 'completely burned' at the end of May, the ashes being 'strewn to the wind'.[186] The body exhumed by the Russians at the beginning of May 1945 from the shell hole in which it had been buried was, to all appearances, quite unidentifiable. According to the information in File No. 12 of the Russian records concerning the autopsy, the remains were burnt beyond recognition. Of the head, nothing remained but 'charred fragments of the occipital bone, the left temporal bone, the lower cheekbones and the upper and lower jaws'. Part of the parietal bone was missing and all the facial skin had been burnt away.[187] The body, arms and legs were in little better case so that the Soviet Investigation Commission's claim to have identified what was 'presumably the corpse of Hitler'[188] rested on the evidence of the teeth alone.[189] The fact that their data concerning bridges, crowns and fillings correspond to Adolf Hitler's dentition does not, in the circumstances, provide adequate evidence. The teeth illustrated in Bezymenski's book and adduced by him as proof of Hitler's identity have nothing in common with those that appear on the X-ray photographs of Hitler's head made by Giesing and von Eicken in September and October 1944. This effectively demolishes Bezymenski's claim. From Professor Blaschke's assistant, Käthe Heusermann, the Russians had obtained the record card containing precise details of Hitler's teeth along with the relevant X-ray photographs, while Fritz Echtmann* who had made some of Hitler's crowns and bridges, had also provided them with information.[190] From May 1945 onwards they used these data, not only to hoodwink such members of Hitler's entourage as they held captive and whom they repeatedly interrogated on the subject of Hitler's death and place of burial[191] but also, in 1968, to support their contention that the body they had found was 'presumably' that of Hitler,[192] and this despite the fact that the corpse's dentition was quite different from his. For the bridge comprising nine teeth in Hitler's upper jaw was held in place by pins on the second left and second right incisors, whereas the bridge in the upper jaw of the Russians' corpse was secured by pins on one second and one middle incisor.[193]

According to information supplied by members of Hitler's imme-

---

*Echtmann expressly told the author on 20 Oct. 1971 that he could not have said for certain that these were Hitler's teeth. But, he went on, there had been another distinctive 'feature' – what, he would not (i.e. obviously could not) say – which indicated that they had belonged to Hitler.

diate entourage who had either witnessed or been immediately concerned with his cremation and burial on 30 April 1943, Hitler's head and body went on burning from four in the afternoon until at least 6.30 (there is no definite information about what happened after that time). The body was buried just before 11 p.m., by which time it was said to have been almost completely consumed.

Nothing of the face was left and only a gruesomely charred remnant of the shattered head. Under a heavy Soviet barrage, the charred remains of the body were rolled onto a piece of tent canvas, which was then lowered into a shell hole in the big burial ground round about the Chancellery building. This shell hole was just outside the exit from the bunker. Earth was then thrown on the body and tamped down with a wooden tamper.

Thus the Führer's personal adjutant, Otto Günsche, who had himself ignited the corpse at 4 o'clock, half an hour after Hitler's suicide.[194] Others involved in the cremation have stated that nothing was left of the head by the time the burial took place – Hitler's servant Heinz Linge, for instance, and his chauffeur Erich Kempka who procured the petrol for the purpose.[195] Harry Mengeshausen of the S S Battle Group Mohnke, one of the men interrogated by the Russians, who had been on sentry duty at the time in the New Reich Chancellery and had watched the cremation from a distance of some ninety yards, declared that Hitler's body was completely 'consumed' before being buried by members of his suite.[196] In addition a policeman (as yet unidentified) belonging to Rattenhuber's security guard, reported to Dr Goebbels some time after 10 p.m. (immediately before Hitler's burial), that the Führer's body had been burnt and 'hardly anything was left of it'.* Certain of the witnesses who later expressed reservations about the total destruction of the body clearly did so because it had been put to them that twenty gallons of petrol would hardly have sufficed to do the job thoroughly. Hitler's personal pilot, Hans Baur, was among these latter witnesses, and it was he who had been entrusted by Hitler with the destruction of his corpse. 'If I had known,' he said later, 'that Kempka wouldn't be able to rustle up more than forty gallons of petrol to pour over the two bodies – Hitler's and his wife's – I would have arranged for him to be burnt in one of our big coke furnaces.'[197] In spite of their subsequent reservations, the surviving witnesses take the view that it would have been impossible after

* Later Rattenhuber tried in vain – as he told Hans Baur – to find out this man's name. Information supplied personally by Hans Baur (10 June 1971).

exhumation to find in Hitler's mouth 'parts of the wall and bottom of a thin-walled ampoule',[198] as is alleged to have been discovered in the mouth of the body described as 'presumably the corpse of Hitler' in the Soviet Commission's file No. 12 of 8 May 1945. This allegation takes no account whatever of Kempka's deposition in which he declared that the head had been shattered by a shot fired into the mouth – a mutilation which caused Linge to wrap the body in a blanket before carrying it out to be burnt.[199]

For a period of twenty-three years Soviet writers, including both Rosanow[200] and Bezymenski,[201] continued to assert that Hitler had committed suicide by shooting himself. This view was supported, not only by every eye-witness account, but also by the findings of non-Russian investigators.[202] Then, in 1968, in his book *The Death of Adolf Hitler*, Bezymenski suddenly declared: 'Our commission could not detect any traces of a gunshot [wound] on 8 May 1945.'[203] Hitherto unpublished documents from the archives in Moscow had, he alleged, refuted the view which he himself had so long 'uncritically' disseminated,[204] namely that Hitler had taken his life by shooting himself in the head. He also quoted the unequivocal statement made by Shkaravski, head of the Soviet team of experts in forensic medicine and a member of the Identification Commission, that examination of the corpse had revealed no traces whatever of gunshot wounds. Yet in the same chapter he speculates[205] about the identity of the person responsible for shooting Hitler in the head – evidence enough of his lack of faith in the Moscow documents and/or their authors. The conflicting information presented by these documents with regard to the 'presumed' identification of Hitler's corpse in 1945 is in itself evidence of uncertainty on the part of the Russians, in turn aggravated by a number of glaring contradictions in the statements made by witnesses. For instance on 30 May Rattenhuber, then in Russian hands, stated that Hitler had ordered someone, presumably Linge, to shoot him after he had taken poison. But if we are to believe Bezymenski, Soviet researchers were of the opinion that the person concerned was Günsche.[206] The inconsistency of the Soviet assumptions concerning the shooting incident is only matched by the falsity of Bezymenski's contention that the state of Hitler's health would almost certainly have precluded his shooting himself. Though a very sick man at the time, Hitler was perfectly capable of eating without assistance; in other words, he was able to spend some twenty minutes several times a day continually raising and lowering a fork or spoon from his plate to his mouth and back again. Hence it must surely have been a comparatively easy matter for him to commit suicide by shooting himself in the mouth. It seems unlikely, though not altogether out of the question, that Hitler shot himself in the temple, as stated by Linge[207] and by Günsche.[208] Baur was also told this by Goebbels immediately after Hitler's suicide.[209]

Bezymenski's assertion that the Russians had delayed publication of their conclusions on the autopsy performed in 1945 because they feared that 'someone might try to slip into the role of the "Führer saved by a miracle"'[210] is nonsense and, moreover, self-defeating. Indeed in 1970 Bezymenski was still patently worried lest valid evidence might have been discovered that would give the lie to Soviet assumptions.[211] Neither he nor Trevor-Roper nor any other writer concerned with Hitler's death and the whereabouts of his remains was aware of the fact that the Russians, conscious of the frailty of their case, had not, as alleged by Bezymenski in 1968, burned the corpse in May 1945 but kept it. Four months after their examination of the body in Berlin they were trying to discover what the Americans and British in the CIC knew about Hitler's death and his remains. They asked the Military Secret Intelligence Unit (MSIU) whether there were any doctors in the custody of the CIC who might be able to identify Hitler's head. The Americans were then holding Dr Erwin Giesing, the ear, nose and throat specialist, who was familiar with Hitler's head and teeth from the frequent examinations and X-ray photographs he had made in 1944.[212] His captors, naturally anxious to elucidate the matter, at once agreed to cooperate. When two American colonels attached to Section 4 of MSIU went to tell Giesing about the Russian 'tests', they found him at work for the CIC, translating entries from his diary along with certain interpolations which he hoped would exonerate him and obtain his early release. On learning, however, that Dr Giesing was in American custody and that he would at any time be ready and willing to identify Hitler's head,[213] the Russians beat a hasty retreat. Nor did they dare show their corpse to the few German prisoners who might have been able to banish all their doubts, especially since one of the bodies they had laid out for identification as being that of Hitler had already been disqualified on 3 May by reason of the much-darned socks on its feet.[214] Evidently the Russians regarded their claim to possess Hitler's corpse – a claim not easy to refute – as a

valuable asset in the game of external politics, and one which, in view
of the growing tension between the Allies, they were unwilling to
relinquish. The Führer's personal pilot, Hans Baur, has stated that
while he was in Russian hands, his captors produced a photograph of
Hitler's teeth, and literally tried to bludgeon him into accepting their
own version. In 1946 he expressed his readiness to have a look
at the body, then still ostensibly in Berlin, with a view to its possible
identification. That was the last he heard of the matter. While
interrogating Baur, a Soviet German-born doctor had remarked
significantly enough that they 'wanted to know at long last' whether
or not 'the corpse could be destroyed'.[215]

The statement in the Russian report that the corpse measured
approximately 5 ft 6 in.,[216] as compared with Hitler's height of
nearly 5 ft 9 in., does not wholly invalidate the Soviet thesis, since the
discrepancy could be attributed to the ravages of the flames. However
the 'findings' of the team of Soviet experts in forensic medicine and
pathology headed by Dr Shkaravski and including Drs Boguslavski,
Krayevski, Marants and Gulkevich, unequivocally refute the Russians' claim that the corpse in their possession was 'presumably' that
of Hitler, for amongst other things the doctors' report declares that
the dead man's 'left testicle' could not be found 'either in the scrotum,
or on the spermatic cord inside the inguinal canal, or in the small
pelvis'.[217] Bezymenski's assertion in 1968 that this allegedly inborn
defect had never previously been mentioned in print because 'the
Führer had always firmly refused to submit himself to medical
examination' is based on assumptions which are totally untrue.[218]
For it can be shown beyond all doubt that between 1934 and 1945
Hitler underwent numerous medical checks and never raised any
objection to an examination of his genitalia. That these were healthy
and in no way abnormal is evident from the testimony of one of the
doctors who, shortly after Hitler's accession to power, examined him
at the Westend Hospital in Berlin and, having heard of his alleged
homosexual tendencies, paid special attention to his penis and testicles. More than once Theodor Morell declared that Hitler's sexual
organs, penis and testicles showed no abnormalities. Upon Baur's
expressing surprise at Hitler's tendency to fight shy of women, the
doctor informed him that 'so far as his sexual organs were concerned'
the Führer was 'completely normal'. In January 1940, when Hitler
already believed himself to be dying, he wished to discover exactly

what the specialists thought of his state of health. On 9, 11 and 15 January he submitted to a searching examination in the course of which serological tests for syphilis produced negative Wassermann, Meinicke and Kahn reactions.

When the Führer was ill in bed on 1 October, Dr Giesing, the ear, nose and throat specialist who treated him between 22 July and 7 October 1944, had no difficulty in obtaining permission to examine all parts of his body, including the penis and testicles. Immediately afterwards the doctor wrote in his dairy: 'I . . . drew the bedclothes right back to uncover the lower part of his body. . . . So far as I could see, the genitals . . . showed no abnormalities. The prepuce was drawn back, the glans showed no signs of irritation, no pyramid signs. . . . Babinsky, Gordon, Rossolimo and Oppenheim [reflexes] . . . negative.'[219] Giesing expressly states that Hitler's testicles were normal and unimpaired.[220] But the dead man laid out by the Russians on the dissecting table in the mortuary of No. 96 Army Surgical Hospital in Berlin-Buch had one testicle missing. Hitler had possessed both testicles, proof of the fact either that his body was never found, or that it had been removed by trusty followers before the arrival of the Russians, as Günsche allegedly once declared.[221]

When on 12 September 1919 Adolf Hitler attended a political meeting in a small Munich public house he was, as he later like to hear himself called, 'an unknown soldier of the common people', an agent of the Bavarian army. The occasion was a gathering of the Deutsche Arbeiter Partei of which before long he was to become member number 555,[222] and his attendance there was his first tangible step on the political ladder which eventually led to the position of 'Führer'. At this gathering he was heard by forty-six politically committed people, disillusioned and embittered by the First World War and its aftermath, who were searching for a leader and redeemer.[223] When on 30 April 1945, after a career unparalleled in history, he committed suicide in the bowels of the earth like a cornered criminal, he was surrounded by very nearly the same number of men and women,* war-weary, embittered, and driven to desperation by the world conflict their Führer had unleashed – a group of people upon whom it had dawned for the first time that they had bound themselves to a false prophet. 'Hitler's death released us from a state of mass hypnosis,'

* Forty-two witnesses were interrogated in connection with Hitler's official death certificate (1956).

Traudl Junge, the secretary who remained with him to the end, was to recall some two decades later. 'Suddenly we rediscovered that we possessed an irresistible urge to live, to be ourselves, to be human beings. Hitler was no longer of any interest to us.'[224]

In 1919 he had been thirty years old and in his prime, eager for action and impelled by an insatiable need to demonstrate to his immediate circle and to the world at large that what he himself deemed possible was indeed a possibility. In 1945, although not more than fifty-six years of age, he was a broken wreck of a man who found it a laborious effort to drag himself a mere forty or fifty yards and who sometimes had to catch hold of his interlocutor to steady himself, doing so with his left hand because he no longer had any command over his right. Till 1941 he had been able to control his facial muscles and his bearing generally as would an experienced actor. By 1945 only his mind remained keen and alert though he was not able to react as he had done four years earlier to what was going on around him. Now he mistrustfully surveyed his surroundings with tired, bleary, bloodshot eyes, saliva dribbling from the corners of his mouth. Yet his astonishing memory continued to function almost unimpaired. Even as the Third Reich crumbled into dust, the intellect that had created it still remained more or less intact. Only Hitler's body, aptly symbolizing the world to which his mind had given birth, was sickly, distorted, finished and done with. And it is well that this was so, for had it been otherwise his supporters could have claimed that everything might have turned out differently and that extremism might yet have prevailed.

Hitler, the man once hailed as a blessed saviour by so many Germans, and not by Germans alone, left 'his' people in a disastrous position unprecedented in their national history. He vanished without trace from a world which, because of him, would never be the same again to the lasting detriment not least of his own country. Where his ashes are interred is today a no-man's-land, a place where even now men are targets for other men's guns. The spot where his body was drenched with petrol and burned by his trusties is today part of the frontier which, through his own fault, has split Germany and the world into East and West. Only when every German, whether from Cologne or Rostock, Hamburg or Schwerin, West Berlin or East Berlin, can visit without risk to life or limb the place where he lies buried will Germany's collective trauma – Adolf Hitler – be overcome.

Appendices, Bibliographies and Index

APPENDIX A

A Chronology of Hitler's life, May 1906 – April 1945

May–June 1906	First visit to Vienna.
Sept. 1907	In company with 112 other candidates at the entrance examination for the Vienna Academy of Fine Arts. Thirty-three failed the first part of the examination (composition) which Hitler passed. Along with fifty-one others he was failed on his 'sample drawings'. Only twenty-eight of the original 113 candidates satisfied the examiners.
Nov. 1907	Hitler returned to Linz (Urfahr) to look after his dying mother.
21 Dec. 1907	His mother died and was buried (23 Dec.) at Leonding.
Feb. 1908	After dealing with matters concerning her estate he returned to Vienna where he shared a room with his Linz friend, August Kubizek, at 29 Stumpergasse. Called on Professor Roller at the School of Handicrafts. On Roller's recommendation he began taking drawing and painting lessons from the sculptor Panholzer.
16 Sept. 1908	Kubizek called up for military service and Hitler left alone in the Stumpergasse.
Sept. 1908	Again sat the Academy entrance examination, but his concentration had been so much impaired by his mother's death and his changed circumstances that he failed the first part and was not admitted to the second (as he had been in 1907).
18 Nov. 1908– 20 Aug. 1909	Lodged at 22 Felberstrasse. In accordance with Statute 41 of the Austrian Miliary Service Act of 11 April 1889 he was required to report for military service. This he omitted to do and from now on changed his lodgings at frequent intervals.
20 Aug.– 16 Sept. 1909	Occupied a room at 58 Sechshauser Strasse.
16 Sept.– Nov. 1909	Subtenant in the Simon-Denk-Gasse.
End of 1909	Spent his nights at the Meidling dosshouse where he made the acquaintance of Reinhold Hanisch, a trained

draughtsman. Since those using the hostel were not permitted to remain there during the day, he may sometimes have worked as an unskilled labourer on building sites.

Dec. 1909   Moved to the men's hostel at 27 Meldemannstrasse where he drew and painted pictures and posters, designed buildings and executed mural reliefs to his own designs. Reinhold Hanisch sold the pictures and took a half share in the profits.

Aug. 1910   Lodged a complaint against Hanisch, accusing him of fraud. This resulted in a week's imprisonment for Hanisch. From then on Hitler sold his pictures himself. He worked in the mornings, sometimes turning out a picture a day which he would deliver in the late afternoon. These would usually have been commissioned by the customers, many of whom were Jewish academics, businessmen and art patrons.

His work brought in so much money (over and above the income from his inheritance) that between May 1911 and April 1913 he voluntarily made over to his sister Paula his orphan's allowance of 25 kronen a month.

24 May 1913   Moved from Vienna to Munich where he lodged in the Schleissheimerstrasse with a tailor called Josef Popp, remaining there until the outbreak of war.

29 Dec. 1913   The Austrian police requested the Munich police to inform them of Hitler's whereabouts, since he was liable for military service.

10 Jan. 1914   The Munich police inform Linz that Adolf Hitler was living in the Schleissheimerstrasse in Munich.

19 Jan. 1914   Hitler brought before the Austrian consul by Munich police officials.

5 Feb. 1914   Travelled to Salzburg to enlist. He was declared unfit and exempted from military service.

1 Aug. 1914   Outbreak of First World War.

16 Aug. 1914   Enlisted as a volunteer in 16 (List) Reserve Infantry Regiment. Joined 6th Recruit Replacement Battalion, 16 (List) Bavarian Infantry Regiment in the Elisabeth-Schule in Munich.

1 Sept. 1914   Transferred to 1 Company, 16 Bavarian Reserve Infantry Regiment.

21 Oct. 1914   Entrained for the front.

29 Oct. 1914   Fought on the Yser.

30 Oct. –	
24 Nov. 1914	Fought at Ypres.
1 Nov. 1914	Promoted to Lance-Corporal.
9 Nov. 1914	Transferred to Regimental HQ.
25 Nov.–	
13 Dec. 1914	Trench warfare in Flanders.
2 Dec. 1914	Awarded Iron Cross, 2nd Class.
14–24 Dec. 1914	Fought in December battle in Flanders.
25 Dec. 1914–	
9 Mar. 1915	Trench warfare in Flanders.
10–14 Mar. 1915	Fought at Neuve Chapelle.
15 Mar.–8 May	
1915	Trench warfare in Flanders.
9 May–23 July	
1915	Fought at La Bassée and Arras.
24 July–24 Sept.	
1915	Trench warfare in Flanders.
25 Sept.–13 Oct.	
1915	Fought at La Bassée and Arras.
7 Oct. 1915	Transferred to 3 Company, 16 Reserve Infantry Regiment.
14 Oct. 1915–	
29 Feb. 1916	Trench warfare in Flanders.
1 Mar.–23 June	
1916	Trench warfare in Flanders (Artois).
24 June–7 July	
1916	6th Army engaged in feint attacks and reconnaissance preparatory to the Battle of the Somme.
8–18 July 1916	Trench warfare in Flanders.
19–20 July 1916	Fought at Fromelles.
21 July–25 Sept.	
1916	Trench warfare in Flanders.
26 Sept.–5 Oct.	
1916	Fought on the Somme.
5 Oct. 1916	Wounded in left thigh at Le Bargur.
9 Oct.–1 Dec.	
1916	Red Cross hospital at Beelitz.
3 Dec. 1916	Transferred to 4 Company, 1st Replacement Battalion, 16 Bavarian Infantry Regiment in Munich.
5 Mar. 1917	At the front with 3 Company, 16 Bavarian Reserve Infantry Regiment.

5 Mar.–26 Apr. 1917	Trench warfare in Flanders.
27 Apr.–20 May 1917	Fought at Arras.
21 May–24 June 1917	Trench warfare in Artois.
25 June–21 July 1917	Operations in Flanders, 1st phase.
22 July–3 Aug. 1917	Operations in Flanders, 2nd phase.
4 Aug.–10 Sept. 1917	Trench warfare in Upper Alsace.
17 Sept. 1917	Awarded Military Service Cross 3rd Class with Swords.
30 Sept.–17 Oct. 1917	Home leave in Spital.
17 Oct.–2 Nov. 1917	Rearguard actions south of the Ailette.
3 Nov. 1917– 25 Mar. 1918	Trench warfare north of the Ailette.
26 Mar.–6 Apr. 1918	The Great Battle on the Western Front.
7–27 Apr. 1918	Fought on the Avre and near Montdidier.
28 Apr.–26 May 1918	Trench warfare north of the Ailette.
9 May 1918	Received a regimental citation for outstanding gallantry at Fontaine.
18 May 1918	Awarded Wounded Badge (Category Black).
27 May–13 June 1918	Fought near Soissons and Reims.
14–30 June 1918	Trench warfare between the Oise and the Marne.
5–14 July 1918	Trench warfare between the Aisne and the Marne.
15–17 July 1918	Offensive operations on the Marne and in Champagne.
18–25 July 1918	Defensive operations between Soissons and Reims.
25–29 July 1918	Mobile defensive operations on the Marne.
4 Aug. 1918	Awarded Iron Cross, 1st Class.
21–23 Aug. 1918	Fought near Monchy-Bapaume.
23–30 Aug. 1918	Leave in Nuremberg.
25 Aug. 1918	Awarded Service Decoration, 3rd Class.
10–27 Sept. 1918	Home leave in Spital.
28 Sept.–15 Oct. 1918	Defensive operations in Flanders.
13–14 Oct. 1918	Gas casualty (eyes) at La Montagne. Initial treatment in the Bavarian Field Hospital at Oudenaarde.

21 Oct.–19 Nov. 1918	Prussian Reserve Hospital in Pasewalk.
21 Nov. 1918	Transferred to 7 Company, 1st Replacement Battalion, 2 Bavarian Infantry Regiment.
12 Sept. 1919	Hitler attends a meeting of the German Workers' Party (DAP) on behalf of No. 4 Reichswehr Group Headquarters.
Sept. 1919	Without having applied for membership, made member (no. 555) of the DAP.
13 Nov. 1919	Becomes one of the DAP's speakers and its chief propagandist.
1 Jan. 1920	First party headquarters established in the *Sterneckerbräu* in Munich.
24 Feb. 1920	DAP announces its programme in the Hofbräuhaus. Soon after this meeting DAP renamed NSDAP.
13–17 Mar. 1920	The Kapp Putsch. At the suggestion of Epp, Mayr and Röhm, Hitler and Dietrich Eckart travel to Berlin with a view to possible collaboration with the Putsch organizers.
31 Mar. 1920	Discharge from the Reichswehr (41 Rifle Regt).
7–8 Aug. 1920	Speaks in Salzburg at the Inter-State Rally of the National Socialists of the German-speaking Area.
29 Sept.–11 Oct. 1920	Speaks at meetings in Austria.
17 Dec. 1920	The NSDAP acquires the *Völkischer Beobachter* (up till 9 Aug. 1919 the *Münchener Beobachter*).
11 July 1921	Hitler resigns so as to put pressure on the party. Delivers ultimatum to the party leadership.
26 July 1921	Rejoins the NSDAP. Membership number 3680.
29 July 1921	Elected first president of the NSDAP at special party meeting.
16 Nov. 1921	In a statement in the Munich Court of Registry he claims to own all the shares of the *Völkischer Beobachter* and the Franz-Eher Publishing House.
12 Jan. 1922	Sentenced to three months imprisonment for breach of the peace (causing a disturbance at a *Bayernbund* meeting).
10 Mar. 1922	The Bavarian government considers deporting Hitler but decides against it.
24 June 1922	Committed to Stadelheim Prison, Munich.
27 July 1922	Released on remission of sentence.
14–15 Oct. 1922	Takes part in German Day at Coburg, organized by the Duke of Coburg in collaboration with the Patriotic

Associations. Political opponents terrorized in the Coburg streets. (This was the first town in which the NSDAP gained an absolute majority in municipal elections – 23 June 1929.)

20 Oct. 1922   Julius Streicher joins the NSDAP, bringing with him his *Deutsche Werksgemeinschaft* and his newspaper *Deutscher Volkswille*.

13 Dec. 1922   The NSDAP holds ten mass demonstrations in Munich.

27–29 Jan. 1923   The NSDAP's first Reich Party Rally in Munich.

15 Mar. 1923   Rejection of the appeals against the proscription of the NSDAP in Prussia, Saxony, Baden, Mecklenburg-Schwerin, Hamburg and Bremen by No. 1 Court of the Reich Court of Justice.

1 May 1923   Armed SA detachments muster on the Oberwiesenfeld. Forced to disperse by state troops.

Aug. 1923   Hitler visits sympathizers and patrons in Switzerland.

1–2 Sept. 1923   German Day in Nuremberg with General Ludendorff. Formation of the German *Kampfbund* in association with other extreme right wing organizations.

25 Sept. 1923   Hitler becomes political leader of the *Kampfbund*.

26 Sept. 1923   End of passive resistance in the Ruhr. State of emergency in Bavaria. Gustav Kahr appointed State Commissioner and given extensive powers (subsequently killed during Röhm affair in June 1934).

27 Sept. 1923   Banning of fourteen NSDAP mass demonstrations in Bavaria.

8–9 Nov. 1923   Differences of opinion with the Bavarian separatists (among them G. Kahr) and others hostile to the Reich are followed by Feldherrnhalle putsch which is balked by force of arms. NSDAP and the *Völkischer Beobachter* banned.

11 Nov. 1923   Hitler escapes to Uffing on the Staffelsee. Is arrested. Death of his friend and mentor Dietrich Eckart.

26 Feb.–1 Apr.
1924   Hitler's trial in Munich.

1 Apr. 1924   Convicted of high treason and sentenced to five years' detention and a fine of 200 gold marks.

7 July 1924   Resigns the leadership of the now banned NSDAP for the duration of his imprisonment in the fortress of Landsberg.

20 Dec. 1924   Sentence remitted.

4 Jan. 1925	Received in Munich by Held, the Bavarian Prime Minister.
26 Feb. 1925	Refounding of the NSDAP. Its organ, the *Völkischer Beobachter* also revived.
9 Mar. 1925	Hitler forbidden to speak in public by the Bavarian cabinet under Held because of his speech on 27 Feb. 1925. He was similarly banned from speaking in Prussia, Baden, Saxony, Hamburg and Oldenburg, but not in Württemberg, Thuringia, Brunswick and Mecklenburg-Schwerin.
11 Mar. 1925	Georg Strasser entrusted with the task of building up and organizing the NSDAP in Northern Germany. After Friedrich Ebert's death, Ludendorff put up by the party for the Reich Presidency but gains only 1·06 per cent of the total votes (as an Austrian Hitler was not eligible).
26 Apr. 1925	Field-Marshal von Hindenburg chosen President at the second election.
27 Apr. 1925	Hitler informs the authorities in Linz that he wishes to renounce Austrian citizenship.
30 Apr. 1925	The Upper Austrian Land government accedes to his request; he remains stateless until 25 Feb. 1932.
18 July 1925	Publication of volume i of *Mein Kampf*.
10–11 Sept. 1925	Formation of the party's 'North-West German Gauleiters' Working Group'.
9 Nov. 1925	Founding of the SS.
28 Feb. 1926	Hitler speaks in Hamburg at the *National-Club von 1919*.
11 May 1926	Assumes leadership of Austrian National Socialists.
3–4 July 1926	Second Party Rally at Weimar. Founding of the Hitler Youth.
1 Nov. 1926	Supreme SA leadership constituted. Goebbels embarks on the 'conquest of Red Berlin'.
10 Dec. 1926	Publication of volume ii of *Mein Kampf*.
30 Jan. 1927	The NSDAP gains two out of fifty-six seats in the Thuringian Landtag.
1 Feb. 1927	Hitler no longer banned from public speaking in Saxony.
5 Mar. 1927	Again permitted to speak in Bavaria.
9 Mar. 1927	First public reappearance in Munich.
1 May 1927	Speaks at a closed meeting of 5000 members in the *Clou* in Berlin.

19–21 Aug. 1927	Third Party Rally in Nuremberg.
9 Oct. 1927	Municipal elections in Hamburg. The NSDAP gains 1·5 per cent of the recorded votes and two out of 160 seats.
27 Nov. 1927	Landtag elections in Brunswick. NSDAP: 3·7 per cent, one out of forty-eight seats.
28 May 1928	NSDAP participation in Reichstag elections, gaining 2·8 per cent of the votes.
28 Sept. 1928	Hitler no longer banned from speaking in Prussia.
16 Nov. 1928	Speaks for the first time in the Berlin Sportpalast.
12 May 1929	Landtag election in Saxony. NSDAP: 4·95 per cent, five out of ninety-six seats.
23 June 1929	Landtag election in Mecklenburg–Schwerin. NSDAP: 4 per cent and two out of fifty-one seats.
9 July 1929	Founding of the *Reichsauschuss für das deutsche Volksbegehren*.
1–4 Aug. 1929	Fourth party rally in Nuremberg.
27 Oct. 1929	Landtag elections in Baden. NSDAP: 6·98 per cent, six out of eighty-eight seats.
10 Nov. 1929	Municipal elections in Lübeck. NSDAP: 8·1 per cent, six out of eighty seats.
8 Dec. 1929	Landtag elections in Thuringia. NSDAP: 11·31 per cent, six out of fifty-three seats.
23 Jan. 1930	Dr Frick becomes first National Socialist minister (Minister for Domestic Affairs and Popular Education in Thuringia).
1 Apr. 1930	First issue of the *Nationalsozialistische Monatshefte* (editor Alfred Rosenberg).
22 June 1930	Landtag elections in Saxony. NSDAP: 14·4 per cent, fourteen out of ninety-six seats. The second strongest party in the Landtag.
14 Sept. 1930	Reichstag elections. NSDAP: 18·2 per cent, 107 out of 577 seats. Second strongest party in the German Reichstag. Landtag elections in Brunswick. NSDAP: 22·2 per cent, nine out of forty seats. Ruling party. The NSDAP appoints the Minister for Domestic Affairs.
15 Sept. 1930	Hitler pledges that his party will respect legality when he appears as witness before the Supreme Court in Leipzig during the trial of the Reichswehr officers Scheringer, Ludin and Wendt. When summing up on 4 October 1930 the President of

No. 4 Criminal Court said of Hitler's testimony: 'Adolf Hitler declared under oath . . . in quite unmistakeable terms that he intended to pursue his aims by strictly legal means, that it was only under duress that he adopted the course he did in Munich in November 1923 and that if he had abandoned that course it was because illegal action was no longer necessary in view of the growing sympathy felt in Germany for the *völkisch* liberation movement; he would he said, attain power in due course by legal means.'

5 Oct. 1930	Received by Reich Chancellor Brüning.
13 Oct. 1930	Opening of the Reichstag. The 107 National Socialist deputies appeared in brown shirts.
9 Nov. 1930	For the first time National Socialist candidates put up for the Austrian National Assembly. NSDAP: 5·4 per cent.
16 Nov. 1930	Volkstag elections in Danzig. NSDAP: 16·1 per cent, twelve out of seventy-two seats.
30 Nov. 1930	Municipal elections in Bremen. NSDAP: 25·6 per cent, 32 out of 120 seats.
5 Jan. 1931	Ernst Röhm appointed SA Chief of Staff.
1 May 1931	Formation in Hamburg of the foreign department of the NSDAP.
3 May 1931	Landtag elections in Schaumburg-Lippe. NSDAP: 26·9 per cent, four out of fifteen seats.
13 May 1931	Landtag elections in Oldenburg. NSDAP: 37·2 per cent, nineteen out of forty-eight seats. For the first time strongest party in the Landtag.
9 Sept. 1931	Talks with Hugenberg about possible cooperation with the Nationalist opposition.
15 Sept. 1931	NSDAP appoints the Minister for Domestic Affairs and Popular Education in Brunswick (Dietrich Klagges).
10 Oct. 1931	Hitler received by Hindenburg, the Reich President.
11 Oct. 1931	Formation of the *Harzburger Front*.
27 Jan. 1932	Hitler speaks at the *Industrie-Club*, Düsseldorf.
25 Feb. 1932	Appointed to the Brunswick Office of Agriculture and Land Survey as the attaché to the Brunswick Legation in Berlin responsible for representing the economic interests of the province. From now on a German citizen.
13 Mar. 1932	Candidate in first presidential election. Gains 30·23 per cent of the poll.

10 Apr. 1932	In second presidential election gains 36·68 per cent of the poll (13·4 million votes as against Hindenburg's 19·4 million and Thälmann's 3·7 million).
1 June 1932	Von Papen Reich Chancellor without a Reichstag majority.
4 June 1932	Dissolution of the Reichstag.
14 June 1932	Ban on SA and SS lifted. In return Hitler agrees to tolerate the government.
15–30 July 1932	Hitler speaks in fifty different towns.
31 July 1932	Reichstag elections. NSDAP gains more than 37 per cent of the votes and becomes the strongest party in the German Reichstag with 230 out of 608 seats.
13 Aug. 1932	Hitler and von Papen visit the Reich President. Having demanded and been refused the Chancellorship, Hitler rejects the offer of the Vice-Chancellorship.
6 Nov. 1932	Reichstag elections. The NSDAP still the strongest party despite loss of votes (down from 37·3 to only 31·1 per cent).
10 Nov. 1932	Hitler renounces the emoluments of his Brunswick appointment during his period of leave.
4 Jan. 1933	Hitler, Hess and Himmler meet von Papen in the house of the Cologne banker von Schröder. They pave the way for the overthrow of Schleicher, Reich Chancellor since 2 December 1932.
15 Jan. 1933	Landtag elections in Lippe (4–14.1.33 in sixteen places). NSDAP: nine out of twenty-one seats.
28 Jan. 1933	Schleicher's government resigns.
30 Jan. 1933	Hindenburg invites Hitler to be Reich Chancellor.
16 Feb. 1933	Hitler asks the Brunswick government to release him from his duties.
5 Mar. 1933	Reichstag elections. NSDAP: 43·9 per cent, 162 out of 422 seats.
17 Mar. 1933	Formation of the SS-Leibstandarte Adolf Hitler.
21 Mar. 1933	Celebrates 'Day of Potsdam' with Hindenburg in the Garrison Church.
24 Mar. 1933	'Law for Relieving the Distress of the People and the Reich' (Enabling Act).
1 Apr. 1933	Boycott of Jewish shops begins.
7 Apr. 1933	The Länder to be compulsorily coordinated (*Gleichschaltung*).
30 Apr. 1933	*Reichsstatthalter* (regional governors) appointed.
14 July 1933	Law for the Reconstruction of the Political Parties.

20 July 1933	Conclusion of the Concordat with the Holy See as a means of winning Catholic support.
31 Aug.–3 Sept. 1933	Fifth Party Rally in Nuremberg.
19 Oct. 1933	Germany leaves the League of Nations.
12 Nov. 1933	Reichstag elections. Also referendum enabling the nation to endorse or otherwise the policy which led to withdrawal from the League. Hitler obtains 92 per cent of the votes. The Reichstag henceforward merely a cipher.
14–15 June 1934	First meeting with Mussolini in Venice.
30 June 1934	'Röhm putsch'. The Reichswehr given priority over the SA. Large numbers of political opponents eliminated with the help of the Gestapo. SA reorganized.
20 July 1934	SS becomes an independent organization within the framework of the NSDAP.
2 Aug. 1934	Death of Hindenburg. Hitler combines offices of President and Chancellor and nominates himself 'Führer and Reich Chancellor'. The Wehrmacht swear an oath of allegiance to 'Adolf Hitler, the Führer of the Reich and of the German people'.
19 Aug. 1934	Plebiscite on the law concerning 'the Supreme Head of the German Reich' ('Führer and Reich Chancellor Adolf Hitler'): 90 per cent of the votes (out of a 99 per cent poll) support Hitler.
4–10 Sept. 1934	Sixth Party Rally in Nuremberg.
31 Jan. 1935	Saar plebiscite results in 91 per cent for the return of the Saar to Germany.
16 Mar. 1935	Promulgation of the 'Wehrmacht Law'. Reintroduction of general conscription.
21 May 1935	Legislation to regulate military service.
18 June 1935	Naval agreement with Great Britain.
9–16 Sept. 1935	Seventh Party Rally in Nuremberg. 'Law for the Protection of German Blood and German Honour' (known as the Nuremberg Laws) of 15 September 1935. Marriage with Jews prohibited. Public appointments dependent on 'Aryan extraction'. 'Reich Flag Law', 'Reich Citizenship Law', and 'Blood Protection Law'.
7 Mar. 1936	Repudiation of the Treaty of Locarno. Occupation of the demilitarized zones in the Rhineland. Full military sovereignty reestablished.
1–16 Aug. 1936	21st Olympic Games in Berlin.

24 Aug. 1936	Introduction of two year period of compulsory military service.
8–14 Sept. 1936	Eighth Party Rally in Nuremberg. Marked anti-Bolshevist emphasis. Announcement of Four Year Plan.
25 Oct. 1936	Rome–Berlin Axis. Anti-Comintern Pact between Germany and Japan.
30 Jan. 1937	Enabling Act extended for a period of four years.
6–13 Aug. 1937	Ninth Party Rally in Nuremberg.
5 Nov. 1937	Hitler's 'political testament' presented in the form of a discourse on foreign policy and military aims (Hossbach Minutes).
4 Feb. 1938	Dismissal of the War Minister, von Blomberg, and of the Commander-in-Chief of the Army, Colonel General von Fritsch. Hitler assumes the office of Reich War Minister. Colonel General von Brauchitsch appointed Commander in Chief of the Army. Creation of a High Command of the Armed Forces under Wilhelm Keitel (later Field-Marshal). Von Ribbentrop replaces Neurath as Foreign Minister, thus extending the influence of the party to the Foreign Office.
11 Mar. 1938	German troops enter Austria.
13 Mar. 1938	Austria becomes part of the German Reich.
2 May 1938	Hitler prepares his will.
3–9 May 1938	Meets Mussolini in Rome.
Sept. 1938	Deliberate intensification of the Bohemian–Moravian crisis.
16 Sept. 1938	Talks with Chamberlain in Berchtesgaden.
22–24 Sept. 1938	Talks with Chamberlain in Godesberg.
26 Sept. 1938	Speech in the Berlin *Sportpalast*. Demands cession of the Sudetenland to Germany. 'Final demand' for a revision.
28 Sept. 1938	Acceptance of Mussolini's proposal, made as a result of British initiatives, for a four power conference in Munich.
29 Sept. 1938	Confers with Mussolini, Daladier and Chamberlain in Munich (Munich Agreement).
1 Oct. 1938	German troops enter the Sudeten German territories.
9 Nov. 1938	*Kristallnacht*. Antisemitic excesses (destruction of Jewish dwellings, businesses, synagogues etc.) after the murder by a Jew of Ernst von Rath, a member of the German Embassy in Paris.
15 Mar. 1939	German troops enter Czechoslovakia (after the Czech

President Hacha and Foreign Minister Chvalkovsky had signed a declaration placing Bohemia and Moravia under German 'protection'). Czech forces disarmed.

16 Mar. 1939	Decree establishing the Protectorate of Bohemia and Moravia. These territories incorporated into the German Reich.
23 Mar. 1939	The Wehrmacht enters Memel.
26 Mar. 1939	Poland rejects the German proposals dated 24 October 1938 and 21 March 1939 for the return of Danzig to the Reich, the concession of an extra-territorial road and railway through the Corridor, and the offer of a lasting guarantee of the German–Polish frontiers.
22 May 1939	'Pact of Steel'. Military alliance between the Reich and Italy.
July 1939	Trade talks with the Soviet Union.
23 Aug. 1939	Non-aggression Pact with the Soviet Union containing an additional secret clause. German–Polish crisis.
1 Sept. 1939	Germany attacks Poland.
3 Sept. 1939	Great Britain, Australia, India, New Zealand and France declare war on Germany.
28 Sept. 1939	Soviet–German Friendship and Frontier Agreement.
6 Oct. 1939	Peace offer to the Western Powers. South Africa declares war on the Reich, followed by Canada on 10 Oct. 1939.
8 Nov. 1939	Speech to the Party veterans in the Bürgerbräukeller in Munich. Failure of Georg Elser's attempt at assassination. Eight killed, sixty-three injured.
9 Apr. 1940	Commencement of German campaigns in Denmark and Norway.
10 May 1940	Germany attacks the Netherlands, Luxemburg, Belgium and France.
22 June 1940	Armistice with France.
6 April 1941	Attack on Yugoslavia and Greece.
10 May 1941	Attack on Soviet Union.
7 Dec. 1941	Japan attacks American fleet in Pearl Harbour.
8 Dec. 1941	Germany at war with China (Chungking government) and France (de Gaulle government). (This chronology omits the dates on which diplomatic relations were broken off.)
11 Dec. 1941	Germany declares war on the USA, turning the conflict into the Second World War. State of hostilities with

	Cuba, the Dominican Republic, Guatemala and Nicaragua.
12 Dec. 1941	Haiti, Honduras and El Salvador declare war on Germany.
16 Dec. 1941	State of hostilities with Czechoslovakia (Czech Government in Exile).
19 Dec. 1941	Dismissal of Field Marshal von Brauchitsch. Hitler now Commander-in-Chief of the Army.
20 Jan. 1942	Wannsee talks on the 'final solution of the Jewish question'.
	Germany at war with Panama (13 January 1942), Luxemburg (Government in Exile) (15 January), Mexico (28 May), Brazil (28 August) and Abyssinia (9 October).
7–8 Nov. 1942	Allied landings in North Africa.
18 Nov. 1942– 2 Feb. 1943	Battle of Stalingrad.
	At war with Iraq (16 January), Bolivia (7 April), Iran (9 September), the Badoglio Government of Italy (13 October) and Colombia.
13 May 1943	Final surrender in North Africa.
6 June 1944	Allies invade France. At war with Liberia (26 January), Romania (16 August), Bulgaria (8 September), San Marino (21 September) and Hungary (31 December).
20 July 1944	Stauffenberg's assassination attempt.
25 Sept. 1944	Organization of the *Deutscher Volkssturm*.
16 Dec. 1944	Opening of Ardennes offensive.
30 Jan. 1945	Last broadcast by Hitler.
	At war with Ecuador (2 February), Paraguay (8 February), Peru (12 February), Chile (14 February), Uruguay (15 February), Venezuela (16 February), Turkey (23 February), Egypt (24 February), Syria (26 February), Lebanon (27 February), Saudi Arabia (1 March), Finland (3 March) and the Argentine (27 March).
25 Apr. 1945	American and Soviet troops link up at Torgau on the Elbe.
29 Apr. 1945	Hitler marries Eva Braun. Writes private and political testaments.
30 Apr. 1945	Suicide in the Chancellery bunker.

Notes for a speech ★

Jewish domination and starvation of the nation.
Unrest
Discontent   Agitation   Mistrust
Intellectual and factual migration.
Catholics become extreme socialists –
Communists revert to being bible students.
                              Everything tends towards
Want – Misery – Scarcity – Famine.
Despite efforts to the contrary.
                              Inadequate means
Whose fault?

     1. A government. (Kahr, Pöhner, Heim)
       in Saxony? Prussia – the Rhineland?

     2. The Prussian. And Austria?

     3. the capitalist system and in Russia?

     Nature?
does not work gradually but by cataclysms
might be parallelized [*sic*] today in transport etc.
               No, it must have more important causes

Kahr – Prussia – Capitalism etc. not
                   universal
                   but
                   the Jew?
Antiquity.
Egypt – Rome – Palestine | Middle Ages – Modern Times
Jewish domination and starvation of the people
Who is invariably to blame for this?
     Never the Jew?

★ Federal Archives, Coblenz, NS 26/49. Hitler's arrangement and punctuation have been retained.

First an analysis.

A thousand years of
wandering

$$\left\{\begin{array}{l}\text{Egypt}\\\text{Palestine}\\\text{Babylon}\\\text{Rome}\\\text{Europe}\end{array}\right.$$

still a people.
Infinitely 'national'
everywhere 'foreigners', –
     just like today in fact.
Gives rise to 'urge for world domination'.
     The Jew as 'world factor = & = power'
     Jahveh's prophecy only the
expression of the obvious end and goal.
Necessary result of Jewish disposition.

Complete domination or nothing
hence all Jewish creations are means towards
          World domination
          ===============
How does he conduct the struggle for this.
economically   and   politically
     Purely intellectual preparation.
     Compassion as a means.
in big things as in small.
          Economically,

I. Devours the economy, the land
                ==============
Control of stock exchange – price fixing.
     Monopoly of raw materials
Not ownership of land but control.
===============   ========
(Land tenure)   (Book of Esther)
Middle Ages   Control of entire production
===========
Land ownership forbidden
Result of the economic struggle is
Scarcity – Withering away of host race
(creeper)
     A people's character the same as a person's.
The Jew is eternally asocial.

That means materialistic:

Attitude to work

| |

Egotism and dedication

Springboard for   Always the same
unearned income   (Berlin garden suburbs)
              Bible

Unearned income of individuals only
   possible as parasite in the body of those who work.

Unearned incomes of peoples only
   possible in 'parasite races'.

Jewish domination and starvation of the people.

Jews poor among themselves.

(Only thrive in foreign bodies)
          (Effect then like a creeper)

Throughout the ages a state within the state

Antiquity – Middle Ages – Modern Times –
          Always persecuted.
          Always equally hated.

Not because the peoples were wicked but in self-defence.

Econ. parasitism is the same as
   domination
   ====

No lasting economic enslavement without
          'political domination'

Political struggle

First   Guardians of the oppressed
                      (as in small things)
                   If aristocracy   then democracy
                   If democracy   then dictatorship
                   If monarchy   then republic
                   If republic   then dictatorship
   Divide the people itself
First divide then conquer.
      The Jew as fission fungus
          Splits the classes.
Creates snobbery on the one side
   and protests on the other.
      (Schoppenhauer [sic] – master of lies)

The Jew as the destroyer of a
nation's inner stability.
(Jericho)   against
                                   1. Character,
                                   2. Decency,
                                   3. Morals
                                   4. Morality (traffic in women)
                                   5. Religion – bible students, reason.
Art,   6. Value of personality,
Science,   7. Belief in the self
Press,   8. Concept of nation
Literature,   9. National values
Theatre,   10. Commercial morality – (Christian–Jewish)
Cinema,   11. destroys sense of justice
etc.   ═══

                                  Jewish rights
                                  Property rights
                                  Human rights (Workers [illegible] –
                                                      'Capitalism')

Destruction of all stability
Fatherland everywhere
Slogan,

                                  the world state,
                                  needs

Miscegenation
Racial pollution = result. –
        World hotch-potch
        World Press
        World literature
        World stock exchange
        World culture
        World language

---

i.e. the world under one master
One thrust to world-mastery
        World revolution
              means:
The oppression of the whole earth
under the dictatorship of the world
stock exchange and its
              masters,
              Judah.

Presupposes
        Elimination of all national
        intelligence.
Racial suicide
        for which prerequisite is
        Mass insanity
        can be fomented.
by mass want – Hunger.
Hunger as a weapon throughout
                        the ages.
Hunger in the service of the Jews,
        destroys physical strength and health
        confuses the mind.

Systematic starvation of a nation
        through shortages.
1. In Germany before the war,
2. During the war.
After the war.
        Causes of shortages –
        Armistice –   Revolution of
        _____   the
                Wasteful economy   stock exchange
                _____   [illegible]

Peace treaty
_____
How can it be solved.

Solution of the Jewish question
Creation of a social state.
                Our programme
                _____
                Apostle of a new truth
                _____
Struggle against us.
Berlin.
Germany will be free notwithstanding.

Daily routine and menu

10 a.m.	Hitler, still in his nightshirt, fetches the morning papers which, together with low priority signals, memoranda, reports, etc., have been placed on the chair outside his door by his manservant (1934–39 Karl Wilhelm Krause; 1939–45 Heinz Linge). He returns to bed to peruse all this material, after which he washes, shaves and dresses. (Later, when illness made his hand tremble, he had somebody else shave him.)
About 11 a.m.	His servant knocks at the locked door and calls out: 'Good morning, my Führer. It's time now!'
Between 11 and 12 a.m.	Hitler rings a bell to summon his breakfast: in the early years a glass of milk, an apple and a piece of crispbread; later a piece of milk bread, and peppermint, apple or camomile tea (with a dash of brandy when he had a cold). Sometimes also a piece of cheese (preferably Gervaise). Later still (1944–45), large portion of cake and a cup of chocolate, or else a mixture of porridge oats, grated apple, nuts, lemon juice and a wheat germ preparation soaked in milk.

The adjutant brings him the more important memoranda and together they arrange the times for the day's conferences. While in the Chancellery bunker he seldom went to bed before 8 a.m. (after a breakfast of cake followed by a game with his Alsatian puppy, Wolf). His short rest was usually interrupted at about eleven o'clock by an air raid alert.

Before the war he would foregather after midday with colleagues and advisers, or receive members of the government and other visitors.

Between 2 and 5 p.m.	Lunch: Fruit, soup (never meat broth), beans, carrots and other vegetables, potatoes and, invariably, salad dressed with lemon juice only. Hitler liked vegetable stew, particularly when made with butter beans, split peas or lentils. He was also fond of baked potatoes which he would dip in butter after peeling them. In order not to embarrass his guests when they were eating steak, Hitler would have a mock steak made entirely of vegetables. Otherwise his food was much the same as theirs. After 1941 he would sometimes eat sardines in oil,

but continued to refuse all food (except for liver dumplings) that contained meat. Vegetables had to be dressed with unsalted butter (when butter became scarce some other form of fat was substituted). At one period he was not averse to eggs stuffed with genuine caviar but, on learning how expensive this was, he no longer allowed it to be served.

Hitler was also fond of fried eggs and bread, the latter baked without leaven and served with the crust removed.

He was quite prepared to eat bread dumplings several days running, provided they were cooked in different ways (roast, baked, boiled, etc.).

Between 8 p.m. and 12 a.m.

Supper, in Hitler's case usually boiled eggs, potatoes in their jackets, and curd cheese.

When supper was over he would take an hour's rest (not always possible in wartime). After Stalingrad he adopted the habit of drinking a glass or two of beer, hoping it would make him sleepy. He gave this up, however, when he realized that he was putting on weight.

Before the war his short rest was followed by a 'fireside chat', and latterly by a situation conference which, as the war progressed, would quite often continue until 6 a.m. or even later. In 1944–45 (particularly in Berlin) he would sometimes still be in session with his female secretaries, his adjutant Schaub or his personal physician, Dr Morell, at 8 a.m.

List of drugs prescribed by Dr Morell, 1936–45

The preparations marked with an asterisk are those shown as still in current use in the *Rote Liste 1969: Verzeichnis pharmazeutischer Spezialpräparate* (Aulendorf 1969).

Brom-Nervacit (Potassium bromide, sodium barbitone, aminopyrine) every other month as a tranquillizer and hypnotic: 1–2 tablets.

Cardiazol (pentamethylenetetrazol) and *Coramine* (diethylnicotinamide) for the stimulation of the circulatory centre in the brain, the vascular nerves and the respiratory centres given at intervals in the form of a solution from 1941 onwards (when oedema of the legs developed): ten drops a week.

Chineurin (product containing quinine, influenza remedy) taken orally to treat colds.

Cortiron (deoxycortone acetate, product of adrenocortical hormone) intended to combat muscular weakness and to influence the absorption of fats and carbohydrate metabolism (alleged by Morell to have been administered once only): intramuscular injection.

Dr Köster's Antigas Pills (extr. nuc. vom. extr. bellad. aa 0.5, extr. Gent.) to combat flatulence; from 1936–43 (with occasional interruptions), before each meal.

Eubasin (sulphonamide) injected to combat infection and colibacilli: 5 ccm intragluteally.

Euflat (active bile extract: radix angelica, papaverine, aloe, coffea tosta, pancreatin and fel tauri) to promote digestion and also to inhibit flatulence; in the form of pills from 1939–44.

Eukodal (chlorohydrate of dihydroxycodeine, produced from thebaine) narcotic, analgesic and anti-spasmodic.

Eupaverin (isoquinoline derivative) for spasms and colic.

Glucose (5–10 per cent in solution added to other injections) to supplement calories and to enhance the action of strophantine, injected from 1937–40 (except for short interruptions): 10 ccm every two or three days.

Glyconorm (metabolic enzymes, containing cozymase I and II, vitamins and amino-acids) to promote the digestion of vegetable foods and reduce flatulence: administered occasionally (rarely, according to Morell), from 1938–40: 2 ccm intramuscular injections.

Homatropin P O S eyedrops (homatropine-hydrobromide. 0·1 g; sod. chlor. 0·08 g; aqua dest. ad 10 ml) for treatment of the right eye.

Intelan (vitamins A, D_3 and B_{12}) to stimulate the appetite, help convalescence, protect against infection, promote physical resistance and combat tiredness, given therapeutically from 1942–44 (like *Vitamultin*): in tablet form, twice daily before meals.

Camomile for enemas: at patient's request.

Luizym (enzyme preparation; digestive enzyme; cellulose, hemicelluloses amylase and proteases) against digestive weakness (disturbance of protein digestion) and flatulence: one tablet after meals.

Mutaflor (emulsion of a strain of Escherichia coli) for causal therapy of symptoms connected with abnormal intestinal flora (e.g. meteorism, eczema and migraine, depressive states), given by Morell from 1936–40 for the regulation of intestinal flora in enteric capsules (colibacilli: normally about 25 thousand million organisms per capsule): on the first day, one yellow capsule, on the second, third and fourth, one red capsule, and from the fifth day onwards, two red capsules. (In 1943 *Trocken-Coli-Hamma* was given for this purpose.)

Omnadin (combination of proteins, lipoids from the bile and animal fat) to inhibit colds in the early stages of infection (sometimes in combination with *Vitamultin-Calcium*): intramuscular injection, 2 ccm.

Optalidon (patent analgesic of barbiturates and amidopyrines: allyl isobutylbarbituric acid = 0·05 g, dimethylaminophenazon, pyramidon = 0·125 g, caffeine = 0·025 g) for headaches: 1–2 tablets taken orally.

Orchikrin (extract of the seminal vesicles and prostate of young bulls, reinforced male sex hormone) to promote potency and combat exhaustion and depression (administered once only, according to Morell): 2·2 cm intramuscular injection.

Penicillin-Hamma: After the assassination attempt of 20 July 1944, over a period of eight to ten days in powder form, for treatment of the right hand.

Progynon B-oleosum (benzoic ester of follicular hormone) to improve the circulation of the gastric mucosa, and to prevent spasms of the stomach walls and vesicles, by intramuscular injection 1937–38.

Prostacrinum (extract of seminal vesicles and prostate) for the prevention of depression, given over a short period in 1943 at two day intervals: 2 ampoules, by intramuscular injection.

Prostrophanta (composite injection: 0·3 mg strophanthin in combination with glucose and Vitamin-B; nicotinic acid) given like strophanthin.

Septoid, for respiratory infections (Morell believed that by administering this drug he could also slow down the progress of arteriosclerosis): maximum dose, 20 ccm, injected.

Strophanthin (glycoside from Strophanthus gratus) for the treatment of coronary sclerosis: from 1941–44, in two to three week cycles, intravenous injections 0·2 mg daily.

Sympatol (p-hydroxyphenyl methylamino ethanol tartrate) to increase the minute volume of the heart, to promote cardiac activity and to help overcome cardiac and vascular insufficiency: from 1942 onwards (with occasional interruptions), 10 drops daily.

Tonophosphan (sodium salt of dimethylaminomethylphenylphosphinic acid) non-toxic preparation of phosphorus used both to supplement phosphorus and to stimulate the smooth muscles. From 1942–44, injected subcutaneously from time to time.

Trocken-Coli-Hamma: see under *Mutaflor*.

Ultraseptyl (sulphonamide) to combat inflammation of the upper respiratory tract: 1–2 tablets orally. To prevent concretions (e.g. kidney stones), taken with fruit juice or water after meals.

Veritol 1(4-hydroxyphenyl)-2-methylamino-propane. In 1 g (20 drops): 0·01 g, in 1 ml ampoule solution: 0·02 g Veritol-sulphate. For the treatment of the left eye, from March 1944.

Vitamultin-Calcium (A, B complex, C, D, E, K, P) injected in combination with other drugs from 1938 to 1944: every other day 4·4 ccm.

The above list is complete save for Morell's product, the 'golden' *Vitamultin* tablets containing *Pervitin* and caffeine.

Locations of headquarters,
September 1939 – April 1945

Polish campaign from 3 Sept. 1939	Accommodated in the Führer's special train (office and living coach for Hitler, several signals and Press coaches, and diners and sleepers for the Staff. A flak truck at either end of the train). Locations: Polzin, Gross-Born, Illnau bei Oppeln, Goddentow-Lanz. Also in the Casino Hotel at Zoppot.
26 Sept. 1939	Return to Berlin.
Campaign in the West (France)	'Felsennest' (from 10 May 1940) at Rodert near Münstereifel (*Führerbunker*). 'Wolfsschlucht' (from 4 June 1940) at Bruly de Pêche where Hitler lived in a hut, his staff in the school house and presbytery. 'Tannenberg' on the Kniebis in the Black Forest (from 25 June 1940). According to Hitler's secretary, Christa Schröder, 'there were a few small, damp bunkers in which life was almost impossible'.
Campaign against Yugoslavia and Greece, April 1941	Special train at Mönichkirchen.
7 July 1940	Return to Berlin.
Campaign against the Soviet Union	'Wolfsschanze' (from 24 June 1941) at Rastenberg in East Prussia. Concrete bunkers above-ground and a few wooden huts. 'Werwolf' at Vinnitsa in the Ukraine (July to October 1942 and February to March 1943). Two concrete bunkers, block-houses and huts in lightly wooded ground.
From October 1942	'Wolfsschanze'. 'Berghof' (Hitler's property since the twenties and enlarged after 1933 with contribution from the 'Adolf Hitler Fund'), situated on the Obersalzberg near Berchtesgaden. Also Schloss Klessheim at Salzburg.
20 Nov.–10 Dec. 1944	Reich Chancellery, Berlin, in the bunker built for the Führer (1943) in the Chancellery garden.

Hitler's secretary, Christa Schröder, writes: 'Hitler's room was very cramped and could accommodate no more than a small desk, a small sofa, a table and three chairs. The room was cold and uncomfortable. A door on the left led into his bathroom and one on the right into his equally small bedroom.'

Dec.1944–Jan. 1945 (Ardennes Offensive) 'Adlerhorst' on the Ziegenberg estate in the Taunus. The manor house was enlarged in 1939 to serve as a headquarters for Hitler.

16 Jan. 1945 until his suicide Reich Chancellery, Berlin (*Führerbunker* in the Chancellery garden).

Notes and references

Abbreviations used in references:

IMT. Record of proceedings against major war criminals, Nuremberg.
Manheim. Hitler's *Mein Kampf*, trans. Ralph Manheim, London 1969.
Picker. Picker, Henry, Hitler's *Tischgespräche im Führerhauptquartier 1941–1942*, Stuttgart 1963.

CHAPTER ONE. *Family and Antecedents*

1. Cf. *Der Spiegel*, 31/67, leading article on some of the author's findings in this field.
2. The entry in the Döllersheim parish register against 'Bride and groom' reads: 'Anna Schicklgruber, resident in her father's house, legitimate daughter of Johann Schicklgruber of this parish . . . and the late Theresia, née Pfeisinger of Dietreichs' (10 Aug. 1842). The entry recording her death: 'Hiedler, Maria, wife of Hiedler,Georg, resident in Klein-Motten no. 4, legitimate daughter of Johann Schicklgruber, formerly farmer of Strones and of Theresia, née Pfeisinger of Dietreichs' (3 Jan. 1847). The cause of death is given as 'Consumption resulting from pectoral dropsy'.
3. Cf. Jetzinger, pp. 16 f. Franz Jetzinger is a former Catholic priest with a provincial background and political ambitions. His book, although in many ways illuminating, is far from objective.
4. There had been another Maria Anna Schicklgruber in Strones, but by this time she had left the village. Cf. Document in Lower Austrian Provincial Archives, Allentsteig Area Court Archives, 8/13, fol. 63 f.
5. Handwritten entries in the Orphans' Fund records, Lower Austrian Provincial Archives, Allentsteig Area Court Archives 8/17, fol. 48.
6. *Ibid*, fol. 23 on which the name appears as Schikelgrueber.
7. Record of transactions for 1793 of the Lordship of Ottenstein.
8. Waldreich Estate Surety Register, Allentsteig District Court Archives, fol. 43.
9. Allensteig District Court Archives, fol. 138.
10. Waldreich Estate Surety Register, Allentsteig District Court Archives, fol. 43.
11. Cf. points 5, 6 and 7 of the NSDAP programme; also Maser, *Die Frühgeschichte der NSDAP*, pp. 468 ff.
12. Manheim, p. 2. Hitler deviated only once from the information given in *Mein Kampf*. On 29 Nov. 1921, in a letter to an unidentified recipient, he stated that his father had been a 'postal official'. Doc: typescript copy of 26 Aug. 1941. The bottom lefthand corner bears the stamp of the NSDAP Central Archives and the name 'Richter' underneath the words 'Authen-

ticated copy'. Former NSDAP Central Archives, Federal Archives, Coblenz, NS 26/17a. *Doc. cit.* Maser, *Frühgeschichte*, pp. 487 ff.

13. Manheim, p. 17.

14. Cf. Maser, *Hitlers Mein Kampf*, pp. 95 ff.

15. See Picker, p. 268, also pp. 199 f. and 232 f. Hitler also refused to let another of his half-brother's sons, Heinz, become a professional soldier on completion of his training at the National-Political Education Centre in 1938; the very name Hitler, he maintained, would evoke toadyism in Heinz's comrades, whether officers or men. In the event the young man was killed in Russia while serving as an NCO with the 23rd Potsdam Artillery Regiment.

16. Letter from Paula Hitler, 10 Jan. 1960.

17. From Probate Certificate, copy in author's possession. Alois Hitler's deceased stepsister and Angela Hammitsch, née Hitler, were each entitled to one sixth of the inheritance. On 25 Oct. 1960, under file entry no. VI 108/60, the Berchtesgaden District Court ruled that 'the heirs to Paula Hitler deceased 1 June 1960 in Schönau . . . shall be her sister's children. . . . Elfriede Hochegger née Raubal . . . Leo Raubal . . . each to inherit one half'.

18. From an entry in the Leonding local records. Also told to the author by the Burgomaster of Leonding, August 1969.

19. Hitler never raised any objection to the documentation of Döllersheim and its surroundings. On the contrary: in 1942, for example, he authorized the publication by the Sudetendeutsche Verlags und Drukkerei GmbH of Eger of a lavish book entitled *Die Alte Heimat. Beschreibung des Waldviertels um Döllersheim (Ancestral Home. Description of the Waldviertel round Döllersheim)*. Containing numerous photographs it gives a detailed account of the region and its history, and revolves round Hitler's forebears, the Schicklgrubers and the Hiedlers. Even at that time it was impossible to identify the house in which Alois Hitler was born in 1837. 'Various attempts have been made', we read, 'to find out which house belonged to the Shicklgrubers. This proved exceptionally difficult because new land registers came into being as a result of the abolition of the Patrimonial Courts (in 1848) so that the holdings in Strones were given entirely new designations. No records appear to have been kept of the former house numbers.' *Die Alte-Heimat*, p. 268.

20. Jetzinger, pp. 34 f.

21. Land Register, 21 Mar. 1961, Vienna, pp. 100–2.

22. 1941, Series 20, no. 226.

23. Register of parishes of Austria, p. 100.

24. Extract from reports of the German Resettlement Association, 1 Sept. 1944, supplied to Theodor Fabian who was responsible for the purchase of villages and for compensating those who had to move out. Reproduction and copies of the reports in possession of the author.

25. Verbal information supplied by Hitler's relations (May 1969).

26. *Die Alte Heimat* contains a picture of the cross on this memorial; p. 62.

27. Written information (26 July 1967) supplied by the former Hitler Youth Hauptjungzugführer Klaus Fabian of 4 Troop, 520 Company, S.E. Lower Danube, who was ordered by his superiors to visit Maria Anna Schicklgruber's grave with his troop.

28. *Ibid.* Klaus Fabian was the son of Th. Fabian (see n. 24 above). Also the documents relating to Theodor Fabian belonging to the German Resettlement Association, Klagenfurt office, including those dated 9 Nov. 1943, 1 Sept. 1944 and 30 Sept. 1945.

29. Letter to the author from Frau Elfriede Binder, Theodor Fabian's secretary.

30. Cf. Maser, *Frühgeschichte*, pp. 270 ff.

31. *Ibid*, p. 271.

32. Konrad Heiden's popular biography of Hitler, in which it is suggested that he might be of Jewish origin, was published in Zürich. The book has had a decisive influence on a whole generation of historians and biographers.

33. Death certificate no. 5653 issued by the Bucharest municipality.

34. *Daily Mirror*, 14 Oct. 1933.

35. *Forward*, 21 Jan. 1966, in which extracts from old newspapers are quoted.

36. Cf. Simon Wiesenthal's account in *Der Spiegel*, no. 33/67, p. 5; also *ibid*, p. 6, an extract from a French periodical of Sept. 1933.

37. Typescript under NSDAP letterhead. Federal Archives, Coblenz, NS 26/14.

38. Typewritten notes by SS leaders concerning investigations into Hitler's antecedents. Federal Archives, Coblenz, NS 26/17a. Appended to one document dated 4 Aug. 1942 is a handwritten message: 'Please send here, Reichsführer wishes to retain.'

39. From unpublished entries in the diary of the German ambassador in Madrid. Document in the possession of the Bechtle Verlag. Cf. also references to this subject in *Der Spiegel*, 31/67, p. 42; also Bezymenski, *The Death of Adolf Hitler*, p. 17.

40. Frank, *Im Angesicht des Galgens*, p. 330.

41. *Ibid*, p. 19.

42. *Ibid*, pp. 330 ff.

43. *Ibid.*

44. Information supplied personally by Leo Raubal in the course of several conversations from May 1969 onwards.

45. Cf. Kessler, 'Familiennamen der Juden in Deutschland', thesis, Leipzig, 1935.

46. The name of Frankenberger does not appear in the records of the Jewish Community in Graz (1864–1938), in those of other religious communities between 1838 and 1900, or again in the records kept up till 1837. Nor does the name occur in the parish registers of the territory annexed in 1938, in the householders' register of the Greater Graz area, in the 1936 registration card indexes or in the census records for the years 1880, 1890 and 1910.

47. Cf. Pirchegger, *Geschichte der Steiermark*, vol. ii, pp. 281–9 and pp. 318 ff.
48. Lower Austrian Provincial Archives, Allentsteig Area Court Archives 8/17, fols 48 ff.
49. *Ibid.*
50. This point was established by the Austrian historian Nikolaus von Preradovich who communicated it to the author in March 1957.
51. Cf. Jetzinger, p. 32.
52. Vol. ii, p. 156, sixth entry.
53. Cf. Frank, p. 431; also I M T, vol. xii. Before the tribunal Frank declared: 'Not even the passage of a thousand years will lift the burden of guilt from Germany.'
54. Letters from Alois Hitler to Frau Veit, 6 and 13 Sept. 1876. Library of Congress. Material not in H A 17, A, R 1.
55. Vol. xiii, 1852–91.
56. Vol. xix.
57. Library of Congress. Material H A 17, A, R 1.
58. Bracher, *Die deutsche Diktatur*, p. 61.
59. For text of regulations see Döllersheim register of births (now in Rastenfeld Presbytery).
60. File ref. 30704/4274 (handwritten), Lower Austrian Provincial Archives.
61. *Ibid.*
62. *Ibid*, file ref. 7845; 35784 and 30704.
63. *Ibid*, file ref. 35784/4956 and 30704.
64. *Ibid*, file ref. 37381/5184 and 30704.
65. Görlitz, p. 14.
66. Koppensteiner, *Die Ahnentafel des Führers*.
67. Manheim, p. 4. The term 'poor cottager' has led unsuspecting National Socialist biographers to describe Alois Hitler as the son of a Spital peasant. But Georg Hiedler was never in fact a cottager. As a journeyman miller he moved about from place to place, lodging in other people's houses, among them the farmhouse in Strones where Maria Anna Schicklgruber was then living with her parents.
68. Because of the close inbreeding in his family, Hitler is known to have been afraid of becoming a father, being tormented by the thought that any child he engendered might be at risk. Yet he so far followed the family pattern as to enter into an incestuous relationship with his niece, Geli Raubal, who was reputedly pregnant by him when she committed suicide in 1931. Cf. *Paris-Soir*, 5 Sept. 1939.
69. Information supplied by descendants, Aug. 1969.
70. Adolf and his mother had a number of features in common, e.g. eyes, eyebrows, mouth and ears. He may have been alluding to this on 24 June 1942 when he said: 'A mother's characteristics are usually to be found in her son' (Picker, p. 413).
71. Cf. also J. Arthur May, *The Habsburg Monarchy, 1867–1914*, Cambridge, Mass., 1951, pp. 173–4, and Geoffrey Drage, *Austria–Hungary, 1909*, p. 58.

72. Deeds shown to the author by the owner of the inn, Aug. 1969.
73. 'Records of house purchases in Spital and Schwarzenbach, 1796–1845', Weitra District Court, fol. 70.
74. Cf. Leo Weber's account of 12 Oct. 1938 and HA 17, R 1. The date is not absolutely certain. Smith (*Adolf Hitler*, p. 31) gives 16 March 1889 as the date on which Alois Hitler paid the purchase price, but this does not alter the case.
75. Cf. also Jetzinger, p. 122.
76. After retirement Alois paid 20 kronen a year; cf. also Jetzinger, p. 123.
77. Handwritten invoice dated December 1907. The cost of Franziska Hitler's funeral and those of her three children would probably have been less than that incurred by Adolf in 1907 when, as eighteen-year-old head of the family, he paid 369·64 kronen (including 110 kronen for a metal-bound coffin) for the conveyance of Klara Hitler's body from Linz to Leonding and its interment there. Handwritten account, Dec. 1907: Federal Archives, Coblenz, N S 26/65.
78. Cf. Smith, p. 46.
79. Cf. also Maser, *Frühgeschichte*, p. 60 and doc. in Federal Archives, Coblenz, N S 26/65.

CHAPTER TWO. *Childhood and Youth*

1. Gustav Hitler died of diphtheria on 8 Dec. 1887, his sister Ida twenty-five days later. Otto, born 1887, lived only a few days.
2. Information supplied by Hitler's cousin in Spital, Anton Schmidt, August 1969. Klara often took Adolf to stay at this cousin's house.
3. Manheim, p. 3.
4. Cf. entry relating to Alois Hitler's departure, reproduced in HA 17, 1. Original probably among the Arlington material.
5. Cf. Central Archive papers, HA 17, R 1 (*Wörnharts*).
6. Photograph by F. Rammer in *Der Spiegel* 33/67, p. 8 and reader's letter from Harry Schulze-Wilde (author of *Die Reichskanzlei*, 4th edition, Düsseldorf, 1960).
7. Rosalia Hoerl's account, HA, 17, R 1.
8. Cf. Kubizek, p. 54.
9. Cf. also Smith, p. 55.
10. Cf. Maser, *Frühgeschichte*, p. 503.
11. Munich police files for 1924, HA, 1760, R 25 A. Cf. also HA, 65, R 13 A.
12. Cf. Manheim, pp. 6 ff.
13. *Ibid*, p. 4.
14. *Ibid*, p. 5.
15. Information supplied by Mgr Haudum (August 1969). See also letter of 10 Nov. 1923 written to Hitler by his boyhood friend Fritz Seidl (Class I, Linz Secondary School), Federal Archives, Coblenz, N S 26/14.
16. Cf. Kubizek, p. 66.

17. Information supplied by Mgr Haudum, August 1969, who relates that she saved the life of an Austrian engineer who had been condemned to death.
18. Cf. Kubizek, pp. 31 and 114.
19. Cf. Patrick Hitler's article in *Paris-Soir*, 5 Aug. 1939.
20. Cf. also Smith, p. 60.
21. Cf. HA, 17, R 1 A.
22. Manheim, p. 6.
23. Kubizek, p. 111. Cf. also Maser, *Frühgeschichte*, pp. 514 f.
24. Orr, *Revue*, no. 40, 4 Oct. 1952, p. 35.
25. Information supplied by the Leonding schoolmaster Alois Harrer and the former Leonding priest Mgr Haudum (August 1969). They both knew Winter personally and had sometimes talked to him about Hitler's childhood.
26. Original typescript. Former NSDAP Central Archives, Federal Archives, Coblenz, NS 26/17a.
27. Manheim, p. 5.
28. Letter from Fritz Seidl to Adolf Hitler, 10 Nov. 1923, typescript, Federal Archives, Coblenz, NS 26/14.
29. Manheim, p. 5.
30. Entry in the Hitler House visitors' book, p. 2.
31. Cf. Kubizek, p. 37.
32. From copy (in author's possession), authenticated by Heim, of the original MS of Heim's record, 8/9 Jan. 1942. Kubizek wrongly avers that Sixtl was headmaster of Leonding Primary School.
33. Kubizek, p. 67.
34. Manheim, pp. 9 and 10.
35. *Ibid*, pp. 7 f.
36. *Ibid*.
37. *Ibid*.
38. *Ibid*, p. 9.
39. Kubizek, p. 64.
40. Manheim, p. 17.
41. Kubizek, p. 63.
42. Cf. *ibid*, pp. 61 *passim*.
43. Letter from Dr Huemer, 28 April 1935. NA. T-84, List no. 4, 3.
44. Kubizek, pp. 69 f.
45. Cf. *Münchner Post*, 27 Nov. 1923 and *Bayerischer Kurier*, 30 Nov. 1923. Hitler repudiated these allegations both publicly and privately, cf. *Bayerischer Kurier*, 5 Dec. 1923.
46. Handwritten report by Professor Gregor Goldbacher, 29 Jan 1941. Orig. in former NSDAP Central Archives, Federal Archives, Coblenz, NS 26/17 a.
47. Heim's record, 8 and 9 Jan. 1942 (author's own copy).
48. Report of 11 Feb. 1905. Published in *Der Spiegel*, 34/66, p. 46, along with pre-publication extracts from Maser, *Hitlers Mein Kampf*.

49. Picker, p. 191.
50. Heim's report, 1942.
51. Hitler's school report, 16 Sept. 1905.
52. Morell's deposition. Information also supplied by Dr Giesing who attended Hitler from July to October 1944.
53. Handwritten account by his teacher, Goldbacher, 29 Jan. 1941.
54. Kubizek, p. 20.
55. Manheim, p. 17.
56. Information supplied by Hitler's cousin, Anton Schmidt (1969).
57. *Ibid.*
58. *Ibid.*
59. Cf. Kubizek, p. 72.
60. Cf. *ibid*, p. 145.
61. *Ibid*, pp. 146 f.
62. Cf. also Manheim, p. 18.
63. Kubizek, p. 75.
64. Record of a statement by Prewatzky-Wendt, former N S D A P Central Archives, Federal Archives, Coblenz, N S 26/65.
65. Cf. Kubizek, p. 97.
66. Handwritten deposition by the surgeon, Dr Urban, 16 Nov. 1938. Federal Archives, Coblenz, N S 26/17 a. The entry concerning the operation reads: 'Sarcoma musculi pectoralis minoris', *ibid*, N S 26/65.
67. Remark made by Klara Hitler to Kubizek in the autumn of 1907. Kubizek, p. 158.
68. *Ibid.*

CHAPTER THREE. *Artist and Architect*

1. Manheim, p. 18. Unlike many of his biographers, Hitler does not dwell in *Mein Kampf* on the subject of this examination. Cf. Josef Greiner, pp. 36 ff, who claims to have sat the examination shortly before the subject of his book. Konrad Heiden (1901–66), a German journalist who emigrated in 1933 and regarded writing about Hitler and National Socialism as his life's work (see bibliography), continued until his death to influence all other writers on these subjects. His writings, by his own admission polemical, were adopted uncritically (though not always acknowledged) by the majority of authors. His access to documents was limited, nor could he easily check the truth of the statements made by the witnesses on whom he relied for much of his material. His chief 'informant' about Hitler's youth was the tramp Reinhold Hanisch, on whose distinctly fantastic stories Heiden continued throughout his life to base his writings. It is to Greiner we must attribute the story recounted by Heiden and others that in his youth Hitler had been a lazy good-for-nothing, living rough or in hostels, and given over to an aimless hand-to-mouth existence. On the subject of Heiden see also Maser, *Frühgeschichte*, p. 512 and Maser, *Neue Deutsche Biographie*, viii, 246 f.

2. Information concerning the 1907 examination candidates at the Vienna Academy of Fine Arts in the 'Classification List of the General School of Painting 1905–1911'. Letter from the head of the Chancellor's office of the Academy of Fine Arts (Dr Alfred Sammer), 6 Sept. 1969.

3. *Ibid.*

4. *Ibid.* Cf. also documents in the Federal Archives, Coblenz, N S 26/36.

5. Picker, p. 324. Cf. also entry in the Classification List for 1905–11 which reads: 'Adolf Hitler, born Braunau/Inn, Upper Austria on 20 April 1889. . . . Catholic, Father: civil servant. Sample drawings, inadequate, few heads.' Also letter from the Vienna Academy of Fine Arts, 24 Feb. 1971, file no. 397/70/11.

6. Manheim, p. 19.

7. *Ibid*, p. 18. Cf. also Kubizek, pp. 159 f.

8. Manheim, p. 19.

9. Article in *Revue* no. 43, 25 Oct. 1952, by Thomas Orr (pseudonym of a historian formerly employed in the N S D A P Central Archives).

10. Handwritten account by Dr Bloch, 7 Nov. 1938. Original in former N S D A P Central Archives, Federal Archives, Coblenz, N S 26/65.

11. *Ibid.*

12. Text of *faire-part* cit. from original in possession of one of Hitler's cousins in Spital.

13. Manheim, p. 17.

14. *Ibid*, p. 18.

15. *Ibid*, p. 20.

16. *Ibid*, p. 114.

17. More especially authors of 'revelations', like Greiner, and of 'memoirs' relating to a period of friendship with Hitler, like Kubizek. Kubizek's memoirs are a medley of truth and fiction in which the latter predominates. As documentary evidence they have value only where Kubizek illustrates his book with facsimiles. I have quoted only such passages as are verifiable. Greiner's account is not worthy of serious attention and his claim to have met Hitler is highly implausible. He is cited here only when his information relates to well-documented circumstances or details. There is some mention of a publication by Greiner in the correspondence files of the former Central Archives of the N S D A P (30 Aug. 1938), Federal Archives, Coblenz, N S 26/36.

18. Kubizek, p. 315. For information about Kubizek, see Maser, *Frühgeschichte*, pp. 514 f.

19. Cf. Manheim, p. 17.

20. Sale contract, 21 June 1905. Documents in Federal Archives, Coblenz, N S 26/65.

21. Handwritten document, Linz Area Court (V), 4 April 1903, assessing Adolf and Paula Hitler's portion of the inheritance at 652 kronen each.

22. Cf. Maser, *Frühgeschichte*, pp. 65 ff.

23. The amount is not ascertainable. Johanna Pölzl (died 1911), one of the three legatees, left 3800 kronen. Cf. Maser, *Frühgeschichte*, pp. 80 f. and

482 f. Documents in the Linz District Court File no. P V 49/3–24 of 4 May 1911. The amount inherited by Klara would probably have been much the same.

24. This will is in the possession of the grandchildren of Walburga Hitler's heirs who loaned it to the author for examination in August 1969. Copy of the original in possession of the author.

25. Letter from Dr Hans Dittrich (27 Jan. 1966). In 1913/14 Dittrich was an assistant master in a Vienna secondary school.

26. Cf. Kirkpatrick, p. 38.

27. Photocopy of a letter in the author's possession. Mistakes corrected by the author.

28. *Ibid.* Cf. also Picker, p. 323. On 10 May 1942 Hitler remarked, in connection with the Vienna Academy and its entrance examination, that he would not have dared approach so great a man on his own initiative.

29. Photocopy of a letter in the author's possession. Correctly written save for the punctuation, amended by the author. Either from excitement or carelessness, Hitler wrote the date wrongly (10 Feb. 1909 for 10 Feb. 1908).

30. Manheim, p. 19.

31. Cf. note 27; as reported by the correspondent to her mother.

32. Remark made by Hitler to Siewert, the stage designer, and repeated to the author in 1970 by Heim who was present at the conversation.

33. Recorded by Heim, 24 Feb. 1942, cit. Picker, p. 182.

34. Letter from the Vienna Academy of Fine Arts, 6 Sept. 1969.

35. Cf. Maser, *Frühgeschichte*, p. 77.

36. *Ibid*, pp. 74 ff.

37. *Ibid*, plate 2, p. 65.

38. Handwritten account by Karl Honisch. Former Central Archives of the NSDAP, Federal Archives, Coblenz, N S 26/17 a.

39. Registration of most of Hitler's works. Federal Archives, Coblenz, N S 26/36 and elsewhere. Favourite themes were the Parliament, the Kärntnerthor Theatre, the Rathaus, the old Ferdinand Bridge, the Heiliger Kreuzerhof, the 'Fisherman's Gate', the Michaelerplatz, the Dreilauferhaus, the Hofburg and a number of churches including the Minoritenkirche, the Michaelerkirche, the Alserkirche, the Karlskirche and the Kirche Maria am Gestade.

40. Hanisch's deposition. Handwritten (undated, original). Former Central Archives of the NSDAP, Federal Archives, Coblenz, N S 26/64.

41. Manheim, p. 32.

42. Handwritten (undated, original). Former Central Archives of the NSDAP, Federal Archives, Coblenz, N S 26/64.

43. *Ibid.*

44. *Ibid.*

45. Cf. Maser, *Frühgeschichte*, p. 69. The picture in question was of the Vienna Parliament building and was alleged by Hitler to be worth at least 50 kronen. Reproduction in the former Central Archives of the NSDAP, no. 213/2, Dr Priesack's file.

46. Maser, *Frühgeshichte*, p. 69.
47. Handwritten (May 1933, original). Former Central Archives of the NSDAP, Federal Archives, Coblenz, NS 26/64. Hanisch's mistakes corrected by the author.
48. Cf. more especially Maser, *Frühgeschichte*, p. 69.
49. A typewritten list of titles, owners and prices (Federal Archives, Coblenz, NS 26/36) reveals that even in 1938, when Hitler's watercolours were at a premium, some of the pictures painted between 1909 and 1913 were still in the hands of Jews, among them Dr Bloch (physician to both Klara and Adolf Hitler), the Hungarian engineer Retschay, the Viennese lawyer Dr Josef Feingold and the picture-dealer Morgenstern. At Longleat the Marquess of Bath's collection contains forty-six signed pictures dating back to the years before 1914 (letter from the Marquess, 2 Oct. 1968).
50. Handwritten (undated original). Former Central Archives of the NSDAP, Federal Archives, Coblenz, NS 26/64. No alteration has been made to Hanisch's style.
51. *Ibid.*
52. Handwritten (May 1933, original), former NSDAP Central Archives, Federal Archives, Coblenz, NS 26/64. *Doc. cit.* Maser, *Frühgeschichte*, p. 477. Cf. also *ibid*, synopsis 3 (facsimile).
53. Handwritten (11 May 1938, original), former NSDAP Central Archives, Federal Archives, Coblenz, NS 16/64.
54. Typescript on headed paper, file entry of 17 Feb. 1944. Former NSDAP Central Archives, Federal Archives, Coblenz, NS 26/64. At this time, when the course of the war was causing Hitler grave concern, Bormann considered the Hanisch affair of sufficient importance to merit the filing of a signed minute.
55. E.g. Rudolf Olden and Konrad Heiden.
56. Manheim, p. 20.
57. *Ibid*, p. 21.
58. Picker, pp. 323 f.
59. *Ibid*, pp. 212 and 323.
60. Manheim, p. 20.
61. *Ibid*, pp. 20 and 22.
62. Cf. Maser, *Frühgeschichte*, pp. 72 ff.
63. Karl Honisch, another temporary inmate of the hostel, recorded that while at work Hitler always wore a 'dark, threadbare suit'. Original MS. Former NSDAP Central Archives, Federal Archives, Coblenz NS 26/17a.
64. Picker, p. 223.
65. *Ibid*, p. 299.
66. *Ibid*, p. 195.
67. Cf. *ibid*, pp. 47 ff.
68. Cf. *ibid*, p. 48.
69. Cf. Picker, pp. 297 ff.

70. *Ibid*, p. 304.

71. Told to the author by Josef and Elisabeth Popp (1966 and 1967).

72. Cf. Maser, *Frühgeschichte*, pp. 315 f.

73. Manheim, p. 116. Some idea of his work at this time can be gained from a handwritten list and typewritten price list in the former Central Archives of the N S D A P, Federal Archives, Coblenz, N S 26/36. This includes the following paintings: *Hofbräuhaus I* (29·4 × 39·9 cm); *Hofbräuhaus II* (27·7 × 22 cm); *Johanniskirche and Asamhaus* (20·6 × 29·5 cm); *Alter Hof* (26·9 × 36·8 cm); *Sendlinger Tor* (27·4 × 37·8 cm); *National-theater* (26·8 × 41 cm); *Feldherrnhalle* (27·6 × 41·7 cm); *Alter Hof* (27 × 37 cm); *Petersbergl I* (28·2 × 22 cm); *Petersbergl II* (26 × 39 cm); *Altes Rathaus* (32·5 × 25 cm); *Johanniskirche and Asamhaus* (22 × 35 cm) and *Viktualienmarkt and Peterskirche* (oil on wood, 13 × 18 cm). In May 1938 one watercolour, *Grosses Standesamt*, fetched 6000 marks and another, *Peterskirche*, 8000 marks.

74. Cit. from original record. Former N S D A P Central Archives, Federal Archives, Coblenz, N S 26/36.

75. *Ibid*.

76. *Ibid*.

77. In 1938, Mend was a prisoner in a concentration camp whose whereabouts is not specified in the relevant document, a typed copy, in the former Central Archives of the N S D A P, Federal Archives, Coblenz, N S 26/64. He gave the commandant of Camp III the names of people who owned pictures by Hitler; these included a Herr Mund, Dachauer Strasse, Munich, and a Frau Inkhofer, wife of one of Hitler's army friends. He suggested that another of Hitler's army friends, Ernst Schmidt, might be able to help and said he believed that a man called Brandmayer, who had written a book about Hitler's army days called *The Runner*, also possessed some pictures (war drawings in charcoal).

78. Communication (16 Feb. 1942) from the Reich Governor in Hessen (Div VII) to the owner of Hitler's watercolour *Altes Hofbräuhaus*. Typescript. Reference no. VII/V. 33 414. Copy in possession of the author. The watercolour was offered for sale in 1970 for 30,000 marks.

79. Nasse, *Die Neue Literatur*, 1936, pp. 736 ff., cit. Wulf, *Die Bildenden Künste in Dritten Reich*, pp. 241 f.

80. *Ibid*.

81. Jetzinger, p. 156.

82. Letter from Cézanne to Zola, 1866, cit. Leymarie, *Impressionismus*, p. 59.

83. Told to the author by Heinrich Heim (6 July 1968). See also Hitler's remark of 24 Feb. 1942, Heim, cit. Picker, p. 182.

84. Told to the author by Henriette von Schirach and others (1966).

85. Information supplied by Edward Carrick (Gordon Craig's son and himself a well-known artist) to Heinrich Heim. On 6 July 1968 the latter placed at the author's disposal a copy, authenticated by E C, of the relevant page from Craig's diary.

86. Rosenberg, *Letzte Aufzeichnungen*, p. 333.

87. Doc. Federal Archives, Coblenz, N S 26/36.

88. Cit. Arno Breker's M S of 1968 (published Paris 1970).

89. *Ibid.*

90. Told to the author by a German diplomat who was present and who wishes to remain anonymous. Cf. also P. Schramm in *Der Spiegel*, 6/64, p. 49.

91. Told to the author by Dr Schmidt(-Carell), 18 March 1969. Dr Schmidt was sitting close to Hitler at the time.

92. Cf. Scully, *Modern Architecture.*

93. Remark made by Hitler to Speer and repeated to the author by the latter (1966); see also Picker, p. 323.

94. Speer interviewed by *Der Spiegel*, 46/66, p. 50. Speer said much the same thing to the author in Dec. 1966.

95. *Cit.* in the *Völkischer Beobachter* of 24 Nov. 1938. See also Wulf, *Die Bildenden Künste*, pp. 220 f.

96. Hitler on 10 May 1942, Picker, p. 323.

97. *Berliner Lokal-Anzeiger*, 2 Sept. 1933, morning edition.

98. Told to the author by Albert Speer, Dec. 1966.

99. *Mitteilungsblatt der Reichskammer der bildenden Künste*, 1 Aug. 1939, also Wulf, *Die Bildenden Künste*, p. 174.

100. *Ibid.*

101. Cf. Zoller, *Hitler privat*, p. 50.

102. *Ibid*, p. 51.

103. *Ibid.*

104. *Ibid.*

105. Told to the author by Heinrich Heim in 1969 and Dr Schmidt(-Carell) (1969–70); see also Speer, p. 57.

106. Told to the author in 1970 by Heinrich Heim who was concerned with the pictures.

107. Cf. Picker, p. 212.

108. Speer in an interview with *Der Spiegel*, 46/66, p. 50. Speer confirmed this in conversation with the author in Dec. 1966.

109. Cf. Hitler's remark of 1 April 1942, cit. Picker, p. 237. Frau Troost, whose husband had informed her about Hitler's taste in art, allegedly told Rosenberg that 'for Hitler, painting had ended in 1890'. Rosenberg, *Letzte Aufzeichnungen*, p. 335.

110. Manheim, pp. 234–5.

111. *Ibid.*

112. Picker, p. 212.

113. Kubizek, pp. 222 f.

114. Manheim, p. 188.

115. Letter from Ernst Schmidt, 16 Aug. 1964.

116. Hans Mend in a handwritten deposition for the Commandant of Camp III (presumably Dachau). Former N S D A P Central Archives, Coblenz, N S 26/84.

117. Told to the author by Ferdinand Staeger (Aug. 1969).
118. Letter from Ernst Schmidt, 16 Aug. 1964. Unmounted etching, 1 copy, in the possession of the author.
119. The lectures were as follows: Müller, 'German history after the Reformation' and 'The political history of the war'; von Bothmer, 'Socialism in theory and practice' and 'The correlation between domestic and foreign policy'; Horlacher, 'German economic conditions and the peace terms'.
120. Told to the author by Heinrich Heim (Feb. 1971). Heim, also an art lover, was then a twenty-year-old student; Hitler, eleven years his senior, was propaganda chief of the German Workers' Party, having been demobilized three months previously. Heim did not know at this time, nor did he learn till much later, that on joining that party Hitler first gave his profession as 'artist', subsequently changing the entry to 'writer'. Heim was later responsible for taking down in shorthand the greater part of Hitler's 'table talk' (see Picker).
121. Told to the author by Albert Speer (Nov. 1966).
122. Recorded by Heinrich Heim, Picker, pp. 167 f.
123. Manheim, p. 241.
124. Zoller, p. 55.
125. Cf. *ibid*, pp. 57 f and 146.
126. Cf. *ibid*, p. 57.
127. *Der Spiegel*, no. 36/69 p. 70. Information also personally supplied by Speer (Nov. 1966).
128. Cf. Schweisheimer's article in *Deutsche Bauzeitschrift*, vol. 5/69, p. 966.
129. *Ibid*.
130. Though it would be possible to give many examples of Hitler's discrimination in technical matters, evidence can only be adduced for the period subsequent to 1924–25. The earlier years are sparsely documented. Nevertheless it seems probable that even before 1914 Hitler was well versed in the details of architectural practice. In 1911 he was commissioned by the Viennese architect, Florian Müller, to make a sketch design for a villa. This pleasing drawing still survives and is reproduced in *Die Lösung des Rätsels Hitler*, Verlag zur Förderung wissenschaftlicher Forschung, Vienna, n.d., p. 107.
131. Told to the author by Speer, Nov. 1966.
132. *Der Spiegel*, no. 46/66, p. 50. In conversation with the author in Nov. 1966, Speer seemed pitifully nervous and unsure of himself.
133. Zoller, pp. 55 and 66.
134. For instance Speer remarked: 'I saw an opportunity of playing a role in the history of art', *Der Spiegel*, no. 46/66, p. 48.
135. *Ibid*.
136. Cf. *ibid*, no. 38/69, p. 68.
137. *Ibid*, p. 78.
138. Thomas Mann, *Bruder Hitler*.

CHAPTER FOUR. *Soldier for the Reich*

1. Manheim, p. 116.
2. Information supplied by J. and E. Popp (1966–67).
3. Cf. Maser, *Frühgeschichte*, p. 115.
4. Hitler, in a letter dated 29 Nov. 1921 to an unidentified correspondent (typewritten copy, 26 Aug. 1941).
5. Told to the author by J. Popp (1966).
6. Cf. Manheim, p. 150, cf. also letter to Hepp, 1915, in this chapter.
7. Told to the author by J. and E. Popp (1966–67).
8. Manheim, p. 116.
9. *Ibid.*
10. Maser, *Frühgeschichte*, pp. 115 f.
11. Manheim, p. 116.
12. Told to the author by J. and E. Popp.
13. Cit. original record in the former Central Archives of the NSDAP, Federal Archives, Coblenz, NS 26/36.
14. Told to the author by J. and E. Popp.
15. Kokoschka in an interview on German television, 7 Feb. 1971.
16. Other neighbouring craftsmen and tradesmen followed Popp's example, cf. Maser, *Frühgeschichte*, p. 117.
17. Manheim, p. 32.
18. Information obtained from, amongst others, Hitler's relations in Spital and Linz (1969–70) and from J. and E. Popp. Also from documentary evidence: record of a declaration made by Prewatzky-Wendt (former NSDAP Central Archives, Federal Archives, Coblenz, NS 26/65) and Karl Honisch's original handwritten deposition (*ibid*, NS 26/17a); see also correspondence between Hitler and his friends prior to 1907 part of which is in the Federal Archives, Coblenz, NS 26/14.
19. Lange-Eichbaum, p. 575.
20. Cf. Maser, *Frühgeschichte*, p. 62.
21. Told to the author by Hitler's relations in Spital, Mistelbach, Weitra and Weiten, Lower Austria (1969–71).
22. Copies of letters in author's possession.
23. Manheim, p. 150.
24. Cf. Maser, *Frühgeschichte*, p. 121.
25. Minute no. 248, 23 Jan. 1914 from the Imperial Austro–Hungarian Consulate.
26. Jetzinger, p. 260.
27. Cf. Maser, *Frühgeschichte*, p. 122.
28. Copy of the official confirmation dated 23 Feb. 1932 in the Federal Archives, Coblenz, NS 26/17a.
29. Handwritten account by Hitler's teacher, Gregor Goldbacher, 29 Jan. 1941. Original. Former NSDAP Central Archives, Federal Archives, Coblenz, NS 26/17a.

30. Cf. Manheim, 150.
31. Cf. *inter alia, Die Grosse Politik der Europäischen Kabinette*, vol. iii, nos. 466, 485, 509, 532, 571.
32. Cf. Manheim, p. 117.
33. *Ibid.*
34. *Ibid*, pp. 117–19.
35. *Ibid*, p. 117.
36. *Ibid*, p. 142.
37. *Ibid*, p. 146.
38. *Ibid*, p. 148.
39. Information supplied by Schmid-Noerr, 1 April 1967.
40. Federal Archives, Coblenz, N S 26/4. Hitler's account has been substantiated by former members of his regiment who had never seen his letter; cf. Meyer, pp. 18 f.
41. Nominal roll of 7 Coy, 1st Replacement Bn, 2 Bavarian Infantry Regt, vol. xxii Federal Archives, Coblenz, N S 26/12; *ibid*, sheet 249, no. e 7111; Nominal Roll 4 Coy, 1st Inf. Rep. Bn, 2 Inf. Regt, no. 204, *ibid*; Nominal Roll 3/16 Res. Inf. Regt sheet 50, no. 718, *ibid*; Nominal Roll 1/16 Res. Inf. Regt sheet 65, no. 166/148, *ibid*; Bavarian Army Casualty List no. 424, 12 April 1919, p. 31 288, *ibid*; 2 hospital strength returns to the Records Section, Royal Bavarian War Ministry, *ibid*; Casualty List, no. 78, *ibid*; Casualty List no. 320, *ibid*; Casualty List no. 233, *ibid*; Official Gazette no. 51 of 25 Nov. 1916, p. 15 366, *ibid*.
    Statements concerning the dates on which Hitler was wounded vary by a day or two. For instance on 29 Nov. 1921 Hitler declared in a short *curriculum vitae* that he had been wounded on 7 Oct. 1916 and 13/14 Oct. 1918 (copy in the Federal Archives, Coblenz, N S 26/17 a), which does not exactly tally with the official records, a fact of no material relevance here.
42. Cf. especially findings of the Hamburg District Court (Z. II 313/32, entry stamp 10 March 1932) in the matter of Hitler *v.* Heinrich Braune and Fa. Auer & Co. Original typescript, former N S D A P Central Archives, Federal Archives, Coblenz, N S 26/17a.
43. Cit. from original letter in possession of the Popp family.
44. Undated letter in possession of the Popp family.
45. Cf. *Vier Jahre Westfront. Die Geschichte des Regiments List R I R 16*, Munich, 1932, p. 381.
46. Account given by Mend to Professor Schmid-Noerr, recorded from memory on 1 April 1967.
47. Verbal and written information supplied by men detained after the July Plot and by German diplomats, all of whom wish to remain anonymous.
48. Letter from Schmid-Noerr, 1 April 1967, who had frequent meetings with Mend.
49. *Ibid.*
50. Mend, pp. 9 and 17.
51. Recorded from memory by Schmid-Noerr, 1 April 1967.

52. Original typescript in the former NSDAP Central Archives, Federal Archives, Coblenz, NS 26/64.
53. Cf. Nominal Roll of 3/16 Res. Inf. Regt, sheet 50, no 718 (for which no. 1062 was later substituted), Federal Archives, Coblenz, NS 26/12.
54. Typescript, copy, Federal Archives, Coblenz, NS 26/17 a.
55. *Ibid.*
56. *Ibid.*
57. *Ibid.*
58. *Ibid.*
59. This account of Hitler's award was given by Gutmann to Ernst Niekisch who in turn retailed it to the author in 1951. In 1953 Max Amann confirmed the story.
60. Cf. Meyer, p. 96.
61. Fragment no. 20, copy in Federal Archives, Coblenz. Cf. also Schramm, *Hitler als militärischer Führer*, p. 61.
62. *Cit.* from Schramm, *Hitler als militärischer Führer*, p. 61.
63. Manheim, pp. 161, 162, 163 and 170, cf. also detailed analysis in Maser, *Hitlers Mein Kampf*, pp. 210 ff.
64. Schramm, *Hitler*, pp. 152 ff.
65. Manheim, pp. 178–9.
66. Authenticated copy of Hitler's letter, Federal Archives, Coblenz, NS 26/17 a. Cf. Manheim, p. 182, for a more detailed account of his gassing.
67. Manheim, p. 184.
68. *Ibid*, p. 187.
69. *Der Hitler-Prozess*, p. 18, cf. also Manheim, pp. 184 ff.
70. Typewritten copy, 26 Aug. 1941, former NSDAP Central Archives, Federal Archives, Coblenz, NS 26/17 a.
71. Told to the author by General Vincenz Müller. Müller was informed by von Bredow that he had initiated investigations.
72. Morell's deposition.
73. Manheim, p. 185.
74. Meyer, p. 72.
75. Manheim, p. 187.
76. *Ibid*, p. 188.
77. Letter from Ernst Schmidt, August 1964.
78. Manheim, p. 188.
79. Cf. Fechenbach, *Der Revolutionär Kurt Eisner*, p. 53.
80. E. Niekisch, *Gewagtes Leben*, p. 49. cf. also H. Speckner, 'Die Ordnungszelle Bayern', p. 3.
81. *Münchener Neueste Nachrichten*, 14 Nov. 1918 and *Bayerische Staatszeitung*, 16 Nov. 1918; cf. also Aretin, 'Die bayerische Königsfrage' *Süddeutsche Monatshefte*, xxx, Jan. 1933, p. 233.
82. Letter from Ernst Schmidt, 1964.
83. Schricker, *Rotmord über München*, p. 21.
84. Manheim, p. 188.
85. Letter from Ernst Schmidt, Aug. 1964.

86. Letter from Ernst Schmidt, 1965.
87. Letter from Ernst Schmidt, 1964.
88. Manheim, p. 187.
89. *Ibid.*
90. *Ibid*, p. 175.
91. Cf. Maser, *Hitlers Mein Kampf*, p. 62.
92. Deutschvölkischer Bund pamphlet, *Von der Hohenzollern- zur Judenherrschaft*, Dec. 1918, cit. Jochmann, *Nationalsozializmus und Revolution*, p. 6.
93. Manheim, p. 152.
94. *Ibid.*
95. Letter from Ernst Schmidt, 1965.
96. Nominal roll, 4/1st Rep. Bn 2 Inf. Regt, no. 204, Federal Archives, Coblenz, NS 26/12.
97. Letter from Ernst Schmidt, Aug. 1964.
98. *Ibid.*
99. Cf. Benoist-Méchin, *L'Histoire de l'armée allemande* . . ., i, p. 176.
100. Information supplied by a former employee of the NSDAP Central Archives, 1953 and 1969. Cf. also Hitler's notes for speeches on the Versailles Treaty, Federal Archives, Coblenz, NS 26/49.
101. Cf. *Weltwoche*, 1944, no. 574, p. 12.
102. Cf. Schricker, *Rotmord über München*, p. 28; also *Münchner Merkur*, 22 Feb. 1954.
103. Cit. H. Speckner, p. 33.
104. *Ibid.*
105. Cf. *Allgemeine Zeitung*, Munich, 25 Jan. 1920.
106. Cf. Maser, *Frühgeschichte*, p. 26.
107. Manheim, p. 188.
108. Entry in nominal roll of 3/16 Res. Inf. Regt, sheet 50, no. 718 (number deleted and replaced by 1062), Federal Archives, Coblenz, NS 26/12.
109. Letter from Ernst Schmidt, 1964.
110. Manheim, p. 188.
111. Letter from Ernst Schmidt, 1965.
112. Reproduced in *Appelle einer Revolution*, Munich 1968, supplement 35.
113. Cf. *ibid*, supplement 67, poster.
114. *Verhandlungen des Bayerischen Landtages*, 1919/20, vol. i, pp. 13 f.
115. Information supplied by Ernst Niekisch, 1965, cf. also Niekisch, *Gewagtes Leben*, p. 63.
116. Cit. Fischer, *Stalin und der deutsche Kommunismus*, p. 126.
117. Cf. Volkmann, *Revolution über Deutschland*, p. 223.
118. Cf. Maser, *Frühgeschichte*, p. 33; also Oertzen, *Die deutschen Freikorps*, p. 328. It would seem that recruiting agents were in fact arrested in Erlangen; see *Escherich-Hefte*, no. 3, p. 18; Oertzen, p. 328; Kanzler, 'Bayerns Kampf', p. 4; Noske, p. 315; also *Verhandlungen des Bayerischen Landtages*, vol. I, p. 161.
119. Cf. Maser, *Frühgeschichte*, p. 33; also Noste, p. 97.

120. *Historisch-politische Blätter für das Katholische Deutschland,* vol. 163 (1919), p. 105.
121. *Ibid.*
122. Cf. also Kanzler, p. 6.
123. Told to the author by Ernst Niekisch, 1964.
124. Cf. Oertzen, *Die deutschen Freikorps,* pp. 336 f., *Escherich-Hefte,* no. 4, pp. 19 f. and Schricker, pp. 83 f.
125. Cf. Hofmiller, pp. 205; also Schricker, pp. 102 f. and *Escherich-Hefte,* no. 5, pp. 12 f.
126. Galéra, vol. i, p. 128.
127. Cf. also Maser, *Frühgeschichte,* p. 33, and Noske, p. 97.
128. Cf. Oertzen, p. 327.
129. Cf. H. Speckner, p. 43.
130. Cf. Franz Schweyer's review of Rudolf Kanzler's 'Bayerns Kampf gegen den Bolschewismus', *Zeitschrift für bayerische Landesgeschichte,* Munich 1932, no. 3, p. 488.
131. Cit. from the proclamation. Photocopy in Erlangen University Library.
132. Text of the proclamation signed by Ernst Toller.
133. Not 35,000 as estimated by Gustav Kahr in his minute (2 Dec. 1920). Cf. dossiers in reconstructed records A.V.XIX, VII, 99 Conv. 1, also Pitrof, pp. 89 f., Galéra, vol. 1, p. 128, Noske, pp. 97 and 315, and Maser, *Frühgeschichte,* p. 37.
134. Cf. Kanzler, p. 16.
135. *Ibid,* pp. 10, 13.
136. Cf. H. Speckner, p. 44.
137. Cf. Karl Speckner, *Die Wächter der Kirche,* p. 23.
138. Maser, *Frühgeschichte,* p. 38.
139. Cf. *ibid,* pp. 146 ff.
140. Cf. Krokow, p. 192.
141. Cf. Maser, *Frühgeschichte,* p. 40.
142. Cf. *Münchener Neueste Nachrichten,* 7 May 1919 and 5 Nov. 1921 and *Bayerische Staatszeitung,* 8, 9, May, 13 Sept. 1919, and 7 Nov. 1921. Also Oertzen, p. 352, Bonn, p. 217 and Pitrof, pp. 102 f.
143. Cf. also Noske, p. 97 and Gumbel, *Verräter verfallen der Feme,* pp. 86 ff.
144. *Bayerische Staatszeitung,* 16 May 1919; see also Gumbel, *Verräter verfallen der Feme,* p. 36.
145. Cf. *ibid,* p. 36.
146. Document in Chief Public Prosecutor's office, Munich Provincial Court II, VI 608/19.
147. Recounted by Thor Goote in *Aus der Geschichte der Bewegung,* Deutsche Arbeitsfront, November 1934.
148. *Ibid.* Hitler did not mention this episode in *Mein Kampf.* It is, however, attested: letter from Ernst Schmidt, 16 Aug. 1962; information also supplied personally by Hermann Esser and Max Amann (1953).
149. In a letter dated 29 Nov. 1921. Copy in Federal Archives Coblenz, NS 26/17 a.

150. Cf. Manheim, p. 188.
151. Letter from Ernst Niekisch, 1964. Also communicated in person to the author, 1965.
152. Letter from Ernst Schmidt, Aug. 1964. There is no truth in any other version of this episode. Cf. Bouhler, *Kampf um Deutschland*, p. 32, for example, or Hasselbach, p. 23. Hitler himself does not enter into any detail on the subject. Cf. Manheim, pp. 188 f.
153. In a letter to the author, 1952, Otto Strasser declared that Hitler had worn a red brassard. In 1953 Hermann Esser agreed that this could have been so.
154. Letter from Ernst Schmidt, Aug. 1964.
155. Told to the author by Ernst Deuerlein.
156. Manheim, p. 189.
157. Letter from Ernst Schmidt, Aug. 1964.
158. Cf. Manheim, p. 189.
159. Viktor von Koerber, *Hitler, sein Leben und seine Reden*. This apologia was confiscated immediately after publication. In 1927 Koerber turned against Hitler and began to attack him publicly, e.g. in the *Vossische Zeitung*, 6 May 1927.
160. Letter from Ernst Schmidt, August 1964.
161. Manheim, p. 189.
162. Cf. Maser, *Frühgeschichte*, p. 133.
163. *Ibid*, p. 134.
164. Manheim, p. 189.
165. Cf. Maser, *Frühgeschichte*, pp. 185 ff.
166. Details in the Munich Central State Archives, section II (former Bavarian War Archives), 4 Group Headquarters, vol. 50/6 (printed). Hereafter the abbreviated German reference will be given for the files in the Central State Archives, namely: HStA. Mü., Abt. II, Gruppen-Kdo. 4, followed by vol. no., ref. no. and the word 'printed' or 'handwritten' where appropriate.
167. Manheim, p. 190.
168. *Ibid*, p. 189.
169. *Ibid*.
170. *Ibid*.
171. *Ibid*, p. 191.
172. Picker, p. 415.
173. Cit. Deuerlein, *Der Aufstieg der NSDAP*, p. 85.
174. Manheim, p. 195.
175. *Ibid*.
176. Authenticated copy of 26 Aug. 1941, Federal Archives, Coblenz, NS 26/17 a.
177. HStA.Mü., Abt. II, Gruppen-Kdo. 4, vol. 50/3; under the note requesting onward transmission to 2 Bavarian Infantry Regiment is written: 'Hitler to be informed of detachment to Demob. Bn (HQ Coy)', and against this the word 'informed', accompanied by an illegible signature.

178. *Ibid.*
179. HStA.Mü., Abt.II, Gruppen-Kdo. 4, vol. 50/8.
180. *Ibid.*
181. Report by Hans Knoden, 24.8.19, HStA. Mü., Abt. II, Gruppen-Kdo. 4, vol. 50/3 (handwritten).
182. Report by Eward Bolle, 24 Aug. 1919, *ibid.*
183. Report by Lorenz Frank, 23 Aug, 1919, *ibid.*
184. Report by Lieutenant Bendt, *ibid.*
185. Report by Karl Eicher, 24 Aug. 1919, *ibid* (handwritten).
186. Report by Lorenz Frank, 23 Aug. 1919, *ibid.*
187. Speech *cit.* Picker, pp. 493 f.
188. *Ibid.*
189. According to HStA.Mü., Abt. II, Gruppen-Kdo. 4, vols. 46/6 and 46/7, 46/8 and 46/9, these included: the Communist Workers' Party, the Red Soldiers' League, the Syndicalists (Anarchists) and their youth organization, the Union of Communist Socialists, the Bible Students, the *Schutz- und Trutzbund*, the *Siegfriedring*, the German Workers' Party and also the larger parties, e.g. the Bavarian People's Party, the Bavarian Centre Party, the Bavarian Monarchist Party and the Farmers' League. Also the Ostara League.
190. Sebottendorff, p. 60. Cf. *ibid*, pp. 57 ff.
191. *Ibid*, p. 92.
192. Birth certificate no. 87/1 875 in the Hoyerswerda Registry Office; copy in author's possession (7 Jan. 1966).
193. Information supplied 4 March 1968 by an ex-S S Standartenführer who wishes to remain anonymous. Like Hitler, he was a political agent in 1919; after 1945 he was engaged in research work for the U S Army.
194. Letter from Rittlinger, 22 June 1968.
195. Told to the author by one of Sebottendorff's influential collaborators, 4 March 1968.
196. Cit. from *Facsimile – Querschnitt durch den Völkischen Beobachter*, p. 5.
197. Sebottendorff, p. 62.
198. Franz-Willing, *Die Hitlerbewegung*, p. 30.
199. Cf. Maser, *Frühgeschichte*, p. 168.
200. Manheim, p. 197.
201. Information obtained from the list, found among the papers of the late Karl Harrer, of those who attended the meeting.
202. Manheim, p. 199.
203. Cf. Maser, *Frühgeschichte*, pp. 160 ff.
204. Manheim, p. 200.
205. *Ibid*, p. 204. Hitler's wrongful claim to have been allotted membership number 7, was later to contribute very materially to the Hitler cult. True, he was the seventh member of the party's working committee, but the fifty-fifth member of the German Workers' Party. Since the enumeration of members began at 501 his membership number was 555. Cf. Maser, *Frühgeschichte*, p. 167; also synopsis 5, *op. cit.*

206. On the development of the German Workers' Party, the structure of its membership etc., cf. Maser, *Frühgeschichte*, pp. 141 ff.
207. Cf. Maser, *Frühgeschichte*, p. 155 and HStA.Mü., Abt II, Gruppen-Kdo. 4, vol. 50/8.
208. HStA.Mü., Abt. II, Gruppen-Kdo. 4, vol. 50/8.

CHAPTER FIVE. *Intellectual Background*

1. Frank, p. 46.
2. Manheim, p. 114.
3. Cf. Kubizek, p. 301.
4. *Der Hitler-Prozess*, p. 18.
5. Manheim, p. 234.
6. Cit. Bullock, *Hitler*, p. 31.
7. Manheim, p. 6.
8. *Ibid*, p. 49.
9. Cf. Kubizek, pp. 226 f. and 37.
10. *Ibid*, pp. 224 f.
11. *Ibid*, p. 226.
12. *Ibid*, p. 37.
13. J. Greiner, p. 83.
14. Dietrich, *Zwölf Jahre mit Hitler*, p. 164. cf. also *Libres propos sur la guerre et la paix*, Paris, 1952, p. 306.
15. Told to the author by a fellow pupil of Heinz Hitler's. The latter was reported missing on the Eastern Front and never returned from the war.
16. Ziegler, *Hitler . . .*, p. 116.
17. Frank, p. 46.
18. Written by Hitler on 29 Nov. 1921 to a correspondent whom he addresses as 'Dear Herr Doktor . . .' but does not name. Former Central Archives of the N S D A P, Federal Archives, Coblenz, N S 26/17 a (typescript copy). Doc. cit. Maser, *Frühgeschichte*, pp. 487 f.
19. Cf. Kubizek, p. 240.
20. Told to the author by Hitler's nephew, Leo Raubal (1967).
21. Cf. Kubizek, pp. 240 ff.
22. Giesing's report (11 Nov. 1945), p. 29 (original). Information also obtained from Dr Giesing in person (June 1971).
23. Cf. Schramm, cit. Picker, p. 69.
24. Cit. from Morell's report.
25. I M T, vol. xv, p. 302.
26. Probably the second edition, published in Vienna in 1912.
27. Cambridge 1920. Cf. Maser, *Mein Kampf*, pp. 91 f.
28. Manheim, p. 585.
29. Information supplied verbally (1966).

30. Cf. also Manheim, pp. 211 and 277; also Picker, pp. 32, 89, 149 and 192.
31. Cf. also Picker, p. 192.
32. Frank, p. 46.
33. Information given by Mend to Schmid-Noerr who recorded it from memory on 1 Apr. 1967.
34. Foreword in the 1818 edition of *Die Welt als Wille und Vorstellung*. Cit. in full in vol. i of the 3rd edition, 1859, p. v.
35. *Ibid*, pp. 165 ff.
36. For instance Schopenhauer writes (*ibid*, p. 409): 'the true purpose of painting, as of art in general, is to make it easier for us to grasp the [Platonic] forms of the beings of this world.'
37. Schopenhauer, *ibid*, pp. 393 ff. and 406 ff.
38. Cf. Ziegler, *Hitler* . . . , pp. 269 ff.
39. Heim's record, cit. Picker, p. 155.
40. *Ibid*, p. 153.
41. *Ibid*, p. 190.
42. Warlimont, p. 401.
43. Cf. Manheim, p. 432.
44. Cf. Picker, p. 348.
45. Cf. Maser, *Hitlers Mein Kampf*, pp. 71 f.
46. Cf. Minder, *Dichter in der Gessellschaft*, p. 219.
47. Müller's published work up to 1964 is extraordinarily comprehensive. In 1928, when he became professor of medieval, modern and Bavarian history at Munich University, Müller already had a distinguished career behind him. From 1935 to 1944 he was editor of the *Historische Zeitschrift*. After 1933 Hitler offered him the post of Reich Minister of Education, an appointment which, on reflection, he refused. (Information supplied by Professor Priesak, 1969.)
48. For example Müller wrote: 'Thus all organic life, including the peoples, remains rooted in the earth and, like the earth, it is bound by certain limitations' (*Die Geltung des Bauern in der Volksgemeinschaft*, 1932 p. 247). In 1933 he demanded that 'the whole life of our people, in its very core and with all its mistakes, must be renewed from the roots up: that is to say from the deepest roots of its national being, in its innermost *völkisch* core' (*Volkserziehung und Volksgemeinschaft*, 1933, p. 269).
49. Cit. from an unpublished M S by Dr Wolfram von Hentig.
50. Cf Maser, *Frühgeschichte* (Index of names, under 'Hess'), p. 512.
51. Cf. *ibid*, Index of names.
52. Cf. *ibid*, pp. 396 ff.
53. Cf. Zoller, p. 50.
54. Cf. *ibid*.
55. Cf. *ibid*, p. 36.
56. Cf. Hanfstaengl, *Hitler*, pp. 48 f.
57. The first edition of *Mein Kampf* had laid down that the sub-leaders were to be elected in accordance with the principles of a 'Germanic democracy' and that after their election all groups were to be subordinate to them. In

the 1930 edition the relevant passage reads: 'In little as well as big things, the movement advocates the principle of unconditional authority of the leader, coupled with the highest responsibility,' Manheim, pp. 312–13.

58. Schramm cit. Picker, p. 69.
59. Cf. Manheim, p. 114.
60. G. W. F. Hegel, *Sämtliche Werke*, Jubiläumsausgabe, Stuttgart, 1928, vol. ii, p. 129.
61. *Ibid*, p. 447.
62. Cf. *inter alia* Compton, pp. 9 ff. and 28 ff.
63. Maser, *Hitlers Mein Kampf*, pp. 182 ff.
64. Schramm, *Hitler : The Man and the Military Leader*, p. 22.
65. Friedländer, pp. 24 f.
66. Cf. *Berliner Illustrierte Zeitung*, 12 March 1889.
67. Cf. 'Politische Bildung: Mangelhalft', *Frankfurter Allgemeine Zeitung*, 28 Nov. 1968.
68. Told to the author by Speer (1967), Heye (1966) and Engel (1968). Cf. also *Der Prozess gegen die Hauptkriegsverbrecher* (containing statements by Keitel, Göring, Jodl and others); also Zoller, p. 38.
69. Told to the author by Heye, 9 July 1966.
70. Letter from Karl Dönitz (10 Jan. 1967).
71. Cf. Zoller, p. 38.
72. Told to the author by Dönitz (1966). Also in a letter of 10 Jan. 1967.
73. Told to the author by Dr Schmidt(-Carell) (1969).
74. Schramm, cit. Picker, p. 98. Cf. also Chapter 9 in this book.
75. Manstein, *Lost Victories*, pp. 274–5.
76. Told to the author by Josef Popp (May 1966). He sometimes acted as prompter to Hitler.
77. Schramm, cit. Picker, pp. 96 f.
78. *Der Spiegel*, library records.
79. Cit. Ziegler, *Wer war Hitler?* p. 222.
80. Article by Veit Harlen, cit. from *Der Spiegel*, 29 Aug. 1966, p. 92.
81. *Ibid*.
82. Picker, p. 382.
83. *Ibid*, pp. 382 f.
84. *Ibid*, p. 383.
85. These were projects evolved by Hitler in the course of conversation on 27 April 1942. Picker, pp. 299 f.
86. Heim's record, cit. Picker, pp. 139 f.
87. Cf. Hitler's remarks on this subject in Picker.
88. Giesing's deposition, 12 June 1945, p. 176.
89. Reader's letter in the *Frankfurter Allgemeine Zeitung*, 6 April 1971,
90. Schramm, cit. Picker, p. 72.
91. Picker, p. 166.
92. Schramm, cit. Picker, p. 73.
93. Picker, p. 166.
94. *Ibid*.

95. *Ibid.*
96. *Ibid*
97. *Ibid.*
98. *Ibid.*
99. *Ibid*, p. 167.
100. *Ibid.* Hörbiger's theory has never received scientific recognition.
101. Cit. Heiber (ed.), *Reichsführer! Briefe an und von Himmler*, p. 57; cf. also Ackermann, *Himmler als Ideologe*, pp. 40 ff.
102. Picker, p. 166.
103. *Ibid*, p. 147.
104. *Ibid.*
105. *Ibid.*
106. *Ibid.*
107. Hitler on 26 July 1942, Picker, p. 478.
108. *Ibid.*
109. *Ibid.*
110. Picker, p. 446.
111. Heim's record, cit. Picker, p. 171.
112. *Ibid.* American research carried out during the 1960s suggests that the fertility of wealthy Romans was reduced by the fact that they drank their wine out of vessels partly made of lead.
113. Heim's record, cit. Picker, p. 172.
114. Hitler in his secret speech to German officer cadets on 30 May 1942; cit. Picker, p. 495.
115. *Ibid.*
116. *Ibid.*
117. Picker, p. 333.
118. Heim's record of 4 Feb. 1942, cit. Picker, p. 174.
119. *Ibid*, p. 173.
120. *Ibid.*
121. *Ibid*, p. 478.
122. *Ibid*, p. 173.
123. *Ibid*, p. 174.
124. Heim's record, cit. Picker, p. 173; cf. Hitler's remarks on 26 July 1942, *op. cit.*, p. 478.
125. *Ibid.*
126. Manheim, p. 598.
127. The first partition took place under Frederick the Great, the last two under Frederick William II.
128. Manheim, p. 591.
129. *Ibid.*
130. Cf. *ibid*, pp. 263 ff.
131. Cf. *ibid*, p. 595.
132. *Ibid*, p. 593.
133. *Ibid*, p. 554 ff.
134. *Ibid*, p. 611.

135. *Ibid.*
136. *Ibid.*
137. *Ibid*, p. 120.
138. *Ibid*, p. 117.
139. *Ibid*, pp. 119–20.
140. *Hitlers Zweites Buch*, p. 90.
141. *Ibid.*
142. *Ibid*, p. 98.
143. Manheim, p. 120.
144. Cf. for instance Hitler's speech of 4 Aug. 1920; cit. *Adolf Hitler in Franken*, p. 10; cf. also Pese, pp. 113 ff.
145. Cf. Maser, *Frühgeschichte*, pp. 273 ff.
146. Cf. *ibid*, p. 356.
147. Cf., *inter alia*, *Hitlers Zweites Buch*, pp. 24 f. and the *Völkischer Beobachter*, 25 May 1928.
148. Cit. Domarus, vol. ii/4, p. 2265.
149. Cf. Manheim, p. 129.
150. *Ibid.*
151. *Ibid*, p. 131.
152. Cf. *Adolf Hitler in Franken*, p. 10, and Pese, pp. 113 ff.
153. Manheim, p. 563; see also p. 565.
154. Cf. *ibid*, p. 565.
155. Cf. Ribbentrop, *Zwischen London und Moskau*, p. 43.
156. Ambassador's reports from Dec. 1936 to the end of Dec. 1937, in the possession of Annelies von Ribbentrop.
157. Letter from Annelies von Ribbentrop, 25 March 1969; cf. also IMT, vol. xxxix, Doc. 075-CT.
158. Kirkpatrick, p. 361.
159. Letter from Annelies von Ribbentrop, 25 March 1969.
160. Cf. *inter alia* Maser, *Hitlers Mein Kampf*, pp. 166 f., Pese, pp. 113 ff. and Ribbentrop, esp. pp. 43 and 59 ff.
161. Cit. from Schubert, p. 57.
162. Cf. *ibid*, pp. 57 f. and Manheim, pp. 563 f.
163. Manheim, p. 569.
164. *Ibid*, pp. 569–70.
165. *Hitlers Zweites Buch*, pp. 194 f.; cf. also Manheim, pp. 571 ff.
166. Cf. also Hitler's remarks about Bertrand de Jouvenel in the *Völkischer Beobachter*, 29 Feb. 1936.
167. Cf. Hitler's speech of 4 Aug. 1920 in *Adolf Hitler in Franken*, p. 10, and Pese, p. 113; cf. also PND report, DC 1478, on Hitler's speech of 24 June 1920.
168. *Völkischer Beobachter*, 24 March 1933.
169. *Akten zur Deutschen Auswärtigen Politik 1918–1945*, Series D, Baden-Baden – Frankfurt/M, 1951–61, vol. vii, p. 131, no. 142.
170. Manheim, pp. 602 f.
171. *Ibid*, pp. 604 f.

172. Ribbentrop, p. 211.
173. Giesing's report, 12 June 1945, p. 122 a. Giesing's somewhat erratic punctuation has been corrected by the author.
174. Manheim, p. 602.
175. Cf. *ibid*, p. 131.
176. Cf. also Friedländer, pp. 208–17 *passim*.
177. Cf. Manheim, p. 601.
178. Cf. Hitler's remark of 25 Feb. 1944, cit. Domarus, ii/4, p. 2265; cf. also Domarus, ii/4, p. 2151.
179. *Manifest der Kommunistischen Partei* (East Berlin, 1955), p. 9.
180. Picker, p. 348.
181. Cf. *ibid*.
182. Heim's record, cit. Picker, p. 169.
183. *Ibid*, p. 173.
184. *Ibid*, p. 235.
185. *Ibid*.
186. *Ibid*, p. 234.
187. *Ibid*, p. 233.
188. *Ibid*.
189. *Ibid*, pp. 233 f.
190. Giesing's report, 11 Nov. 1945, p. 29,
191. Cf. also Speer, p. 94.
192. *Ibid*, pp. 94 f.
193. Cf. also Hillgruber, *Hitlers Strategie*, incl. the foreword.
194. Hammann, *Der neue Kurs*, p. 165.
195. Salomon, *Die deutschen Parteiprogramme*, cit. from Schreiner, *Zur Geschichte der deutschen Aussenpolitik 1871 bis 1945*, p. 173.
196. Cf. Maser, *Frühgeschichte*, pp. 93 ff.
197. Manheim, p. 13. On 20 June 1929, twenty-five years after their last meeting, Poetsch wrote to say that 'he had pleasant recollections of his pupil' and asked him to send him a copy of the passage mentioning him in *Mein Kampf*, so that he could hand it down as a 'family heirloom'. (Letter from Poetsch to Hitler, 20 June 1929; copy in the former Central Archives of the NSDAP, Federal Archives, Coblenz, NS 26/15). See also Maser, *Hitlers Mein Kampf*, p. 260.
198. Hitler in conversation on 23 April 1942; cf. Picker, p. 289.
199. Hitler on 2 July 1942; cf. Picker, p. 429.
200. Manheim, pp. 15–16.
201. Cit. from the copy of the original MS of Heim's record, authenticated by Heim in July 1968.
202. Manheim, p. 10.
203. *Ibid*, p. 13.
204. Maser, *Frühgeschichte*, p. 99.
205. Cit. from the copy of the original MS of Heim's record, authenticated by Heim in July 1968.
206. Manheim, p. 591.

207. *Ibid.*
208. *Ibid.*
209. *Ibid*, p. 266.
210. Picker, p. 230.
211. *Ibid.*
212. Hitler put this over very impressively in a speech on 30 May 1942. Cit. Picker, pp. 493 ff.
213. Manheim, p. 163.
214. Heim's record, cit. Picker, p. 493.
215. *Ibid*, p. 172.
216. *Ibid*, p. 153.
217. Cf. also Manheim, p. 138, where he speaks of the state as a 'folkish organism'.
218. Heim's record, cit. Picker, p. 171.
219. 28 Jan. 1942 in the Wolfsschanze, cit. Picker, p. 172.
220. Cf. the article 'Führt Überbevölkerung zu Unruhen?', *Die Welt*, 12 April 1967.
221. Ploetz, *Die Tüchtigkeit unserer Rasse und der Schutz der Schwachen.*
222. *Ibid*, p. 136.
223. *Ibid*, p. v.
224. *Ibid*, p. 147.
225. Hanfstaengl, *Hitler*, pp. 40 and 47.
226. Cf. also Heiber in his introduction to *Hitlers Lagebesprechungen*, p. 30.
227. Told to the author by Dönitz (1966 and 1967). Also by Blumentritt (13 Jan. 1964) and Manstein (12 Feb. 1964). Information also derived from a letter written by Liss to N. Krüger on 9 Jan. 1964.
228. Cf. *inter alia* Krause, p. 48, Zoller, pp. 49 f., Kubizek, pp. 75, 111 and 226, and P. E. Schramm in his introduction to Picker, *Hitlers Tischgespräche*, pp. 67 ff. For a contrary view see also Hanfstaengl, *Hitler*, p. 47.
229. Warlimont to Krüger, 12 Nov. 1963.
230. Clausewitz is mentioned in a number of Hitler's speeches and writings, as for example in a speech on 18 Sept. 1922, in his final submission to the People's Court in Munich on 27 March 1924, in *Mein Kampf* (1924–25), in his *Zweites Buch* (1928), in public speeches on 27 Jan. 1932, 1 Sept. 1933, 8 Nov. 1934, 14 Sept. 1936 and 8 Nov. 1938, in his proclamation (read by Gauleiter Wagner) at the 1938 Party Rally, in a signal to General Paulus on 30 Jan. 1943, in a recorded broadcast on 10 Sept. 1943, at a situation conference on 25 April 1945 and, on 29 April 1945, in his political testament. Bibliographical data in order of quotation: Boepple, *Hitlers Reden*, p. 38; *ibid*, p. 140; Manheim, p. 612; *Hitlers Zweites Buch*, p. 142; *Parteigenosse! Der Führer spricht zu Dir*, p. 26; *Völkischer Beobachter*, 2 Sept. 33; Domarus, *Hitler – Reden und Proklamationen*, i/1, pp. 457 f., *ibid*, i/2, p. 647; *Völkischer Beobachter*, 11 Nov. 1938; Hitler, *Reden des Führers am Parteitag Grossdeutschland 1938*, p. 18; Wieder, *Stalingrad und die Verantwortung des Soldaten*, 2nd edn, pp.

316 f.; Domarus, ii/2, p. 2038; *Der Spiegel*, 3/69; Domarus, ii/2, p. 2237.

231. Cf. Hanfstaengl, *Hitler*, pp. 40 and 47–8.
232. Cit. Domarus, i/1, p. 457.
233. Carell, *Unternehmen Barbarossa*, p. 92.
234. Cf. Guderian, *Erinnerungen eines Soldaten*, pp. 342 f, cf. also Domarus, ii/4, p. 2171.
235. Heim's record, cit. Picker, p. 152.
236. Manheim, p. 286.
237. *Ibid*, p. 287; cf. also pp. 272–99.
238. *Ibid*, p. 51. On Hitler's attitude to Jewry see also Maser, *Hitlers Mein Kampf*, pp. 190 ff; also Maser, *Frühgeschichte*, pp. 155 f; cf. also Nolte, *Der Faschismus in seiner Epoche*, esp. pp. 500 f.
239. Manheim, pp. 47 ff.
240. Kubizek, p. 112.
241. *Ibid*, p. 113.
242. Cf. also Smith, p. 88.
243. Cit. from the copy of the original M S of Heim's record, authenticated by Heim in July 1968 (reproduction in the possession of Heinrich Heim).
244. Manheim, p. 49.
245. *Ibid*, pp. 50 f.
246. *Ibid*.
247. *Ibid*.
248. *Ibid*.
249. *Ibid*, pp. 51 f.
250. Cf. Kubizek, p. 299.
251. Cf. *ibid*, p. 300.
252. Manheim, p. 52.
253. *Ibid*.
254. No. 29, 1908, inside of front cover.
255. Cf. Daim, p. 21.
256. *Theozoologie oder Naturgeschichte der Götter IV : Der neue Bund und neue Gott*, Vienna 1929, p. 11.
257. *Theozoologie V : Der Götter-Vater und Götter-Geist oder die Unsterblichkeit in Materie und Geist*, Vienna 1929, p. 15.
258. Cf. Daim, pp. 21 ff.
259. The title of Daim's book.
260. Stein, *Adolf Hitler, Schüler der 'Weisen von Zion'*.
261. Cit. from the *Südmark-Kalender* for 1904.
262. Cf. Werner, *Der Alldeutsche Verband. Historische Studien*, p. 127.
263. Hasse, *Deutsche Weltpolitik*, vol. i, no. 4, p. 46.
264. Werner, p. 82.
265. Cf. Kuczynski, *Studien zur Geschichte des deutschen Imperialismus*, p. 28, cf. also Werner, p. 127.
266. Cf. Maser, *Frühgeschichte*, pp. 253 ff.
267. Cf. Manheim, pp. 276 ff.

268. *Ibid*, p. 296.
269. *Ibid*, p. 276.
270. *Ibid*, p. 54.
271. *Ibid*, p. 296.
272. *Ibid*, p. 60.
273. Bölsche, *Vom Bazillus zum Affenmenschen*, 2nd edn., Jena 1921. This is the edition cited.
274. *Ibid*, foreword. 'I use the word bacillus . . .', Bölsche writes on p. 5, 'as the most convenient comprehensive term [since it] expresses most adequately the menacing quality I wish to convey.'
275. *Ibid*, p. 35.
276. *Ibid*, p. 11.
277. *Ibid*, pp. 35 f.
278. *Ibid*, p. 19.
279. Cf. *Libres propos sur la guerre et la paix*, Paris 1952, p. 321.
280. Manheim, pp. 276 f.
281. *Ibid*, p. 60.
282. Cf. Warlimont, esp. p. 314
283. Cf. Maser, *Frühgeschichte*, p. 287.
284. Cf. Hoffmann, *Widerstand – Staatsstreich – Attentat*, 2nd edn, pp. 628 and 879. Photographs of the executions were still to be seen on Hitler's desk in mid-August.
285. Told to the author by Schmidt-Carell (5 April 1971).
286. Account given by Dr Brandt to Heinrich Heim (spring of 1945). Information also personally supplied to the author by Heim (1971), Arno Breker and Gerhard Engel (1967); also by Hans Baur (1971).
287. Told to the author by Heinrich Heim (1971), Ilse Braun (1971), Gerhard Engel (1967) and Dr Schmidt(-Carell) (1971).
288. Cf. Warlimont, p. 423.
289. 'Zidé a zidovské . . .', pp. 255 f.
290. *Ibid*, p. 536.
291. *Ibid*, p. 258.
292. Cf. Heer, *Gottes erste Libber*, p. 205.
293. Cf. Wolf, *Geschichte der Juden*, p. 109; also Kessler, p. 93.
294. Kessler, p. 81, note 7.
295. Manheim, p. 60. Cf. Maser, *Hitlers Mein Kampf*, pp. 190 ff.
296. Told to the author by Heinrich Heim, 6 July 1968. Hitler's inmost thoughts were recorded by Heim, with Martin Bormann's connivance.
297. Cit. from Domarus, ii/4, p. 2239.
298. Heim's record, cit. Picker, p. 155.
299. Cf. Heim's record, cit. Picker, p. 149.
300. *Ibid*, p. 235.
301. Cf. *ibid*, p. 150.
302. *Ibid*, p. 149.
303. *Ibid*, p. 151.

304. *Ibid*, p. 148.
305. *Ibid*, p. 151.
306. Giesing's deposition, 12 June 1945, p. 73.
307. *Ibid*, p. 131.
308. *Ibid*, p. 176.
309. Heim's record, cit. Picker, pp. 147 f.
310. *Ibid*, pp. 167 f.
311. Cf. Engels, *Anti-Dühring*.
312. Heim's record, p. 151.
313. Schramm, cit. Picker, p. 84.
314. Heim's record, cit. Picker, p. 167.
315. *Ibid*, p. 154.
316. *Ibid*, p. 167. On 13 Dec. 1941 (Picker, p. 155) Hitler said that if he were in Mussolini's place, he would 'march into the Vatican and fetch out the whole lot of them. Then I'd say: "Sorry, I've made a mistake!" – but they'd be out.'
317. In *Mein Kampf*, p. 5, he writes: 'at Lambach I had excellent opportunity to intoxicate myself with the solemn splendour of the brilliant church festivals. As was only natural, the abbot seemed to me ... the highest and most desirable ideal.' Cf. also Manheim, p. 9, and Maser, *Hitlers Mein Kampf*, pp. 97 f.
318. Told to the author by one of Hitler's Linz schoolmates (1969). Cf. also Kandl, pp. 44 f.
319. Cit. from the copy of the original M S of Heim's record, authenticated by Heim in July 1968.
320. Manheim, p. 99.
321. *Ibid*.
322. Cf. Maser, *Hitlers Mein Kampf*.
323. Picker, p. 235.
324. Cf. Picker, pp. 258 f.
325. Hitler himself has stated that he investigated the question of Protestantism in the period 1908–13. Manheim, p. 103.
326. Cf. Picker, p. 260. However fifteen years later the Protestant bishops were criticized by the Socialist Unity Party (SED) for allying themselves with Catholicsm 'which for centuries has organized war and death, witch burning and excommunication' (Gute and Ritter, *Glauben und Wissen*, pp. 20 f); cf. Maser, *Genossen beten nicht*, pp. 134 ff.
327. Manheim, p. 103.
328. Picker, p. 260.
329. Cf. *ibid*, p. 259.
330. *Ibid*.
331. *Ibid*, p. 388.
332. *Ibid*, p. 259.
333. Heim's record, cit. Picker, p. 153.
334. *Ibid*, p. 150.
335. *Ibid*, p. 149.

336. *Ibid*, p. 154.
337. Heim's record, cit. Picker, p. 155.
338. Written statement by Ribbentrop, 23 Sept. 1946. Typescript with three handwritten insertions, two sets of initials, and J. von Ribbentrop's signature. Original in the possession of Robert M. W. Kempner.
339. Heim's record, cit. Picker, p. 155.
340. *Ibid*, p. 154.
341. *Ibid*, p. 150.
342. *Ibid*, p. 154.
343. Picker, p. 388.
344. Heim's record, cit. Picker, p. 154.
345. *Ibid*, p. 155.
346. *Ibid*, p. 151.
347. *Ibid*, p. 155.
348. *Ibid*, p. 149.
349. Told to the author by Ilse Braun (24 May 1971).
350. Among the writers and thinkers who meant most to Hitler the following stand out: Thomas Robert Malthus (1766–1834), Karl von Clausewitz (1780–1831), Arthur Schopenhauer (1788–1860), Charles Darwin (1809–82), Gregor Mendel (1822–84), Robert Hamerling, a relative of Hitler's (1830–89), Alfred Ploetz (1860–1940), Wilhelm Bölsche (1861–1939), Houston Stewart Chamberlain (1855–1927), Ernst Haeckel (1834–1919), Gustave Le Bon (1841–1931), Sigmund Freud (1856–1939), Rudolf Kjellén (1864–1922), William McDougall (1871–1938), Sven Hedin (1865–1952), Fridtjof Nansen (1861–1930), Hanns Hörbiger (1860–1931) and Alexander von Müller (1882–1964).
351. Schramm, *Hitler*, p. 125.
352. Cf. Manheim, p. 9.
353. Cf. Kubizek, pp. 68 f.
354. Told to the author by Josef Popp Jr, 1966.
355. Cf. Maser, *Hitlers Mein Kampf*, pp. 91 f.
356. Cf. *inter alia* Schramm in the introduction to Picker, p. 32.
357. Ziegler, *Hitler . . .* , p. 130.
358. Prof. K. Brandt, cit. Schramm, *Hitler*, p. 21, footnote 1.
359. Picker, p. 192.
360. Frank, p. 45.
361. See Eckart, *Der Bolschewismus von Moses bis Lenin. Zwiegespräche zwischen Adolf Hitler und mir*, also Maser, *Frühgeschichte*, pp. 88 ff., Maser, *Hitlers Mein Kampf*, pp. 80 f; Nolte, 'Eine frühe Quelle zu Hitlers "Antisemitismus" ', pp. 584 ff.
362. Eckart, p. 26.
363. Cf. Schoeps, *Paulus. Die Theologie des Apostels im Lichte der jüdischen Religionsgeschichte*, p. 13.
364. Eckart, p. 26.
365. *Ibid*, p. 33.
366. Cf. Maser, *Frühgeschichte*, pp. 405 and 517.

367. Told to the author by Hermann Esser in 1953.
368. Picker, p. 191.
369. *Ibid*, p. 193.
370. Cf. Zoller, p. 155.
371. Schmidt (interpreter), p. 295.
372. Hitler's letters quoted and reproduced by Kubizek.
373. Cf. Maser, *Hitlers Mein Kampf*, pp. 13 ff. and 22 f.
374. Cf. *ibid*, pp. 37 ff., 49 f., 54 f. and 60.
375. Original of letter in the possession of the Bechtle Verlag. No corrections were made to Hitler's punctuation in the passage quoted.
376. Original of the undated letter (probably 1915) in private ownership, text unamended.
377. Cit. from Kubizek, pp. 310 f.
378. Translated from the original (undated, in the possession of the Bechtle Verlag).
379. Cf. Zoller, pp. 13 ff.
380. When questioned by Kempner on 1 July 1947, Hitler's secretary Johanna Wolf provided independent confirmation of what Christa Schröder had said. Sometimes referred to by Hitler as 'Wölfin' or she-wolf, Johanna Wolf had once been in the employ of his friend, Dietrich Eckart. Cf. Kempner, *Das Dritte Reich im Kreuzverhör*, pp. 33 ff.
381. The handwritten notes for his speeches of the early twenties are perfectly legible but this is not the case with the corrections and insertions made after 1933. Hence age and deteriorating eyesight were perhaps not wholly to blame for his occasional inability to decipher what he had written only a short while before.

CHAPTER SIX. *Women*

1. Cit. from Gun, *Eva Braun-Hitler*. Ilse Braun has confirmed the authenticity of the text.
2. *Ibid*.
3. Told to the author by Frau Winter (1969). In his will of 2 May 1938 Hitler left her 'a pension of 150 marks a month for the remainder of her life'.
4. Cf. Picker, p. 323.
5. *Ibid*.
6. Cf. Kubizek, pp. 78 ff. and Jetzinger, pp. 142 ff., also Stephanie's comments as a mature woman, Jetzinger, pp. 143 f.
7. Photocopy of a written statement by Stephanie; cf. also Jetzinger's correspondence with her, Jetzinger, p. 144.
8. Including those given by Kubizek, Greiner, Dr Bloch, Prewatzky-Wendt, Hanisch, Honisch, teachers and fellow-pupils. Cf. also documentary and bibliographical data in Maser, *Frühgeschichte*.
9. Manheim, p. 32.
10. Cf. Kubizek, pp. 282 f.

11. *Ibid.* Kubizek leans so heavily on *Mein Kampf* and embroiders on it to such an extent that the information he provides is of little more than secondary importance. The minutes written in 1938 by the historians of the NSDAP Central Archives (Federal Archives Coblenz, NS 26/17 a) prove conclusively that there had already been exhaustive correspondence and discussions with Kubizek about the kind of book he was to produce. A file entry (dated 8 Dec. 1938) by one of the archivists concerned reads: 'If Kubizek can write down his recollections of the Führer just as he relates them, this account might well be one of the most important documents in the Central Archives. . . . It can safely be said that the reconstruction of the Greater German Reich was already the stuff of the Führer's youthful daydreams.'

12. Information personally supplied by the doctor in 1952 (name and address lodged in the Munich District Court under sealed cover).

13. Cit. from Picker, p. 165.

14. *Ibid*, p. 194.

15. Told to the author by Josef and Elisabeth Popp (May 1966).

16. Meirowsky and Neisser, 'Eine neue sexualpädagogische Statistik', *Zeitschrift für die Bekämpfung der Geschlechtskrankeiten*, 1912, no. 12, pp. 1–38; cf. also Giese and Schmidt, *Studenten – Sexualität*, pp. 231 ff.

17. Of the 300 doctors to whom Meirowsky and Neisser sent questionnaires, 90 replied (86 being married men).

18. Nominal roll of 7 Coy, 1st Replacement Bn, 2 Bavarian Inf. Regt, vol. xx, Federal Archives, Coblenz, NS 26/12.

19. *Ibid.*

20. *Ibid.*

21. Told to the author by Hitler's Spital relations, 1969.

22. Cit. from the copy of the original MS of Heim's record, authenticated by Heim, July 1968 (reproduction in possession of Heinrich Heim).

23. Among these were Hermann Esser (information personally supplied, 1953), and Henriette von Schirach, née Hoffmann (information supplied May 1966).

24. Cf. for instance the *Münchner Post*, 3 April 1923.

25. Cf. Gun, pp. 56 f.

26. Maria Kubisch, née Reiter, first met Hitler in 1926. During 1931–34 and also in 1938 she had several further meetings with him. Cf. also Günter Peis, 'The Unknown Lover' with a commentary by Eugen Kogon, *Der Stern*, Hamburg 1959, no. 24.

27. Cf. Gun, p. 64.

28. *Ibid*, p. 62.

29. Cf. Heinrich Hoffmann, *Erzählungen*. The woman eventually married and Hoffmann therefore withheld her name for fear of possible repercussions.

30. Told to the author by Geli's brother, Leo Raubal, in the course of several meetings, 1967; Raubal maintained that his uncle, Adolf Hitler, had been entirely innocent of Geli's death.

31. Cf. Hanfstaengl, *Hitler*, p. 205.

32. Cf. report of the Public Prosecutor's inquiry, 2 Jan. 1924 (Munich Police Headquarters); also Maser, *Frühgeschichte*, p. 406.
33. Ciano incorrectly gives her name as 'von Lappus'. A native of Mecklenburg, she was born on 28 Dec. 1916.
34. Eleonore Bauer later gave birth to a child which was educated at the Party's expense. For a time she worked in the editorial office of the NSDAP's *Völkischer Beobachter*.
35. Cit. from Picker, p. 193.
36. Cf. Maser, *Frühgeschichte*, p. 408.
37. Frau von Seidlitz's statement at Munich Police Headquarters on 13 Dec. 1923.
38. Cf. Maser, *Frühgeschichte*, p. 409.
39. Cit. from Picker, p. 164.
40. *Ibid.*
41. *Ibid*, p. 188.
42. *Ibid*, p. 194.
43. *Ibid*, p. 269.
44. *Ibid*, p. 188.
45. Information personally supplied by Henriette von Schirach, (née Hoffmann) and Dr Paul Karl Schmidt(-Carell). Their statements have been confirmed by Hitler's secretaries. Also by his dentist, SS Brigadeführer Dr Hugo Blaschke, when examined by R. M. W. Kempner on 19 Dec. 1947. Unpublished record of examination, original in Kempner's possession.
46. Told to the author by Ilse Braun (1969).
47. Told to the author by Henriette von Schirach (née Hoffmann) (1965).
48. Told to the author by Ilse Braun (1969).
49. Told to the author by Leo Raubal (1967).
50. Told to the author by Anny Winter (1969).
51. Told to the author by Ilse Braun (1969).
52. Told to the author by Henriette von Schirach (1967).
53. Told to the author by Anny Winter (1969).
54. Cf. Gun, pp. 78 ff. These particulars were confirmed by Eva Braun's sister Ilse in conversation with the author on 18 March 1969.
55. Told to the author by Ilse Braun (18 March 1969).
56. Told to the author by Luis Trenker (1967).
57. Heim's record, cit. Picker, p. 189.
58. Cf. also Hanfstaengl, *Hitler*, p. 192.
59. Told to the author by Luis Trenker (1967).
60. In conversations with the author in September 1970, Leni Riefenstahl was extremely reserved.
61. Mady Rahl showed herself no less reserved when questioned by the author in October 1969.
62. Cf. Bezymenski, *Der Tod des Adolf Hitler*, pp. 67 and 77 *passim*.
63. Published in the Federal Republic in the autumn of 1968; cf. bibliography, Bezymenski, *op. cit.*

64. E.g. in the 'Erotik-Lexikon', *Jasmin*, no. 24/1968, pp. 191 f.
65. US record of Morell's interrogation.
66. Morell documents: results of examination by Drs Brinkmann and Schmidt-Burbach. US record of doctors' interrogations.
67. Röhrs, pp. 100 f.
68. Told to the author by Ilse Braun (18 March 1969).
69. Cit. from Gun, p. 75.
70. Morell's deposition (urological data: sexual characteristics).
71. Cf. Chap. 7, pp. 209 ff.
72. Told to the author by Dr Paul Karl Schmidt(-Carell), 17 Feb. 1971.
73. Cf. also the 'Erotik-Lexikon', *Jasmin*, no. 24/1968, p. 192.
74. Blaschke, examined by R. M. W. Kempner, 19 Dec. 1947; cf. note 45.
75. On 3 Sept. 1939 after Britain's declaration of war, Unity Mitford shot herself twice in the head but survived. She died in 1948.
76. Told to the author by Henriette von Schirach (née Hoffmann) May 1966.
77. Cit. from Gun, p. 77. The 'Valkyrie' to whom Eva Braun refers is almost certainly Unity Mitford.
78. Cit. from Picker, p. 194.
79. *Ibid*, pp. 164 f.
80. Baur, p. 89.
81. *Ibid*, p. 90.
82. Recorded by Heinrich Heim, cit. Picker, p. 189. Cf. also *op. cit.*, pp. 292 ff.
83. Picker, p. 335.
84. Cf. Picker, p. 164.
85. Told to the author by Eva Braun's sister, Ilse (1969). Cf. Gun; also Kempner, *Das Dritte Reich im Kreuzverhör*, p. 39.
86. Cf. Manheim, pp. 7 ff.
87. Information supplied by Anny Winter (1969).

CHAPTER SEVEN. *The Ailing Führer*

1. Manheim, p. 372.
2. Morell's deposition.
3. Told to the author by Hermann Esser, 1953–54.
4. Morell's deposition.
5. Speer, *Inside the Third Reich*, p. 104.
6. Cf. *ibid*, pp. 104 f.
7. US record of doctors' interrogations.
8. Hanfstaengl, *Zwischen Weissem und Braunem Haus.*
9. Morell's deposition.
10. Speer, p. 104.
11. Morell's deposition.
12. *Ibid.*

13. Told to the author by Ilse Braun.
14. US record of doctors' interrogations.
15. Morell's deposition.
16. Cf. also Speer, p. 106.
17. Told to the author by Ilse Braun, 1969.
18. Hossbach transcript.
19. Told to the author by Luis Trenker, 1967, and Leni Riefenstahl, 1970.
20. Morell documents. Results of examination by Drs Brinkmann, Schmidt-Burbach and Nissle. US record of doctors' interrogations.
21. *Ibid.*
22. Morell's deposition.
23. Morell documents.
24. Morell's deposition.
25. Cf. DNB release, 4 Sept. 1940; also cit. Domarus, ii/3, pp. 1575 ff.
26. Cit. from Kempner, *Eichmann und Komplizen*, p. 97.
27. *Ibid.*
28. Told to the author by Ilse Braun (1969).
29. Cf. Speer, p. 104.
30. Cf. Röhrs, pp. 53 ff.
31. Kempner, *Eichmann und Komplizen*, pp. 97 ff.
32. *Ibid*, pp. 101 ff.
33. Cf. Ullrich von Hassell, *Vom anderen Deutschland*, p. 183.
34. Cf. Heim, cit. Picker, pp. 139 f.
35. Told to the author by Heim, 22 Oct. 1970.
36. Cf. DNB release and photographs, 6 Aug. 1941.
37. Cf. Picker, pp. 140 ff.
38. Morell's deposition.
39. *Ibid.*
40. Führer Directive, 21 Aug. 1941; cf. entry in Halder's diary for 22 Aug. 1941, Federal Archives, Coblenz.
41. Cf. Heim, cit. Picker, pp. 143 ff.
42. Heim's record, cit. Picker, pp. 143 ff.
43. Picker, p. 432.
44. Morell's record.
45. Manstein, *Lost Victories*, p. 365.
46. Morell's report.
47. *Ibid.*
48. Cf. *Hitler's War Directives*, p. 199.
49. Cf. Ciano, *Tagebücher 1939–1943*, p. 455.
50. Doc. in Federal Archives, Coblenz, NS 26/17 a.
51. *Ibid.*
52. Cf. Kersten, pp. 209 f.
53. Morell documents and US record of doctors' interrogations.
54. Cf. Zoller, p. 65.
55. *Ibid*, pp. 67 f.
56. Cf. *ibid*, p. 67.

57. Morell-Löhlein correspondence: Morell's report and US records of doctors' interrogations.
58. *Ibid.*
59. Result of Dr Löhlein's examination, cf. note 57.
60. *Ibid.*
61. *Ibid.*
62. *Ibid.*
63. *Ibid.*
64. Irving, 'Hitlers Krankheiten', *Der Stern*, 26/69, p. 42.
65. Cf. *Neue Zürcher Zeitung*, 13 April 1944, and Domarus, vol. ii/4, p. 2091.
66. Cf. Manstein, *Lost Victories*, pp. 535 f.
67. Hitler, on 12 Dec. 1942 at the midday conference in the Wolfsschanze: cf. Warlimont, p. 308.
68. At the evening conference on 31 Aug. 1944; cit. Schramm, *Hitler als miltärischer Führer*, p. 93.
69. Cf. *Hitler's War Directives*, pp. 239 f.
70. Cit. Domarus ii/4, pp. 2069 and 2073.
71. DNB release, 23 July 1944.
72. Hitler's remark has since been confirmed by Morell (Morell's report).
73. US record of the doctors' investigations. Four drawings of noses by Dr Giesing (the normal nose being Hitler's) on an A4 sheet of paper. For Hitler's case history after July 1944 see also Chap. 9.
74. Trevor-Roper, *The Last Days of Hitler*, p. 70.
75. Morell's report.
76. *Ibid.*
77. Cf. Blaschke's statement in Kempner, *Das Dritte Reich im Kreuzverhör*, p. 65. Hugo Blaschke had become Hitler's dentist soon after 1933. Hitler's teeth had been bad for years. Such as he had, yellowing and worn down, were much filled and were supplemented by crowns and bridges. In his upper jaw he had nine gold and porcelain teeth: four incisors and both the canines, the first left molar and first and second right molars, these being comprised in a gold bridge held in place by pins on the second left and second right incisors. Ten of the fifteen teeth in the lower jaw were false.
78. Cf. Kempner, *ibid*, p. 62.
79. Morell documents and US record of doctors' interrogations. On 21 Oct. 1944 two more X-ray photogaphs were taken of Hitler's head.
80. Giesing's deposition, 12 June 1945, pp. 150 ff.
81. In his depositions Giesing enlarges on the danger of these pills.
82. Cf. Trevor-Roper, *The Last Days of Hitler*, p. 94.
83. Cf. *ibid*, p. 72.
84. Cit. from Röhrs, p. 41.
85. Giesing's deposition, 12 June 1945, pp. 175 f.
86. Cit. from Schramm, *Hitler als militärischer Führer*, pp. 134 ff.
87. Cit. from Bullock, p. 706.
88. Cf. Trevor-Roper, *The Last Days of Hitler*, p. 97.
89. Cf. *Der Spiegel*, no. 3/66.

90. Letters reproduced in Gun (unnumbered).
91. Cf. Bezymenski, *The Death of Adolf Hitler*, p. 70.
92. Cf. Zoller, pp. 67 f.
93. Told to the author by Dr Schmidt(-Carell), 1971. Schmidt visited Morell three or four times. On the last occasion he was told by a German medical orderly: 'The professor was taken away early this morning.'
94. These were given to the author by Dr Kempner who had acted as US chief prosecutor in some twelve court cases arising out of the Nuremberg trials.
95. Trevor-Roper, *The Last Days of Hitler*, p. 66. Most critics have adopted his version of the events.
96. Told to the author by Heinrich Heim, 22 Oct. 1970, who had heard it from Dr Brandt.
97. Cf. Trevor-Roper, p. 68.
98. *Ibid*, p. 66.
99. *Ibid*, p. 65.
100. *Ibid*, p. 66. After 1945 Brandt declared: 'When I asked Morell the name of the drug he had prescribed, he refused to tell me.'
101. Giesing's deposition, 11 Nov. 1945, pp. 4 f.
102. Morell's deposition. The author is indebted to the physician, Dr Fritz Ehlers, and the chemist, Dr Adolf Wenz, for their expert and disinterested help in the evaluation of this document.
103. Cit. Röhrs, pp. 110 f.
104. Told to the author by members of Hitler's entourage (1969 and 1970). Christa Schröder, Hitler's secretary, has also made this known. Cf. Zoller, pp. 67 *passim*. In 1945 Morell told Dr P. K. Schmidt that Eva Braun had sometimes urged him to prescribe drugs to revive the ailing and overworked Führer's sexual appetite and had not always shown herself amenable to medical arguments. Told to the author by Dr Schmidt (-Carell), 12 Feb. 1971.
105. Cf. Trevor-Roper, p. 68.
106. Cf. *ibid*, p. 99.
107. Cf. also Schramm, in Picker, pp. 109 f.
108. Morell's deposition.
109. Schramm in Picker, p. 110.
110. Morell's deposition.
111. *Ibid*.
112. *Ibid*.
113. Cf. his remark on 31 Aug. 1944; cit. Schramm, *Hitler als militärischer Führer*, p. 93.
114. Hitler on 12 Dec. 1942 during the midday conference in the Wolfsschanze; cf. Warlimont, p. 308.
115. It is clear that Hitler never suffered from nervous palsy during the First World War, the whole of which he spent on active service with his unit save for well-attested periods in hospital (9 Oct. 1916 to 1 Dec. 1917: shell splinter in left thigh; 15–16 Oct. 1918 and 21 Oct. 1918 to 19 Nov.

1919: gas casualty): nominal roll of 7 Coy 1. Replacement Bn, 12 Bavarian Inf. Regt (vol. xxii, Federal Archives, Coblenz, NS 26/12); home leave (30 Sept. to Oct. 17 1917; 10–27 Sept. 1918), and short leave (23–30 Aug. 1918): *ibid*. It seems quite probable that, after he had been gassed in October 1918, his reactions were oversensitive (hysterical).

CHAPTER EIGHT. *The Politician*

1. Manheim, p. 187.
2. Told to the author by Hitler's fellow-soldier Ernst Schmidt, Aug. 1964.
3. Manheim, p. 62.
4. Ernst Schmidt, Aug. 1964.
5. Manheim, p. 187.
6. *Ibid*, p. 266.
7. *Ibid*, pp. 191–2.
8. *Ibid*, p. 192.
9. *Ibid*, p. 244.
10. *Ibid*, pp. 207 ff.
11. *Ibid*, p. 603: cf. also *Hitlers Zweites Buch*, p. 94.
12. Cf. also Harold J. Gordon.
13. Manheim, p. 193.
14. *Ibid*, p. 191.
15. *Ibid*, pp. 191, 192.
16. Cf. Jacobsen, *Nationalsozialistische Aussenpolitik 1933–1938*, pp. 618 ff. *passim*.
17. *Ibid*.
18. *Ibid*.
19. Told to the author by Josef Popp, the son of Hitler's Munich landlord.
20. Cf. Hammann, *Deutsche Weltpolitik 1890–1912*, p. 232.
21. The signatories comprised 352 academics, 148 members of the legal profession, 158 clergymen, 145 senior civil servants, 40 parliamentarians, 182 businessmen, 18 serving generals and admirals, 52 landowners, 252 artists, writers and publishers. Cf. also Töpner, *Gelehrte Politiker und politisierende Gelehrte*, p. 114.
22. Cit. from Krummacher, *Die Auflösung der Monarchie*, 5th edn, pp. 14 f. In 1914, the German historian Friedrich Meinecke, as respected then as he was after 1945, declared that Germany should pursue an imperialist policy, and considered the war to be a defensive one. This undoubtedly corresponded to the views Hitler had held from the time of his youth. Cf. also *Süddeutsche Monatshefte*, vol. xi (September 1914), pp. 796 ff.
23. Manheim, pp. 148 ff.
24. *Ibid*, p. 594. In March 1938 Neville Chamberlain was prepared to reach a compromise over the African colonies. In the face of stiff opposition from his colleagues in the Cabinet he proposed firstly that Germany should participate in the administration of a colonial zone extending from South-

388 HITLER

West Africa to the Sahara, and secondly that her former colonies, administered as mandates by Britain, France, Belgium and Portugal, should be returned.

25. Cf. Jacobsen, *Nationalsozialistische Aussenpolitik*, pp. 331 f.
26. *Ibid*, p. 332.
27. Cf. Hillgruber, *Kontinuität und Diskontinuität in der deutschen Aussenpolitik von Bismarck bis Hitler*, p. 17.
28. *Ibid*, p. 20.
29. *Ibid*, p. 21.
30. For instance on 8 July 1930 Brüning publicly demanded a just and lasting order in Europe and 'sufficient natural living-space' for the Reich; cf. *ibid*, p. 21. Brüning regarded the question of reparations as crucial by comparison with German rearmament which he relegated to second place.
31. Chancellor, von Papen; Foreign Minister, von Neurath; Minister of Food, von Braun; Minister of the Interior, von Gayl.
32. Cf. also Hitler's speech of 1 May 1933, cit. Domarus, vol. i/1, pp. 259 ff.
33. Cf. Brüning's declarations on 8 July 1930, cit. Lipgens, 'Europäische Einigungsidee 1923–1930', and Briand, 'Europaplan im Urteil der deutschen Akten' in *Historische Zeitschrift* 203 (1966), p. 339.
34. Cit. Domarus, vol. i/1, pp. 271 ff.
35. Speech of 10 Nov. 1938, cit. *Vierteljahrshefte für Zeitgeschichte*, 6/1958, vol. ii, pp. 175 ff. Two years previously Hitler had told Koczma, the Hungarian Minister of the Interior, that he could only proceed step by step and that he must be prepared to protect each one of them 'with his sword'; cf. Jacobsen, *Nationalsozialistische Aussenpolitik*, p. 332, n. 15.
36. Speech at Erlangen University, 13 Nov. 1930, cit., *Adolf Hitler in Franken*, p. 171.
37. Cf. Hillgruber, '"Die Endlösung" und das deutsche Ostproblem', pp. 133 ff.
38. Manheim, p. 620.
39. Cit. Domarus, ii/3, p. 1058; cf. also Hitler's speeches of 30 Jan. 1941 and 30 Jan 1942, *ibid*, pp. 1663 and 1829.
40. Cf. also Höhne, *Der Orden unter dem Totenkopf*, pp. 290 ff.
41. Federal Archives, Coblenz, LXIV B 22, fol. 1–72, p. 11.
42. Letter dated 12 Oct. 1940 from the General Public Prosecutor, Stuttgart, to the Minister of Justice, LXIV b 25, fol. 1–175; letter marked 'Top Secret, Personal' and dated 4 March 1941 from the Minister of Justice to the Head of the Reich Chancery (p. 47); also a declaration by Pastor Braune, director of the Hoffnungstal Institute and head of the eastern section of the Home Mission's Central Committee, *ibid*, p. 134; also sworn statement (12 Oct. 1946) by Viktor Hermann Brock, Bouhler's personal representative, *ibid*, p. 18.
43. Cf. also Secret Report on Monale, 17 Oct. 1941, Federal Archives, Coblenz LXIV B 25, fol. 1–175, p. 34, part of which runs: 'the asylums now have their own registry offices where documents are deliberately falsified by the officials' (p. 34).

44. *Ibid*, LXIV B 25, fol. 1–175, p. 40. On 7 Dec. 1940 Walter Buch, Chief Justice of the NSDAP, wrote to Himmler: 'The kind of thing we're handling today . . . so as to achieve eternal life for our nation . . . must remain a close secret.'
45. Cf. *ibid*, also letter, 12 Oct. 1940, from the General Public Prosecutor, Stuttgart, to the Minister of Justice, LXIV B 25, fol. 1–175; also interrogation record, 4 July 1945, of Dr Otto Schliemann, LXIV B 26, p. 149.
46. Letter from L. Schleich, 6 Sept. 1940, Federal Archives, Coblenz, LXIV B 24, fol. 1–82, p. 41.
47. Cf. *ibid*, pp. 65–7.
48. *Ibid*, LXIV B 25, p. 34.
49. LXIV B 25, p. 34.
50. *Ibid*, fol. 1–175, p. 41.
51. Cf. also Hillgruber, ' "Die Endlösung" . . .', pp. 133 ff.
52. Two Secretaries of State, Franz Schlegelberger and Wilhelf Stuckart, had attended the Wannsee Conference on 20 Jan. 1942. After examining them at Nuremberg, R. M. W. Kempner felt convinced that it had not been Hitler's intention to wait until the end of the war before exterminating the Jews. This view was subsequently borne out when the minutes of the conference were discovered. (Information supplied by Kempner, 22 July 1972; cf. also his book *Eichmann und Komplizen*, pp. 126 ff.)
53. Cf. also *Kriegstagebuch der OKW*, vol. iv, Frankfurt/M, 1961, p. 1505.
54. Statement by Kurt Gerstein, 26 April 1945. Federal Archives, Coblenz, LXIV B 26, fol. 1–160.
55. Cf. Höhne, *Der Orden unter dem Totenkopf*, p. 291.
56. Federal Archives, Coblenz, LXIV B 26, fol. 1–160.
57. *Reichsgesetzblatt I*, p. 535, cit. from *Gesetze des NS-Staates*, pub. Ingo von Münch, p. 115.
58. Cf. *Völkischer Beobachter*, no. 79, 20 March 1934; also Domarus, vol. i/1, p. 371.
59. Cf. Maser, *Frühgeschichte*, pp. 357 ff. Also Appendix A, pp. 323–4.
60. Cf. Jacobsen, *Nationalsozialistische Aussenpolitik*, p. 320.
61. *Ibid*, p. 599.
62. Maser, *Frühgeschichte*, pp. 307 ff.
63. Manheim, pp. 619 f. At a time of national emergency those communists – accused in *Mein Kampf* of treason – allowed their well-known apologist, Ruth Fischer, to tell an audience of *völkisch*-minded students: 'Whoever protests against Jewish capital . . . thereby joins the class struggle. . . . Tread the Jewish capitalists underfoot, string them up on lampposts, trample upon them': Maser, *Frühgeschichte*, pp. 337 f.
64. The accusation persisted, even after his trial. He repudiates it in *Mein Kampf* and elsewhere; cf. Maser, *Frühgeschichte*, pp. 369 ff.
65. Heim's record, cit. Picker, p. 171.
66. Russo–German Pact, concluded 23 Aug. 1939.
67. Cit. Jacobsen, *Nationalsozialistische Aussenpolitik*, p. 339.
68. Cf. Maser, *Hitlers Mein Kampf*, pp. 41 ff.

69. Jacobsen, *Nationalsozialistische Aussenpolitik*, p. 339.
70. Maser, *Hitlers Mein Kampf*, pp. 47 f. Interview published in the *Völkischer Beobachter*, 29 Feb. 1936.
71. Cf. Maser, *Hitlers Mein Kampf*, p. 31.
72. Picker, p. 268.
73. Jacobsen, *Nationalsozialistische Aussenpolitik*, p. 599.
74. Trevor-Roper, 'Hitlers Kriegsziele'.
75. Manheim, p. 189.
76. Maser, *Frühgeschichte*, p. 157.
77. Manheim, p. 202.
78. Maser, *Frühgeschichte*, p. 166.
79. *Ibid*, pp. 169 ff. and 263 ff.
80. *Ibid*, pp. 334 ff.
81. *Die Justiz*, no. 11, Aug. 1939.
82. R. M. W. Kempner, *Research Studies of the State College of Washington*, vol. xiii, June 1945.
83. File entry made by Boden, the Brunswick envoy, on 26 Feb. 1932, Federal Archives, Coblenz, N S 26/6.
84. On 24 Feb. 1933 Hitler formally resigned from the Brunswick state service (Correspondence of the Brunswick State Ministry, N S 26/6).
85. Maser, *Frühgeschichte*, p. 270.
86. *Ibid*, p. 275.
87. *Ibid*, p. 229.
88. Buchheim, 'Hitler als Politiker', *Der Führer ins Nichts*, pp. 12 f.
89. Cit. from Freund, *Deutschland unterm Hakenkreuz*, p. 361.
90. *Der Hitler-Prozess*, p. 267.
91. Cit. *Der Führer ins Nichts*, p. 26.
92. Cf. *inter alia* Greiffenhagen, Müller and Kühnl, *Totalitarismus*.
93. Cf. Nolte, *Three Faces of Fascism*, and *Der Faschismus. Von Mussolini bis zu Hitler*.
94. Goebbels, *Goebbels Reden, 1932–39*, ed. Heiber, p. 224.
95. Manheim, p. 431.
96. *Ibid*, p. 162.
97. *Ibid*. p. 164.
98. *Ibid*, p. 166.
99. *Ibid*.
100. *Ibid*, pp. 166–7.
101. Cf. Le Bon, *The Crowd. A Study of the Popular Mind*, p. 17 *passim*.
102. Manheim, p. 167.
103. *Ibid*, p. 169.
104. *Ibid*, p. 167.
105. Cf. Le Bon, p. 10 *passim*.
106. Cf. *ibid*.
107. Cf. *ibid*.
108. Manheim, p. 165.
109. *Ibid*, pp. 163–4.

110. *Ibid*, p. 165.
111. *Ibid*, p. 167.
112. *Ibid*, p. 164.
113. *Ibid*, p. 167.
114. *Ibid*, p. 169.
115. Cf. Picker, p. 265.
116. Hitler on 4 April 1942, cf. Picker, p. 248.
117. *Ibid*.
118. *Ibid*.
119. Cf. *ibid*; also p. 338.
120. *Ibid*, p. 265.
121. Cf. *ibid*, p. 248.
122. *Ibid*, p. 338.
123. *Ibid*, p. 248.
124. *Ibid*.
125. Cf. *ibid*, p. 305.
126. *Ibid*, pp. 264 f.
127. Manheim, p. 62.
128. *Ibid*, p. 482.
129. Cit. from Kramarz, *Claus Graf Stauffenberg*, 1965, p. 11.
130. Cit. from Domarus, vol. i/1, p. 207.
131. Cf. the *Völkischer Beobachter*, 25/26 Feb. 1933.
132. Cf. *ibid*, 26 Oct. 1933.
133. Cf., *inter alia*, Buchheim, 'Hitler als Politiker', *Der Führer ins Nicht*, p. 11.
134. *Ibid*, p. 19.
135. Cf. Picker, pp. 311 f.
136. Cf. *ibid*; also Bollmus, *Das Amt Rosenberg und seine Gegner*. The amount of the national debt in 1933 is given variously as 12,000 million marks (Bollmus) and 15,000 million marks (Picker). At the end of the war Bollmus declares that it amounted to 379·8 thousand million and Picker 390 thousand million.

CHAPTER NINE. *The Strategist and Warlord*

1. Recorded by Lieutenant-General Liebmann, *Vierteljahrshefte für Zeitgeschichte*, 1954, pp. 434 f.
2. Respectively Foreign Minister and Minister of Defence under Papen.
3. Cf. Maser, *Hitlers Mein Kampf*, pp. 249 ff.
4. Part of the wording of the oath.
5. Cit. from Schramm, *Hitler als militärischer Führer*, p. 48.
6. Cf. Manstein, *Lost Victories*, pp. 29 ff. and pp. 81 f., also Jodel, cit. Schramm, *Hitler: The Man and the Military Leader*, p. 198.
7. DNB release, 1 Sept. 1970.
8. Hjalmar Schacht was the last exponent of a 'liberal-imperialist' course. Cf. Hildebrand, *Vom Reich zur Weltreich, NSDAP und koloniale Frage*

1919–1945, pp. 204 ff., also Hillgruber, *Kontinuität and Diskontinuität in der deutschen Aussenpolitik.*

9. Cf. Hillgruber, *Kontinuität und Diskontinuität*, p. 24; also Hillgruber, *Hitlers Strategie*, p. 34 and pp. 581 ff.

10. Hitler alleged that the Germans' lack of resolution in the prosecution of the war in 1918 had led to the Second World War: cf. his New Year Proclamation of 1 Jan. 1943, cit. Domarus, vol. ii, p. 1967.

11. Speech of 19 Sept. 1939, cit. Domarus, ii/3, pp. 1357 f.

12. On Hitler's interpretation of the Non-Aggression Pact cf. Maser, *Hitlers Mein Kampf*, pp. 177 ff.

13. Speech of 23 Jan. 1943, cit. Domarus, ii/4, p. 2000.

14. Cit. *ibid*, p. 2236.

15. Speech cit. Domarus, ii/3, p. 1639.

16. Cit. *ibid*, ii/4, p. 2208.

17. Cf. Gunzenhäuser, 'Die Bibliographien zur Geschichte des zweiten Weltkrieges' in *Jahresbibliographie 1961 der Bibliothek für Zeitgeschichte Stuttgart*, p. 529. Also Hillgruber, *Hitlers Strategie*, p. 13. In 1961 some 50,000 serious books and articles on World War II had already appeared. By now the number must exceed 100,000 to which should be added the important records in the Military Archives in Freiburg relating to the reconstruction of the army, navy and air force up to 1939, and the files in the British Public Record Office concerning the rearmament question. The French records have not yet been released and there is little likelihood that the Russian primary sources will be made available in the foreseeable future. The lack of French documents is not of great importance since all the major decisions were taken in London. Despite the unusually large number of publications on the Second World War, no overall view of the history of the conflict has appeared that is worthy of mention. In this connection see H. A. Jacobsen's proposals on the subject in *Zur Konzeption einer Geschichte des Zweiten Weltkrieges 1939–45*, also Müller, 'Gedanken zum Problem einer Geschichts-schreibung über den Zweiten Weltkrieg' in *Wehrwissenschaftliche Rundschau*, 1962, pp. 634–51 and 729–36. Cf. also Hillgruber, *Hitlers Strategie*, pp. 588 f.

18. Cf. IMT vol. xv,

19. Cf. Schramm, *Hitler*, p. 168.

20. IMT, vol. x, pp. 600 f.

21. Cit. in Giesing's report of 11 Nov. 1945, pp. 13 ff. Quoted from the original.

22. Clausewitz, *Vom Kriege*, p. 151.

23. Cf. also Hillgruber, *Hitlers Strategie*, p. 23.

24. Cit. Schramm, *Hitler*, p. 197.

25. Manstein, *Lost Victories*, p. 287.

26. Bezymenski, *Sonderakte Barbarossa*, p. 195; cf. also *ibid*, p. 296.

27. Cf. Rohwer, 'Zeitgeschichte, Krieg und Technik', *Wehrwissenschaftliche Rundschau*, 1964, pp. 205–14.

28. Cf. official accounts of the war in all countries during 1962. See J. C.

Allmeyer-Beck, 'Die Internationale amtliche Krieggeschichtsschreibung über den Zweiten Weltkrieg', pp. 507–40.

29. Cf., for instance, F. H. Hinsley, *Hitler's Strategy*, Cambridge, 1951; Buchheit, 'Hitler als Soldat', *Der Führer ins Nichts*; Trevor-Roper, 'Hitlers Kriegsziele'; Schramm, *Hitler als militärischer Führer*, bibliography; Hillgruber, *Hitlers Strategie*, bibliography; Bullock, 'Hitler and the origins of the Second World War', *Proc. British Academy*, xiii, pp. 259–87 (henceforward referred to as Bullock, 'Second World War').

30. Hitler's comments were made in the course of his meeting with the Foreign Minister, the War Minister and the Commanders-in-Chief of the three Services, as reported by Hossbach; see also Bullock, 'Second World War', pp. 270 ff.

31. Bullock, 'Second World War', pp. 271 ff.

32. Hillgruber, *Hitlers Strategie*, p. 593.

33. Cf. Clausewitz, *Vom Kriege*, pp. 65–77.

34. Cf. *ibid*, p. 67.

35. An entry in Goebbel's diary on 9 March 1943 is particularly instructive in this context: 'The Führer's opinion of the generals is wholly negative. According to him they deceive him whenever they can. . . . Apart from that they are uneducated and not even au fait with their own military craft which is the least that could be expected. . . . The fact that they are so badly informed about the purely material aspects of the war speaks volumes. He feels that for generations their upbringing has been wrong . . .' Cit. Schramm, *Hitler als militärische Führer*, p. 48.

36. Cit. from Warlimont, *Im Hauptquartier der Wehrmacht*, p. 342. It was a faculty also noted by Speer. During a conversation with the author in November 1967 he said: 'Hitler always had a sixth sense.'

37. Cf. Buchheit, 'Hitler als Soldat', p. 48.

38. IMT, vol. xv.

39. Verbal account given by E. von Breitenbuch on 8 Sept. 1966 to Prof. Peter Hoffmann who passed the information on to the author on 7 June 1971.

40. Cit. Schramm, *Hitler*, p. 200.

41. Giesing's deposition of 11 Nov. 1945, pp. 13 ff.

42. *Ibid*.

43. Document filed under 'Bormann' at the US Berlin Document Center. Attached to this there is a typewritten letter to Himmler covering three sheets of A4, dated 30 July 1944 and signed by Martin Bormann.

44. Giesing's deposition of 11 Nov. 1945, pp. 13 ff.

45. *Ibid*.

46. *Der Spiegel*, no. 3/66. Situation conference of 25 April 1945.

47. *Ibid*, p. 41. The Red Army comprised two and a half million men, 41,600 guns, 6250 tanks and 7560 aircraft. Opposing them were a mere 44,630 German regular troops, 42,531 Volksturm, 3532 Hitler Youth (of whom only 50 per cent were armed) and other auxiliaries.

48. Cf. *ibid*, p. 37.

49. *Ibid*, pp. 49 f.
50. Cf. Warlimont, *Im Hauptquartier der Wehrmacht*, p. 290.
51. Hitler on 20 May 1943; transcript cit. Warlimont, p. 343; cf. also *ibid*, p. 344.
52. Related by the interpreter in the course of a television programme ('Valkyrie') on 20 July 1971 (Programme 1).
53. Told to the author by Dr Giesing in June 1971.
54. Account given on the television programme 'Valkyrie' on 20 July 1971 by von Gersdorf, one of the conspirators in the July plot, who stated that in March 1943 it had been his intention to blow himself up at the same time as Hitler.
55. Cf. Höhne, p. 479.
56. Cf. *Hitler's War Directives*, pp. 198 ff.
57. Cf. Schellenberg, pp. 279 and 283. Schellenberg's account is clearly in accordance with the facts. As early as August 1942 Himmler had instructed the Gestapo to collect information about Hitler's origins.
58. Jacobsen, *1939–1945*, p. 532, cf. also Höhne, pp. 534 ff.
59. Cit. Warlimont, p. 341.
60. Cf. Speer, *Inside the Third Reich*, p. 364.
61. Cf. also Bullock, 'Second World War', p. 268.
62. Cf. Speer, p. 364.
63. Cf. *ibid*.
64. Cf. *ibid*.
65. Cf. *ibid*.
66. Cf. *ibid*, p. 366.
67. Cf. *ibid*.
68. Cf. Bullock, 'Second World War', p. 269.
69. Cf. *Hitler's War Directives*, p. 135. The Wehrmacht was only equipped for a summer campaign. On the day the operation began Hitler ordered a cut back in armaments production and in his Directive 32a of 14 July 1941 spoke of a reduction in the strength of the army.
70. Cf. Manstein, pp. 72–3. Hans Baur, Hitler's personal pilot, recalls a conversation between Hitler and Ribbentrop on the morning of the day war was declared: 'In my opinion,' he writes, 'Hitler did not decide upon war until he felt it was safe to assume that Britain and France would not intervene.' Cf. Baur, p. 179. In the course of conversations between December 1970 and February 1971 Baur confirmed a number of Manstein's observations.
71. Cf. also *Hitler's War Directives*, pp. 276 *passim*.
72. Cit. Warlimont, p. 524.
73. Cit. Zoller, p. 35.
74. Cit. Schramm, *Hitler*, p. 197.
75. Cf. Jacobsen, *Fall 'Gelb'*, p. 21.
76. Cf. also Manstein, p. 51. 'Indeed as far as its speed of execution and the outcome were concerned, it [the campaign] did constitute something almost unique.'

77. Cit. Schramm, *Hitler als militärischer Führer*, p. 49.
78. Cf. Schramm, *Hitler*, pp. 199 ff.
79. *Hitler's War Directives*, p. 51.
80. E.g. Manstein, *Lost Victories*, p. 535.
81. Cf. *ibid*, p. 536.
82. Cit. Schramm, *Hitler*, pp. 199 ff.
83. Cit. Warlimont, pp. 66 f.
84. Cf. Bullock, 'Second World War', p. 268.
85. On the question of German rearmament cf. *inter alia* Milward, *The German Economy at War*; Klein, *Germany's Economic Preparations for War*, Cambridge, Mass., 1959, and Stübel, 'Die Finanzierung der Aufrüstung im Dritten Reich', *Europa-Archiv*, no. 6/1951, pp. 4128 ff.
86. Hitler's instructions to Göring. After the war the documents were found amongst Speer's papers. Cf. *Documents on German Foreign Policy*, Ser. C, vol. v, no. 490; also Meinck, *Hitler und die deutsche Aufrüstung*, p. 164, and Tessin, *Formationsgeschichte der Wehrmacht 1933–39*.
87. Cf. Bullock, 'Second World War', p. 268.
88. Figures for subsequent years were as follows: 1941, 19 per cent; 1942, 26 per cent; 1943, 38 per cent; 1944, 50 per cent. Cf. Hans Kehrl, 'Kriegswirtschaft und Rüstungs-industrie', *Bilanz des Zweiten Weltkrieges*, p. 272. According to Speer's *Memoirs*, p. 548, 'the index for the production of explosives rose from 103 in 1941 to 131 in 1942 to 191 in 1943 to 226 in 1944. But the index for munitions production including bombs rose from 102 in 1941 to 106 in 1942 to 247 in 1943 to 306 in 1944.'
89. Speech in the Reichstag, cit. Domarus ii/3, pp. 1112 ff.
90. Hillgruber, *Hitlers Strategie*, p. 31.
91. On this aspect of the Hitler–Stalin pact, cf. F. Friedensburg, 'Die sowjetischen Kriegslieferungen an das Hitlerreich', *Vierteljahrshefte für Wirtschaftsforschung*, 1962, pp. 331 ff.; also Faby, *Der Hitler–Stalin Pakt 1939–41*, pp. 168 ff.
92. Cf. Treue, *Gummi in Deutschland*; also 'Gummi in Deutschland zwischen 1933 and 1945', *Wehrwissenschaftliche Rundschau*, 1955, pp. 169 ff.
93. Cf. Birkenfeld, *Der synthetische Treibstoff 1933 bis 1945*.
94. Cf. Hillgruber, *Hitlers Strategie*, p. 34.
95. Cf. Weidemann, 'Der rechte Mann am rechten Platz', in *Bilanz des Zweiten Weltkrieges*, pp. 215 ff.
96. Cf. Manstein, *Lost Victories*, p. 71.
97. Cit. Domarus, i/2, p. 968.
98. In late September 1938 a rising against Hitler had been planned by a number of senior army commanders, among them von Witzleben, but because of the successes scored by Hitler at the talks in Berchtesgaden, Godesberg and Munich, the scheme came to nothing.
99. Churchill was advocating the occupation of Norwegian ports such as Narvik and Bergen. Cf. Hubatsch, *Die deutsche Besetzung von Dänemark und Norwegen 1940*, p. 15.
100. Cf. Warlimont, pp. 86 f. and 89. On 13 Dec. 1940 Hitler's order 'that

the means of occupying Norway be studied by the smallest possible staff', was transmitted by Jodl, contrary to established custom, to the Senior Air Staff Officer in Section L.

101. Cf. *ibid*, p. 88.
102. Cit. *ibid*, p. 87; see also Domarus, ii/3, p. 1149.
103. Entry in Jodl's diary, cit. Warlimont, p. 87.
104. Cf. Jodl's statement of 1946, cit. Schramm, *Hitler*, p. 199.
105. *Ibid.* Even Jodl described Hitler's order as 'the most daring of solutions'. Warlimont, p. 97, speaks of the campaign as an adventure.
106. Cf. Hubatsch, *Die deutsche Besetzung*, pp. 40 f. Cf. also Warlimont, p. 85.
107. Cf. Warlimont, p. 84.
108. *Hitler's War Directives*, p. 62.
109. Cf., *inter alia*, Warlimont, p. 86.
110. Cf. *ibid*, pp. 92 ff. It was thanks to Jodl that Hitler persisted with his Norwegian campaign.
111. Warlimont, p. 92.
112. Cf. *ibid*, p. 96.
113. Cf. Warlimont, p. 64. At Nuremberg, however, Jodl expressly declared that, before reaching a decision, Hitler had asked for and studied 'the relevant documents such as maps, strength returns and reports on the enemy' (IMT, vol. xv).
114. During a television programme on 18 Sept. 1969, Warlimont spoke of these predictions of Hitler's.
115. Guderian, 'Erfahrungen im Russlandkrieg', in *Bilanz des Zweiten Weltkrieges*, p. 86.
116. Cit. from Schramm, *Hitler*, p. 200.
117. *Hitler's War Directives*, pp. 74 and 75.
118. Told to the author by Arnold Breker 1969. Cf. also Giesler cit. Ziegler, *Wer war Hitler?* p. 330, and Speer, *Inside the Third Reich*, p. 170.
119. Cf. Speer, p. 173.
120. Cf. Buchheit, *Hitler, der Feldherr*, p. 50.
121. *Hitler's War Directives*, pp. 86 and 87.
122. DNB release, 4 May 1941.
123. Guderian, 'Erfahrungen im Russlandkrieg', p. 87.
124. Cf. also Bezymenski, *Sonderakte Barbarossa*, p. 263.
125. According to Russian sources the victims of the purge included 3 of the 5 marshals, 14 of the 16 army commanders Ranks I and II, all 8 admirals Ranks I and II, 60 of the 67 (commanding) generals, 136 of the 199 divisional commanders and 221 of the 397 brigade commanders. All 11 deputy defence commissars and all but 5 of the 80 members of the Supreme War Soviet were eliminated. In addition some 35,000 junior officers, or about half the entire officer corps, were either shot or imprisoned. Cf. *Der Spiegel*, vol. 7, 8 Feb. 1971, p. 121.
126. Guderian, *Erinnerungen*, p. 89.
127. Directive, cit. Domarus, ii/4, p. 1748.

128. Heusinger, in his review of Hillgruber, *Hitlers Strategie*, in *Der Spiegel*. Cit. from Bezymenski, *Sonderakte Barbarossa*, p. 298.
129. Bezymenski, *Sonderakte Barbarossa*, pp. 299 f.
130. *Ibid*, p. 300.
131. *Ibid*, pp. 300 ff.
132. *Hitler's War Directives*, pp. 154 f.: Directive for 6 Sept. 1941.
133. *Ibid*, p. 159.
134. Cit. Domarus, ii/4, p. 1753.
135. Hitler's comments made on 30 March 1941. Entry for that date in Halder's diary. Cit. Domarus, ii/4, pp. 1681 f.
136. On the 'Commissar Order' see also Hillgruber, *Hitlers Strategie*, and Jacobsen, 'Kommissarbefehl und Massenexekution sowjetischer Kriegsgefangener', *Anatomie des SS-Staates*, ii, pp. 167–279.
137. IMT, vol. ix, p. 92.
138. Schramm, *Hitler*, p. 161.
139. Told to the author by Heinrich Heim, who was standing beside Hitler when the news was announced (18 Aug. 1961).
140. *Hitler's War Directives*, p. 178.
141. Dr Giesing's deposition, 12 June 1945, pp. 72 f.
142. Cf. Kesselring, p. 153.
143. Manstein, *Lost Victories*, p. 289.
144. Cf. Warlimont, p. 289. A possible exception was the Ardennes offensive at the end of 1944, the mounting of which was due to Hitler's own initiative.
145. Manstein, p. 280.
146. *Ibid*, p. 277. Manstein does, however, make some exception in the case of the Norwegian campaign.
147. Cf. Bullock, 'Second World War', p. 235.
148. Picker, p. 381.
149. Giesing's deposition, 12 June 1945, p. 176.
150. Cf. Schramm, *Hitler*, p. 163.
151. IMT, vol. xv, p. 375.
152. IMT, vol. x, p. 485. Keitel's remark applies equally to political decisions.
153. Cf. also Hillgruber, *Die Räumung der Krim*, p. 51.
154. Cf. *ibid*, p. 76, and Schramm, *Hitler*, p. 151.
155. Cf. also *Der Spiegel*, no. 12/71, p. 161.
156. Hitler to Manstein. Cf. Manstein, p. 540.
157. *Ibid*, p. 542.
158. *Ibid*, p. 547.
159. *Ibid*, p. 547 ff.
160. Cf. Schramm, *Hitler*, p. 169
161. *Ibid*, p. 165.
162. *Ibid*, pp. 169–70.
163. *Ibid*, p. 177.
164. *Ibid*, p. 181.
165. *Ibid*.

166. Giesing's deposition, 12 June 1945, pp. 13 f.
167. *Ibid*, 11 Nov. 1945, pp. 1 f.
168. Told to the author by Dr Giesing in June 1971.
169. Giesing's deposition, 11 Nov. 1945, pp. 12 f. Here Giesing draws on information supplied to him by Hitler's servant, Linge, and his orderlies, Fehrs and Arndt.
170. Told to the author by Dr Giesing in June 1971.
171. Giesing's deposition, 12 June 1945, p. 11.
172. Cf *ibid*, 11 Nov. 1945, p. 16.
173. Cf. *ibid*, 12 June 1945, pp. 9 and 10.
174. *Ibid*.
175. Cf. Warlimont, p. 505.
176. *Ibid*, p. 524.
177. Extracted from an article, 'US Foreign Relations – diplomatic papers', *Frankfurter Allgemeine Zeitung*, 15 Dec. 1966.
178. Cit. Schramm, *Hitler*, p. 171.
179. At his situation conference, 27 May 1945. Cit. from *Der Spiegel*, no. 3/66, p. 42.
180. *Ibid*, p. 37.
181. Schramm, *Hitler*, p. 179.
182. Told to the author by G. Engel in 1968.
183. Cf. *Der Spiegel*, no. 3/66, p. 42.
184. Trevor-Roper, *The Last Days of Hitler*.
185. Bezymenski, *The Death of Adolf Hitler*; cf. also *Der Spiegel*. no. 32, 5 Aug. 1968.
186. Bezymenski, *The Death of Abolf Hitler*, p. 66.
187. Cf. *ibid*, p. 45.
188. *Ibid*, p. 44.
189. Cf. *ibid*, pp. 45 f. and 55 f.
190. Cf. *ibid*, pp. 54 f.
191. Baur himself told the author (10 June 1971) about the interrogations to which he was subjected after May 1945.
192. Cf. Bezymenski, *The Death of Adolf Hitler*, p. 45.
193. See also photograph of Hitler's teeth in Bezymenski and illustrations in this volume.
194. Information supplied to Dr Giesing, Giesing's deposition, 8 June 1971.
195. Information supplied to Dr Giesing by Kempka and passed on to the author 8 June 1971.
196. Bezymenski, *op. cit.*, p. 36. Mengeshausen's assertion that Hitler's corpse had taken half an hour to be consumed is untrue and can only be ascribed to his agitation at the time.
197. Told to the author by Harry Baur on 10 June 1971.
198. Bezymenski, *op. cit*, p. 46.
199. Cf. also Trevor-Roper, *The Last Days of Hitler*, p. 219 and Bezymenski, p. 71.
200. Rosanow, *Das Ende des Dritten Reichs*.

201. Bezymenski, *Auf den Spuren von Martin Bormann.*

202. Cf. also Trevor-Roper, p. 217 and the same author's article in *Der Monat,* no. 92/1956, pp. 3 ff.

203. Bezymenski, *The Death of Adolf Hitler,* p. 75.

204. Bezymenski, *Der Tod des Adolf Hitler,* p. 89, note 63.

205. Cf. Bezymenski, *The Death of Adolf Hitler,* pp. 72 ff.

206. *Ibid,* p. 7.

207. *Der Spiegel.* no. 22/1965.

208. Bezymenski, *The Death of Adolf Hitler,* p. 71.

209. Told to the author by Hans Baur, 10 June 1971.

210. Bezymenski, *op. cit.,* p. 66.

211. Evident from the tone of Bezymenski's reply to a letter (4 March 1970) from the author giving a more or less generalized account of his own findings.

212. Letter from Giesing, 21 May 1971, and information supplied in person on 25 May 1971. In his letter Giesing wrote: 'The passages marked with a red cross . . . do not represent a true account of what happened but were intended for the C I C with my early release in view.'

213. Told to the author by Dr Giesing, 8 June 1971.

214. Cf. Bezymenski, *op. cit.,* p. 32.

215. Told to the author by Hans Baur, 10 June 1971.

216. Cf. Bezymenski, *op. cit.,* pp. 45 and 49.

217. *Ibid,* p. 49.

218. *Ibid,* pp. 57/8.

219. Giesing's translation of his own diary.

220. Told to the author by Giesing, 8 June 1971. Cf. also Giesing's account of this examination written on 12 June 1945 and quoted in Chapter 7 above.

221. Information supplied by a number of Günsche's friends (1966–71). Cf. also Trevor-Roper, *The Last Days of Hitler,* p. 196.

222. Maser, *Frühgeschichte,* p. 167.

223. *Ibid.*

224. Gun, p. 207.

Bibliography

The most important sources for this biography consist of unpublished material and verbal testimony supported by documentary evidence. Published works have been drawn on as and where necessary either to supplement the above or by way of comparison; they are listed below, after *Unpublished Sources* and *Published Files and Documents*, in the alphabetical order of their authors' names. Theses are included in the same category. The final section of this bibliography comprises learned journals and reviews.

UNPUBLISHED SOURCES

Documents of the NSDAP Central Archives, and of various Reich and NSDAP agencies; also of the Foreign Office, the SS, the Wehrmacht, the economic administration, the police and the judiciary. The documents evaluated prior to May 1961 at the US Berlin Document Center are quoted as 'Berlin Document Center' with the appropriate number; those examined after 1961 are identified by their then location, e.g. Federal Archives, Coblenz (1429 vols), or HStA. Munich and BHStA. Munich (494 vols). Other documents are referred to by their catalogue numbers in the *NSDAP Hauptarchiv Guide to the Hoover Institution Microfilm Collection*. Details of all documents and of information personally supplied to the author are given in the notes. An outline of the main sources is given below.

Church records relating to Hitler's ancestors in the parish of Döllersheim, Lower Austria.
Church records, Braunau am Inn.
Records connected with the Hitler family in the Lower Austrian Provincial Archives (Vienna).
All documents connected with Alois Schicklgruber's change of name.
Records of the municipal authorities in Graz, Linz, Braunau and Vienna.
Verbal and written information supplied by Hitler's surviving relations, including family documents.
Letters from Hitler's half-brother Alois giving autobiographical details.
Letters and biographical details from Paula Hitler.
Files in the Munich City Archives.
Documents from Hitler's *Nachlass*.
Verbal and written information supplied by close associates in the years after 1919.
Information, including documents, supplied by schoolmates and fellow soldiers.

Verbal information and documents supplied by Hitler's landlords.

Verbal and written information supplied by a senior S S officer who, shortly before the war, had been commissioned by Goebbels to collect material for a biography of Hitler covering the years 1889 to 1918; also documents filed by Goebbels for this purpose.

Statements made by Hitler's teachers; also letters, some addressed to Hitler himself.

Documents relating to Hitler's examinations in 1907 and 1908 at the Vienna Academy of Fine Arts.

The Leonding records relating to Hitler and his parents.

Report of investigation concerning Hitler by the Austrian Provincial Administration (1932).

Some 250 documents relating to Hitler's appointment as attaché to the Brunswick Legation.

Nominal Roll of 3 Coy, 16 Res. Inf. Regt.

Documents and records relating to Hitler's military service, 1914–19.

Hitler's correspondence 1905–45.

Diaries of politicians, writers and senior officers during the period after 1918.

Verbal and written information supplied by historians in the former N S D A P Central Archives.

Records kept by Heinrich Heim in 1941 and 1942 in the Führer headquarters; also information supplied by Heim in person to the author.

Verbal and written informatin supplied *inter alia* by Hans Baur, Albert Speer, Hans-Dietrich Röhrs, Annelies von Ribbentrop, Gerhard Engel, Ilse Braun, Arno Breker, Heinrich Hoffman jr, Henriette von Schirach (née Hoffmann), Ferdinand Staeger, Hans Severus Ziegler, Wilhelm Zander, Ludwig Wemmer, Robert M. W. Kempner, Generals Blumentritt, Hauck, Warlimont, Gause, von Manstein, Liss and Halder and also Admiral Dönitz.

Entries in the diary of a German diplomat concerning a conspiracy to abduct Hitler.

Gestapo files, correspondence etc., including Himmler's secret directives.

Findings of the People's Court.

Correspondence between the author and journalists and other writers at home and abroad on the subject of Hitler.

Medical documents: Reports of official interrogations of Hitler's medical and dental attendants, Morell, Giesing and Blaschke and of Drs Löhlein, Weber, Nissle and Brinkmann. Correspondence between Morell and the doctors he called in for consultation.

Report made by Dr Giesing in diary form (quoted as 'Giesing's deposition, 12 June 1945'). The report, which runs to 177 folios, concerns his treatment of Hitler between 22 July 1944 and 7 October 1944 and also records some fifty-five conversations with his patient. He also wrote a second report of thirty-two folios (quoted as 'Giesing's deposition, 11 November 1945').

Verbal information supplied by Dr Giesing, May and June 1971, and by Fritz Echtmann, October 1971.

PUBLISHED FILES AND DOCUMENTS

Files of 4 Reichswehr Group Headquarters in the Munich State Archives, Section II (former Bavarian War Archives).
Der Hitler-Prozess, Auszüge aus den Verhandlungsberichten, Munich, 1924.
Dokumente der deutschen Politik und Geschichte, 3 vols, Berlin and Munich (undated)
Hitler und Kahr. Aus dem Untersuchungsausschuss des bayerischen Landtags. Bavarian SPD Provincial Committee, Munich, 1928.
Hitlers Weisungen für die Kriegsführung 1939 bis 1945. Dokumente des Ober- kommandos der Wehrmacht, edited by Walter Hubatsch, Frankfurt/M, 1962. Cit. from unabridged paperback edition, Munich 1965. Translated as *Hitler's War Directives 1939–1945*, edited by H. R. Trevor-Roper, London, 1964. The Pan Books edition of 1966 has been used here for reference except when otherwise specified in the notes.
NSDAP Hauptarchiv Guide to the Hoover Institution Microfilm Collection, Grete Heinz and Agnes F. Peterson (Hoover Institute Bibliographical Series XVII), Stanford University.
Proceedings of the German National Assembly.
Minutes of the proceedings of the National Assembly: 'The German National Assembly ', Berlin.
Minutes of the proceedings of the Reichstag: 'Proceedings of the Reichstag', Berlin.
Proceedings of the provisional National Soviet of the Bavarian People's State for the year 1918–19.
Proceedings of the Bavarian Landtag, Munich.
Record of the proceedings against the major war criminals at Nuremberg, quoted as IMT, with volume and page number where available.
Vier Jahre Westfront. Die Geschichte des Regiments List. RIR 16, Munich, 1932.

PUBLISHED SOURCES

ACKERMANN, JOSEF. *Himmler als Ideologe*, Göttingen, Zürich and Frankfurt, 1970.
ADLER, H. G. *Jews in Germany*, Notre Dame, Illinois and London, 1970.
Adolf Hitler in Franken, Reden aus der Kampfzeit, collected and edited by Heinz Preiss on the instructions of Julius Streicher, n.d. (foreword by Ostern, 1939).
ALLMEYER-BECK, J. 'Die Internationale amtliche Krieggeschichteschrei- bung über den zweiten Weltkrieg', *Jahresbibiliographie 1962 der Bibliothek für Zeitgeschichte Stuttgart*, Frankfurt, 1964.
Die Alte Heimat. Beschreibung des Waldviertels um Döllrsheim, Eger, Sudeten- deutsche Verlag und Drukkerei GmbH, 1942.
ANSCHÜTZ. *Die Verfassung des Deutschen Reiches*, 3rd and 4th edns, Berlin, 1926.
ARENDT, HANNAH. *Origins of Totalitarianism*, London, 1967.

ARETIN, ERWEIN VON. 'Die bayerische Königsfrage', *Suddeutsche Monatshefte*, xxx, Jan. 1933.
— *Krone und Ketten*, Munich, 1955.

BÄTHE, KRISTIAN. *Wer wohnte wo in Schwabing? Wegweiser für Schwabinger Spaziergänge*, Munich, 1965.

BAEUMLER, ALFRED. *Das mythische Weltalter, Bachofens romantische Deutung des Altertums*, Munich, 1965 (first published under the title *Bachofen der Mythologe der Romantik*, the introduction to the Bachofen anthology, *Der Mythus von Orient und Occident*, Manfred Schroeter, Munich, 1926).

BAUER, OTTO, MARCUSE, HERBERT, and ROSENBERG, ARTHUR. *Faschismus und Kapitalismus. Theorien über die sozialen Ursprünge und die Funktion des Faschismus*, Frankfurt and Vienna, 1967.

BAYER, ERNST. *Die SA-Geschichte. Arbeit, Zweck und Organisation der SA*, Berlin, 1938.

BECKMANN, EWALD. *Der Dolchstossprozess*, Munich, 1925.

BENNECKE, HEINRICH. *Hitler und die SA*, Munich and Vienna, 1962.
— *Die Reichswehr und der 'Röhm-Putsch'*, Munich and Vienna, 1964.

BENNEWITZ, GERT. *Die geistige Wehrerziehung der deutschen Jugend*, Berlin, 1940.

BENOIST-MÉCHIN, JACQUES. *L'Histoire de l'armée allemande depuis L'Armistice*, 2 vols, Paris, 1936–38; English translation, *History of the Germany Army since the Armistice*, vol. 1 only, Zürich, 1939.

BERBER, FRITZ. *Die völkerreschtspolitische Lage Deutschlands*, Berlin, 1936.

BERNADOTTE, COUNT FOLKE. *The Fall of the Curtain. Last Days of the Third Reich*, London, 1945.

BERNDORFF, H. R. *General zwischen Ost und West*, Hamburg, 1951.

BERNETT, HAJO. *Nationalsozialistische Leibeserziehung*, Schorndorf bei Stuttgart, 1966.

BESGEN, ACHIM. *Der stille Befehl. Medizinalrat Kersten und das Dritte Reich*, Munich, 1960.

BESSER, JOACHIM. 'Die Vorgeschichte des Nationalsozialismus im neuen Licht', *Die Pforte* 2 (1950), pp. 763–84.

BEYER, HANS. *Von der Novemberrevolution zur Räterepublik in München*, East Berlin, 1957.

BEYERLE, KONRAD. *Föderalistische Reichspolitik*, Munich, 1924.

BEZYMENSKI, LEW. *Auf den Spuren von Martin Bormann*, Zurich, 1966.
— *Der Tod des Adolf Hitler*, Hamburg, 1968; English translation, *The Death of Adolf Hitler*, London and New York, 1968.
— *Sonderakte Barbarossa*, Stuttgart, 1968.

BINDER, GERHARD. *Lebendige Zeitgeschichte 1890–1945*, Munich, 1961.

BIRKENFELD, W. *Der synthetische Treibstoff 1933 bis 1945*, Göttingen, 1964.

BISS, ANDREAS. *Der Stopp der Endlösung. Kampf gegen Himmler und Eichmann in Budapest*, Stuttgart, 1966.

BLOCH, CHARLES. *Hitler und die europäischen Mächte 1933/1934. Kontinuität oder Bruch*, Frankfurt, 1966.

BLÜCHER, WIPERT VON. *Deutschlands Weg nach Rapallo*, Wiesbaden, 1951.
BOEHRINGER, ROBERT. *Mein Bild von Stefan George*, Munich, 1951.
BOEPPLE, ERNST. *Hitlers Reden*, Munich, 1933.
BOLDT, GERHARD. *In the Shelter with Hitler*, ed. Ernst A. Hepp, London, 1948.
— *Die letzten Tage der Reichskanzlei*, Reinbek bei Hamburg, 1964.
BOLLMUS, . *Das Amt Rosenberg und seine Gegner*.
BÖLSCHE, WILHELM. *Vom Bazillus zum Affenmenschen*, 2nd edn, Jena, 1921.
BONN, M. J. *So macht man Geschichte*, Munich, 1953.
BORKENAU, FRANZ. *The Communist International*, London, 1938.
BOTHMER, KARL GRAF VON. *Bayern den Bayern*, Diessen vor München, 1920.
BOTT, MAXIMILIAN. 'Das bayerische Generalstaatskommissariat und Bayerns Konflikt mit dem Reich', thesis, Giessen, 1927.
BOUHLER, PHILIPP. *Der grossdeutsche Freiheitskampf* (Hitler's speeches), 2 vols, Munich, 1940, 1941.
— *Kampf um Deutschland*, Munich, 1938.
BRACHER, KARL DIETRICH. *Adolf Hitler*, Berne, Munich and Vienna, 1964.
— 'Das Anfangsstadium der Hitlerschen Aussenpolitik', *Vierteljahrshefte für Zeitgeschichte* (1957), pp. 63 ff.
— *Die Auflösung der Weimarer Republik. Eine Studie zum Problem des Machtverfalls in der Demokratie*, 1st edn, Stuttgart and Düsseldorf, 1955; 3rd edn, Villingen, 1960.
— *Die Deutsche Diktatur. Entstehung, Struktur, Folgen des Nationalsozialismus*, Cologne, 1969; English translation, *The German Dictatorship. The origins, structure and effects of National Socialism*, London, 1971.
— 'Das "Phänomen" Adolf Hitler', *Pol. Lit.*, 1952, pp. 207 ff.
— 'Die völkische Ideologie und der Nationalsozialismus', *Deutsche Rundschau*, 1958, pp. 53 ff.
BRACHER, KARL DIETRICH, SAUER, WOLFGANG, and SCHULZ, GERHARD. *Die nationalsozialistische Machtergreifung. Studien zur Errichtung des totalitären Herrschaftssystems in Deutschland 1933/34*, Cologne and Opladen, 1960.
BRANDMAYER, B. *Mit Hitler Meldegänger 1914–1918*, Überlingen, 1940.
BRAUN, OTTO. *Von Weimar bis Hitler*, New York, 1940; Hamburg, 1949.
BRAUWEILER, HEINZ. *Generäle in der deutschen Republik. Groener, Schleicher, Seeckt*, Berlin, 1932.
BRECHT, ARNOLD. *Prelude to Silence. The end of the German Republic*, New York, 1944.
BRONDER, DIETRICH. *Bevor Hitler kam*, Hanover, 1964.
BROSS, WERNER. *Gespräche mit Hermann Göring während des Nürnberger Prozesses*, Flensburg/Hamburg, 1950.
BROSZAT, MARIN. *Der Nationalsozialismus. Weltanschauung, Programm und Wirklichkeit*, Stuttgart, 1960.
— *Nationalsozialistische Polenpolitik 1939–1945*, Stuttgart, 1961.
— 'Die völkische Ideologie und der Nationalsozialismus', *Deutsche Rundschau* I (1958).

BUCHHEIM, HANS. 'Ernst Niekischs Ideologie des Widerstands', *Vierteljahrshefte für Zeitgeschichte* 5 (1957), pp. 334–61.
— *Glaubenskrise im Dritten Reich. Drei Kapitel nationalsozialistischer Religionspolitik*, Stuttgart, 1953.
BUCHHEIM, HANS. 'Hitler als Politiker' in *Der Führer ins Nichts*, Rastatt-Baden, 1960.
— *SS und Polizei im NS-Staat*, Duisburg, 1964.
BUCHHEIM, HANS, BROSZAT, MARTIN, JACOBSEN, HANS-ADOLF, and KRAUSNICK, HELMUT. *Anatomie des SS-Staates*, 2 vols: 1, *Die SS – Das Herrschaftsinstrument, Befehl und Gehorsam;* 2, *Konzentrationslager, Kommissarbefehl, Judenverfolgung*, Olten and Freiburg/Br., 1965.
BUCHHEIT, GERT. *Der deutsche Geheimdienst. Geschichte der militärischen Abwehr*, Munich, 1966.
— *Hitler, der Feldherr. Die Zerstörung einer Legende*, Rastatt, 1958.
— 'Hitler als Soldat', in *Der Führer ins Nichts*, Rastatt-Baden, 1960.
BUCHNER, EBERHARD. *Revolutionsdocumente*, vol. 1, Berlin, 1921.
BUCHRÜCKER, BRUNO ERNST. *Im Schatten Seeckts*, Berlin, 1928.
BULLOCK, ALAN. *Hitler. A study in Tyranny*, revised edn, London, 1964.
— 'Hitler and the Origins of the Second World War', Raleigh Lecture on History, London, Oxford University Press, *Proceedings of the British Academy*, vol. xiii, 1968, pp. 259–87. Cited as Bullock, 'Second World War'.
BURKE, KENNETH. *Die Rhetorik in Hitlers 'Mein Kampf' und andere Essays zur Strategie der Überredung*, Frankfurt, 1967.

CARELL, PAUL. *Hitler's War on Russia: the Story of German Defeat in the East. 2. Scorched Earth*, London, 1970.
— *Unternehmen Barbarossa. Der Marsch nach Russland*, Frankfurt, Berlin and Vienna, 1963.
CIANO, GALEAZZO. *Tagebücher 1939–43*.
CILLER, ALOIS. *Deutscher Sozialismus in den Sudetenländern und in der Ostmark*, Hamburg, 1944.
— *Vorläufer des Nationalsozialismus. Geschichte und Entwicklung der nationalen Arbeiterbewegung im deutschen Grenzland*, Vienna, 1932.
CLASS, HEINRICH. *Zum deutschen Kriegsziel*, Munich, 1917.
CLAUSEWITZ, KARL VON. *Vom Kriege*, Leipzig, 1935; English translation *On War*, 3 vols, London, 1962.
COMPTON, JAMES V. *The Swastika and the Eagle: Hitler, the United States and the Origins of the Second World War*, London, 1968. (Ref. to German edn.)
CRAIG, GORDON A. *The Politics of the Prussian Army, 1640–1945*, New York and Oxford, 1964.

DAIM, WILFRIED. *Der Mann, der Hitler die Ideen gab*, Munich, 1958.
DALLIN, ALEXANDER. *German Rule in Russia, 1941–4*, London, 1957.
DAMASCHKE, ADOLF. *Ein Kampf um Sozialismus und Nation*, Dresden, 1935.
DARRÉ, WALTHER R. *Neuadel aus Blut und Boden*, Munich, 1935.
DEAKIN, F. W. *The Brutal Friendship*, London, 1962.

DE MAN, HENDRIK. *Sozialismus und National-Faschismus*, Potsdam, 1931.

DEUERLEIN, ERNST. *Der Aufstieg der NSDAP 1919–1933 in Augenzeugen-berichten*, Düsseldorf, 1968.

— *Hitler – Eine politische Biographie*, Munich, 1970.

DEUERLEIN, ERNST *Der Hitler-Putsch. Bayerische Dokumente zum 8./9. November 1923*, Stuttgart, 1962 (= *Quellen und Darstellungen zur Zeitgeschichte*, vol. 9).

— 'Hitlers Eintritt in die Politik', *Vierteljahrshefte für Zeitgeschichte* 7 (1959), p. 2.

DIETRICH, OTTO. *Zwölf Jahre mit Hitler*, Munich, 1955; English translation, *The Hitler I Knew*, Chicago, 1955; London, 1957.

— *Mit Hitler in die Macht. Persönliche Erlebnisse mit meinem Führer*, Munich, 1934.

DOMARUS, MAX. *Hitler. Reden und Proklamationen 1932–1945*, 4 vols, Munich, 1965.

DÖNITZ, CARL. Memoirs. *Ten years and twenty days*, London, 1959.

DORMANNS ALFRED. *Die Bevölkerung hatte Verluste*, Hamburg, 1947.

DRESSLER, ADOLF, and MAIER-HARTMANN, FRITZ. *Die Sammlung Rehse. Dok. der Zeitgeschichte*, 1st vol, Munich, 1940. Cited as 'Sammlung Rehse'.

DREXLER, ANTON. *Mein politisches Erwachen*, Munich, 1919.

DÜHRING, EUGEN. *Die Judenfrage*, Leipzig, 1930.

DWINGER, EDWIN ERICH. *Die 12 Gespräche 1933–1945*, Velbert and Kettwig, 1966.

ECKART, DIETRICH. *Der Bolschewismus von Moses bis Lenin. Zwiegespräche zwischen Adolf Hitler und mir*, Munich, 1925.

EDER, KARL. *Der Liberalismus in Altösterreich, Geisteshaltung, Politik und Kultur*, Vienna, 1955.

EHLERS, DIETER. *Technik und Moral einer Verschwörung. 20 Juli 1944*, Frankfurt and Bonn, 1964.

ENGELS, F. *Anti-Dühring*, London, 1959.

ERFURTH, WALDEMAR. *Die Geschichte des deutschen Generalstabes von 1918 bis 1945*, Göttingen, Berlin, Frankfurt, 1957.

EYCH, ERICH. *A History of the Weimar Republic*, I, London and Harvard, 1962.

FABRICIUS, HANS. *Dr Wilhelm Frick*, Berlin, 1938.

FABY, PHILIPP W. *Der Hitler–Stalin Pakt 1939–41*, Darmstadt, 1962.

— *Mutmassungen über Hitler. Urteile von Zeitgenossen*, Düsseldorf, 1967.

FECHENBACH, FELIX. *Der Revolutionär Kurt Eisner*, Berlin, 1929.

FEDER, GOTTFRIED. *Der deutsche Staat auf nationaler und sozialer Grundlage*, Munich, 1923.

— *Das Manifest zur Brechung der Zinsknechtschaft*, Munich, 1926.

— *Der Staatsbankerott die Rettung*, Diessen vor München, 1924.

FEIL, JENNY. 'Bayerischer Separatismus zur Eisner-Zeit', thesis, Munich, 1939.

FEST, JOACHIM C. *Face of the Third Reich*, London, 1970.

FISCHER, RUTH. *Stalin und der deutsche Kommunismus*, 2nd edn, Frankfurt 1948; English translation, *Stalin and German Communism. A study in the origins of the State Party*, London, 1948.

FISHMAN, JACK and JUTTON, JOSEPH BERNARD. *The Private Life of Josef Stalin*, London, 1962.

FLECHTHEIM, OSSIP. *Die KPD in der Weimarer Republik*. Offenbach/M., 1948.

FOCH, FERDINAND. *The Memoirs of Marshal Foch*, London, 1931.

FRANÇOIS-PONCET, ANDRÉ. *The Fateful Years*, London and New York, 1949.

FRANK, HANS. *Im Angesicht des Galgens*, München-Gräfelfing, 1953.

FRANZ-WILLING, GEORG. *Die Hitlerbewegung. Der Ursprung 1919–1922*, Hamburg and Berlin, 1962.

FREUD, ARTHUR. 'Zur Gemeinde und Organisation. Zur Haltung der Juden in Österreich', *Publikationen des Leo-Baeck-Instituts, Bulletin für die Mitglieder der Gesellschaft der Freunde des Leo-Baeck-Instituts*, Tel-Aviv, July 1960.

FREUD, SIGMUND. *Group Psychology and the Analysis of the Ego*, London and Vienna, 1922.

FREUND, MICHAEL. *Deutschland unterm Hakenkreuz. Die Geschichte der Jahre 1933–1945*, Gütersloh, 1965.

FRIEDENSBURG, FERDINAND. 'Die sowjetischen Kriegslieferungen an das Hitlerreich', *Vierteljarhrshefte für Wirtschaftsforschung*, 1962.
— *Die Weimarer Republik*, Berlin, 1946.

FRIEDLÄNDER, SAUL. *Auftakt zum Untergang. Hitler und die Vereinigten Staaten von Amerika 1939–41*, Stuttgart, 1965; English translation, *Prelude to Downfall: Hitler and the US., 1939–41* (translated from the French edn), London, 1966.

FUNDER, FRIEDRICH. *Vom Gestern ins Heute. Aus dem Kaiserreich in die Republik*, Vienna, 1952.

GALÉRA, KARL SIEGMAR, BARON VON. *Geschichte unserer Zeit*, 4 vols, Leipzig, 1932.

GELLERT, WILHELM. *Der Zusammenbruch der Demokratie*, Berlin, 1922.

GENGLER, LUDWIG FRANZ. *Die deutschen Monarchisten 1919–1925*, Kulmbach, 1932 (also an Erlangen thesis).

GENSCHEL, HELMUT. *Die Verdrängung der Juden aus der Wirtschaft im Dritten Reich*, Göttingen, 1966.

Gesetze des NS-Staates, pub. Ingo von Münch, Bad Homburg, Berlin and Zürich, 1968.

GESSLER, OTTO. *Reichswehrpolitik in der Weimarer Zeit*, Stuttgart, 1958.

GEYER, KURT. *Drei Verderber Deutschlands*, Berlin, 1924.

GIESE, HANS, and SCHMIDT, GUNTER. *Studenten – Sexualität. Verhalten und Einstellung*, Hamburg, 1968.

GILBERT, G. M. *Nuremberg Diary*, New York, 1947; London, 1948.

GISEVIUS, HANS-BERND. *Adolf Hitler. Versuch einer Deutung*, Munich, 1963.

GLUM, FRIEDRICH. *Der Nationalsozialismus. Werden und Vergehen*, Munich, 1962.

GOEBBELS, JOSEPH. *The Goebbels Diaries, 1942–1943*, ed. Louis P. Lochner, New York, 1948; London, 1949,
— *Goebbels Reden 1932–39*, ed. Helmut Heiber, Düsseldorf, 1972.

GÖRING, HERMANN. *Germany Reborn*, London, 1934.

GÖRLITZ, WALTER. *Generalfeldmarschall Keitel. Verbrecher oder Offizier? Erinnerungen, Briefe, Dokumente des Chefs OKW*, Göttingen, Berlin, Frankfurt, 1961.

GÖRLITZ, WALTER and QUINT, HERBERT. *Adolf Hitler. Eine Biographie*, Stuttgart, 1952.

GORDON, HAROLD J. *The Reichswehr and the German Republic*, Princeton, 1957.

GREBING, HELGA. *Der Nationalsozialismus. Ursprung und Wesen*, Munich, 1959.

GREINER, HELMUTH. *Die Oberste Wehrmachtführung 1939–1943*, Wiesbaden, 1951.

GREINER, JOSEPH. *Das Ende des Hitler-Mythos*, Zürich, Leipzig and Vienna, 1947.

GROENER, WILHELM. *Lebenserinnerungen*, ed. Freiherr Hiller v. Gaertringen, Göttingen, 1957.

GRÜN, WILHELM. *Dietrich Eckart als Publizist*, Part 1: Introduction, with a genealogical tree and a bibliography of Dietrich Eckart 1868–1938, Munich, 1942.

GUDERIAN, HEINZ. 'Erfahrungen im Russlandkrieg', *Bilanz des Zweiten Weltkrieges*, Oldenburg, 1953.
— *Erinnerungen eines Soldaten*, Heidelberg, 1951: English translation, *Panzer Leader*, London, 1952.

GUMBEL, EMIL JULIUS. *Verräter verfallen der Feme. Opfer/Mörder/Richter 1919–1929*, Berlin, 1929.
— *Vier Jahre politischer Mord*, Berlin, 1923.

GUN, NERIN E. *Eva Braun-Hitler. Leben und Schicksal*, Velbert and Kettwig 1968; English translation, *Eva Braun: Hitler's mistress*, London, 1969.

GUNZENHÄUSER. 'Die Bibliographien zur Geschichte des zweiten Weltkrieges', in *Jahresbibliographie 1961 der Bibliothek für Zeitgeschichte Stuttgart*, Frankfurt, 1963.

Gutachten des Instituts für Zeitgeschichte (Preface by Paul Kluke), Munich, Selbstverlag des Instituts für Zeitgeschichte, 1958 (= *Veröffentl. des Instituts für Zeitgeschichte*).

GUTE, HERBERT, and RITTER, HANS. *Glauben und Wissen*, East Berlin, 1956.

HALDER, FRANZ. *The Halder Diaries* (The private war journal of Generaloberst Franz Halder, from 14 August 1939 to 24 September 1942), ed. Arnold Lissance, 7 vols, Washington, 1950.

HALLGARTEN, GEORGE W. F. *Hitler, Reichswehr und Industrie. Zur Geschichte der Jahre 1918–1933*, Frankfurt, 1962.

HAMMANN, OTTO. *Deutsche Weltpolitik 1890–1912*, Berlin, 1925.
— *Der neue Kurs*, Berlin, 1918.

HAMMER, HERMANN. 'Die deutschen Ausgaben von Hitlers "Mein Kampf"', *Vierteljahrshefte für Zeitgeschichte* 4 (1956), pp. 161–78.

HAMMER, WOLFGANG. *Adolf Hitler – ein deutscher Messias?*, Munich, 1970.

HANFSTAENGL, ERNST. *Hitler. The Missing Years*, London, 1957.
— *Zwischen Weissem und Braunem Haus. Erinnerungen eines politischen Aussenseiters*, Munich, 1970.

HANNOVER, HEINRICH and ELISABETH. *Politische Justiz 1918–1933*, Frankfurt, 1966.

HANSEN, REIMER. 'Albert Speers Konflikt mit Hitler', *Geschichte in Wissenschaft und Unterricht* 10/1966, pp. 596–621.

HARAND, IRENE. *His Struggle – an answer to Hitler*, Chicago, 1937.

HART, F. TH. *Alfred Rosenberg. Der Mann und sein Werk*, 5th edn, Munich and Berlin, 1942.

HARTUNG, FRITZ. 'Zur Geschichte der Weimarer Republik', *Historische Zeitschrift* 181 (1956).

HASSE, ERNST. *Deutsche Weltpolitik*, Munich, 1897.

HASSELL, ULLRICH VON. *Vom anderen Deutschland. Aus den nachgelassenen Tagebüchern 1938–1944*, Frankfurt, 1964.

HASSELBACH, ULRICH VON. 'Die Entstehung der nationalsozialistischen deutschen Arbeiterpartei 1919–1923', thesis, Leipzig, 1931.

HAUSSER, PAUL. *Soldaten wie andere auch. Der Weg der Waffen-SS*, Osnabrück, 1966.

HEER, FRIEDRICH. *Der Glaube des Adolf Hitler. Anatomie einer politischen Religiosität*, Munich and Esslingen, 1968.
— *God's First Love: Christians and Jews over two thousand years*, London, 1970. (Ref. to German edn, 1967.)

HEIBER, HELMUT. *Adolf Hitler: a short biography*, London, 1961.
— (ed.) *Hitlers Lagebesprechungen*, Stuttgart, 1962.
— (ed.) *Reichsführer! Briefe an und von Himmler*, Stuttgart, 1968.
— *Walter Funk und sein Reichsinstitut für Geschichte des neuen Deutschlands*, Stuttgart, 1967.

HEIDEN, KONRAD. *Geburt des Dritten Reiches*, 2nd edn, Zürich, 1934.
— *A History of National Socialism*, London, 1934.
— *Hitler. A biography*, London, 1936.

HEROLD, EMIL. *Ein Jahr bayerische Revolution im Bilde*, Munich, 1919; 3rd unchanged edn, 1937.

HERRE, PAUL. *Die Südtiroler Frage*, Munich, 1927.

HERZFELD, HANS. 'Die deutsche Kriegspolitik im Ersten Weltkrieg', *Vierteljahrshefte für Zeitgeschichte* 3 (1961), pp. 224 ff.

HESS, ILSE. *Gefangener des Friedens*, Leoni am Starnberger See, 1962.

HEUSS, THEODOR. *Hitlers Weg*, Stuttgart, Berlin and Leipzig, 1932.

HILDEBRAND, K. *Vom Reich zur Weltreich, NSDAP und koloniale Frage 1919–45*, Munich, 1969.

HILLGRUBER, ANDREAS. *Chronik des Zweiten Weltkrieges* (with Gerhard Hümmelchen), Frankfurt, 1966.

— 'Deutschlands Rolle in der Vorgeschichte der beiden Weltkriege' in *Die deutsche Frage in der Welt* (ed. W. Conze, P. Kluke and Th. Schider), vol. 7, Göttingen, 1967.

HILLGRUBER, ANDREAS. '"Die Endlösung" und das deutsche Ostproblem als Kernstück des rassenideologischen Programms des Nationalsozialismus', *Vierteljahrshefte für Zeitgeschichte*, 2 (1972), pp. 133 ff.

— *Hitlers Strategie, Politik und Kriegführung 1940–41*, Frankfurt, 1965.

— *Kontinuität und Diskontinuität in der deutschen Aussenpolitik von Bismarck bis Hitler*, Düsseldorf, 1969.

— (ed.) *Probleme des Zweiten Weltkrieges*, Neue Wissenschaftliche Bibliothek, vol. 20, Cologne and Berlin, 1967.

— *Staatsmänner und Diplomaten bei Hitler. Vertrauliche Aufzeichnungen über Unterredungen mit Vertretern des Auslands* (ed. and commentary by Hillgruber): vol. I, *1939–1941*, Frankfurt, 1967; vol. II, *1942–1944*, Frankfurt, 1970.

— 'Südost-Europa im Zweiten Weltkrieg. Literaturbericht und Bibliographie', *Schriftenreihe der Bibliothek für Zeitgeschichte Stuttgart* 1, Frankfurt, 1962.

HILPERT, FRIEDRICH. 'Die Grundlagen der bayerischen Zentrumspolitik 1918–1921', thesis, Munich and Berlin, 1941.

HITLER, ADOLF. *Hitlers Zweites Buch. Ein Dokument aus dem Jahre 1928*, introduction and commentary by Gerhard L. Weinberg, Stuttgart, 1961; English translation, *Hitler's Secret Book*, New York, n.d.

— *Mein Kampf*, trans. Ralf Manheim, London, 1969, cited in notes as 'Manheim'.

— *Reden des Führers am Parteitag Grossdeutschland 1938*, Munich, 1938.

— *Die Südtiroler-Frage und das deutsche Bundnisproblem*, Munich, 1926.

HITLER, WILLIAM PATRICK, *Paris Soir*, 5 Aug. 1939.

Hitler's Table Talk, 1941–1944, translated from *Bormann Vermerke*, recorded by Martin Bormann, with introductory essay on 'The Mind of Adolf Hitler' by H. R. Trevor-Roper, London, 1953.

Hitler's War Directives, 1939–1945, ed. H. R. Trevor-Roper, London, 1964; edition used here, Pan paperback, 1966.

HOEGNER, WILHELM. *Der schwierige Aussenseiter*, Munich, 1959.

— *Die verratene Republik*, Munich, 1958.

HOESS, RUDOLF. *Commandant of Auschwitz. The autobiography of Rudolf Hoess*, London, 1957.

HOFFMAN, HEINRICH. *Erzählungen, Münchner Illustrierte*, 1954–55.

— *Hitler was my Friend*, London, 1955.

HOFFMANN, PETER. *Widerstand – Staatsstreich – Attentat*, 2nd edn, Munich, 1970.

HOFMANN, HANS HUBERT. *Der Hitler-Putsch, Krisenjahre deutscher Geschichte, 1920–1924*, Munich, 1961.
HÖHNE, HEINZ. *Der Orden unter dem Totenkopf. Die Geschichte des SS*, Hamburg 1966 and Gütersloh, 1967; English translation, *Order of the Death's Head: the story of Hitler's S.S.*, London, 1969.
HÖRBIGER-FAUTH, *Glazial = Kosmogonie*, Leipzig 1912; new edn, unrevised, 1925.
HOFMILLER, JOSEF. *Revolutionstagebuch 1918/19. Aus den Tagen der Münchener Revolution*, Leipzig, 1938.
HOSSBACH, FRIEDRICH. *Zwischen Wehrmacht und Hitler 1934–1938*, 2nd edn, Göttingen, 1965.
HUBATSCH, WALTER. *Die deutsche Besetzung von Dänemark und Norwegen 1940*, Göttingen, 1952.
— (ed.). *Hitlers Weisungen für die Kriegführung 1936 bis 1945*, Frankfurt, 1962.
HUMBERT, MANUEL. *Hitlers 'Mein Kampf'. Dichtung und Wahrheit*, Paris, 1936.
HUNDHAMMER, ALOIS. 'Geschichte des bayerischen Bauernbundes', thesis, Munich, 1924.

IRVING, DAVID. 'Hitlers Krankheiten', *Der Stern*, 26, 1969.
— *Mare's Nest: German Secret Weapons Campaign and British Counter Measures*, London, 1964.

JÄCKEL, EBERHARD. *Frankreich in Hitlers Europa*, Stuttgart, 1966.
— *Hitlers Weltanschauung. Entwurf einer Herrschaft*, Tübingen, 1969.
JACOBSEN, HANS-ADOLF. *Deutsche Kriegführung 1939–1945*, Hanover, 1961.
— *The Diplomacy of the Winter War. An Account of the Russo–Finnish War 1939–40*, Cambridge (Mass.), 1961.
— *Dünkirchen*, Neckargemünd, 1958.
— *Fall 'Gelb'. Der Kampf um den deutschen Operationsplan zur Westoffensive*, Wiesbaden, 1957.
— *Nationalsozialistische Aussenpolitik 1933–1938*, Frankfurt, 1968.
— *1939–1945. Der Zweite Weltkrieg in Chronik und Dokumenten*, Darmstadt, 1959.
— 'Kommissarbefehl und Massenexekution sowjetischer Kriegsgefangener', *Anatomie des SS-Staates*, vol. ii, pp. 167–279.
— *Zur Konzeption einer Geschichte des Zweiten Weltkrieges 1939–45*, Frankfurt, 1964.
— *Der Zweite Weltkrieg. Grundzüge der Politik und Strategie in Dokumenten*, Frankfurt, 1964.
— *Der Zweite Weltkrieg in Dokumenten*, Frankfurt, 1965.
JACOBSEN, HANS-ADOLF and DOLLINGER, H. *Der Zweite Weltkrieg in Bildern und Dokumenten*, 3 vols, Munich-Vienna-Basle, 1962–63.
JETZINGER, FRANZ. *Hitlers Jugend. Phantasien, Lügen- und die Wahrheit*, Vienna, 1956; English translation, *Hitler's Youth*, London, 1958.

JOCHMANN, WERNER. *Im Kampf um die Macht. Hitlers Rede vor dem Hamburger Nationalklub von 1919*, Frankfurt, 1960.
— *Nationalsozialismus und Revolution, Ursprung und Geschichte der NSDAP in Hamburg 1922–1933*, Frankfurt, 1963.
JUNG, RUDOLF. *Der nationale Sozialismus – Seine Grundlagen, sein Werdegang und seine Ziele*, Munich, 1922.

KANDL, ELEONORE. 'Hitler's Österreichbild', thesis, Vienna, 1963.
KANZLER, RUDOLF. 'Bayerns Kampf gegen den Bolschewismus', *Zeitschrift für bayerische Landesgeschichte*, Munich, 1932, no. 3.
KELLEY, DOUGLAS M. *22 Cells in Nuremberg*, New York, 1947.
KEMPNER, ROBERT M. W. *Das Dritte Reich im Kreuzverhör*, Munich and Esslingen, 1969.
— *Eichmann und Komplizen*, Zürich, Stuttgart, Vienna, 1961.
— *SS im Kreuzverhör*, Munich, 1964.
KERSTEN, FELIX. *Totenkopf und Treue. Heinrich Himmler ohne Uniform. Aus den Tagebüchern des finnischen Medizinalrates.*
KESSEL, EBERHARD. 'Zur Geschichte und Deutung des Nationalsozialismus. Literaturbericht und Stellungnahme', *Archiv für Kulturgeschichte*, vol. 45, Cologne and Graz, 1963, pp. 357–394.
KESSLER, GERHARD. 'Die Familiennamen der Juden in Deutschland', thesis Leipzig, 1935.
KIRKPATRICK, IVONE. *Mussolini*, Berlin, 1965.
KLAGES, LUDWIG. *Der Geist als Widersacher der Seele*, vol. 3, Leipzig, 1932.
— *Der Geist als Widersacher der Seele*, vols 2, 3 (revised edn), Bonn, 1954.
— *Rhythmen und Runen. Nachlass*, Leipzig, 1944.
KLAMPFER, JOSEF. *Das Eisenstädter Ghetto*, Eisenstadt, 1965.
KLEIN, BURTON H. *Germany's Economic Preparations for War*, Cambridge, Mass., 1959.
KLEIST, PETER. *The European Tragedy*, Douglas, IOM, and London, 1965.
KLEMMT, ALFRED. *Volk und Staat*, Berlin, 1936.
KLEMPERER, KLEMENS VON. *Germany's New Conservatism: its history and dilemma in the twentieth century*, Princeton, 1968.
KLUKE, PAUL. 'Nationalsozialistische Europaideologie', *Vierteljahrshefte für Zeitgeschichte*, Stuttgart, 1955.
KOELLRETUER, OTTO. *Grundfragen unserer Volks- und Staatsgestaltung*, Berlin, 1936.
KOERBER, VIKTOR VON. *Hitler, sein Leben und seine Reden*, Munich, 1923.
KOGON, EUGEN. *The Theory and Practice of Hell*, London 1950; New York, 1951.
KOPPENSTEINER, RUDOLF. *Die Ahnentafel des Führers*, Leipzig, 1937.
KOTZE, HILDEGARD, KRUMMACHER, F.A. *et al. Es spricht der Führer. Sieben exemplarische Hitler-Reden*, Gütersloh, 1966.
KRAMARZ, JOACHIM. *Claus Graf Stauffenberg. 15. November 1907–20. Juli 1944. Das Leben eines Offiziers*, Frankfurt, 1965; English translation, *Stauffenberg: the life and death of an officer*, London, 1967.

KRANNHALS, HANNS VON. *Der Warschauer Aufstand 1944*, Frankfurt, 1962.

KRAUSE, KARL WILHELM. *Zehn Jahre Kammerdiener bei Hitler*, Hamburg, 1949.

KREBS, ALBERT: FRITZ-DIETLOF GRAF VON DER SCHULENBURG. *Zwischen Staatsräson und Hochverrat*, Hamburg, 1964.

— *Tendenzen und Gestalten der NSDAP. Erinnerungen an die Frühzeit der Partei*, with a foreword by Hans Buchheim, Stuttgart, 1959 (= *Veröffentlichungen des Instituts für Zeitgeschichte in München. Quellen und Darstellungen zur Zeitgeschichte*, vol. 6).

KROKOW, MARTIN. *Vom Novemberstaat zum Grossdeutschen Reich*, Breslau, 1942.

KRUCK, ALFRED. *Geschichte des Alldeutschen Verbandes*, Wiesbaden, 1954.

KRUMM, PAUL. *Der Sozialismus der Hitlerbewegung im Lichte der Spenglerschen Geschichtsforschung oder die tiefste Ursache für den Aufstieg des Nationalsozialismus in Deutschland*, Geldern, 1932.

KRUMMACHER, F. A. *Die Auflösung der Monarchie*, 5th edn, Hanover, 1960.

KRUMMACHER, F. A. and LANGE, HELMUT. *Krieg und Frieden. Von Brest-Litowsk zum Unternehmen Barbarossa*, Munich and Esslingen, 1970.

KRUMMACHER, F. A., SCHEURIG, BODO, BRACHER, KARL DIETRICH, JACOBSEN, HANS-ADOLF, and JÄCKEL, EBERHARD. *Die totale Verführung. Propaganda und Wirklichkeit im Dritten Reich*, television programmes of Zweites Deutsches Fernsehen, 4, 8 and 10 May 1970, script in the author's possession.

KUBIZEK, AUGUST. *Adolf Hitler – Mein Jugendfreund*, Graz and Göttingen, 1953; English translation, *Young Hitler – the story of our friendship*, London, 1954. Published in the USA as *The Young Hitler I Knew*, Boston, 1955.

KUCZYNSKI, JÜRGEN. *Studien zur Geschichte des deutschen Imperialismus*, East Berlin, 1948–50.

KÜHNL, REINHARD. *Das Dritte Reich in der Presse der Bundesrepublik*, Frankfurt, 1966.

LANG, SERGE, and SCHENCK, ERNST VON (eds). *Memoirs of Alfred Rosenberg*, Chicago and New York, 1949.

LANGBEIN, HERMANN. *Im Namen des deutschen Volkes. Zwischenbilanz der Prozesse wegen nationalsozialistischer Verbrechen*, Vienna, Cologne, Stuttgart and Zürich, 1963.

LANGE, KARL. *Hitlers unbeachtete Maximen. 'Mein Kampf' und die Offentlichkeit*, Stuttgart, 1968.

LANGE-EICHBAUM, WILHELM. *Genie. Irrsinn und Ruhm*, 3rd edn, Munich, 1942.

LE BON, GUSTAVE. *The Crowd. A Study of the Popular Mind*, London, 1896 (French original entitled *Psychologie des Foules*, Paris, 1895).

LEHMANN-RUSSBÜLDT. *Der Kampf der Liga für Menschenrechte, vorm. Bund Neues Vaterland für den Weltfrieden 1924*, Berlin, 1927.

LEISER, ERWIN. *Mein Kampf, Eine Dokumentation*, Frankfurt and Hamburg, 1961.

LEVERKUEHN, PAUL. *Posten auf ewiger Wache. Aus dem abenteuerlichen Leben des Max von Scheubner-Richter*, Essen, 1938.

LEYMARIE, JEAN. *Impressionismus*, Geneva, 1955.

LITTNANSKI, EUGEN. *Hochverrat in Revolutionszeiten*, Bamberg and Greifswald, 1926.

LÖWITH, KARL. *From Hegel to Nietzsche*, London, 1965.

LUDENDORFF, ERICH. *Der totale Krieg*, Munich, 1936.

LUEDECKE, KURT. *I knew Hitler*, London, 1938.

LURKER, OTTO. *Hitler hinter Festungsmauern. Ein Bild aus trüben Tagen*, 2nd edn, Berlin, 1933.

MCDOUGALL, WILLIAM. *The Group Mind. A Sketch of the Principles of Collective Psychology*, Cambridge, 1920.

MALANOWSKI, WOLFGANG. 'Der Widerspruch von Tradition und Doktrin in der deutschen Aussenpolitik von der Revisionspolitik zur einseitigen Liquidierung des Vertrages von Versailles', D. Phil. thesis, Hamburg, 1955–56.

MANHEIM: see HITLER, ADOLF, *Mein Kampf.*

MANN, THOMAS. *Bruder Hitler*, vol. xii of *Gesammelte Werke*, 12 vols, Frankfurt, 1960.

MANN, VIKTOR. *Wir waren fünf*, Konstanz, 1949.

MANSTEIN, ERICH VON. *Verlorene Siege*, Bonn 1958; English translation, *Lost Victories*, London and Chicago, 1958.

MANVELL, ROGER, and FRAENKEL, HEINRICH. *Heinrich Himmler*, London, 1965.

MARTIN, BERND. *Deutschland und Japan im Zweiten Weltkrieg*, Zürich and Frankfurt, 1969.

MASER, WERNER. *Die Frühgeschichte der NSDAP. Hitlers Weg bis 1924*, Frankfurt and Bonn, 1965.

— *Hitlers Mein Kampf*, Munich and Esslingen, 1966.

— *Hitler's Mein Kampf: An Analysis*, London, 1970. The text of this edition has been considerably cut from that of the German edition of 1966, though not in substance.

— *Neue Deutsche Biographie*, vol. viii, Berlin, 1969.

— 'Die Organisierung der Führerlegende. Studien zur Frühgeschichte der NSDAP bis 1924', thesis, Erlangen, 1954.

MATZERATH, HORST. *Nationalsozialismus und kommunale Selbstverwaltung, Schriftenreihe des Vereins für Kommunalwissenschaften e. V.*, vol. 29, Stuttgart, 1970.

MAXIMILIAN FREDERICK WILLIAM, PRINCE OF BADEN. *The Memoirs of Prince Max of Baden*, 2 vols, London, 1928.

MAY, J. ARTHUR. *The Habsburg Monarchy 1867–1914*, Cambridge, Mass., 1951.

MEIER-BENNECKENSTEIN, PAUL (ed.) *Grundfragen der deutschen Politik*, vol. 1, Berlin, 1939.

MEINCK, GERHARD. *Hitler und die deutsche Aufrüstung*, Wiesbaden, 1959.

MEINECKE, FRIEDRICH. *The German Catastrophe*, Cambridge, Mass., 1950.

MEIROWSKY, E., and NEISSER, A. 'Eine neue sexualpädagogische Statistik', *Zeitschrift für die Bekämpfung der Geschlechtskrankheiten*, 1912, no. 12, pp. 1–38.

MEISSNER, OTTO. *Staatssekretär unter Ebert-Hindenburg-Hitler. Der Schicksalsweg des deutschen Volkes von 1918 bis 1945, wie ich ihn erlebte*, 3rd edn, Hamburg, 1950.

MEND, HANS. *Adolf Hitler im Felde 1914–1918*, Diessen vor München, 1931.

MEYER, ADOLF. *Mit Adolf Hitler im Bayerischen Reserve-Infanterie-Regiment 16 List*, Neustadt/Aisch, 1934.

MILTENBERG, WEIGAND VON. *Adolf Hitler – Wilhelm III*, Berlin, 1930–31.

MILWARD, A. S. *The German Economy at War*, London, 1965.

MINDER, ROBERT. *Dichter in der Gesellschaft*, Frankfurt, 1966.

MOELLER-BRUCK, ARTHUR. *Germany's Third Empire*, condensed edn. by E. O. Lorrimer etc., London, 1934.

MÖHL, WOLFGANG. 'Bayern in Deutschland', thesis, Erlangen, 1928.

MOHLER, ARMIN. *Die konservative Revolution in Deutschland 1918–1932. Grundriss ihrer Weltanschauungen*, Stuttgart, 1950.

MOSER, JONNY. 'Von der Emanzipation zur antisemitischen Bewegung. Die Stellung Georg Ritter von Schönerers und Heinrich Friedjungs in der Entwicklungsgeschichte des Antisemitismus in Österreich (1848–1896)', thesis, Vienna, 1962.

MÜLLER, KARL ALEXANDER VON. *Deutsche Geschichte und Deutscher Charakter*, Berlin and Leipzig, 1927.

— *Mars und Venus. Erinnerungen 1914–1919*, Stuttgart, 1954.

MÜLLER, K. J. 'Gedanken zum Problem einer Geschichtsschreibung über den Zweiten Weltkrieg', *Wehrwissenschaftliche Rundschau*, 1962, pp. 634–51 and 729–36.

MÜLLER-MEININGEN, ERNST. *Aus Bayerns schwersten Tagen*, Berlin and Leipzig, 1923.

NAUMANN, FRIEDRICH. *Demokratie und Kaisertum*, 4th edn, Berlin, 1905.

NIEKISCH, ERNST. 'Bayern', *Die Weltbühne*, 5 April–7 June, 1923.

— *Gewagtes Leben. Begegnungen und Begebnisse*, Cologne and Berlin, 1958.

— *Hitler – ein deutsches Verhängnis*, Berlin, 1932.

— *Das Reich der niederen Dämonen*, Hamburg, 1953.

— 'Unveröffentlichte Aufzeichnungen'. Cited as Niekisch, M S.

NOLLER, SONJA, and KOTZE, HILDEGARD VON. *Facsimile–Querschnitt durch den Völkischen Beobachter*, Munich, Berne and Vienna, 1967.

NOLTE, ERNST. *Der Faschismus. Von Mussolini bis zu Hitler*, Munich, 1968.

— 'Eine frühe Quelle zu Hitlers "Antisemitismus"', *Historische Zeitschrift*, 192 (1961), pp. 584–606.

— *Der Faschismus in seiner Epoche*, Munich 1963; English translation, *Three Faces of Fascism*, London, 1965.

NORDEN, ALBERT. 'Hinter den Kulissen des ersten westdeutschen Separatstaates', *Neue Welt* (East Berlin) 7 (1952), no. 4.

NOSKE, GUSTAV. *Erlebtes aus Aufstieg und Niedergang einer Demokratie*, Offenbach/M, 1947.

OERTZEN, F. W. VON. *Die deutschen Freikorps 1918–1923*, Munich, 1936.

OLDEN, RUDOLF. *Hitler, the Pawn*, London, 1936.

ORR, THOMAS. 'Das war Hitler', series of articles in *Illustrierte Revue*, 1952.

Parteigenosse! Der Führer spricht zu Dir, Wuppertal, 1943–44.

PAULUS, GÜNTER. 'Reichswehr und Freikorps', *Geschichte in der Schule* (East Berlin) 3 (1950), no. 1.

PECHEL, RUDOLF. *Deutscher Widerstand*, Elenbach-Zürich, 1947.

PEIS, GÜNTER. 'The Unknown Lover', commentary by Eugen Kogon, in *Der Stern*, Hamburg, 1959, no. 24.

PESE, WALTER WERNER. 'Hitler und Italien 1920–1926', *Vierteljahrshefte für Zeitgeschichte* 3 (1955), pp. 113–26.

PHELPS, REGINALD. 'Aus den Groenerdokumenten', *Deutsche Rundschau* 96 (1950).

— 'Before Hitler Came. Thule Society and German Orden', *Journal of Modern History*, 1936.

— 'Dokumente aus der "Kampfzeit" der NSDAP – 1923', *Deutsche Rundschau* 84 (1948), pp. 459 ff. and 1034 ff.

PICKER, HENRY. *Hitlers Tischgespräche im Führerhauptquartier 1941–1942*, Stuttgart 1963; references are to the 2nd edn of 1965, ed. Schramm, Percy Ernst.

PICKER, HENRY and HOFFMANN, HEINRICH. *Hitlers Tischgespräche im Bild*, ed. von Jochen von Lang, Oldenburg, 1969.

PIRCHEGGER, HANS. *Geschichte der Steiermark*, 2 vols, Graz, 1931.

PITROF, RITTER VON. *Gegen Spartakus in München und im Allgäu. Erinnerungsblätter des Freikorps Schwaben*, Munich, 1937.

PLOETZ, ALFRED. *Die Tüchtigkeit unserer Rasse und der Schutz der Schwachen – Ein Versuch über Rassenhygiene und ihr Verhältnis zu den Humanen Idealen, besonders zum Sozialismus*, Berlin, 1895.

PLÜMER, FRIEDRICH. *Die Wahrheit über Hitler und seinen Kreis*, Munich, 1925.

POLIAKOV, LÉON, and WULF, JOSEF. *Das Dritte Reich und die Juden*, Berlin-Grunewald, 1955.

— *Das Dritte Reich und seine Denker*, Berlin-Grunewald, 1959.

— *Das Dritte Reich und seine Diener*, Berlin-Grunewald, 1956.

PRANCKH, HANS FREIHERR VON. *Der Prozess gegen den Grafen Anton Arco-Valley*, Munich, 1920.

PROEBST, HERMANN, and UDE, KARL (ed.) *Denk' ich an München. Ein Buch der Erinnerungen*, Munich, 1966.

PROSS, HARRY. *Die Zerstörung der deutschen Politik. Dokumente 1871 bis 1933*, Frankfurt, 1959.

PULZER, P. G. J. *The Rise of Political Anti-Semitism in Germany and Austria*, New York, 1964.

RABENAU, FRIEDRICH VON. *Seeckt. Aus seinem Leben 1918–1936*, Leipzig, 1940.

RABITSCH, H. *Aus Adolf Hitlers Jugendzeit*, Munich, 1938.

RADEK, KARL. *Rosa Luxemburg, Karl Liebknecht, Leo Jogiches*, Hamburg, 1921.

RAUSCHNING, HERMANN. *Conversations with Hitler*, London, 1939.

— *Die Revolution des Nihilismus. Kulisse und Wirklichkeit im Dritten Reich*, 5th edn, Zürich and New York, 1938.

— *The Revolution of Nihilism*, New York 1939; published in England as *Germany's Revolution of Destruction*, London, 1939.

RECKTENWALD, JOHANN. *Woran hat Adolf Hitler gelitten?* Munich and Basle, 1963.

REDLICH, J. *Das österreichische Staats- und Reichsproblem. Geschichtliche Darstellung der inneren Politik der Habsburger Monarchie von 1848 bis zum Untergang des Reiches*, 2 vols, Leipzig, 1920–26.

REICH, ALBERT, *Dietrich Eckart*, Munich, 1934.

REITLINGER, GERALD. *The Final Solution – The attempt to exterminate the Jews of Europe, 1939–1945*, London and New York, 1953.

— *The House Built on Sand. Conflicts of German policy in Russia, 1939–1945*, London, 1960.

— *The S.S. Alibi of a Nation, 1922–1945*, London, 1956; New York, 1957.

RIBBENTROP, JOACHIM VON. *Zwischen London und Moskau. Erinnerungen und letzte Aufzeichnungen*, ed. Annelies von Ribbentrop, Leoni am Stamberger See, 1961.

RIEHL, WALTER. 'Die deutsche nationalsozialistische Partei in Österreich und der Tschechoslowakei', *Deutschlands Erneuerung*, 3, 1920.

RITTER, GERHARD. *Europa und die deutsche Frage*, Munich, 1948.

— *The German Resistance. Carl Goerdeler's struggle against tyranny*, abridged edn, London, 1958.

RÖHRS, HANS-DIETRICH. *Hitler – die Zerstörung einer Persönlichkeit. Grundlagen der Feststellungen zum Krankheitsbild*, Neckargemünd, 1965.

ROEPKE, FRITZ. *Von Gambetta bis Clemenceau*, Stuttgart and Berlin, 1922.

RÖHM, ERNST. *Die Geschichte eines Hochverräters*, Munich, 1933.

ROHWER, J. 'Zeitgeschichte, Krieg und Technik', *Wehrwissenschaftliche Rundschau*, 1964.

ROSANOW, GERMAN L. *Das Ende des Dritten Reichs*, Berlin, 1965.

ROSEN, EDGAR R. 'Mussolini und Deutschland 1922–1923', *Vierteljahrshefte für Zeitgeschichte* 5 (1957), pp. 17–41.

ROSENBERG, ALFRED. *Letzte Aufzeichnungen, Ideale und Idole der nationalsozialistischen Revolution*, Göttingen, 1955.

— '*Mythus*' etc. (extracts only), London, 1936–7.

— *Wesen, Grundsätze und Ziele der Nationalsozialistischen Deutschen Arbeiterpartei*, Munich, January, 1923.

ROSSBACH, GERHARD. *Mein Weg durch die Zeit*, Weilburg/Lahn, 1950.

ROTHENBÜCHER, KARL. *Der Fall Kahr*, Tübingen, 1924 (=*Recht und Staat in Geschichte und Gegenwart. Eine Sammlung von Vorträgen und Schriften aus dem Gebiet der gesamten Staatswissenschaften*, no. 29).

ROTHFELS, HANS. *The German Opposition to Hitler*, Ninsdale, Illinois, 1948; London, 1961.

RUPPRECHT, KRONPRINZ VON BAYERN. *Mein Kriegstagebuch*, 2 vols, Munich, 1929.

SAGITZ, WALTER. *Bibliographie des Nationalsozialismus*, Cottbus, 1933.

SAILER, J. B. *Des Bayernkönigs Revolutionstage*, Munich, 1919.

SALOMON, ERNST VON. *The Answers of Ernst von Salomon to the 131 Questions in the Allied Military Government 'Fragebogen'*, London, 1954.

SALOMON, F. *Die deutschen Parteiprogramme*, Berlin, 1932.

SANDVOSS, F. *Hitler und Nietzsche. Eine bewusstseinsgeschichtliche Studie*, Göttingen, 1969. Cited from the publisher's proofs (1967).

SCHÄFER, WOLFGANG. *NSDAP. Entwicklung und Struktur der Staatspartei des Dritten Reiches*, Hanover and Frankfurt, 1956.

SCHEIDEMANN, PHILIPP. *Memoirs of a Social Democrat*, 2 vols, London, 1929.

SCHELLENBERG, WALTER. *The Schellenberg Memoirs*, ed. Louis Hagen etc., London, 1956.

SCHILLING, ALEXANDER. *Dr Walter Riehl und die Geschichte des Nationalsozialismus*, Leipzig, 1933.

SCHLABRENDORFF, FABIAN VON. *Revolt against Hitler*, London, 1948.

SCHLOTTNER, ERICH HEINZ. 'Stresemann, der Kapp-Putsch und die Ereignisse in Mitteldeutschland und in Bayern im Herbst 1923', thesis, Frankfurt, 1948.

SCHMALIX, ADOLF. *Gerechtigkeit für Kapitän Ehrhardt*, Leipzig, 1923.

SCHMIDT, PAUL. *Hitler's Interpreter*, abridged edn, London and New York, 1951 (the English translation omits about half of the original version, which also covers the pre-Hitler period).

SCHMITT, FRANZ AUGUST. *Die neue Zeit in Bayern*, Munich, 1919.

SCHOEPS, HANS JOACHIM. *Paulus. Die Theologie des Apostels im Lichte der jüdischen Religionsgeschichte*, Tübingen, 1959.

SCHRAMM, PERCY ERNST. *Hitler als militärischer Führer. Erkenntnisse und Erfahrungen aus dem Kriegstagebuch des Oberkommandos der Wehrmacht*, Frankfurt, 1962.

— *Hitler : The Man and the Military Leader*, London, 1972. References are to this English translation, as *Hitler*, except where the German title is given.

SCHREINER, ALBERT. *Zur Geschichte der deutschen Aussenpolitik, 1871 bis 1945*, East Berlin, 1952.

SCHRICKER, RUDOLF. *Rotmord über München*, Berlin, n.d.

SCHUBERT, GÜNTER. *Anfänge nationalsozialistischer Aussenpolitik*, Cologne, 1963.

SCHÜDDEKOPF, OTTO-ERNST. *Linke Leute von rechts – Die national-revolu-*

tionären Minderheiten und der Kommunismus in der Weimarer Republik, Stuttgart, 1960.

SCHÜRER, HEINZ. 'Die politische Arbeiterbewegung Deutschlands in der Nachkriegszeit 1918–1923', thesis, Leipzig, 1933.

SCHULER, ALFRED. *Fragmente und Vorträge. Aus dem Nachlass*, with an introduction by Ludwig Klages, Leipzig, 1940.

— 'Einige Gedanken über Ibsens neuestes Werk *Baumeister Solness*', *Die Gesellschaft. Monatsschrift für Literatur, Kunst und Sozialpolitik* (founded and ed. by M. G. Conrad) 9, Leipzig, 1893.

SCHWARZ, GEORG. *Völker höret die Zentrale : KPD bankerott*, Berlin, 1933.

SCHWARZ, HERMANN. *Zur philosophischen Grundlegung des Nationalsozialismus*, Berlin, 1936.

SCHWEND, KARL. *Bayern zwischen Monarchie und Diktatur. Beiträge zur Bayerischen Frage in der Zeit von 1918 bis 1933*, Munich, 1954.

SCHWEISHEIMER, W. Article in *Deutsche Bauzeitschrift : Fachblatt für Architektur*, Gutersloh, vol. 5 (1969).

SCHWEYER, FRANZ. 'Rudolf Kanzler, Bayerns Kampf gegen den Bolschewismus' (review), *Zeitschrft für bayerische Landesgeschichte*, Munich, 1932.

SCULLY, VINCENT. *Modern Architecture. The architecture of democracy*, New York, 1961.

SEBOTTENDORFF, RUDOLF VON. *Bevor Hitler kam*, Munich, 1934.

SENDTNER, KURT. *Rupprecht von Wittelsbach, Kronprinz von Bayern*, Munich, 1954.

SERAPHIM, HANS-GÜNTHER (ed.) *Das politische Tagebuch Alfred Rosenbergs aus den Jahren 1934-35 and 1939-40*, Göttingen, Berlin and Frankfurt 1956; Munich, 1964.

SHIRER, WILLIAM L. *The Rise and Fall of the Third Reich*, London, 1964.

SKORZENY, OTTO. *Skorzeny's Special Missions etc.*, London, 1957.

SMITH, BRADLEY F. *Adolf Hitler, His Family, Childhood and Youth*, Stanford California, 1967.

SONTHEIMER, KURT. 'Antidemokratisches Denken in der Weimarer Republik', *Vierteljahrshefte für Zeitgeschichte* 5 (1957), pp. 42–62.

— *Antidemokratisches Denken in der Weimarer Republik. Die politischen Ideen des deutschen Nationalismus zwischen 1918 und 1933*, Munich, 1962.

SPECKNER, HERBERT. 'Die Ordnungszelle Bayern. Studien zur Politik des bayerischen Bürgertums, insbesondere der Bayerischen Volkspartei, von der Revolution bis zum Ende des Kabinetts Dr von Kahr', thesis, Erlangen, 1955.

SPECKNER, KARL. *Die Wächter der Kircher. Ein Buch vom deutschen Episkopat*, Munich, 1934.

SPEER, ALBERT. *Erinnerungen*, Frankfurt and Berlin, 1969; English translation, *Inside the Third Reich : memoirs*, London, 1970.

SPEIDEL, HANS. *Invasion 1944*, Chicago, 1950; published in England as *We Defended Normandy . . .*, London, 1951.

SPENGLER, OSWALD. *Politische Schriften*, Munich, 1924.

STADTLER, EDUARD. *Weltrevolution = Krieg*, Düsseldorf, 1937.

STAFF, ILSE. *Justiz im Dritten Reich. Eine Dokumentation*, Fischer Bücherei, February 1964.

STAMPFER, FRIEDRICH. *Die ersten 14 Jahre der Deutschen Republik*, Offenbach, 1947.

STEIN, ALEXANDER. *Adolf Hitler, Schüler der 'Weisen von Zion'*, Karlsbad, 1936.

STEIN, GEORGE H. *Waffen SS: Hitler's Elite Guard at War, 1939–45*, Cornell, 1966.

STEINER, FELIX. *Die Armee der Geächteten*, Göttingen, 1963.

— *Von Clausewitz bis Bulganin. Erkenntnisse und Lehren einer Wehrepoche*, Bielefeld, 1956.

STRASSER, OTTO. *Hitler and I*, London, 1940.

STÜBEL, HEINRICH. 'Die Finanzierung der Aufrüstung im Dritten Reich', *Europa-Archiv* 1951, no. 6, pp. 4128 ff.

TAYLOR, TELFORD. *Die Nürnberger Prozesse. Kriegsverbrechen und Völkerrecht*, Zürich, 1951.

TESSIN, GEORG. *Formationsgeschichte der Wehrmacht 1933–39*, Federal Archives Publications, vol. vii, Boppard-Rhein, 1959.

TOBIAS, FRITZ. *The Reichstag fire : legend and truth*, London, 1963.

TOLLER, ERNST. *Deutsche Revolution*, Berlin, 1933.

— *I was a German*, London, 1934.

TÖPNER, KURT. *Gelehrte Politiker und politisierende Gelehrte*, Zürich and Frankfurt, 1970.

TORMIN, WALTER. *Zwischen Rätediktatur und sozialer Demokratie*, Düsseldorf, 1954.

TREUE, W. *Gummi in Deutschland*, Munich, 1955.

TREVOR-ROPER, H. R. Article in *Der Monat*, no. 92, 1956, pp. 3 ff.

— *The Bormann Letters. The Private Correspondence between Martin Bormann and his Wife from January 1943 to April 1945*, London, 1954.

— 'Hitlers Kriegsziele', *Vierteljahrshefte für Zeitgeschichte*, April 1960.

— *The Last Days of Hitler*, 3rd edn, London, 1956.

UNGER, ERICH. *Das Schrifttum zum Aufbau des neuen Reiches*, Berlin, 1934.

VALENTIN, VEIT. *Chapters of German History*, London, 1940.

VOGELSANG, THILO. *Reichswehr, Staat und NSDAP. Beiträge zur deutschen Geschichte 1930–1932*, Stuttgart, 1962.

VOLKMANN, E. O. *Revolution über Deutschland*, Oldenburg, 1930.

VOLZ, HANS. *Daten der Geschichte der NSDAP*, Berlin and Leipzig, 1943.

— *Die Geschichte der NSDAP*, Leipzig and Berlin, n.d.

WARLIMONT, WALTER. *Im Hauptquartier der deutschen Wehrmacht 1939 bis 1945. Grundlagen, Formen, Gestalten*, Frankfurt and Bonn, 1964.

WEDEL, HASSO VON. *Das grossdeutsche Heer*, Berlin, 1939.

WERNER, LOTHAR. *Der Alldeutsche Verband. Historische Studien,* Berlin, 1935.

WHEELER-BENNETT, JOHN W. *The Nemesis of Power. The German Army in Politics, 1918–1945,* London, 1953.

WIEDEMANN, FRITZ. *Der Mann, der Feldherr werden wollte. Erlebnisse und Erfahrungen des Vorgesetzten Hitlers im Ersten Weltkrieg und seines späteren persönlichen Adjutanten,* Velbert and Kettwig 1964.

WIEDER, JOACHIM. *Stalingrad und die Verantwortung des Soldaten,* 2nd edn, Munich, 1962.

WIESER, FRIEDRICH. *Das Gesetz der Macht,* Vienna, 1926.

WILLI, M. *Hakenkreuz und Rutenbündel,* Berlin, 1924.

WOLF, DIETER. *Die Doriot-Bewegung. Ein Beitrag zur Geschichte des französischen Faschismus,* Stuttgart, 1967.

WOLF, G. *Geschichte der Juden in Wien 1156–1876,* Vienna, 1876.

WULF, JOSEPH. *Literatur und Dichtung im Dritten Reich,* Gütersloh, 1963.

— *Musik im Dritten Reich,* Gütersloh, 1963.

— *Presse und Funk im Dritten Reich,* Gütersloh, 1964.

— *Theater und Film im Dritten Reich,* Gütersloh, 1964.

WULZ, GUSTAV. 'Die Familie Kahr', *Archiv für Rassenund Gesellschaftsbiologie,* vol. 18, pt 3.

'Zidé a zidovské abee v Ceehách v minulosti a v pritomnosti. V dubnu 1934' ('The Jews and the Jewish community in Bohemia in the past and at present'), April, 1934.

ZIEGLER, HANS SEVERUS. *Hitler aus dem Erleben dargestellt,* Göttingen, 1964.

— *Wer war Hitler?* Tübingen, 1970.

ZIMMERMANN, WERNER GABRIEL. *Bayern und das Reich 1918–1923,* Munich, 1953.

ZINK, ADOLF VON. *Gustav Ritter von Kahr, Dr med. h.c. Festschrift zur Feier des fünfzigjährigen Bestehens des Bayerischen Verwaltungsgerichtofes,* Munich, Berlin and Leipzig, 1929.

ZITTEL, BERNHARD. 'Rätemodell München 1918/19', *Stimmen der Zeit* 165 (1963).

ZOLLER, ALBERT. *Hitler privat. Erlebnisbericht seiner Geheimsekretärin,* Düsseldorf, 1949.

Quellen und Darstellungen zur Zeitgeschichte als Veröffentlichungen des Instituts für Zeitgeschichte:

BÖHOME, HERMANN. *Der deutsch-französische Waffenstillstand im Zweiten Weltkrieg,* pt 1, Stuttgart, 1966.

ECHTERHÖLTER, RUDOLF. *Das öffentliche Recht im nationalsozialistischen Staat,* vol. 2, Stuttgart, 1970.

GROSCURTH, HELMUTH. *Tagebücher eines Abwehroffiziers 1938–1940* (with other documents. Ed. Harold Deutsch and Helmut Krausnick with Hildegard Kotze), Stuttgart, 1970.

LOOCK, HANS-DIETRICH. *Quisling, Rosenberg und Terboven*, Stuttgart, 1970.
WEINKAUFF, HERMANN and WAGNER, ALBRECHT. *Die Umgestaltung der Gerrichtsverfassung und des Verfahrens- und Richterrechts im national-sozialistischen Staat*, vol. I, Stuttgart, 1968.

Essays on the Second World War in: *Bilanz des Zweiten Weltkrieges*, Oldenburg, 1953; among the contributors:

TIPPELSKIRCH, KURT VON. 'Operative Führungsentschlüsse in Höhepunkten des Landkrieges', pp. 47 ff.
KESSELRING, ALBERT. 'Der Krieg im Mittelmeerraum', pp. 65 ff.
GUDERIAN, HEINZ. 'Erfahrungen im Russlandkrieg', pp. 81 ff.
RENDULIC, LOTHAR. 'Der Partisanenkrieg', pp. 99 ff.
ASSMANN, KURT. 'Die deutsche Seekriegführung', pp. 115 ff.
GODT, EBERHARD. 'Der U-Boot-Krieg', pp. 135 ff.
KESSELRING, ALBERT. 'Die deutsche Luftwaffe', pp. 145 ff.
RUMPF, HANS. 'Luftkrieg über Deutschland.', pp. 159 ff.
WEIDEMANN, ALFRED. 'Der rechte Mann am rechten Platz', pp. 213 ff.
SCHNEIDER, ERICH. 'Technik und Waffenentwicklung im Kriege', pp. 223 ff.
KEHRL, HANS. 'Kriegswirtschaft und Rüstungsindustrie', pp. 265 ff.
KUMPF, WALTER. 'Die Organisation Todt im Kriege', pp. 287 ff.
KROSIGK, GRAF SCHWERIN VON LUTZ. 'Wie wurde der Zweite Weltkrieg finanziert?', pp. 311 ff.
RIECKE, HANS-JOACHIM. 'Ernährung und Landwirtschaft im Kriege', pp. 329 ff.
PFEFFER, KARL HEINZ. 'Die Deutschen und die anderen Völker im Zweiten Weltkrieg', pp. 365 ff.
SULZMANN, RUDOLF. 'Die Propaganda als Waffe im Kriege', pp. 381 ff.
LATERNSER, HANS. 'Der Zweite Weltkrieg und das Recht', pp. 403 ff.
LÜDDE-NEURATH, WALTER. 'Das Ende auf deutschem Boden', p. 421.
ARNTZ, HELMUT. 'Die Menschenverluste im Zweiten Weltkrieg', p. 439.

Index

424 INDEX

Mittermaier, Karl, 25
Möhl, von, 112
Molotov, V. M., 262
Moltke, Helmuth, Count von, 159, 163, 288, 290
Morell, Dr Theodor, 93, 122, 153, 181, 204–5, 210–14, 218–25 passim, 228–31 passim, 275, 311, 316, 339, 340
Mühsam, 99
Müller, Hermann, 242
Müller, Karl Alexander von, 105, 106, 126–7, 128, 160, 163
Müller, Bishop Ludwig, 181
Müller, Sigurd, 345
Münchener Beobachter, 112
Mund, 65
Munich, 51, 52, 53, 61, 64, 65, 70–1, 74, 76, 77, 84, 93, 94, 97, 98, 101–4 passim, 113, 117, 121, 126, 133, 143, 163, 171, 196, 198–200, 262
Munich Agreement, 136, 283, 330
Munich putsch, 208, 209, 218, 232, 278, 327
Munich trial (1924), 33, 117, 324
Mussolini, Benito, 43, 60, 61, 145–6, 187, 262, 278, 329, 330

Nagel, Siegfried, 165
Napoleon, 154, 159, 287, 294, 297
Nasse, Hermann, 53, 54
National Association of German Officers, 110
National Socialist Women's Organization, 10
National Socialists (Austrian), 255
National Socialists, 88, 140, 141, 180, 241, 247, 250, 258
aggressive policy of, 236
foreign policy, 248, 250
Hitler's achievement of, 268
NSDAP, 4, 9, 49, 59, 87, 96, 110, 111, 127, 152, 248, 253, 254–5, 257, 262, 279, 287, 323–9
Nationalsozialistische Monatshefte, 326
Neuberger, burgomaster of Vienna, 57
Neue Freie Presse (Austrian), 118, 166
Neuhaus, Walter, 112
Neumann, 48, 50, 53
Neurath, Konstantin von, 148, 241, 267, 330
Niekisch, Ernst, 97, 103
Nissle, Dr, 212, 214
Nolde, Emil, 63
Nolte, Ernst, 118
Norway, 135, 290
Noske, Gustav, 98, 100, 101, 102, 103
NSDAP, see National Socialists
Nuremberg, 68, 88, 97, 324, 329
Nuremberg trials, 11, 68, 236, 256, 268

O'Connor, Fr Sixtus, 11, 14
Old Reich Flag Association, 109
Olden, Rudolf, 49
Operation Barbarossa, 215, 262, 281, 283, 295, 300, 304
Operation Citadal, 305
Ostara, 167
Ostermayer, Herta, 194, 229
Ostpolitik, 140, 142
Ottenstein, house of, 2–3, 13
Oven, Gen. von, 102

Pan-Germanism, 77, 111, 114, 115, 117, 142, 155–6, 157–8, 169, 179, 237, 241
Panholzer, sculptor, 46, 319
Papen, Franz von, 242, 254, 328
Pasewalk, 92, 93, 94, 323
Passau, Bavaria, 24–5
Paulus, Gen. Friedrich, 301
Peter, King of Yugoslavia, 154
Petz, Maj.-Gen. Friedrich, 87

73 74 75 76 77 10 9 8 7 6 5 4 3 2